Microsoft®
Publisher 2000
Bible

Microsoft® Publisher 2000 Bible

Sue Plumley

IDG Books Worldwide, Inc.
An International Data Group Company

Foster City, CA ✦ Chicago, IL ✦ Indianapolis, IN ✦ New York, NY

Microsoft® Publisher 2000 Bible
Published by
IDG Books Worldwide, Inc.
An International Data Group Company
919 E. Hillsdale Blvd., Suite 400
Foster City, CA 94404
www.idgbooks.com (IDG Books Worldwide Web site)

ISBN: 0-7645-3343-6

Printed in the United States of America

10 9 8 7 6 5 4 3 2 1

1B/QS/QX/ZZ/FC

Distributed in the United States by
IDG Books Worldwide, Inc.

Distributed by CDG Books Canada Inc. for Canada; by Transworld Publishers Limited in the United Kingdom; by IDG Norge Books for Norway; by IDG Sweden Books for Sweden; by IDG Books Australia Publishing Corporation Pty. Ltd. for Australia and New Zealand; by TransQuest Publishers Pte Ltd. for Singapore, Malaysia, Thailand, Indonesia, and Hong Kong; by Gotop Information Inc. for Taiwan; by ICG Muse, Inc. for Japan; by Norma Comunicaciones S.A. for Colombia; by Intersoft for South Africa; by Eyrolles for France; by International Thomson Publishing for Germany, Austria and Switzerland; by Distribuidora Cuspide for Argentina; by Livraria Cultura for Brazil; by Ediciones ZETA S.C.R. Ltda. for Peru; by WS Computer Publishing Corporation, Inc., for the Philippines; by Contemporanea de Ediciones for Venezuela; by Express Computer Distributors for the Caribbean and West Indies; by Micronesia Media.Distributor, Inc. for Micronesia; by Grupo Editorial Norma S.A. for Guatemala; by Chips Computadoras S.A. de C.V. for Mexico; by Editorial Norma de Panama S.A. for Panama; by American Bookshops for Finland. Authorized Sales Agent: Anthony Rudkin Associates for the Middle East and North Africa.

For general information on IDG Books Worldwide's books in the U.S., please call our Consumer Customer Service department at 800-762-2974. For reseller information, including discounts and premium sales, please call our Reseller Customer Service department at 800-434-3422.

For information on where to purchase IDG Books Worldwide's books outside the U.S., please contact our International Sales department at 317-596-5530 or fax 317-596-5692.

For consumer information on foreign language translations, please contact our Customer Service department at 800-434-3422, fax 317-596-5692, or e-mail rights@idgbooks.com.

For information on licensing foreign or domestic rights, please phone +1-650-655-3109.

For sales inquiries and special prices for bulk quantities, please contact our Sales department at 650-655-3200 or write to the address above.

For information on using IDG Books Worldwide's books in the classroom or for ordering examination copies, please contact our Educational Sales department at 800-434-2086 or fax 317-596-5499.

For press review copies, author interviews, or other publicity information, please contact our Public Relations department at 650-655-3000 or fax 650-655-3299.

For authorization to photocopy items for corporate, personal, or educational use, please contact Copyright Clearance Center, 222 Rosewood Drive, Danvers, MA 01923, or fax 978-750-4470.

Library of Congress Cataloging-in-Publication Data

Plumley, Sue.
   Microsoft Publisher 2000 bible / Sue Plumley.
      p.   cm
   ISBN 0-7645-3343-6 (alk. paper)
   1. Microsoft Publisher.   2. Desktop publishing
   I. Title
Z253.532.M53P58 2000
686.2'25445369 - - dc21   99-30304
                                                            CIP

ABOUT IDG BOOKS WORLDWIDE

Welcome to the world of IDG Books Worldwide.

IDG Books Worldwide, Inc., is a subsidiary of International Data Group, the world's largest publisher of computer-related information and the leading global provider of information services on information technology. IDG was founded more than 30 years ago by Patrick J. McGovern and now employs more than 9,000 people worldwide. IDG publishes more than 290 computer publications in over 75 countries. More than 90 million people read one or more IDG publications each month.

Launched in 1990, IDG Books Worldwide is today the #1 publisher of best-selling computer books in the United States. We are proud to have received eight awards from the Computer Press Association in recognition of editorial excellence and three from Computer Currents' First Annual Readers' Choice Awards. Our best-selling ...For Dummies® series has more than 50 million copies in print with translations in 31 languages. IDG Books Worldwide, through a joint venture with IDG's Hi-Tech Beijing, became the first U.S. publisher to publish a computer book in the People's Republic of China. In record time, IDG Books Worldwide has become the first choice for millions of readers around the world who want to learn how to better manage their businesses.

Our mission is simple: Every one of our books is designed to bring extra value and skill-building instructions to the reader. Our books are written by experts who understand and care about our readers. The knowledge base of our editorial staff comes from years of experience in publishing, education, and journalism — experience we use to produce books to carry us into the new millennium. In short, we care about books, so we attract the best people. We devote special attention to details such as audience, interior design, use of icons, and illustrations. And because we use an efficient process of authoring, editing, and desktop publishing our books electronically, we can spend more time ensuring superior content and less time on the technicalities of making books.

You can count on our commitment to deliver high-quality books at competitive prices on topics you want to read about. At IDG Books Worldwide, we continue in the IDG tradition of delivering quality for more than 30 years. You'll find no better book on a subject than one from IDG Books Worldwide.

John Kilcullen
Chairman and CEO
IDG Books Worldwide, Inc.

Steven Berkowitz
President and Publisher
IDG Books Worldwide, Inc.

*Eighth Annual
Computer Press
Awards ≥1992*

*Ninth Annual
Computer Press
Awards ≥1993*

*Tenth Annual
Computer Press
Awards ≥1994*

*Eleventh Annual
Computer Press
Awards ≥1995*

Credits

Acquisitions Editor
Andy Cummings

Development Editors
Greg Robertson
Kenyon Brown

Technical Editor
John Preisach

Copy Editors
William F. McManus
Corey Cohen
Amanda Kaufmann
Ami Knox
Michael Welch

Production
IDG Books Worldwide Production

Proofreading nad Indexing
York Production Services

Cover Design
Murder By Design

About the Author

Sue Plumley is a partner in Humble Opinions, a consulting firm in southern West Virginia. Sue works with her husband, Carlos, to provide software training, computer consulting, and network installation and maintenance to businesses and corporations. Sue's degree is in art education. She worked for four years as a professional typesetter and graphic artist, and has been writing books since 1992. Sue has written more than 35 books on operating systems, Microsoft Office products, Lotus products, Windows NT networking, and network administration. In addition, Sue has cowritten an additional 35 books about various software products and procedures.

To my dad (in-law), Carlos Plumley, from whom I've learned so much about life and who is an inspiration to our whole family

Preface

Microsoft Publisher 2000 is a desktop publishing program. With Publisher you can create your own publications — newsletters, flyers, letterheads, brochures, and the like — and make them attractive and professional in appearance.

You've probably heard of PageMaker, a desktop publishing program; or perhaps you've seen the Ventura desktop publishing program. These programs are created for professional typesetters and are difficult to use. This is not so with Publisher.

Publisher was created for you, the everyday user who just wants to produce letterhead and an envelope, or a monthly company newsletter. Publisher is easy to use, yet it includes some advanced tools and features. Produce publications for printing at a commercial print shop; perform a mail merge to print your envelopes or labels; or create your own Web page and publish it on the Internet.

Publisher includes wizards to help you. Follow a wizard's step-by-step instructions to create your documents. Using Publisher's tools, you can change the formatting, designs, and even the graphics in any wizard publication. Or design your own publications from scratch.

Publisher enables you to format text, check your spelling, create drawings, enhance photographs, use clip art, and more. Publisher includes the tools you need to quickly and efficiently produce the business and personal documents you use every day.

Why This Book?

So, if Publisher includes wizards that help you produce your documents, why do you need this book? The *Microsoft Publisher 2000 Bible* shows you how to use Publisher to its fullest capabilities. You learn more than just how to run a wizard. You learn how to change a wizard's designs to better suit your needs, as well as how to produce documents for which there are no wizards.

Moreover, you learn about document design. On its own, a desktop publishing program cannot create quality designs and professional-looking documents. Even if you use one of Publisher's wizards, the final layout, the page design, the font formatting, and other design elements all can be improved.

These days it's easy to produce a flyer, pamphlet, or newsletter. Anyone with a computer and printer can create his or her own documents. At the same time, there are many documents on the market today that look unprofessional and unattractive. They may attract attention, but not the desired kind.

You want your documents to look their best. A well-designed document impresses current and prospective customers. Your documents should make a good first impression. This book helps you create that kind of document.

As a professional typesetter, I designed documents of all kinds: newsletters, catalogs, programs, books, reports, magazines, and more. I worked at a commercial print shop as a graphic artist, typesetter, and then as production manager. I learned to produce quality designs, work with color, apply special printing techniques, and more. In this book, I share that knowledge with you.

Who Can Use This Book?

The *Microsoft Publisher 2000 Bible* offers information for the beginning user of the program, as well as for the advanced user. The beginning user who wants to use Publisher but knows nothing about the mouse, toolbars, dialog boxes, and other program basics can learn from this book.

Intermediate users who are familiar with Windows and general Windows applications, but not with Publisher, can learn to use the program by reading this book. The text quickly develops from the beginning level to the intermediate level after the first few chapters.

Advanced users can find program tips and design advice in the early chapters, and information about more advanced procedures and processes at the end of the book. If you're familiar with Publisher but want to learn more, *Microsoft Publisher 2000 Bible* offers information about design, program enhancements, Publisher interaction with Internet technologies, and more.

Whether you're using Publisher for personal publications such as letterhead, flyers, signs, and Web pages, or company documents such as newsletters, Web sites, forms, and brochures, you can benefit from this book. All the examples are business-oriented, but you can adapt the designs, layouts, and advice to any document.

What's Different in Publisher 2000?

Publisher 2000 now has more Office commands, tools, and features. If you're familiar with Office's Word, Excel, or PowerPoint, you'll get up to speed more quickly with Publisher.

Microsoft has made Publisher 2000 more like other Office programs. Not only is the interface more familiar, but many procedures are similar to those in other Office programs. For example, entering and editing text in Publisher is more like Word than ever before. Also, many keyboard shortcuts and toolbars work as they do in other Office programs.

Another new feature is the improved commercial printing technologies added to the program. If you plan to take your publication to a commercial print shop, Publisher offers you more control over your documents. For example, now you can reliably set up spot-color and process-color printing for your documents. Publisher also offers process-color models, including CMYK and Pantone. Create separations and composites to take to the shop. You'll be sure the printer understands what you want.

Publisher also includes graphics linking and font embedding features that enable you to take your publication to the print shop with all the images and fonts included—no more font substitutions or rushing around to get an appropriate piece of clip art to replace the one you left on your computer. The Pack and Go feature makes putting your files on disk easier, too.

Publisher's new Web features and tools make your Web site look professional. Publisher includes new designs and backgrounds for use with the Web, more GIFs and animations for your Web pages, and easy Web page previewing and design troubleshooting.

Finally, Publisher 2000 is easier to use than the preceding version. Things such as the zooming and scrolling features simplify getting around in Publisher. The Quick Publications Wizard makes it easy to build a document base using color schemes, various layouts, and design sets. Add to these improvements additional fonts, more clip art files, and new master design sets, and you'll be even happier with this version of Publisher.

How Is the Book Organized?

The *Microsoft Publisher 2000 Bible* is organized such that the material covers the process of creating a publication in sequential order: from considering the design to designing the page, formatting and adding graphics, to printing the document. The introductory procedures appear at the front of the book, and the more advanced features appear at the back.

You can read the book sequentially or use it as a reference, looking up processes and procedures as you need them. If you read the book sequentially, you learn to design your own documents step by step. If you use the book as a reference, you can go directly to the help you need and apply it right away.

The *Microsoft Publisher 2000 Bible* is organized into eight parts and one appendix. Each part covers one process of creating publications in Publisher.

The book starts with a **Quick Start** chapter for those who are new to the program and want quick results.

Part I, "**Publisher Basics**," introduces you to Publisher's screen and tools, selecting and editing techniques, and Help feature. You also learn how to save and organize files, apply good design strategies to a publication, and do some basic program customization.

Part II, "**Working with Page Layout**," introduces Publisher's page layout tools and features. Chapters teach how to arrange page elements, work with multiple pages, design by using a background and a foreground, use and edit frames, change page setup, and use advanced page features.

Part III, "**Working with Text**," shows you how to use text in your publications. Chapters cover entering and editing text, revising and correcting text, basic text formatting, font formatting and styles, paragraph formatting and line spacing, and creating special text effects such as text rotation, watermarks, and logos.

Part IV, "**Adding Graphics, Objects, and Images**," covers the use of various graphics in your publications. Chapters cover adding clip art, sounds, and motion clips; drawing with Microsoft Draw; using WordArt to create special text effects; creating tables; and linking and embedding objects from other programs.

Part V, "**Producing Publications**," shows you how to use Publisher's wizards. You learn to use the Design Gallery to add elements to a document, and then you learn to create various document types, such as letterhead, flyers, calendars, business cards, newsletters, greeting cards, brochures, and more. You learn to create these documents with a wizard, and from scratch.

Part VI, "**Printing**," includes information on installing printer drivers, using various types of printers, using a service bureau, and printing various types of publications. You also learn how to use Publisher's commercial printing tools, including the spot- and process-color tools, print separation proofs and composites, and trap objects and text for a commercial printer.

Part VII, "**Using Mail Merge**," explains how to merge an address list or other data source with a publication, such as a letter or mailing labels. You learn to create a data source and then perform a mail merge. You learn what to check before you print to make sure your publications look right, and then print the merged documents for easier mailing and handling.

Part VIII, "**Designing for the Web**," presents information on how to prepare a Web page and a Web site. Learn to use the Web Wizard to create your own Web page, and learn to design a Web page from scratch. Add hyperlinks, buttons, and other icons to the page to make navigation easier for Web visitors. Learn to plan and organize your site, add navigation bars and other links, create electronic forms, and publish your Web site to the Internet.

The Appendix, "**Publisher and Windows 95/98**," explains how best to use Windows features to make your work in Publisher easier. Learn to find files by using wildcards, organize folders and files by using Windows Explorer, use Internet Explorer, and set up dial-up networking.

What Are the Conventions Used in This Book?

The *Microsoft Publisher 2000 Bible* conventions include step-by-step instructions for performing most procedures in Publisher. Choosing menus and commands is represented as "Choose Insert ➪ Picture ➪ Clip Art." You choose these commands in sequence.

Sidebars represent extra information that's related to the text but not integral to Publisher procedures. Tips present advice and shortcuts that help you complete your work in Publisher. Notes offer information related to the text as well.

To Summarize . . .

Publisher is a fine program, and with some help, you can create professional-looking and attractive documents to represent your company. I hope you find this book helpful in your work. I welcome all comments from my readers. E-mail me at splumley@citynet.net.

Acknowledgments

I'd like to thank all the people who helped me in this venture. Thanks to Andy Cummings, my acquisitions editor, for finding the perfect topic for my first book with IDG Books Worldwide. His patience and perseverance are greatly appreciated. Thanks to Ken Brown for his guidance. I also want to thank Greg Robertson for his dedication, support, and wonderful sense of humor. It's strange how our paths have crossed several times in the past, but we never met before this project. My thanks also go to the book's technical reviewer, John Preisach, for his help in ensuring the accuracy of the text; to the book's copy editors, William F. McManus, Corey Cohen, and Amanda Kaufmann; and to the indexer, York Production Services. Thanks, too, to Microsoft's Katie Jordan and Richard Okazaki for their interest and counsel. Finally, I want to thank my family — especially my husband, Carlos — for their love, patience, and commitment.

Contents at a Glance

• •

Contents

• •

Part V: Producing Publications   559

Part VIII: Designing for the Web — 761

Chapter 33: Preparing a Web Page 763

Chapter 34: Preparing a Web Site 787

Appendix: Publisher and Windows 95/98 817

Index 847

Quick Start with Publisher

Starting Publisher

Publisher is a desktop publishing program. That is, it's a program that enables you to create various documents to use in your personal life or in your business. For example, you can create your own letterhead with a matching envelope, or create invitations to a bridal shower. If you're in business, you can also use Publisher to create documents. You can produce a newsletter, brochure, and even a catalog of your products.

To give you a sample of how Publisher works, this chapter guides you through the process of creating a personal letterhead and a matching envelope. Your first step is to start Publisher, by following these steps:

1. Choose Start ➪ Programs.

2. Choose the folder in which you installed Publisher. That folder might be Microsoft Office, MS Office, Office 2000, or some other folder.

   Alternatively, Publisher may appear on the Programs menu.

3. Click Microsoft Publisher to start the program.

Publisher opens, displaying the program window in the background and a box called the Microsoft Publisher Catalog in the foreground, as shown in Figure 1. You can read more about the Catalog in Chapter 3, "Understanding the Catalog."

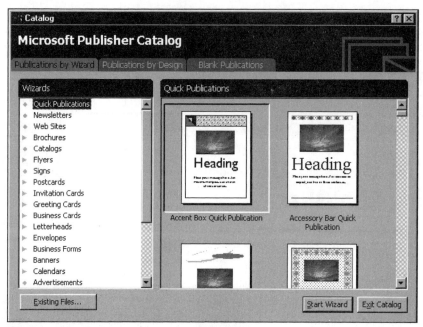

Figure 1: Publisher opens with myriad options.

Using a Wizard

Publisher's Catalog offers numerous options for creating publications. You can create a newsletter, Web site, brochure, or other document. You can choose from many different designs, colors, and layout options. For the purpose of this first exercise, you'll choose one of the easier publications to create. You'll learn about all of the options in the following chapters of the book.

The list that appears in the Catalog is a collection of available wizards that you can use to help you build a document. Some wizards guide you, step by step, through the process of creating the type of publication that you want. These wizards ask you questions and then use your answers to make decisions about color, layout, and design.

Other wizards simply create a document for you, including some borders, pictures, and text. After the wizard creates the document, you can go into the document and make changes to suit your purposes.

Creating a letterhead

The first document that you will create in Publisher is a letterhead. You can use this letterhead for your personal or business needs. After you learn more about Publisher and its features and tools, you can make changes to your letterhead to suit your tastes better.

Running the Letterhead Wizard

To start the Letterhead Wizard, follow these steps:

1. From the Wizards list in the Catalog, choose Letterheads. The Catalog changes in appearance to offer several options, as shown in Figure 2.

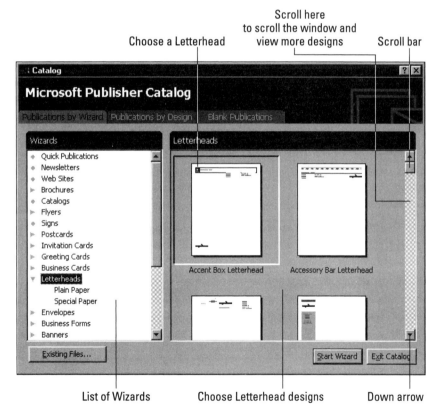

Figure 2: Publisher offers a variety of letterhead designs.

2. You can view the letterhead designs by clicking the down arrow on the scroll bar. Click the up arrow to view previous designs.

3. Choose the letterhead design called Accessory Bar Letterhead, in the upper-right corner of the Letterheads box.

4. Click the Start Wizard button. Publisher creates the letterhead and displays it onscreen, as shown in Figure 3.

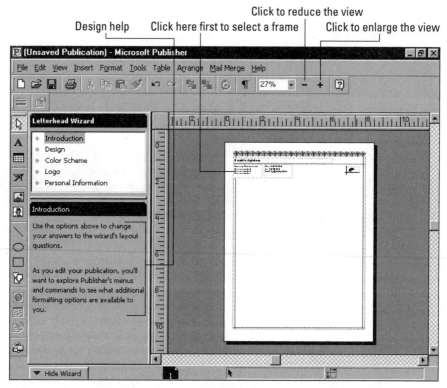

Figure 3: The Letterhead Wizard creates a design; now you simply fill in the text.

Note

A pop-up information dialog box tells you that the Wizard wants to gather information about you. Click OK. A dialog box appears, asking you for information; cancel that box for now. You can fill it out later in the book.

Also, the appearance of your wizard may be different, depending on any preferences that you've selected. If the Wizard displays the Letterhead Wizard Introduction, click the Finish button at the bottom of the Wizard box to continue with Step 5.

5. The view of the letterhead is too small for you to read the text, so you need to enlarge the view. Click the text anywhere near the top part of the letterhead page. Clicking the text displays a rectangle around the text. This rectangle is called a *text frame*. Small black boxes appear around the edge of the frame.

Note

Publisher places all text, pictures, and other items in frames, or boxes, on the page. You can move, copy, delete, and otherwise manipulate these frames. You'll learn more about frames later in the book.

6. Click the plus button on the toolbar, as marked in Figure 3. This button enlarges the view so that you can see the frame that you chose. Click the button a second, third, and even fourth time, if necessary, to see the text clearly in the frame.

If you enlarge the text too much, click the button with the minus (-) sign to reduce the view a little. Figure 4 illustrates the page after clicking the button five times.

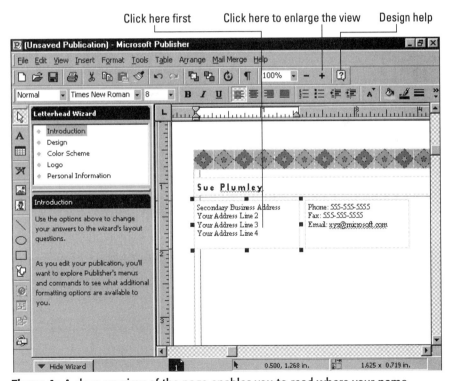

Figure 4: A close-up view of the page enables you to read where your name and address should be entered.

Note   Publisher may put your name into the first frame for you.

Entering your name and address

Next, you need to enter your name (if it's not already entered by Publisher), address, phone number, and any other information that you want in your letterhead. Publisher displays some placeholder text in the frames, to show you where your text goes.

You need to delete Publisher's text before you enter your own. To delete the text, you first need to *select* it. You select text with the mouse. Click at the beginning of the text and then drag the mouse I-beam to the end of the text. The text appears in *reversed video* (white text on a black background), as shown in Figure 5. If dragging the mouse over the text is difficult for you, you can click the mouse I-beam at the beginning of the text, press and hold down the Shift key, and then click the mouse at the end of the text, which gives you the same results as dragging the mouse. (Other ways of selecting text are described later in the book.)

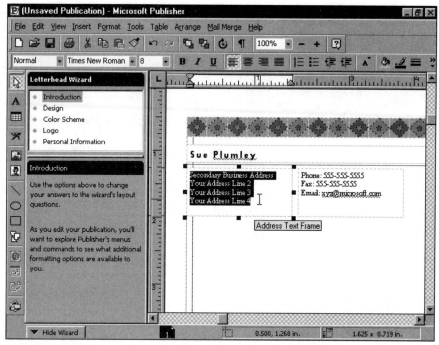

Figure 5: Select the text by using your mouse, and then delete it.

After you select the text, press the Delete key on your keyboard to remove the text. Alternatively, you can just begin typing and the selected text disappears. You'll notice a blinking vertical line in the text box; this is called the *insertion point,* which indicates the point where you can begin typing.

To enter text in a frame, follow these steps:

1. Select and delete the text in the frame.

2. Make sure the insertion point is in the frame; if it is not, click the mouse in the frame to insert it.

3. Enter the appropriate information in the frame.

4. Enter your phone number and e-mail address in the second frame, after deleting the existing text. Figure 6 illustrates the text in the appropriate boxes.

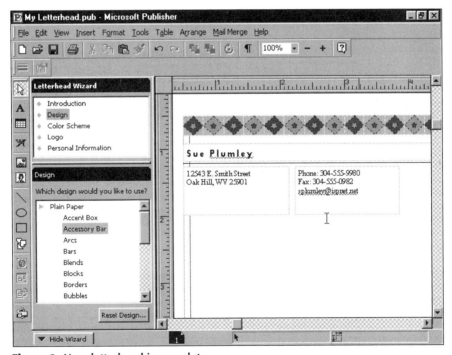

Figure 6: Your letterhead is complete.

Changing the design

You can change the design of your letterhead a bit, if you want. You may not care for the border at the top of the page, for example. Publisher offers hundreds of designs and colors, all of which you'll learn to access throughout the book; however, for this sample, you'll just change the border design.

To change the design, follow these steps:

1. The Letterhead Wizard box to the left of your letterhead contains a top and a bottom window pane. In the top pane, click the word Design. Multiple options appear in the bottom pane, as shown in Figure 7.

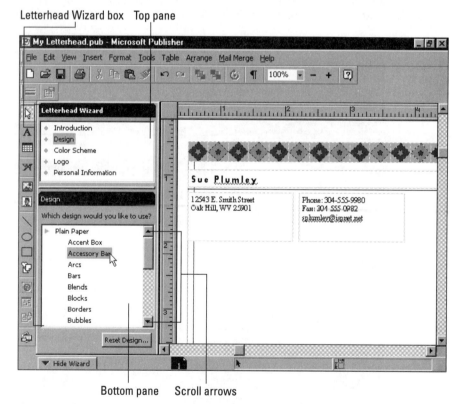

Figure 7: Alter the design of the letterhead to suit your taste.

2. Choose the third option in the bottom pane (Accessory Bar). See the difference in the letterhead. You can use the scroll arrows to move around on the page. Alternatively, you can use the minus button to reduce the view a bit.

3. Try at least three or four of the design options and then choose the one that you like best. Remember the name of the design so that you can use it to create matching envelopes.

Saving the letterhead

If you don't save your letterhead, you'll lose your work. If you save your letterhead to your hard disk, you can open it at any time to modify or print it. For now, you'll use the default technique for saving a publication. You can learn more about saving a publication in Chapter 4, "Working with Files."

To save your letterhead, follow these steps:

1. Press Ctrl+S. The Save As dialog box appears, as shown in Figure 8.

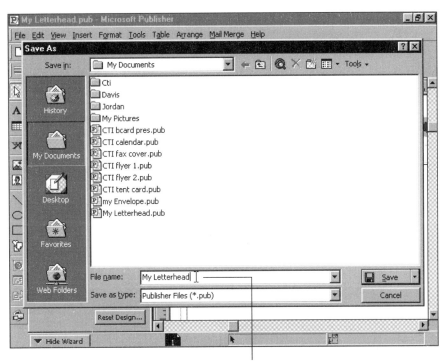

Enter a file name here

Figure 8: Give your letterhead a name under which you can save it.

2. Enter a filename in the File name text box. You can use the name My Letterhead, as shown in Figure 8, if you want.

3. Press the Enter key. Publisher saves the document, but the page remains onscreen.

Printing the letterhead

You can print the letterhead so that you can write a letter on it or use it in a typewriter. Naturally, you also can create a letter in Publisher, by typing the text directly onscreen. For more information about entering text in a document, see Chapter 13, "Entering and Editing Text."

To print the letterhead, follow these steps:

1. Press Ctrl+P. The Print dialog box appears, as shown in Figure 9.

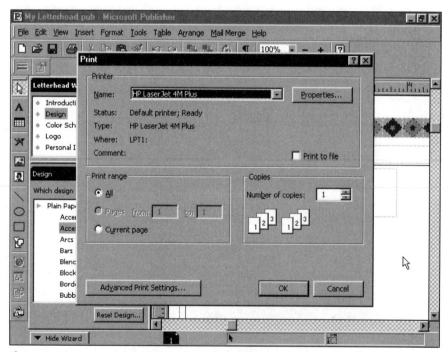

Figure 9: You can print your letterhead in Publisher quickly and easily.

2. Press the Enter key to print one copy of the letterhead.

Creating a matching envelope

Creating an envelope to match your letterhead is easy. The envelope can use the same design that you applied to the letterhead, and can contain your return address. Publisher provides another wizard to help you create an envelope.

Using the Envelope Wizard

To create an envelope, follow these steps:

1. Choose File ➪ New. If Publisher displays the warning box shown in Figure 10, click Yes. The Wizards list then appears onscreen.

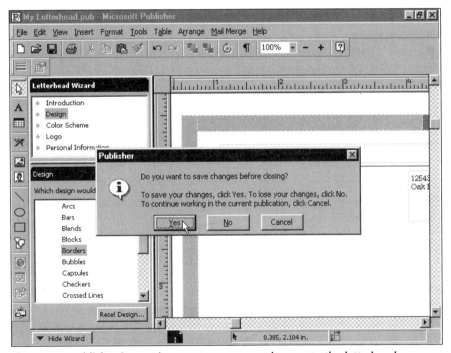

Figure 10: Publisher is warning you to save your changes to the letterhead.

2. In the Wizards list, choose Envelopes.

3. Scroll to find the envelope design that matches your letterhead design. Choose it.

4. Click Start Wizard. Publisher applies the design to an envelope and displays it onscreen, as shown in Figure 11.

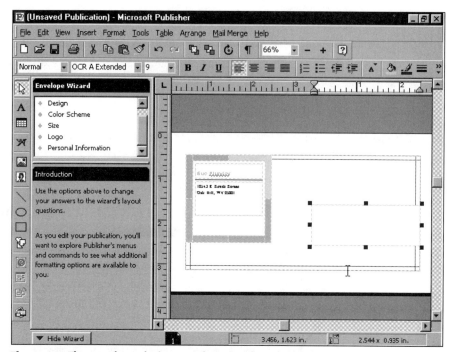

Figure 11: The envelope design matches your letterhead design.

Note   If you haven't entered your personal information, you'll be prompted again to do so. Cancel the dialog box for now.

5. Choose a frame by clicking it, and then use the Zoom tool (+) to enlarge the view so that you can type.

6. Select and delete the text in the frame.

7. Enter your address in the return address box.

8. If you want, you can enter a mailing name and address in the box provided. Alternatively, you can simply delete the text and fill it in later by hand or typewriter. You can delete the text in the mailing address and leave the empty frame in place; however, it won't print.

Saving and printing the envelope

You can save the envelope just as you saved the letterhead. After saving it, you can print or modify it whenever you want. You also can print the envelope now, just as you printed the letterhead.

To save the envelope, follow these steps:

1. Press Ctrl+S. The Save As dialog box appears.
2. Enter a filename in the File name text box. You can use the name My Envelope, if you want.
3. Press the Enter key. Publisher saves the document, but the page remains onscreen.

To print the envelope, follow these steps:

1. Press Ctrl+P. The Print dialog box appears.
2. Press the Enter key to print one copy of the envelope.

Exiting Publisher

After you finish using Publisher, you can exit the program. Before you exit the program, always make sure that you save any document that is onscreen. Publisher automatically closes the saved document as it exits.

To exit Publisher, choose File ⇨ Exit. If you have not saved your document, Publisher prompts you to save it. The program window then closes.

Summary

In this chapter, you've had a quick start with using Publisher. You learned how to do the following:

✦ Start Publisher
✦ Create a letterhead
✦ Create a matching envelope
✦ Print and save the documents
✦ Exit Publisher

The next chapter explains many basics, such as various methods of starting Publisher and how to use the basic program features.

✦ ✦ ✦

Publisher Basics

This part introduces you to Publisher's tools and features. You learn how to operate the mouse, menus, and toolbars, as well as save and close a publication. You may need to use Publisher's online help feature from time to time; this part shows you how to find the information you need. You also learn about Publisher's wizards and designs, and how to use them to create a document quickly and efficiently. Additionally, this part discusses key design considerations that can give you ideas for changing publications to better suit your needs and desires. Finally, you learn to customize some of Publisher's features, such as start-up and editing options.

Getting Started with Publisher

Publisher is a desktop publishing program (a program for formatting text and graphics on the page) that's intuitive and easy to use. You can produce professional-looking newsletters, business cards, brochures, and business forms, for example, quickly and effortlessly by using Publisher's many templates and wizards. Additionally, you can add your own special touches — drawings, custom headlines, WordArt designs, and other elements — to any Publisher document to make it better suit your purposes.

This chapter covers the fundamentals of operating Publisher and creating and saving a publication. You'll also learn about the program window and some of the tools that Publisher provides for your use.

Starting Publisher

You start Publisher similarly to other Windows programs. You can use the Start menu, a desktop shortcut to the program, or Windows Explorer to open the program. No matter how you open the program, you need to know where the program files are located. Publisher may be located in the Microsoft Office folder, in a Publisher folder, or in another folder that you specified for the program files when you installed the program. You can find the program files by using the Windows Find File feature. Look for the Mspub.exe file. See the Appendix for information about using the Find File feature.

The following are the three methods for starting Publisher, each of which is described, in turn, in the sections that follow:

   ✦ Double-click the Publisher program icon in the Windows Explorer window.

✦ Choose Start ⇨ Programs ⇨ MS Office ⇨ Microsoft Publisher.

✦ Double-click the Publisher shortcut on the desktop.

Using Windows Explorer

You can open any program in Windows by activating the program's EXE (executable) file in Windows Explorer. (For more information about using Windows Explorer, see the Appendix.) After you locate the Mspub.exe filename in Explorer, you can activate the Publisher program by double-clicking this filename. You also can start the program by selecting the filename in Explorer and pressing Enter.

Figure 1-1 shows the Publisher program icon in Windows Explorer. The location of the file depends on your installation of the program.

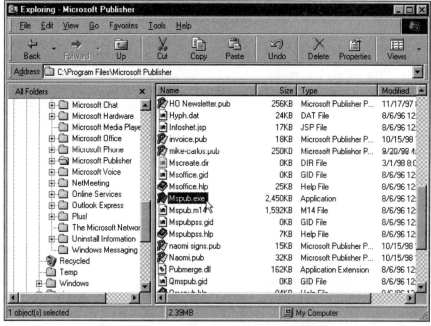

Figure 1-1: Open the Publisher program from Windows Explorer.

Using the Start menu

To use the Start menu, you must know the folder in which Publisher is installed. You can look in any of the folders in the Programs menu; for example, the file may be in either the Microsoft Office, MS Office, or Office folder. Click the Publisher entry on the menu to start the program.

Creating a shortcut

You can create a Publisher shortcut for the desktop so that you can quickly open Publisher without going through menus or the Explorer. You must first find the program files. In Windows Explorer, right-click the Publisher icon. A Windows quick menu appears, as shown in Figure 1-2.

Figure 1-2: Use the quick menu to create a shortcut to the program.

Click Create Shortcut. The shortcut appears in Explorer's window. You then can move the shortcut to the desktop by dragging it. To drag an item — such as a file, shortcut, folder, and such — you click the item and continue to hold down the mouse button while dragging the item to a new position onscreen. To open the program, double-click the shortcut.

Creating a New Publication

When Publisher opens, a dialog box called Microsoft Publication Catalog appears. The Catalog offers a variety of publication sizes, styles, and templates. *Templates* are files that contain basic formatting—such as page size and orientation, fonts, pictures, and so on—for a certain type of document. From the Publisher Catalog, you can start, for example, a new blank publication, newsletter, or letterhead. Figure 1-3 shows the Catalog dialog box with the Publication by Wizard tab selected, listing the various wizards that you can use as a foundation for your publication.

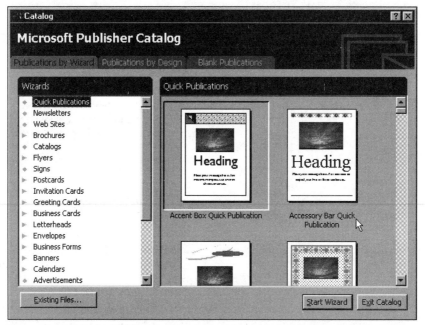

Figure 1-3: Use the Publication Catalog to choose a publication foundation.

The following lists the three tabs of the Publisher Catalog and provides brief descriptions of the options the Catalog offers under each tab (Chapter 3 describes these options in detail):

✦ **Publications by Wizard:** *Wizards* are guides that lead you, step by step, through creating a publication. The Letterheads wizard, for example, asks you to enter your name, address, phone number, and other information that commonly appears on a letterhead. It also lets you choose a design, decide whether to use a logo, and offers other options for creating an attractive and useful letterhead for your business or personal concerns. Other wizards include Newsletters, Brochures, Flyers, Envelopes, Labels, and so on.

✦ **Publications by Design:** Each design set includes several document templates that use the same or similar colors, images, lines, and other design elements. When you use a design set, you create a set of documents that are consistent, which enables you to present the same styles throughout your company documents. For example, you might create a business card, letterhead, brochure, and newsletter using a design set. All of these documents will then use the same colors, image placement, fonts, and other elements. All you do is enter the text.

✦ **Blank Publications:** Publisher offers a variety of preset blank publications. You can choose a blank page for use with a business card, an invitation, a Web page, or a letter. From these blank pages, you can build your own designs by adding elements and text.

Note   Publisher uses the term *publication* to describe any document that you create, whether it's a blank page, a letterhead, or a book. You can use the words *publication* and *document* interchangeably in Publisher.

You also can open Publisher and bypass the Catalog, if you want to work with a standard blank page or create your own publication with no help from the Publisher wizards or templates. To get started with Publisher and learn about its tools and program window, exit the Catalog by clicking the Exit Catalog button. A blank page appears in the program window.

Getting to Know the Program Window

The program window contains many tools that you can use to create, edit, and format Publisher documents. Many of the tools are the same as in any Windows program — such as the Close button, scroll bars, mouse arrows, and so on — and other tools are specific to the Publisher program.

Figure 1-4 illustrates the Publisher program window. You see this window every time that you open Publisher. The document that appears depends on whether you exit the Catalog or choose a wizard or template.

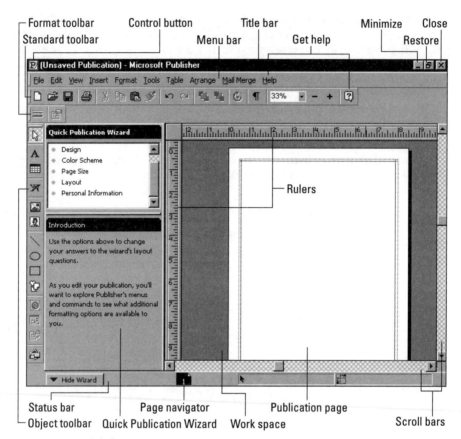

Figure 1-4: Elements in the Publisher program window

Depending on the work you're doing in Publisher, the program adds some tools or other elements. For example, when you create text in the publication, Publisher adds more buttons to the Formatting toolbar. These added tools and elements are examined as they surface throughout the book. For now, concentrate on familiarizing yourself with the common window elements.

Understanding How Publisher's Features Work

Each program window element has its own purpose and use. If you're familiar with other Windows applications, you'll easily understand these uses. This section covers the basic uses of the program window elements and any special processes within Publisher.

Mouse

The mouse is a tool for selecting text and objects, entering and inserting items into the window, moving items, and other manipulation of the publication and program components. The actions you perform with the mouse — clicking, double-clicking, dragging, and right-clicking — are the same as in other applications.

Additionally, the Publisher mouse pointer acts similarly to the mouse pointer in other Windows applications. The arrow enables you to select items, the I-beam means that you can enter text or values, and so on. Publisher presents other mouse pointers for resizing an object, moving an object, and other special procedures. The pointers specific to Publisher are described when appropriate elsewhere in the book.

Title bar

The Title bar contains the name of the program and the name of the publication after you save it. Until you save a file, (Unsaved Publication) appears in the Title bar. You'll also notice the following buttons in the Title bar (refer to Figure 1-4):

✦ **Control:** Controls the program window. Click this button to display a drop-down menu with the Restore, Move, Size, Minimize, Maximize, and Close commands.

✦ **Minimize:** Click to reduce the window to a button on the Taskbar (which appears by default at the bottom of your screen). Click the Program button on the Taskbar to restore the window to its previous size.

✦ **Restore/Maximize:** If the program window is at its maximum size, the Restore button is displayed; if the window is at a restored size, the Maximum button is displayed. Click the Maximum button to enlarge the window to fill the entire screen. Click the Restore button to display the program window at a smaller size and with window borders.

✦ **Close:** Click to close the program window.

Tip   You can click the mouse arrow in the title bar of a restored window and drag to move the window onscreen. You also can position the mouse arrow over a window border (restored window) and, when the mouse changes to a double-headed arrow, drag the border to resize the window (see Figure 1-5).

Window border   Double-headed arrow

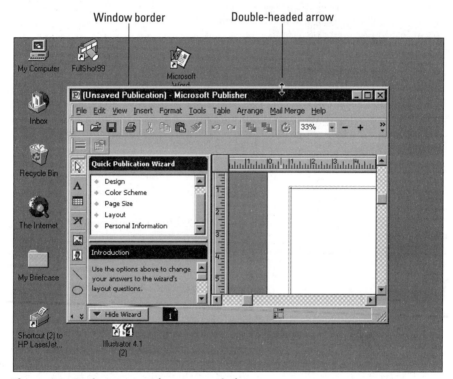

Figure 1-5: Resize a restored program window

Menu bar

The Menu bar contains menus and commands that you need to use to create and format a variety of publications in Publisher. To open a menu, either click the menu name or press the Alt key plus the underlined letter in the menu name. You can open the File menu, for example, by clicking File or by pressing Alt+F. Cancel a menu by clicking the mouse anywhere in the program window or by pressing the Esc key. Figure 1-6 shows the open File menu.

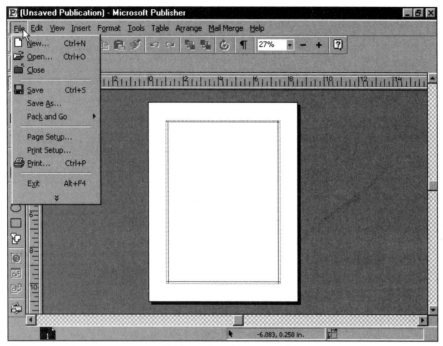

Figure 1-6: Open a menu to display related commands.

Menus

Each menu contains commands related to that menu. Table 1-1 lists the menus in Publisher, with a brief description of the commands contained in each menu, plus a reference to the chapter where you can learn more detailed information about each menu's commands.

Table 1-1
Publisher Menus and Commands

Menu	Commands	More Information
File	Contains commands that enable you to control, open, save, and close files. Commands include Open, New, Close, Save, Page Setup, Exit, and so on. The File menu also contains a list of the last four documents or publications that you opened. If you click one of these filenames, you can quickly open that file.	See Chapter 4, "Working with Files."

Continued

Table 1-1 *(continued)*

Menu	Commands	More Information
Edit	Contains commands that you can use to edit documents, such as Undo, Cut, Copy, Paste, Find, Replace, and so on.	See Chapter 14, "Revising and Correcting Text."
View	Contains commands that control what you see on the screen. Commands include Picture Display, Toolbars, Rulers, Zoom, and so on.	See Chapter 8, "Using Page Layout Tools."
Format	Contains commands that enable you to format text and objects, such as Line/Border, Shadow, Color Scheme, and Text Style.	See Chapter 16, "Formatting Characters."
Tools	Contains tools that enable you to check the publication or modify the program options, including the Spelling, Language, Design Checker, and Options commands.	See Chapter 14, "Revising and Correcting Text."
Table	Contains commands that enable you to format and edit tables. Commands include Insert Rows or Columns, Delete Rows or Columns, Merge Cells, and the like.	See Chapter 22, "Creating a Table."
Arrange	Contains commands that enable you to rearrange the position of objects and tools, such as Layout Guides, Ruler Guides, Rotate, or Flip.	See Chapter 20, "Drawing with Microsoft Draw."
Mail Merge	Contains commands that enable you to work with *mail merge*, a feature that enables you to create mailing labels for your publications, among other things. Commands include Open Data Source, Merge, Show Merge Results, and so on.	See Chapter 32, "Merging an Address List with a Publication."
Help	Contains commands that enable you to get help on the Publisher program and its features and tools.	See Chapter 2, "Performing Basic Tasks."

Commands

Commands, in general, have several common characteristics as well as some specific ones. For example, all commands contain an underlined letter. As with menus, you can use the underlined letter as a keyboard shortcut. To use the File ⇨ New command, for example, you press Alt+F to open the File menu and then press N to activate the New command.

Commands help you to perform or complete a task. The File ⇨ New command, for example, opens the Catalog so that you can choose the type of publication that you want to create. Some commands lead to a dialog box in which you can choose additional options related to that command. Other commands lead to a submenu, and yet others perform a task immediately. You can tell which action a command performs by the way it looks.

Figure 1-7 shows the View menu with the common characteristics and features of commands. The following list describes those characteristics:

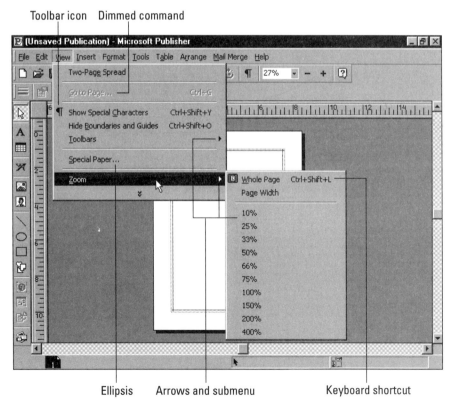

Figure 1-7: Most menus and commands have common characteristics.

✦ An icon to the left represents the picture that you see for that command on a toolbar. The File ➪ New and File ➪ Open commands each display an icon in the File menu, with a matching icon in the Standard toolbar.

✦ Many commands list a keyboard shortcut to the right of the command, such as Ctrl+N for the File ➪ New command. You must close the menu to use this keyboard shortcut. As you use a menu command, you can note whether a keyboard shortcut exists and then use it the next time, instead of clicking the menu.

✦ A command that is dimmed, or gray, indicates that the action or task cannot be performed at this time. For example, the Edit ➪ Cut and Edit ➪ Copy commands are dimmed when nothing has been selected to cut or copy. Similarly, Table commands are dimmed when you have not yet drawn or selected a table.

✦ An ellipsis following a command indicates that a dialog box containing more options will appear when you select that command.

✦ An arrow following a command indicates that a submenu will appear, offering more options related to the command, if you hover the mouse pointer over the command.

✦ A check mark appearing in front of a command indicates that the option is active. Clicking a command either displays (activates) or hides (deactivates) the check mark. You usually can check more than one option at a time on a menu.

Dialog boxes

When you choose a command that is followed by an ellipsis, a dialog box appears. The dialog box offers additional, related options from which to choose. After a dialog box appears, you must click either OK or Cancel before you can continue with your work.

Certain characteristics are common to all dialog boxes, and others appear in some boxes but not in others. Figure 1-8 illustrates the Options dialog box (Tools ➪ Options). This dialog box shows several of the common characteristics in a dialog box.

Tabs　　　　Title bar　　　　Help

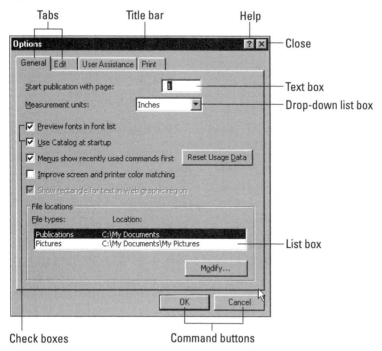

Figure 1-8: Dialog boxes offer options and choices
related to the command.

Following are the common characteristics in dialog boxes:

✦ **Title bar:** Lists the title of the dialog box.

✦ **Tabs:** Represent "pages" of options. Click a tab to display related options.

✦ **Help button:** Click to activate help, and then click the option about which you have a question. This displays a definition, comment, or procedure regarding that option.

✦ **Close button:** Click to cancel the dialog box.

✦ **Text box:** A box in which you can enter a value or text.

✦ **Drop-down list box:** Click the down arrow to display available choices. Choose one of the options.

✦ **List box:** Similar to a drop-down list box, but you can see more options at one time. Sometimes, a list box has a scroll bar beside it that enables you to view all the choices. (See the next section, "Scroll bars.")

✦ **Check boxes:** Click to check the box and activate the option. Click again to clear the box and turn off the option. You can check as many or as few options as you want. Check boxes are always square, and they contain a check mark if they are activated.

✦ **Option buttons:** (Not shown in Figure 1-8.) Click to select one of two or more options. Option buttons are round, and when you choose one option, a small black dot appears inside the option button. All other options are not active when you choose one. Option buttons are sometimes called *radio buttons* because they work the same way buttons for choosing preset radio stations worked on older car radios, in which only one button could be selected at a time.

✦ **Command buttons:** Click to continue. Click OK to accept the changes that you have made in the dialog box. Click Cancel to close the dialog box without making changes. Some dialog boxes contain other command buttons that perform other actions, such as display another dialog box (those that have an ellipsis after the command button name) or apply changes only in one tab.

Scroll bars

Each Windows program uses scroll bars to navigate the document window, and Publisher is no different. A horizontal scroll bar is located at the bottom of the work area; a vertical scroll bar is located to the right of the work area. Use these arrows to move around when the page is enlarged. Figure 1-9 shows horizontal and vertical scroll bars and their components.

Scroll box

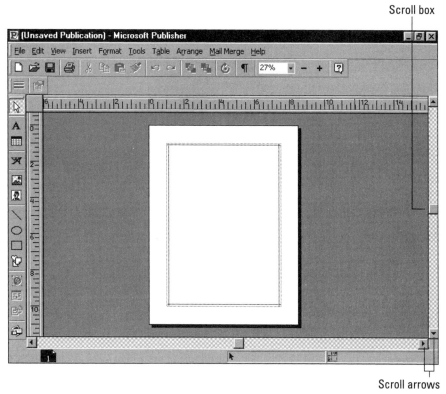

Scroll arrows

Figure 1-9: Scroll so that you can view everything on the page.

To navigate by using the scroll bars, follow these instructions:

✦ For horizontal scroll bars, click the left or right scroll arrow to move character by character to the left or right.

✦ For vertical scroll bars, click the up or down scroll arrow to move line by line up or down the page.

✦ Drag the scroll box to the left or right (horizontal scroll bar) or up or down (vertical scroll bar) to make larger jumps in the move. For example, drag the vertical scroll box to the top of the scroll bar to move to the top of the publication page.

✦ Click anywhere in the scroll bar to jump to that position on the page. This method isn't easy to control, but it will get you there quicker than using the arrow.

Note   You also can use the PgUp and PgDn keys or the directional keys on your keyboard to navigate around the publication page.

Toolbars

Publisher toolbars provide shortcuts to common tasks. For example, you can click the New tool on the Standard toolbar to display the Catalog, from which you can choose a format for a new publication. Most toolbar tools represent menu commands and are just a way of helping you work more efficiently.

The following are some additional things that you need to know about toolbars and tools:

✦ Some tools on any toolbar may be dimmed. As with commands, the tools are dimmed when not available at that time.

✦ To activate a tool, click the tool's button. A dialog box may appear or the command may be performed, just as with menu commands.

✦ To cancel a tool, press Esc.

✦ Use a toolbar's handle to move the toolbar or to display additional buttons.

✦ You can move toolbars around on the screen for your convenience.

Standard and Object toolbars

The Standard toolbar contains many of the same tools that other Windows programs contain. Figure 1-10 illustrates the Standard toolbar. Any time that you want to know the name of a tool on the toolbar, hold the mouse pointer over the tool, and a ToolTip appears with the name. (For more information, see Chapter 2, "Performing Basic Tasks.")

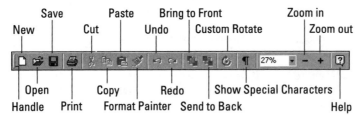

Figure 1-10: Standard tools provide shortcuts to tasks.

The Object toolbar, located by default on the left side of the screen, contains tools for creating objects, such as text boxes, tables, pictures, and drawings. Figure 1-11 shows the Object toolbar and its tool buttons. Don't worry if you're unfamiliar with the tool names, because each tool button is explained in more detail later in the text, when appropriate.

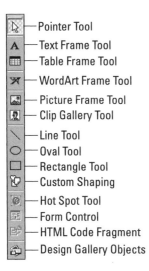

— Pointer Tool
— Text Frame Tool
— Table Frame Tool
— WordArt Frame Tool
— Picture Frame Tool
— Clip Gallery Tool
— Line Tool
— Oval Tool
— Rectangle Tool
— Custom Shaping
— Hot Spot Tool
— Form Control
— HTML Code Fragment
— Design Gallery Objects

Figure 1-11: Use toolbars to perform tasks and procedures quickly.

Moving toolbars

To move a toolbar, drag the toolbar handle. If you drag the handle to the left or right, the toolbar simply moves to the left or right. If one toolbar is layered on top of another, dragging the handle to the left or right displays the tools of the toolbar underneath.

If you drag the toolbar handle down and away from where the toolbar is located, or *docked,* the toolbar becomes a floating toolbar. Floating toolbars (see Figure 1-12) have title bars, and you can alter their shape. To return a floating toolbar to its original position, drag the title bar of the toolbar back to the original position and release the mouse.

Figure 1-12: Float a toolbar so that it's closer to or out of the way of your work.

Status bar

The status bar displays information that you may need as you work in Publisher: Object Position and Object Size. As your mouse pointer moves, the status bar displays the position of the mouse or object that you're moving. This Object Position describes the distance from the top and left edge of the page, in inches. When you draw an object, its size appears in the Object Size area of the status bar, again in inches.

The status bar also displays the Quick Publication Wizard button. When the Wizard is displayed, click the Hide Wizard button to hide it; when the Wizard is hidden, click the Show Wizard button to show it. Finally, a page navigator appears on the status bar. Each publication starts with at least one page. If multiple pages exist, or if you add additional pages, icons representing those pages also appear on the status bar. Figure 1-13 illustrates the items on the status bar.

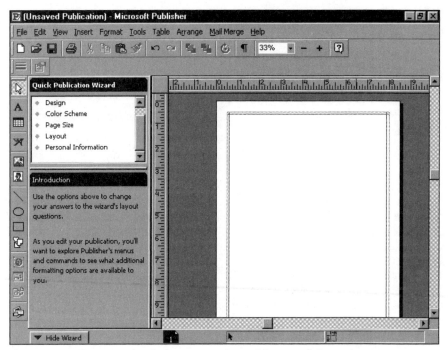

Figure 1-13: The status bar helps you to place objects and choose pages.

Note   The other items in the publication window—rulers, Change Pages box, Format toolbar, and Select Zoom mode—are each covered in detail in the following chapters.

Using the Quick Publication Wizard

One last screen element that Publisher includes by default when you open a blank publication is the Quick Publication Wizard. You also can choose the Quick Publication Wizard from the Catalog. Use the Wizard to add professional design, page layout, color schemes, and such to your blank document. For more information about the Wizard, see Chapter 3, "Understanding the Catalog."

To turn off the Quick Publication Wizard when you're not using it, click the Hide Wizard button, located on the status bar. To display it again at any time, click the Show Wizard button on the status bar.

Saving a Publication

You save a publication so that you can open it and modify or print it at a later date. When you save a publication, you give it a name. By default, Publisher places a saved file in the My Documents folder, although you can save the file in other folders or drives. For more information, see Chapter 4, "Working with Files."

You can use any descriptive name that you want to save your file, preferably something that's easily recognizable. Because Windows now enables the use of long filenames, you no longer need to limit a name to the 8.3 DOS naming convention (eight characters for the filename plus a three-character extension). For example, a file named Bender03.pub can now be named Bender letter-advertisement.pub. Publisher automatically adds the .pub extension when you save a file.

Publisher provides two Save commands: Save and Save As. Save As enables you to name the file and place it in a specific location. You might, for example, save a file a second time to place it on a floppy or zip disk. You might save a file under a different name and then make some revisions to it. You use the Save command when you've made changes to a file that you want to preserve. Saving a file by using the Save command doesn't change the file location or the name.

You can save a file in several different ways:

1. Choose File ➪ Save As. The Save As dialog box appears (see Figure 1-14).

Figure 1-14: The Save As dialog box

2. Enter a name in the Filename text box.

3. Click the Save button. The dialog box closes, and the name of the publication appears in the program's Title bar.

You also can save a file by doing either of the following:

✦ Click the Save button on the Standard toolbar.

✦ Press Ctrl+S.

Closing a Publication

You can have only one publication open at a time in Publisher. When you start a new publication, Publisher prompts you to close any publication that's already open. It also prompts you to save the open publication, if it has not already been saved.

To close a publication, choose File ➪ Close. Save the file if prompted to do so.

Exiting Publisher

Exit Publisher when you're finished working in the program. You can exit Publisher in several ways, as follows:

✦ Choose File ➪ Exit.

✦ Press Alt+F4.

✦ Click the Close (X) button.

✦ Click the program's Control button and then select Close.

Summary

In this chapter, you learned the basics of using Publisher, including the following:

✦ Starting and exiting Publisher.

✦ Creating a new publication and saving it.

✦ Using common features, such as toolbars and dialog boxes.

In the next chapter, you learn to perform basic tasks in Publisher, such as getting help. You also learn about rudimentary text editing and selection.

✦   ✦   ✦

Performing Basic Tasks

✦ ✦ ✦ ✦

In This Chapter

Getting help

Selecting text and objects

Learning editing basics

Using multiple pages

✦ ✦ ✦ ✦

As with other Windows programs, some tasks in Publisher are essential to creating a publication successfully. You'll need help from time to time with a term, procedure, or problem that you can't solve on your own. Publisher's online help can lend the assistance that you need, if you know how to use it. Other Publisher basics include selecting text and objects, copying and pasting, undoing actions, adding pages, and navigating through a publication.

Even if you're already familiar with performing these tasks in other programs, you'll want to check out this chapter so that you can see how Publisher treats these essential procedures.

Getting Help

Publisher offers online help consisting of tutorials, troubleshooters, definitions, and step-by-step procedures. You can use the Office Assistant for help, or you can search for specific topics by using the Index Help or Contents Help. Each type of help displays topics and terms in a different way. After you get used to the various help methods, you may choose one method as your favorite.

Contents Help displays help divided into major topics — such as Troubleshooting, Print Help, and so on. Index Help enables you to enter a keyword or keywords, and then displays topics related to the word that you entered. Like other Microsoft Office programs, Publisher provides an Office Assistant to help answer questions and view topics. You can even get additional help from the Office Update Web site.

Starting with the Office Assistant

Microsoft Office supplies an Office Assistant as the default Help tool. The user-friendly Assistant provides a place to type a question and then presents multiple subtopics from which you can choose. For example, if you type the word "help" in the Assistant's bubble, it offers a variety of Help topics, as shown in Figure 2-1. Note that the default Office Assistant is a paper clip and sheet of paper.

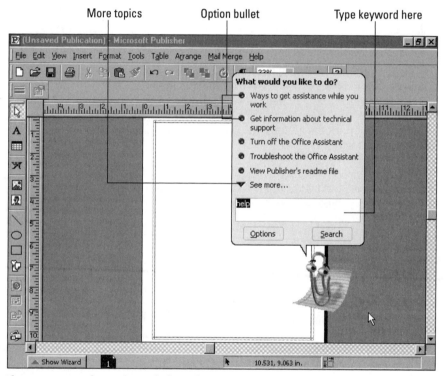

Figure 2-1: Let the Assistant help with your questions.

Using the Office Assistant

To display the Office Assistant, do any of the following:

✦ Press F1.

✦ Choose Help ⇨ Microsoft Publisher Help.

✦ Choose Help ⇨ Show the Office Assistant, and then click the Assistant.

To use the Assistant to get help, follow these steps:

1. Type a question or keyword in the Assistant's bubble and press Enter. The Assistant displays a variety of Help topics.

2. Click an option bullet. The Publisher Help window appears (see Figure 2-2). You may need to drag the Office Assistant out of the way so that you can read the Help window. Drag the Assistant to the program window.

Note

Publisher may prompt you to connect to the Internet; you can either connect to view Help topics online or cancel the connection dialog box to view Help topics locally.

Show Content and Index help
Options menu
Print to pic

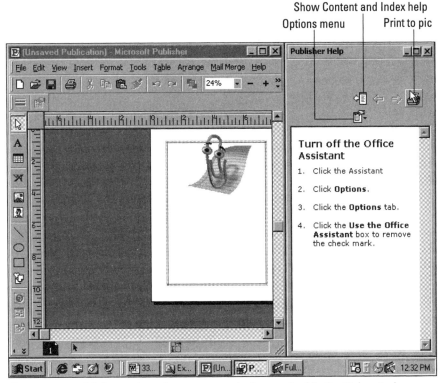

Figure 2-2: Publisher resizes the program window and adds the Help window.

Note

The Options menu, available in the Publisher Help dialog box, contains commands for Internet options, printing, hiding tabs, and so on.

3. Scroll the window to read about the topic.

4. Optionally, click the Print button to print the topic.

5. If you want more information on the topic, click the Office Assistant to display the Help bubble. Choose a topic or enter a new topic in the bubble. To view Help options about another topic, enter the topic and click Search.

6. To close Help, click the Close (X) button.

The Assistant remains onscreen as you work. You can hide the Assistant by right-clicking it and then choosing Hide.

Choosing another Office Assistant character

If you don't like the animated Office Assistant character, you can change it to another character. Office offers a variety of characters to represent the Office Assistant, including a dog, a cat, and Einstein. To change the Office Assistant character, follow these steps:

1. Right-click the Assistant. From the quick menu, select Choose Assistant. The Office Assistant dialog box appears with the Gallery tab showing, as shown in Figure 2-3.

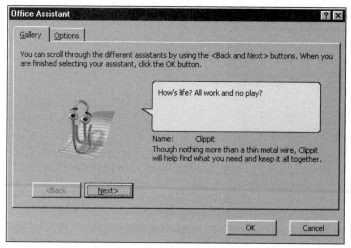

Figure 2-3: Use any of a variety of Office Assistant characters to help in your work.

2. Click the Next button. The second character choice for Office Assistant appears.

3. Continue to click Next until you find an Assistant character that you like. You can click the Back button to see previous Assistants.

4. When you find the character that you want, click OK.

Note Depending on your installation of Office and Publisher, a message may appear, telling you that the Assistant character isn't installed. You can install it by clicking Yes. You may need to insert your Office CD-ROM. Follow the directions onscreen.

Setting Office Assistant options

You can set various options for the Office Assistant, such as the sounds that the Assistant makes and the help that it displays. You can even turn off the Assistant, if you want, and use Contents and Index Help, as explained in the next section.

To set Office Assistant options, follow these steps:

1. Right-click the Assistant. Choose Options from the quick menu. The Office Assistant dialog box appears with the Options tab showing, as illustrated in Figure 2-4.

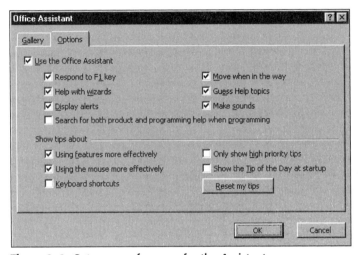

Figure 2-4: Set your preferences for the Assistant.

2. In the Options tab, choose the options that you want to activate by placing a check mark in the box. Clear the check box to turn off that option.

3. The lower section of the Options tab — Show tips about — enables you to choose options about the Publisher Tip of the Day. If selected, this option displays a tip — each time that you start the program — about working more efficiently within Publisher.

4. When you're finished, click OK.

Using Contents Help

Publisher offers other help besides the Office Assistant. You can view the contents of the Publisher Help program and choose from those topics. The Contents tab of Publisher Help lists major topics, under which are more-detailed, related topics. For example, if you choose the Print Publications topic, several additional topics appear, such as Text, Pictures, Tables, and so on. Choose a topic under the Text heading, and additional topics appear, such as Add or replace text, and Arrange text.

Figure 2-5 illustrates this set of contents under the Contents tab. Note the icons to the left of the Help topics. A book indicates a major topic, and a document page represents a specific Help topic.

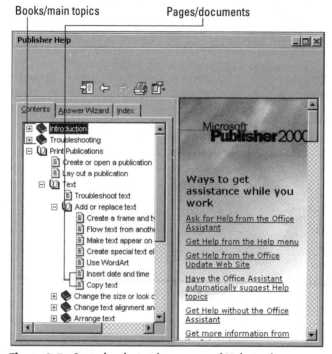

Figure 2-5: Open books to view pages of Help topics.

When you choose a document in the left window, the help appears in the right window. You can scroll the help as you read it, you can print it, or you can click any links to view related topics. Publisher represents links by underlining them and using a different color of text, as shown in Figure 2-6. Note that when you point the mouse at a link, a pointing hand appears, indicating that you've found a link.

To use Contents Help, follow these steps:

1. Press F1 or choose Help ➪ Microsoft Publisher Help.

   If the Assistant appears, choose a bulleted topic. The Publisher Help window appears. Click the Show button.

If you turned off the Assistant, the Publisher Help dialog box appears with the entire dialog box showing.

2. Choose the Contents tab.

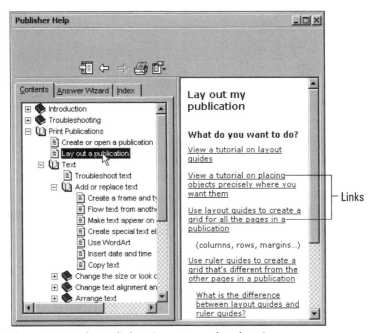

Figure 2-6: Select a link to jump to a related topic.

3. Choose the book representing the topic that you want to view, and then do one of the following:

- Double-click the book.
- Click the plus (+) sign next to the topic.

4. From the list, choose either another book topic or the Help document that you want to view.

5. When you're finished with the Help window, click the Close button.

Note   The Answer Wizard tab of the Publisher Help dialog box is similar to the Office Assistant. You enter a question or keyword, and the Answer Wizard displays various related topics from which you can choose.

Using Index Help

The Index tab in the Publisher Help window enables you to find every occurrence of a keyword. For example, if you type "help," every occurrence of that word appears in the Index tab, as shown in Figure 2-7.

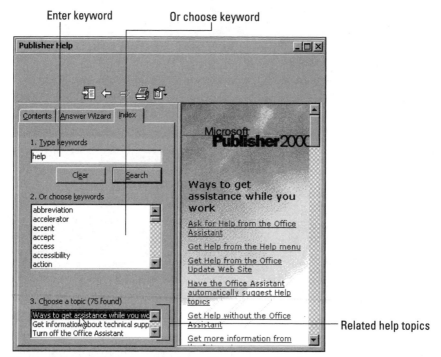

Figure 2-7: Use the Index to find specific terms and topics.

To use Index Help, follow these steps:

1. Press F1 or choose Help ➪ Microsoft Publisher Help.

   If the Assistant appears, choose a bulleted topic. The Publisher Help window appears. Click the Show button.

   If you turned off the Assistant, the Publisher Help dialog box appears with the entire dialog box showing.

2. Choose the Index tab.

3. Enter a keyword in the Type keywords text box. Click the Search button.

4. Alternatively, double-click a word in the Or choose keywords list.

5. Choose the topic from the Choose a topic list.

6. When you're finished, click the Close button.

Getting help with ScreenTips and TipPages

ScreenTips and TipPages are two forms of help that Publisher provides. ScreenTips help you to identify toolbar buttons and other objects onscreen. TipPages are helpful hints that Publisher displays as you work, such as "If the text you are typing is too small to read, press the F9 key to zoom in."

Figure 2-8 shows the ScreenTip for the Print button. Holding the mouse over any tool button displays a yellow label describing the tool. ScreenTips don't stay onscreen forever. They disappear after a few seconds, as do TipPages.

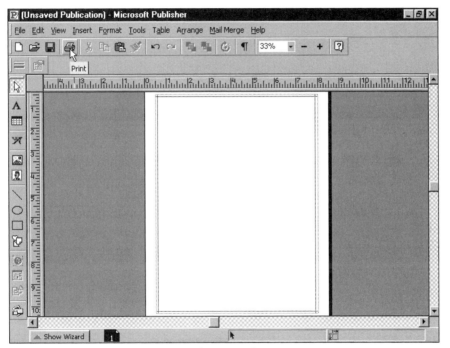

Figure 2-8: ScreenTips help you to identify tools.

One other type of help that Publisher offers is via the question mark in the Title bar of any dialog box. Clicking the question mark icon enables you to get help regarding any items in that dialog box. Click the question mark button and then point to the item about which you have a question. A box appears with an explanation of the item, as shown in Figure 2-9.

To remove the explanation box, click anywhere else in the dialog box.

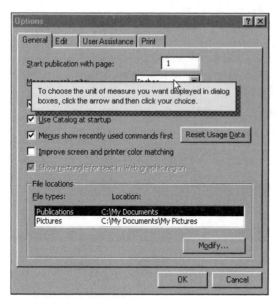

Figure 2-9: Get quick help in a dialog box by clicking the question mark icon.

Trying the troubleshooters

Publisher's Help offers several different troubleshooters — most dealing with Web preview and printing. The Print Troubleshooter also contains help with document design and layout. The troubleshooters pose several problem scenarios, from which you can choose the scenario that best describes the trouble that you are experiencing. After you choose a scenario, the troubleshooter offers various explanations and solutions.

For example, you might choose "I cannot print my publication" as your print problem. Publisher then poses two more selections: "I cannot print a specific publication" and "I cannot print any publication." Each of these options guides you to a different solution. The troubleshooter helps you to figure out just what the problem is.

To use a troubleshooter (for example, the Print Troubleshooter), follow these steps:

1. Choose Help ➪ Print Troubleshooter.

   Alternatively, you can press F1 or choose Help ➪ Microsoft Publisher Help. In the Assistant bubble or the Answer Wizard text box, type **troubleshooter** and then click Search. A list of available troubleshooters appears, as shown in Figure 2-10.

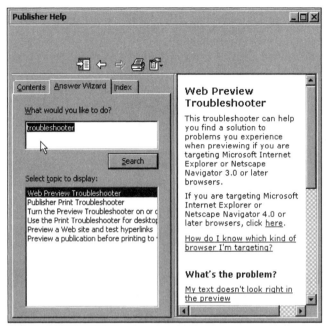

Figure 2-10: Choose a troubleshooter to help solve your problem.

2. Choose the troubleshooter in the Publisher Help window then and view the help in the right window.

3. Click the Close button when you're finished.

Selecting Text and Objects

Selecting text and objects in Publisher is similar to selecting these items in other Windows programs. You select an item so that you can edit, delete, move, or format it. Usually, you select items by using the mouse, but you can also select some items, such as text, with the keyboard.

You might select text, such as the headline in a newsletter, to enlarge the text and change the font or color. You might select an object — such as a table, drawing, or logo — to move it, change its color, or edit it. Text and objects in Publisher are contained in frames. A *frame* is a box that you can also select, move, edit, and format. Each type of object or text is contained in its own frame. For more information about frames, see Chapter 10.

Selecting an object

Selecting an object is different from selecting text, but after you select either, you can format, edit, and manipulate the item. When you select an object, eight small black boxes, called *handles,* appear around the edges and corners, to indicate that the object is selected, as shown in Figure 2-11. You can also use these handles to resize the object; for example, Figure 2-11 shows a text frame being resized. When you select an object, you can make changes to that object's characteristics.

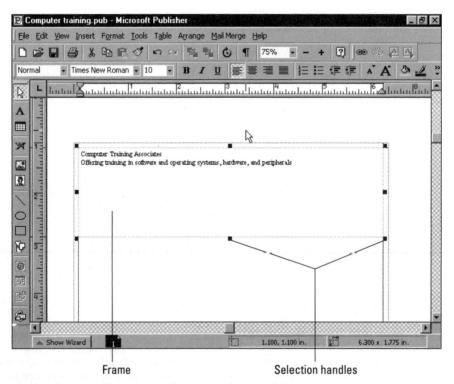

Figure 2-11: Handles appear when you select an object.

Select an object by clicking the object with the mouse.

Selecting text

When you select text, the text appears highlighted (in *reverse video,* such as white text on a black background) to indicate the selection, as shown in Figure 2-12. You format only the selected text by changing alignment, font, size, spacing, and so on. For more information about formatting text, see Chapter 15.

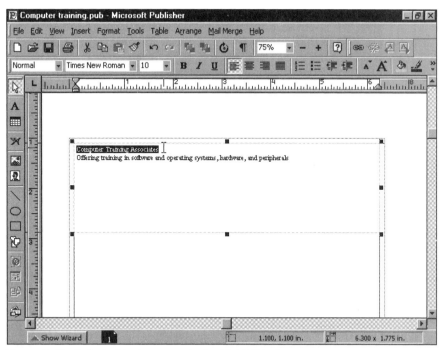

Figure 2-12: Selected text appears to be highlighted.

Select text by doing one of the following:

✦ Click and drag the mouse I-beam across the text that you want to select.

✦ Click the mouse at the beginning of the text that you want to select, press and hold down the Shift key, and then click the mouse at the end of the text that you want to select.

✦ Click the mouse at the beginning of the text that you want to select, press and hold the Shift key, and then press either the PgDn key, the down arrow, or the right arrow until the text is selected.

✦ Click the mouse at the beginning of the text that you want to select, and then press and hold down Shift+Ctrl while pressing either the right-arrow key, to select a word at a time, or the down-arrow key, to select a paragraph at a time.

✦ Double-click one word to select it. Triple-click a paragraph to select it.

Selecting multiple items

You can select one item or multiple items in Publisher. When you select multiple items, you can delete, move, or format those items at the same time. For example, select all the text in a frame to change alignment or text size. Select all objects in a drawing to change their color or size.

When you select text in Publisher, you can select text to format only within one frame at a time. You select text by clicking and dragging the mouse I-beam over all text in the frame.

To select multiple objects in a publication, do one of the following:

✦ Click the first object, press and hold down the Shift key, and then click the second and any other items you want to select.

✦ Choose Edit ⇨ Select All to select all objects on the page.

Figure 2-13 shows three objects selected in a publication. Note that handles appear around each of the two text frames — the company name frame and the address frame — and around the picture frame.

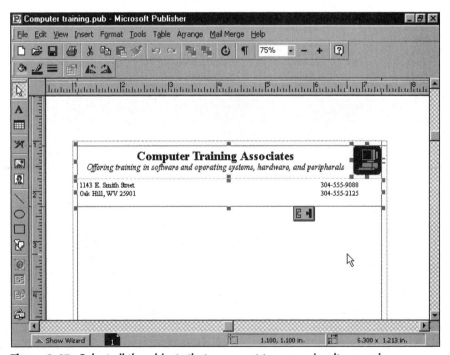

Figure 2-13: Select all the objects that you want to move simultaneously.

Deselecting

You also can *deselect* an object or text. And you can deselect one object of several selected ones. To deselect selected object(s), do one of the following:

✦ To deselect text, simply click the mouse anywhere on the page or within the frame.

✦ To deselect one selected object, click the mouse anywhere on the *blank* page. If you click within another object, that object becomes selected.

✦ To deselect one or more objects from several selected objects, press and hold down the Shift key, and then click the object that you want to deselect.

Moving selected objects

After you select one or more objects — including text frames — you can move them around on the page or to another page in the publication. You may want to move two text frames closer together, for example, or select several frames and move them to another position on the page. When moving items to another page, you use the cut-and-paste technique. See the next section for more information.

To move an item, select it and then position the mouse over the object until you see the MOVE mouse pointer (a moving van), as shown in Figure 2-14. Drag the icon and the objects to the new location.

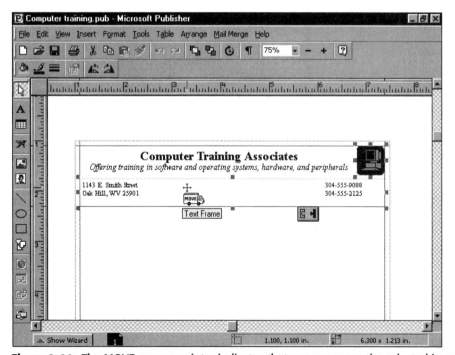

Figure 2-14: The MOVE mouse pointer indicates that you can move the selected items.

Learning Editing Basics

Several editing techniques are the same for Publisher and other Windows applications, including the following actions:

✦ **Copy and paste:** A handy technique for duplicating text or an object on one page and placing the copy on another page, another publication, or even within another program.

✦ **Cut and paste:** Similar to copy and paste, but you use it to *move* text or an object to another location.

✦ **Undo:** Enables you to reverse the most recent action. In Publisher, you can undo actions such as moving an object, deleting text, formatting text and objects, and so on. You cannot undo some tasks; the Undo command or tool is dimmed for tasks that you cannot undo. Unfortunately, no way exists to know whether an action is "undoable" until after you do it. You can undo the last 20 changes to your publication.

✦ **Redo:** Enables you to recover the last 20 tasks that you used the Undo command to undo.

You can use a menu, toolbar tool, or keyboard shortcuts to perform any of these tasks. You can use Undo/Redo by choosing Edit ➪ Undo or Edit ➪ Redo. Alternatively, you can click the Undo or Redo toolbar button. Finally, you can press Ctrl+Z to Undo or Ctrl+Y to Redo the most current action.

One other important component to editing basics are the *defaults,* the settings that Publisher uses for fonts, page sizes and orientation, line and shape sizes and colors, printer configuration, toolbar button sizes, and many, many other settings throughout the program. You can change most defaults to better suit your working style, and Publisher enables you to change back to its normal defaults in most cases, as well.

Copy, cut, and paste

When you cut or copy an object or text, you can paste that item to another location, either within the current publication, in another publication, or in another Windows program. You can copy or cut text, table text, tables, drawings, clip art, pictures, sound clips, lines, borders, and many other objects in Publisher.

In most cases, you can select the text or object to be copied or cut (moved), choose the appropriate command, choose an insertion point, and then choose the Paste command to accomplish the copy or cut process. In some cases, copying and cutting can be a bit more complex.

To cut or copy text or an object, select the item and then do one of the following:

✦ Choose Edit ➪ Cut or Copy.

✦ Click the Cut or Copy tool on the Standard toolbar.

✦ Press Ctrl+X to cut or Ctrl+C to copy.

To paste text or an object, move to the new page, publication, or program, locate the insertion point, and then do one of the following:

✦ Choose Edit ➪ Paste.

✦ Click the Paste tool on the Standard toolbar.

✦ Press Ctrl+V.

You can also use drag-and-drop text editing to move or copy an item. To move text, for example, select the text and then drag it to another location onscreen. To copy text, select it, press and hold down the Ctrl key, and then drag the text to another location onscreen.

The following are some techniques for copying or moving special items:

✦ To copy an entire Publisher publication, save the publication under a different name by using File ➪ Save As.

✦ To copy an entire Publisher page, choose Insert ➪ Page. In the Options section, choose Duplicate all objects on page. Enter the page number of the page that you want to copy. Choose where to add the pages, and then click OK.

✦ To copy text formatting, use the Format Painter. For more information, see Chapter 16.

Note   Copying, cutting, and pasting are also covered in other chapters in this book, when the procedures are different from the basic editing presented here.

Undo and Redo

You can undo most changes that you make simply by using the Undo command in Publisher. Additionally, you can undo up to 20 changes, one at a time. These changes include text formatting, object rotation, resizing and scaling, deleting objects and text, and others. Also, you can Redo any recent Undo action. You may only Redo the subject of the Undo command.

The Undo and Redo commands on the Edit menu display the action within the command — for example, Undo Create Object or Undo Delete Text.

To Undo an action, do one of the following:

✦ Choose Edit ➪ Undo.

✦ Press Ctrl+Z.

✦ Click the Undo button on the Standard toolbar.

To Redo an action, do one of the following after using the Undo command:

✦ Choose Edit ➪ Redo.

✦ Press Ctrl+Y.

✦ Click the Redo button on the Standard toolbar.

Defaults

Publisher contains many defaults — for text, object formatting, printing configurations, and so on — that you can use. You also can change many of the defaults to better suit your working methods. After you set defaults, you can usually change back to Publisher's defaults when necessary.

The following are a few examples of default settings that you can change. To find other defaults, look in the dialog box when making changes. Often, you'll see a command button that says Restore Defaults or Set Defaults.

✦ In the Tabs dialog box, you can change the default tab stops from half an inch to any setting that you prefer.

✦ In the Print Properties dialog box, you can make changes and restore the defaults for paper, fonts, graphics, or device options for a specific printer at any time by clicking the Restore Defaults button.

Using Multiple Pages

Most publications contain more than one page. Some of the Publisher wizards, for example, start with two or four pages or more. Most newsletters are two or four pages, brochures often are two pages (front and back), and catalogs, business forms, and calendars may also contain multiple pages.

You can easily add pages to and delete pages from a publication. When you have multiple pages, you need to move from page to page to enter text and format the document.

Adding and copying pages

You can add any number of pages in Publisher. You can also choose where to place the pages — before or after the current page. Publisher also offers options for inserting pages, as shown in Figure 2-15. Within these options is a choice for copying an entire page. Note that you choose the number of pages to insert and their placement. You then choose one of the following options:

✦ **Insert blank pages:** Pages contain only the design elements from the template or background designs; no text, frames, or objects.

✦ **Create one text frame on each page:** Each page has one text frame to give you a head start on entering text.

✦ **Duplicate all objects on page:** Choose the page that you want to duplicate (copy), and Publisher inserts all objects — such as a logo, clip art, headline, and so on — onto the new pages.

Figure 2-15: Insert pages and choose options for content.

To insert pages in a publication, follow these steps:

1. Choose Insert ➪ Page or press Ctrl+Shift+N. The Insert Page dialog box appears.

2. In the Number of new pages text box, enter a value.

3. Choose either Before current page or After current page.

4. Choose one of the options in the Options section of the dialog box. If you choose Duplicate all objects on page, then enter the page number of the page to be duplicated.

5. Click OK.

After you insert pages, page icons appear in the status bar, as shown in Figure 2-16.

Figure 2-16: Icons represent pages in the publication.

Deleting a page

You can delete any page in your publication. When you delete a page, all objects and text on that page are deleted as well, unless your text is located in connecting frames. If the page contains a frame as part of a chain of frames, the text in that frame moves to connected frames on other pages. See Chapter 10 for more information.

To delete a page, choose Edit ⇨ Delete Page.

If you want to keep some of the objects or text on a page, but you want to delete the page, you can select the items and move them to the work area (the gray area around the page) until you need them later.

Moving from page to page

The page navigation feature, located in the status bar, enables you to move from page to page by clicking page icons. If you have more pages than the page navigation feature can show, Publisher supplies forward and backward scroll arrows that you can use to view the rest of the pages, as shown in Figure 2-17.

Scroll arrows

Figure 2-17: Scroll to find your page.

To use the page navigator, do one of the following:

✦ Click the page that you want to view. To use the scroll arrows, click the arrow once, or hold down the arrow to move quickly from beginning to end.

✦ Press Shift+F5 to move to the beginning of the pages; press Ctrl+F5 to move to the end of the pages.

✦ Press Ctrl+G to display the Go To Page dialog box. Enter the number of the page and then click OK.

Tip

Using the PgUp and PgDn keys moves the view up and down the page, but not from one page to the next.

Summary

In this chapter, you've learned some basic tasks and features of Publisher that you can use as you create your publications. Following are some of the procedures that you've learned:

✦ Getting help by using the Office Assistant, Contents Help, and Index Help

✦ Selecting text and objects

✦ Basic editing with the Copy, Cut, and Paste tools

✦ Adding, copying, and deleting pages and moving from page to page

In the next chapter, you learn about Publisher's wizards and templates. The Catalog supplies step-by-step guidance for creating publications or simply a publication foundation, depending on your needs and choices.

✦   ✦   ✦

Understanding the Catalog

When you first open Publisher, the Microsoft Publisher Catalog dialog box appears, containing several options for creating publications. You can base your publication on a template for a newsletter, Web site, brochure, or other common document. You also can choose from design sets that base several documents on a similar design, so that your publications present a consistent and professional look. Or, you can choose any of several blank templates as a foundation for your publication, and create the layout and design yourself.

This chapter covers each of these options in detail, presenting clear explanations of each option, instructions for using the Catalog, and examples created by using various options as a base.

Learning About the Catalog

The Catalog is a dialog box that opens when you start Publisher. The Catalog provides various publication wizards and designs on which you can base your new publication. Additionally, you can open an existing file from the Catalog.

The Catalog presents three tabs containing options:

+ **Publications by Wizard:** Wizards are step-by-step guides to building a specific publication type, such as a business form or catalog. Within each publication type, Publisher offers various designs and layouts from which you can choose. As the wizard runs, it asks questions and then bases your document on those answers.

+ **Publications by Design:** Offers several design sets — including color schemes, page layout, graphic designs, and so on—on which you can build a set of documents. Most businesses use many different types of documents, such as a brochure, business cards, and a newsletter. Design sets enable you to match the designs and layout of your business documents.

✦ **Blank Publications:** Offers various sizes of blank pages. Some sizes are appropriate for a Web page, whereas others are appropriate for programs or invitations. You can also create your own custom size.

The Catalog opens when you start Publisher. You can also open the Catalog at any time by doing either of the following:

✦ Choose File ➪ New

✦ Press Ctrl+N

Figure 3-1 illustrates the Catalog, which has three tabs from which to choose a publication base. Alternatively, you can click the Existing Files button to open an existing file. For more information, see Chapter 4.

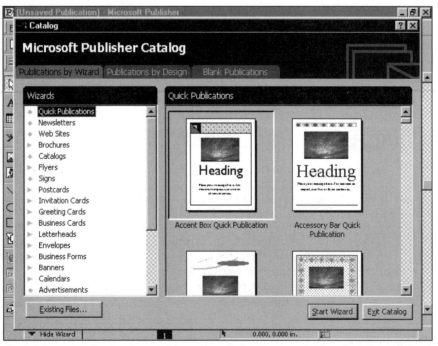

Figure 3-1: Use the Catalog to choose a style, layout, or template for your publication.

You can close the Catalog without choosing an option by clicking the Exit Catalog button. You can also close the Catalog so that it doesn't open when you start Publisher. If you close the Catalog, Publisher starts with a new blank publication instead. To close the Catalog so that it doesn't appear when you start Publisher, follow these steps:

1. Choose Tools ⇨ Options.

2. Choose the General tab.

3. Remove the check mark in the Use Catalog at startup check box.

4. Click OK.

Working with the Quick Publication Wizard

When you first open Publisher, the Catalog appears by default. The first tab — Publications by Wizard — includes as its first wizard Quick Publications. Additionally, when you exit or cancel the Catalog, the Quick Publication Wizard automatically appears in the Publisher program window. Figure 3-2 shows the Quick Publication Wizard with Design and Blends selected in the wizard window. Note the result of the design choice in the publication window.

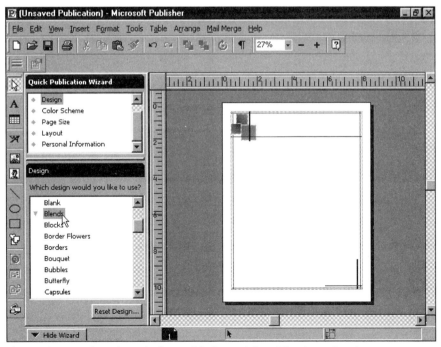

Figure 3-2: Apply various designs with the Quick Publication Wizard.

Using the Quick Publication Wizard, you can apply various design elements to the page as a base for your new publication. The following list provides an explanation of each design element available in the Quick Publication Wizard. You can use any one of the elements or a combination of several; for example, use one of the designs as the default, but use a different color scheme than Publisher displays.

✦ **Design:** Presents multiple graphics, such as borders, lines and shapes, backgrounds, arrows, art, and so on, in various colors and color schemes. Figure 3-2 shows the Blends design.

✦ **Color Scheme:** The design that you choose appears in a default color scheme (set of matching colors). You can apply a different color scheme to any design. Figure 3-3 illustrates the Color Scheme window in the Quick Publication Wizard.

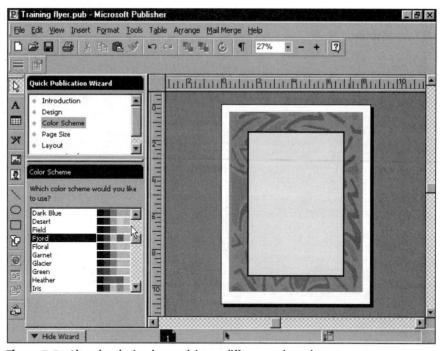

Figure 3-3: Alter the design by applying a different color scheme.

✦ **Page Size:** You can change the size and orientation of the paper so that it works with the type of document that you want to create. For example, you might want a brochure to be *landscape* (long) orientation rather than *portrait* (tall) orientation. For more information about page size and orientation, see Chapter 7. Figure 3-4 illustrates the selected page in landscape orientation.

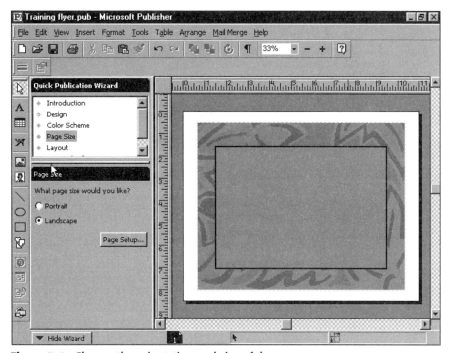

Figure 3-4: Change the orientation and size of the page.

✦ **Layout:** Enables you to add nearly any combination of picture and text that you want. Add, for example, a picture, heading, and a smaller heading or text. Or, add only the heading and text, as shown in Figure 3-5. After choosing the layout, you can enter your own text and pictures.

✦ **Personal Information:** Finally, you can enter any personal information, such as your company's name and address, e-mail addresses, phone numbers, fax numbers, and other information. Personal Information is perfect to use when you create publications for yourself or your company. It saves you from repeatedly typing the same information. For more about using the Personal Information feature, see Chapter 13.

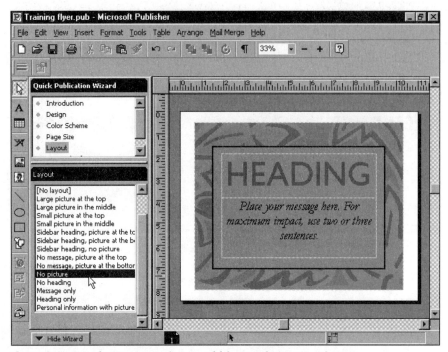

Figure 3-5: Use the Layout option to add frames for text or pictures.

Figure 3-6 shows the same page as previous figures, but with a new design, color scheme, page size, and layout applied. You can easily completely change the look of your document in a matter of seconds.

As you enter text into the Quick Publication Wizard's document, the text automatically resizes to fit the page and layout. Also, you can double-click any picture frame to view the Clip Art Gallery and insert a different picture than the default.

You might want to use the Quick Publication Wizard after you're more familiar with formatting text and adding objects. For more information, see Part III, "Working with Text," and Part IV, "Adding Graphics, Objects, and Images."

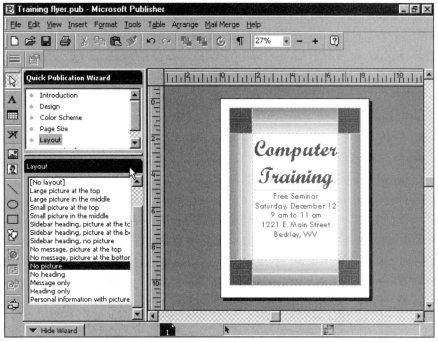

Figure 3-6: Apply various designs and schemes to see which fits your message.

You can display the Quick Publication Wizard that appears with a new publication by following these steps:

1. Click the Show Wizard button on the status bar. The Show Wizard button changes to the Hide Wizard button.

2. Choose the Design, Color Scheme, Page Size, Layout, and Personal Information, as you desire.

3. Hide the wizard window when you're finished.

You can also display the Quick Publication Wizard from the Catalog. This wizard presents the same options in a different manner. Follow these steps:

1. Choose File ➪ New to display the Catalog.

2. Choose the Publications by Wizard tab and then choose Quick Publications.

3. Click the Start Wizard button.

Note The first time you use the Quick Publication Wizard, it asks you to fill in your Personal Information. You can enter your name, address, and other information if you want, or you can choose Cancel and fill it in later.

4. The introduction to the Quick Publication Wizard appears in the wizard window, as shown in Figure 3-7. Follow the steps indicated by the Wizard and then click the Next button to continue choosing the color scheme, page size, and layout.

Figure 3-7: Let the Wizard step you through the process of creating a publication.

5. When the Wizard finishes, you can choose Design and other options from the Quick Publication Wizard dialog box.

Using a Publication Wizard

Publisher provides publication wizards that help you to create the type of document that you want, such as a newsletter, Web site, brochure, or catalog. A wizard guides you, step by step, through setting up the document; for example, a wizard might ask how many pages you want, or the name and address of your company. A wizard displays various styles of a document and asks you to choose the style that best suits your purpose.

The following lists and describes the various Publisher wizards:

✦ **Newsletters:** Wizards that present layout designs for single- and multiple-page newsletters that include a masthead (or newsletter name), headers and footers, columns, and graphics. Publisher presents more than 30 different designs for newsletter publications. For more information, see Chapter 28.

✦ **Web Sites:** More than 40 wizards presenting design and layout options for a Web page, complete with graphics and text. You can easily add navigation buttons and hyperlinks to the pages to make your site more intuitive to the viewer. For more information, see Part VIII, "Designing for the Web."

✦ **Brochures:** More than 70 brochure designs give you a wide choice of foundations for a brochure publication. You can choose from informational, price list, event, or fund-raiser brochures, with layouts and graphics to suit each purpose. For more information, see Chapter 28.

Tip   In the list of wizards, some categories are preceded by a diamond and others are preceded by an arrow. An arrow signifies additional groups of related wizards. For example, under Brochures, you can choose from Informational, Price List, Event, and so on.

✦ **Catalogs:** Wizards that present a design and layout suitable for a large document. Twenty different designs present graphics and text areas for each page. You see only the title page of the catalog in the wizard window.

✦ **Flyers:** More than 80 flyer designs with various layouts to represent such things as Informational, Special Offer, Sale, and Event flyers. Sell your house or dog, or advertise a play or music lessons. For more information, see Chapter 25.

✦ **Signs:** Wizards that present various signs, such as Beware of Dog and Out of Order. You can use the sign as is or add to it to make it more suitable for your purposes.

✦ **Postcards:** More than 100 post card designs and topics from which you can create such things as holiday greetings, sale announcements, reminder cards, and thank you notes. Use special paper to create several postcards on a page; special papers make cards easy to print and easy to tear out. For more information about special papers, see Chapter 11.

✦ **Invitation and Greeting Cards:** A variety of card wizards that can help you to create party invitations and greeting cards. Choose from more than 60 invitation designs and topics, including birthday parties, housewarmings, and other events. Choose from more than 80 designs for greeting cards, such as thank you cards, reminders, get well cards, and such.

✦ **Business Cards:** Designs are based on various arrangements of a company name, personal name, address, phone numbers, and other contact information. Print cards on special paper that you can easily tear cards from or take the final print to a commercial print shop for printing.

✦ **Letterheads and Envelopes:** Choose from designs so that your letterheads and envelopes match. The wizards help you to format and arrange the text on the page to create an attractive and professional-looking letterhead. For more information, see Chapter 25.

✦ **Business Forms:** Wizards that make it easy to create expense reports, fax cover sheets, invoices, and other forms that you use in business every day. You should be able to find the exact form you need; Publisher presents ten types of forms in more than 150 different designs. For more information about business forms, see Chapter 28.

✦ **Banners:** Wizards that enable you to create large documents for various events, including sales, congratulations, welcome, birthdays, and so on. After printing a banner, you have to piece it together. For more information, see Chapter 26.

✦ **Calendars:** Wizards to create either full-page calendars or wallet-sized calendars that you can use for personal or business purposes or give out to customers. Various designs use borders, pictures, and different layouts. For more information, see Chapter 26.

✦ **Advertisements:** Wizards that produce ads you can use in magazines, newspapers, or newsletters. Eye-catching headlines and clip art make the ad stand out.

✦ **Award and Gift Certificates:** Use Award wizards with or without special paper to present a certificate for best of show, special achievement, sports activities, and so on. Gift certificates include interesting designs and areas to fill in necessary information.

✦ **Labels:** Mailing, Shipping, Cassette, Video, and other Label wizards provide an easy layout for most Avery brand labels. For more information, see Chapter 26.

✦ **With Compliments Cards:** Various designs enable you to make up the With Compliments card to suit your business.

✦ **Menus:** Designs include regular menus, takeout menus, and wine/dessert menus. Print your own, or take the layout and design to a commercial print shop for professional printing.

✦ **Programs:** Layouts include graphics and text areas for a play, music program, or religious service program.

✦ **Airplanes and Origami:** These fun wizards enable you to produce paper airplane models and origami instructions for paper folding.

When working with a wizard, you'll notice that even within one type of publication, options and questions may change. Each question that a wizard asks may contain several solutions, each depending on the way you answer the preceding question or the design of the publication.

Just as wizards help you to develop entire publications, Publisher provides wizards, called *smart objects,* to help you add elements to a publication. These smart objects include logos, coupons, ads, and a calendar. For more information about using these publication elements, see Chapter 24.

Starting a wizard

You use a wizard by answering the wizard's questions as you move from one wizard dialog box to another. After Publisher displays your publication, you can begin to enter text and create your document. You can go strictly by the wizard, retaining all layout, color schemes, designs, and font formatting, or you can make changes in any publication to make it more your own.

To use a wizard, follow these steps:

1. Open the Catalog.

2. Choose the Publications by Wizard tab.

3. Choose the wizard category in the left window of the Catalog.

4. Choose the design and layout that you want in the right window.

5. Click Start Wizard. Publisher closes the Catalog window, and the wizard starts. If you haven't filled in your personal information, the wizard prompts you to do so, as shown in Figure 3-8. For more information, see Chapter 13.

6. Follow the instructions in the wizard window on the left. Move from page to page by clicking the Next and Back buttons.

7. Answer any special questions that the wizard asks.

8. Click Finish to complete the publication. The publication appears in the work area, and the wizard window appears to the left, as shown in Figure 3-9.

9. Similar to the Quick Publication Wizard, use the current wizard to choose the color scheme, layout, page size, and to add other items to the document.

10. You're ready to fill in the text that you want for your publication.

You can also delete or add items, change the text formatting and placement of objects on the page, and otherwise customize the publication. For information about customizing a publication, see Part II, "Working with Page Layout," Part III, "Working with Text," and Part IV, "Adding Graphics, Objects, and Images."

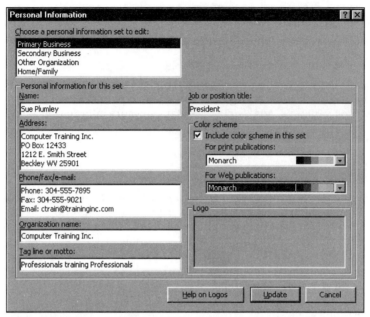

Figure 3-8: Fill in your personal information once, and several different wizards can use it.

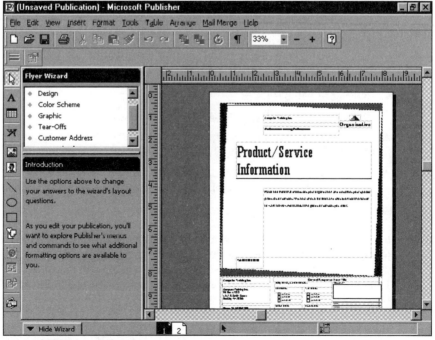

Figure 3-9: The publication base is complete.

Tip You'll also want to save the publication. Immediately after the wizard completes the document base, save it and give it a name, using one of the Save techniques described in Chapter 1. Then, as you add text and other objects to the document, save it often.

Turning off step-by-step questions

You can turn off the step-by-step questions in any wizard if you prefer to work without it. After you turn off the wizard's steps, you can still use the publication design, but no wizard will ask questions and display dialog boxes, even in future sessions. Naturally, you can always turn on the step-by-step option again.

To turn off the option, follow these steps:

1. Choose Tools ⇨ Options. The Options dialog box appears.

2. Choose the User Assistance tab, as shown in Figure 3-10.

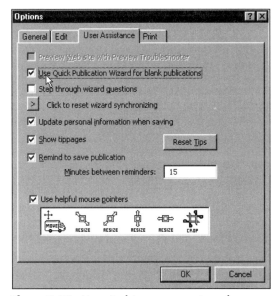

Figure 3-10: User Assistance presents various options to help you work in Publisher.

3. Remove the check mark in the Step through wizard questions check box.

4. Click OK.

After turning off this option, when you open a wizard, Publisher displays the default elements for that wizard, as well as the wizard window containing various designs, layouts, color schemes, and so on. You can make changes and additions as before, but you don't see the step-by-step questions.

Looking at examples

After you create a publication, you can make any changes that you want. You've seen how changes in design, color schemes, layout, and so on completely change a document. In addition to changes to the wizard, you can make changes to the placement and formatting of the text, and to object placement.

To give you an idea of how these changes affect your publication, Figures 3-11 and 3-12 illustrate changes made to the flyer created with a Publisher wizard. Each flyer uses different fonts, type sizes, logo and type placement, graphic sizes, and elements.

Using a Design Set

Design sets are collections of related publication types that share a consistent design and layout. One set might contain a letterhead, fax cover sheet, brochure, and business card, for example.

Design sets are also wizards that help you to create the publication of your choice. Design sets are simply a different way of looking at publication wizards. Figure 3-13 illustrates the Publications by Design tab of the Microsoft Publisher Catalog.

Following is a description of each design set:

✦ **Master Sets:** A collection of 20 different designs applied to various documents. Designs consist of images, graphics, borders, colors, and text layouts. Each design set contains between 26 and 30 document types, such as letterheads, business forms, invitation cards, and business cards.

✦ **Special Event Sets:** A collection of three different designs applied to documents such as brochures, flyers, postcards, and Web sites. These design sets are more limited in the types of documents included in each set.

✦ **Fundraiser Sets:** A collection of three designs applied to a limited number of document types: brochures, flyers, and Web sites.

✦ **Holiday Sets:** Three design sets applied to postcards, greeting cards, newsletters, Web sites, and invitations. The holiday is mainly Christmas, although a winter/New Year's design is included.

✦ **We've Moved Sets:** Four design sets applied to postcards, announcements, and invitations.

✦ **Restaurant Sets:** Two design sets applied to menus of all types: daily special, takeout, wine/dessert, and Web site.

✦ **Special Paper Sets:** Designs for use with preprinted paper designs from Paper Direct. The set includes nine different designs.

Figure 3-11: Keep the basic flyer layout but change some fonts and object placement.

Figure 3-12: Change text alignment and placement, resize the graphic, and add a coupon.

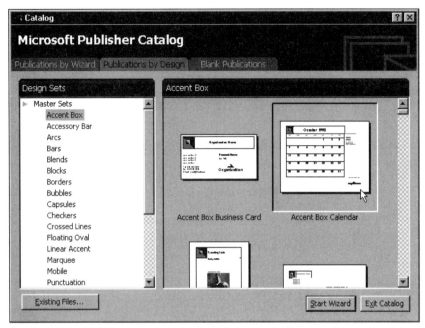

Figure 3-13: Design sets present various documents that use the same color scheme, design, and layout.

Creating a publication

To create a new publication using design sets, open the Catalog and choose the Publications by Design tab. Follow these steps:

1. In the left pane of the Catalog window, choose a design set.

2. In the right pane, choose the document type.

3. Click Start. The wizard creates the document, using the selected design set, as shown in Figure 3-14.

You can modify designs, colors, layout, and add various elements by using the wizard window, or you can modify the publication on your own without using the wizard's help. Remember that if you change design, color, or other elements of the publication, you'll want to change those same elements in any other documents that you want to match the publication.

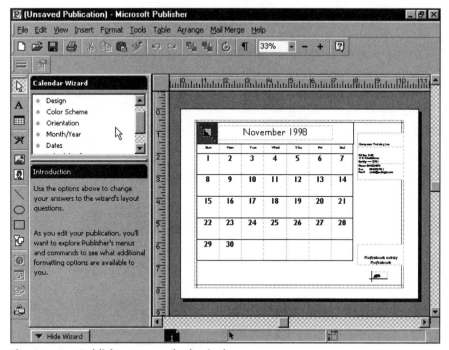

Figure 3-14: Publisher creates the basic document.

Looking at examples

You use design sets to create publications with consistent and matching designs, which makes your documents and your company appear more professional and organized.

Figure 3-15 shows a calendar that was created by using a design set and then modified by changing the size of graphics and altering font sizes and types. Additionally, the original design set has been changed.

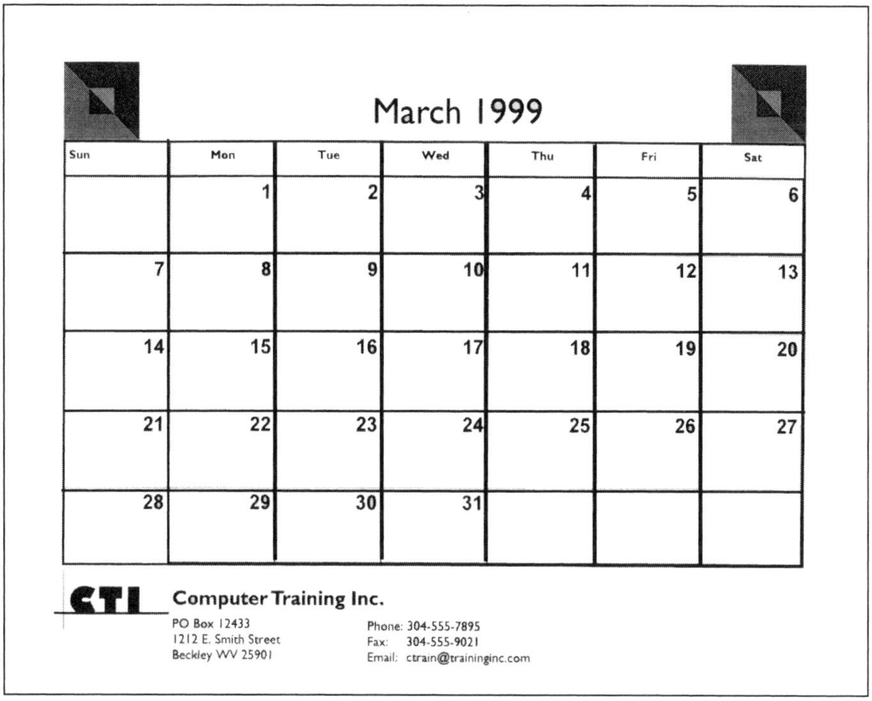

Figure 3-15: Base a document on a design set and then modify it.

Figure 3-16 illustrates a fax cover sheet based on the same design set but modified to match the calendar. The graphic design is repeated, as are vertical lines in the document. The font type and size match those used in the calendar, and the same logo is repeated in the fax cover sheet.

Figure 3-17 shows a business card design that uses the same design set and modifications. A customer will likely remember the company that uses consistent design and document layout.

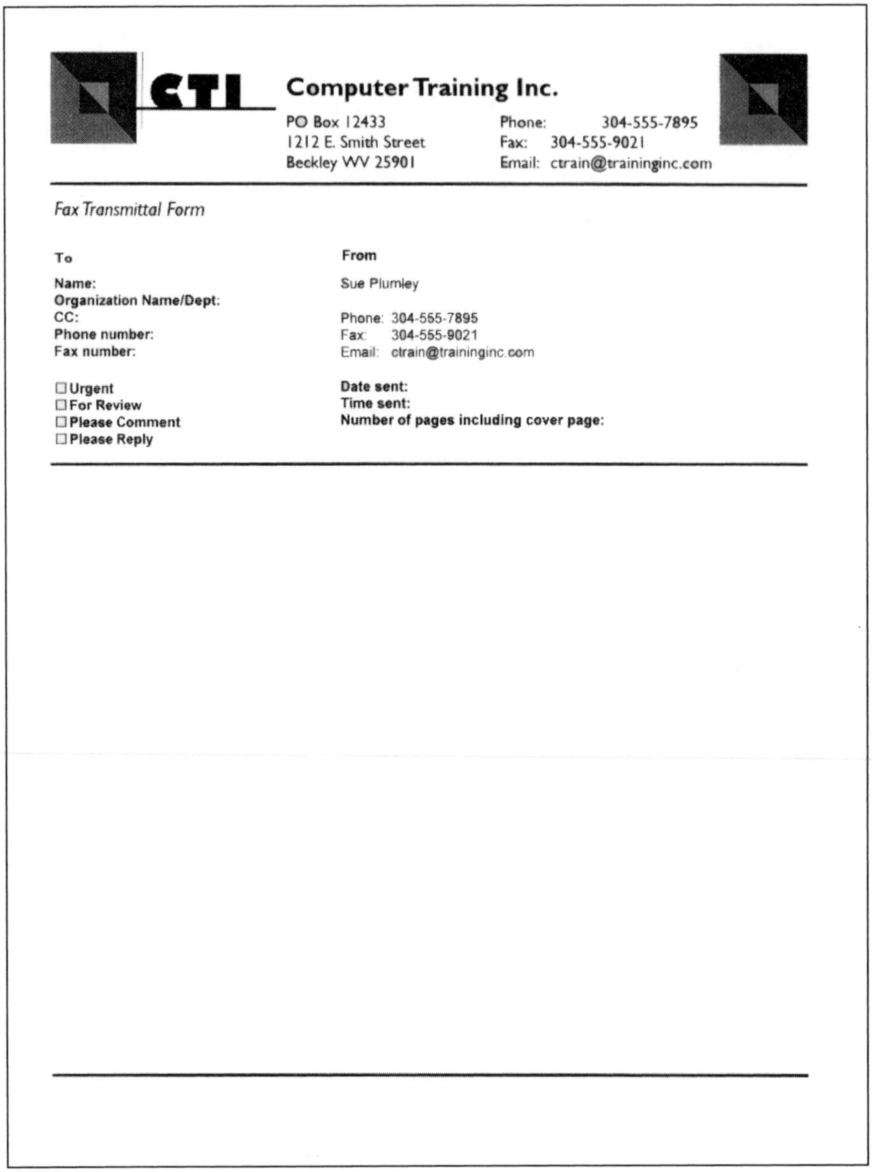

CTI Computer Training Inc.

PO Box 12433   Phone: 304-555-7895
1212 E. Smith Street Fax: 304-555-9021
Beckley WV 25901   Email: ctrain@traininginc.com

Fax Transmittal Form

To   **From**

Name: Sue Plumley
Organization Name/Dept:
CC: Phone: 304-555-7895
Phone number: Fax: 304-555-9021
Fax number: Email: ctrain@traininginc.com

☐ Urgent   **Date sent:**
☐ For Review   **Time sent:**
☐ Please Comment   **Number of pages including cover page:**
☐ Please Reply

Figure 3-16: A matching design set applied to a fax cover sheet.

Figure 3-17: Matching business cards complete the look of the company documents.

Starting a Blank Publication

You can create a document based on a blank publication and then use any of Publisher's tools and features to design the document on your own, from scratch. Publisher's blank publications include a page size and page margins. You provide any other design elements that you want to add.

The Blank Publications tab of the Catalog includes the following publications foundations:

✦ **Full Page:** An 8.5×11-inch page with one-inch margins.

✦ **Web Page:** A 6×15-inch page with negligible margins.

✦ **Postcard:** A 5.5×4.25-inch page with half-inch margins on the left and right and quarter-inch margins on the top and bottom.

✦ **Business Card:** A 3.5×2-inch page with quarter-inch margins.

✦ **Book Fold:** A 4.25×11-inch page with two pages printed on each sheet of paper. This publication prints pages in groups of four. You use the book fold as a base for greeting cards, tent cards, and book-fold publications. Margins are half an inch.

✦ **Side Fold Card:** A 4.25×5.5-inch page with four pages printed on each sheet of paper and then folded. Margins are one inch. This publication prints pages in groups of four. Use for greeting cards and invitations. The fold is on the side.

✦ **Top Fold Card:** The same as Side Fold Card, except the fold is on the top.

✦ **Tent Card:** An 8.5×5.5-inch card that folds on top. Two pages are printed on each piece of paper. Margins are one inch.

✦ **Poster:** Overall size is 18 × 24 inches. The poster consists of nine 8.5×11-inch pages that are combined to make one large poster. Margins are half an inch.

✦ **Banner:** Overall size is 8.5 inches × 5 feet. Nine pages combine to create the banner.

✦ **Index Card:** A 5×3-inch page with one-inch margins.

Note   Any time that you print a page size that is smaller than 8.5 × 11 inches, Publisher automatically prints crop marks. For more information, see Chapter 12.

Using the blank publication

To start a blank publication, follow these steps:

1. Open the Catalog and choose the Blank Publications tab.

2. Choose the publication from either the left or right pane.

3. Click the Create button. Publisher displays the blank page plus the Quick Publication Wizard.

You can use the options in the Quick Publication Wizard to add color, designs, layout, and so on. Alternatively, you can use other Publisher tools — such as the Text Frame and Picture Frame tools — to create your publication.

Looking at examples

Although you can create hundreds of designs by using the wizards and publication elements in Publisher, you also can create your own designs from scratch. You may, for example, need a simple design to match other materials in a presentation, or you may have the time and inclination to draw and lay out your own documents. You can design your own documents, using blank publications as a base.

Figure 3-18 illustrates a tent card created from a blank publication. A simple design makes the text easy to read and useful for displaying on tables at a business dinner.

Figure 3-19 illustrates a design created for a side-fold invitation. The color scheme consists of various shades of blue. The type is blue as well. Figure 3-20 illustrates the inside panel of the card. Colors in the design and type are repeated.

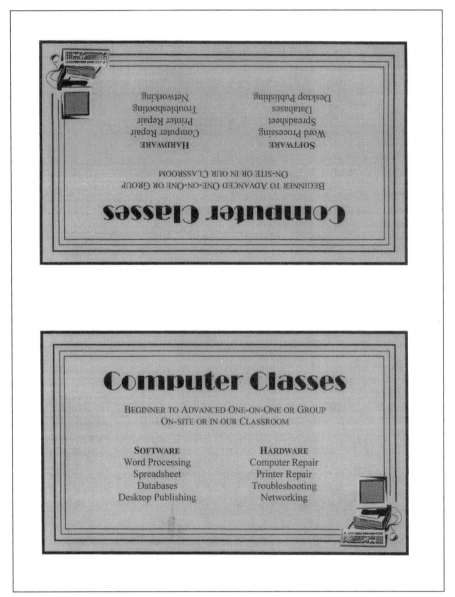

Figure 3-18: Use line, color, and clip art to create your own layout and design.

Figure 3-19: Make up your own designs and use any colors you want for graphics and text.

Figure 3-20: Repeat designs and color to make the two pages of the card match.

Summary

In this chapter, you learned about the Microsoft Publisher Catalog and how to use it to create a variety of publications. You can consider the Catalog a beginning, with which you create a base on which to build; or, you can consider the choices in the Catalog to constitute a final product, and simply add text.

In this chapter, you learned how to use the following:

✦ Quick Publication Wizard

✦ Publication wizards

✦ Design sets

✦ A blank publication

In the next chapter, you learn about working with files. You'll discover how to save a publication in various ways, how to open an existing publication, and how to organize and print your files.

✦   ✦   ✦

Working with Files

After you create a publication, you save it for later use. You might want to open the publication to edit or modify its contents, or you might want to print another copy of the documents. Storing your publication files so that they're easy to find is important. If you lose a file after you save it, you can waste a lot of time trying to find it again.

In this chapter, you learn how to work with files in Publisher. You learn how to save files, open and print files, and organize your publication files.

Saving a Publication

In Chapter 1, you learned the basic method of saving a publication. However, Publisher has additional options and procedures for saving files. First, you want to make sure of the locations to which you are saving your files. You may want to save some publications to special folders, so that you can keep them organized, and save other files to floppy or zip disks, for storage.

File naming is another factor when saving a file. Unlike the old 8.3 DOS conventions, Windows 95, 98, and NT offer long filenames for easy identification purposes. The so-called "8.3 DOS" naming convention refers to using eight characters for the filename followed by a period and a three-character extension (smith101.doc, for example). Naturally, you can still use this convention with your Publisher files, if you want, but it is limiting, especially when you want to identify a file. Long filenames free you from these limits.

Another Publisher feature enables you to easily make backup copies of your files. Backups are handy in case you lose, damage, or overwrite a file. You certainly don't want to lose all of your hard work.

Understanding the Save As dialog box

Choose File ➪ Save when a publication already has a name and you simply want to save changes to that publication. Using the Save command displays the Save As dialog box if the publication that you're saving hasn't been named.

However, getting in the habit of using the Save As command to name your files is a good idea. Otherwise, you might intend to rename a file, but accidentally save it under its old name by using the Save command. Using the Save As command enables you to name the file and choose its location and file type.

To save a file, choose File ➪ Save As. The Save As dialog box appears, as shown in Figure 4-1. Note that, unless you specify otherwise, Publisher saves your file in the default folder, My Documents.

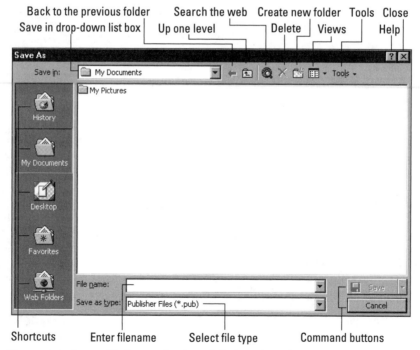

Figure 4-1: Save a file by naming it and designating a location.

Tip To save a file quickly that you have already named, press Ctrl+S.

The following list describes the components of the Save As dialog box:

◆ **Save in drop-down list box:** Displays the current folder. Click the down arrow to display a list of available folders and drives on the computer.

◆ **Shortcuts:** Click My Documents, Desktop, or Favorites to quickly open that folder. Click History to see a list of recently saved files. Click Web Folders to open a folder located on the Web.

◆ **File name:** Enter the name of the file that you want to save. Click the down arrow to view a list of recent filenames.

◆ **Save as type:** Describes the file type, such as a Publisher file, template, or something else.

◆ **Command buttons:** Click Save to save the file in the selected location and under the selected name. Click Cancel to close the dialog box without saving changes.

◆ **Back button:** Click to open the last folder that you viewed in the Save in list.

◆ **Up one level button:** Click to move to the parent folder of the current folder. For example, if My Pictures is the current folder in C:\My Documents\My Pictures, clicking the Up one level button moves you to My Documents. Clicking the button again moves you to the root folder, which is drive C.

◆ **Search the Web button:** Click to display Microsoft Internet Explorer and connect to Microsoft's home page.

◆ **Delete button:** Click to remove the selected file.

◆ **Create new folder button:** Click to add a new folder in the current folder. For example, if the current folder is My Documents and you click this button, the new folder appears as a subfolder of My Documents.

◆ **Views button:** Click to display a Views menu containing the List, Details, Properties, and Preview views. When you display files in Details view, you can click Arrange Icons to arrange the files by name, size, type, or date. Figure 4-2 shows the Details view in the Save As dialog box. Use this view to review the files that you have recently saved.

◆ **Tools button:** Click to display a menu containing the following commands: Delete, Rename, Add to Favorites, and Map Network Drive.

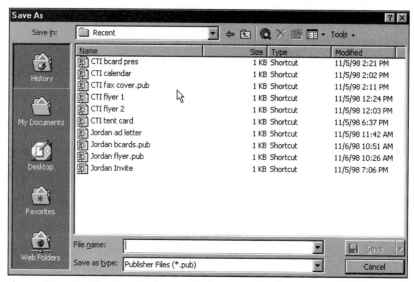

Figure 4-2: Use the Details view to find out details about the files that you've saved.

Saving a file

When you save a file, you choose a location in which to store the file, assign a filename, and save the file as a specific type. Save any publication that you may later want to reference, edit, modify, or print.

> **Tip**   You can save a file under a new name and then customize or modify that file while keeping the original intact.

Choosing a file location

Publisher enables you to store files in any drive or folder on your computer, on the Web, or on a network (if you're attached to one). Using the Save in drop-down list box, you can choose any location for your files. Figure 4-3 illustrates the choices in the Save in list box. (The drives — 3½ Floppy (A:), 5¼ Floppy (B:), and so on — may differ on your computer from the one shown in this figure.)

The following list is a description of the possible locations to save a file:

✦ **Desktop:** Places an icon of that file on your Windows desktop. You might want to do this for quick access to the file, for easy printing or copying of the file, or as placement for a temporary file.

✦ **My Computer:** Includes all drives and folders that are local to your computer, as well as any connected drives and folders, such as a local or remote network and the Internet.

Drives   Web location

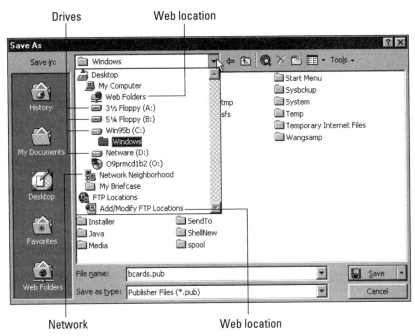

Figure 4-3: Save your files in any location on your computer.

✦ **Web Folders:** Includes drives and folders located on the Web. You use URL (*Uniform Resource Locator*) addresses to map your way to Web folders. (See Part VIII, "Designing for the Web," for more information.)

✦ **Drives:** Refers to all disk drives connected to your computer, including hard drives, floppy drives, CD-ROM drives, Zip drives, tape drives, and more. When you select a drive, all folders on that drive are displayed.

✦ **Network Neighborhood:** Refers to all servers and other computers attached to your computer. After you open a connection to any computer attached to the network, you can view all drives and folders on that computer, as long as you have permission to do so. Figure 4-4 illustrates two networked computers. The user may access drives on either computer, as long as she or he has permission; *permissions* refer to the rights that a network administrator assigns to users of the network.

✦ **FTP Locations:** Lists any FTP (*File Transfer Protocol*) sites to which you can attach. FTP sites are usually located over the Internet, although they may be located over private networks. FTP sites are used for the sole purpose of transferring files between two computers. You can upload (save) your file to an FTP site instead of saving it to your hard drive. You use FTP, for example, when you upload a Web site to the Internet. (See Chapter 34, "Preparing a Web Site," for more information.)

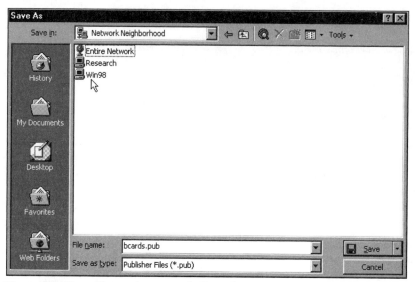

Figure 4-4: Save files to the network, if you have permission.

After you choose the location for the file and verify that the location is able to accept the file, you're ready to name the file.

Naming a file

You can name your files in any way that enables you to recognize easily the file's contents. You might use words, abbreviations, a numbering system, or any combination of these. You can use long filenames with Publisher and Windows, so choosing filenames that you can easily recognize should be easy.

Consider using a naming convention for your files, to make them easier to find and recognize. You might use a company's initials within the name, for example, or the date the file was created. You might use a customer's last name within the filename, or the name of the document. However you name your files, try to be consistent and descriptive.

For example, consider having to view the following filenames in a list:

      advertising letter for J

      calendar

      Card design

      card for table

      fax cover

Flyer for Jordan

flyer for training

Invitation for dinner and lecture

Press cards

second training flyer

Even though these filenames appear in alphabetical order, they are difficult to read and understand. These filenames sometimes are initial capped and sometimes not; similar documents aren't grouped together; and the filename lengths even vary considerably. In contrast, consider the way the filenames are listed in Figure 4-5. The naming convention that is used divides the documents created for each customer by name—CTI and Jordan. Also, short yet descriptive filenames are easier to read and understand.

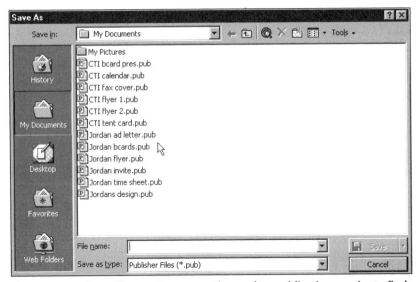

Figure 4-5: Using a file-naming convention makes publications easier to find.

When you're ready to name a file, enter the filename in the File name text box.

Choosing a file type

Generally, you'll want to save each of your publications as a Publisher file type. Publisher files have a .pub extension at the end of the filename; you must keep that extension instead of using one of your own. Only files with the .pub extension appear in the Open dialog box by default. If you use any other extension, you will have trouble finding the files that you saved.

You can save Publisher files in other file formats. You might do this if you plan to use the text in another Windows application or need to send the file to someone who does not use Publisher. Also, you can save a publication as a template that you can open and use later as a basis for a different publication. You can even save files in Publisher 98 format, so that you can open them in the older version.

Note   When you save files in any format other than as Publisher files, you will most likely lose much or all of the text and page formatting in your publication.

The following are the file formats (and extensions) in which you can save your publications:

+ Publisher Template (.pub)
+ Publisher 98 (.pub)
+ PostScript (.ps)
+ Plain Text (.txt)
+ Rich Text Format (.rtf)
+ Word 2.*x* for Windows (.doc)
+ Word 97, Word 98, Word 2000, and 6.0 (.doc) with various language converters
+ Works 3.0 and 4.0 for Windows (.wps)
+ Word 6.0/95 (.doc)
+ WordPerfect 5, 5.0, 5.1, and 5.*x* (.doc)
+ Word 4, 5, and 5.1 for Macintosh (.mcw)
+ Windows Write (.wri)

Making a backup copy

You can make a backup copy as you save a file, just in case the original becomes corrupted. Making backup copies of important publication files is always a good idea. Remember, however, that saving backup files takes up double the disk space, because you are saving two copies of the file. Also, if a problem with a corrupted folder occurs or your hard disk crashes, the backup copy is useless if it is saved in the same folder as the original.

Tip   Consider saving a copy of important files to a floppy disk, Zip drive, or other storage media as a backup, in case of a hard disk crash.

After you indicate that you want to save a backup copy, the backup that you save in the Save As dialog box appears in the file list with the filename "Backup of *name*.pub," so that you can distinguish between the original and the backup. The backup copy is saved the next time that you save your original file. In other words, each time you save your publication, Publisher updates the backup.

To save a backup copy of a publication as you save the original, click the drop-down arrow beside the Save button in the Save As dialog box. From the drop-down menu, choose Save with Backup. From that point on, every time that you choose to save the publication, Publisher updates the backup copy.

To stop updating the backup copy, return to the same drop-down menu and click the Save command.

Note   You open a backup copy as you would any other publication; however, be careful when saving the backup copy, because you could save another backup of the backup (see the next section).

Opening an Existing Publication

You open a publication to modify, edit, review, or print its contents. You can open any publication that you have saved. When you open a publication in Publisher while another publication already is open, the current publication automatically closes. If you have not saved the current publication, Publisher prompts you to do so.

Tip   Even though you can have only one open publication at a time in Publisher, you can open a second Publisher program for copying and pasting between publications, if you want. You should not, however, open more than two Publisher programs at one time, because doing so greatly taxes your computer system's resources.

Opening a file

To display the Open Publication dialog box in Publisher, press Ctrl+O or choose File ➪ Open. The Open Publication dialog box appears, as shown in Figure 4-6. Note that the Open Publication dialog box is similar to the Save As dialog box. Again, My Documents is the default folder for storing Publisher files.

Note   You can also open an existing publication from the Catalog dialog box. Click the Existing Files button in the lower-left corner of the Catalog to display the Open Publication dialog box.

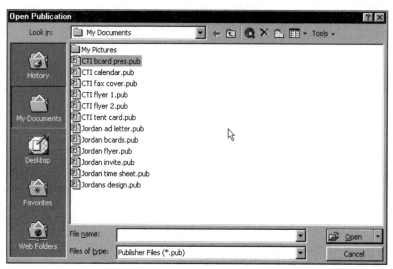

Figure 4-6: Use the Open Publication dialog box to open existing publications.

Many of the contents and tools in the Open Publication dialog box are the same as in the Save As dialog box. Use the Look in drop-down list box to locate the file; or, you can click one of the shortcuts — History, My Documents, Desktop, Favorites, or Web Folders — to help you locate a file. Use the tools to navigate the drives and folders, show different views of files, search the Web, or create a new folder.

To open a file in the Open Publication dialog box, follow these steps:

1. Select the type of file that you want to open, if it is something other than a Publisher file. Only Publisher files appear in the dialog box.

2. Locate a file by first finding the drive and then the folder containing the file. Use the Look in drop-down list box or the shortcuts on the left side of the window.

3. You can enter the filename in the File name text box. You must locate the drive and folder that contain the file before you can open it, however. Alternatively, you can select the file in the list.

4. With a file selected, click the Open button. Alternatively, double-click the selected file. The dialog box closes and the publication file opens.

Using Floppy Disks

Although you might save publication files to floppy disks either as a backup or to use on another computer, you should not work on a file that is stored on a floppy disk. When you're making changes, adding information or objects, or formatting a publication, the computer must perform read and write operations to the file on which you're working. If the file on which you're working is on a floppy disk, the computer takes longer to access the file and make the changes.

If you have a publication file saved to a floppy disk, copying that file to a folder on your hard drive, such as a temporary folder, and making any changes to it there is faster and easier than making the changes on the floppy disk. Then, you can save the file back to the floppy disk and delete it from the hard drive, if you want. Using this procedure will save you a lot of time and aggravation.

Understanding miscellaneous opening scenarios

Generally, you open a publication, do your work, close it, and then continue with your day. However, a few special circumstances for opening files exist that you should understand. For example, you might want to share your files with someone on the network, or you might want to open a file and make no changes, simply to review or print it. Publisher provides for these special scenarios.

Opening a read-only file

If you want to open a file to read it only and not make any changes, click the down arrow beside the Open button in the Open Publication dialog box and choose Open Read-Only. The file opens, but you cannot save the file under the same name. You can, however, make changes and save the file under a new name; the changes apply to the new file only, not to the original one. Each time that you want to open a file as read-only, you must choose Open Read-Only from the Open Publication dialog box.

Sharing files

When you work on a network, you may share the files that you use every day with others who also have access to the network. If you're having trouble opening a network file, someone else may be using it; or, you may not be able to open a file if it is already open in a second copy of Publisher running on your computer. You cannot open a file that is already open.

When a file is already in use by someone else, Publisher displays the message shown in Figure 4-7. Only one copy of any Publisher file can be open at a time.

Figure 4-7: Check whether you have two copies of Publisher open or whether someone else is using the file.

You can prevent coworkers from changing your publications, if you want, by applying the read-only attribute to your files.

To make a file read-only, follow these steps:

1. In Publisher, close the file in question.

2. In Windows Explorer or My Computer, locate the file that you want to change and then select it.

3. Choose File ➭ Properties. The publication's Properties dialog box appears, as shown in Figure 4-8. If not already showing, choose the General tab.

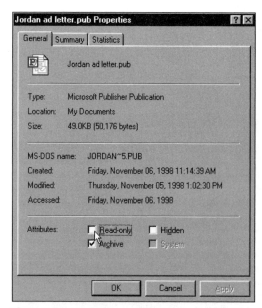

Figure 4-8: Protect your files from changes made by coworkers.

4. Click Read-only to place a check mark next to its name.

5. Choose OK. When you or anyone else tries to save changes to the file, the message in Figure 4-9 appears.

Figure 4-9: No one can make changes to a read-only file.

You can, of course, remove the read-only attribute from the file. Go through the preceding steps, but *remove* the check mark in Step 4 instead.

Opening a backup copy

As previously mentioned, you can open a backup copy of your publication in case something within the original file becomes corrupted. Be careful how you save it, however.

If you want to save the backup copy in place of the original, use the Save As command and change the name to the original publication's name or to another name, deleting Backup Of from the name. You then can choose to save normally. You also can choose to save by using a backup copy of the newly saved file.

If you want to save a backup of the new original file, then in the Save As dialog box, click the down arrow beside the Save button. Click Save with Backup. If you want to save only the original file and stop making backups, click only the Save button.

Opening two publications simultaneously

Publisher does not allow you to open two publications within one program. As previously mentioned, however, you can open two publications at one time by opening two program windows simultaneously (that is, start Publisher two times). Although you can open two Publisher programs at a time, opening more than two Publisher programs simultaneously isn't a good idea. Doing so may use up your system resources and thus slow your computer considerably.

When you open two program windows, you can easily copy, cut, and paste objects and text between the two windows. Windows enables you to display two windows on the screen at one time, or you can easily switch between the windows.

To copy text and objects between two Publisher program windows, follow these steps:

1. With one Publisher program open, open the second Publisher program.

2. Select the text or object(s) that you want to cut or copy, and then copy or cut the text or object(s) to the Clipboard.

3. To switch between the open windows, click the Publisher button on the Windows taskbar (you can also press Alt+Tab).

4. Position the insertion point in the second window at the point where you want to locate the text or object(s), and then click the Paste button.

5. When you're finished, save and close your publications; then, exit each Publisher program in the normal manner.

To view the two program windows onscreen simultaneously, follow these steps:

1. Close all programs except for the two Publisher programs.

2. Right-click the Windows Taskbar. A shortcut menu appears.

3. From the menu, choose either Tile Horizontally or Tile Vertically. Figure 4-10 illustrates two program windows tiled horizontally.

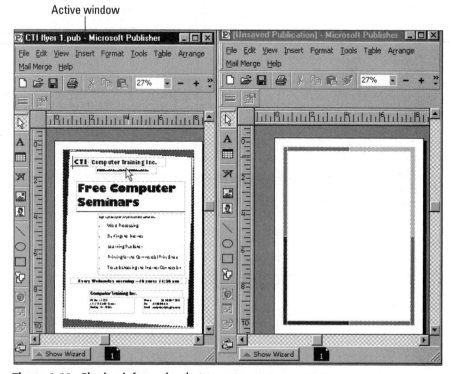

Figure 4-10: Sharing information between two open programs

When working in the Publisher programs, click the mouse in a program window to activate that window. Any menus, commands, selection or editing techniques, or other actions that you take affect only the active window. To switch windows, click anywhere within the second program window.

Alternatively, you can cascade the two program windows. Figure 4-11 illustrates two open Publisher programs that are cascaded. To activate a window, click within it. To move a window, drag the title bar. To resize the window, drag a border or click the Minimize or Maximize button in the window's title bar.

Figure 4-11: Using cascading windows is similar to switching between maximized windows.

Organizing Files

If you use Publisher only occasionally, to create a few files, you don't have much need to organize your files. However, if you create several publications a week and use other software applications on your computer, you should organize your files periodically, for efficiency. The time that you save will be worth the time that you spend organizing files.

Organize your files either in My Computer or in Windows Explorer. You can use either of these programs to delete, copy, move, and otherwise manage your files. The following sections present some ideas for managing files in Windows Explorer. For more information on the basic operation of Windows Explorer, see the Appendix.

Using the My Documents folder

If you want to store your files in the My Documents folder, where Publisher saves files by default, you can create multiple folders within that folder to help you organize your files. Adding new folders as you create new publications will help you to manage your files quickly and easily.

How you organize the files depends on the work that you do. If you have multiple customers, for example, you might want to name a folder for each customer, as shown in Figure 4-12. The next step is to move the files to their appropriate folders.

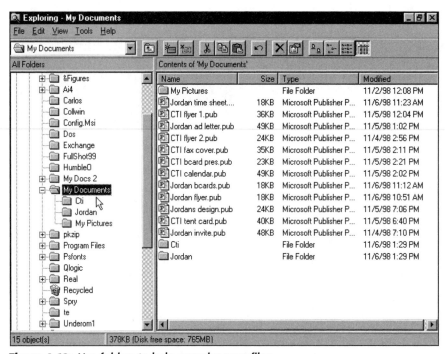

Figure 4-12: Use folders to help organize your files.

You can use other naming techniques with folders, just as you used a naming convention for files. Use account numbers for folders, for example, or use document types as folder names, such as Letters, Forms, Invitations, and so on. The method that you use to name your folders is up to you; try to find a method that is clear, easily recognizable, and efficient.

Note You can create a set of folders on your hard drive instead of in the My Documents folder. Name the folder Publisher Files, for example. Then, create several subfolders that represent specific document files.

To create a new folder and move files to the folder, follow these steps:

1. In Windows Explorer, select the My Documents folder. Alternatively, select the folder or drive where you want to store the new folder.

2. Choose File ⇨ New ⇨ Folder. A new folder appears in the right window of the Explorer pane. Windows highlights the New Folder name.

3. Enter the new name of the folder and then press Enter.

4. Move files by first selecting the files that you want to move.

Tip Select files that are contiguous by clicking the first file and then pressing and holding down the Shift key. Then, click the last file. Select files that are not adjacent by pressing and holding down the Ctrl key as you click each file.

5. Choose Edit ⇨ Cut.

6. Open the new folder and choose Edit ⇨ Paste. A confirmation message appears. Choose Yes to All.

Another way to move files to a new folder is to select them and simply drag them to the new folder's window or icon.

Finding files

If, after all of your organizing efforts, you lose a file, Windows makes finding any file easy. Rather than search through list after list, folder after folder for that file you lost, use the Windows Find feature. Following is a brief overview of the feature; for more information, see the Appendix.

To find a file, follow these steps:

1. Choose Start ⇨ Find ⇨ Files or Folders. The Find: All Files dialog box appears.

2. In the Name & Location tab, enter the filename in the Named text box.

3. In the Look in drop-down box, choose the drive or folder in which the file resides. If you're not sure of the folder, choose your local hard drive and then click Include subfolders, so that a check mark appears in the box.

4. Click the Find Now button. The Find feature locates all files with that filename and displays the found files in the Find dialog box, as shown in Figure 4-13.

5. Note the file's location, or double-click the file to open it and Publisher simultaneously.

6. Click the Close button to exit the Find dialog box.

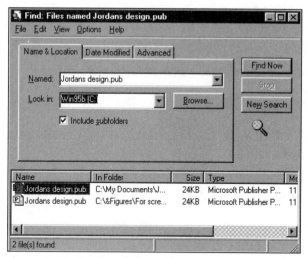

Figure 4-13: Finding all files with a specific name

Find Files enables you to look for files and folders by using a variety of methods. For example, you can look for all PUB files or all files that start with CTI. For more information, see the Appendix.

Printing Files

After you create your publication, you'll want to print it. You can proofread the printed document, have it printed commercially, or make copies of the document to distribute. Because Publisher offers various page sizes, color options, and picture file types, printing a publication can be a fairly complicated process. This section covers basic printing of Publisher publications, but Part VI, "Printing," covers all of these topics in more detail.

Understanding the Print dialog box

Open the Print dialog box by doing one of the following:

✦ Choose File ➪ Print

✦ Press Ctrl+P

✦ Click the Print button on the Standard toolbar

Figure 4-14 illustrates the Print dialog box. The printing options are similar to those found in other Windows applications.

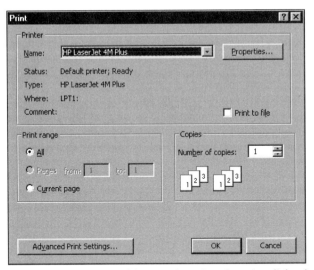

Figure 4-14: Print a publication by using the Print dialog box.

Following is a description of the elements in the Print dialog box:

✦ **Name:** The printers attached to your computer or network appear in the Name drop-down list box. You can choose the printer to which you want to send your publication. Generally, the printer set as Windows' default printer is the one selected. (For more information about Windows printers and printer properties, see the Appendix.)

✦ **Print to file:** Check this box to print the publication as a file that you can save to the hard disk or a floppy disk. Use this option to take the publication to a service bureau or commercial print shop. (For more information, see Chapter 30, "Printing in Publisher.")

✦ **Print range:** Choose the publication pages that you want to print. You can print all pages, the current page only, or a range of pages. To print a range of pages, choose Pages and then enter the first and last pages to print.

✦ **Copies:** Enter the Number of copies that you want to print.

✦ **Advanced Print Settings:** Options in this dialog box relate to resolution of graphics, crop marks, bleeds, and so on. (See Chapter 30 for more information.)

Choosing paper size and orientation

When you set the printer's paper size, you're setting the printer configuration to agree with the size of the paper in the paper tray. You might use the letter size paper (8½ by 11 inches) or a legal size paper (8½ by 14 inches). You can also set your printer to print envelopes and custom sizes of paper.

Generally, however, you'll want to leave your printer settings at letter size and adjust the page size in Publisher. You've seen how some wizards offer various page sizes. You can also set a custom size for the page. If the page size that you choose is different from the printer's paper size, Publisher either prints marks that you can use to cut the paper down to size or prints sections of the page on several pieces of paper. (For more information, see Chapter 12, "Considering Advanced Page Issues.")

You can also set the orientation of the paper that the printer uses. For example, if you choose landscape orientation, all pages you print will end up in that orientation, no matter what you set in Publisher. Again, unless you have a specific reason for doing so, leave the printer set at portrait orientation and change page orientation within Publisher. (For information about setting your publication's page size and orientation in Publisher, see Chapter 7, "Understanding Page Design.")

If you *do* need to change your paper size or page orientation in your printer settings, you can accomplish that task by following these steps:

1. In Publisher, choose File ➪ Print Setup. The Print Setup dialog box appears, as shown in Figure 4-15.

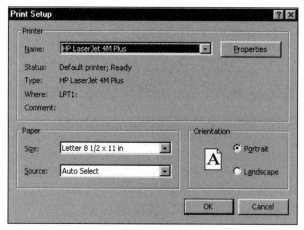

Figure 4-15: Setting printer defaults

2. In the Paper section, select the Size from the drop-down list box.

3. In the Orientation section, choose either Portrait or Landscape.

4. Click OK.

Finding the image area

When you print a page to a printer, a small area around the edge always exists, called the *unprintable area*, on which the printer cannot print. The size of this area depends on the type of printer that you're using. Laser printers, for example, leave a .25-inch or .30-inch edge around the page on which they cannot print. So, if you create a shape or line that goes off the edge of the paper, the image stops before it gets to the edge of the paper. The rest of the page is the printer's image area.

To find out your printer's unprintable area, follow these steps:

1. Choose Start ➪ Settings ➪ Printers.

2. Right-click the printer and choose Properties from the shortcut menu. The printer's Properties dialog box appears.

3. Choose the Paper tab, as shown in Figure 4-16. If your printer's Properties dialog box has no Paper tab, look for a tab with an area or button labeled Unprintable Area or something similar.

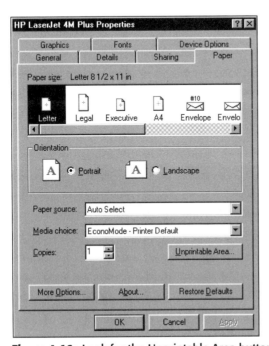

Figure 4-16: Look for the Unprintable Area button

4. Click the Unprintable Area button. The Unprintable Area dialog box appears, as shown in Figure 4-17.

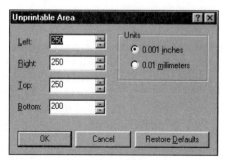

Figure 4-17: Discovering your printer's margin or unprintable area

5. Note the left, right, top, and bottom measurements so that you'll know how close to the edge you can get when you lay out a publication.

6. Click the Cancel button.

Summary

In this chapter, you learned how to work with files, including the following:

✦ Saving files

✦ Opening files

✦ Organizing files

✦ Printing files

In the next chapter, you learn about design strategies and using color in your publications.

✦   ✦   ✦

Considering Design in Your Publication

Publisher provides publication wizards, design sets, color schemes, and layouts to help you create attractive and professional-looking publications. Created by experts, Publisher's wizards and other similar features use certain fundamental design elements to arrange text and graphics on the page.

Note   *Graphics* refers to lines and shapes used in a publication for design purposes. For example, you can use lines to separate major topics, or use a border to spice up a page or paragraph. *Graphics* may also refer to the use of objects, such as tables, pictures, clip art, charts, and so on.

If you plan to stick with Publisher's designs and never make a change, add a picture, or delete a text frame, then your publications will employ winning designs. More likely than not, however, you will want to add to Publisher's designs by modifying, adding, moving, and otherwise manipulating text, graphics, and objects. You may also want to start with a blank page and create page designs of your own. Acquiring an understanding of basic design techniques is a good idea, so that when you *do* make changes to your documents, the results will be attractive and professional looking.

Planning the Content

Before you choose the type of document that you want to create or the design and layout of that document, you should consider several content issues. For example, decide on the purpose of your document — should it sell a product or announce a grand opening? Will the document inform employees of a change of policy or present a calendar of events? The purpose of your publication determines the size, design, and layout of the page. Other issues that you should consider include your audience and the method of distributing the document.

After you make these basic decisions, you can gather information and organize the content of your publication.

Document purpose

To determine the purpose of your document, take a look at the content. What is the desired end result? Are you going to sell, inform, gather information, or do you have a combination of purposes? Consider the following when planning your publication:

✦ Are you trying to sell a product or service? Are you selling to individuals or to businesses? Will you advertise the price? What other details should you include? What makes your product or service special?

✦ Are you informing employees about a new process, procedure, or guidelines? How much information do they need? How technical will the information be? Will it include illustrations?

✦ Perhaps you're offering other information, such as facts about your company or information that a customer might want or need. What is the best way to present that information?

✦ Do you need to collect information from your audience? How many questions will you present? What type of questions will you use?

After you decide on your document's purpose, you can begin planning your content. Base all the information in your publication on promoting your purpose and achieving the desired results. Additionally, you'll want to consider a few other issues when planning your publication—your audience and the method of distribution.

Audience

As you plan your publication, think about your intended audience. Who are you trying to reach with this document? Will it be employees, coworkers, customers, prospective customers, or the general public? You should prepare your publication's content to match your audience.

First, identify your audience. Next, learn more about it. Each audience has its own communication needs. You might use different rhetoric, for example, with an older group of people than with young professionals. Your publication may present a different message to women than to men, or to white-collar workers than to those who perform more physical labor.

Research your audience and adapt your content to it. Address the readers directly and focus on their interests.

Method of distribution

The method by which you distribute your publication relates to its size and format. For example, if you plan to mail the publication, consider the folded size and the weight of each piece. If you plan to hang the document in store windows or on bulletin boards, the piece can be larger and more noticeable.

Consider, too, how readers will carry or store the document. Some documents may need to fit in a notebook or on a clipboard, for example, whereas others may need to fit in a file folder or on an index card.

Gathering and organizing content

As you create or copy your content, keep in mind the purpose and audience for the publication. Outline your main topics first, and then form them into well-written and interesting text. Remember, you want to persuade the audience to read the copy as much as you want to get a message across.

Make sure that the text is clearly written and that spelling and grammar are impeccable. Experiment with phrasing. Consider using the most eye-catching words and phrases as headings in your publication.

A next step is to gather any objects and pictures that you want to use in your publication. Use any images, charts, tables, or other objects that reinforce your message. Often, an image or graphic of some type will grab the reader's attention.

Planning the Publication

Now that you have your content, you can plan the type of publication. Formats are easy to plan because certain types of documents fit specific purposes; a flyer, for example, is a good format for selling a product or service. Choosing the size of the publication goes hand in hand with the format, although you must also consider the method of distribution and the amount of content.

Choosing a format

The format of a document is the same as the document type. The publication could be a flyer, newsletter, brochure, invitation, booklet, or something else. To decide the format, consider the document's purpose, required size, copy (text, figures, charts, and other graphics), and method of distribution.

The following is a brief description of the most common document types:

✦ **Flyers:** Quick-sell advertisements that can be used to announce, introduce, or remind people of a new product, sale, grand opening, or other event. Flyers use short phrases, lists, or single words, and perhaps pictures or clip art. Use descriptive adjectives and a minimum of text on one side of a sheet of paper. Common flyer sizes are letter size (8½×11 inches) or legal size (8½×14 inches). Figure 5-1 illustrates a flyer. Note how the graphics and image attract attention while the brief text tells the audience all it needs to know.

Figure 5-1: A flyer is a quick-sell method of advertising.

✦ **Brochures:** Used to explain or inform. Brochures detail information, such as presenting facts about a service, product, or company. The text generally consists of sentences and paragraphs, as opposed to short phrases. You can use pictures, graphic designs, tables, charts, and so on. A brochure also can include a mailing panel. Brochures generally are printed on two sides and normally are letter or legal size. Figure 5-2 illustrates a three-panel brochure for the same artist advertised in the flyer in Figure 5-1. Note the consistency of designs.

Figure 5-2: A brochure enables you to describe more details than you can in a flyer.

✦ **Newsletters:** Used to inform, instruct, announce, or explain information. You might send newsletters to employees, coworkers, customers, or prospective customers. The content, then, covers anything that interests the audience. Coupons, articles, product information, news about people, and so on, are likely topics for a newsletter. Newsletters often include a title, headers and footers, and a logo, and sometimes include a table of contents. Usually, the final size of a newsletter is letter size, printed on both sides of the paper, and often ranges from two to eight pages. However, a newsletter can be any size that you want. Figure 5-3 illustrates the cover page of a newsletter for a computer consultant. Newsletters provide more room for detailed articles than do other documents.

✦ **Programs:** Usually describe a play, dinner, agenda, or other event. A program's finished size is often $5\frac{1}{2}\times8\frac{1}{2}$ inches — a letter-sized page that is folded in half to create a booklet, and thus creates four pages.

✦ **Booklets:** Publications that describe a topic in detail. Whether describing products, services, history, or other information, a booklet can consist of four or more pages. Commonly, the booklet's finished size is $5\frac{1}{2}\times8\frac{1}{2}$ inches or $8\frac{1}{2}\times11$ inches.

Figure 5-3: Newsletters can consist of two, four, eight pages or more.

Planning size

The size of your publication depends on the amount of content, method of distribution, and type of document that you're planning. However, the size also depends on which paper sizes are commonly available. Most printers, for example, print to letter-size or legal-size paper. Some printers work with other sizes, larger or smaller.

If you plan to take your publication to a commercial print shop, you'll have a bit more flexibility in size; however, sticking with commonly used sizes of documents costs less. Commercial print shops purchase paper in standard sizes — $8\frac{1}{2} \times 11$ inches, 11×17 inches, and several larger sizes. The paper is sized so that standard cuts waste no paper; custom cuts may take twice as much paper as standard cuts. For example, an $8\frac{1}{2} \times 9$-inch cut may cost you as much as an $8\frac{1}{2} \times 11$-inch cut, and an $8\frac{1}{2} \times 12$-inch cut may cost twice as much.

So, when you plan the size of your publication, consider how you will print the publication, before you make any decisions.

Applying Design Strategies

Within the format and size of the publication are certain design strategies that you can apply to nearly any document. With each publication, consider using the design strategies of consistency, emphasis, balance, and white space to make the publication interesting, readable, and eye-catching.

Each element contributes to a pleasing composition. If you omit one element from your design, the publication suffers.

Consistency

Consistency creates unity within the publication. You can create consistency by repeating elements, by not introducing too many different fonts or type sizes, and so on. For example, if you use a graphic line to separate stories in a newsletter, repeat that same line at the end of each story. If you use a certain font size for a headline, use that same font size for all headlines. If you add a small piece of clip art to one story, add another small piece of clip art to another story elsewhere in the newsletter. Repetition of objects, images, and fonts creates consistency.

Emphasis

Although consistency is important to the design of the piece, you may want to introduce one or two alternative points of emphasis, to add interest and pizzazz. For example, to make one headline in a newsletter stand out, you can emphasize it by making its text larger or by using a different font. Or, to emphasize an important story, you can include it within a large, screened box. Other ways to catch the reader's attention include adding a splash of color or a large graphic or image.

Emphasize only one item on a page, though; if you emphasize everything, then nothing is emphasized.

Figure 5-4 illustrates the cover page of a newsletter that uses both consistency and emphasis. The headlines are the same font, and body text is formatted in the same way for each article; however, the callout, or *pull quote,* adds a point of emphasis. The eye focuses on that item first.

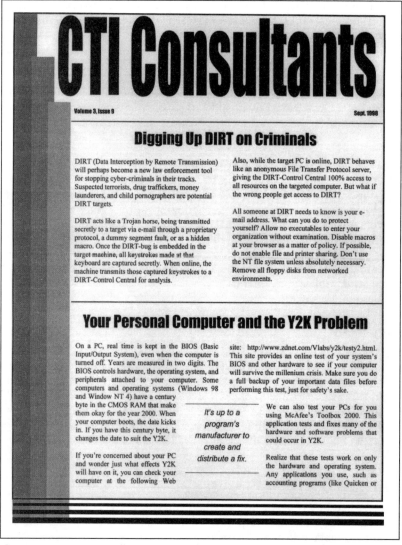

Figure 5-4: Even a small point of emphasis breaks up the consistency.

White space

White space describes any area of the page that is left blank, with no text or graphics. Margins, gutter space between columns, the space around one-word headings, and so on create white space. White space provides contrast to the text and graphics on a page and offers a rest for the reader's eyes.

As a general rule, white space should be balanced with text and graphics at a 50-50 ratio. This may sound excessive, but by adding space to a page design, you make the text and graphics easier to read. Note in Figure 5-5, for example, that the text is crowded onto the page, and the graphic lines make the page even more packed. The page has an overall gray look to it, which just might discourage a reader from tackling the text.

As a contrast, Figure 5-6 shows the same page with white space added. The margins are a little larger, additional space is added between bulleted text and paragraphs, and a piece of clip art is substituted for the text box, which also provides more white space. The extra text is either moved to another page or simply cut out.

So, how do you increase white space? The following are some suggestions:

✦ Use less text

✦ Add more pages

✦ Enlarge margins

✦ Left-align text (as opposed to using justified text)

✦ Add extra space between paragraphs

✦ Add extra space after a heading

Using Color in a Publication

Designing a publication in color is fun. Publisher offers line color, fill color, and color clip art and photographs. Nearly all the designs and wizards use various colors, and you can easily and quickly change color schemes within any publication. Printing is the main problem when working onscreen with color.

If you use only a black-and-white printer, all of your publications print in black and white. The colors that are so vivid onscreen print in various shades of gray and black. You can apply color to the printed page only if you print to a color inkjet or laser printer or take your document design to a commercial print shop for printing on a press.

Benefits of Networking

The reason you connect your PCs to a network is to benefit your business, to maintain a competitive edge. No matter what your business goals are, using a client/server system enables better information sharing, communications, and organization within your company. Following are some of the benefits of client/server networking.

Using the client/server model of networking enables your employees to collaborate easily and efficiently. In addition to sharing documents over the network, employees can also e-mail ideas, questions, and suggestions to each other; access sales, inventory, and manufacturing information; and gather, store, and share customer feedback and information. During all of this collaboration, you have the control of who is authorized to access information and data.

Networking also enables your employees to access current customer account records and service records to track customer needs and anticipate market trends. Productivity also improves immediately after e-mail and scheduling programs are made available to your staff. You might even want to establish an intranet (internal web site for your company's use only) on which you can publish and update information quickly and efficiently.

Following are a few more of the advantages to using a network in your business:

* Share files electronically. Whether your network users work with 1-2-3 or Excel, WordPerfect or Word for Windows, they can share files of all types with each other over the network. Store files on the server for easy access by all users or just those users you specify. Share directories and folders as well.

* Back up critical data electronically to the network. You can back up data on the server from individual workstations connected to the network. Back up to a tape drive, network drive, or other data storage component.

* Share printers, CD-ROM drives, modems, and other peripherals. You can connect expensive laser printers, for example, to the network so everyone can access them.

* Share ideas, requests, questions, and so on. E-mail or an intranet within your company enables people to connect to each other when it's most convenient, providing a method by which individuals can exchange text files, image files, and others to one or more of their co-workers on the network.

* The administrator can limit access to shared data so that users' access to sensitive files and directories is limited; and he/she can reserve resources for use by specific personnel only.

* The administrator can remotely support users of the network. Use a workstation anywhere on the network or even a dial-up connection to troubleshoot user's problems.

You'll find your employees are more productive when they use a network. They can collaborate with their co-workers, complete their work more efficiently, and they are happier in the working environment.

Networking Clients

If you're already using computers in your business, you may be wondering if you'll need to change the operating systems already in use. Most likely, you will not.

Windows 95, a most popular operating system, is also the perfect networking client for both NT Server and NetWare networks.

A few additions in hardware—a network card and a cable connection—and a few configuration changes to the operating system, are all that is needed to change a PC into a network client.

Naturally, you may also want to employ a server and depending on your needs, some other hardware to complete the network; but transformation of your clients is fairly easy and usually quite inexpensive. Call Humble Opinions to find out more.

Windows 95 A or B?

There are two versions of Windows 95 floating around out there—Windows 95 A and Windows 95 B.

Windows 95 A, the original release, had a lot of bugs. Luckily, Microsoft released a Service Pack 1 that can help correct many of the problems discovered in that operating system. Among other things, the service pack includes the 32-bit DLC Protocol, a Microsoft Exchange update, Microsoft Internet Explorer 2.0, Support for Dial-Up Networking, and Microsoft Word Viewer. You can download Service Pack 1 from Microsoft's Web site.

You can view the Windows 95 version by opening the System icon in the Control Panel. In the System Properties dialog box, General tab, the version is listed under System. Version 4.00.950 refers to Windows 95 A and 95 A with the service pack installed. Version 4.00.950 B refers to Windows 95 B, also called OSR-2 (operating system release 2).

Windows 95 OSR-2 is only available preinstalled on new PCs and not as an upgrade to Windows 95 A. The reason for Windows 95 OSR-2 is to supply PC manufacturers with the latest available updates and supports for hardware advances. Microsoft states that it will not release a Windows 95 OSR-2 upgrade for Windows 95 A. One probable reason for this is that Microsoft anticipates 95 B may not work well on a lot of older computers.

Windows 95 OSR-2 includes, among other things: FAT32 file system, Internet Explorer 3.0, Internet Mail and News, IDE busmastering support, ActiveMovie and DirectX 2.0, additional support for printing, faxing, and networking. To get it, you'll have to purchase a new computer, a new controller, or a new hard drive.

All in all, you will likely be happier with Windows 95B. Even when compared to Windows 98, 95B may be best.

Humble Opinions offers a monthly newsletter to our customers. Included in the newsletter is information about networking, Windows 95, betas, recent technologies, and fun facts.

Figure 5-5: Too much text and not enough white space looks crowded.

Benefits of Networking

The reason you connect your PCs to a network is to benefit your business, to maintain a competitive edge. No matter what your business goals are, using a client/server system enables better information sharing, communications, and organization within your company. Following are some of the benefits of client/server networking.

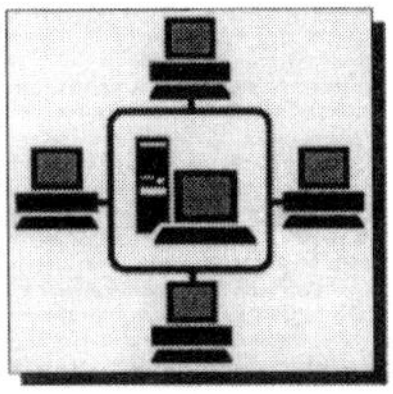

Using the client/server model of networking enables your employees to collaborate easily and efficiently. In addition to sharing documents over the network, employees can also e-mail ideas, questions, and suggestions to each other; access sales, inventory, and manufacturing information; and gather, store, and share customer feedback and information. During all of this collaboration, you have the control of who is authorized to access information and data.

Networking also enables your employees to access current customer account records and service records to track customer needs and anticipate market trends. Productivity also improves immediately after e-mail and scheduling programs are made available to your staff.

You might even want to establish an intranet (internal web site for your company's use only) on which you can publish and update information quickly and efficiently.

Following are a few more of the advantages to using a network in your business:

- Share files electronically. Whether your network users work with 1-2-3 or Excel, WordPerfect or Word for Windows, they can share files of all types with each other over the network. Store files on the server for easy access by all users or just those users you specify. Share directories and folders as well.

- Back up critical data electronically to the network. You can back up data on the server from individual workstations connected to the network. Back up to a tape drive, network drive, or other data storage component.

- Share printers, CD-ROM drives, modems, and other peripherals. You can connect expensive laser printers, for example, to the network so everyone can access them.

- Share ideas, requests, questions, and so on. E-mail or an intranet within your company enables people to connect to each other when it's most convenient, providing a method by which individuals can exchange text files, image files, and others to one or more of their co-workers on the network.

- The administrator can limit access to shared data so that users' access to sensitive files and directories is limited; and he/she can reserve resources for use by specific personnel only.

- The administrator can remotely support users of the network. Use a workstation anywhere on the network or even a dial-up connection to troubleshoot user's problems.

Windows 95 A or B?

There are two versions of Windows 95 floating around out there—Windows 95 A and Windows 95 B.

Windows 95 A, the original release, had a lot of bugs. Luckily, Microsoft released a Service Pack 1 that can help correct many of the problems discovered in that operating system. Among other things, the service pack includes the 32-bit DLC Protocol, a Microsoft Exchange update, Microsoft Internet Explorer 2.0, Support for Dial-Up Networking, and Microsoft Word Viewer. You can download Service Pack 1 from Microsoft's Web site.

You can view the Windows 95 version by opening the System icon in the Control Panel. In the System Properties dialog box, General tab, the version is listed under System. Version 4.00.950 refers to Windows 95 A and 95 A with the service pack installed. Version 4.00.950 B refers to Windows 95 B, also called OSR-2 (operating system release 2).

Windows 95 OSR-2 is only available preinstalled on new PCs and not as an upgrade to Windows 95 A. The reason for Windows 95 OSR-2 is to supply PC manufacturers with the latest available updates and supports for hardware advances. Microsoft states that it will not release a Windows 95 OSR-2 upgrade for Windows 95 A. One probable reason for this is that Microsoft anticipates 95 B may not work well on a lot of older computers.

Windows 95 OSR-2 includes, among other things: FAT32 file system, Internet Explorer 3.0, Internet Mail and News, IDE busmastering support, Ac-

Humble Opinions offers a monthly newsletter to our customers. Included in the newsletter is information about networking, Windows 95, betas, re-

Figure 5-6: White space makes the page more attractive and easier to read.

Printing in black and white

Color printing is expensive, especially when compared with black-and-white printing on your laser printer. If you don't have a color printer and don't want to take your publication to a commercial print shop, you can apply various shades of gray to a publication to make it more interesting. Use screened text boxes and even screened borders and lines to add interest to the publication.

You can also print black ink on various colors of paper to add color to your publication. Printing black on orange, yellow, red, or blue paper, for example, produces an extremely intriguing piece.

Finally, you might want to look into specialty papers and foils for color printing on a black-and-white page. You can purchase papers with multiple colors, specialty borders, and so on, to add color to your publications. You can also purchase special foils that you run through the printer with paper to heat-seal color onto the page. Be careful with these products, however. A little color on the page may not be worth a ruined laser printer. For more information about paper, see Chapter 11, "Working with Page Elements."

Printing in color

If you do use a color printer or plan to take your publication to a print shop for commercial printing, you should consider some color issues before you apply color in a publication. Remember, you want your text to be readable, and too many colors may detract from the piece rather than add to it.

Stick with Publisher's color schemes, unless you're artistic and knowledgeable about color printing. Publisher's color schemes apply matching and contrasting colors that work well together. If you don't know what you're doing, you may add a color scheme to your publication that is less compatible than the color schemes offered by Publisher, thus making your publication less attractive than it could be.

The following are some other issues to consider regarding color printing:

✦ You can imitate multiple colors in your print jobs if you use one color of ink on another color of paper. Red ink on blue paper or green ink on yellow paper creates a nice contrast and provides inexpensive color printing.

✦ If you're using two colors, use contrasting colors for the best results — blue and red, red and green, and blue and orange are all good examples.

✦ If you use white type on a dark background, use bold type so that the letters are thick enough to be read easily.

✦ Never use yellow or another light color for text unless it is on a dark background. You can use yellow for screens, lines, and shapes, however.

For more information about printing in color, color separations, spot color, and full-process color, see Chapter 31, "Using Commercial Printing Tools."

Summary

In this chapter, you learned to plan and design your publication before working with Publisher. In addition, you learned the importance of the following:

✦ Deciding on a purpose for your publication

✦ Identifying the audience

✦ Deciding on format and size

✦ Using color in a publication

In the next chapter, you learn about customizing Publisher by setting options for measurement units, editing, and toolbars.

✦   ✦   ✦

Customizing Publisher

Before you continue working with Publisher, you may want to set some customizations and preferences to improve your working environment. Publisher enables you to set certain options for working, such as previewing fonts and setting measurement units in the program. You may be satisfied with the defaults, but just in case you want to make a change at some point, this section explains setting general options in Publisher.

To open the Options dialog box, choose Tools ➪ Options. The Options dialog box appears with the General tab displayed, as shown in Figure 6-1.

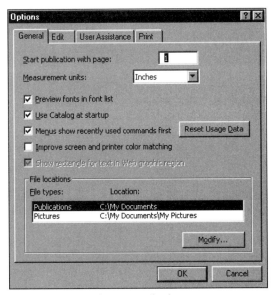

Figure 6-1: Use the General tab to set a variety of options.

Setting Startup Options

The General tab enables you to set your preferences for the way things look and work when you first open Publisher. The following is an explanation of those options:

✦ **Start publication with page:** Enter the page number with which to start the document. Page 1 is the default.

✦ **Measurement units:** Inches, the default measurement unit, are used in the ruler, in spacing, tab settings, and other settings in Publisher. You can change the measurement units to centimeters, picas, or points. Picas and points are printer's measurements; 6 picas are in an inch, and 72 points are in a pica. Points are commonly used for measuring type.

✦ **Preview fonts in font list:** By default, the fonts in the font list on the Formatting toolbar appear in the actual typeface, instead of all fonts appearing in one typeface. This way, you can see what a font looks like before you apply it to your text. Figure 6-2 shows the font list from the Formatting toolbar. (For more information about changing fonts, see Chapter 16, "Formatting Characters.")

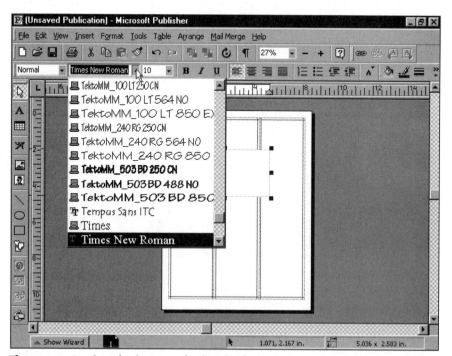

Figure 6-2: Preview the fonts on the font list before you apply a font to your text.

✦ **Use Catalog at startup:** By default, the Catalog appears when you start Publisher. If you prefer to display a blank page and the Quick Publication Wizard, clear the check box for this option.

✦ **Menus show recently used commands first:** When you first display a menu, a short list of recently used commands appears, as shown in Figure 6-3. You can click the arrow at the bottom of the menu to display all the commands on that menu. If you prefer, clear the check box to display all the commands all the time. To reset the menu commands to the default settings, click the Reset Usage Data button in the Options dialog box.

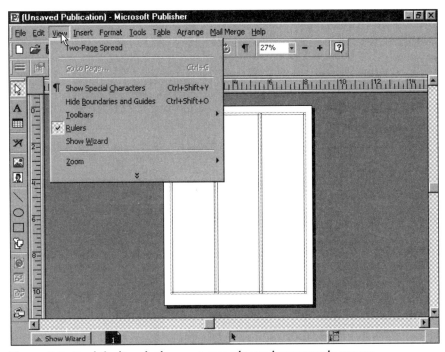

Figure 6-3: By default, only the most recently used commands appear.

✦ **Improve screen and printer color matching:** Add a check to the check box to make your printed colors appear more like the colors you view onscreen. You must be running Windows 95 or 98, and your monitor must support ICM color profiles. (For more information, see Chapter 31, "Using Commercial Printing Tools.")

✦ **Show rectangle for text in Web graphic region:** This is a tool for locating problem areas in your Web pages. When text is located too close to a picture or other object on the Web page, the text may take longer than normal to appear. This tool draws a rectangle around any problem areas on the page. (For more information about Web pages and Web sites, see Part VIII, "Designing for the Web.")

Setting File Locations

The other part of the General tab in the Options dialog box concerns the default folders that Publisher displays in the Open and Save As dialog boxes. By default, Publisher saves files to the My Documents folder, which also is the folder Publisher displays when you want to open a file. Also by default, Publisher stores pictures and images in the My Documents\My Pictures folder. You can, however, make changes to these file locations.

In the Options dialog box, select the item that you want to change (in the File locations section of the dialog box) and then click the Modify button. The Modify Location dialog box appears, as shown in Figure 6-4. Note that the dialog box looks and behaves similarly to the Save As and Open dialog boxes. In the Look in drop-down list, locate the folder that you want to make the default, and then select it so that its name is in the Folder name text box. Click OK.

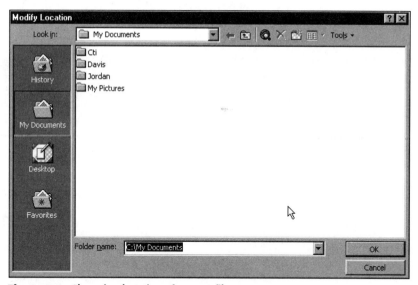

Figure 6-4: Changing locations for your file storage

Setting Edit Options

The Edit tab of the Options dialog box enables you to set your editing preferences in Publisher. You can choose options for text editing, formatting, and object editing. Figure 6-5 illustrates the Edit tab. The following sections describe the options in the Edit tab of the Options dialog box.

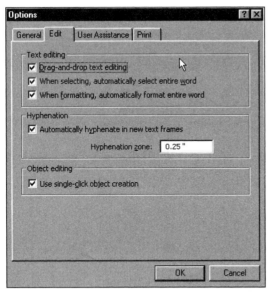

Figure 6-5: Use the Edit tab to control text and object editing.

Setting text editing options

The Text editing section includes options for copying, pasting, selecting, and formatting text. If you're not familiar with editing text, you may want to read Part III, "Working with Text," before you change any of the default options.

✦ **Drag-and-drop text editing:** When checked, enables you to select text in a document and then drag that text to a new location. Clear the check box to turn off the feature.

✦ **When selecting, automatically select entire word:** When checked, the entire word automatically highlights as you select it. You can still select only one letter, for example, but this option makes whole words easier to select. (For more information about selecting text, see Chapter 13, "Entering and Editing Text.")

✦ **When formatting, automatically format entire word:** When checked, this handy option, by default, enable you to click anywhere within a word and format the entire word with a font, type size, or type style. If you clear this check box, you must select the entire word to format it. (For more information, see Chapter 16, "Formatting Characters.")

Setting hyphenation

Hyphenation automatically divides words that are too long to fit entirely at the end of a text line, inserts a hyphen, and then continues that word on the next line. Automatic hyphenation saves a lot of time and trouble when you're entering text in Publisher. The Hyphenation options are as follows:

✦ **Automatically hyphenate in new text frames:** By default, Publisher automatically divides with a hyphen long words at the end of a line in any new text box. Clear the check box if you prefer not to hyphenate your text automatically.

✦ **Hyphenation zone:** Controls the "raggedness" of the text on the right margin. If you use a large zone—say, one inch—then words that could be hyphenated but fall in that one inch of space on the right are forced to the next line. Using too large of a hyphenation zone results in large gaps in the text. Too small a hyphenation zone may result in more hyphenated words.

Figure 6-6 illustrates both instances of hyphenation, as well as the proper use of the hyphenation zone. The paragraph of text on the left uses too large a hyphenation zone, and the paragraph on the right uses no hyphenation zone. The paragraph in the middle uses Publisher's default, quarter-inch hyphenation zone. Note that very little difference exists between the default hyphenation zone and the no hyphenation zone; the main difference is that more words will be hyphenated when you have no zone, or too small a zone.

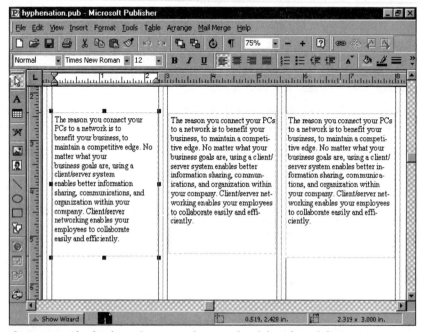

Figure 6-6: The hyphenation zone changes the right edge of the text.

For more information about hyphenating text, see Chapter 15, "Basic Text Formatting."

Setting object editing options

The last area of the Edit tab is Object editing. You can create various objects, such as text frames or picture frames, by dragging a tool to size and place the frame. Alternatively, you can click the mouse, and a default frame appears. Generally, you must resize and relocate this frame after you create it.

By default, Publisher offers you the option of using this click-once feature to create objects. You can also use the other method with this option checked. If you prefer not to use this single-click method, clear the check box labeled Use single-click object creation.

For more information about object creation, see Chapter 10, "Using Frames."

Setting User Assistance Options

User Assistance options include choices for using the Quick Publication Wizard, getting help in Publisher, and saving your publication. You can choose the options that will make your work easier. Figure 6-7 shows the User Assistance tab of the Options dialog box.

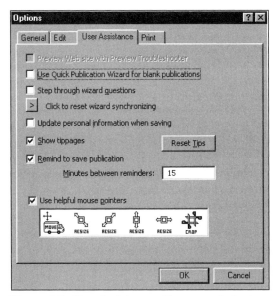

Figure 6-7: User Assistance offers a reminder to save your publication.

The following are the options in the User Assistance tab of the Options dialog box:

✦ **Preview Web site with Preview Troubleshooter:** When checked, the Preview Troubleshooter for Web sites appears after you preview your site. You can use the Help screen to solve any problems with display, graphics, page formatting, and other Web-related issues.

✦ **Use Quick Publication Wizard for blank publications:** By default, the Quick Publication Wizard appears when you choose to use a blank publication. Clear the check box to turn off that feature. You can still display the Quick Publication Wizard from the Catalog at any time.

✦ **Step through wizard questions:** When you choose a wizard from the Catalog, by default, it asks questions so that it can help you to create your publication. If you prefer to display the publication without answering the questions, clear this check box.

✦ **Click to reset wizard synchronizing:** When you change formatting of certain objects, such as smart objects, or when you change your personal information, Publisher automatically changes any information in similar objects. This synchronization saves time and energy. If you don't like the changes that Publisher makes, however, you can use the Undo command to cancel the synchronization for that publication.

If you want to turn on synchronization again for a publication, you use this check box to reset the wizard's synchronization.

✦ **Update personal information when saving:** When checked, Publisher saves any changes to your personal information whenever you save a publication. (For more information about personal information, see Chapter 13, "Entering and Editing Text.")

✦ **Show tippages:** TipPages are the balloon Help screens that appear when you work in Publisher. If you prefer to not show TipPages as you work, clear the check box. A TipPage for any one action or process appears only one time. You can, however, reset the tips so that you can view them again, even on procedures that you've performed previously. Click the Reset Tips button to do so.

✦ **Remind to save publication:** By default, Publisher reminds you every 15 minutes to save your publication. If you prefer not to receive save reminders, clear this check box. If you want reminders but would prefer them every 30 or 60 minutes, for example, enter the new value in the Minutes between reminders text box.

✦ **Use helpful mouse pointers:** By default, Publisher uses a variety of mouse pointers to help you move and resize objects. If you clear this check box, Publisher uses a different set of mouse pointers for these procedures. Clear the text box to view the substitute pointers.

For information about the Print tab of the Options dialog box, see Chapter 30, "Printing in Publisher."

Changing Toolbar Options

You can change various toolbar options, including whether to show ScreenTips and whether to show animations on the menus. You might want to turn off ScreenTips, for example, after you're more familiar with the program.

To change toolbar options, choose View ➪ Toolbars ➪ Options. The Toolbar Options dialog box appears, as shown in Figure 6-8.

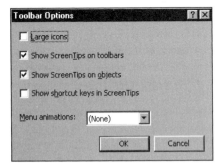

Figure 6-8: Choose options for the toolbars in Publisher.

The following is a description of the toolbar options:

✦ **Large icons:** If you have trouble seeing the buttons on the toolbars, check this box to use large icons. Figure 6-9 shows the screen with enlarged toolbar buttons. Use the arrows at the end of the toolbars to view the rest of the buttons.

✦ **Show ScreenTips on toolbars:** By default, Publisher displays small tips when you place your mouse pointer over a toolbar button. These tips identify the tool, as shown in Figure 6-10. If you prefer to hide the ScreenTips, clear the check box for this option.

✦ **Show ScreenTips on objects:** By default, Publisher displays a ScreenTip when your mouse pointer pauses over an object in your publication. If you prefer to hide the ScreenTips, clear this check box.

✦ **Show shortcut keys in ScreenTips:** Check this box if you want to include keyboard shortcuts in your tool ScreenTips. For example, the Paste ScreenTip shown in Figure 6-10 would read Paste (Ctrl+V) with this option checked.

✦ **Menu animations:** You can change the way a menu appears onscreen. Instead of simply dropping down, you can change to one of the following animations: Random, Unfold, or Slide. You might try each one to see whether you prefer an animation instead of the drop-down menu.

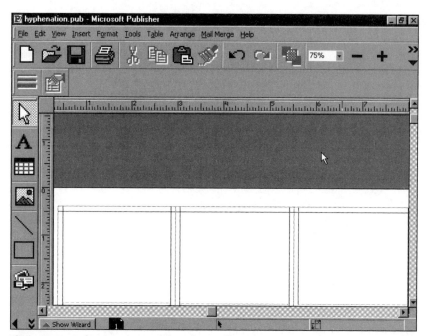

Figure 6-9: Enlarging the tools on the toolbars

Screen Tip

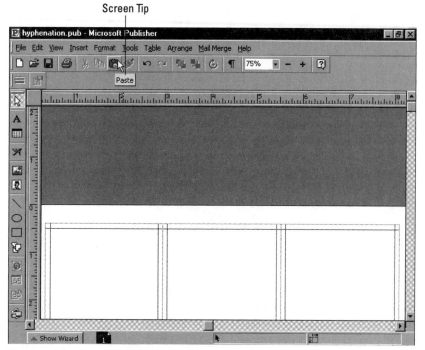

Figure 6-10: Use ScreenTips to identify tools.

Summary

You can set several options within Publisher to make your work environment better suit your working style. In this chapter, you learned to set options for the following:

✦ Measurement units

✦ Previewing fonts

✦ Reminders to save publications

✦ Editing options

✦ Selecting Publisher tools and features to appear onscreen when the program starts

✦ Toolbar options

In the next chapter, you learn about page layout and page design, including orientation, page size, and balancing elements on the page.

✦   ✦   ✦

Working with Page Layout

The page is the foundation to any document or publication. In this part you learn about working with pages in Publisher. You learn to understand page layout and design, and you learn about page elements such as margins, headers, columns, and so on. You learn to use Publisher's rulers, toolbars, and zoom feature. You learn to understand foregrounds and backgrounds in Publisher, and how those views affect document design. One of the most important features in your document is the frame. You learn to create and format frames for text, graphics, and other images. Page setup includes information about planning your document's size, margins, and working with advanced page elements such as crop marks and first pages.

Understanding Page Design

This chapter explains the basics of page design, detailing the elements that make up page design and how best to work with them. Specifically, you learn what page layout is, what page orientation may be best for your publication, what page elements are and how to manipulate them to produce a pleasing layout, and how to work with multiple pages.

Understanding Page Layout

As far as professional design and page layout is concerned, *page layout* refers to the way text and objects are arranged on the page. However, *page layout* also refers to page format and size, the design of the page — white space, use of color, use of emphasis, and so on — and the basic page elements, including margins, columns, headings, and other text items.

In Publisher, *page layout,* or *publication layout,* refers to actual placement of text and objects. In the Quick Publication Wizard, for example, the layout option displays a list of possible placements for text and figures, such as Large picture at the top or Sidebar heading, picture at the bottom. When you select a layout option from the list, Publisher creates the text and picture frames, plus the formatting that you need to create the publication based on that option. Figure 7-1 shows the Layout options in the Quick Publication Wizard.

Even though the Quick Publication Wizard lists various layout options, it omits many other layout possibilities. For example, no layout option exists for three columns on a page or for multiple pictures. If you want to add those items, you must either do it yourself or locate a wizard to do it for you.

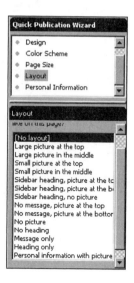

Figure 7-1: Choose a layout in Publisher with the Quick Publication Wizard.

As you become more familiar with Publisher, you'll learn it can't supply every possible page layout option that you need. When you choose to create your own page layout, you need to understand the basics of page design. Knowledge about components such as balance, using margins and columns, applying page orientation, and so on, can help you design your own pages in Publisher. The purpose of this chapter is to help you understand some of these page layout components.

Using Page Orientation

Page orientation describes the way that you view the page—portrait (tall) or landscape (long). The orientation you choose depends on your document's purpose, and the text and graphics that you plan to use.

Understanding orientation

Traditionally, the purpose of a publication dictates its shape. For example, newsletters are generally portrait-oriented, whereas a travel log or expense form might be better suited to a landscape format. Some document types can be either portrait or landscape, but some of the design elements must change to fit the orientation.

Programs, brochures, signs, invoices, statements, banners, advertisements, calendars, and other publications may also fit the landscape format. Catalogs, flyers, greeting cards, letterheads, fax cover sheets, time billing forms, menus, and other publications fit the portrait format.

Figure 7-2 shows an advertisement in landscape orientation. The large text and background design suits the orientation. The design is bold and the advertisement is definitely eye-catching.

Figure 7-3 illustrates the same advertisement in portrait orientation. Note that the type sizes are smaller and that the design has changed somewhat. Although the advertisement still looks good in portrait orientation, it's not quite as exciting as the landscape sample.

In the preceding examples, the ad copy fits into either orientation, even though it may look better in landscape orientation. Some copy, however, doesn't fit into one orientation or the other. Suppose that you have a photograph that is longer than it is tall. Rather than squeeze it into portrait orientation, landscape orientation might work better.

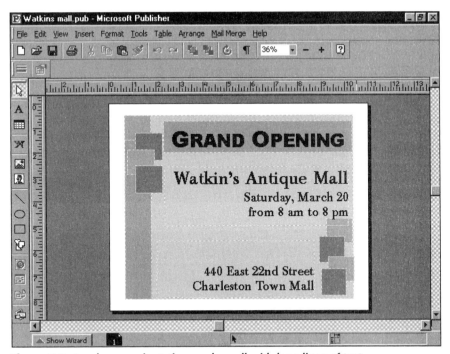

Figure 7-2: Landscape orientation works well with long lines of text.

Figure 7-3: Portrait orientation works well with lists and phrases.

You also must consider the text that you plan to put into one orientation or another. For example, short lists and narrow columns of text suggest portrait orientation. Long paragraphs of text may suggest landscape orientation.

Setting orientation in Publisher

You can set the orientation of a page in Publisher. If you're using the Quick Publication Wizard, click Page Size and then choose either Portrait or Landscape. If you're not using a wizard, follow these steps:

1. Choose File ➪ Page Setup. The Page Setup dialog box appears, as shown in Figure 7-4.

2. In the Choose an Orientation section, choose either Portrait or Landscape. The selected orientation appears in the Preview section of the dialog box.

3. Click OK.

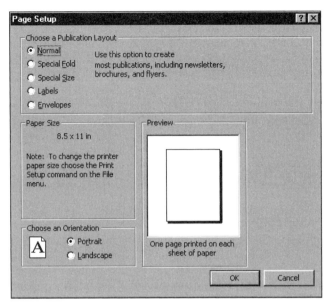

Figure 7-4: Set orientation in the Page Setup dialog box.

Balancing Elements on the Page

Balance is a method by which you distribute text and graphics on the page. Think of the page as a set of scales. No one element should outweigh or dominate another.

Balance leads the reader's eyes through a publication, helping him or her mentally organize the elements on the page and retain more of the message. Page layout generally employs two types of balance: symmetrical and asymmetrical. You should use only one type of balance throughout any publication.

When balancing page elements in a publication, equalize the elements on the page by visual weight. Consider the elements as blacks, whites, and grays. White areas are the margins and other white space. Black areas are either very dark graphics or actual black lines and shapes. Gray is generally the text, or any light screens or images.

Symmetrical balance

Symmetrical balance distributes the page elements — text, graphics, white space, images, and so on — equally on either side of a center point. This invisible center line could be drawn from top to bottom or from left to right. What appears on one side of the center line appears exactly the same on the other side — in visual weight, of course.

Symmetrical balance is formal. Although you could use symmetrical balance on any publication, it's commonly used in reports, books and booklets, formal invitations, and so on. Symmetrical balance also guarantees consistency within a document.

Figure 7-5 illustrates a symmetrically balanced newsletter page. If you draw a line from top to bottom in the center, you can see how the left side balances with the right side. The headlines are the same size and type of font, body text is the same size throughout, and white space is similarly distributed.

Asymmetrical balance

Asymmetrical balance distributes the visual weight differently. No center lines are necessary, because asymmetrical balance isn't as strict as symmetrical balance. One large gray area, for example, can balance multiple smaller gray areas.

Asymmetrical balance is informal, more relaxed than symmetrical. Asymmetrical is also more interesting visually. You can use asymmetrical balance in any document, but especially for advertisements, flyers, newsletters, brochures, and any unconventional publications.

Figure 7-6 illustrates visual weight in a newsletter using the same text as the preceding example. Note that the visual weight of the screened text box helps to balance the black and darker grays of the clip art.

> **Note**   Learn about design by studying various documents. Pick up brochures, flyers, and other documents whenever you run across them. You will find both good and bad designs in your studies. Identify the design elements in each document that attract or offend your aesthetic sensibilities. This knowledge will give you a head start on creating attractive designs for your publications.

Understanding Page Elements

Page elements are physical components that make up a page. Frames, margins, columns, and headers and footers are all page elements that you can add to your publications in Publisher. Each of these page elements is described in the following sections.

Frames

When you enter text, pictures, clip art, tables, charts, or other objects in Publisher, you place these objects in frames. Frames make editing, sizing, and moving their contents easy. In addition to putting objects and text into frames, you can format frames with borders and *fill* (colors or patterns that fill the frame background), divide frames with columns, and set margins for a frame.

Humble Opinions

Volume 3, Issue 11   November, 1998

Y2K
Ready or Not

To prepare for the year 2000, you will need to check your computer hardware, operating system, and software. Some manufacturers are certifying their products as Y2K ready, others are not, yet.

For example, all NT 4 Server and Workstation operating systems are Y2K ready. All Windows 98 operating systems are okay, too. If you plan to purchase any hardware or software from this point on, make sure it too is Y2K compatible, or that the manufacturer has a plan for the year 2000.

What can you do in the mean time? You can test the equipment and software already in place to see if your office is ready for the millenium.

Humble Opinions can test your equipment for you, using McAfee's Toolbox 2000. Toolbox 2000 is a diagnostic application that not only tests hardware, operating systems, and software for Year 2000 compliance, but can also fix many problems it runs into.

As the program tests your equipment, it creates a report about your PC's compliancy. We analyze the report and list, in a more readable format, the problems with each computer and suggested fixes for those problems.

Following are some of the problems the Toolbox 2000 can discover:

Application compliance—It searches the PC for programs that have Y2K issues and lists those issues.

Database and Spreadsheet Analyzer—It studies each database and

Troubleshooting

First Print Job of the Day Takes Longer than Subsequent Jobs
The print spooler must be started the first time you print a file. Depending on your system configuration, this can take several seconds (that add time to your first print job). After the print spooler is started, subsequent print jobs take less time.

Purge Print Jobs Command Won't Stop a Print Job
Purging print jobs stops Windows from sending the print jobs in the queue to the printer. However, it cannot purge print jobs that are currently being processed by the printer. You'll need to reset the printer to terminate any print jobs already in process.

System Hangs During Shutdown
This problem can occur when a system BIOS expects a PS/2-style mouse port to occupy IRQ 12, but a software-configured plug-and-play adapter occupies it instead. You can change the software-configurable device in Device Manager to another IRQ number. Or you could reserve IRQ12 in the Device Manager, so plug-and-play doesn't assign a device to that resource.

Windows Doesn't Start Correctly
If you've just placed one or more applications in the Startup folder so they open on startup, they may be causing the problem.

Windows 95
Tips and Tricks

Videos Don't Play Smoothly
Videos don't play well over a network, so make sure you're running them locally. Also, if your CD-ROM drive is using real-mode drivers, this could be causing your problem. You'll get the best performance from the drive by installing a 32-bit driver; contact the drive's manufacturer to update.

Hardware Device Not Working
If you find that a hardware device—modem, sound card, CD-ROM drive, network card, and such—you can check the status of the device Windows System folder. Choose Start, Programs, Settings, and Control Panel. Double-click the System icon. Select the Device Manager tab. Any device that has an X through it means it is disabled. Double-click the device to check its settings. If the icon has a circled exclamation point, there is a problem. Double-click the icon to find out about the problem.

Excel Doesn't Open to Edit an Embedded Object
If Excel doesn't open when you double-click an embedded object, in Excel, choose Tools, Options and then click the General tab. Clear the Ignore Other Applications check box.

Display and Mouse Act Erratically
If you've just installed a new video card, this problem may occur because you need an updated driver from the vendor. You may be able to download the driver from the Web, or call the manufacturer of the card. If you haven't just installed a new video card but your display and/or mouse are acting erratically, you may need a new

Figure 7-5: Symmetrical balance guarantees consistency.

Humble Opinions

Volume 3, Issue 11   November, 1998

Y2K—Ready or Not

To prepare for the year 2000, you will need to check your computer hardware, operating system, and software. Some manufacturers are certifying their products as Y2K ready, others are not, yet.

For example, all NT 4 Server and Workstation operating systems are Y2K ready. All Windows 98 operating systems are okay, too. If you plan to purchase any hardware or software from this point on, make sure it too is Y2K compatible, or that the manufacturer has a plan for the year 2000.

What can you do in the mean time? You can test the equipment and software already in place to see if your office is ready for the millenium.

Humble Opinions can test your equipment for you, using McAfee's Toolbox

2000. Toolbox 2000 is a diagnostic application that not only tests hardware, operating systems, and software for Year 2000 compliance, but can also fix many problems it runs into.

As the program tests your equipment, it creates a report about your PC's compliancy. We analyze the report and list, in a more readable format, the problems with each computer and suggested fixes for those problems.

Following are some of the problems the Toolbox 2000 can discover:

Application compliance—It searches the PC for programs that have Y2K issues and lists those issues.

Database and Spreadsheet Analyzer—It studies each database and

Troubleshooting

First Print Job of the Day Takes Longer than Subsequent Jobs
The print spooler must be started the first time you print a file. Depending on your system configuration, this can take several seconds (that add time to your first print job). After the print spooler is start-ed, subsequent print jobs take less time.

Purge Print Jobs Command Won't Stop a Print Job
Purging print jobs stops Windows from sending the print jobs in the queue to the printer. However, it cannot purge print jobs that are currently being processed by the printer. You'll need to reset the printer to terminate any print jobs already in process.

System Hangs During Shutdown
This problem can occur when a system BIOS expects a PS/2-style mouse port to occupy IRQ 12, but a software-configured plug-and-play adapter occupies it instead. You can change the software-configurable device in Device Manager to another IRQ number. Or you could reserve IRQ12 in the Device Manager, so plug-and-play doesn't assign a device to that resource.

Windows Doesn't Start Correctly
If you've just placed one or more applications in the Startup folder so they open on startup, they may be causing

Windows 95 Tips and Tricks

Videos Don't Play Smoothly
Videos don't play well over a network, so make sure you're running them locally. Also, if your CD-ROM drive is using real-mode drivers, this could be causing your problem. You'll get the best performance from the drive by installing a 32-bit driver; contact the drive's manufacturer to update.

Hardware Device Not Working
If you find that a hardware device—modem, sound card, CD-ROM drive, network card, and such—you can check the status of the device Windows System folder. Choose Start, Programs, Settings, and Control Panel. Double-click the System icon. Select the Device Manager tab. Any device

that has an X through it means it is disabled. Double-click the device to check its settings. If the icon has a circled exclamation point, there is a problem. Double-click the icon to find out about the problem.

Excel Doesn't Open to Edit an Embedded Object
If Excel doesn't open when you double-click an embedded object, in Excel, choose Tools, Options and then click the General tab. Clear the Ignore Other Applications check box.

Display and Mouse Act Erratically
If you've just installed a new video card, this problem may occur because you need an updated driver from the vendor.

Figure 7-6: Asymmetrical balance is more interesting than symmetrical balance.

Figure 7-7 illustrates one of three text frames in a publication. The active frame is the middle one, which displays eight small boxes, or *handles*, on the corners and edges of the text frame. (For more information about frames, see Chapter 10, "Using Frames.")

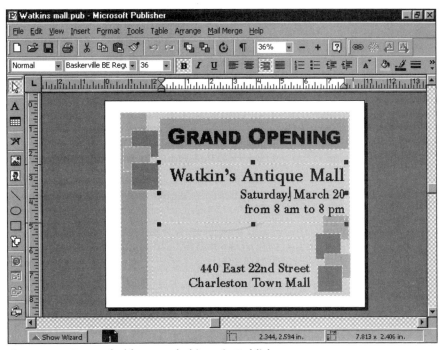

Figure 7-7: Frames hold text and objects in Publisher.

Margins

Margins are the areas of white space around the edge of the page. Margins make the text easier to read, because they give the reader's eyes a rest at the end of a sentence or paragraph. The contrast between the gray of the page and the white of the margin also makes the page more attractive and pleasant to look at.

Margins provide consistency from page to page. After you set the margins for a publication, maintain those same margins throughout the entire document.

Additionally, remember the *unprintable area* set by certain printers (refer to Chapter 4). Check your printer for the minimum amount of necessary margin, and then build the margins in your publications from that starting point. However, including margins that are larger than the quarter-inch or so margins required by most printers is better. The following are a few general guidelines for setting margins:

✦ Use less margin on the top of a page than on the bottom.

✦ Side margins should measure the same as the top margin, unless you're producing a book, in which case you should leave a wider margin for binding.

✦ Uneven margins that employ white space are usually interesting and eye-catching if done well.

Publisher's layout guides

In Publisher, you set the size of margins by using *layout guides*. The default margins of a blank page are one inch for the top, bottom, left, and right. You can change the margins for any publication at any time by following these steps:

1. Choose Arrange ➪ Layout Guides. The Layout Guides dialog box appears, as shown in Figure 7-8.

2. Enter the values, in inches, in the following text boxes: Left, Right, Top, and Bottom.

3. Click OK. Figure 7-9 illustrates an 8.5×11-inch page with half-inch left, right, and top margins and an inch-and-a-half bottom margin.

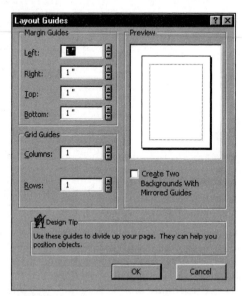

Figure 7-8: Set margins in Publisher by using layout guides.

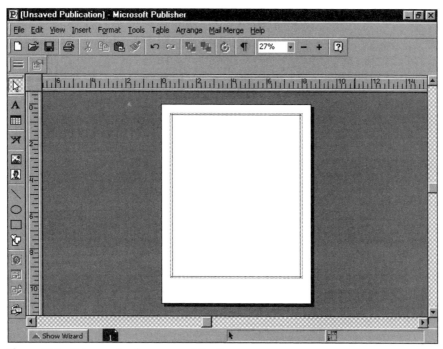

Figure 7-9: Set margins for your publication.

Binding margins

Some documents require a *binding margin* to allow room for fastening together the documents. Books, reports, and some papers might require a wider left margin for staples, punched holes, or the type of stitching used in bookbinding. If the pages are printed on both sides, the front page uses a binding edge on the left, and the back page uses a binding edge on the right, as evident in the pages of this book.

When designing the publication, consider the type of binding that you might use. Generally, you can add an extra inch to the margin to accommodate the binding margin.

Headers and footers

Headers and *footers* are informational sections of the page that are placed in the top (header) or bottom (footer) margin of the page. Headers and footers usually describe the document or its elements, such as the title, author's name, page number, company name, date, and so on. If you plan to use a header or footer in a document, make sure that you leave additional top or bottom margin space; don't squeeze the text into an already confined space.

Note   Use headers or footers, or both, in newsletters, catalogs, books, reports, and other such publications. Format headers and footers in type that is a point size or two smaller than your body text, and usually in bold or italic text. You may also use a horizontal line to separate the header or footer from the text of the document.

To create headers or footers, you draw a frame across the top or bottom of the page. In that frame, you enter the text that you want to use for the header or footer. (For more information, see Chapter 11, "Working with Page Elements.")

Columns and gutters

Columns enable a division of the text and graphics on the page. Documents such as newsletters, brochures, and catalogs commonly use columns. You can use from three to six columns per page, depending on the orientation, page size, and column width.

Gutters are the vertical spaces between columns. Consider gutters extra white space in your documents. Gutters that are too narrow make reading the text difficult, because the columns run together. Gutters that are too wide may separate the ideas of a continued story. Limit gutters to .25 to .35 inch and keep them consistent throughout the publication.

Publisher enables you to insert nonprinting vertical guides to help you lay out the columns on the page. Figure 7-10 illustrates a portrait-oriented page with guides for a three-column format. You can also change gutter width; for more information, see Chapter 11, "Working with Page Elements."

When placing text and graphics in the columns on the page, you use Publisher frames. Publisher provides a method by which you can connect the frames so that a story or article can continue from one column to another. As a general rule, text should flow from the left column to the right.

Your column widths can be either equal or unequal. Be consistent, however, and remember that the most important goal is for the text to flow logically so that readers can understand it; too much distraction in layout or design makes reading the text difficult.

To create columns in Publisher, follow these steps:

1. Choose Arrange ➪ Layout Guides. The Layout Guides dialog box appears, as shown in Figure 7-11.

2. In the Grid Guides area of the dialog box, enter the number of columns in the Columns text box.

3. Click OK. Publisher creates the columns and automatically enters gutter space between the columns.

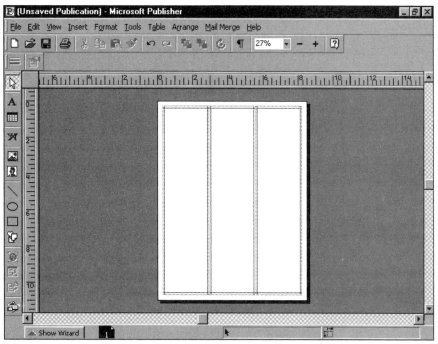

Figure 7-10: Create columns in Publisher by using layout guides.

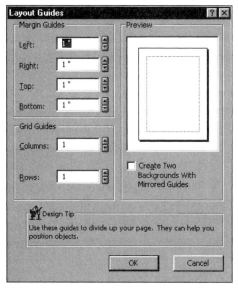

Figure 7-11: Publisher sets gutter space automatically.

Line Length

One factor to consider when creating columns is the length of the line of text. The width of the column determines line length, which influences readability. Lines that are too long or too short can be difficult to read. The general rule to remember is that the smaller the type size, the shorter the line length; the larger the type size, the longer the line length.

You must also consider the font that you use. Some fonts are naturally wider than others. Condensed fonts, such as Bernard MT Condensed or Placard Condensed, require a narrow column, whereas expanded fonts—Braggadocio or Impact—may require a wider column width.

Working with Multiple Pages

Many of your publications will consist of one page; however, many others will use two or more pages. You can easily insert pages as you need them and then move from page to page within the publication.

Inserting a page in Publisher

To insert a page in Publisher, follow these steps:

1. Choose Insert ➪ Page. Alternatively, press Ctrl Shift N. The Insert Page dialog box appears, as shown in Figure 7-12.

Figure 7-12: Add one or multiple pages to your publication.

2. In Number of new pages, enter a value.

3. Choose either Before current page or After current page.

4. You also can choose from the following Options:

   • **Insert blank pages:** The pages you insert will be blank, but they will use the same layout guides and margins as previous pages.

   • **Create one text frame on each page:** The pages you insert will contain one text frame, ready for the insertion of text.

   • **Duplicate all objects on page:** The pages you insert will contain all text and objects that appear on the page whose page number you indicate in the box.

5. Click OK.

Note Many times, you'll print a publication on both the front and the back. Newsletters, brochures, catalogs, and so on are examples of this type of publication. Although readers won't see the front and back simultaneously, and thus can't compare designs, you should still be consistent with columns, margins, and other page elements.

Facing pages

When a publication contains four or more pages, you must arrange those pages as *facing* (or double-sided) pages. A four- or eight-page newsletter, for example, contains facing pages. Whenever you use facing pages, the right-hand pages are always odd-numbered, and the left-hand pages are always even-numbered.

Figure 7-13 illustrates the inside of a four-page newsletter. These facing pages use a mirrored design, whereby the left page is a mirror reflection of the right page. Note how the screened columns and the two-column headlines in page two are reflected in page three.

With facing pages — as with any design — be consistent with columns, margins, gutters, and other page elements. Also, consider the two pages together when you lay out the page. One page's design may work on its own, but you must consider the facing page, too, as you work.

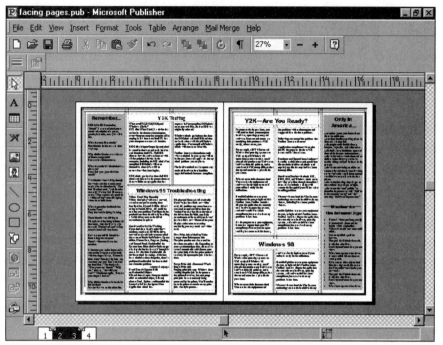

Figure 7-13: A facing page can mirror the other page's design.

Summary

In this chapter, you learned about page layout elements and the basic methods of laying out a page in Publisher. Additionally, you learned about the following:

✦ Using page orientation

✦ Balancing elements on a page

✦ Applying page elements

✦ Working with multiple pages

In the next chapter, you learn about using Publisher's page layout tools, such as rulers, guides, and the Zoom feature.

✦   ✦   ✦

Using Page Layout Tools

Publisher's default view is full page. When you start a new publication or open an existing one, Publisher displays the document so that you can see the entire page and the workspace around it, which is called *Whole Page view*. Figure 8-1 illustrates this view with a newsletter. You can read the newsletter title, or *masthead,* and the large headline; however, you cannot read the text in this view.

Tip Whole Page view is perfect for determining whether the balance, white space, margins, and other design elements need any adjustments.

Understanding Zoom

Publisher provides a variety of views in addition to Whole Page. You'll want to change the view to read and format the text, or enlarge the view to work on a drawing or picture. Publisher's view tool is called Zoom.

Zoom provides you with multiple choices for how to view the page. You can zoom to a certain percentage of the screen, or use the View menu to choose from the three views: Whole Page, Page Width, and Selected Objects.

The Zoom tool offers a range of screen percentages, from 10 percent to 400 percent. You also can type any nonstandard size, such as 73 percent. As Figure 8-2 shows, 100-percent view is perfect for drawing objects or placing graphics and lines. You also can format text in this view.

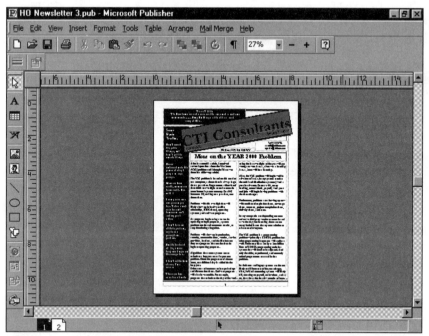

Figure 8-1: Use Whole Page view to check the layout of the page.

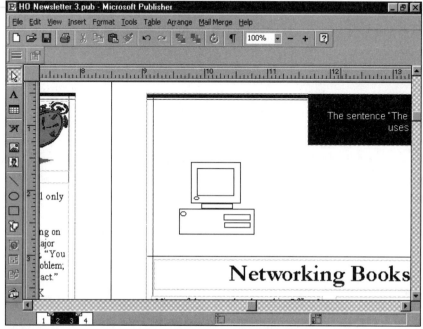

Figure 8-2: Zoom to 100 percent to see the sections of the page.

To do close work with objects and drawings, 400-percent view works well, as shown in Figure 8-3.

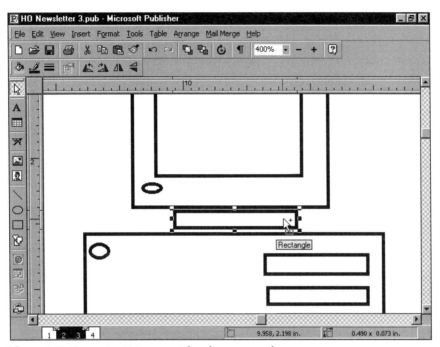

Figure 8-3: Zoom to 400 percent for close-up work.

You also may choose Whole Page, Page Width, or Selected Objects view. Whole Page is the default view that you see when you start Publisher.

Page Width view, shown in Figure 8-4, displays a section of the page from the left edge of the left page to the right edge of the right page. You can read the text, format it, insert objects, and comfortably perform other tasks in this view.

Selected Objects view zooms in to the selected item—text or object—so that you can work on only that object. Figure 8-5 illustrates Selected Objects view; the object fills the entire screen.

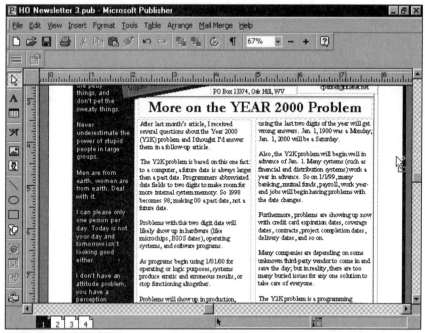

Figure 8-4: Page Width view is a good view for reading the text.

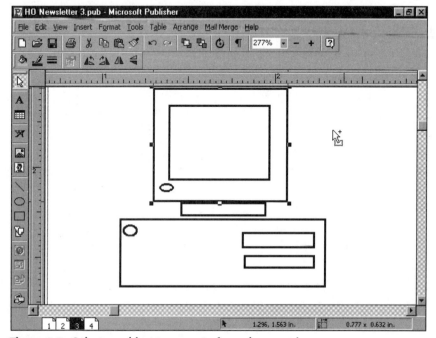

Figure 8-5: Select an object to zoom to for a close-up view.

If you select a frame of text and choose Selected Objects, Publisher zooms in so that you can see the entire frame of text, not any specific text within the frame, as shown in Figure 8-6.

Selected Objects view appears as an option in the menu only when something on the page is selected.

Tip Press the F9 key to switch between the current view and actual size. Press Ctrl+Shift+L to switch to Whole Page view.

Using Zoom

Publisher offers three methods of changing the view of the publication. The variety of views enables you to see any text or object in the publication.

To use the Zoom menu, follow these steps:

1. Choose View ⇨ Zoom and then choose the view from the resulting menu, as shown in Figure 8-7.

2. Choose the view that you want to use.

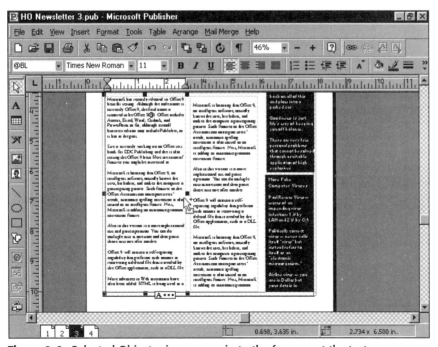

Figure 8-6: Selected Objects view zooms in to the frame, not the text.

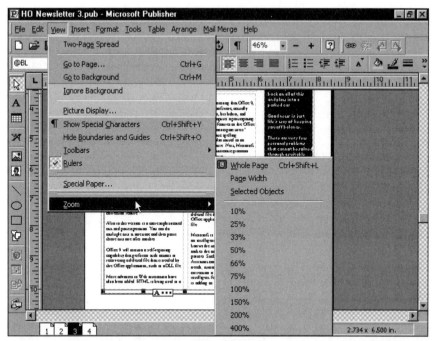

Figure 8-7: Choose from a variety of views.

To use the Zoom button on the Standard toolbar, use one of the following methods:

✦ Type the percentage into the Zoom tool's text box.

✦ Click the down arrow beside the tool's text box and select from the drop-down menu, as shown in Figure 8-8. Note that the ten listed percentages are the same as in the Zoom menu.

Figure 8-8: Change views with the Zoom tool on the Standard toolbar.

To zoom in and out quickly by using the Zoom feature's incremental percentages — 10, 25, 33, and so on — click the Zoom Out or Zoom In buttons on the Standard toolbar (see Figure 8-9).

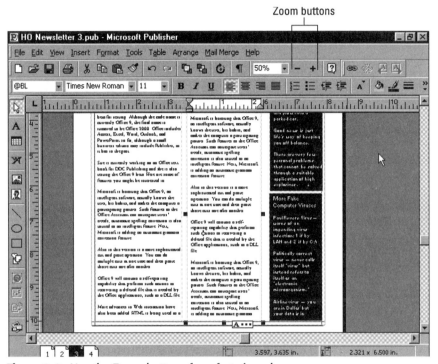

Figure 8-9: Use the Zoom buttons for a fast view change.

Using Rulers

Publisher provides both a horizontal and a vertical ruler to help you measure objects and text and place elements on the page. The rulers are marked with the default measurement of inches, but you can change measurements in the Options dialog box to display centimeters, picas, or points. The horizontal ruler also enables you to set tabs and indents for text quickly and easily. (For more information, see Chapter 15, "Basic Text Formatting.")

Note   To change ruler measurements, choose Tools ⇨ Options. In the Options dialog box, select the General tab. In Measurement units, choose the measurement that you prefer from the drop-down list.

Miscellaneous View Points

Publisher provides a view—the Two-Page Spread—that changes the way the Zoom feature works. If you're using the Two-Page Spread view, Publisher treats both pages as one. For example, choosing the Page Width option yields the following result:

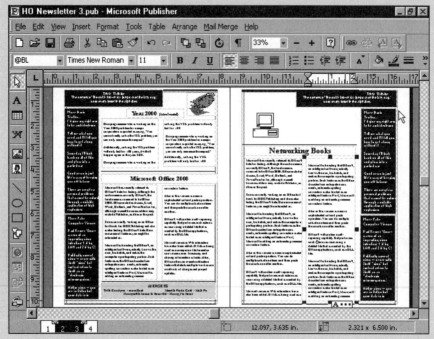

The page width changes when you use Two-Page Spread view.

Publisher shows the "page" in this view from the left page edge to the right page edge. The Page Width option is the only view affected by the Two-Page Spread feature. Percentages and Whole Page view are the same as when viewing one page.

To use the Two-Page Spread feature, choose View ➪ Two-Page Spread. A check mark appears beside the option. To turn off the option, choose View ➪ Two-Page Spread a second time to remove the check mark.

When you select a frame in a publication, Publisher displays the frame's size on the horizontal ruler, as shown in Figure 8-10. The selected frame's width appears in white on the ruler. Note that you can also find the size of the selected frame in the status bar in the Object size area.

Note   To expand the viewing area to see more of the publication, you can always hide the rulers. Choose View ⇨ Rulers to remove the check mark and hide the rulers. Choose View ⇨ Rulers again to add the check mark and show them again.

Selected object   Frame width   Horizontal ruler

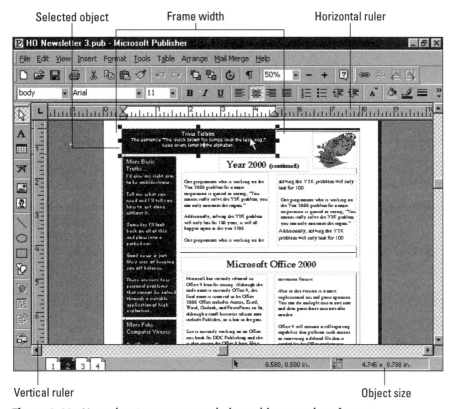

Vertical ruler   Object size

Figure 8-10: Use rulers to measure and place objects, such as frames.

To show rulers, choose View ⇨ Rulers. A check mark appears beside the command. To hide rulers, choose View ⇨ Rulers again to remove the check mark on the View menu.

Moving a ruler

You can move either ruler onscreen so that it's closer to the object that you want to measure. You can also move both rulers at the same time. Additionally, each ruler has a zero point, which corresponds with the upper-left corner of the page. You can move the zero point for one or both rulers, or for both rulers simultaneously.

To move either ruler while leaving the zero point as is, follow these steps:

1. Position the mouse pointer over the ruler border until the mouse changes to a double-headed arrow, as shown in Figure 8-11.

2. Drag the ruler to the new position.

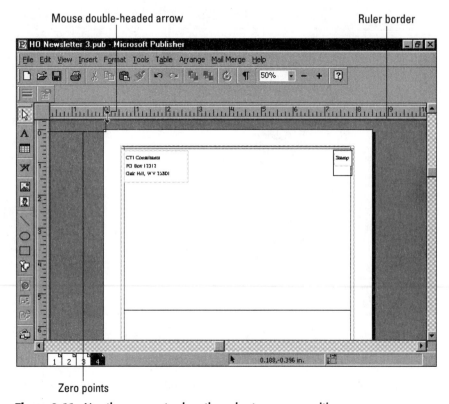

Figure 8-11: Use the mouse to drag the ruler to a new position.

To move both rulers simultaneously while leaving the zero point as is, follow these steps:

1. Position the mouse pointer in the box joining the two rulers. The pointer changes to a diagonal, double-headed arrow.

2. Drag the rulers to a new position, as shown in Figure 8-12. Note the double-headed arrow in the box.

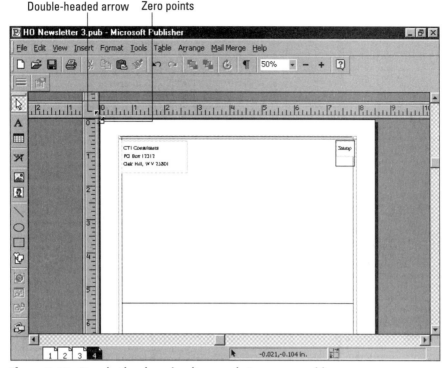

Figure 8-12: Drag both rulers simultaneously to a new position.

To move either ruler and its zero point to a new location, follow these steps:

1. Press and hold down the Shift key.

2. Position the mouse pointer over the vertical ruler border to move the horizontal zero point. Alternatively, position the mouse pointer over the horizontal border to move the vertical zero point.

3. Press and hold down the Ctrl key while you move the ruler and the zero point, as shown in Figure 8-13. Note that the vertical ruler has moved along with the zero point on the horizontal ruler.

4. You can return the zero point to its original position by holding down the Ctrl key while moving the vertical ruler back to the edge of the page. Then, release the Ctrl key and continue moving the vertical ruler back to the edge of the window, if you want.

Horizontal zero point

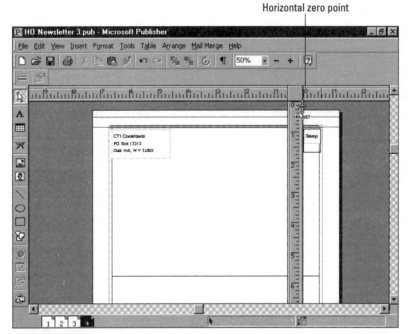

Figure 8-13: Move the horizontal ruler's zero point with the vertical ruler.

To move both rulers and both zero points, follow these steps:

1. Position the mouse pointer in the corner box joining the rulers.

2. Press and hold down the Ctrl key while dragging the box and the zero points to the new location, as shown in Figure 8-14.

Note

To return the zero points and rulers to their original position, press Ctrl and drag the box back to the top-left corner of the page. Release the Ctrl key and then move each ruler back to the edge of the window.

Using guides

Publisher provides various guides to help you place objects, such as frames, tables, pictures, and text. You can create nonprinting ruler guides to help you at any time. Ruler guides appear only on one page, not throughout the publication.

Figure 8-15 illustrates four ruler guides: two horizontal and two vertical. Move the guides to any location with the help of the ruler marks. Ruler guides appear as green dotted lines on the page.

Zero points

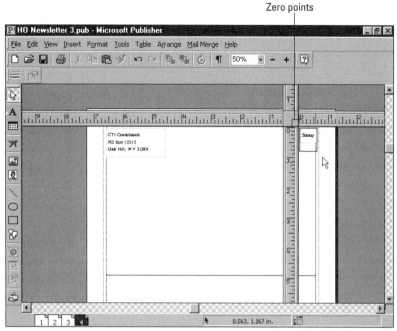

Figure 8-14: Move the zero points to help you measure or place objects.

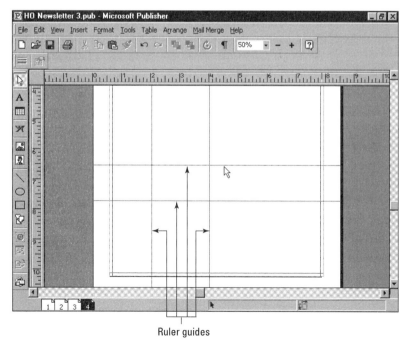

Ruler guides

Figure 8-15: Use ruler guides to help you line up objects or text.

To create a ruler guide, follow these steps:

1. Press and hold down the Shift key.

2. Position the mouse pointer over the ruler until you see the Adjust pointer, shown in Figure 8-16.

3. Drag the pointer to where you want the new guide to be. You can create as many vertical and horizontal guides as you need.

Adjust pointer

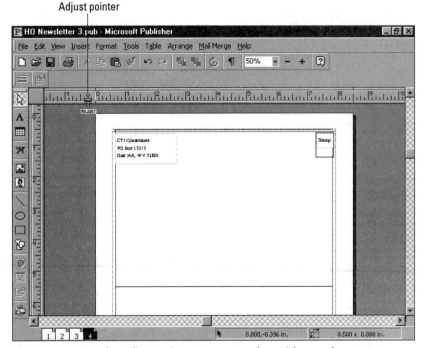

Figure 8-16: Use the Adjust pointer to create ruler guides on the page.

To remove any ruler guide from the page, follow these steps:

1. Press and hold down the Shift key and position the mouse pointer over the guide, to display the Adjust pointer.

2. Drag the guide off the page.

To delete quickly all ruler guides on the page, choose Arrange ➪ Ruler Guides ➪ Clear All Ruler Guides.

To move a guide after it is created, press and hold down the Shift key. Position the mouse pointer to display the Adjust pointer, and then drag the guide to a new position.

Understanding Snap To

To help you position objects, Publisher includes ruler guides and layout guides (see the following section). To make placement even easier, Publisher includes a feature called *Snap To* for each of these guides. Snap To makes the guide or ruler work like a magnet, to pull any line, frame, shape, or other object to the guide. For example, if you create guides for your columns, using Snap To makes any frame that you draw conform to those guides.

The following list provides some information about the Snap To feature:

✦ Three Snap To tools are available: Snap to Ruler Marks, Snap to Guides, and Snap to Objects.

✦ Publisher first snaps to a guide, and then to the nearest object, and then to the closest ruler mark.

✦ The Snap to Ruler Marks feature works even when rulers are hidden.

✦ If Snap to Ruler Marks is on, ruler guides snap to a ruler mark; if Snap to Ruler Marks is off, the guides snap to the nearest object.

To use Snap To, choose either Tools ⇨ Snap to Ruler Marks, Tools ⇨ Snap to Guides (or press Ctrl+W), or Tools ⇨ Snap to Objects.

A check mark appears beside the command on the Tools menu. You can turn off the feature by selecting it again to remove the check mark.

Using Layout Guides

Layout guides differ from ruler guides. Whereas ruler guides appear only on one page, layout guides appear on all pages within the publication. Use layout guides to establish margins, columns, gutters, and other guidelines that you need to use to position text and objects on the page.

Layout guides are nonprinting lines that appear as pink and blue dotted lines on the page, as shown in Figure 8-17. Note that layout guides can create rows as well as columns. In the figure, the three rows help you to lay out a mailing panel for the back of the newsletter.

When you apply layout guides to form rows and columns, you're creating a grid on which you can work. Grids simply divide the page so that you can more accurately place the text and objects. Using grids helps you to control the placement on the page and to create consistency and interest.

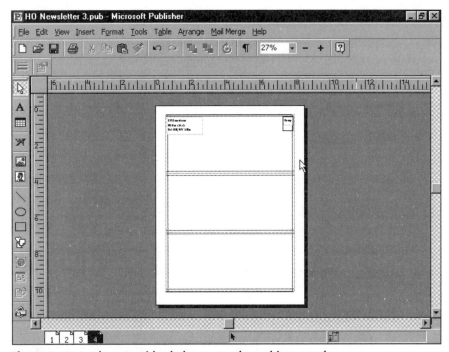

Figure 8-17: Let layout guides help you to place objects on the page.

Understanding layout guides

You create layout guides either by setting a page margin or by creating columns or rows (or both) on the page. Using the Layout Guides dialog box, you can set your margins and insert as many columns or rows as you want, as shown in Figure 8-18. To display the Layout Guides dialog box, choose Arrange ⇨ Layout Guides.

Guides and boundaries

As mentioned previously, layout guides consist of pink (boundaries) and blue (guides) dotted lines on the page. The pink dotted lines represent the measurement that you set; for example, if you divide an 8.5×11-inch page into three vertical columns, the pink dotted lines fall at the 2.5- and 4.75-inch marks. The blue dotted lines create a measure of extra space on either side of the pink line. You use the blue dotted lines as your boundaries for frames, so that they don't bump against each other and appear too crowded or make text difficult to read.

As Figure 8-19 illustrates, the text and picture frames fit inside the blue dotted lines, leaving a margin, or gutter space, between the objects. The grid in the figure creates an interesting layout for the sale items.

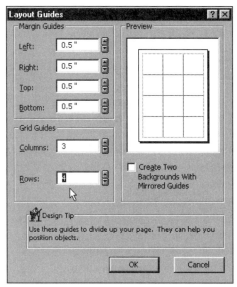

Figure 8-18: Set a grid to help you place objects and text on the page.

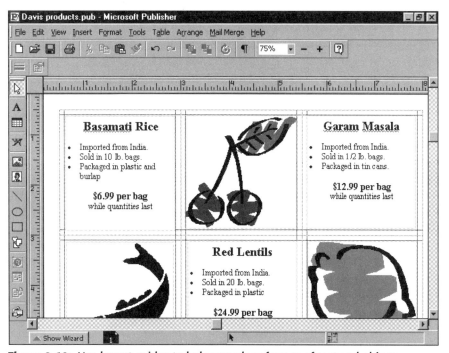

Figure 8-19: Use layout guides to help you place frames of text and objects.

Background view

Sometimes, you may need to adjust the layout guides — move them to create an asymmetrical column layout, for example. But, you'll notice that you can't move layout guides in a normal Publisher view. Publisher provides another view, called Background, that you can use. In Background view, you can move the layout guides.

Publisher provides the background as an area that you can use to create repeating elements, such as headers or footers, a company logo or name, text that you want to appear on every page, and so on. Whatever you place on the background page shows up in the foreground and prints the same as any other object or text. The layout guides are another element found in the background; they also repeat on every page.

You can add, move, delete, or work with an item in the background only by going to Background view. Similarly, you can work with objects in the foreground only when you're in Foreground view. For more information about the foreground and background, see Chapter 9, "Working with Foregrounds and Backgrounds."

To switch between the background and foreground, choose View ➪ Go to Background, or press Ctrl+M. To switch back to the foreground, choose View ➪ Go to Foreground, or press Ctrl+M again. When you switch to the background, Publisher hides items that are located in the foreground.

To move guides, follow these steps:

1. Press Ctrl+M to go to the background.

2. Press and hold down the Shift key.

3. Position the mouse pointer over the guides, to display the Adjust mouse pointer, as shown in Figure 8-20.

4. Drag the guide to its new location.

5. Press Ctrl+M to return to the foreground.

Figure 8-21 illustrates the final page design with the altered guides. Instead of using 12 boxes of equal size, this layout varies the size of the boxes and their content. Also, the change in the guide placement makes room for the store's name and address.

Other great background design ideas are discussed in Chapter 9, "Working with Foregrounds and Backgrounds."

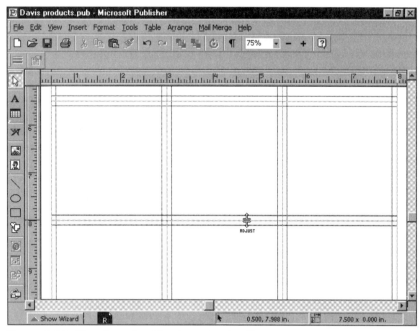

Figure 8-20: Drag layout guides to customize the page.

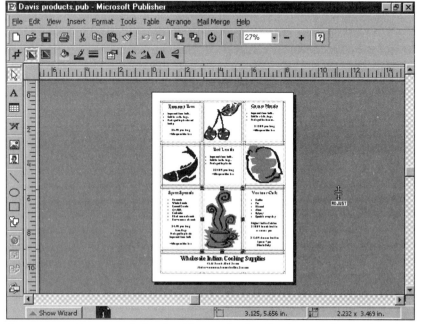

Figure 8-21: The page design is still attractive but fits the copy better than the original layout.

If you have trouble seeing the layout guides, check whether your frame overlaps the guide. Text and object frames are not transparent, unless you make them transparent. (For more information, see Chapter 10, "Using Frames.") Figure 8-22 illustrates the text frame overlapping and hiding the layout guides.

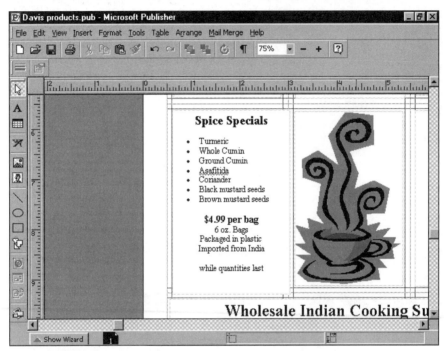

Figure 8-22: If you lose a guide, check for overlapping frames.

Hiding guides

As you work, you might want to hide the layout guides. Sometimes, the guides can distract from the design, especially if you don't plan to use lines and borders in your document. You can hide the guides and then show them again at any time. When you hide guides, the page looks quite different than it did in Figure 8-21, as shown in Figure 8-23. Note that the divisions aren't as clear as they are with the guides showing; you might decide the document needs some borders and lines to spice it up. However, the white space really opens up when no lines or boundaries are used.

To hide the boundaries and guides, choose View ➪ Hide Boundaries and Guides, or press Ctrl+Shift+O. To show the boundaries again, choose View ➪ Show Boundaries and Guides, or press Ctrl+Shift+O a second time.

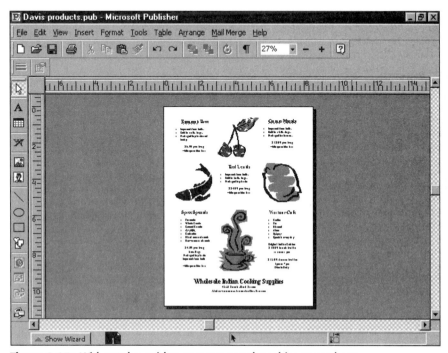

Figure 8-23: Without the guides, you can see the white space better.

Examples of documents using grids

You can use layout guides to create grids of rows and columns on the page. These grids can help you to place text and objects so that the design is consistent and interesting. You can apply grids to any type of document.

Newsletters can use grids that consist of two or three columns and anywhere from two to six or more rows. The rows that you create in a newsletter apply to the newsletter's name, headlines, headers or footers, a contents box, and so on. A flyer might have only one column, or it may have three. In a flyer, rows may apply to the placement of the company's name and address, a large headline, and other items on the page.

Figure 8-24 illustrates a simple layout for a newsletter. The grid clearly consists of two columns and two rows. The balance is symmetrical, and the design is plain yet effective for the copy.

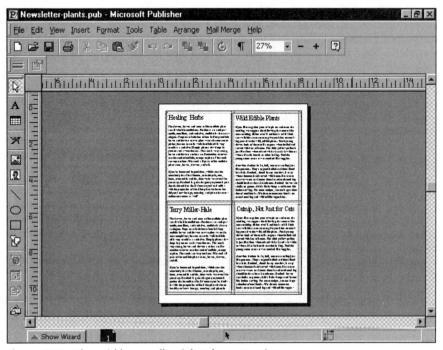

Figure 8-24: The grid keeps all articles the same size.

Figure 8-25 shows the same grid altered to create a more interesting page. The balance is asymmetrical. The text, of course, was altered to suit the layout; but, you can either continue a story on the next page or add or delete some of the text to make it fit the layout.

Using three columns and four rows creates an exciting design for the flyer in Figure 8-26. Instead of fitting the text into strict column boundaries, each text box covers two columns in one row, and the clip art fills in the final column.

Figure 8-27 illustrates the same flyer but in landscape orientation. Three columns and three rows give a different look to the flyer. Again, you don't have to be rigid with the layout guides; use them only as a general design suggestion.

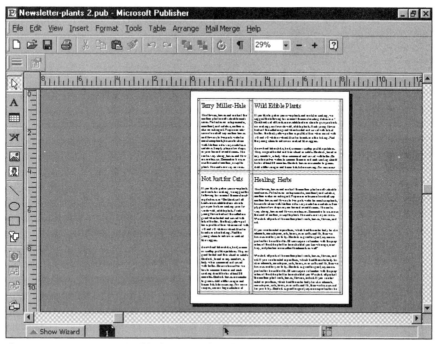

Figure 8-25: Asymmetrical balance and grids make the page interesting.

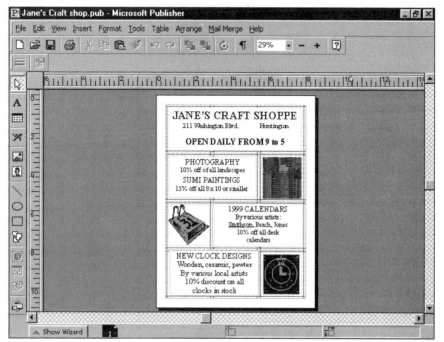

Figure 8-26: You don't have to stick to the exact grids; use them only as a base.

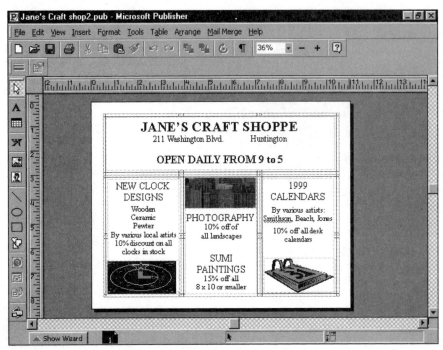

Figure 8-27: Use the grid as a starting point for creating a document.

Summary

In this chapter, you learned about using Publisher's page layout tools when designing a publication. You learned how to do the following:

✦ Use the Zoom feature

✦ Use rulers

✦ Apply layout guides

✦ Create grids for design purposes

In the next chapter, you learn more about working with foregrounds and backgrounds in Publisher.

✦   ✦   ✦

Working with Foregrounds and Backgrounds

Each page in Publisher has a foreground and a background. The foreground is where you work the most. Actually, you don't even have to go to the background, if you don't want to.

You create text and objects on the foreground of every page. You can produce headlines, body text, page borders, tables, pictures, and any other page element on the foreground. You can apply colors and patterns, and you can even layer objects. For example, you might want to layer a set of rectangles, or other shapes, to create a background design on the page.

Figure 9-1 shows three rectangles of varying shades of gray stacked on top of each other to create a background page design. If you want all the pages in your document to contain the same exact design, you can simply copy the rectangles, or other elements, and paste them to each page. (For more information about layering objects, see Chapter 10.)

Note   Boundaries and guides are the only page elements that you can't reproduce in the foreground. You can, however, create ruler guides to help you place elements on the page.

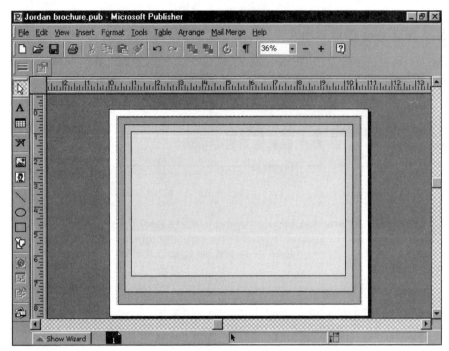

Figure 9-1: You can create any page element in the foreground.

Placing Text in the Foreground

After you create your layout guides on the page, you can use text frames to create any text on the page. In general, the text that you create on each page of a publication changes. You might have various articles in the pages of a newsletter, different details on each page of a brochure, and various tables on each form that you produce. Additionally, you can create the same or similar text on each page for certain page elements.

If you're creating a logo or header, for example, you can copy and paste that text to all other pages in the publication. The handy thing about working in the foreground is that if you want the text to have even the slightest change from page to page — such as page numbers — it's easy to accomplish. You just type in the new text.

Figure 9-2 illustrates the top of a catalog page. The header contains the name of the catalog and the page number. Depending on how you set up a catalog, you might want to copy the exact text frame and use it as a header on the other pages, changing only the page number. Alternatively, you might switch the catalog name and the page number for the left-hand page if you're creating facing catalog pages. (For more information about headers and footers, see Chapter 11.)

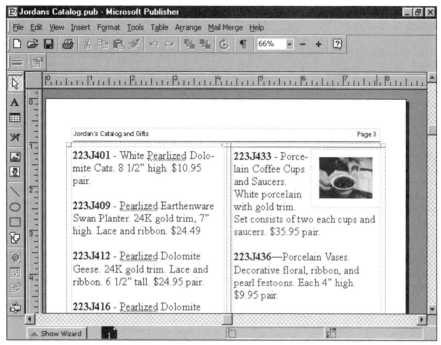

Figure 9-2: Headers are common text frames that appear on every page of the publication.

Another type of text that you can copy and paste to each page is a logo. *Logo text* is the name of a company or product that is specially formatted to stand out from the text around it. Logos may include only text, text and images, or images (pictures, clip art, animations) and graphics (lines, fills, flourishes) only.

You can apply a logo to a publication in a variety of ways. You might place a small logo beside the name of the company, or even in a header or footer. Figure 9-3 illustrates catalog pages in which a text logo is used as a *watermark*—text or a picture that is a light shade of gray or other color so that it remains behind the actual text on the page. In this figure, the logo is the name of the company, and the watermark is large, light gray, and recedes to the background so that you can read the catalog entries.

In this case, the watermark is in the background, defined as one layer down from the actual catalog text; the logo is still in Publisher's foreground page. You can copy this logo to every page in the document. (For more information about watermarks, see Chapter 17.)

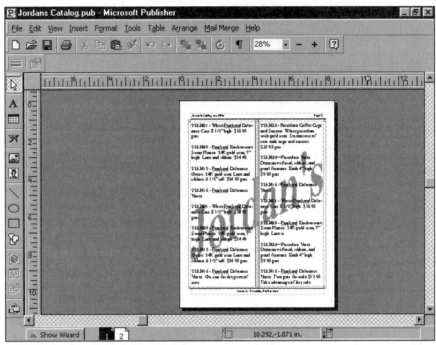

Figure 9-3: The watermark appears behind the catalog text.

Placing Objects in the Foreground

You will place most objects—including pictures, drawings, shapes, lines, clip art, and tables—in the foreground of your publication. Each page of the publication will display different objects; a table, for example, might appear on only one page of the document. Headlines vary from page to page; you also change pictures and clip art to suit the text on each page.

You might want to repeat some objects from page to page, such as lines, shapes, or logos, but you need most objects in the foreground, so that you can adjust the placement of each page's design. If you place horizontal lines within a newsletter page to separate articles, for example, the lines might fall in different places on each page, depending on the length of the stories. If you decide to repeat any objects from page to page, you can easily copy and paste them.

Figure 9-4 illustrates the cover of Jordan's Catalog. Objects on the page include a piece of clip art, two rectangles, three graphic lines, a WordArt logo, and a table in which the contents of the catalog are listed. (For more information about WordArt, see Chapter 21.)

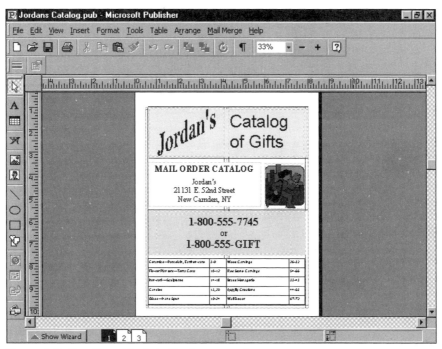

Figure 9-4: Creating objects in the foreground

Understanding the Background

So, if you can place all of your text and objects on the foreground, why use the background at all? You use the background to save time. You use the background for items that you want to repeat on every page. You might want a logo to appear on every page of the publication, for example. A header using the title could appear on every page of the publication. A watermark is another candidate for placement on the background.

How do you use the background if you want some changes in the text? Suppose that you want both the page number and the publication's title in the header. Simple. Place the title of the publication — and any other information that doesn't change — on the background. Create a text box for the page number in the appropriate place in the foreground.

Figure 9-5 illustrates the background of the catalog. You can cut and paste from the foreground to the background such items as the publication's title, the watermark, and even any lines that you want to repeat on every page. These items don't change from page to page.

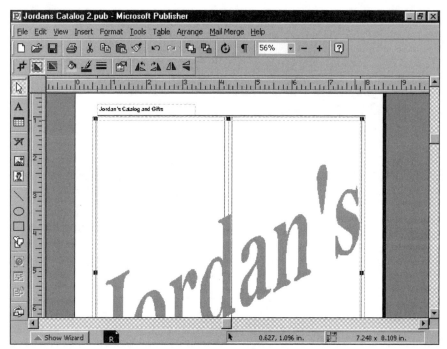

Figure 9-5: Place items that do not change in the background.

Figure 9-6 illustrates the view of the foreground of the publication. The items in the background appear with the text and graphics in the foreground. You can add the page number to the foreground, and any text that changes from page to page.

The background consists of one page if your publication is based on a single-page layout, and consists of two pages — one left and one right — if you're viewing your page in a two-page spread (choose View ➪ Two-Page Spread).

Using the background

You can use the background in Publisher in two different ways:

✦ Switch to the background and then create the objects or text that you want to repeat on every page.

✦ Create the objects in the foreground and then, with a command, send the objects to the background.

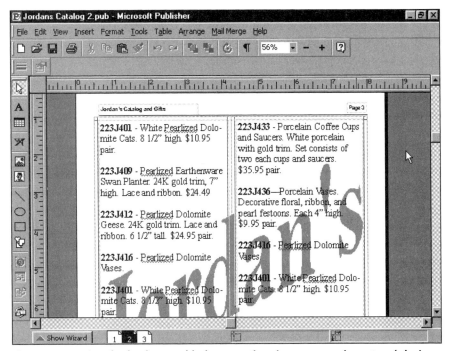

Figure 9-6: Using the background helps save time in your page layout and designs.

Anything in the background is not available for editing in the foreground; therefore, you cannot accidentally delete, modify, or move background objects. You must move to the background to edit the objects. Similarly, any items in the foreground are not available in Background view, so they don't get in your way while you're designing your page. But, you have to go to the foreground to edit those objects.

To view the background, choose View ➪ Go to Background (or press Ctrl+M). To return to the foreground, choose View ➪ Go to Foreground (or press Ctrl+M again).

When you're in the background, you can add frames and objects — text, tables, logos, pictures, colors, shapes, lines, and so on — just as you would in the foreground. The only difference is that those things that you place in the background will show on every page in the publication.

Alternatively, you can transfer objects from the background to the foreground, and vice versa, while you're working. To perform this procedure, follow these steps:

   1. In the foreground, select the item that you want to send to the background.

2. Choose Arrange ⇨ Send to Background. The item moves to the background. A Publisher confirmation dialog box appears (see Figure 9-7).

3. Click OK.

Figure 9-7: Confirm the move to the background.

To move an object from the background to the foreground, you must first move to the background. Remember, the background consists of only one (single-page layout) or two (two-page spread) pages. So, you must select the page to which you want to send the object while in the foreground, if you want the object transferred to the appropriate page. To move the object from the background to the foreground, follow these steps:

1. In the foreground, select the page by clicking anywhere on the page to which you want to send the object.

2. Move to the background.

3. Select the object that you want to move.

4. Choose Arrange ⇨ Send to Foreground. The confirmation dialog box appears, telling you the page number to which Publisher sent the object.

5. Click OK.

Hiding elements in the background

Your next question might be what to do if you don't want a background object on one page to show. You can draw a text frame over the object, or you can hide all the background objects on that page.

Foreground objects, or frames, can cover background objects. A text or other type of frame is opaque, by default. Unless you make it transparent, you can draw a frame in the foreground and hide one or more objects, as shown in Figure 9-8. This frame covers only part of the watermark, but you could make the frame the size of the background frame to cover it all. Naturally, you can enter text or another object in that frame. You can even layer another frame on top of the text frame. (For more information about frames, see Chapter 10.)

To make a frame transparent, select it and then press Ctrl+T. To make it opaque again, press Ctrl+T again.

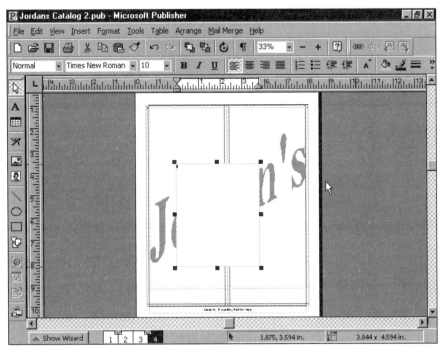

Figure 9-8: Hide one background object by drawing a frame in the foreground.

You might want to hide all objects in the background for one page. Or, you may want to hide all objects on only left pages or only right pages. You can easily do either. To hide all objects on a page, follow these steps:

1. Choose View ➪ Ignore Background. The Ignore Background dialog box appears, as shown in Figure 9-9.

Figure 9-9: Ignore the background on the left, right, or both pages of the publication.

2. Choose Left page, Right page, or both check boxes to hide the background, as shown in Figure 9-10. Note that the watermark and both the header and footer are hidden on the left page.

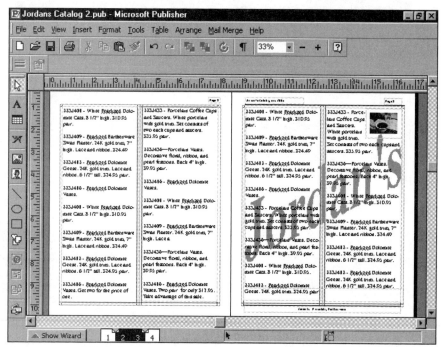

Figure 9-10: Hiding all objects on the left page, for example, might make the watermark on the right page more interesting.

3. Click OK.

To show the background objects again, reverse the steps. When you choose View, a check mark appears beside the Ignore Background command. Choose the command again to turn it off. The Ignore Background dialog box appears again, and you select the background that you want to view.

Designing Publications with Backgrounds

You've seen how a watermark can enhance the background pages of a catalog or other publication. Many other designs can be accomplished by using the background feature.

Using fills

You can draw any number of shapes in the background of your publication and then fill the shapes with various colors or patterns. Even though you can create some interesting and novel backgrounds, don't make the backgrounds so distracting that you can't read the text in the foreground.

Figure 9-11, for example, shows a rectangle filled with color as a background for the catalog. Note that the header and footer still show, but outside the rectangle, to distinguish them from the text.

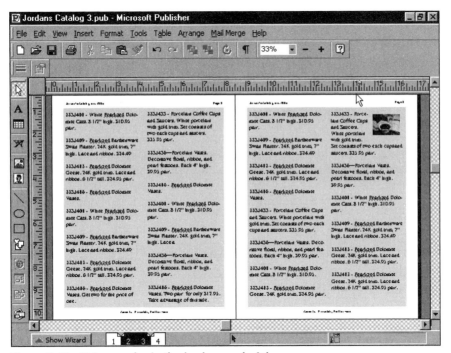

Figure 9-11: Using a color in the background of the page.

Tip   Light colors, such as light gray or yellow, are best for backgrounds when you use black type in the foreground.

Gradients and patterns are interesting for backgrounds, too. Make sure, however, that the text is still readable when you use any kind of background color or design. Figure 9-12 illustrates a gradient fill for the rectangle. (For more information about filling shapes and objects, see Chapter 20.)

You can also vary the shapes in the background, as shown in Figure 9-13. These shapes fit the columns and layout guides, but also add a bit of excitement.

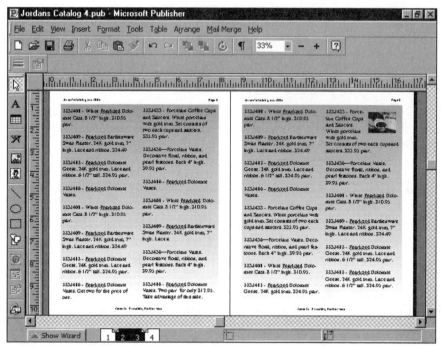

Figure 9-12: Variety in the background should be interesting but not distracting.

Using borders

You can also use a series of lines or borders to add to the background layout of your publication. Often, when you're working with your boundaries and guides showing, you forget that the page may look empty without them.

Use the guides to help you place text, but when you're looking at the design, turn off boundaries and guides (press Ctrl+Shift+O). Figure 9-14 illustrates a border and gutter line drawn in the background. With boundaries turned off, you can better see the effect of the lines in the document.

Adding logos

You can create company or product logos by using text, graphics, or both. You might want to use the company name, initials, or a symbol to represent the company. A logo is a symbol of identity; it projects an image for the company or product. When designing a logo, you might stretch or condense the text, rotate the text, place the logo on a curve, and so on. You can add one or more lines or shapes to the logo, or use a picture or other image. (For more information, see Chapter 17 and Chapter 22.)

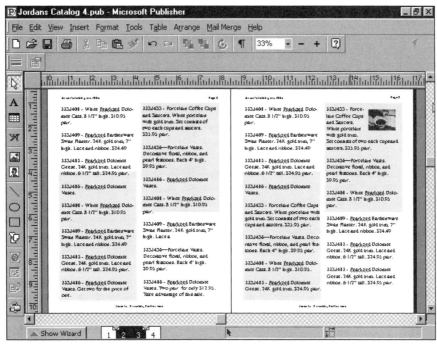

Figure 9-13: Use shapes that reflect the column or grid layout of the page.

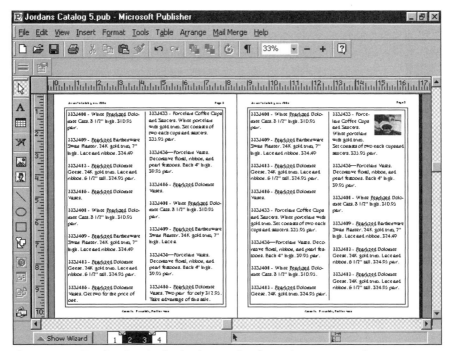

Figure 9-14: Use borders in the background to keep the pages consistent.

A logo is the perfect element to add to the background of a publication. Likely candidates for the logo include company forms, reports, fax cover sheets, memo sheets, and product information sheets. Also, you can place a logo on all right-hand pages, for example, of a catalog or newsletter. The logo helps identify the company or product and keep it foremost in the customer's mind.

Figure 9-15 illustrates a text logo on a form. The logo includes the name of the printing company, so both are located in the background. The publication file contains various forms for the company, each bearing the same logo.

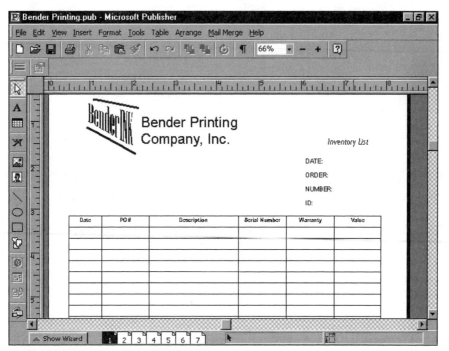

Figure 9-15: The logo identifies the company.

Figure 9-16 shows a text and image logo on a business card. The publication file holds four different business cards, all using the same logo. Placing the logo in the background makes it easy to create additional cards.

Another handy use for dividing background and foreground elements is in a set of advertisements. Figure 9-17 shows an ad for a newspaper. Each Wednesday, the ad copy changes, but the size of the ad, the border, and the logo and address remain the same. Using the background for the repeated elements makes creating an ad each week quick and easy. Keeping the ads in a file helps the owner remember what was on sale last week.

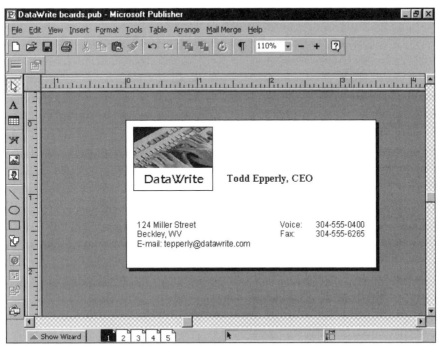

Figure 9-16: A picture makes the logo more interesting.

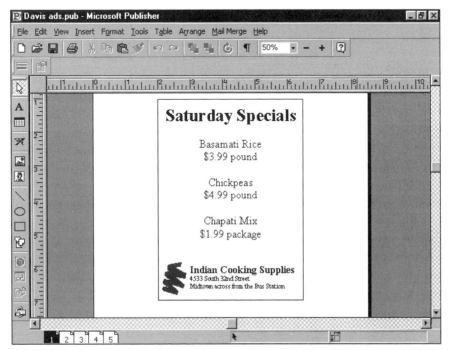

Figure 9-17: Use repeated elements in the background of an advertisement.

You can use the background with any number of documents. Your goal is to make creating the document easier while maintaining a professional and consistent look to your publications. Using the background can help you accomplish these goals.

Summary

In this chapter, you learned how to use foregrounds and backgrounds effectively. You also learned about the following:

✦ Displaying the background

✦ Ignoring the background

✦ Designing documents by using the background

In the next chapter, you learn about using frames to hold text, pictures, and objects.

✦   ✦   ✦

Using Frames

Frames are "boxes" in which you place text or objects. Nearly everything that you place on a page in Publisher — text, pictures, clip art, tables, and so on — must use a frame. About the only things for which you don't need a frame are those shapes and lines that you draw by using the line, oval, or rectangle tools. You can place these objects in a frame, but you don't have to. (For more information about drawing shapes and lines, see Chapter 20.)

Figure 10-1 shows the beginnings of a publication. The page contains two frames — one text and one clip art. Note that the clip art frame overlaps the text frame, but the text wraps around the clip art so that you can still read it.

You can move frames on the page, or copy and paste frames to other pages in a publication. You can resize frames to make them larger or smaller than their contents, or size them to fit their contents exactly. You can apply borders and fills (color or patterns) to frames in addition to the text or other elements. You also can apply margins and columns to a frame.

Figure 10-2 illustrates three frames. The first (left) is a plain frame with a border; the second (center) frame contains a gradient fill; and the third (right) frame uses a solid gray fill with a border on the top and bottom of the frame.

Thus far, "text and objects" have been discussed as two elements in Publisher. Objects include tables, pictures, and elements other than text. A frame is also an object, however, because you can format, resize , and otherwise treat it the same as you treat other objects. (For more information about objects, see Chapter 18.)

When you work with frames, you'll find that the default frame is opaque. However, you can make any frame transparent. Opaque and transparent frames come in handy when you overlap text and graphic frames for special effects, such as when you use a watermark in the background of a text page, as shown in Figure 10-3.

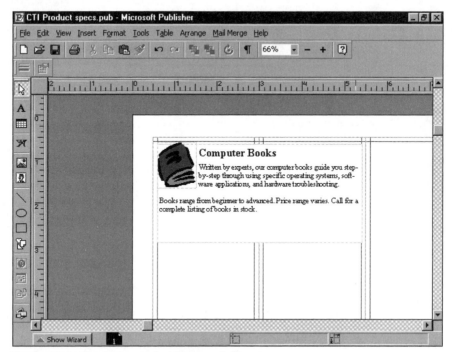

Figure 10-1: Use frames to hold text and clip art.

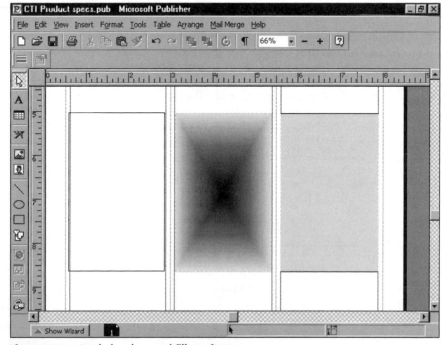

Figure 10-2: Apply borders and fills to frames.

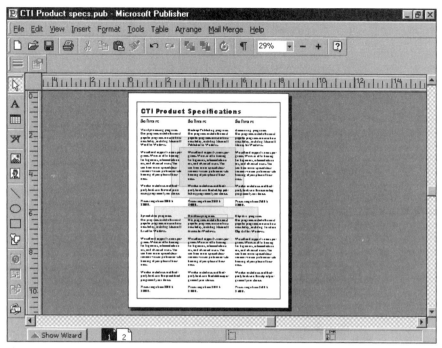

Figure 10-3: A watermark can consist of text, an image, or a combination of both.

Defining Frame Types

Publisher provides various frame types for you to use on the page, including text, table, picture, WordArt, and clip art frames. You must choose the tool for a specific frame type and then draw that frame on the page. You may enter only one type of element within each frame. For example, you cannot create text within a picture frame.

The following is a description of the various frame types available with Publisher.

✦ **Text frame tool:** Creates a frame for use with text of any kind. After you draw the frame, you type in it and then format the text as you want. (For more information about entering and formatting text, see Part III, "Working with Text.")

✦ **Table frame tool:** Creates a frame and a table, using the number of rows and columns that you specify, plus a table format that you select. After you create the frame and table, you enter values in the table cells. (For more information about tables, see Chapter 22.) Figure 10-4 shows a simple table in a Publisher publication. You can choose from various table formats or design your own table.

	1996	1997
Software	65%	50%
Books	25%	42%
Misc	10%	8%

Figure 10-4: Use tables in publications to display information in an easy-to-understand format.

✦ **WordArt frame tool:** Creates a frame and then opens the WordArt program, in which you enter and format special text for logos or fanciful headlines. (For more information about WordArt, see Chapter 21.) Figure 10-5 illustrates a WordArt frame and logo for CTI Technologies. You can choose from many shapes and fonts to create a logo or other word design.

Figure 10-5: WordArt enables you to fill a frame with fancy text.

✦ **Picture frame tool:** Creates a frame in which you can import a photograph, clip art, or other picture files. (For more information, see Chapter 19.) Figure 10-6 shows a picture in a frame. You can insert into a picture frame any picture from a file, scanner, camera, and so on.

✦ **Clip Gallery frame tool:** Creates a frame and opens the Microsoft Clip Gallery, from which you can insert sound, motion, and clip art clips. (See Chapter 19 for more information.) Figure 10-7 shows two clips: the left clip is a pine tree, and the right clip is an animated motion clip of a cat. You also can acquire various clips from the Internet.

Figure 10-6: The picture fills the frame.

 Tip   You might want to use sound or motion clips for publications that you send via e-mail or display on the Internet, such as on a Web site. For more information, see Part VIII.

Figure 10-7: Use various clips in your publications.

Creating a Frame

To create a frame, you first click the frame tool that you want to create. The mouse pointer changes to a cross, as shown in Figure 10-8. Drag the mouse over the page until the frame is the size that you want; then, release the mouse button.

Defining Frame Elements

Even though you must use different frames to hold different objects, all frames have basic characteristics in common. You have to select a frame to edit it, for example. You can move, copy, cut, and delete any frame. You can make all frames transparent or opaque, although the contents may or may not follow suit. The following sections describe some of the common frame characteristics.

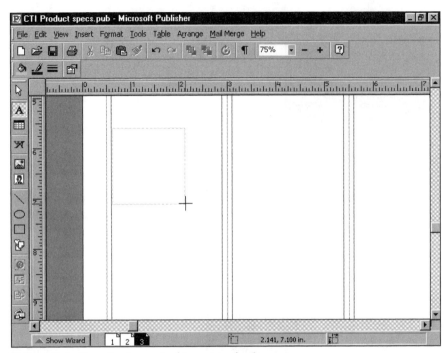

Figure 10-8: Drag the frame tool to create the frame.

Selecting frames

You select a frame to edit it in some way, such as to move, cut, copy, or format it, or insert text or an object into it. To select a frame, click the frame with the mouse pointer.

When you select a frame, eight small black boxes, called *handles*, appear on the corners and edges of the frame, as shown in Figure 10-9. This figure illustrates the frame and handles with the Boundaries and Guides showing so that you can also see the outline of the frame. The clip art of the book also has an outline, but it has no handles around its outline, which indicates that it isn't selected.

To deselect a frame, click the mouse anywhere outside the object, such as at the edge of the page or in the workspace. The handles disappear when you deselect a frame.

Selecting multiple frames

To select two or more frames simultaneously, click the first frame, press and hold down the Shift key, and then click the other frames. Figure 10-10 illustrates two selected frames: the text frame and the clip art frame. Note that both frames have handles around them; the frame outlines don't show because the Boundaries and Guides are hidden.

Handles

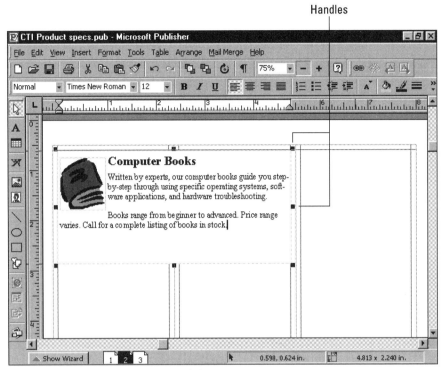

Figure 10-9: Select one frame by clicking it.

When you select multiple frames, one larger frame, or box, appears around all of them. You can easily move, delete, or perform other actions on all selected frames simultaneously.

To deselect one frame from several that you have selected, press and hold down the Shift key and then click the frame that you want to deselect. To deselect all selected frames, click the side of the page or inside the workspace.

Grouping frames

Notice the Group Objects button when you select multiple frames. If you click the button, Publisher *locks*, or groups, together the frames. Grouping the frames means that they act as one frame; so, the next time that you click the frame, both objects are selected. Also, if you edit the grouped frame, such as add a fill to the frame, the fill covers both frames.

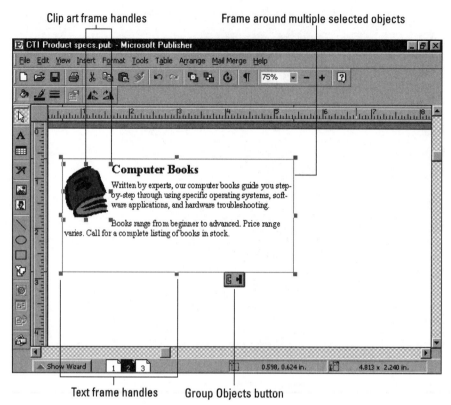

Figure 10-10: Select multiple frames to edit them together.

Figure 10-11 shows the two frames grouped together, with a fill added. Note that the Group Objects button is now locked, the fill covers the entire frame, and the frame border is different from the border for a single object.

To ungroup frames that you have grouped together, select the frames and then click the Ungroup Objects button.

You can select all frames on a page quickly by choosing Edit ➪ Select All. Publisher draws a frame around all objects on the page. Deselect one or all objects as described previously.

Positioning frames

As with other objects, Publisher can help you to position frames. You can use the following Snap To tools with frames:

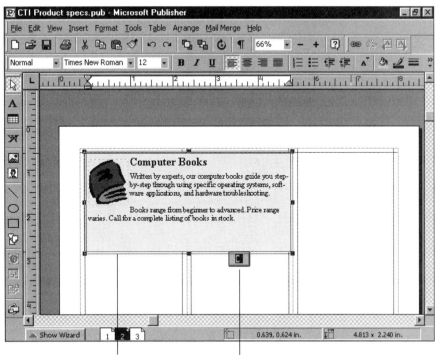

Grouped frame border   Ungroup Objects button

Figure 10-11: Group frames together so that they act as one frame.

- ✦ Snap to Ruler Marks
- ✦ Snap to Guides
- ✦ Snap to Objects

See Chapter 8 for more information.

Creating frame margins

For any frame that you create, you can also create margins within that frame. You might want to add margins so that a frame border doesn't run up against the text or picture, for example. You might want to add a frame margin to employ extra white space in your document. Figure 10-12 illustrates a text frame and a picture frame. The margin in the picture frame (around the picture itself) separates the text from the frame, thus avoiding a crowded look.

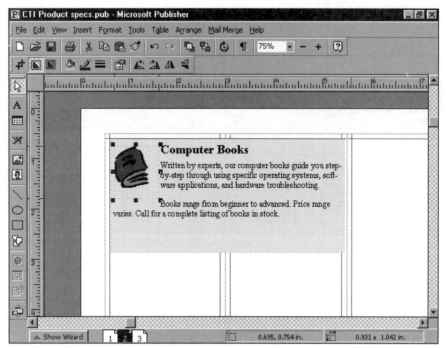

Figure 10-12: When you add margins to the picture frame, Publisher reduces the picture to make room for the margins.

Publisher considers frame margins to be a *property,* or characteristic, of the frame. Therefore, you can find the dialog box for changing frame margins in the Format menu under the Frame Properties command. The command for each type of frame varies a bit. Select the frame and then choose the appropriate command for the frame type, as set forth here:

Frame Type	Command
Text	Format ⇨ Text Frame Properties
Clip or Picture	Format ⇨ Picture Frame Properties
WordArt	Format ⇨ Object Frame Properties
Table	Format ⇨ Table Cell Properties

Note   The Table Cell Properties dialog box works a bit differently than the dialog boxes for the other frame margins. For the table, you set the margins for each individual cell in the table, not for the frame that holds the table.

In the Properties dialog box, enter the value for each margin, or click the spinner arrows to set the value.

Setting frame margins for an object

An object's Frame Properties dialog box looks a bit different than the Text Frame Properties dialog box. Figure 10-13 shows the Picture Frame Properties dialog box, in which you can set the margins and text wrap. (For information about text wrap, see the next section.) You can set one margin, two margins, or all margins for the graphic. When you set a margin, the picture or object reduces in size to make room for the margin.

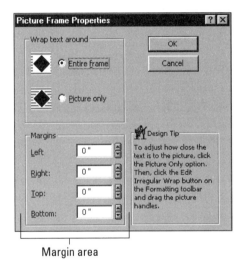

Margin area

Figure 10-13: Set the margins for a frame in the Frame Properties dialog box.

Setting frame margins and columns for a text frame

The Text Frame Properties dialog box, shown in Figure 10-14, includes more options than the object's Properties dialog box. In the text frame, you can also set columns and text wrap options.

The default margin for any text frame is .04 inch, but you can change that for one or all of the frame's margins.

You also set a frame's columns and gutter space in the Text Frame Properties dialog box. In the Columns area, enter the number of columns and the amount of space that you want to apply to the gutter between the columns. The default spacing is .08 inch, but you can change it to any amount that you want.

Tip

For readability, you should use at least $^1/_5$-inch gutter space, but $^1/_4$-inch gutter space is better.

Figure 10-15 shows a text frame with two columns of text. The gutter space is $^1/_4$ inch in the figure.

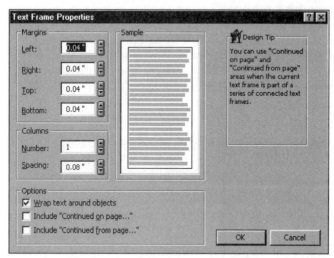

Figure 10-14: Set a frame's margins and columns.

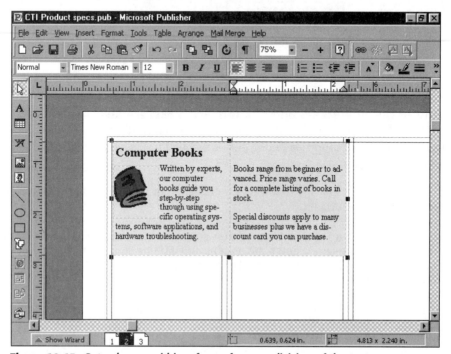

Figure 10-15: Set columns within a frame for easy division of the text.

Wrapping text around a frame

Wrapping text describes how the text around a frame behaves. In Figure 10-15, the text wraps around the book clip art. Text can either wrap around the picture frame or wrap around the object itself, for a more interesting effect. By default, Publisher wraps text in a text frame around the frame of any objects that you place within that frame.

Figure 10-16 shows a piece of clip art with a border and a photograph each inserted into text frames. Both pictures have margins set, and the text wraps around them for a nice effect.

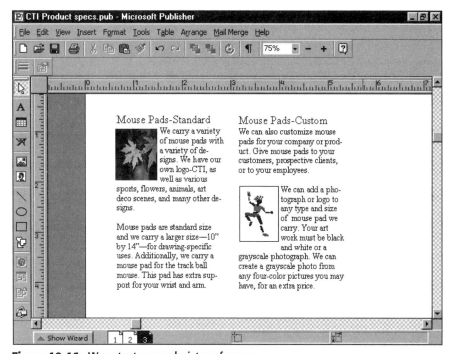

Figure 10-16: Wrap text around picture frames.

You also can wrap text around the *object*—a picture or clip art, for example—within the frame, as shown in Figure 10-17. The text borders the clip art of the computer instead of the clip art's frame. You can still set a margin around the object so that the text doesn't crowd the picture.

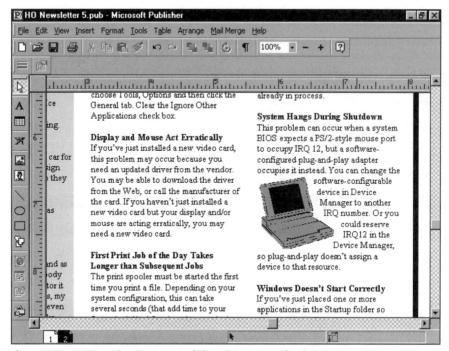

Figure 10-17: Wrapping text around the picture, not the frame

To set the text wrap options, follow these steps:

1. Select the picture frame.

2. Choose Format ➪ Picture Frame Properties. The Picture Frame Properties dialog box appears.

3. To wrap text around the frame, choose Entire frame, and then set the frame margins in the Margins area of the dialog box.

   To wrap text around the picture's shape, choose *Picture only*. Set the outside margin in the Outside text box, as shown in Figure 10-18.

4. Click OK.

You must also set the text frame to wrap around the objects. To do that, follow these steps:

1. Select the text frame.

2. Choose Format ➪ Text Frame Properties. Alternatively, you can click the Text Frame Properties button on the Formatting toolbar. The Text Frame Properties dialog box appears, as shown in Figure 10-19.

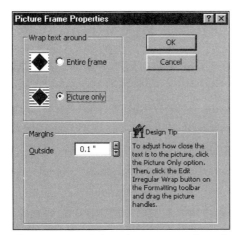

Figure 10-18: Select the text wrap by using the picture frame's properties.

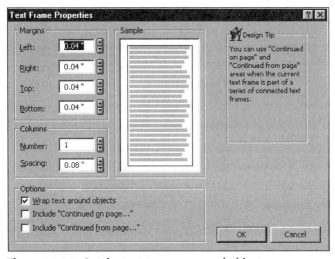

Figure 10-19: Set the text to wrap around objects.

3. In the Options section, check the Wrap text around objects check box.

4. Click OK.

Using Frame Borders and Fills

You can use borders and fills to divide and organize the elements within text and object frames. Borders and fills also add emphasis to the publication and add interest to the page. *Borders* are lines that you apply to the top, bottom, left, right, or all edges of the frame. *Fills* are colors and patterns that you apply to a frame background.

Figure 10-20 illustrates a pull quote, or callout. The frame uses a top and bottom border plus a light-gray fill to pull attention to it. Note, too, that the text in the frame wraps around the quote's frame to create an interesting effect.

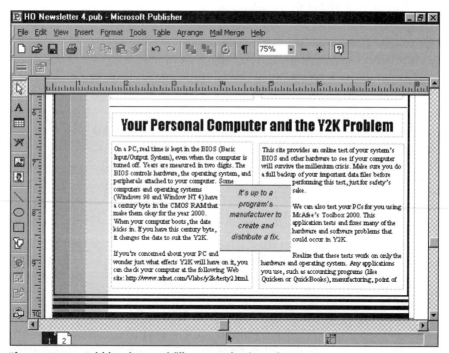

Figure 10-20: Add borders and fills to emphasize a frame.

Using borders

Publisher offers various thicknesses and colors for your borders. You can apply a color that matches your color scheme, or choose another color or pattern. A *color scheme* is a set of six or so colors that look good together. Publisher uses color schemes in its design wizards, and you can use them in your documents, regardless of whether you use Publisher's designs.

Publisher also offers fancy borders that contain flowers, animals, shapes, and colors. You might want to apply Publisher's border art to a page frame for a sign or poster, for example. You can also add a shadow to the frame border, to give the frame the illusion of depth.

Line borders

Line borders consist of a thick or thin line that surrounds the frame or appears only on one, two, or three sides of the frame. You can apply any thickness or color to the line border.

To add a line border to a frame, follow these steps:

1. Select the frame.

2. Choose Format ➪ Line/Border Style. A cascading menu appears, as shown in Figure 10-21. Alternatively, you can click the Line/Border Style button on the Formatting toolbar to display the menu.

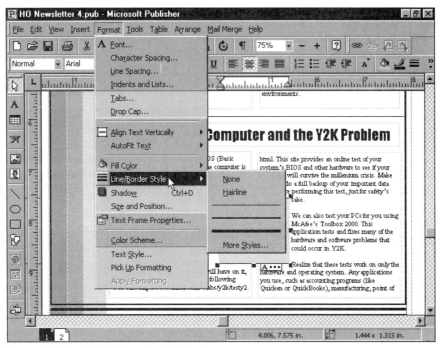

Figure 10-21: Select a border for the frame.

3. Choose a border, or choose More Styles to display the Border Style dialog box, as shown in Figure 10-22.

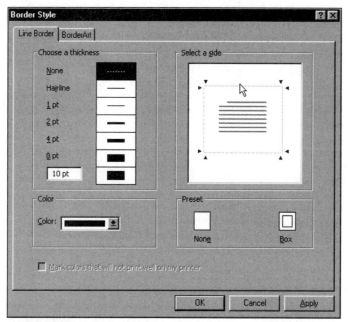

Figure 10-22: The Line Border tab enables you to choose the thickness of your border.

4. In the Line Border tab, choose the line that you want in the Choose a thickness area. You can also enter a value in the text box, to specify a different line thickness.

5. In the Select a side area, click the sides where you want the border to appear. If you want the border on all sides, click Box in the Preset area.

6. If you want to apply a color, click the Color drop-down arrow to display the color menu (see the following section).

7. Click OK to close the dialog box.

Border color

You can apply any color in your scheme, or some other color, to a line border. To apply a line border color, follow these steps:

1. In the Border Style dialog box, click the Color drop-down arrow. Alternatively, click the Line Color button on the Formatting toolbar to display the color menu, shown in Figure 10-23.

2. Choose a Scheme color from the ones shown, or choose More Color Schemes to display the Color Schemes dialog box. Alternatively, choose More Colors to display the Colors dialog box, shown in Figure 10-24.

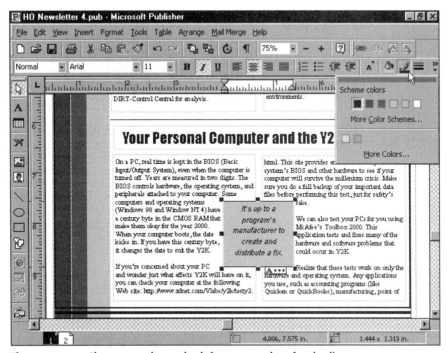

Figure 10-23: Choose a color, or look for more colors for the line.

3. Choose a color from box 1. If necessary, choose a color from box 2, which shows a range of colors related to the one that you selected in box 1.

4. Click OK to apply the color.

Tip

If you're familiar with color models, you can enter a value for red, green, and blue to create an exact color of line. For more information about color models, see Chapter 31.

Border art

As an alternative to a line border, you can apply a decorative border to a frame. Publisher offers various border art designs to choose from, such as apples, balloons, and baby rattles. Also included in the list are double-line borders and coupon cutout dashes. Be careful with these borders, however; some are large and can be quite distracting. Figure 10-25 illustrates the BorderArt tab of the Border Style dialog box.

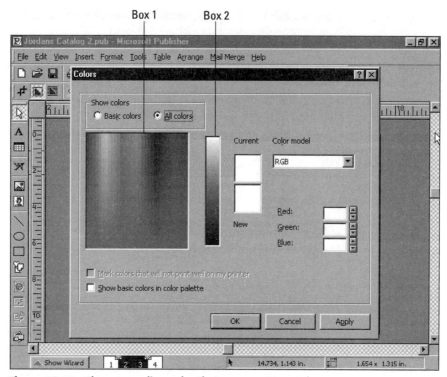

Figure 10-24: Choose any line color that you want to apply.

To use border art, follow these steps:

1. Select the frame.

2. Choose Format ⇨ Line/Border Style. The cascading menu appears. Alternatively, you can click the Line/Border Style button on the Formatting toolbar to display the menu.

3. Choose More Styles to open the Border Style dialog box.

4. Choose the BorderArt tab.

5. In the Available Borders area, select the border that you want to use. A preview appears in the Preview area.

6. In the Border size box, adjust the size of the border. As a border gets smaller, the number of items in the border increases. For example, a smaller border means more apples or balloons appear in the border.

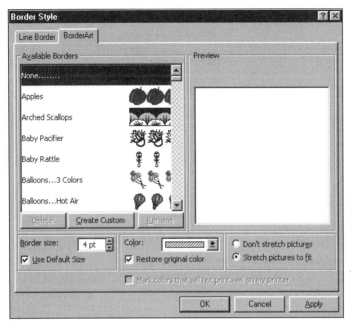

Figure 10-25: Use border art to attract attention to your publication.

7. In the Color drop-down box, select a color to apply to the objects. If you select one color, Publisher uses various tints and shades of that color to create the border. If you want to revert back to the original color, check the Restore original color check box.

8. If a picture is in the frame, you can choose whether or not to distort the picture to fit the border art frame. Choose either Don't stretch pictures or Stretch pictures to fit from the radio buttons located below the Preview area.

9. If you want to select one or more sides for the border instead of using it on all four sides, click the Apply button and then select the Line Border tab.

   If you want the border to apply to all four sides, click OK.

10. In the Line Border tab, select the side(s) for the border art, and then click OK.

Figure 10-26 illustrates decorative border art on a frame. The size of the frame, the contents of the frame, and the border art make the frame look too crowded.

Figure 10-27 illustrates border art used in a sign. With the border reduced in size and the color changed to a light gray, it adds to the message instead of distracting from it.

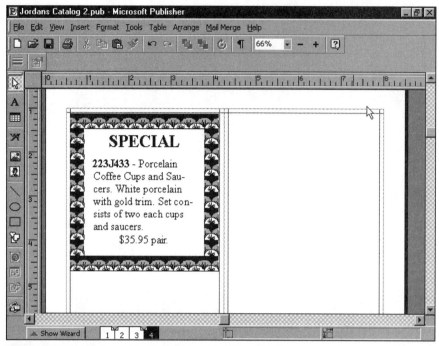

Figure 10-26: Border art is nice, but not in this situation.

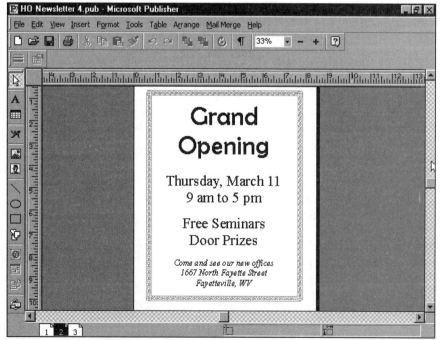

Figure 10-27: Border art can add emphasis and interest.

Another example of border art is the coupon shown in Figure 10-28. Add a coupon to a flyer, newsletter, or other publication and use coupon border art to identify it.

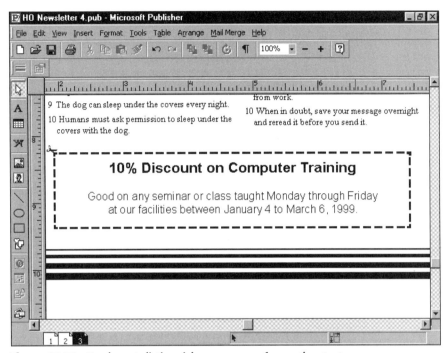

Figure 10-28: Border art distinguishes a coupon from other text.

Border shadows

You can add a shadow to any frame—text or object—to add depth to the frame. Publisher applies a $1/_8$-inch dark-gray shadow to the right and left side of a frame, as shown in Figure 10-29. Note the margin added between the picture and its frame. You set the inside margin in the Picture Frame Properties dialog box. The margin around the frame and the shadow on the right and bottom sides add an air of distinction to the photograph.

To add a shadow to a frame, follow these steps:

1. Select the frame.

2. Choose Format ⇨ Shadow. Alternatively, press Ctrl+D.

To remove the shadow, press Ctrl+D again, or choose Format ⇨ Shadow to deselect the option.

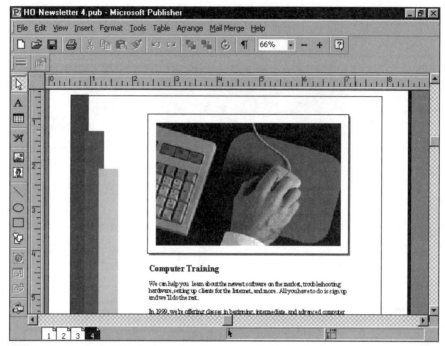

Figure 10-29: Add a shadow to give the page a little depth.

Using fills

In addition to adding a border to a frame, you can fill the frame with a color or pattern. Colors for fill are similar to colors for lines. You can choose a scheme color to fill a frame, or you can choose another color from the Colors dialog box.

Tip   When you use a fill in a frame, especially a text frame, make sure that the fill doesn't overwhelm the text. You must be able to read the text. Also, fills can be overwhelming. Bright colors or strong patterns may obstruct the text view.

Border Tips

Never draw a border past the column or layout guides into the gutters and margins. If you do, the publication will look cluttered and unbalanced.

Include white space with all borders, if applicable, both on the inside and the outside of the frame.

Use borders to emphasize or isolate messages.

You can use the drawing rectangle tool to create a second or third border around the outside of a frame, just for a different look.

Fill effects include tints and shades, patterns, and gradients. Tints and shades are variations on one color. Suppose you choose blue as your color; you then can choose from more than ten tints and shades of that color. A *tint* is the color plus white; a *shade* is the color plus black. *Patterns* are combinations of two colors; one acts as a background and the other creates a pattern, or design, on top. Some patterns include checks, lines, stripes, bricks, and so on. *Gradients* are blends of two colors on the page.

Color

You can add any color that you want as a fill for a text or object frame. If you have a photograph in the frame, no color shows unless you have a margin in the frame. If you're using a piece of clip art or some other image in the frame, the fill acts as a background to the image, but doesn't change the colors of the image. If you're filling a text frame, the text remains readable as long as the fill is light.

Note   Remember that if you're not using a color printer, you should use a black-and-gray color scheme for better results on a black-and-white printer.

To add a color fill to a frame, follow these steps:

1. Select the frame.

2. Choose Format ➪ Fill Color. Alternatively, click the Fill Color button on the Formatting toolbar. The cascading menu in Figure 10-30 appears.

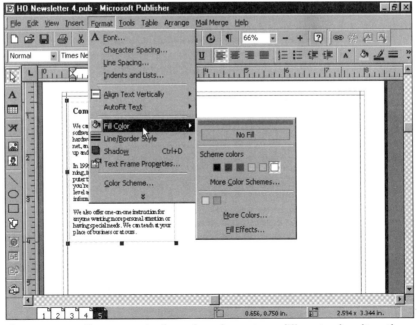

Figure 10-30: Choose a color from the scheme, or a different color altogether.

3. Do one of the following:

- Choose a color from the color scheme.

- Choose More Color Schemes and then choose one of Publisher's color schemes. Figure 10-31 illustrates the Color Scheme dialog box. If you choose this option, you must click OK to close the dialog box and apply your changes.

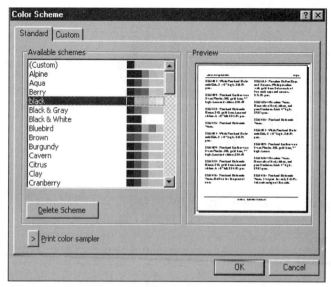

Figure 10-31: Choose a color scheme from Publisher's available schemes.

- Choose More Colors to display the Colors dialog box, as described in the previous section, "Border color." If you choose this option, you must click OK to close the dialog box and apply your changes.

- Choose Fill Effects to display the Fill Effects dialog box, as shown in Figure 10-32. From this box, choose a tint or shade of the color that you want to use. If you choose this option, you must click OK to close the dialog box and apply your changes.

Note

When you choose a new color scheme, Publisher changes the scheme colors on the cascading menu to match that scheme. When you choose a color from the Colors dialog box, Publisher adds that color to the cascading menu, as well. You can then quickly choose these same colors from the menu if they are repeated in your publication.

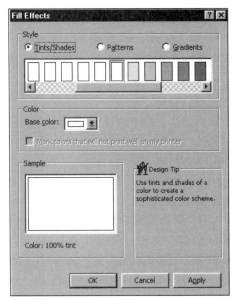

Figure 10-32: Choose a tint or shade of the selected color.

Patterns

You can apply patterns to text and object frames as a background. You might want to add an empty frame with only a pattern fill, for a decorative effect. If, however, you add a pattern to a text or picture frame, make sure that you can still read the text and that the frame and picture don't look too cluttered.

To use patterns, follow these steps:

1. Select the frame.
2. Choose Format ⇨ Fill Color. Alternatively, click the Fill Color button on the Formatting toolbar. The cascading menu appears.
3. Choose Fill Effects. The Fill Effects dialog box appears.
4. In the Style area, choose Patterns. The dialog box changes to offer pattern choices.
5. In the Color area, choose a Base color and then choose a Color 2. Select a pattern to see how it looks in the Sample box, as shown in Figure 10-33.
6. Click OK to accept the changes and return to the publication.

Figure 10-34 illustrates three examples of using patterns as fills in frames. Naturally, you wouldn't use all three patterns on one page, but this illustration gives you an idea of ways to use patterns. You can use them for headlines, logos, or picture backgrounds, for example.

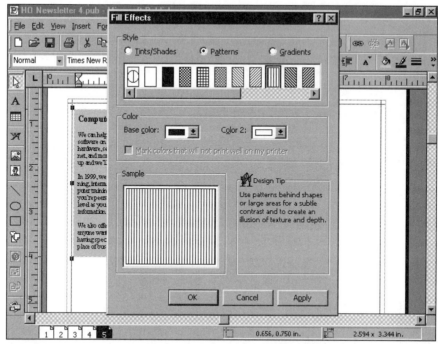

Figure 10-33: Choose the colors and patterns that you want to use.

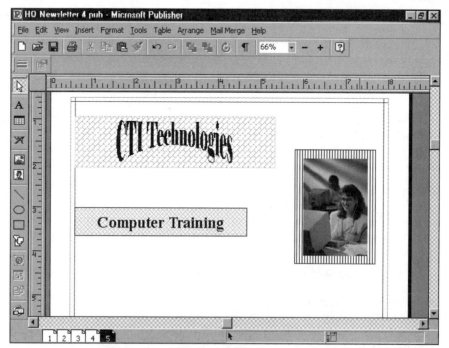

Figure 10-34: The tasteful use of patterns is best.

Gradients

The way in which you use gradients is similar to how you use patterns. A gradient can be quite distracting in a small frame; in a large frame, however, it may be perfect. Publisher includes gradients that start in the center and fan out, as well as gradients that start at one corner of the page. Publisher also includes vertical and horizontal patterns, curves, stars, and other patterns. Figure 10-35 illustrates the Fill Effects dialog box with a fill showing in the Sample area. Note, too, the various gradients in the Style area.

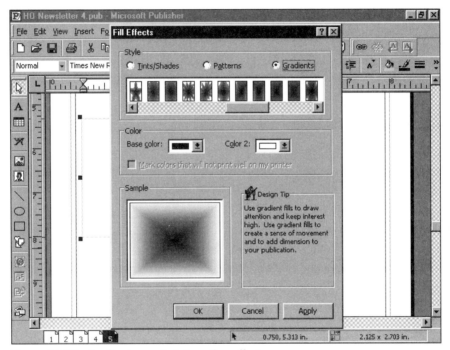

Figure 10-35: Gradients create interesting effects.

You can use light gradients (two light colors) and easily read the text on the frame; however, using colors that are too dark might make reading difficult. Figure 10-36 shows a letterhead with two light colors — white and a medium gray — in the gradient. The letterhead is quite striking.

To use gradients, follow these steps:

1. Select the frame.

2. Choose Format ➪ Fill Color. Alternatively, click the Fill Color button on the Formatting toolbar. The cascading menu appears.

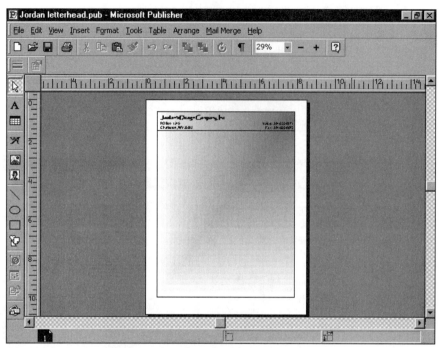

Figure 10-36: Use gradients to create emphasis.

3. Choose Fill Effects. The Fill Effects dialog box appears.

4. In the Style area, choose Gradients and then choose the gradient that you want to use.

5. Choose the Base color and the Color 2.

6. Click OK.

Working with Frames

Now that you are familiar with the types of frames and frame elements, you need to know a few methods of manipulating frames on the page. You can copy and move frames. You also can layer frames and connect them. All of these procedures help you to create and format your publications.

You can drag any handle to resize the frame. A side handle enables you to enlarge or reduce one side of the frame. A corner handle enables you to resize two sides at the same time. If you want to enlarge or reduce a frame so that it remains proportional, press and hold down the Shift key as you drag a corner handle.

Sizing frames

When you select a frame, eight handles appear on the corners and edges of the frame, to indicate that it has been selected. These handles also enable you to resize a frame after you draw it.

You size a frame by positioning the mouse pointer over a handle until the pointer changes to the Resize mouse pointer, as shown in Figure 10-37. Drag the handle toward the center of the frame to make it smaller, or away from the center of the frame to make it larger.

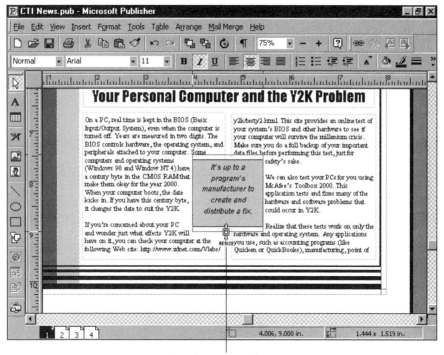

Resize mouse pointer

Figure 10-37: Resize a frame by using its handles.

When you make a text frame smaller, the Text in Overflow button appears. The text in overflow remains until you either enlarge the frame or dump the text into another frame. For more information, see the forthcoming section "Connecting frames."

When you make a picture frame larger or smaller, you also enlarge or reduce the picture size. The same is true for a table frame and a clip frame.

Copying, moving, and deleting a frame

You can copy, cut and paste, and delete a frame as you would any other object. You can copy or move a frame on the same page, within the same publication, and between publications.

To copy and paste a frame, follow these steps:

1. Select the frame.

2. Choose Edit ⇨ Copy or press Ctrl+C.

3. Move to another area of the page, to another page, or to another publication.

Note   If you move to another publication, you need to save the current one first, because Publisher closes the current publication before opening a new file.

4. Choose Edit ⇨ Paste or press Ctrl+V.

To move a frame, follow these steps:

1. Select the frame.

2. Choose Edit ⇨ Cut or press Ctrl+X.

3. Move to the page or publication to which you want to move the frame.

4. Choose Edit ⇨ Paste or press Ctrl+V.

You can also move a frame by positioning the mouse pointer over the frame until it changes to the MOVE pointer. Drag the frame to another position on the same page.

To delete a table or picture frame, select the frame and then press either the Delete key or Ctrl+X.

To delete a text frame, select the frame and then press Ctrl+X. Pressing the Delete key deletes the text within the selected frame.

Layering frames

You can place one frame on top of another frame, in a stack, when necessary. You've already seen how you can place a picture frame on top of a text frame and then flow the text around it. You might also want to stack additional frames to create a design of some sort.

Figure 10-38 illustrates three stacked frames. The text, computer, and clock frames are stacked one on top of the other.

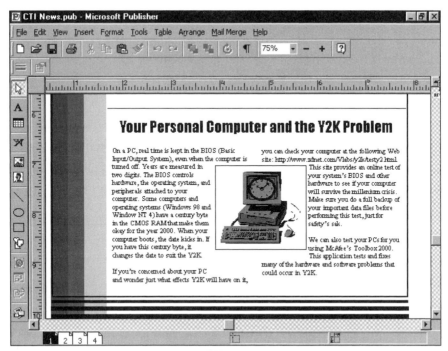

Figure 10-38: Layer frames to create different effects.

When you stack one frame on top of another, the new frame covers the current one. Frames are opaque by default, so you cannot see one through the other. Granted, with a text frame, you can wrap the text around the object placed on top. With picture frames, however, one frame *covers* another.

Tip If you want to make a text frame transparent, select the frame and then press Ctrl+T. Press Ctrl+T again to change the frame back to opaque.

When you layer frames, you can change the order of each frame in the stack. For example, you can bring one frame to the front or send it to the back, enabling you to create the effect that you want. You also can bring a frame one layer forward in the stack or send it one layer back in the stack.

To rearrange a frame within the stack, select the frame and then choose Arrange from the menu. Then, choose one of the following:

✦ Bring to Front (or press F6) to bring the frame to the top layer of the stack

✦ Send to Back (or press Shift+F6) to send the frame to the bottom of the stack

✦ Bring Forward to bring the frame one layer forward

✦ Send Backward to send the frame one layer back

Tip When you create a text frame on top of a picture frame, use the Arrange ➪ Send to Back command instead of making the frame transparent. If the text frame is on the bottom layer, the text wraps around the picture; if the text frame is transparent, however, the text shows through the picture frame.

Connecting frames

The previous section on sizing frames mentioned that you can connect two text frames so that you can continue text from one frame to the other. You can connect two or more frames so that a story or article flows between them. When two frames are connected and you enlarge the first frame, the text automatically flows to the enlarged frame. Similarly, when you make a frame smaller, the text automatically flows to the second frame.

You need to understand the difference between frames that are connected and frames that are grouped. When you *group* frames — text, picture, or other object frames — the frames act as one. If you delete one frame, you delete all frames. If you copy one frame, you copy all frames in the group.

When you *connect* frames, each frame is independent of the other. The only thing that connected frames share is a string of text. If you delete one frame, the text reverts to other connected frames or to the overflow area. Connected frames are not grouped, and vice versa.

Connecting two frames

When you have more text than will fit into one frame, you can enlarge the frame or dump the text into another frame. To dump text into another frame, you click the Text in Overflow button. The mouse pointer changes to a cup icon. Move the cup icon to an empty frame and click it. The text flows into the second frame. You can connect any number of frames together in a string by following this procedure.

Jumping from frame to frame

After you connect frames, you can move from frame to connected frame quickly and easily. You use the Go to Next Frame or Go to Previous Frame buttons attached to the bottom of any connected frame.

Figure 10-39 shows a selected frame. You can tell the frame is connected by the Go to Next Frame button. If you click the button, Publisher jumps to the next connected frame and selects it, whether that frame is on the same page or on another page in the publication.

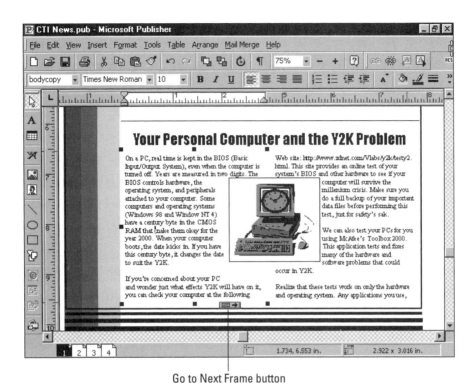

Go to Next Frame button

Figure 10-39: Jump from one connected frame to another.

Some frames cannot be connected to others. One example is a frame in which the automatic copyfitting feature is being used (see Chapter 13 for more information). When a frame cannot be connected, the cup icon remains horizontal when the mouse pointer is over that frame. Otherwise, the cup tilts to indicate that you can use that frame to connect.

Copying connected frames

Connected text frames behave a bit differently than other frames when you copy and paste them. You can copy and paste connected frames; however, you get two different results, depending on what you copy. If you copy and paste all connected text frames in a string (that is, all frames sharing one string of text), then Publisher copies all text and frames to the other location. If you copy and paste only a few of the connected frames, Publisher copies only the frames, not the text.

Summary

In this chapter, you learned about the basic element in any Publisher publication — the frame. You learned the following about frames:

✦ Identifying types of frames

✦ Adding margins to a frame

✦ Using a frame's handles

✦ Selecting frames

✦ Sizing frames

✦ Wrapping text around frames

✦ Connecting frames

In the next chapter, you learn more about working with page elements, such as margins, columns, headers and footers, and first pages.

✦   ✦   ✦

Working with Page Elements

This chapter introduces you to the finer points of setting up pages to suit your particular publication. In particular, you learn what the common document sizes are, how to choose the layout that is best for your publication, how to match your printer setup, and how to choose and work with the right paper for your publication.

Understanding Common Document Sizes

Traditional document sizes developed for many reasons. The commercial printing industry, for example, buys paper in standard, large sizes and then cuts it down to document size. Buying large paper sizes saves money for the printing company.

Additionally, standard-size envelopes fit certain document sizes. A commercial (size 10) envelope fits an $8^1/_2 \times 11$-inch or $8^1/_2 \times 14$-inch document perfectly. Post office regulations, shelving at libraries and bookstores, and other factors also help to determine the traditional sizes of documents.

Note   Paper measurements are always listed with the width first and then the height. An $8^1/_2 \times 11$-inch page, then, is $8^1/_2$ inches wide by 11 inches tall. When you see a measurement such as $11 \times 8^1/_2$ inches, the page is in landscape orientation — 11 inches wide by $8^1/_2$ inches tall.

In the last 15 years or so, common sizes have changed a bit with the development of printers attached to computers. The dot matrix, or impact, printer used paper sizes larger than the standard $8^1/_2 \times 11$-inch size; but, with the popularity of inkjet and laser printers, standard sizes have returned. Most inkjet and laser printers print to $8^1/_2 \times 11$-inch and $8^1/_2 \times 14$-inch paper sizes.

Table 11-1 describes common sizes of paper found in commercial print shops. These paper sizes are multiples of $8^1/_2$×11 inches and $8^1/_2$×14 inches for a reason. The more pieces that can be cut from a large sheet, with the least amount of wasted paper, the more money that can be saved.

Table 11-1		
Common Paper Sizes		
Original Size	*Cut Sizes*	*Document Types*
$8^1/_2$×11	$8^1/_2$×11, $4^1/_4$×$5^1/_2$, $8^1/_2$×$3^1/_2$, $2^1/_2$×3	Most documents, postcards, rack cards, business cards
$8^1/_2$×14	$8^1/_2$×14, 5×7	Legal-size documents, newsletters, reports
11×17	$8^1/_2$×11 and its smaller sizes	Most documents
17×28	$8^1/_2$×14 and its smaller sizes	Legal-size documents
17×22	$8^1/_2$×11 sheets	Most documents
23×35	$8^1/_2$×11, 11×17	Most documents
25×38	$8^1/_2$×14	Legal-size documents

Many paper sizes can also be folded to a common document size. An $8^1/_2$×11-inch page, for example, can be folded to $8^1/_2$×$5^1/_2$ to create a program, or to $8^1/_2$×$3^2/_3$ to create a brochure. An 11×17 page can be folded to $8^1/_2$×11 to create a four-page newsletter.

Choosing a Publication Layout

When you start a new publication in Publisher, you choose your publication layout, whether you create a publication by wizard, by design, or by basing your document on a blank publication. Publisher assigns a page size and layout to your document according to traditional paper sizes and design principles.

If you choose to open a newsletter wizard, for example, the common size is $8^1/_2$×11 inches in portrait orientation. If you choose a brochure, the size is 11×$8^1/_2$ inches in landscape orientation. When you choose to start a blank publication, Publisher presents several sizes and layouts from which you can choose a foundation for your document. Naturally, you can change any page layout that you choose.

Whether you're using one of Publisher's document layouts or one of your own, you'll want to know how to change the publication's layout. You might find that you need to use a different orientation or size while you're working on the document—

to fit the copy, for example. Publisher enables you to set the publication layout in any document.

Understanding publication layouts

Publisher offers five different publication layouts. Each document type, wizard, template, or other publication that you create fits into one of these publication layouts. You can change the publication layout for documents that you create on your own, such as when you choose for your document base a blank publication in the Catalog.

You choose publication layouts in the Page Setup dialog box. Each layout type presents its own layout options from which you can choose. Figure 11-1 shows the Page Setup dialog box with the default publication type — Normal — selected. Options are very few with this particular publication layout.

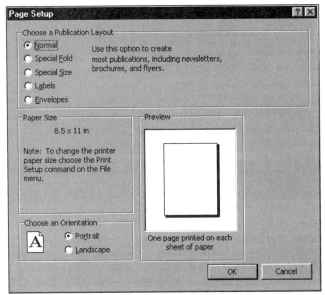

Figure 11-1: The Normal publication layout is the default, because it's used in most documents.

Normal publication layout

The Normal publication layout is the one that you'll use for most documents. The Normal layout creates an $8^1/_2$×11-inch page, which is the base for most documents, including newsletters, flyers, letterheads, brochures, reports, catalogs, and so on. The default orientation is portrait.

Note The Normal layout also easily fits most printer specifications.

Figure 11-2 shows one page of a marketing report. The page is $8^1/2 \times 11$ inches in size and uses portrait orientation.

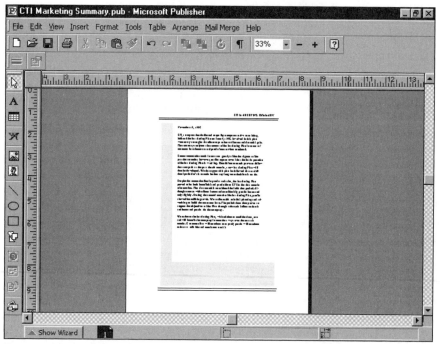

Figure 11-2: The Normal publication layout is perfect for most documents.

Special Fold publication layout

The Special Fold publication layout offers four different folds from an $8^1/2 \times 11$-inch sheet of paper. You can create invitations, tent cards, programs, and other documents by using this layout. The Page Setup dialog box also lists the finished size of the folded document, as shown in Figure 11-3.

The following list provides a description of the Special Fold publication layouts offered:

✦ **Book Fold:** Uses an $8^1/2 \times 11$-inch page and folds it one time, lengthwise, as shown in Figure 11-3. The final size of the folded document is $4^1/4 \times 11$ inches. You print on both sides of the page. Figure 11-4 shows pages 2 and 3 (the inside) of the book fold publication. You may more likely use the book fold layout in landscape orientation, which has a finished (folded) size of $5^1/2 \times 8^1/2$ inches.

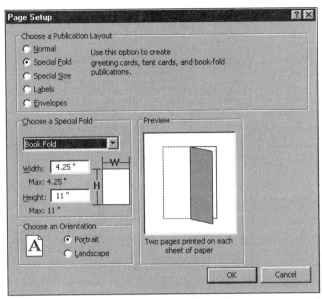

Figure 11-3: Choose the Special Fold publication layout and then either accept the default size or change it.

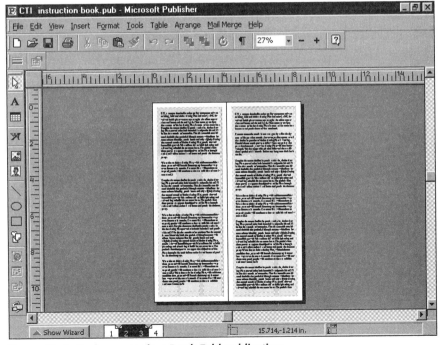

Figure 11-4: Facing pages in a Book Fold publication

You can use a title page on the first page, or you can combine two $8^1/2$×11-inch pages for an 8-page book, combine three $8^1/2$×11-inch pages for a 12-page book, and so on. Use this layout for books, booklets, or a 2-page (front and back) rack card.

✦ **Tent Card:** An $8^1/2$×11-inch page folded in half from top to bottom, as opposed to the book fold, which is folded side to side. Figure 11-5 shows the illustration of the tent card fold in the Page Setup dialog box. You can use this layout for invitations and other cards, or for cards that you place on tables as an advertisement, announcement, or offer of other information. The finished size of the tent card publication is $8^1/2$×$5^1/2$ inches.

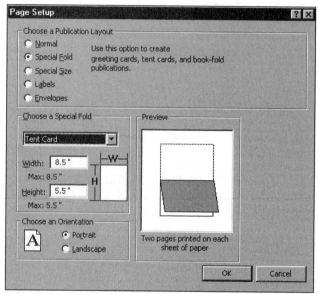

Figure 11-5: A tent card folds from top to bottom.

✦ **Side-Fold Card:** Perfect for greeting cards and note cards. The cards are folded once from top to bottom and then folded once from side to side. The finished size of the side-fold card is $4^1/4$×$5^1/2$ inches. The card displays four pages in Publisher; when you print it, however, all pages appear on one side of the paper, as shown in Figure 11-6. You create four pages when you fold the sheet of paper.

Page 3   Page 2

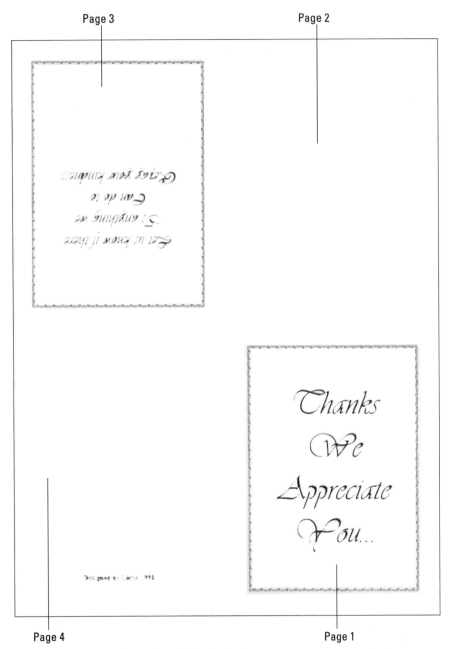

Page 4   Page 1

Figure 11-6: Side-fold works well for invitations, announcements, and other greeting cards.

✦ **Top-Fold Card:** A variation of the side-fold card. With the top-fold card, you first fold the card from side to side and then fold it from top to bottom. Again, you print on only one side of the paper, and Publisher creates four separate pages on which you can work. The final measurement of the folded publication is $4^1/4$×$5^1/2$ inches. Figure 11-7 shows the cover page of the top-fold card. Note that the page measures $4^1/4$×$5^1/2$ inches, as indicated by the rulers, even though it looks like a larger sheet. Also note that the publication has four pages, each representing one side of the card: front, back, inside-left, and inside-right pages.

Figure 11-7: Use the top-fold card for invitations or thank-you cards.

Naturally, you can change the orientation from portrait to landscape on any Special Fold layout to get a completely different finished size. In landscape orientation, the book fold layout becomes $5^1/2$×$8^1/2$ inches, which is better suited to a program or booklet than is 8$^1/2$×11 inches. The tent card changes to 11×$4^1/4$ inches in landscape orientation, and the side-fold and top-fold cards each change to $5^1/2$×$4^1/4$ inches.

After you select the fold, you can change the size of the page by making it smaller than the default size. Note in the Choose a Special Fold area (refer to Figure 11-3) that Publisher lists the maximum height and width. You can enter any size that better suits your purpose.

When you change the size, the layout guides change on the page, and crop marks appear, indicating where you should cut the paper to fit the size. Figure 11-8 illustrates the top-fold card printed to one sheet of paper. The crop marks appear on the page because the card is a custom size — 3×5 inches.

Page 1   Page 2

Crop marks   Page 4   Page 3

Figure 11-8: Cut between the crop marks and then fold the sheet.

For more information about crop marks, see Chapter 12, "Considering Advanced Page Issues." For more information about printing, see Part VI, "Printing."

Special Size publication layout

You can use the Special Size publication layout to produce large or very small publications. Posters and banners are the larger-than-standard sheet size publications. Index cards, postcards, or business cards are the smaller publications. Publisher lists various sizes for each publication type in the Choose a Publication Size area, or you can specify a custom size for the publication. Additionally, you can specify either Portrait or Landscape orientation in the Choose an Orientation area.

Figure 11-9 illustrates the Special Size publication layout of the Page Setup dialog box, with Banner (10 ft) selected. For information about banners, see Chapter 26, "Producing Specialty Publications."

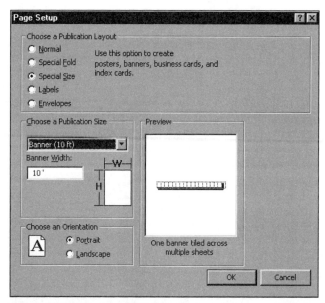

Figure 11-9: Create publications that are larger or smaller than the standard, common sizes.

Table 11-2 provides a description of the various publication sizes offered in the Special Size publication layout.

Table 11-2
Special Size Publication Layouts

Description	Size
Printer sheet size	$8^1/_2 \times 11$
Index card	5×3
Business card	$3^1/_2 \times 2$
Poster	18×24
Poster	24×36
Custom	You set the dimensions
Banner	5 feet
Banner	10 feet
Banner	15 feet
Custom banner	You set the dimensions
Postcard	$5^1/_2 \times 4^1/_4$
Postcard	5.85×4.13
Postcard	3.94×5.83

Labels publication layout

Use the Labels publication layout to create various labels, including address labels, diskette labels, stickers, shipping labels, name tags, and so on. Publisher's page setup for each label fits various sizes, as listed in the Choose a Label area of the Page Setup dialog box, shown in Figure 11-10. The sizes listed match the Avery brand labels, available in most office supply stores; Publisher even lists the Avery stock number for each size, so that you can easily find the labels that you need.

When you select a label size, Publisher displays only one label onscreen, but can print multiple labels to the page, so that you can run a sheet of labels through the printer and print 10, 20, or 30 labels at a time.

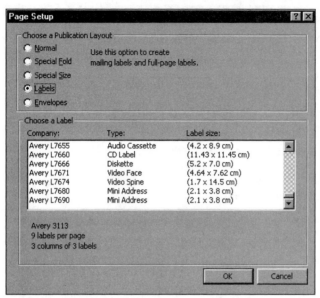

Figure 11-10: Use a Label publication layout to fit the exact size and shape of your Avery labels.

Envelopes publication layout

Publisher offers two common envelope sizes: a number 10 envelope and a number 6 envelope. You can also enter a custom size envelope in the Envelopes publication layout. After you choose an envelope layout, you can then enter your return address, a design or logo, and even the recipient's address, if you want.

Figure 11-11 shows a commercial number 10 envelope layout for Jordan's Designs. When you design envelopes, be careful to follow all postal regulations. For example, don't print a design or text in the lower-right half of the envelope. Also, good design dictates that you should match the envelope design to any letterhead or invoice that you plan to mail, for consistency's sake. Finally, if you design a custom envelope, make sure that your printer can print that envelope size. Some smaller envelopes may jam your printer instead of printing correctly.

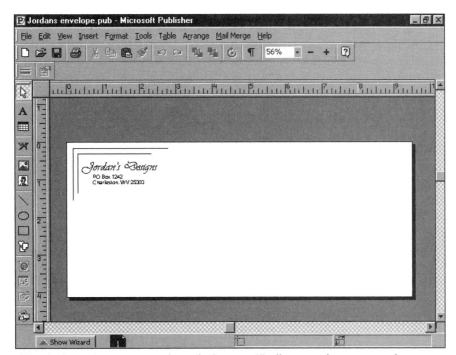

Figure 11-11: Create an envelope design specifically catered to your needs.

Using the Page Setup dialog box

You use the Page Setup dialog box to set the publication layout size and orientation. You can change the layout for any wizard, design, or blank publication that you create.

To change the page setup, follow these steps:

1. Choose File ➪ Page Setup. The Page Setup dialog box appears.

2. In the Choose a Publication Layout area, choose from one of the following: Normal, Special Fold, Special Size, Labels, Envelopes.

3. Choose either Portrait or Landscape in the Choose an Orientation area of the dialog box.

4. Click OK.

Note   You should make sure that your printer setup matches the page setup, as explained in the next section.

Using the Quick Publication Wizard

When you work with the Quick Publication Wizard, you can easily change the orientation and publication layout of your document. You can apply the Wizard's options to any document that you create based on a wizard, design template, or blank publication. For more information on starting a new publication, see Chapter 3, "Understanding the Catalog."

To change the page size and orientation in the Quick Publication Wizard, follow these steps:

1. In the top pane of the Quick Publication Wizard window, choose Page Size.

2. In the bottom pane of the window, choose either Portrait or Landscape orientation.

3. Click the Page Setup button, if you want to change the publication's layout. Make any changes by using the options presented in the previous section.

4. Click OK.

Matching Printer Setup

You may need to match your printer setup to your publication layout size and orientation, depending on your printer. Some printers, especially newer ones, can print to a variety of sizes without a change in the printer setup. Other printers may need the configuration or setup changed. To find out whether your printer setup needs to be changed, see your printer's documentation before you change anything in Publisher.

If you're sure that you need to change the printer setup, you can do so by using the Print Setup dialog box in Publisher. To change the printer setup, follow these steps:

1. Choose File ⇨ Print Setup. The Print Setup dialog box appears, as shown on the following page.

2. In the Paper area, you can change the paper size, if necessary, for your printer. Click the Size drop-down list to display the various available paper and envelope sizes.

   The sizes listed depend on the default printer that you use. Check the Paper Size drop-down list to see what sizes of paper — and especially envelopes — your printer can handle.

3. If you need to use a different paper source than the one listed, choose that paper source from the Source drop-down list.

4. Choose either Portrait or Landscape in the Orientation area of the dialog box. When you change the orientation in this dialog box, all documents print in that orientation, no matter what your page size or layout indicates. Check your printer documentation for more information.

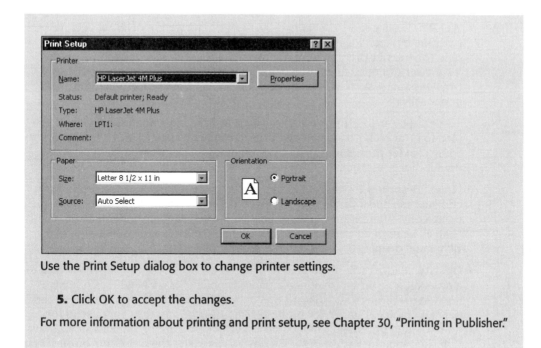

Use the Print Setup dialog box to change printer settings.

5. Click OK to accept the changes.

For more information about printing and print setup, see Chapter 30, "Printing in Publisher."

Choosing Paper

The paper that you use for your printer can be as plain as copy paper or as fancy as linen. Paper comes in various sizes, finishes, colors, and weights. You must make sure that your printer works with a particular paper type before you purchase the paper. Most printers suggest the appropriate paper to use with them. Read your printer's documentation for more information.

If you plan to take your print job to a commercial print shop, you can use most, if not all, kinds of paper that the shop offers. Ask to see samples before you choose one for the job.

Characteristics of paper

The following are the characteristics of paper:

✦ **Size:** As discussed in a previous section, "Understanding Common Document Sizes," the paper sizes available are many and varied. However, choosing a large paper size and cutting smaller sizes out of it at a print shop usually is less expensive. The most important factor is that you keep the *trim* size (the final cut size of the paper) of your documents within the common size ranges.

✦ **Weight:** Calculated by the *ream* (500 sheets). The weight of 500 sheets of 23×35-inch paper, for example, may be 24# (also called *fifty pound*), 28#, or 32#. The heavier the weight of the ream, the heavier each individual sheet. Most laser printers can handle paper that is 24# or 28#; some can print to heavier papers, such as 32# or slightly more. As a reference point, most copy paper is 20#.

Test a paper in your printer before you purchase large quantities. Also, if you plan to print on both sides of the paper, test a few sheets before you buy. Some heavier papers may print okay on one side but wrinkle badly with double-sided printing.

✦ **Finish:** Describes the texture of the paper, which affects how the printed text and images appear on the page. A printed image on a smooth finish looks completely different on a linen or enamel finish. Photographs print well on an enamel, smooth, or vellum finish, for example, because the dark tones look richer and deeper.

✦ **Opacity:** Matters when you plan to print on both sides of the paper, such as in a newsletter or brochure. When a paper is opaque, dark headlines or images don't show through and disrupt the text or image on the opposite side of the paper. Parchment paper, for example, isn't opaque and thus isn't useful for double-sided printing; a linen paper is perfect for printing on both sides. Consider, too, the weight of the paper — the heavier the paper, the more opaque it is.

✦ **Brightness:** Describes how well the paper reflects light. Paper is rated from brightest (1) to least bright (3). If you can find a brightness rating on your paper, consider using a brightness rating of 1 for photographs, to make them appear more detailed.

✦ **Grain:** Describes the direction in which the majority of the paper fibers run. All papers have a grain. If possible, the grain should run parallel to the spine fold of a newsletter, book, catalog, or magazine. You are more likely to differentiate the grain of the paper if you take your print job to a commercial printing shop.

✦ **Color:** Can add to your printed piece. By using your laser printer and colored paper, you can create an exceptional publication simply by using black on one color. White paper is the most common color for publications, but you might consider buying some ivory paper for a change. Also use any pastel colors — pink, green, blue, and so on — for different accents on your publications.

Fluorescent and metallic colors of paper are also very popular. However, if you use these colors in your publications, be careful of two things: don't overwhelm the message of your publication with bright colors, and make sure that any metallic or specialty papers won't ruin your printer.

Types of paper

The paper types you can choose from are as numerous as types of printers. Basically, you'll likely choose desktop publishing papers, such as book, bond, or cover paper. Each paper type has a weight, finish, opacity, grain, brightness, and color attached to it. You need to take all of these characteristics into consideration when purchasing paper. The following are the common paper types.

Note

Depending on where you purchase your paper, the name may be different. If you have a commercial print shop close to you, but you plan to print on your own laser printer, for example, you can still buy the paper from the print shop — and likely save money. They can cut the paper to any size and amount that you need.

✦ **Book:** The most commonly used paper, it comes in three types: offset, coated, and text. Offset, which is fairly inexpensive, is perfect for newsletters, booklets, and programs. Common finishes of offset are smooth, linen, vellum, and laurentine.

✦ **Coated book:** Great for photographs. Can be bought in a glossy or matte finish, usually in white or ivory, and in various weights. Coated papers are reasonably priced, costing no more than offset paper.

✦ **Text book:** A heavier and more deeply finished paper than the previous two listed. The finish is rough, and therefore unsuitable for photographs. Good for invitations, booklets, and programs. It is also quite expensive.

✦ **Bond:** A very inexpensive and lightweight paper that comes in 16# and 20#. If you purchase 16#, make sure that you test it with your printer, because most printers can't handle very lightweight papers. Available in most colors very inexpensively. Use bond papers for printing on one side only.

✦ **Letterhead:** With matching envelopes, it is usually 20# or 24#, and comes in a variety of colors and finishes. A good quality usually contains a percentage of *rag* (the cotton content), and as much as 25 to 100 percent of the paper might be rag. Comes in a variety of finishes, including linen, laid, and smooth.

✦ **Cover:** A heavier, "board" grade used for business cards, postcards, booklet covers, and so on. Comes in either coated or uncoated varieties, in weights of 65# to 80#. You can get a variety of finishes, including linen and smooth, and can buy colors to match your letterhead paper, so that your business documents all match.

You can find many other paper types, such as label paper, index paper, and so on. You need to make sure that the paper you purchase works with your printer, so check weights, finishes, and other characteristics before you buy.

Working with Inks

Whether you use a black printer, color printer, or take your publications to a commercial or quick-print shop, you need to consider ink colors. Black ink on any color of paper is always very attractive. You can create variety by adding shades and tints of gray in your publication. You can also create variety by printing black ink on a colored paper.

If you use a color inkjet or laser printer, you'll most likely have three colors (in addition to black) to use in your publication. If you take your job to a print shop, you'll have the same three colors and black inks to choose from. However, with each color of ink that you add at a print shop, you also add to the price.

You can tastefully apply color to your publications. Some areas where you can add color include lines, borders, fills, headlines, and so on. Try to use contrasting colors together, such as black and yellow, or red and blue. Be careful, however, about using light colors for text; yellow, light blue, and pink make the text difficult to read.

Another idea for using color in your documents is to use tints and shades of one color. For example, you can apply dark blue to the text and then apply lighter tints of blue to graphics, lines, and so on.

Working with Special Papers

Publisher includes several designs and wizards for use with special papers produced by PaperDirect, a company that produces paper for desktop publishing and printing on laser printers. PaperDirect's designs include borders, backgrounds, and patterns for many business uses and a variety of document types.

Publisher has wizards that fit several document types from PaperDirect. When you open the wizard or design publication, PaperDirect's design appears on the screen. You can create your document around the design, but the design doesn't print. Instead, you use PaperDirect's paper with the publication (the paper will have the design on it).

Publisher contains wizards for the following PaperDirect document types:

- ✦ Brochures
- ✦ Flyers
- ✦ Postcards
- ✦ Business cards
- ✦ Letterheads
- ✦ Envelopes
- ✦ Certificates

You can also apply some of PaperDirect's designs to a blank, $8^1/2 \times 11$-inch publication. To use PaperDirect's paper designs, open the wizard for the document type and look for Special Papers. To apply PaperDirect's designs to a standard page size, follow these steps:

1. Choose View ➪ Special Paper. The Special Paper dialog box appears, as shown in Figure 11-12.

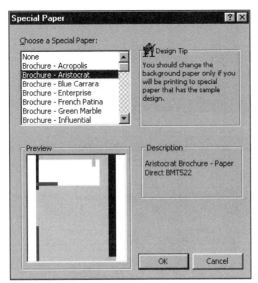

Figure 11-12: PaperDirect designs help you lay out your publication.

2. Select the design that matches the design on the paper that you purchased from Paper Direct, and then click OK.

3. Publisher displays an information dialog box, as shown in Figure 11-13.

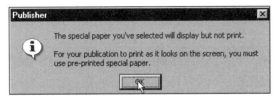

Figure 11-13: A reminder about the page design appears.

4. Click OK. You can now design your document to fit the page design.

Figure 11-14 illustrates a letterhead created on the Aristocrat design. The entire design appears on the paper; all you add is the type.

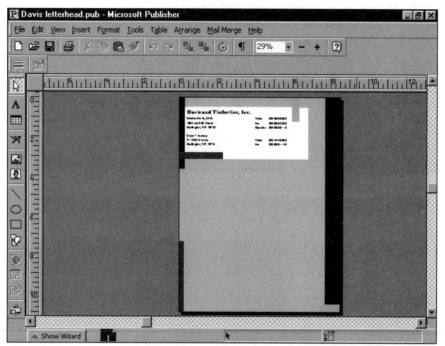

Figure 11-14: Use a PaperDirect design for an easy and professional-looking publication.

Summary

In this chapter, you learned about changing page setup to suit your own publications. Specifically, you learned about the following:

✦ Understanding common document sizes

✦ Choosing a publication layout

✦ Matching the printer setup

✦ Choosing paper

✦ Working with special papers

In the next chapter, you learn about some advanced page issues, including working with crop marks, designing first pages, and setting up a publication for color.

✦   ✦   ✦

Considering Advanced Page Issues

This chapter covers some of the advanced page issues—
crop marks, first pages, and spot color—you need to
know to produce a more professional-looking publication.

Understanding Crop Marks

In Chapter 11, you saw an invitation card that used a publication
layout smaller than an $8^{1}/_{2}\times11$-inch page. When you print a
publication that is smaller, or larger, than the standard page
size, Publisher adds crop marks to the page. Crop marks appear
outside the actual document but right on the corners, so that
you can locate the edges of the document. Crop marks define
the trim size, or actual size, of the document.

Crop marks are also called *printer's marks,* which refers to any
directions to a press operator or commercial printer who
helps print the document. Printer's marks include the
following:

 ◆ **Crop marks:** Define the trim size of the document

 ◆ **Registration marks:** Help the commercial printer align
 color separations

 ◆ **Color bars:** Help the commercial printer monitor color

 ◆ **Bleed marks:** Identify where the image extends from the
 edge of the page

 ◆ **Any job information:** Such as page, date, plate name,
 and so on

For more information about color registration, see Chapter 31,
"Using Commercial Printing Tools."

Looking at examples

Figure 12-1 illustrates an advertisement for a newspaper or magazine. This ad is smaller than an 8½×11-inch page, so when you print it, it displays crop marks.

Figure 12-1: Crop marks define the trim edge on a small publication.

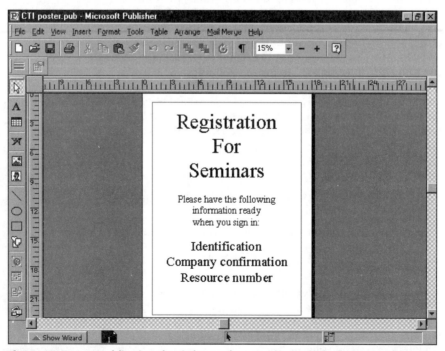

Figure 12-2: Any publication that is larger than an 8½×11-inch sheet must be cropped and then pieced together.

Figure 12-2 shows a design for a poster in Publisher. The final poster size is 18×24 inches. When you print this publication, Publisher sends nine pages to your printer, each with a part of the poster on it. To assemble the poster, you must cut each piece by using the crop marks, and then piece together the pages. Figure 12-3 shows the top-left corner of the poster printed, with crop marks.

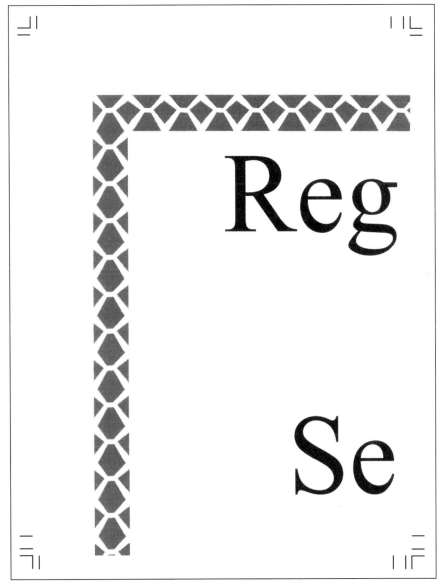

Figure 12-3: Crop each sheet and then piece together the poster.

Note   If you create a publication with crop marks, you need to cut the document down to size. You can, of course, use a ruler to connect the lines and then cut with scissors, but this works only with one or two publications. You could also use a paper cutter. If, however, you have multiple publications that need cutting, you can take your documents to a commercial printer, quick-print shop, or even a copy shop. These businesses have commercial paper cutters that can cut your documents quickly. Your publication will look better, too.

Printing crop marks

You can print crop marks only if the document is smaller than the paper size. Publisher prints crop marks by default. To turn off the print crop marks option, or to turn it on again, follow these steps:

1. Choose File ⇨ Print. The Print dialog box appears.

2. Click the Advanced Print Settings button. The Advanced Print Settings dialog box appears, as shown in Figure 12-4.

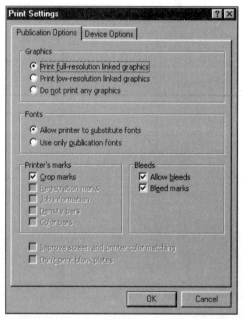

Figure 12-4: Make sure that crop marks will print.

3. Select the Publication Options tab.

4. In the Printer's marks area, put a check mark in the Crop marks check box to print crop marks; or, remove the check mark to turn off the option.

5. Click OK and then click OK to print.

Working with First Pages

When you create a publication that contains more than one page, you must consider the differences in layout and design between the first page and the other pages in the document. Usually, first pages contain elements that the other pages don't need. For example, a first page of a newsletter may contain a nameplate (or the name of the newsletter), a date line, and a table of contents. The first page of a catalog should also include a name or logo, and perhaps an address or phone number. You might even want to add a large photo or other image to the catalog's cover.

Likewise, several elements aren't added to a first page but should appear in the rest of the document, such as page numbers, headers and footers, a background, and perhaps other special elements.

Removing elements from first pages

First pages usually contain a different type and format of text, so the first page design generally leaves out many of the elements that the other pages need. Most pages in a catalog, newsletter, book, or other multiple-page publication use headers and footers, for example. These elements present useful information, such as page numbers, titles, dates, author's names, and other material the reader might need. However, you shouldn't use a header or footer on the first, or *cover*, page of a document. The first page should contain a title and other information that the reader needs.

Page numbers are another element that you don't want on the cover page, but that are handy on all other pages, especially if the document is large or if you have a table of contents. Similarly, some backgrounds may not be suitable for the first page but work perfectly well for the rest of your publication's pages.

So, how do you deal with this dilemma? Publisher doesn't provide any special "first pages" options, per se. You can work around these obstacles, however, by using various Publisher tools.

First, you can set up the items that you want to repeat on every page — such as the headers, footers, page numbers, watermark or other background, and any other elements — on the background. This procedure displays all items on every page. On the first page, then, you ignore the background (choose View ➪ Ignore Background), and Publisher hides everything in the background on that one page. (For more information about backgrounds and foregrounds, see Chapter 9, "Working with Foregrounds and Backgrounds.")

If you want some of the background items to show on the cover page of your publication, you can block other items from the page by using a white text block. Remember, by default, all text blocks are white. Carefully place a blank text frame over the items that you want to hide on the cover page.

One final suggestion: Create the items that you want on the second page, or on pages 2 and 3 (for facing page view), in the foreground. Then, copy and paste them to the other pages in the publication. This procedure, of course, will be time-consuming if your document is very long.

Figure 12-5 illustrates pages 2 and 3 of a multiple-page document. The double lines at the top and bottom of the page, the page numbers, headers, and the colored designs are in the background. The white text block and the text are in the foreground.

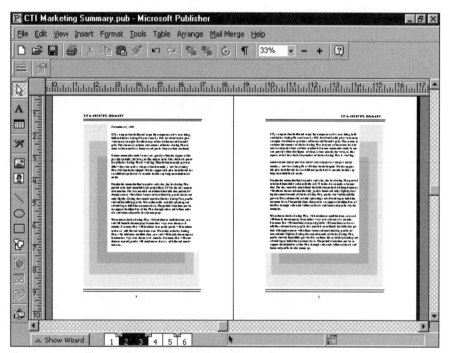

Figure 12-5: All pages but the first look similar to these.

Figure 12-6 illustrates the report's cover page. The headers and page numbers were hidden by using a white text block in the foreground. The background design, however, was incorporated in the first page to make the cover more interesting. Note, too, that the double lines from the background also show on the cover.

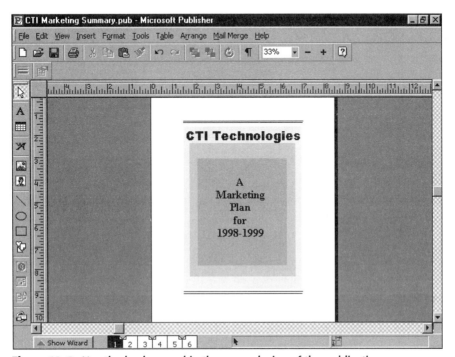

Figure 12-6: Use the background in the cover design of the publication.

Adding elements to first pages

You can choose to add design elements to the first page rather than use the background design. Naturally, you should try to make the design compatible with the rest of the publication. For example, you might want to repeat lines, shapes, or colors in the cover page design, even if you don't use the exact shapes and placement.

Figure 12-7 illustrates the cover page of the marketing report with a different, but compatible, design. The double lines and repeated colors keep the document consistent. And, by ignoring the background, you're free to add any graphics or images you want to the cover.

Figure 12-7: Create a different cover page design by ignoring the background.

Considering Color Before Designing a Publication

As you gather your contents for a publication and consider its size, layout, paper types, and other key design elements, also consider how you will use color in your publication. You have three primary choices when designing your publication:

✦ **Blacks and grays:** Can produce an attractive and professional-looking publication. Black type, black and various grays of graphics, gray screens behind the type, and the use of colored papers produce good-looking publications. Whether you're using a printer that prints only black ink or having your job printed at a commercial print shop, using black and grays is an excellent, and standard, design solution.

✦ **Spot-color:** Use one or two colors in your publication to emphasize a logo, headline, borders, or screens in the document. You can use spot-color regardless of whether you print to a color inkjet or laser printer, or if you plan to take your print job to a commercial print shop.

✦ **Process-color:** Use four semitransparent colors printed over each other to produce realistic color photographs or works of art. Commercial print shops produce this process-color, also called *four-color process,* by using an offset printing press and several press runs. The result is a high-quality and extremely professional-looking product. You can emulate a process-color result by using a color inkjet or laser printer; however, the results are not nearly as admirable as true process-color.

For a more thorough discussion of spot-color and process-color printing and preparations, see Chapter 31, "Using Commercial Printing Tools."

Planning for spot-color

Spot-color emphasizes certain items in your publication. For example, you could print only a logo, or only one border and headline, in a color that contrasts with the rest of your document. You could use red as the spot-color in a document printed in black, or use yellow in a document printed in dark blue or green. The splash of color attracts attention and accentuates that part of the document.

You can also use spot-color as part of the design. Use orange, for instance, to print all borders and screens in a newsletter that prints text and the nameplate in dark green. The orange adds to the design and makes the page more interesting and attractive.

When designing for spot-color printing, remember all the elements of design — balance, white space, emphasis, and consistency. Just as you would balance the blacks and grays on the page, so should you balance your use of color. Figure 12-8 illustrates a newsletter in which the light-gray text and graphics represent the areas of spot-color — say, red. The rest of the text and graphics are printed in black. The varying tints and shades of gray print as varying tints and shades of red.

In Figure 12-8, the color and black elements are well-balanced. A black border and multiple black lines at the bottom of the page balance the large red nameplate of the newsletter. The page also uses plenty of white space around headlines and in margins. Likewise, the pull quote uses a tinted box for accentuation. Proper use of all the design elements is represented on this page.

Figure 12-9 shows a different use of spot color. All text is black, but the background designs are printed in tints and shades of yellow. The design certainly catches your attention and is easy to read both from a distance and close up.

Figure 12-10 illustrates an example of using spot-color to emphasize one item on a page. Applying a color to the screened article makes it stand out, thus highlighting that story. You can apply spot-color to only one item, for emphasis, or spread it around as part of the design.

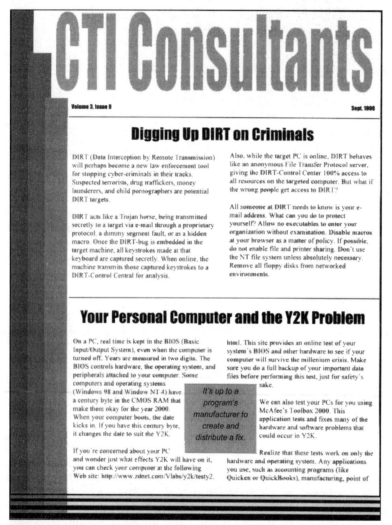

Figure 12-8: Use spot-color to spice up your publication.

When you print spot-color to a color inkjet or laser printer, the printing process applies the color for you. When you take your printed publication to a commercial print shop, you need to take along an extra copy of the document that is marked up for color. *Marking up* the document means that you circle or otherwise distinguish the areas to be printed in a different color.

Tip   Depending on your screen resolution and your method of printing, the colors onscreen may not match exactly the printed result. You might want to test certain colors with your printer, or choose the colors that you want from samples at the print shop.

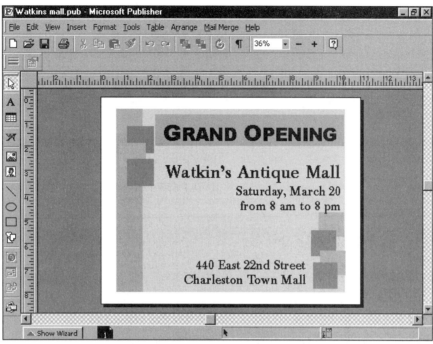

Figure 12-9: Use a contrasting color in the background to attract attention.

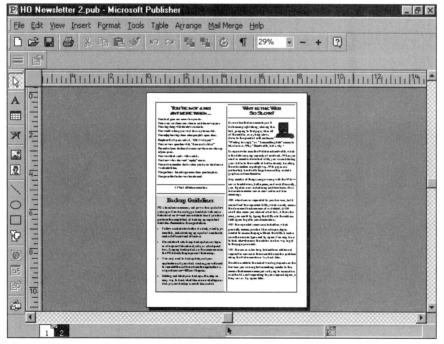

Figure 12-10: Emphasize one item on the page with spot-color.

Planning for process-color

Process-color printing generally is used for photographs or artworks that require a wide range of colors. Process-color printing is also called CMYK, or four-color, printing. CMYK stands for cyan (C), magenta (M), yellow (Y), and black (K). The process uses semitransparent process inks that overprint to create the various colors.

Process printing at a commercial print shop is more expensive than spot-color printing, but produces a professional, high-quality product. Although you can create a simulated process-color product with a color inkjet or laser printer, the output will not be nearly as good as a commercial print shop produces.

When you print process-colors, the colors onscreen won't exactly match the colors that print. Check with a commercial printing service to find out what color system it uses, before you take your print job to it; that way, you can better match the colors onscreen. (See Chapter 31, "Using Commercial Printing Tools," for more information.)

The colors used in process-color differ greatly from those used in spot-color printing. When you're printing process-color, the goal is to successfully blend the four colors to create realistic colors and results; you're not simply printing four spots of color. Figure 12-11 shows a photograph that you might want to print by using process-colors.

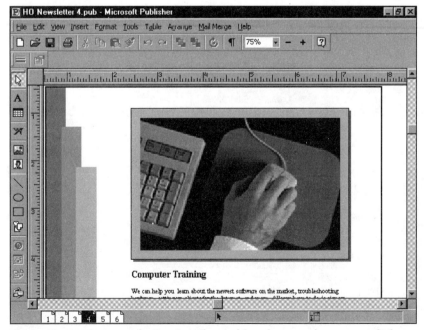

Figure 12-11: Process-color is primarily used for photographs or artwork that must use specifically mixed colors.

Summary

In this chapter, you learned a little about advanced page issues, including the following:

✦ Crop marks

✦ First pages

✦ Spot-color and process-color design

In the next chapter, you learn about entering and editing text in a publication.

✦ ✦ ✦

Working with Text

In this part you learn about entering, editing, and formatting text in Publisher. Basic editing procedures — such as copying and moving text, inserting the current date, and checking spelling — are similar to other Office programs, but nevertheless are described in this part. Formatting text is one of the major reasons you'll want to use Publisher. A document that presents well-formatted text is attractive and professional-looking. You learn how to create tabs, indents, bullets, and numbered lists. In addition, you can format characters and paragraphs in Publisher. Character formatting includes changing fonts and type size; paragraph formatting includes setting text alignment, line spacing, and text styles.

Entering and Editing Text

You must use a frame to hold any text, or other element, that you add to a Publisher publication. A text frame is similar to other frames — picture, table, and object frames — in many ways. Text frames use handles for resizing and selection purposes; you can add fill and borders to text frames; and you can edit, delete, and otherwise manipulate and format text frames. Text frames also differ a bit from other frame types; for example, you can add columns to text frames.

The major difference between text frames and other frames is that text frames hold text. You treat the text in a text frame just as you would treat text in other programs, such as Microsoft Word for Windows. You can enter and edit text in a frame. You can format text in text frames by changing the size, font, and style of the text. You can apply color, tabs, indents, and otherwise edit the text in a frame. But first, you have to create the text frame.

Creating a Text Frame

To create a text frame, you first click the Text Frame Tool button on the Object toolbar. The mouse pointer changes to a cross, and you drag the mouse to create the frame, as shown in Figure 13-1.

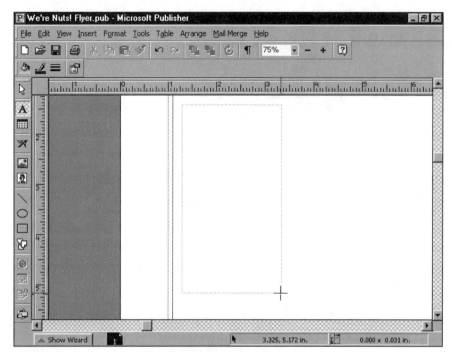

Figure 13-1: Draw a text frame before creating text.

After you draw the frame, it remains selected and displays a blinking vertical line in the upper-left corner of the frame. This vertical line is the text *insertion point*. Note that you cannot type anywhere else in the blank frame but at the insertion point. If you press the Enter key, however, you can type at the beginning of any line that you create.

You can create the frame in any zoomed view, and you can make the frame as small or as large as you want. You can use the handles in the frame to resize it later, or you can drag and move the frame to a new position. This chapter concentrates more on text than on frames; for more information about frames, especially text frames, see Chapter 10.

Entering Text

You can enter text in any selected text frame. When you finish drawing a text frame, it's automatically selected, so it displays the insertion point. If you want to enter text in a frame that you drew previously, click anywhere in that frame to determine the insertion point.

Typing in a frame

When typing text in a frame, you are limited by the frame's boundaries. As you type to the right boundary of the frame, the text wraps automatically to the next line.

If you want to start a new line, or paragraph, of text, you press the Enter key. Pressing the Enter key creates a *hard return,* also called a *paragraph return.* You can press Enter to start a new paragraph, or press Enter twice to skip a line between lines of text, as shown in Figure 13-2.

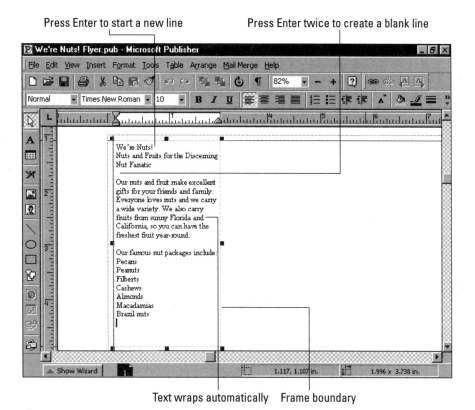

Figure 13-2: Press Enter to start a new line of text.

You can continue to type until you get to the bottom of the frame; Publisher automatically adds the text, line by line. When your text reaches the bottom of the frame, you simply resize the frame to fit the text better, as shown in Figure 13-3. Additionally, if your text takes up more of the frame than is showing, you can click the Text in Overflow button to continue the text from one frame to another. (For more information, see Chapter 10.)

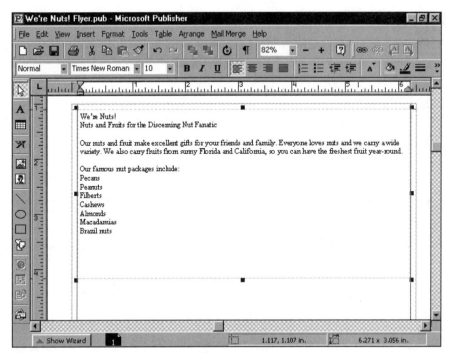

Figure 13-3: Enlarge the frame to add more text.

If you want to move the insertion point to a different position within the text, you can use your mouse to reposition the I-beam, as shown in Figure 13-4. Click the mouse anywhere within existing text to reposition the insertion point.

The following are some other methods of entering and deleting text in a frame:

✦ Reposition the insertion point by pressing a directional arrow key or by pressing the PgUp or PgDn key.

✦ Press the Home key to go to the beginning of a sentence; press the End key to go to the end of the sentence.

✦ Press Ctrl+Home to go to the beginning of the text in a frame. Press Ctrl+End to go to the end of the text in a frame.

✦ As you type, you can use the Backspace key to erase characters to the left of the insertion point.

✦ Position the insertion point and press the Delete key to erase characters to the right of the insertion point.

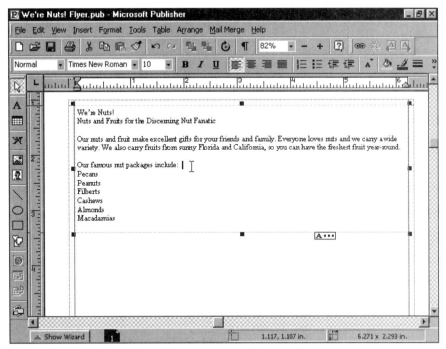

Figure 13-4: Click the mouse I-beam to move the insertion point

Tip

As you type text, avoid typing two spaces in a row at the end of a sentence after a period or other punctuation. It may look okay on the page to do that now, but after you format your text, the two spaces may end up looking like a huge gap in the text. Try to get into the habit now of typing only one space after a sentence.

Adding special characters

Naturally, you're familiar with the keyboard characters — letters, numbers, and symbols such as the dollar sign. But, several special characters also are available that you can add to your text.

You can enter a tab easily by pressing the Tab key. Publisher's default tab stops appear at half-inch marks on the ruler. For information about setting tab stops, see Chapter 15.

The following list explains how to add two common symbols to your text. If you don't want your typing to be converted to these symbol, but instead want to use the characters that you actually type, press the Backspace key once after the text changes to a symbol, and your text changes back to what you typed.

✦ Typing **(C)** produces the copyright symbol.

✦ Typing **(R)** produces the registered trademark symbol.

You also can insert other special characters, such as arrows, letters with accent marks, and various small pictures, such as cars or planes, astrological signs, decorative numbers, and more.

To insert special characters in your text, follow these steps:

1. Position the insertion point in your document.

2. Choose Insert ➪ Symbol. The Symbol dialog box appears, as shown in Figure 13-5.

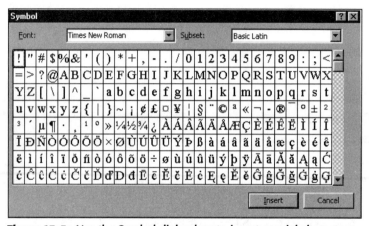

Figure 13-5: Use the Symbol dialog box to insert special characters.

3. Select the symbol that you want to use. If you click the mouse and hold it over any symbol in the box, the symbol enlarges so that you can better see it.

4. If you don't see the symbol that you want, click the down arrow beside the Font box and then choose another font.

Note
If you need a different subset of the selected font, such as mathematical operators, geometric shapes, or Greek, Latin, or Arabic forms, click the drop-down arrow beside the Subset text box. Only some fonts display the Subset box.

5. Click the Insert button to close the dialog box and insert the symbol.

Each font that you have on your computer produces different symbols. You can explore the possibilities as you need the characters. The Greek or Latin symbols may not be something you need very often; however, some of the other pictures may be useful as bullet shapes or other special characters in your publication. (For more information about bullets, see Chapter 15.)

Figure 13-6 shows just a few of the symbols that you can insert into a document. Beside each set of symbols is the name of the font, as listed in the Symbol dialog box. You can use any of these symbols in your publications, and you can enlarge them to make a better picture, if you want. (See Chapter 16.)

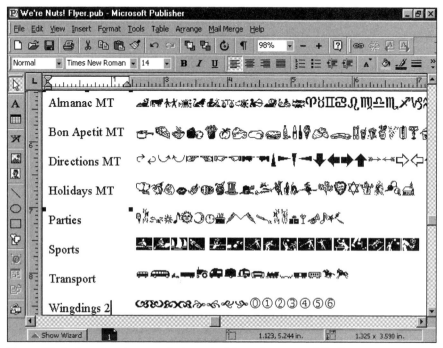

Figure 13-6: Insert various symbols and pictures in your publication.

Inserting Personal Information

Publisher enables you to record your personal information — about your company, your home or family, and any other organization with which you're affiliated — so that you can quickly enter that information in any document at any time.

Your personal information in Publisher consists of four information sets: Primary Business, Secondary Business, Other Organization, and Home/Family. You can choose to fill in one or all of these sets. For each of these sets, you can enter a name, address, phone, fax, e-mail, organization name, motto, and job title. You can also choose a color scheme to use, in general, with each information set, and you can include a logo if you want.

After you create the personal information, you can insert any part of it into a publication without retyping it. You can insert just your name, for example, or just your company logo, as you need it.

Creating the personal information

When you run one of Publisher's wizards, Publisher prompts you to fill in the personal information. You can do it at that time or at a later date.

To enter or edit your personal information, follow these steps:

1. Choose Edit ➪ Personal Information. The Personal Information dialog box appears, as shown in Figure 13-7.

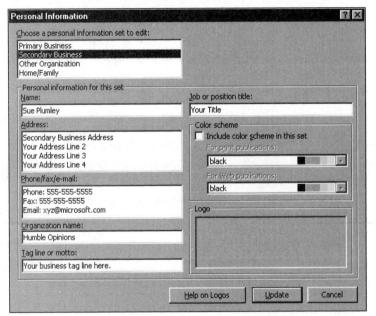

Figure 13-7: Enter your personal information now to enter it quickly and easily in documents later.

2. Choose the information set that you want to fill in.

3. Enter the information that you want to use, such as name, address, and so on. You don't *have* to enter all of the information, but you can.

4. Optionally, choose a color scheme to use any time that you use the information.

5. Optionally, create a logo. For information about creating logos, see Chapter 25.

6. Choose one of the following:

- Select another personal information set to enter or edit.

- Choose Update to update the information and close the dialog box.

Adding personal information to a publication

After you create your personal information, you can add it quickly and easily to any publication — signs, letterheads, newsletters, forms, or other publications.

To add personal information to a publication, follow these steps:

1. If you use multiple personal information sets, choose Edit ➪ Personal Information and then select the personal information set that you want to use. Click Update.

2. Choose Insert ➪ Personal Information. The cascading menu shown in Figure 13-8 appears.

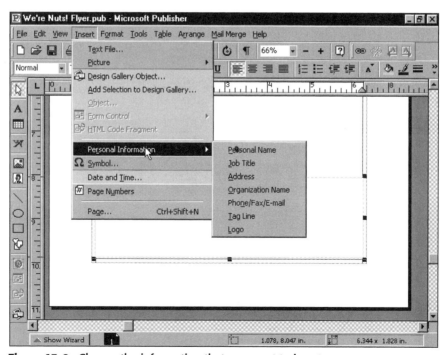

Figure 13-8: Choose the information that you want to insert.

3. Choose the personal information that you want to insert; Publisher places that information in the center of the page in a frame.
4. You can continue to select information to insert by repeating Step 2. Publisher places each subsequent frame of information on top of the previous frame. You have to move the text frames to their final location, as shown in Figure 13-9.

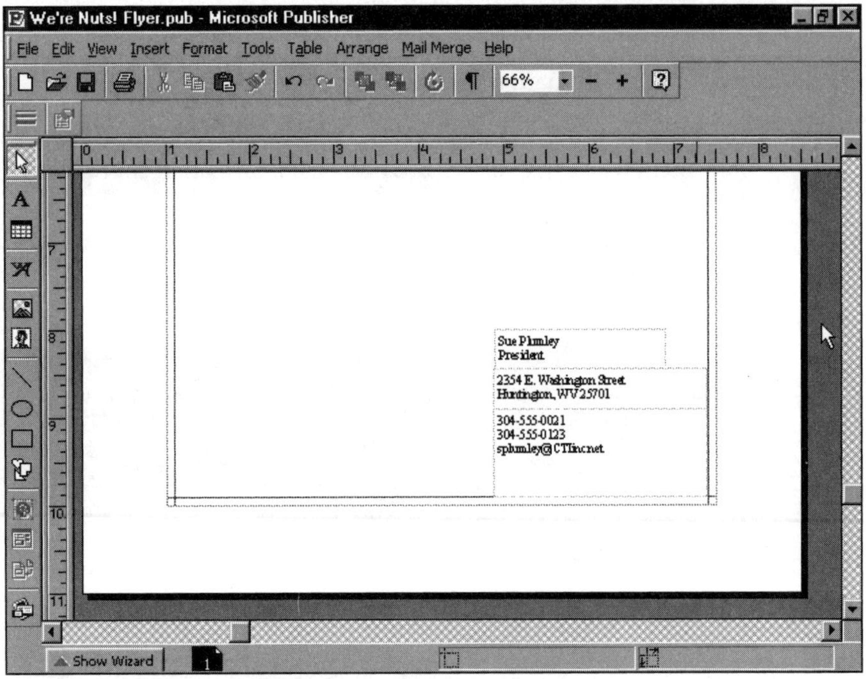

Figure 13-9: Enter the personal information quickly.

After you enter the personal information, you can move or resize the frames, add or delete text, and format the text as you want.

Basic Text Editing in Publisher

As you enter text into a frame, you can navigate around the text by using the keyboard and mouse. You can also navigate and edit text after you enter it. To edit text in Publisher, you must learn how to select the text, hide and display returns and special characters, enter line breaks, and so on. Editing also includes copying, moving, pasting, and deleting text.

Selecting text

Before you can edit text, you need to select it. As you learned previously, you can select a frame and then format or edit the frame, but that has no effect on the text. When you select text, you also select the frame that holds the text.

To select text, you do one of the following:

✦ Drag the mouse across the text to highlight it.

✦ Double-click a word to select it; triple-click a paragraph to select it.

✦ Click at the beginning of the text that you want to select, press and hold down the Shift key, and then click at the end of the text that you want to select.

✦ Position the insertion point at the beginning of the text that you want to select, press and hold down the Shift key, and then use the PgUp, PgDn, or directional arrows to move across the text to the end of the selection.

Note   A *paragraph* is defined as any amount of text with a paragraph mark at the end. You create a paragraph mark by pressing Enter. A paragraph, in Publisher, can consist of a blank line, one letter, one word, or several sentences.

Figure 13-10 illustrates selected text. Note that the text appears highlighted, or in *reverse video*.

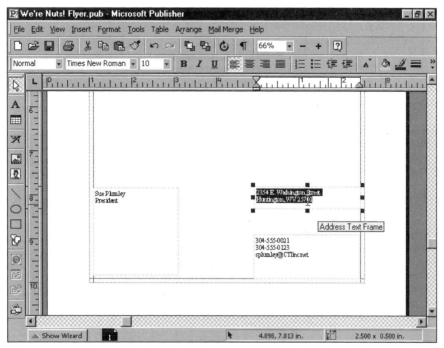

Figure 13-10: You must select text before you can edit or format it.

Tip If you select text and then type a character on the keyboard, that one character replaces the selected text. If you replace the text accidentally, press Ctrl+Z or choose Edit ➪ Undo.

Copying, moving, or deleting text

After you select text, you can copy, cut, paste, or delete it. When you copy text, you make a duplicate of the text, which you can then insert someplace else — in the same text frame, somewhere else on the page, on another page, or in another publication. You can even place the copy in a document in another Windows program. When you cut text, you can move it to another location. When you delete text, you remove it from the document permanently.

To copy and paste text, follow these steps:

1. Select the text.

2. Choose Edit ➪ Copy or press Ctrl+C.

3. Reposition the insertion point to another frame, page, or document.

4. Choose Edit ➪ Paste or press Ctrl+V.

You can continue to paste the text over and over again, if necessary, until you copy or cut something else to Windows Clipboard.

To move text, follow these steps:

1. Select the text.

2. Choose Edit ➪ Cut or press Ctrl+X.

3. Reposition the insertion point to another frame, page, or document.

4. Choose Edit ➪ Paste or press Ctrl+V.

To delete text, follow these steps:

1. Select the text.

2. Press the Delete key.

Hiding/showing special characters

By default, Publisher hides special characters, which are marks of various types that show where spaces, tabs, and paragraph returns are located in the text. If you're having trouble locating a character or formatting text, you can show these special characters onscreen, as shown in Figure 13-11.

Tip   The end of file marker indicates the point at which you can no longer enter text. You can, however, insert paragraph marks just before the end of file marker and continue to enter text on those blank lines.

To show special characters in the text, do one of the following:

✦ Choose View ➪ Show Special Characters.

✦ Press Ctrl+Shift+Y.

✦ Click the Show Special Characters button.

To hide special characters, do one of the following:

✦ Choose View ➪ Hide Special Characters.

✦ Press Ctrl+Shift+Y.

✦ Click the Hide Special Characters button.

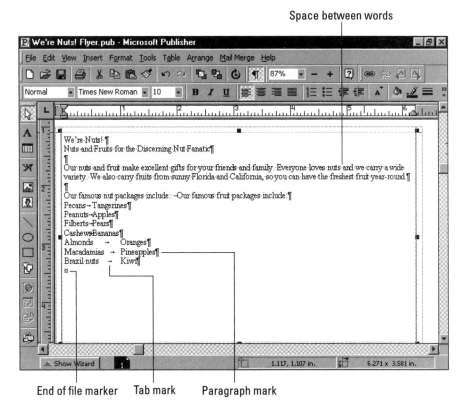

Figure 13-11: Showing special characters in the text

Entering line breaks

A *line break* is a way of splitting a line in two. Two types of line breaks exist: one type moves the following text to the next line; the other type moves the following text to another column.

You might want to insert a line break that moves text to the next line for formatting purposes, for example. Suppose that you want to change where the hyphen falls in a particular line of text. If you insert a line break, the text retains the paragraph formatting but still splits at the point where you insert the line break, as shown in Figure 13-12. (For more information about hyphenating text, see Chapter 15.)

Note in Figure 13-12 that you also can insert line breaks that send the text to the text overflow area. You might do this if you want to keep together a list of items or a paragraph of text instead of splitting it between pages or columns.

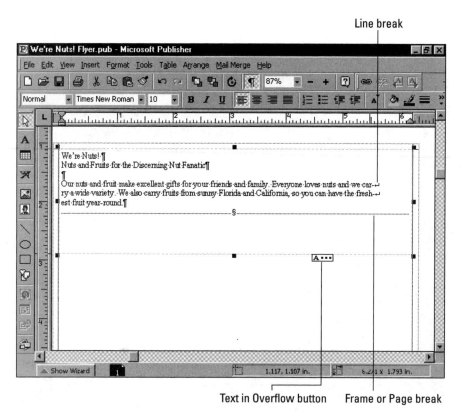

Line break

Text in Overflow button   Frame or Page break

Figure 13-12: Use line breaks to control the text.

The text in the overflow area is easy to send to another frame, on the same page or on another page in the publication. Click the Text in Overflow button and then click the text frame in which you want to continue the text. (For more information, see Chapter 10.)

To enter a line break that sends the text to the next line, position the insertion point and then press Shift+Enter.

To enter a line break that sends the text to another frame, position the insertion point and then press Ctrl+Enter.

To remove either line break, position the insertion point just before the line break and then press the Delete key. You can use the Show/Hide Special Characters button to locate the line break easily in the text.

Copyfitting Text

Many methods are available by which you can fit your text on the page, most of them include formatting changes, such as reducing text size or reducing line spacing. Find out more about manually fitting your copy in Chapter 17.

Publisher also offers automatic *copyfitting,* or *AutoFit*. Publisher's copyfitting resizes the text to make it fit the amount of space in the frame. You can use copyfitting, for example, to make a headline fit onto one line instead of two, or to squeeze one more line of text into a frame when you have no room left. AutoFit continues to work in a frame as you enter more text, delete text, resize the frame, or make the text bold.

You can choose to AutoFit the text in either of two methods:

✦ **BestFit**: Shrinks or expands the text to fit the allotted space; reduces line and character spacing as well as type size.

✦ **Shrink Text on Overflow**: Decreases the size of the type to make excess text fit into the allotted space.

Figure 13-13 shows two frames of text that are the same size and contain the exact same text. The frame on the left uses the BestFit copyfitting feature, and the frame on the right uses the Shrink Text feature. The BestFit text is a little larger than the Shrink Text frame. The option you choose is a matter of preference.

Note   You should try to keep your text sizes and line and character spacing the same for your text throughout a publication, for consistency. You might use Publisher's copyfitting features for minor changes on body text or headlines, but if the change is too noticeable, your publication looks unprofessional. You lose consistency in your document.

Hiding/Displaying Text Frames

At some point, you may create some text that you want to hide from view. You might not want to print the text but you want to keep it for later. You might want to display certain text for some letters, for example, but hide it for others. You can hide and display any text frame without deleting it and retyping it. Publisher offers two methods of performing this task:

✦ **Draw another text frame over the text that you want to hide.** Text frames are opaque, so you can easily hide any text or graphic with another text frame. You then can enter text in the frame on top, or leave it blank for extra white space.

✦ **Move the text frame off the page and into the workspace area.** The following figure illustrates two text frames in the workspace. When you save your publication, you save these text frames. The next time that you open your publication, the text frames are still in the workspace. You can move them back to the page at any time.

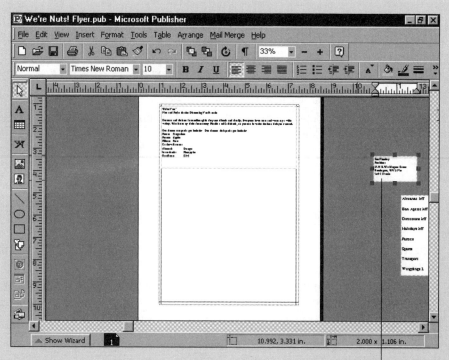

Hidden text frames

You can hide text frames in the workspace.

To copyfit text automatically in a frame, follow these steps:

1. Choose Format ➪ AutoFit Text. The cascading menu appears.

2. Choose one of the following:

   • None

   • Best Fit

   • Shrink Text on Overflow

The frame retains the copyfitting feature until you turn off the formatting by choosing None in the AutoFit Text cascading menu. When you choose None after copyfitting text in a frame, the frame maintains the last size and spacing assigned to it by the copyfitting procedure. If you want to return the text to its original size and spacing, you can click the Undo button up to 20 times to undo the copyfitting formatting.

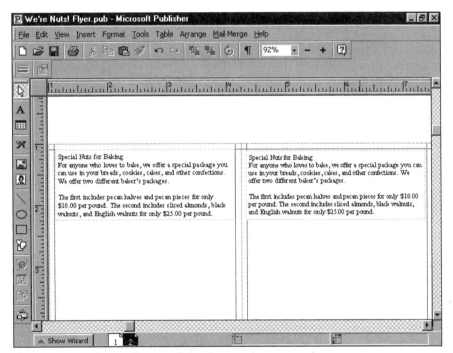

Figure 13-13: Choose the copyfitting feature that you prefer.

Summary

In this chapter, you learned about entering and editing text in Publisher. Specifically, you learned about the following:

✦ Creating a text box

✦ Entering and editing text

✦ Inserting personal information

✦ Copyfitting text

In the next chapter, you learn about revising and correcting text.

✦   ✦   ✦

Revising and Correcting Text

Publisher helps make the tasks of revising and correcting text a bit easier, and this chapter shows you how. Specifically, you learn how to insert the current date and time into your publication automatically, how to use the AutoCorrect and AutoFormat features, how to find and replace text, how to check spelling, and how best to edit the text in your publication.

Inserting the Date and Time

Often, you'll need to add the date to a document, such as a letter, report, form, or other publication. Publisher provides a command that enables you to enter the date and time, and automatically update the date when you open the document again.

You can insert the date and time into the background of your document so that it appears on every page. Alternatively, you can insert the date and time into the foreground of your document.

Looking at date and time options

Publisher offers a variety of options for inserting the date and time. First, you can choose the language that you prefer, including English, French, German, Italian, and many more. Publisher uses the language and the common format of the country that you choose; for example, in French (Swiss), you can choose lundi, 23, novembre 1998 or 1998-11-23, among other formats.

Another option is to choose from a list of available formats. You can use 11/23/98 or Monday, November 23, 1998. You might choose 23-Nov-98 or 11.23.98, or any of a host of other formats. You can also include the time in your date, such as 11/23/98 11:12 AM. Alternatively, simply insert the time: 11:12 AM or 11:12:29 AM.

Finally, you can choose whether to update the date automatically each time that you open the document. If you do not choose to update, the date and time remain the same as when you first insert them.

Adding the date and time

You can add the date and time to any publication, in either the background or the foreground. To insert the date and time, follow these steps:

1. Position the insertion point in a text frame.

2. Choose Insert ➪ Date and Time. The Date and Time dialog box appears, as shown in Figure 14-1.

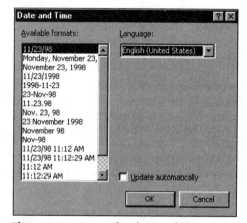

Figure 14-1: Insert the date and time and, optionally, have them updated automatically.

3. In the Language drop-down list, select a language, if you want something other than English.

4. In the Available formats list, select the date/time format that you want to use.

5. Check the Update automatically check box if you want the date to change each time you open the document.

6. Click OK.

Using AutoCorrect

You can use AutoCorrect, a Publisher tool, to correct common mistakes that you might make as you type. Suppose that you consistently make the same typographical error, such as typing **teh** instead of **the** or **aganist** instead of **against**. AutoCorrect can automatically correct the error right after you type it.

AutoCorrect includes a list of many common typographical errors, but you can also add your own. If you find a particular word that is difficult to type correctly, you can enter it into the AutoCorrect dialog box and let Publisher take care of it for you.

Another handy use of AutoCorrect is to substitute shortcuts for company names or long phrases. Suppose your company's name is CTI Technologies, Inc. You can set AutoCorrect to fill in the entire name for you whenever you type **CTI**, for example. If you find a phrase or product name that you often use in your documents, you can create a shortcut for it. Suppose that you use the word "Microsoft" a lot; simply enter a shortcut for that word, such as **MSS**.

Note   If you sometimes type a shortcut (such as **CTI** or **MSS**) and want it to remain as you type it rather than use AutoCorrect's substitution, you have to edit AutoCorrect's substitution. First, type the shortcut and press the spacebar. When you enter a space, the AutoCorrect substitution appears. Use the mouse to move back into the word and correct it with the appropriate letters.

Understanding the AutoCorrect options

AutoCorrect also offers other options and common substitutions. Figure 14-2 illustrates the AutoCorrect dialog box. Note that it offers some general editing substitutions, plus a list of misspellings that you can replace.

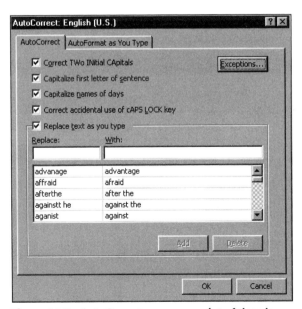

Figure 14-2: AutoCorrect saves you a lot of time in editing and revising your work.

The following is a description of the AutoCorrect options:

✦ **Correct TWo INitial CApitals:** Check this box to automatically correct the mistake when you accidentally hold down the Shift key too long and end up with two initial capital letters (*initial caps*) in a word. To negate this action when you need two initial caps in a word, type the word, press the spacebar, and then go back and capitalize the second letter.

✦ **Capitalize first letter of sentence:** Often, you may type so quickly that you miss the Shift key when you start a sentence. Checking this box capitalizes the first letter of any sentence when you miss it. Naturally, it also capitalizes the first letter of phrases that you may not want capitalized. To negate this action when you want the first letter of a phrase or sentence to remain lowercase, type the word, press the spacebar, and then go back and replace that one letter.

✦ **Capitalize names of days:** Publisher substitutes an initial cap for a lowercase letter in the name of any day of the week.

✦ **Correct accidental use of cAPS LOCK key:** Publisher can tell when you accidentally use the Caps Lock key—indicated by an initial lowercase letter followed by all caps—and automatically changes the text to initial cap, otherwise known as *sentence case*.

✦ **Replace text as you type:** This option governs the lists labeled Replace and With in the AutoCorrect dialog box. To add words to the list, first enter in the Replace text box the typo or abbreviation that you want replaced, and then enter the correct spelling or full word or phrase in the With box. Also, you can scroll through the list of common typographical errors and remove any that you don't want to use.

Making exceptions

The Exceptions button in the AutoCorrect dialog box enables you to enter any exceptions that you want to the First Letter and the INitial CAps options.

Figure 14-3 shows the First Letter tab of the AutoCorrect Exceptions dialog box. Publisher capitalizes the first letter in a sentence, which it identifies as any letter that follows a period and a space. However, when you use an abbreviation that ends with a period, Publisher mistakes the first letter of the next word as the beginning of a new sentence and thus automatically capitalizes that letter. To avoid this from occurring, you can add to the list any abbreviations that you frequently use, as well as delete any from the list that don't apply to you. Publisher then knows not to capitalize the next word following the abbreviations that you add to this list.

Figure 14-4 shows the INitial CAps tab of the AutoCorrect Exceptions dialog box. You can add any abbreviations or acronyms that you commonly use so that Publisher doesn't automatically correct them as you type.

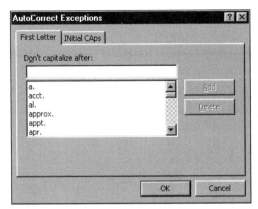

Figure 14-3: Enter any exceptions to the Capitalize first letter of sentence rule.

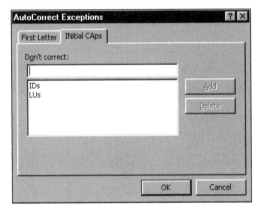

Figure 14-4: Enter exceptions to the Correct TWo INitial CApitals rule.

Configuring AutoCorrect

You can accept the defaults in the AutoCorrect dialog box or customize AutoCorrect to suit your personal needs. To set options for AutoCorrect, follow these steps:

1. Choose Tools ➪ AutoCorrect. The AutoCorrect dialog box appears.

2. In the AutoCorrect tab, check the options that you want to apply.

3. Click Exceptions to enter any exclusions to the INitial CApitals or First Letter rules.

4. In Replace, enter any typos that you commonly make or enter an abbreviation of your name, company, or other text.

5. In With, enter the correction or long name that you want to use to replace the typo or abbreviation.

6. Click the Add button to add the new typos and abbreviations to the list.

7. Optionally, select a word in the Replace list and click the Delete button to remove it.

8. Click OK.

See the next section for information about the AutoFormat tab.

Using AutoFormat

AutoFormat is included in the AutoCorrect dialog box. In reality, however, it applies to formatting more than to editing and revising text. AutoFormat deals with smart quotes, en and em dashes, and formatting bulleted and numbered lists. AutoFormatting corrections apply as you type.

Using smart quotes, em dashes, and en dashes

Smart quotes (also called *curly* quotes or *typographical* quotes), em dashes, and en dashes are tools that typesetters use to make a document look professional. Smart quotes replace inches marks (" ") with quote marks (" ").

En dashes and em dashes replace the hyphen(s) in your text. An en dash is equal in width to a capital N in the typeface that you're using; it replaces the use of one hyphen in the text. An em dash is a longer dash, used to separate phrases; it replaces the use of two hyphens when you're typing. The name indicates that it is the width of the capital M in the current typeface. Figure 14-5 illustrates the smart quote and em dash typographical marks.

Automatically formatting lists

You can also choose to let Publisher automatically convert lists that you want to be bulleted or numbered. Suppose that you want to create a bulleted list. If you type an asterisk and spaces for two items, Publisher replaces the asterisks with bullets and the spaces with tabs. Also, if you type a numbered list, Publisher begins to number automatically when you press Enter on the second item. It also replaces the spaces with tabs.

Figure 14-6 illustrates both a bulleted list and a numbered list. To the right of the bulleted item is what was actually typed, in parentheses. When you press Enter and type another asterisk, Publisher changes the asterisks to the bullets that are shown on the left.

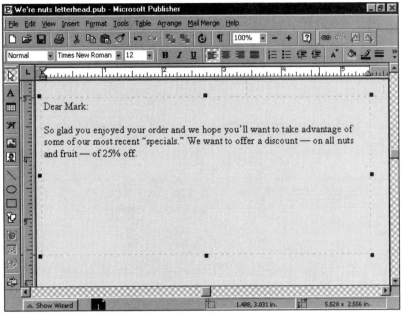

Figure 14-5: Make your publication look more professional by using typographical marks.

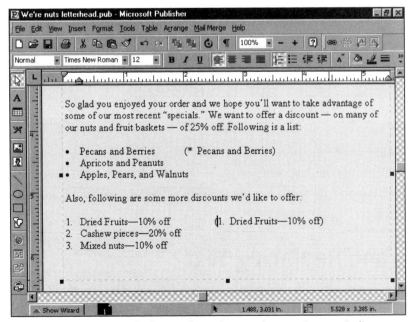

Figure 14-6: Automatic bullets and numbers make entering text in lists quick and easy.

In the numbered list, the situation is similar. To the right of the first number is what was actually typed, in parentheses. When you press Enter, Publisher automatically enters the number 2 and a tab.

Setting options for AutoFormat

Set the options for AutoFormat in the AutoCorrect dialog box, as follows:

1. Choose Tools ➪ AutoCorrect. The AutoCorrect dialog box appears, as shown in Figure 14-7.

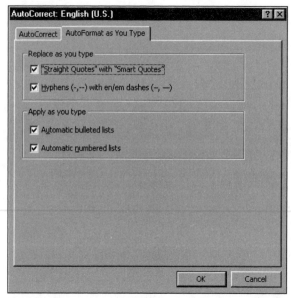

Figure 14-7: Setting AutoFormat options

2. Select the AutoFormat as You Type tab.

3. Check the options that you want to apply in the Replace as you type area.

4. Check the options that you want to apply in the Apply as you type area.

5. Click OK.

Finding and Replacing Text

Many times, especially in very long documents, you may need to search for a word or phrase. You might want to edit the word or phrase. Or, you might want to add text to that area, change a figure caption, print that page, or otherwise manipulate the text.

Frequently in your text, you may enter a word or a phrase that you later decide to change. For example, you might have entered the wrong name for a company or product or used a word that you wish you could replace with a different word.

Publisher includes a find-and-replace feature that you can use both to find text in a document and to replace text in a document. Publisher can find, or find and replace, text in only one text frame at a time.

Note
Publisher can't find text in the text overflow area. To find or replace in that text, you have to either enlarge the frame or continue the story into another frame.

Finding text

You can search for a word or a phrase in the text. Publisher searches in the selected frame and any frame connected to it. You can find characters, partial words, whole words, and so on by using the Find dialog box. You can also find words that match the case of the word that you enter; for example, you can choose to find instances of "Packages" only, and not "packages."

Finally, you can search up or down in the document. If you search up, for example, Publisher notifies you when it reaches the top of the publication, and asks you whether you want it to continue searching the rest of the document.

Figure 14-8 shows the Find dialog box in Publisher.

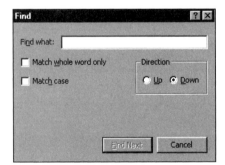

Figure 14-8: Searching for words in the text

Special characters

You also can find special characters, such as question marks and hyphens. Table 14-1 lists the keystrokes for finding special characters.

Table 14-1 Finding Special Characters	
To Find:	**Type:**
Question mark	^?
Optional hyphen	^-
Line break	^N
Paragraph mark	^P
Tab stop	^T

Partial and whole words

You can search for only parts of a word if you want. Suppose that you want to search for "Microsoft" but you're in a hurry; type **Micro**. Or, if you cannot remember how a word is spelled, enter any part of the word that you do know how to spell. The Find feature searches for word pieces as well as whole words and phrases.

This feature can be troublesome, however. If you want to find every occurrence of the word "the" in the text, for example, the Find feature also finds words such as "their," "there," "theory," and so on. In such a case, you can specify to match only whole words, and the Find feature will return only words that match exactly what you type.

Steps to find text

To find text, follow these steps:

1. Select the frame that you want to search.

2. Choose Edit ➪ Find or press Ctrl+F.

3. In the Find what text box, enter the word, character, or phrase that you want to find.

Note

The last word you entered in the Find what text box remains there until you enter a new word or end the Publisher session.

4. Choose either of the following Direction options:

   • Up

   • Down

5. Check options as they apply.

6. Click the Find Next button.

When Publisher reaches the end or the beginning of the selected frame, it displays an information dialog box like the one shown in Figure 14-9. Choose Yes to continue searching or No to cancel the search.

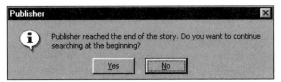

Figure 14-9: Continue the search by clicking Yes.

The following are the possible results of the search, and your next step for each situation:

1. If Publisher finishes the search and cannot find the requested item, it displays the dialog box shown in Figure 14-10. Click OK.

Note

If you didn't find the text for which you're searching, you might try again in a different text frame or end the Publisher session.

Figure 14-10: Publisher couldn't find the search item.

If Publisher *does* find the text for which you're searching, the Find dialog box remains onscreen and Publisher highlights the word in the text, as shown in Figure 14-11.

2. When Publisher finds the text, you can either click the Find Next button, to find the next occurrence of the text, or click Close to cancel the dialog box and proceed with editing the found text.

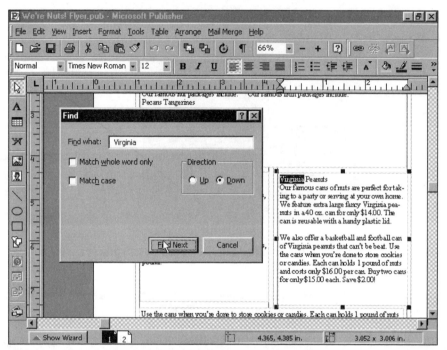

Figure 14-11: Publisher highlights the found text.

Replacing text

Publisher also can replace any text that you find, either one occurrence at a time or all occurrences simultaneously. You can replace words, phrases, capitalization, and so on. You can replace only one instance or every occurrence in your document.

Figure 14-12 illustrates the Replace dialog box with a sample of text that you might want to replace. Note that the dialog box is similar to options found in the Find dialog box.

Heading for disaster

Be careful if you choose to replace all occurrences in the publication. Just in case you make a mistake, it's a good idea to save your document before you do an automatic find-and-replace procedure. Additionally, you should always manually replace the first few occurrences, to make sure that you're replacing the correct words.

You might, for example, forget to check the Match whole word only box and consequently replace something such as all instances of "can" with "can't." Without choosing the Match whole words only option, words like "cannot," "candy," and "canoe" change to "can'tnot," "can'tdy," and "can'toe." If you save the publication before you run the Replace procedure, you can revert back to the correct document and try again. If you notice a problem with any find-and-replace operation, you should immediately Undo the Replace procedure and try again, being careful not to repeat the same mistake.

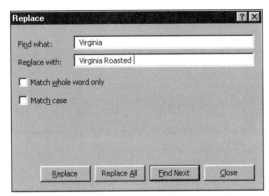

Figure 14-12: Finding and replacing text in a publication

Steps for replacing text

To replace text, follow these steps:

1. Choose Edit ➪ Replace or press Ctrl+H. The Replace dialog box appears.

2. In the Find what text box, enter the exact text that you want to find, making sure to use the appropriate capitalization.

3. In the Replace with text box, enter the exact text that you want to substitute.

4. Check the Match whole word only check box, if appropriate.

5. Check the Match case check box, if appropriate.

6. Click one of the following buttons:

   - **Find Next:** To locate the next occurrence of the text in the Find what text box.

   - **Replace:** To substitute only that one occurrence with the text in the Replace with text box.

   - **Replace All:** To substitute all occurrences in the publication.

7. When Publisher has finished replacing text, it displays an information dialog box telling you it's finished. Click OK.

8. Click Close when you're finished with the Replace procedure.

Checking Spelling

As you type your text into a text block, Publisher marks misspelled words with a wavy red underline, as shown in Figure 14-13. These underlined words are easy to spot, whether your Zoom view is 100% or Whole page. You can correct the words as you work, or you can correct the spelling mistakes later.

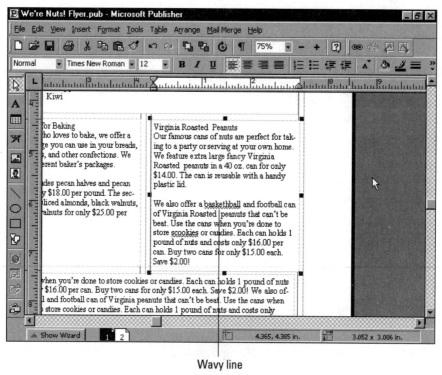

Wavy line

Figure 14-13: Publisher checks your spelling as you type.

Publisher's spelling feature checks for misspelled words and words that are repeated in text and table frames. Publisher doesn't check the spelling in WordArt frames or mail merge fields. (For more information about mail merge, see Part VII, "Using Mail Merge.")

If you choose to check spelling manually, Publisher displays any words that are not listed in its dictionary. The Spelling feature suggests possible spellings and offers multiple options and solutions.

You also can hide spelling errors while you're working in a publication, and check them later. You also can change Spelling options.

Hiding spelling errors

By default, Publisher checks your spelling as you enter text in a text frame, and notifies you of misspelled or repeated words by underlining that text with a red wavy line.

If you prefer, you can hide spelling errors so that you can concentrate on entering text, formatting text, or designing the page. To hide spelling errors, choose Tools ⇨ Spelling ⇨ Hide Spelling Errors. To show the spelling errors again, choose Tools ⇨ Spelling ⇨ Show Spelling Errors.

The option applies only to the current publication. The errors will show again, by default, in the next publication that you open or start new.

Manually checking spelling

You have more control over the spelling checker if you manually check spelling in a document. For example, Publisher may question a word or name when it's spelled correctly, just because that word isn't in Publisher's dictionary. You can add that word to the dictionary so that Publisher doesn't question it any more, or you can simply tell Publisher to ignore the word within the current publication.

To check the spelling of a publication manually, follow these steps:

1. Select the frame that you want to check.

2. Choose Tools ⇨ Spelling ⇨ Check Spelling; alternatively, press F7. The Check Spelling dialog box appears, as shown in Figure 14-14. The misspelled or otherwise unknown word appears in the Not in dictionary text box.

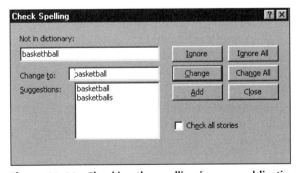

Figure 14-14: Checking the spelling in your publication

3. Choose the appropriate option, all of which are explained in Table 14-2.

4. Publisher continues to check the spelling. If it finds a word that is repeated, as shown in Figure 14-15, you can click either Ignore, to ignore the repeated word, or Delete, to delete the repeated word.

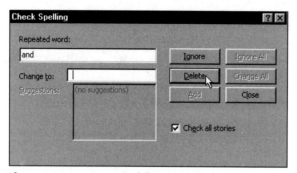

Figure 14-15: Ignore or delete repeated words.

5. When Publisher has finished checking the spelling, it displays a dialog box telling you the spelling check is complete. Click OK.

| | Table 14-2 |
| | **Check Spelling Dialog Box Options** |

Option	Description
Change to	Accept the suggestion in this text box or enter your own corrected spelling
Suggestions	Select one of the words; it appears in the Change to text box
Ignore	Click to disregard the spelling of the word and continue checking the document
Ignore All	Click to disregard all occurrences of the word in this publication
Change	Click after you choose a suggestion or enter the correct spelling in the Change to text box, to modify the selected word in the text
Change All	Click to change all occurrences of the word to the spelling in the Change to text box
Add	Click to add the word to the dictionary, so that Publisher will not question its spelling again
Close	Click to close the Check Spelling dialog box
Check all stories	Check this box to check the spelling in all text and table frames in the publication

Note

Publisher checks the spelling in all text frames, even the frames in the workspace area, if you choose to check all stories. Publisher also checks text in the text overflow area, unlike the find-and-replace feature.

Changing spelling options

You can change some Spelling options to suit your working style better. By default, Publisher checks spelling as you type, notifies you of a repeated word, and ignores words in uppercase. You can choose to ignore words in all caps, such as acronyms. You can also choose to ignore repeated words or turn off the function that checks spelling as you type.

To change Spelling options, follow these steps:

1. Choose Tools ➪ Spelling ➪ Spelling Options. The Spelling Options dialog box appears, as shown in Figure 14-16.

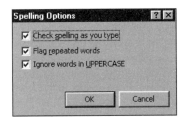

Figure 14-16: Customize the spelling checker.

2. Clear the check box of any of the following:
   - **Check spelling as you type:** To hide spelling errors in all publications as you type. To check spelling, you have to do it manually.
   - **Flag repeated words:** To ignore repeated words in the text.
   - **Ignore words in UPPERCASE:** To question all misspelled words, even acronyms.
3. Click OK.

Omitting words from the spelling check

You can choose to exclude certain words from a spelling check, such as a product or company name, an acronym, a person's name, and so on. When you mark a word as no proofing, Publisher ignores it in all publications. To omit a word from the spelling check, follow these steps:

1. Select the word to be omitted.
2. Choose Tools ➪ Language ➪ Set Language. The Language dialog box appears, as shown in Figure 14-17.

Figure 14-17: Mark text as no proofing to ignore it in a spelling check.

3. In the Mark selected text as list box, scroll to the top and select (no proofing).

4. Click OK. Publisher ignores that word in all documents and publications.

Editing Text in Word

Publisher contains many of the same proofing tools as you find in Microsoft Word for Windows, including the spelling checker, find-and-replace feature, AutoCorrect, AutoFormat, and so on. You might, however, prefer to enter and edit your text in Word and then import it into Publisher when you're finished.

Note

To use Word to edit Publisher documents, you must have Word version 6.0 or later installed on your computer.

You can also import a text file from Word, as well as from many other programs (see the sidebar "Converting Files to Publisher Format"). For example, you might have a text file consisting of a report or other document that you created in Word that you now want to import to use in a Publisher publication.

Editing publisher text in Word

After you create a story in Publisher, you can edit it in Word. You might have a long story that spans several text frames and pages in Publisher, for example. To edit a story in Word, follow these steps:

1. Right-click the text frame. A quick menu appears.

2. Choose Change Text ⇨ Edit Story in Microsoft Word, as shown in Figure 14-18. Word opens and displays the text.

3. Edit the text in Word, as shown in Figure 14-19.

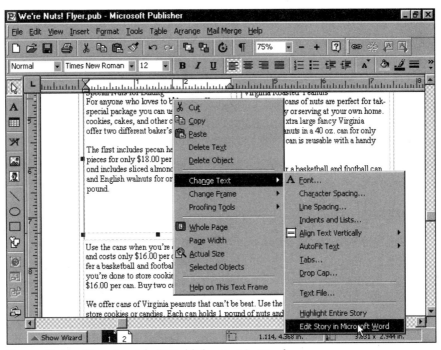

Figure 14-18: Choosing to edit Publisher text in Word

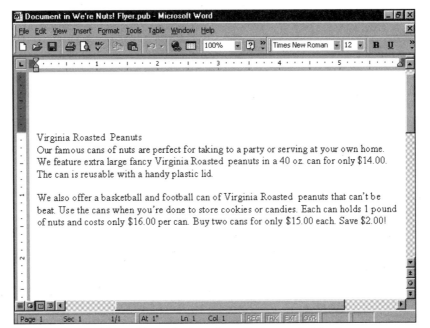

Figure 14-19: Add, modify, and otherwise edit the text in Word.

4. When you're finished, choose File ➪ Update.

5. Choose File ➪ Close & Return to *filename* in Publisher. The Word file closes, but the program remains open.

Writing in Word

If you prefer to write your text in Microsoft Word and then convert it to a Publisher publication, you can do that, too. Publisher can convert Word files, as well as many other file types, to files that you can use in your publications.

You can import a file into any text frame in Publisher, regardless of whether that frame already has text in it or is a new frame.

To import a file from Word, follow these steps:

1. Position the insertion point in a text frame in Publisher.

2. Choose Insert ➪ Text File. The Insert Text dialog box appears, as shown in Figure 14-20.

3. In the Look in drop-down list box, locate the folder and the file.

4. Select the file and click OK.

5. Publisher imports the file into the specified text frame.

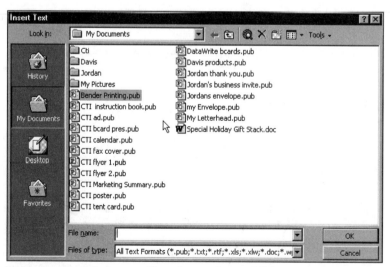

Figure 14-20: Select a text file to import into Publisher.

Converting Files to Publisher Format

Publisher can convert many file formats from other programs. In many cases, Publisher maintains the character and paragraph formatting, as well. The following is a list of file types that Publisher can convert:

✦ Any Publisher files (PUB)

✦ Plain text (TXT)

✦ Rich Text Format (RTF)

✦ Microsoft Word for Windows, versions 2 and 6, Word 95 and 97, and Word 2000 (DOC and DOT)

✦ Microsoft Word for Macintosh, versions 4, 5, 5.1, 6, and Word 98 (DOC)

✦ Microsoft Works for Windows, versions 3 and 4 (WPS)

✦ WordPerfect for MS-DOS, version 5.1 (WP)

✦ WordPerfect for Windows, versions 5, 5.1, 6, 7, and 8 (WP)

✦ Microsoft Excel for Windows, versions 2, 2.1, 3, 4, 5, Excel 95, and Excel 97 (XLS)

To convert files to a Publisher format, follow these steps:

1. Choose File ➪ Open. The Open dialog box appears.

2. In Files of type, choose the file type — PUB, TXT, RTF, XLS, or other.

3. Locate the folder and select the file. Click the Open button. Publisher converts and opens the file in a new blank document.

Summary

In this chapter, you learned about revising and correcting text. Specifically, you learned about the following:

◆ Inserting the date and time

◆ Using AutoCorrect

◆ Using AutoFormat

◆ Finding and replacing text

◆ Checking spelling

◆ Editing text in Word

In the next chapter, you learn about basic text formatting.

✦   ✦   ✦

Basic Text Formatting

Publisher enables you to apply basic formatting to the text of your publication. For instance, you can change text indents, create bulleted or numberred lists, insert or delete tabs, and hyphenate text automatically, all while working in Publish. This chapter shows you how.

Inserting and Deleting Indents

An *indent* is an extra margin set on the left or right edge (or both) of text in a frame. Several different types of indents can be set: first-line indent, hanging indent, quotation indent, left-edge indent, and right-edge indent. Figure 15-1 illustrates these five common indents.

You generally use a first-line indent to announce the beginning of a new paragraph of text. Each paragraph uses a ¼- or ½-inch indention on the first line, to make the text easier to read and to provide a brief rest for the reader's eyes.

Hanging indents are perfect for numbered and bulleted lists. *Quotation* indents set off excerpts and quotes from the rest of the text so that they're easier to locate and identify. *Left-* and *right-edge* indents also set off text.

You can indent text in Publisher by using a preset default or by setting your own custom indents. The preset indents make applying text formatting easy, but custom indents may suit some text requirements better than the preset indents.

Publisher also provides a dialog box in which you can set indents, and set indent markers on the ruler, which make indents quick and easy to complete.

Hanging indent   First line indent

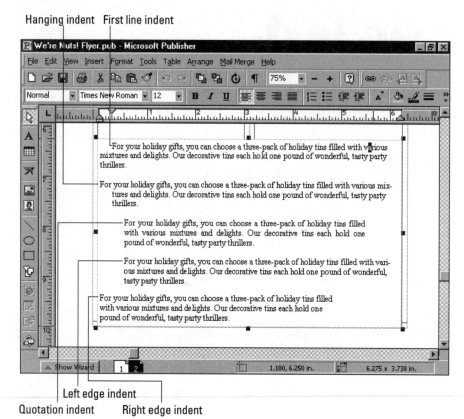

Left edge indent

Quotation indent   Right edge indent

Figure 15-1: Each indent has certain uses within your document.

Using preset indents

Publisher provides the most common indents for you, measured and formatted, so that you simply have to choose the indent that you want. You can either adjust the indents to suit yourself or accept the defaults that Publisher presents. The following are the preset indents and Publisher's measurements for each:

✦ **First-line indent:** Indents only the first line, at ¼ inch. The left and right edges are flush with the edge of the text frame.

✦ **Hanging indent:** The left edge of the text is indented ¼ inch, the first line of the paragraph is *outdented* ¼ inch (hangs over into the left margin, whereas the rest of the lines are indented), and the right edge is flush.

✦ **Quotation indent:** The left and right edges of the text are indented ½ inch.

Applying the indent

To apply a preset indent, follow these steps:

1. Select the paragraph(s) of text to be indented.

2. Choose Format ⇨ Indents and Lists. The Indents and Lists dialog box appears, as shown in Figure 15-2.

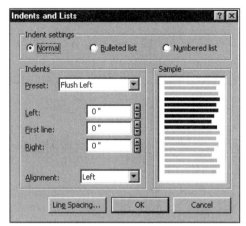

Figure 15-2: Applying preset indents quickly to your text

Note Other elements appear in the Indents and Lists dialog box. Bulleted and numbered lists are discussed later in this chapter; alignment and line spacing are covered in Chapter 17.

3. In the Indent settings area, choose the Normal option, if it is not already selected.

4. In the Indents area, click the Preset drop-down arrow and choose one of the following preset indents: First Line Indent, Hanging Indent, or Quotation.

5. Click OK. Publisher applies the indent to the text.

Removing the indent

To remove a preset indent, follow these steps:

1. Select the paragraph(s) of text from which to remove the indent.

2. Choose Format ⇨ Indents and Lists. The Indents and Lists dialog box appears.

3. In the Indents area, click the Preset drop-down arrow. From the list, choose Flush Left.

4. Click OK to close the dialog box. Publisher removes the indent.

Setting custom indents

Publisher provides preset first line, quotation, and hanging indents; however, you can also set your own custom indents. You can create any indent that you want, including a left- or right-edge indent.

Tip   You can create your own custom indents by using either the Indents and Lists dialog box or the horizontal ruler in Publisher. For more information about using the ruler to create and adjust indents, see the next section.

To set your own custom indents, follow these steps:

1. Select the paragraph(s) of text to be indented.

2. Choose Format ➪ Indents and Lists. The Indents and Lists dialog box appears.

3. In the Preset drop-down list, select Custom.

4. Enter values in the Left, First line, and Right text boxes, as applicable to the indents that you want to make.

5. Click OK.

If you need to adjust the indents, you can either open the Indents and Lists dialog box and adjust them or use the horizontal ruler to adjust them, as shown in the next section.

Using a ruler to create and adjust indents

You can move the paragraph markers on the horizontal ruler in Publisher to quickly set any type of indent that you want. You can create or adjust indents with the ruler. Figure 15-3 illustrates a hanging indent and the paragraph markers on the ruler.

Figure 15-4 shows a 1-inch left indent on the ruler. The indent applies to the text that is selected. Indent both the first line and subsequent lines by dragging the left and first-line indent markers.

First line indent marker   Left indent marker   Right indent marker

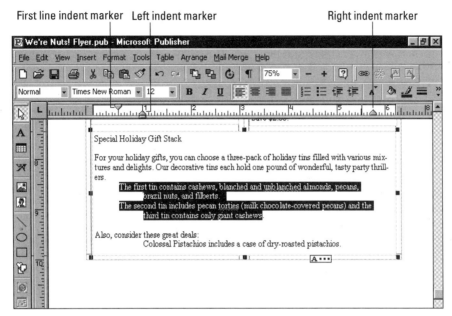

Figure 15-3: Creating custom hanging indents

Click here to drag both the first line and the left indent markers

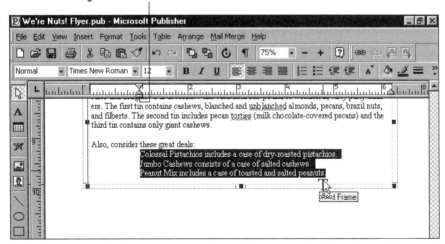

Figure 15-4: Indenting the left edge of the text by using the ruler

So far, all you've seen of hanging indents is the first line of text hanging over the second and subsequent lines of text. Figure 15-5 illustrates a better use for hanging indents. You can insert special characters to create the bullets. For more information about bullets and lists, see the next section, "Working with Lists."

To create a custom indent, follow these steps:

1. Select paragraph(s) of text.

2. On the ruler, drag the indent markers of choice to a new position.

Tip

If indent markers are dimmed, you've selected more than one paragraph, and they have different indents. You can either select each paragraph and adjust the indents or set new indents for all selected paragraphs.

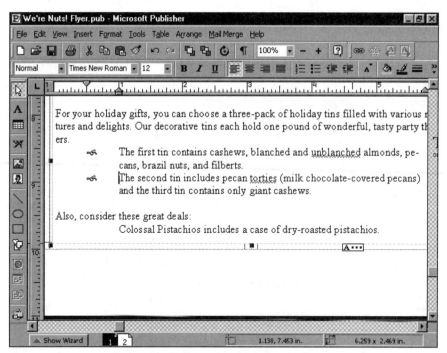

Figure 15-5: Create interesting bullets with the help of a hanging indent.

Using tool buttons to indent text

Using the Decrease Indent or Increase Indent buttons on the Formatting toolbar is one other method that you can use to indent text in Publisher. Each time that you click the Increase Indent button, the indent of the selected text moves one tab stop away from the left edge of the frame. Each time that you click the Decrease Indent button, the indent moves one tab stop toward the left edge of the frame.

By default, the tab stop is set at $1/2$ inch, but you can change the tab stops, which also changes the indent amount. For more information about tabs, see "Inserting and Deleting Tabs," later in this chapter.

Working with Lists

You can create lists within your publications. For example, you can create a list by indenting each item on the list $1/2$ inch or 1 inch to set it off from the rest of the text. Alternatively, you can apply bullets or numbers to a list.

You apply bullets to a list when all items on the list are of equal importance. You apply numbers to a list when the items are of varying importance—number one is more important than number two, and so forth. You might also apply numbers to a list when you must follow a step-by-step procedure, such as perform step one, and then step two, and so on.

Whether you're creating bulleted or numbered lists, you use the hanging indent to do it. You can create the hanging indent yourself or let Publisher do it. Publisher offers some standard bullet and numbering schemes that you can use with your lists.

Creating bulleted lists

Publisher presents three methods by which you can create a bulleted list:

✦ Use the Bullets button on the Formatting toolbar

✦ Use the Indents and Lists dialog box

✦ Type an asterisk and a space before you enter the list, and Publisher automatically inserts bullets for you

The Formatting Toolbar

Previously in this book, the Formatting toolbar has contained only two buttons, both of which were dimmed. The first time that you created a text box and clicked the mouse in that text box, the Formatting toolbar became active, displaying multiple buttons you can use for formatting text. From this point forward, you'll be using buttons on the Formatting toolbar. The following list briefly describes each tool's job and tells where you can find more information about the tool; each tool is explained in more detail, where appropriate, in the text in this part of the book.

✦ **Style:** Enables you to choose from a list of various styles—say, one for headlines, another for bullets—from a list of available styles. For more information, see Chapter 7.

✦ **Font:** Presents a list of available fonts, or typefaces, that you can apply to selected text. For more information, see Chapter 16.

✦ **Font Size:** Presents a list of common text sizes from which you can choose. For more information, see Chapter 16.

✦ **Bold:** Makes the selected text bold (see Chapter 16 for more information).

✦ **Italic:** Makes the selected text italic (see Chapter 16 for more information).

✦ **Underline:** Underlines the selected text (see Chapter 16 for more information).

✦ **Align Left:** Arranges the selected text so that it is flush with the left edge of the frame (see Chapter 17 for more information).

✦ **Center:** Arranges the selected text so that it is centered in the middle of the frame (see Chapter 17 for more information).

✦ **Align Right:** Arranges the selected text so that it is flush with the right edge of the frame (see Chapter 17 for more information).

✦ **Justify:** Arranges the selected text so that it has flush-left and flush-right edges (see Chapter 17 for more information).

✦ **Numbering:** Changes the selected text so that it is a numbered list (see the next section for more information).

✦ **Bullets:** Changes the selected text so that each item is preceded by a bullet (see the next section for more information).

✦ **Decrease Indent:** Reduces the indent of the selected text by one tab stop (see the preceding section for more information).

✦ **Increase Indent:** Expands the indent of the selected text by one tab stop (see the preceding section for more information).

✦ **Decrease Font Size:** Reduces the size of the selected font, or text, by one or two sizes, depending on the starting size of the text (see Chapter 16 for more information).

The default bulleted list looks the same no matter which method you use. Figure 15-6 illustrates Publisher's default bulleted list. The bullet symbol is flush left with the frame and the text indents are $1/4$ inch. Note the hanging indent for the bullets on the horizontal ruler.

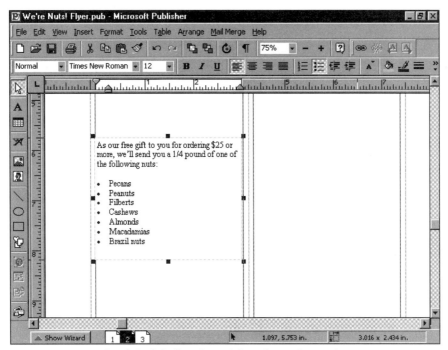

Figure 15-6: Use the default bullets for quick and easy formatting.

Using the default bullets

You can choose any of three methods to create a default, or preset, bulleted list in Publisher.

To create the list as you type, follow these steps:

1. Type an asterisk, followed by a space or a tab, and then type the first item on the list.

2. Press Enter and type another asterisk. Publisher changes both asterisks to the bullet symbol and changes the text indents to a hanging indent.

3. To add more bulleted items to the list, press Enter and type the item. To enter a line of text that does not use a bullet, press Enter twice after the last bulleted item.

To create a bulleted list by using the Bullets button on the Formatting toolbar, you can either enter the text first, select it, and then click the button, or you can click the button and then begin to type the list. To create a bulleted list by using the Bullets button on the Formatting toolbar, follow these steps:

1. Select the text or position the insertion point.

2. Click the Bullets button.

3. Click the Bullets button again to remove the bullet from a selected item or the last line of text.

To use the Indents and Lists dialog box to create a default bulleted list, follow these steps:

1. Select the list.

2. Choose Format ⇨ Indents and Lists. The Indents and Lists dialog box appears.

3. In the Indent settings area, choose the Bulleted list option.

4. Click OK.

Modifying bullets

You can create new bullets or modify existing bullets so that they have different characteristics than the default bullets. You can change the indent, for example, or change the bullet type and size. Figure 15-7 illustrates the Indents and Lists dialog box with the Bulleted list options.

Figure 15-7: Creating custom bullets

Publisher offers six bullet symbols that you can use. Alternatively, you can open the Symbol dialog box to choose from numerous bullet symbols. (For more information about using the Symbol dialog box, see Chapter 13.)

You can also change the size of the bullet. The bullet symbol size is measured in points, just as type is. By default, Publisher makes the bullet the same size as the text around it; however, you can change that size, if you want.

Tip   If you change the size, change it only by 2 points at a time, to see how it looks. Bullets that are too large are distracting.

Finally, you can change the bullet indent. When you change the indent in the Indents and Lists dialog box, only the text is indented; the bullet remains flush left. You can, however, adjust the bullet's indent by using the ruler and indent markers, as shown in Figure 15-8. Note the indent markers on the ruler. You move each indent marker $^1/_4$ inch to the right, and the hanging indent remains, but the bullet symbols and the text move in $^1/_4$ inch.

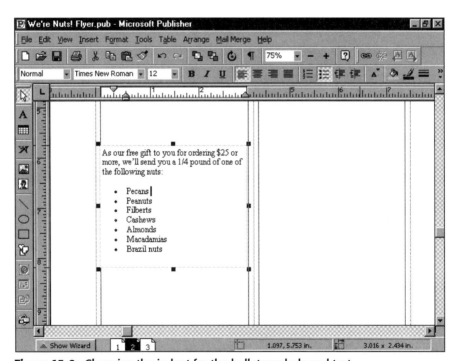

Figure 15-8: Changing the indent for the bullet symbols and text

To create bullets or modify existing bullets, follow these steps:

1. Select the text.

2. Choose Format ⇨ Indents and Lists. The Indents and Lists dialog box appears.

3. In the Indent settings area, select the Bulleted list option.

4. Choose a Bullet type. If you prefer, click the New Bullet button to view the Symbol dialog box. Select any font and any symbol and then click the Insert button. Publisher replaces one of the bullet types with the new bullet.

5. Optionally, change the bullet size in the Size text box.

6. If you want to change the indent of the text, enter the value in the Indent list by text box.

Note Note the Line Spacing button in the Indents and Lists dialog box. Normally, you also change line spacing in a bulleted list. For more information, see Chapter 17.

7. Check the Sample box to see whether this is the format that you want. Click OK to accept your changes.

Figure 15-9 illustrates a customized bulleted list. Note that the bullet symbol indent was modified on the ruler, not in the Indents and Lists dialog box. However, the space between the bullet and the text was changed in the dialog box.

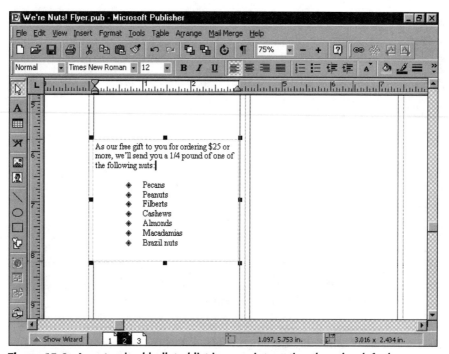

Figure 15-9: A customized bulleted list is more interesting than the default.

Tip When you choose a symbol for a bulleted list, use that same symbol for all bulleted lists in that publication, for consistency of design.

Adding a bullet to a hanging indent

The reason you use a hanging indent for bulleted text is so that the second and subsequent lines of text align with the beginning of the first line of text, as shown in Figure 15-10. You can add an extra line of space between bullets to make them easier to read. Just press Enter and then click the Bullets button on the toolbar to remove the bullet from the blank line.

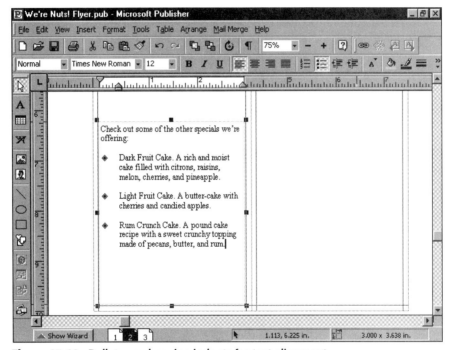

Figure 15-10: Bullets use hanging indents for text alignment.

To set a standard hanging indent and add a bullet, follow these steps:

1. Select the paragraphs of text.

2. On the ruler, set the left indent marker to 1 inch.

3. On the ruler, set the first-line indent marker to $1/2$ inch.

4. Position the insertion point in front of the first indented item.

5. Choose Insert ➪ Symbol. The Symbol dialog box appears.

6. Select a font and then a symbol. Click the Insert button.

7. Press the Tab key once.

8. Select the bullet and the tab, and then copy them.

9. Paste the bullet and tab in front of each item that should be bulleted.

Creating numbered lists

You number a list when you want to prioritize items in a group by order of importance. Similar to when you're creating bulleted lists, Publisher presents three methods of creating numbered lists:

✦ Use the Numbering button on the Formatting toolbar

✦ Use the Indents and Lists dialog box

✦ Type a number and space before you enter the list, and Publisher automatically inserts numbers for you

The default numbered lists look the same no matter which method you use. Figure 15-11 illustrates Publisher's default numbered list. The number is flush left with the frame, and the text is indented $1/4$ inch. Note the hanging indent for the text on the horizontal ruler.

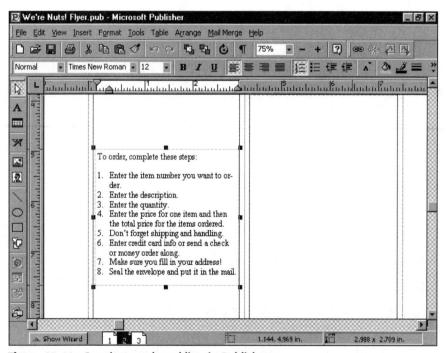

Figure 15-11: Creating numbered lists in Publisher

Using the default numbered list

You can choose any of three methods to create a default, or preset, numbered list in Publisher.

To create the list as you type, follow these steps:

1. Type the number **1** and a period, followed by a space or a tab, and then type the first item on the list.

2. Press Enter. Publisher enters the number 2 for you and changes the text indents to a hanging indent.

3. To add more numbered items to the list, press Enter and type the item. To enter a line of text that does not use a number, press Enter twice after the last numbered item.

To create a numbered list by using the Numbering button on the Formatting toolbar, you can either enter the text first, select it, and then click the button, or you can click the button and then begin to type the list. To create a numbered list by using the Numbering button on the Formatting toolbar, follow these steps:

1. Select the text or position the insertion point.

2. Click the Numbering button. Enter text for the first numbered item. Press Enter to create the second item, press Enter again to create the third item, and so on.

3. Click the Numbering button again to remove the number from the last line of text.

To use the Indents and Lists dialog box to create a default numbered list, follow these steps:

1. Select the list.

2. Choose Format ➪ Indents and Lists. The Indents and Lists dialog box appears.

3. In the Indent settings area, select the Numbered list option.

4. Click OK.

Modifying numbered lists

You can use the Indents and Lists dialog box to modify numbered lists. You can change the format of the numbers, the separator, the starting number, and the indent of the list. Figure 15-12 illustrates the Indents and Lists dialog box with the Numbered list option selected. A description of the Number options follows.

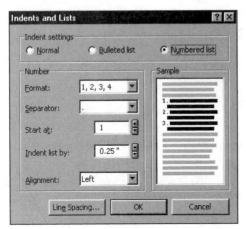

Figure 15-12: Use the Indents and Lists
dialog box to modify numbered lists.

The Number Format drop-down list box offers you three choices for your list: 1, 2,
3; a, b, c; and A, B, C. By default, Publisher uses numbers for the number format.

The *separator* refers to the character that follows the number or letter on the list.
By default, Publisher uses a period, but you can choose no separator, a colon,
parentheses around the number or letter, or some other symbol.

Publisher enables you to choose the starting point for the numbers. By default, the
numbers start at 1 or A, according to whichever format you chose. You may want to
insert between two numbered items some text that is not numbered. Figure 15-13
illustrates a situation in which you might use this feature.

You also can indent the list by more than ¹/4 inch. Just as with bullets, this setting
only increases the distance between the number and the text; it doesn't indent the
numbers from the edge of the frame. You can indent the number by using the ruler,
as shown in Figure 15-14. Note that the text between numbers 5 and 6 now uses a
hanging indent to align it with the rest of the bullets. Insert a tab in front of the text
on the first line to make the overhang line up too.

Note   As with bulleted lists, you can modify the text alignment and the line spacing from
within the Indents and Lists dialog box. For more information about text alignment
and line spacing, see Chapter 17.

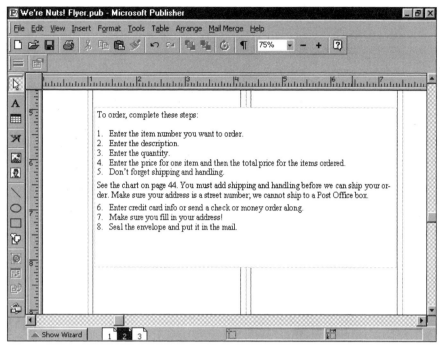

Figure 15-13: Stopping the numbering scheme and starting it again

To create or modify numbered lists, follow these steps:

1. Select the text.

2. Choose Format ⇨ Indents and Lists. The Indents and Lists dialog box appears.

3. In the Indent settings area, select the Numbered list option.

4. In the Format drop-down list, choose a number format.

5. In the Separator drop-down list, select a separator for the numbers.

6. In the Start at text box, enter a number or letter to start the list.

7. In the Indent list by text box, enter a value, if you want.

8. View the sample in the Sample box. Click OK to accept the changes.

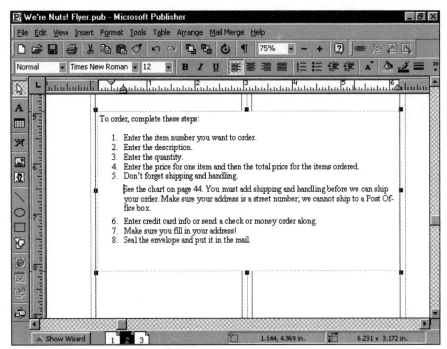

Figure 15-14: Indenting numbers and text by using the ruler

Inserting and Deleting Tabs

You use tabs to align text in lists that appear side by side. When you use tabs, you're assured that each item lines up directly below the preceding one. Figure 15-15 illustrates tab settings used to align two lists that appear on the same lines. Note the tab markers on the ruler.

By default, Publisher sets tab stops at $1/2$-inch increments. A *tab stop* is the ruler marking on which the tab appears. Each time you press the Tab key, the insertion point moves $1/2$ inch. Rather than pressing the Tab key several times to move the insertion point, however, you can change the tab stops by using the ruler or the Tabs dialog box.

Tab markers

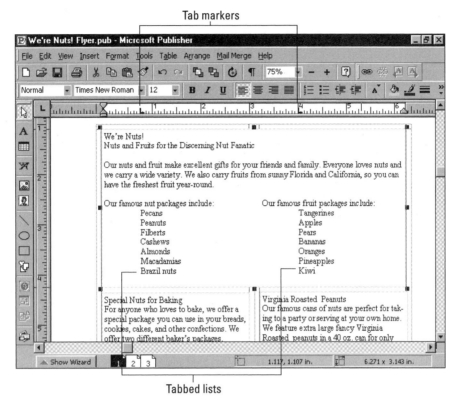

Tabbed lists

Figure 15-15: Lining up lists of items by using tabs

Understanding tabs

In addition to positioning a tab stop, or a ruler measurement on which the tabbed text rests, you can set a tab alignment and a tab leader. *Tab alignment* is the definition of the text edge: flush left, flush right, centered, or on a decimal point. A *tab leader* is a symbol—dot, dash, line, or bullet—that fills the space between a tab and the following text.

Figure 15-16 illustrates tab alignments. Note the tab marks on the ruler. The headings for each tab type in the figure are all on a centered tab.

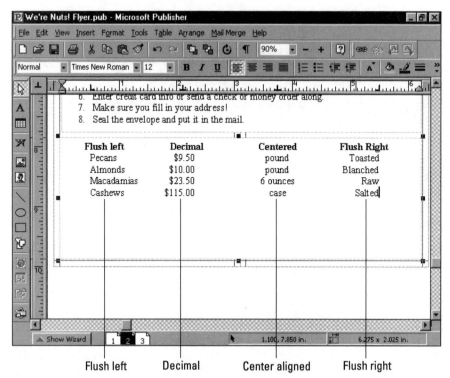

Figure 15-16: Aligning text by using the appropriate tab alignment

The following list describes each tab and some common uses:

✦ **Flush left:** Aligns the tabbed text along the left edge of the text and creates a ragged right edge. You can use flush left tabs for most any text, especially in forms, programs, lists of items, and so on.

✦ **Decimal:** Aligns the text on the decimal, no matter what type of text appears to the left or right of the decimal. Use decimal tabs when typing currency, percentages, and other values that contain decimals.

✦ **Centered:** Aligns the text on an imaginary center line, so both the right and left edges of the text are ragged. Use center tabs only for single words or short phrases, invitations, greeting card text, and so on. Large amounts of centered text is difficult to read.

✦ **Flush right:** Aligns text on the right edge, producing a ragged left edge. You can use flush right for currency, in programs, or for limited text use. Again, large amounts of flush right text is difficult to read.

Figure 15-17 illustrates two types of tab leaders: line leaders and dotted leaders. Generally, you use leaders to separate items such as names. However, you can use a line leader to create lines for filling in information on forms, in a coupon, or in another area of a publication. Note the tab markers on the ruler for the dotted leader tabs.

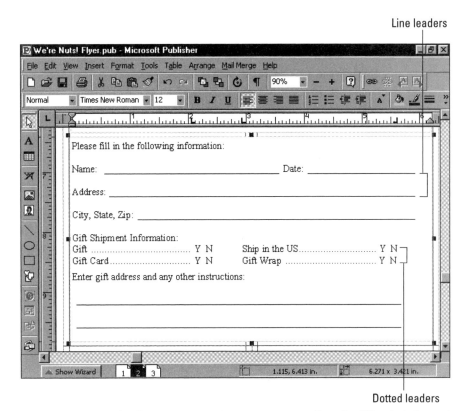

Figure 15-17: Use leaders to separate items or to create lines for filling in information.

Inserting tabs by using the ruler

You can create quick tabs by using any alignment on the ruler in Publisher. You cannot, however, insert leaders for the tabs that you set on the ruler. You must use the Tabs dialog box to set leaders for tabs. See the following section, "Using the Tabs dialog box," for information.

Publisher's horizontal ruler includes a tab alignment box that you can use to set the alignment of each tab that you add to the ruler. By default, the tab alignment is flush left. When you click the tab alignment box, the alignment changes. As you continue to click the box, the tab alignment cycles from flush left to centered to flush right to decimal. Figure 15-18 illustrates the ruler, the tab alignment box, and the representative alignment markers.

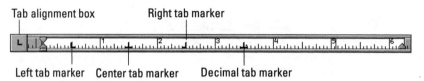

Figure 15-18: Add tabs to the ruler, using any of the four alignments.

To insert a tab by using the ruler, follow these steps:

1. Select the text to which the tabs will apply.

2. Click the tab alignment box to display the appropriate alignment. If the alignment that you want is already displayed, do not click the box.

3. Click the ruler at the point you want to position the tab. You can add as many tabs as you want, just by clicking the ruler.

To reposition a tab with the ruler, select the text and then drag the tab marker to a new position. To delete a tab from the ruler, select the text and then drag the tab marker down and off the ruler.

Note
If you select two or more lines of text that use different tab settings, the tabs appear dimmed on the ruler. If you insert new tabs or move the dimmed tabs, the new positions appear for all selected text.

Using the Tabs dialog box

You can set tabs, apply alignment, and add tab leaders to the text by using the Tabs dialog box. By using the Tabs dialog box, shown in Figure 15-19, you can simultaneously set multiple tab stops, apply any formatting, and change the measurement of the default tab stops (if you want).

Tip
Planning the tab stops before you open the Tabs dialog box is recommended; you might want to use the ruler onscreen. Until you become accustomed to setting tabs with the Tabs dialog box, you may need to close the box and view the changes, and then open the box again to correct or modify the settings.

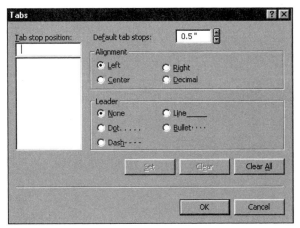

Figure 15-19: Setting tab stops and formatting the tabs simultaneously

Understanding the Tabs dialog box options

The following is a description of each of the elements in the Tabs dialog box:

✦ **Default tab stops:** Enter a value to use as tabs for all text, by default. You can change the 0.5 inch to .25 or 1 inch, for example. Each time that you press the Tab key in text that isn't specially formatted with tab stops, the text moves the default amount of your tab setting. Also, changing the default tab stops changes the amount of indent that you get when clicking the Increase Indent or Decrease Indent tool buttons on the Formatting toolbar.

✦ **Tab stop position:** Enter the ruler measurement for the first tab. You might, for example, enter **.5** in the Tab stop position box. You can then choose the alignment and a leader, if you want. But, you must set the tab for it to take effect. Clicking the Set button sets the tab, and the measurement appears in the list box below the Tab stop position text box. You can then enter a new Tab stop position and format it, using the steps just described.

✦ **Alignment:** This area governs only the individual tab stop. After you enter the tab stop, select the alignment that you want and set the tab. You can set a second, third, or multiple tab stops, but with each one, you need to choose the appropriate alignment — Left, Center, Right, or Decimal.

✦ **Leader:** This area controls the repeated symbol that appears between the point at which you press the Tab key and the left edge of the tabbed text. You can use no leader or any leader listed — Dot, Dash, Line, or Bullet.

✦ **Set:** Click to set the tab that you entered in the Tab stop position box.

✦ **Clear:** Click to clear any single selected tab stop.

✦ **Clear All:** Click to clear all set tabs for the selected text.

Figure 15-20 illustrates the set tab stops in the list box. Figure 15-21 shows the resulting tabbed text. Note that the tab markers appear on the ruler. You could select the text and adjust the tab markers on the ruler, if necessary, or you could open the Tabs dialog box to modify any tab stops or formatting.

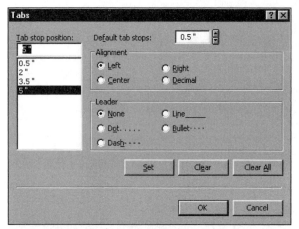

Figure 15-20: Set each tab after entering the ruler measurement, alignment, and leader.

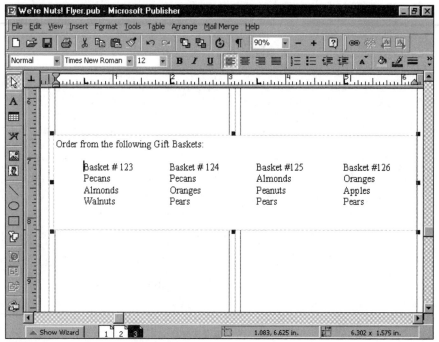

Figure 15-21: Adjust the tab markers if the tabs aren't exactly where you want them.

Setting tabs

To use the Tabs dialog box, follow these steps:

1. Select the text.

2. Choose Format ⇨ Tabs. The Tabs dialog box appears.

3. Enter a measurement in the Tab stop position text box.

4. Optionally, choose one of the following from the Alignment area: Left, Right, Center, or Decimal.

5. Optionally, choose one of the following from the Leader area: None, Dot, Dash, Line, or Bullet.

6. Click the Set button.

7. Enter another tab stop and choose the alignment and a leader, if you want. Click the Set button after each addition.

8. Click OK when you're finished.

Removing and repositioning tabs

If you make a mistake when creating a tab and you haven't set it yet, just clear the Tab stop position text box and enter a new value. If you already set the tab (clicked the Set button), select the tab from the list and then click the Clear button.

If you want to remove one tab, select it in the Tab stop position list and then click the Clear button. If you want to remove all tabs from the selected text, click the Clear All button.

Setting a Line Leader

If you have an area in your publication for information collection—such as name, address, date, phone number, or other data—you can create line leader tabs instead of creating a line with the Shift+underline character on the keyboard. Using the underline isn't always efficient, and most times you can't get the line endings the same for multiple lines. Setting line tabs guarantees that the line endings remain the same.

To set tabs using line leaders, follow these steps:

1. Determine the length of the text frame by checking the ruler. If the frame is 6.5 inches long, for example, you might want the line leaders to end at 6 inches.

2. Enter any text—such as **Name**—and press the spacebar once. Then press the Tab key once.

3. Select the text and then choose Format ⇨ Tabs. The Tabs dialog box appears.

Continued

(continued)

4. In the Tab stop position text box, enter the measurement for the end of the line — say, 6 inches.

5. In the Alignment area, choose Right.

6. In the Leader area, choose Line.

7. Click Set and then click OK. The line appears in the text. If you press Enter, the next line of text is formatted the same. You can enter another item, such as Address, and then press Tab again to create a line.

If you're creating lines for people to fill in, double-space between the lines so that they have room to write. Just press Enter twice after each line to provide that space.

If you want to create more than one line leader on each line of text, as shown in the last line of the following figure, you can set multiple tabs using line leaders for just that line. Note in the figure that the Show Special Characters option is turned on, so that you can see where the tabs are located in the text. The tab stops are marked on the ruler.

One tab

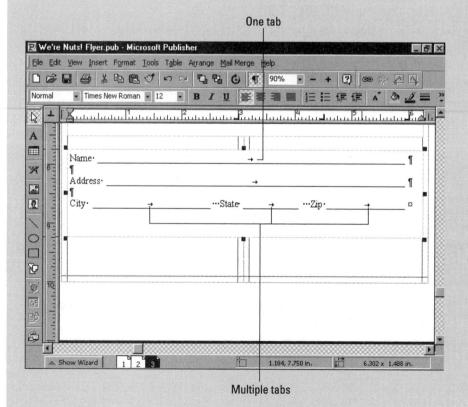

Multiple tabs

To create multiple line leader tabs on one line, follow these steps:

1. Select only the lines to which you want the multiple tabs to apply.

2. Check the ruler to see where the tabs should appear.

3. Choose Format ⇨ Tabs to open the Tabs dialog box.

4. Using the measurements in the figure, enter the first measurement (3 inches) in the Tab stop position text box. Choose Right alignment and Line leader. Click the Set button.

5. Enter the next measurement (4.5 inches) in the Tab stop position text box. The Right alignment and Line leader options remain selected. Click Set.

6. Enter the final measurement (6 inches) in the Tab stop position text box. The Right alignment and Line leader options remain selected. Click Set.

7. Click OK.

Hyphenating Text

Hyphenation is a program feature that automatically hyphenates words based on program rules (*algorithmic* hyphenation) or a list of hyphenated words (*dictionary* hyphenation).

Publisher hyphenates the text in a text frame by default. Hyphenation occurs in standard divisions of words and syllables. For example, Publisher hyphenates the following words in this manner: mix-ture, thrill-er, thir-teen, con-tain, and so on.

You can let Publisher hyphenate your text for you or you can perform manual hyphenation. You are advised *not* to insert hyphens (-) at the end of lines manually. If you add or remove text, change the frame size, or add a piece of clip art or other image to the frame, you change where the lines end and thus where the hyphens fall. You may end up with hyphens in the middle of lines instead of at the end of lines.

In general, consider the following hyphenation guidelines, which make the text easier to read and the document more professional-looking:

✦ **Don't hyphenate words at the end of more than two consecutive lines of text.** Too many hyphens in a row doesn't look attractive and makes the text hard to read.

✦ **Don't hyphenate titles or headlines.** Make room for the text by making the frame larger or the text smaller.

✦ **Don't hyphenate the last word in a text frame, column, or page.** Continuing to read at the top of a text frame, column, or page is difficult if the first word is only a part of a word.

Using automatic hyphenation

By default, Publisher hyphenates all text in your document. You also can turn off automatic hyphenation and manually hyphenate the text, or change the hyphenation zone.

Turning off automatic hyphenation

If you turn off automatic hyphenation, Publisher removes all hyphens from the text frame. You can either leave the text as is, manually hyphenate the text, or turn on automatic hyphenation again.

Tip   You might prefer not to hyphenate certain text, but consider that the right edge of the text might become too ragged to be read comfortably. Also, always hyphenate justified text (see Chapter 17 for information about text alignment and justified text).

To turn off automatic hyphenation, follow these steps:

1. Select the text frame.

2. Choose Tools ⇨ Language ⇨ Hyphenation; alternatively, press Ctrl+Shift+H. The Hyphenation dialog box appears, as shown in Figure 15-22.

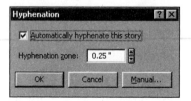

Figure 15-22: Turn off automatic hyphenation to hyphenate the text manually.

3. Click OK.

Figure 15-23 illustrates text in which automatic hyphenation was turned off. Note the right edge of the text; it's a bit ragged. If you prefer, you could avoid using hyphenation in this text frame by inserting a line break or two in the last paragraph, to make the right edge seem less ragged.

To turn on automatic hyphenation again, simply open the Hyphenation dialog box and check the Automatically hyphenate this story check box.

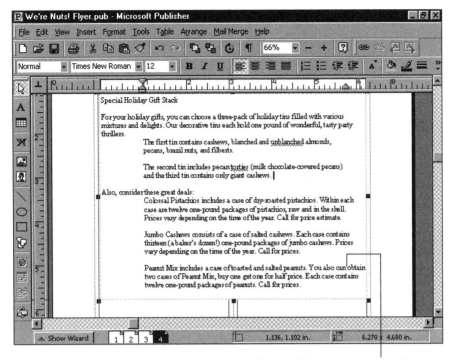

Insert a line break here to even up the right edge

Figure 15-23: No hyphenation may be your choice for the text in some frames.

Changing the hyphenation zone

The *hyphenation zone* governs the raggedness of the right edge of the text. A larger hyphenation zone increases the raggedness of the right margin; a smaller zone lessens the raggedness. You measure the hyphenation zone from the right edge of the frame to the right edge of the text. Publisher's default is $1/4$ inch, which is a good standard to observe.

If you want to change the hyphenation zone, however, follow these steps:

1. Select the text frame.

2. Choose Tools ⇨ Language ⇨ Hyphenation; alternatively, press Ctrl+Shift+H. The Hyphenation dialog box appears.

3. Make sure that Automatically hyphenate this story is checked.

4. In the Hyphenation zone box, use the up or down arrow to enter the new amount for the zone.

5. Click OK.

Hyphenating text manually

You can hyphenate the text in a frame manually, so that you can decide which words to hyphenate and where to hyphenate them. Naturally, where you hyphenate the words depends somewhat on the hyphenation zone that you set.

To hyphenate the text manually, follow these steps:

1. Select the text frame.

2. Choose Tools ➪ Language ➪ Hyphenation; alternatively, press Ctrl+Shift+H. The Hyphenation dialog box appears.

3. Remove the check mark from the Automatically hyphenate this story check box.

4. Click the Manual button. Publisher locates the first word that, according to its rules, it would hyphenate. It displays the Hyphenate confirmation dialog box, as shown in Figure 15-24.

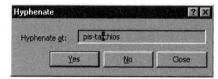

Figure 15-24: Choosing whether or not to hyphenate a word

5. Choose one of the following: Yes, to accept the hyphenation; No, to cancel that particular hyphenation, or — if offered multiple choices for hyphenation — select the hyphen that you want to use and then click Yes. Publisher continues to search the document and display possible solutions to hyphenating the text.

6. When Publisher finishes, it closes the Hyphenation confirmation dialog box.

Inserting nonbreaking and optional hyphens

You can insert "codes" for nonbreaking or optional hyphens in your text, to help Publisher decide what to do when it's hyphenating your text. You insert a nonbreaking hyphen to prevent a word from being hyphenated. You insert an optional hyphen to instruct Publisher where a word can alternatively be hyphenated if necessary.

Nonbreaking hyphens show up on the page. Use a nonbreaking hyphen, for example, with a name such as David Charles-Bender. The hyphenated second name shouldn't be split at the end of a line, so you insert a nonbreaking hyphen in place of the current hyphen. If the word comes to the end of a line, Publisher forces the entire name — Charles-Bender — to the next line.

Optional hyphens don't appear on the page unless hyphenating the word is necessary or you choose the Show Special Characters option, so that you can see optional hyphens.

Figure 15-25 illustrates both a nonbreaking hyphen and two optional hyphens in the text. You can't identify the nonbreaking hyphen simply by looking at it; however, it forces the hyphenated name to the next line. With special characters showing, you can see the two optional hyphens. If using the optional hyphens isn't necessary, their presence in the text doesn't cause any harm.

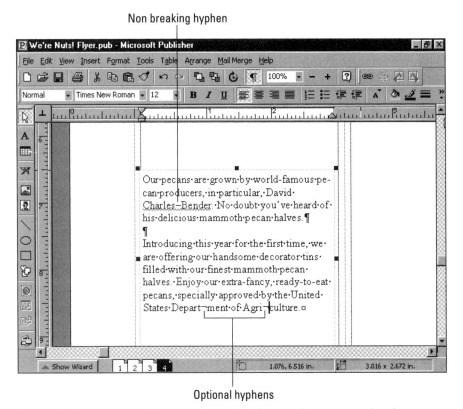

Figure 15-25: Use special hyphens to control the way that your text breaks.

To enter a nonbreaking hyphen, position the insertion point and press Ctrl+Shift+- (hyphen). To insert an optional hyphen, position the insertion point and press Ctrl+- (hyphen). To view optional hyphens, choose View ➪ Show Special Characters.

Summary

In this chapter, you learned about basic text formatting, including the following:

✦ Inserting and deleting indents

✦ Working with bulleted and numbered lists

✦ Inserting and deleting tabs

✦ Hyphenating text

In the next chapter, you learn how to format characters.

✦   ✦   ✦

Formatting Characters

*T*ypography refers to the style, arrangement, and appearance of the text on the page. Typography isn't just about the font, type style, or size of the text; it's also about the readability of the text and the overall design of the page. You've already learned about consistency, emphasis, white space, and balance. Add the skillful use of typography to your knowledge of design, and your publication will look attractive and professional. The purpose of any printed document is to deliver a message to the reader; typography and good page design can help you convey your message.

Understanding Typefaces and Fonts

Type generally refers to printed characters. In the past, handset type applied to blocks of type—usually one letter per block—that the typesetter placed in position to create the page on the press. The term now has many derivatives: typeface, type style, font, and type family. The traditional terms have changed with the onset of computers, desktop publishing, and programs such as Publisher.

Typeface

A *typeface* is a specific style of type. Arial, Times New Roman, and Courier are all typefaces. A typeface is a collection of letters that share a common stroke, serif, and stress. The *stroke* describes the thickness of the lines that form the letter. Some typefaces use a combination of thick and thin strokes; others use a uniform stroke throughout.

A *serif* is a fine cross-stroke at the ends of the main strokes of a character, such as the cross-strokes on the Times New Roman typeface, as shown in Figure 16-1. Serifs may be rounded, curved, or abrupt. *Stress* refers to the distribution of weight in an individual letter.

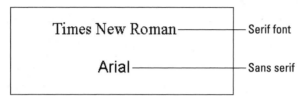

Figure 16-1: Serif and sans serif typefaces

Some typefaces don't have any serifs, such as the Arial typeface. These typefaces are called *sans serif* (literally, "without serif"). Sans serif fonts are usually a uniform stroke with a vertical emphasis, whereas serif typefaces use a varied stroke and have serifs to soften the vertical emphasis.

Tip   Using a serif and a sans serif typeface together in a document creates an attractive page. Use a serif typeface for the body text of the publication, and the sans serif typeface for all headlines in the piece. To maintain consistency, avoid using more than two or three typefaces for the entire publication.

Font

Font originally meant a collection of all characters of one size and typeface, such as 10-point italic Times. But, with desktop publishing, font packages, and computerized typesetting, *font* has become a catch-all term that encompasses all sizes and styles of a particular typeface.

So, Times New Roman that is italic, regular, or bold qualifies as a font. Whether the type is 10-point or 96-point doesn't matter; as long as it's Times New Roman, it's all part of the same font. "Font" has pretty much become synonymous with "typeface."

Styles

The *style* of a font denotes the characteristics, or attributes, such as bold, italic, regular, condensed, and such, and any combination of these characteristics. Most fonts include regular, bold, and italic styles; many other fonts include condensed and extra bold, as shown in Figure 16-2.

Publisher also includes effects that you can apply to most fonts, including superscript, subscript, outline, and others. For more information, see "Implementing Attributes," later in this chapter.

Note   You should never use a bold or italic type for the body of your publication. Use these styles to emphasize text, such as one or two words in the body, for example, or headlines. Too much bold or italic type is difficult to read.

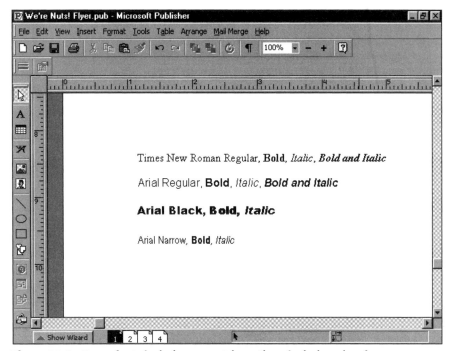

Figure 16-2: Some fonts include many styles; others include only a few.

Understanding Type Sizes

Font size is measured in *points*. Twelve points equal a *pica*; 6 picas equal an inch. Therefore, 1 point equals 1/72 inch. *Picas* are standard measures in typesetting and printing. Often, measuring gutters, spaces, margins, and the like in picas is easier. Many desktop publishing programs offer the choice of measurement units, as does Publisher. The measurement unit that you use is a matter of personal preference.

 Tip   You can use picas or points in Publisher for your measurement units — on the ruler, in dialog boxes, and so on — instead of using inches. Choose Tools ➪ Options to change measurement units.

Although you can make your type any size — from 2 points to 200 points, for example — certain type sizes are standard for certain uses of type. You use common type sizes to give your document the best look. These standard uses of type include body text, subheads, headlines, and display type.

In general, the larger the document size, the larger the text size. For instance, a business card may use 9- and 11-point text, whereas a newsletter would use 12-point body text and 18- or 24-point headlines.

Some fonts are larger than others, even when you assign the same point size. Serif fonts are often slightly smaller than the same size of sans serif font. Script fonts are often smaller than any of the other fonts. To get an idea of the size of the fonts, click the Font drop-down arrow on the Formatting toolbar. As you scroll through the fonts, you can see a definite difference in size, as well as stroke, stress, and other characteristics.

Body text

The *body text* is the main portion of your publication. Paragraphs of text, bullets and numbered lists, text in tables, and other large sections of type are called body text. The body text in a document might range from 9-point to 12-point type.

Type that is smaller than 9 points is too small to read comfortably; it's commonly referred to as the "fine print" in contracts. Type larger than 12 points is also difficult to read in sentences or paragraphs, and usually is reserved for subheadings in the text. The size of body text that you choose depends on the size of the document.

Tip

Choosing one size of body text and using that size throughout the entire publication is important. Using varying sizes of body text makes the document inconsistent and unprofessional.

Figure 16-3 illustrates the common sizes used for body text, subheads, headings, and display type.

Subheads and headings

Subheads usually categorize main topics, whereas *headings* announce the main topics. You may use one or both levels of headings in your document, depending on the type of information and how much division you want in your information.

Subheads are more significant than the body text, yet not as important as a heading. Usually, subheads are bold or italic and 12- or 14-point. If you use 12-point type for the body text too, set the subhead apart by making it all uppercase, bold, or italic.

Headings, or *headlines,* can be bold, bold italic, or all uppercase. The standards are 18-, 24-, 28-, 32-, 36-, and 48-point headings. Even though Publisher enables you to create 19-, 23-, 37-, or 41-point type, avoid using these odd sizes. Your screen may not display the exact size, so although they may look okay onscreen, on the printed page, they may look strange. Sticking with the time-tested, proven standard sizes of text is recommended.

Body Text
This is 9-point type
This is 10-point type
This is 11-point type
This is 12-point type

Subheads
12-POINT BOLD
14-Point *Italic* or **Bold**

Headings or Headlines
18-Point Regular, **Bold,** or *Italic*
24-Point Regular, **Bold,** or *Italic*

36-Pt. Regular, **Bold,** or *Italic*

48 Pt. Reg., **Bold,** or *Italic*

Display Type

60 Pt. Regular, **Bold,** or *Italic*

72 Pt. Regular, **Bold,** or *Italic*

Figure 16-3: Standard type sizes used in documents

Display type

Display type is very large and is used for larger documents, such as posters and banners, and occasionally for signs and fliers. Use display type sparingly in a smaller document, to grab attention. Display type can be, depending on the size of the document, 48-, 56-, 60-, 72-point, or even larger.

Figure 16-4 illustrates the letter *N* in Times New Roman, regular type, at 700 points. The letter is nearly seven inches tall when printed.

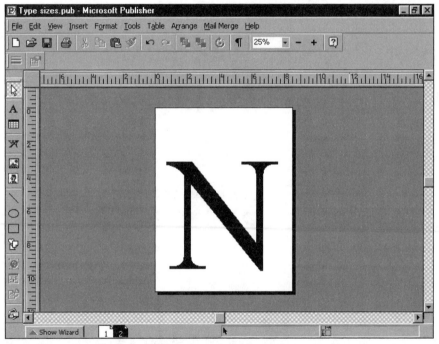

Figure 16-4: Use display type for banners or posters, for example.

Applying Fonts

You can apply fonts to your documents to make them more interesting and attractive. Publisher includes a variety of fonts that you can use, including multiple types of serif and sans serif fonts, script and text, and even decorative fonts.

As previously mentioned, avoid using more than two or three different fonts in each publication. Perhaps choose a serif font for the body text and a sans serif for the headings. Times New Roman and Arial work very well together, for example, as do Bookman and Lucida.

Which Fonts to Use?

Fonts that work well for body text include Bookman Old Style, Century Schoolbook, Garamond, Georgia, Goudy Old Style, and Times New Roman.

Fonts that work well for subheads and headings include Arial and Arial Black, Bauhaus, Bernard MT Condensed, Elephant, Eras, Franklin Gothic, Lucida, Rockwell, and Verdana.

Use the following fonts for invitations, certificates, and other short documents: Algerian, Bradley Hand ITC, Brush Script MT, Forte, Freestyle Script, French Script, Lucida Calligraphy, Old English Text MT, and Papyrus.

Fonts for display type include Arial Black, Bauhaus 93, Bernard MT Condensed, Braggadocio, Britannic Bold, Broadway, Cooper Black, Desdemona, Eras Ultra ITC, Franklin Gothic Heavy, Goudy Stout, Impact, Rockwell Extra Bold, Showcard Gothic, Stencil, and Wide Latin.

You shouldn't use Courier font in a professional-looking document. Courier is the typeface used in typewriters and it's far outdated in the age of computers and laser printers. Courier is a *monospaced* font, meaning that each letter takes up the same amount of space; for example, an *m* takes up as much space as an *i* or a period. Courier looks unprofessional and is unsuitable for any publication, unless you want the document to look like a typewriter produced it.

Looking at Publisher's font defaults

Each Publisher wizard that you use and each blank document that you open gives you the base for a publication. Each publication uses a different font; for example, one newsletter wizard opens using Gill Sans MT for both body text and headlines; another newsletter wizard uses Bookman Old Style for both body and headlines. Publisher's blank publication uses 10-point Times New Roman as the default body text.

You can make any changes to the fonts, sizes, and attributes that Publisher assigns, both in the wizards and in the blank publications. When you create a document within Publisher, you can either accept the defaults and create an attractive document or modify the fonts to suit your own tastes and style.

Looking at the fonts on your computer

Which fonts are available on your computer depends on several factors. You may have fonts that were installed with your printer that you can use in a document. You may have installed fonts from a third-party package, such as Adobe Type Manager. You may have downloaded font packages, or added fonts from another application that you installed on your computer. Publisher also installs fonts on your computer, for use with your publications.

To find out which fonts are installed on your computer, follow these steps:

1. Choose Start ➪ Settings ➪ Control Panel.

2. In the Control Panel, double-click the Fonts folder. The folder opens with a list of the fonts that are installed on your computer (see Figure 16-5).

TrueType Fonts

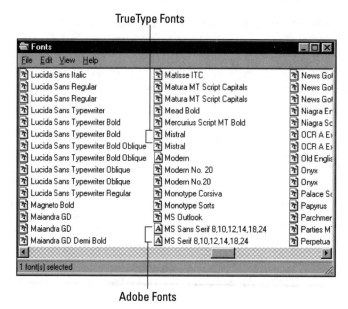

Adobe Fonts

Figure 16-5: Fonts are listed in alphabetical order in the Fonts folder.

3. To see a page that describes a font's version and copyright and displays samples of the font, double-click the font name. Figure 16-6 illustrates the font description and samples for the Castellar font.

4. Print the font page by clicking the Print button.

5. Click Done when you're finished with the font page.

6. Close the Fonts folder and the Control Panel by clicking the Close (X) button in the title bar.

Understanding TrueType fonts

Many brands of fonts are available. Manufacturers sell font packages in software stores, over the Internet, and through software catalogs. Many fonts come with each program that you purchase. And, you can often obtain free fonts over the Internet or through shareware.

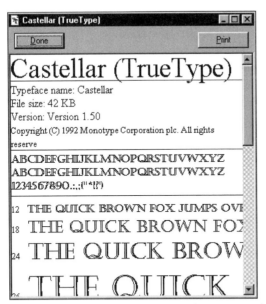

Figure 16-6: Print the font page to have a record of all styles and attributes related to the font.

The most popular and common Windows font is the TrueType brand. You already have TrueType fonts on your computer from Publisher, Word, and many other applications that you've installed.

The method by which TrueType fonts are created, both onscreen and by your printer, makes most of them appear in print exactly as they appear on your screen. TrueType fonts are created first by outline and then by filling in that outline. Therefore, the outer edges of the font are clear and concise. Printed publications look best when you use TrueType fonts with Publisher.

Previewing fonts

You can preview the available fonts before you apply them to your documents. When you turn on the Preview fonts option, the font names in the Font box on the Formatting toolbar, in the Insert Symbol dialog box, and in the Drop Cap dialog box are displayed in their respective actual font. (For more information about drop caps, see the section "Creating Drop Caps and Fancy First Words," later in this chapter.)

Screen Fonts Versus Printer Fonts

Screen fonts and printer fonts are two separate things. *Screen fonts* appear onscreen, but may not look the same when printed. *Printer fonts* are installed by the software that comes with your printer; the printer font that you see onscreen may or may not look the same as the font that is printed.

One problem between screen and printer fonts, as well as many third-party font packages, is that if your computer doesn't have an image of the font that you've chosen, the computer uses a font that's close to the one that you chose. Also called *font substitution,* this process means that what you see onscreen may not be what you get on paper.

Fortunately, TrueType fonts very seldom have this problem. What you see onscreen is what prints, in most cases. Sometimes, however, a TrueType font isn't licensed or is installed only as a preview font. This means the font appears onscreen and will likely print, but the printed font may look ragged or otherwise different than it does onscreen.

If you plan to have your publication printed at a commercial printing service, you need to know whether or not the fonts that you choose will print correctly. See Chapter 31 for more information.

Figure 16-7 illustrates the Font box on the Formatting toolbar, with a listing of available fonts shown in their actual font. This makes choosing a font so much easier as you work on your publication. Note that the letters TT appear beside TrueType fonts, and a small printer icon appears beside printer fonts on the list.

To turn on the Preview fonts option, follow these steps:

1. Choose Tools ➪ Options. The Options dialog box appears, as shown in Figure 16-8.

2. In the General tab, click the Preview fonts in font list check box so that a check mark appears.

3. Click OK to close the dialog box.

Applying fonts to your text

You can modify any font in a publication, whether a wizard applied the font or you changed it and want to make another change to the font. Publisher provides two methods of applying fonts to your text: the Font dialog box and the Font box on the Formatting toolbar.

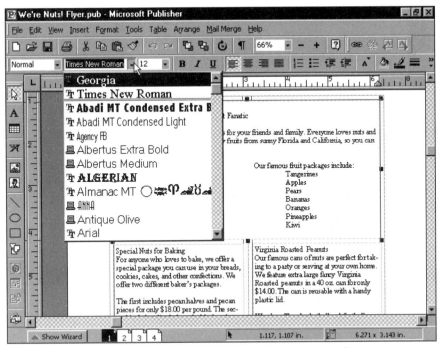

Figure 16-7: You can preview your fonts from the Formatting toolbar.

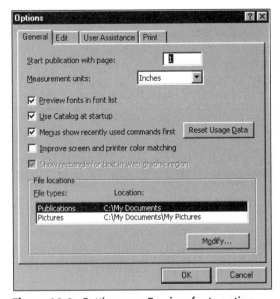

Figure 16-8: Setting your Preview fonts option

Using the Font box tool

You can apply a different font to any selected text by clicking the Font box tool on the Formatting toolbar. Follow these steps:

1. Select the text that you want to change.

2. Click the drop-down arrow beside the Font box tool.

3. Scroll through the fonts in the box until you find the font that you want to use. Click that font.

When you choose a font from the list, that font also appears at the top of the list, so that you can quickly and easily apply it again within the current publication.

Using the Font dialog box

The Font dialog box offers simultaneously many choices concerning your fonts. You can change only the font, or you can change the size and attributes, too, or apply additional effects to the font for the selected text. Each option in the Font dialog box is explained in the following sections. This section describes using the Font selection options.

To change the font by using the Font dialog box, follow these steps:

1. Select the text.

2. Choose Format ➪ Font. The Font dialog box appears, as shown in Figure 16-9.

3. In the General area, click the drop-down arrow beside the Font list box. A drop-down list of fonts appears.

4. Select the font that you want to use. An example of that font appears in the Sample box at the bottom of the dialog box.

5. Click OK to accept the changes.

Changing Type Size

As previously mentioned, each type of text that you use — body, headings, subheads, and so on — have suggested common, standard sizes of type. You can, of course, apply any size of type that is appropriate to your document, the size of the publication, and the importance of the type.

Figure 16-10 illustrates a flyer using various type sizes and fonts. The heading and subhead are 24-point Arial Rounded MT, the body text is 12-point Times New Roman, and subheads are 14-point Times New Roman.

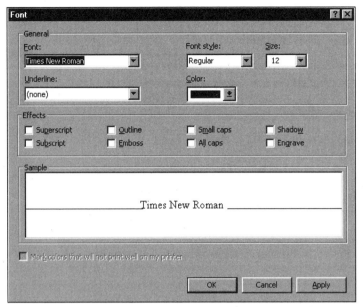

Figure 16-9: Use the Font dialog box to change one text characteristic, or multiple characteristics simultaneously.

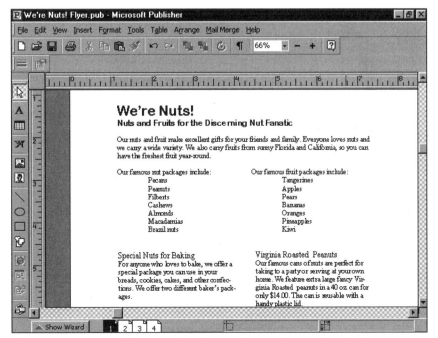

Figure 16-10: Formatting text using fonts and type sizes makes the document more attractive.

> **Tip**
> Formatting text as you work in a document is better, because you know how much space it takes up, and copyfitting is easier. For example, enlarging the text means that you must enlarge the frame.

Increasing or reducing text sizes

You can change type sizes by using any of three different tools in Publisher:

✦ The Font Size tool on the Formatting toolbar

✦ The Decrease Font Size button on the Formatting toolbar

✦ The Font dialog box

To change type sizes by using the Formatting toolbar tools, follow these steps:

1. Select the text.

2. Click the drop-down arrow beside the Font Size list box. Scroll the list of sizes until you find the one that you want.

3. Select the size.

Alternatively, you can select the number in the Font Size list box and then enter a new size for the selected text.

To decrease the text quickly by 2 points when the text is larger than 12 points, or by 1 point when the text is 12 points or smaller, click the Decrease Font Size button on the Formatting toolbar.

Copyfitting tricks

Although Publisher includes a Copyfitting feature that you can use to squeeze that last little bit of text into your frame, changing the size of your body text really isn't the best idea. Body text, in particular, should be consistent throughout the document.

However, you can use a few tricks to fit the copy to the page. First, reduce the size of your headings and headlines. Making headings uppercase and reducing their size makes them stand out from the surrounding text without taking up much room. If you have subheads, keep them the same size as the body text, but make them all uppercase and bold so that they stand out.

Using a smaller font is another trick that you can use to fit too much copy into a smaller area. Arial, for example, is a much larger font than Times New Roman. Book Antiqua is similar to Bookman Old Style, but is a smaller font. Condensed fonts, such as Anna or Franklin Gothic Medium Condensed, are great for long headlines, because they compress the type.

Implementing Attributes

Attributes, also called *font styles* or *characteristics,* include bold, italic, underline, superscript, and subscript. Publisher offers these attributes, as well as special effects, such as outline, shadow, embossed, and engraved fonts. In many instances, the case of the text — uppercase, title case, and so on — is also a point of emphasis.

You use attributes and special effects to emphasize text. You can attract attention to a word or phrase in your document, but never use any attribute or special effect for more than a phrase or two of text. The same goes for uppercase text. Too much italic, bold, uppercase, or other attribute is difficult to read.

Figure 16-11 illustrates text that is all uppercase and another text frame that contains all italic text. Realize that a person reads by recognizing letter forms and word shapes. When readers see text with *ascenders* (the upper half of b, d, f, h, k, l, and t) and *descenders* (the lower half of g, j, p, and y), they recognize it more quickly than when they see text in all uppercase. Reading uppercase takes longer and is more tedious. Italic or boldfaced text presents a similar problem; it's hard to read. When text is hard to read, the reader may give up before finishing the message.

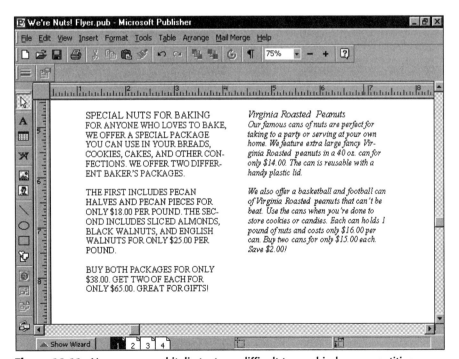

Figure 16-11: Uppercase and italic text are difficult to read in large quantities.

Tip   Any attribute or special effect that you apply to a font creates a slightly different effect if you change fonts. If you don't like it in Times New Roman, for example, try it in Georgia or Impact.

Understanding the uses of attributes

So, when should you use attributes? When you want to accentuate a word or phrase in your text, or for headings, subheadings, and display type. The following sections provide some general guidelines that professional typesetters follow regarding the use of attributes in printed documents.

Using italic and bold

Use italic and bold to emphasize words in the body text of a publication. You can use them to emphasize one word or phrase in a paragraph, for example. The reader sees the word and stresses that word in his or her mind.

You might also use italic in the text to set off a book or article title from the rest of the text. You can also use italics for a short introduction to an article or report; however, don't italicize more than a sentence or two of the text.

Naturally, you can use italic and bold in headings, display type, and subheads to emphasize that text. The limit to using attributes comes into play with body text.

Excluding underlining

Underlining text generally isn't accepted as an attribute that you apply to your publications. As with Courier type, underlining was used with a typewriter to emphasize text. You don't need to emphasize text with underlines any more; use italic or bold text instead. You can use an underline, however, before you enter a sum below a column of numbers.

Note   Don't confuse the underline with a line that is used as a graphic, for emphasis, above or below a heading. An underline normally goes from the beginning to the end of a word or group of words. A line added as a graphic under a heading, for example, usually stretches from margin to margin.

Applying superscript and subscript

Superscript and subscript are particularly useful in formulas and mathematical equations, footnotes, and other similar circumstances. You generally don't apply these effects to any other situations.

Superscript text appears above the baseline, higher and smaller than the normal text. *Subscript* text is written below the baseline of the text and is usually smaller than the normal text. Figure 16-12 illustrates the use of superscript and subscript.

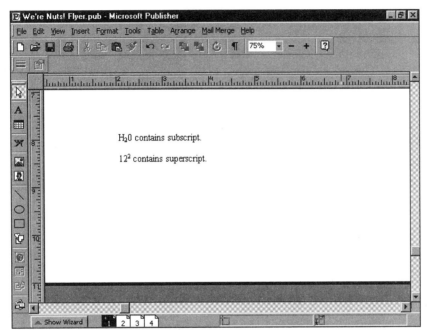

Figure 16-12: Use superscript and subscript only in special situations.

Applying special effects

Publisher includes various special effects, including outline, emboss, small caps, all caps, shadow, and engrave. Each of these effects has a use. Some work for headings or display type, and others work for emphasizing text. Figure 16-13 shows each special effect.

Four of the special effects — outlined, shadowed, embossed, and engraved — show up better if you use them with large headings or display type. You also should limit your use of these effects within one publication.

You can use small caps and uppercase with any subhead, heading, or display type, although small caps are hard to recognize when the text is very small.

Using Cases

Publisher doesn't offer a feature that enables you to change the case of your text quickly and easily. For example, if you enter type and then decide you want to capitalize each letter in the heading, you must go back and type the capitals yourself.

Publisher *does* offer the All Caps effect in the Font dialog box. When you apply all caps to text, however, you must remove the check mark from the All Caps check box in the Font dialog box before you can type text in lowercase again. If you delete the text and type new text, or continue to type on the same line as the formatted text, it will remain in uppercase.

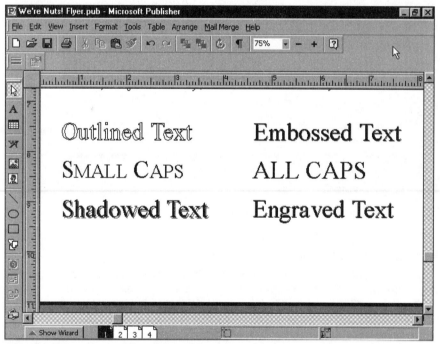

Figure 16-13: Use special effects to grab attention.

Applying attributes and special effects to your text

To apply an attribute to text, you first must select the text. Alternatively, you can activate the attribute, type the text, and then deactivate the attribute. You can apply attributes in Publisher in three different ways:

✦ **Use keyboard shortcuts**: Possibly the easiest way to apply the bold, italic, and underline attributes. Press the shortcut key combination to apply the attribute to the selected text. Press the keyboard shortcut again to remove the attribute from the selected text. The following are the keyboard shortcuts:

- Bold   Ctrl+B
- Italic   Ctrl+I
- Underline Ctrl+U

✦ **Use the buttons on the Formatting toolbar:** Click the appropriate button to apply the attribute to the selected text. Click the button again to remove the attribute from the selected text. The following are the buttons:

- Bold
- Italic
- Underline

✦ **Use the Font dialog box:** This also is how you apply special effects. The Font dialog box is especially useful when you want to change several things simultaneously, such as the font, type size, and an attribute or effect. To apply attributes or special effects to text, follow these steps:

1. Select the text.

2. Choose Format ➪ Font. The Font dialog box appears (see Figure 16-14).

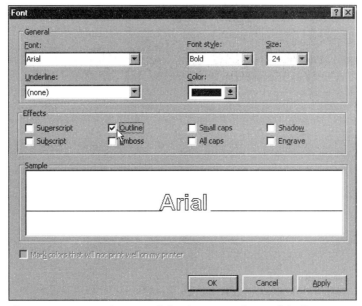

Figure 16-14: Use the Font dialog box to apply special effects.

3. In the General area, click the drop-down arrow for Font style and choose the style from the drop-down list.

4. In the Effects area, add a check mark to the effect that you want to use.

5. Click OK.

Tip   To remove text formatting, select the text and then choose Format ➪ Font. In the General area of the Font dialog box, choose Regular in the Font style drop-down list.

Creating Drop Caps and Fancy First Words

You might want to use a drop cap or fancy first word in a report or a book, to denote the beginning of a chapter or section. *Drop caps* emphasize the first letter of the first paragraph on the page. The drop cap might be a larger letter, a different font, or a decorative letter that starts the first word on the first page. Publisher also enables you to include more letters than the first, thereby enabling you to create a fancy first word instead of just a drop cap.

Don't use more than one drop cap or fancy word per page. You might prefer to use only one drop cap or fancy word per section or chapter of the publication. Figure 16-15 illustrates a document with a fancy first word that indicates the beginning of a section of the report. The first word in this case is CTI, the name of the corporation, which is perfect for the fancy first word.

Using preset drop caps

Publisher offers 16 different preset drop caps that you can apply to your document. Each drop cap uses a different font and style, so you are likely to find one that best suits the body text and layout of your document. Publisher also includes a Preview box that displays your text and the drop cap that you choose. That way, you can tell exactly what it looks like before you accept the changes to the dialog box.

To insert a drop cap, follow these steps:

1. Position the insertion point anywhere in the paragraph to which you want to add the drop cap.

2. Choose Format ➪ Drop Cap. The Drop Cap dialog box appears with the Drop Cap tab showing, as shown in Figure 16-16.

3. In Available drop caps, click any one to see how it looks in the Preview box. Scroll through the box to choose a different drop cap.

4. When you find the right drop cap for your text, click OK.

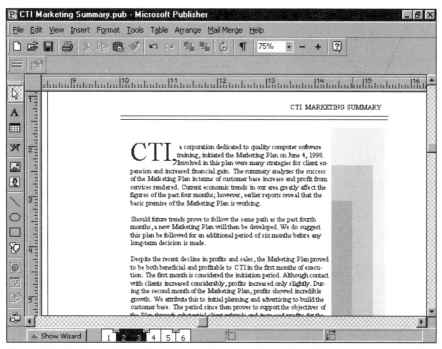

Figure 16-15: Use a fancy first letter or first word to make the page more attractive.

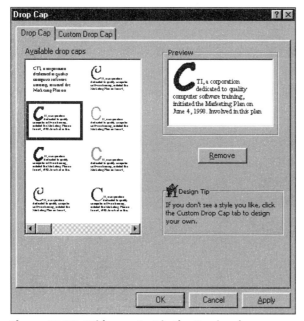

Figure 16-16: With your text in the Preview box, you can choose the drop cap that looks right.

To remove a drop cap, follow these steps:

1. Position the insertion point in the paragraph containing the drop cap.

2. Choose Format ➪ Change Drop Cap. The Drop Cap dialog box appears, with the Drop Cap tab showing.

3. Click the Remove button. The dialog box closes, and the drop cap in your text disappears.

Customizing drop caps and fancy words

You can create customized drop caps by changing the position of the cap, the size of the letters, or the font, font style, and font color. You can also add letters to the initial drop cap to create a fancy first word. The Custom Drop Cap tab of the Drop Cap dialog box enables you to make these changes, as shown in Figure 16-17.

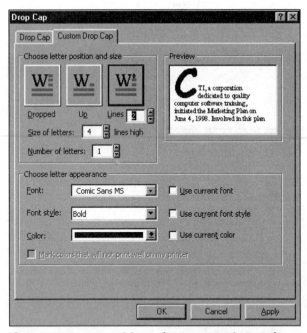

Figure 16-17: Customizing a drop cap to suit your document

Using the custom drop cap options

This section contains descriptions of the options in the Drop Cap dialog box. In the Choose letter position and size area, you have the following options:

✦ **Dropped/Up/Lines:** Either drop the letter so that it falls within subsequent lines of text, raise the letter to extend above the text, or enter the number of lines that you want to move the letter up or down. You can move the letter only 1, 2, or 3 lines up or down. You can experiment with the number of lines, though, and see the results in the Preview box.

✦ **Size of letters:** Choose the size of the drop cap. For example, you might want to make the cap only 2 lines tall, 12 lines tall, or even 24 lines tall. Making the drop cap 24 lines tall greatly changes your design, centering the entire page around the drop cap. However, you can make it very large, if you want.

✦ **Number of letters:** Add letters to your drop cap to create the fancy first word (if you add enough letters to include the first word). You could, alternatively, include one, two, three, or even more letters in the drop cap. Again, consider your design and the message of the document; you want to enhance the message, not destroy it.

In the Choose letter appearance area of the Drop Cap dialog box, you can change the font, style, and color of the drop cap with the following options:

✦ **Font:** Choose any font that's available on your computer. Alternatively, you can choose to use your document's font, by checking the Use current font check box.

✦ **Font style:** Choose any available font style — bold, italic, or regular. Again, you can choose to use the current style of the text, by checking Use current font style.

✦ **Color:** Use a scheme color or any other color or pattern of your choice. The color box works the same as the frame fill color box. If you check the Use current color check box, the drop cap remains the same color as the type in the paragraph.

Creating your own drop cap or fancy word

You can apply any number of options and formatting to your drop cap or fancy first word. Figure 16-18 illustrates one way of customizing a drop cap. Note that the color is lighter than the rest of the text, but the font uses a broader stroke to balance the use of the drop cap and match the colors in the page design.

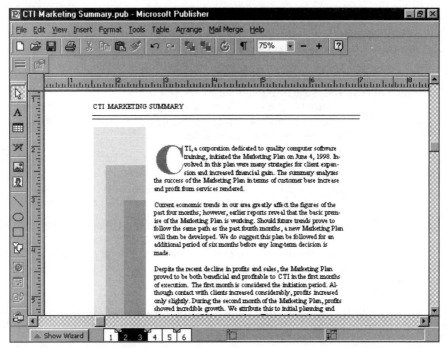

Figure 16-18: Customize the drop cap to suit your document and its style.

To create a custom drop cap, follow these steps:

1. Position the insertion point anywhere in the paragraph to which you want to add the drop cap.

2. Choose Format ⇨ Drop Cap. The Drop Cap dialog box appears with the Drop Cap tab showing.

3. Select a style of drop cap from the Drop Cap tab, as a base for your custom style.

4. Select the Custom Drop Cap tab and click the Apply button. The changes you make from this point on are optional.

5. Choose one of the letter positions — Dropped, Up, or Lines — and enter a value.

6. In Size of letters, enter a number between 2 and 32.

7. In Number of letters, enter a number between 1 and 15. If the first word includes an apostrophe, that counts as one of the letters.

8. In the Choose letter appearance area, select any font from the Font drop-down list box. Alternatively, you can choose Use current font.

9. Select a Font style, or choose Use current font style.

10. Select a Color or pattern, or choose Use current color.

11. Click OK.

Setting Character Spacing

When a person reads, his or her eyes don't look closely at each word; instead, they note the shapes of words — the presence of ascenders and descenders in relation to the body of the word — to recognize the words. The spacing between the letters in a word can make it easier or more difficult to read.

Certain letters fit together in recognizable pairs, such as *th, er, sp,* and *ly.* When too much space appears between letters, recognizing those letter pairs is more difficult. The Courier font is a good example of a font that's difficult to read; because it is monospaced, each letter takes up the exact same amount of space and letter pairs are difficult to recognize.

Figure 16-19 illustrates the Courier and Times New Roman fonts. Note how difficult Courier is to read, because of the letter, or character, spacing.

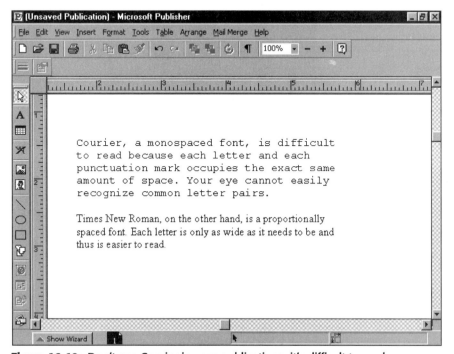

Figure 16-19: Don't use Courier in your publications; it's difficult to read.

Publisher automatically spaces the characters in proportionally spaced fonts, such as Times New Roman or Century Schoolbook. Publisher uses *kerning,* a method of adjusting the character space between two adjacent letters so that they look proportional. Publisher also enables you to adjust spacing in your characters by using kerning, tracking, and scaling.

Understanding kerning

Kerning is a process that brings two letters in a word closer together so that they are more appealing to the eye. Letter pairs such as AV, WA, or RY are letters for which you often need to adjust kerning. Publisher automatically kerns letters in your text, but also enables you to kern text manually.

You can also kern letters so that they are expanded rather than condensed. You might use expanded kerning, for example, when two letters in a specific font look too close together in a heading or display type.

Automatic kerning applies to text that is 14-point or larger; smaller text generally doesn't need to be kerned. The text that you use in headings or display type is the most likely to require kerning. Also, uppercase letters usually require more kerning than lowercase characters.

Figure 16-20 shows the word AVANT in 48-point, regular, Times New Roman. The top example is how the word would normally appear; the second example is how the word appears with 1.5-point condensed kerning applied to AVA. The difference is slight, but the bottom word does look better.

You might also want to use kerning to apply a different look to letters either for the design's sake or to create a logo. Figure 16-21 illustrates two examples of kerning with the logo designs for CTI Technologies. The top example uses normal kerning, the second uses expanded kerning, and the third uses condensed kerning.

Tip   When copyfitting headings, you can use kerning to add or remove space between the letters so that the heading better fits the available space.

Publisher automatically kerns text larger than 14-point. You can kern letter pairs from 0 to 600 points. If you want to expand the selected letters, enter a number between 0 and 600 points, and that is the amount of space Publisher inserts. If you want to condense the letters, enter a number between 0 and 600 points, and Publisher removes that amount of space from between the letters. Remember: 1 point equals ½ of an inch.

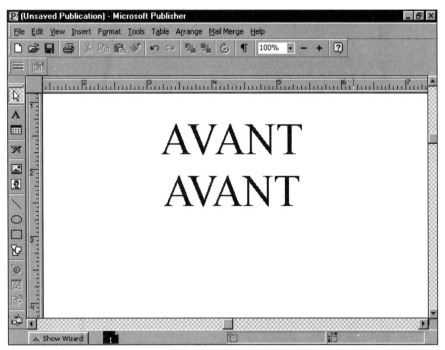

Figure 16-20: Kern large, uppercase headings to make the word more readable and attractive.

To apply automatic or manual kerning, follow these steps:

1. Select the letters or the words that you want to kern.

2. Choose Format ⇨ Character Spacing. The Character Spacing dialog box appears, as shown in Figure 16-22.

3. In the Kerning area, choose the kerning option that you want to apply: Normal (no kerning), Expand, or Condense. When you choose Expand, Publisher enters the default, 3 points, in the By this amount text box. When you select Condense, Publisher enters the default, 1.5 points.

4. You can accept Publisher's default amount or enter your own. Publisher displays a sample of the kerned text in the Sample box.

5. Click OK.

To change the font size for Automatic pair kerning, click the Kern text at check box, so that a check mark appears in the box, and then enter the size of the text in the text box by clicking the up or down arrow.

Figure 16-21: Use kerning to change the look of the text or to create logo text.

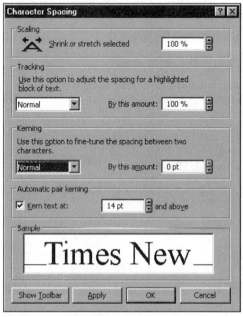

Figure 16-22: Use the Character Spacing dialog box to kern characters in your text.

Note If you use automatic kerning for a large amount of text, such as body text, Publisher may work more slowly, because it has more letter pairs to kern. Text smaller than 14-point generally doesn't need to be kerned, so you can start automatic kerning at 14- or 18-point to keep Publisher's speed normal.

Tracking characters

Tracking is a method of adjusting spacing between all letters in a word. In Publisher, you can adjust letter tracking from very tight to very loose. You can adjust custom tracking between .1 percent and 600 percent.

Publisher provides the following tracking options:

Very Tight	75 percent
Tight	87.5 percent
Loose	112.5 percent
Very Loose	125 percent
Custom	Set the percentage yourself

Figure 16-23 illustrates normal text on the first line, and then the four preset tracking settings in Publisher: Very Tight, Tight, Loose, and Very Loose. You can enter any percentage from .1 to 600 percent in the Custom setting. Use tracking to fill available space or to create a text design, such as a logo.

To apply tracking to letters or words in a document, follow these steps:

1. Select the letters or text to which you want to apply tracking.

2. Choose Format ➪ Character Spacing. The Character Spacing dialog box appears.

3. In the Tracking area, select the tracking that you want to apply from the drop-down list labeled Use this option to adjust the spacing for a highlighted block of text: Normal, Very Tight, Tight, Loose, Very Loose, Custom.

4. Accept the default or enter a new amount in the By this amount text box. View the sample in the Sample box.

5. Click OK.

Figure 16-23: Use tracking to change the look of headings and display type.

Scaling characters

Scaling is a method of stretching or shrinking the width of the characters, as opposed to the space between the characters. You can change the width of one or more selected letters. You can change the width of the selected letters from .1 to 600 percent. You can use scaling along with tracking to create some very interesting designed type.

Figure 16-24 illustrates some scaling changes to the text. The first example is normal text; the second example shows 150-percent scaling; the third shows 75-percent scaling; the fourth shows 150-percent scaling with tight tracking; and the fifth example shows 75-percent scaling with very loose tracking.

Note   When using kerning, scaling, or tracking, make sure that you apply the same effects to all headings in a document. For example, if you apply 150-percent scaling to one headline in a newsletter, you should apply the same scaling to all headlines in that newsletter.

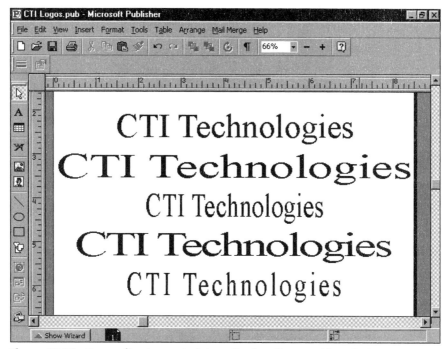

Figure 16-24: Use scaling to create interesting headings and logo text.

To scale characters, follow these steps:

1. Select the letters or text to which you want to apply scaling.

2. Choose Format ➪ Character Spacing. The Character Spacing dialog box appears.

3. In the Scaling area, enter the percentage that you want in the Shrink or stretch selected text box. View the sample.

4. Click OK.

Using the Measurements toolbar

Publisher provides the Measurements toolbar for you to use to kern, track, or scale text. Using a toolbar makes the process easier if you have several letters or words to modify. The Measurements toolbar also enables you to set the exact horizontal and vertical positions of the frame, the precise width and height of the frame, a rotation for the frame, and line spacing for the selected text.

Figure 16-25 illustrates the Measurements toolbar. By default, the measurements appear in inches, but you can change the measurements in the General tab of the Options dialog box (choose Tools ➪ Options).

Horizontal Position   Width   Text Scaling   Kerning

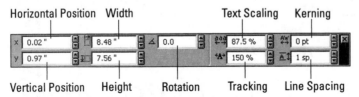

Vertical Position   Height   Rotation   Tracking   Line Spacing

Figure 16-25: Use the Measurements toolbar to scale, track, or kern letters quickly onscreen.

Note   For more information about frame position and size, see Chapter 10. For more information about text rotation and line spacing, see Chapter 17.

To display and use the Measurements toolbar, follow these steps:

1. Choose View ➪ Toolbars ➪ Measurements. Alternatively, click the Show Toolbar button in the Character Spacing dialog box.

2. Select the text to be scaled, tracked, or kerned.

3. Enter the percent or point size in the Text Scaling, Tracking, or Kerning text boxes.

4. To close the toolbar, click the Close (X) button.

Using Color with Text

In Publisher, you can apply a color fill to any text in your document. You might want to apply one or two colors to all the headings in your newsletter, for example, or apply one color to subheads and another to headings in a report or flyer.

To take full advantage of the colors, you should use a color printer, have a commercial print shop print your publication, or distribute your publication over the Internet or via e-mail. If you plan to print to a black-and-white printer, however, you can use black and gray to create an interesting variation to all black text.

Choosing colors

When choosing colors for text, you should follow a few guidelines to ensure readability of the text:

✦ **Don't use a light text on a light background.** For example, don't use yellow, pink, or light blue on a background of white or a pastel color. You don't want the reader to strain to read the text. Instead, use yellow or white text on a black background. Make sure that the text is large enough to read — at least 12-point for body text — and make it bold if the font uses thin strokes (such as Times New Roman). Larger text — for headings and display type — works fine with a light text on a dark background. You may also want to apply a bold attribute to larger fonts. Figure 16-26 illustrates a light tint of gray used in the CTI Technologies heading, on a black background. The text in the second frame is 12-point, white, and bold.

Figure 16-26: Make sure that the text is readable when applying color to the fonts.

✦ **Don't use colors that offer too much contrast between the text and the background.** For example, if you plan to use a bright-blue background, don't use text that is bright red or orange to place on that background. Too much contrast can be difficult to read. You can use contrasting colors; just keep the contrast at a lower level. For example, use a bright-blue font on a background that is a tint, or light color, of yellow, blue, or red. You still have the contrast and can read the text.

✦ **Use the Publisher color schemes or carefully choose colors that match for a multiple-color document.** Don't use colors that oppose each other, such as lime green and kelly green, or pink and orange.

Using color with text effects

Using color in any font makes the document more attractive. You can also apply any of Publisher's text effects to add to the interest of the colored fonts. For example, adding embossing or engraving effects to the text applies a darker line to the text. Figure 16-27 illustrates the original text with only a tint applied. The second line shows embossed text; the third shows engraved text; and the fourth shows a shadow applied to the colored text.

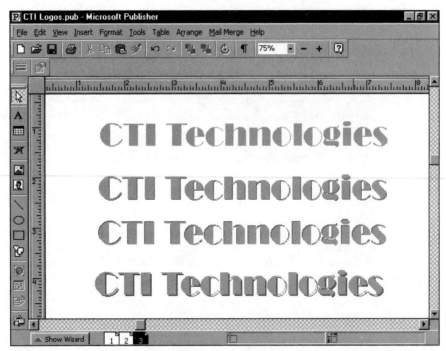

Figure 16-27: Experiment with different text effects when using color in your type.

Tip

In addition to applying color and a text effect, try applying scaling or tracking to the text, to create an interesting effect.

Using Format Painter

Publisher includes a tool called Format Painter that you can use to copy the formatting of text and apply it to other text in your publication. Suppose that you apply a font, size, color, and shadow to a heading in a report. You want to repeat that format to each heading of the same level throughout the report, but you don't want to select and change all the font characteristics for each heading. You can use Format Painter instead.

Using Format Painter, you can apply fonts, type size, attributes, color, and special effects to any text in the document. In Figure 16-28, the heading on the left is formatted with a different font, color, and text effect than the heading on the right. The formatting of the heading on the left has been copied with Format Painter and is about to be applied to the heading on the right.

Format Painter pointer

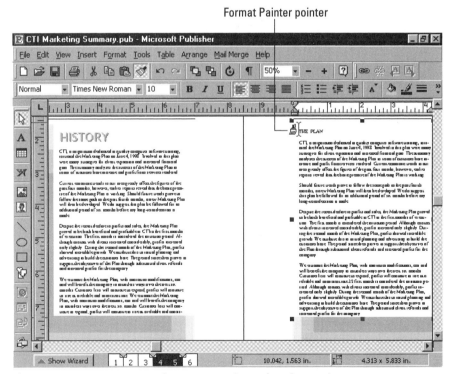

Figure 16-28: Use Format Painter to save time when formatting text.

To use Format Painter, follow these steps:

1. Select the text with the formatting that you want to copy.

2. Click the Format Painter button on the Standard toolbar. The mouse pointer changes to a paintbrush.

3. Click the word or select the words to which you want to copy the formatting. The formatting of the selected words changes.

Summary

In this chapter, you learned how to format characters in your publication. You learned how to do the following:

✦ Apply fonts

✦ Change type size

✦ Apply attributes and special text effects

✦ Create a drop cap and fancy first word

✦ Set character spacing

✦ Use color with text

✦ Use Format Painter

In the next chapter, you learn how to format paragraphs of text, including tasks such as text alignment, line spacing, and using styles.

✦   ✦   ✦

Formatting Paragraphs

Publisher enables you to set the alignment of paragraphs, specify line and paragraph spacing, create and use text styles, and create special paragraphs. This chapter shows you how.

Setting Alignment

You use text alignment as a method of organizing your text. No matter what text you use — body text, headings, tabs, or other — all text has some sort of alignment assigned to it. By default, Publisher left-aligns the text in a blank publication. You also can choose to right-align, center-align, or justify text.

Figure 17-1 illustrates the four text alignments — left, right, centered, and justified. Although all four alignments appear in this flyer, you wouldn't normally use more than two alignments in one document. You could, perhaps, use center alignment for headings and left-aligned text for the body. Or, you could use right-aligned headings and justified body text, for example.

Understanding text alignment

Each of the four text alignments has a standard use. Justified and left-aligned text are used primarily for body text. Left-aligned and centered text are often used for headings, subheads, and display type. Right-aligned text is not often used; however, when it is used, it's for headings and subheadings only.

Left-aligned text

Left-aligned text has a flush left edge and a ragged right edge. It is commonly used for body text, headings and subheads, and nearly any type of text. It's one of the most popular and common alignments for body text, because left-aligned text offers so many advantages.

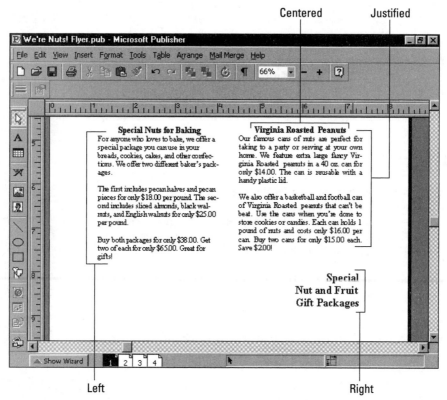

Figure 17-1: Use text alignment to make your publications look more professional.

The following are the advantages of left-aligned text:

✦ Provides consistency throughout the document

✦ Readers always know where the next line begins

✦ Equalized word spacing occurs naturally, providing better readability to the text

✦ Works well in narrow columns, because it directs the reader's eye quickly and easily to the next line of text

✦ Ragged right line endings provide additional white space in the document

If the right ending to a column of left-aligned text is too ragged, it can distract from the page design. Using hyphenation to control the right line endings, however, can eliminate the problem. (For information about hyphenating text, see Chapter 15.)

Tip   If the right line ending is too ragged and has too many hyphens, you need to adjust the column width.

The main disadvantage to using left-aligned text is that you cannot fit as much text on the page as you can with justified text.

Figure 17-2 illustrates a newsletter that uses left-aligned body text and headlines. Note the white space between columns and to the right of the headings. The page is neat, attractive, and well balanced.

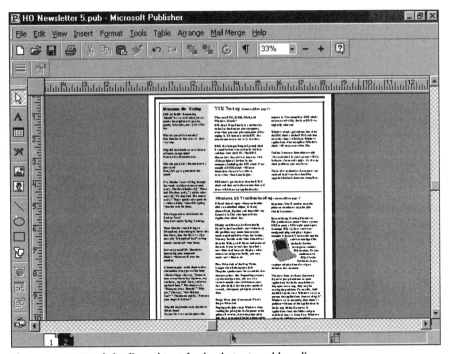

Figure 17-2: Use left-aligned text for body text and headings.

Right-aligned text

Right-aligned text provides a flush right edge and a ragged left edge. The ragged left edge makes finding the beginning of the line difficult. For that reason, format only short phrases with right-aligned text, such as headings and subheads; never use it for body text. When using it for headings, remember to keep the alignment of headings consistent throughout the publication.

Tip   When using right-aligned heads, consider mixing uppercase and lowercase letters (or use small caps). Reading right-aligned text often is difficult, but using all uppercase makes reading it nearly impossible.

Figure 17-3 illustrates a flyer that uses right-aligned text throughout. Each line is short, and the text uses uppercase and lowercase letters. "Grand Opening" is formatted in small caps, which uses a large cap for the first letter of each word and small caps for the rest of each word; small caps makes right-aligned text easier to read than all uppercase would be.

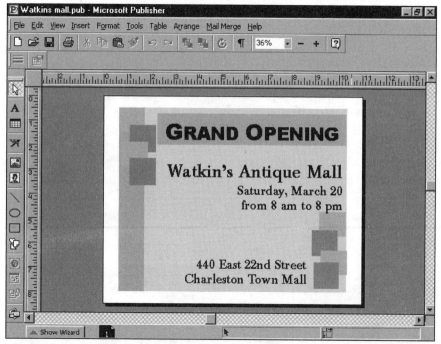

Figure 17-3: Use right-aligned text as part of the design of the publication.

Center-aligned text

Center-aligned, or *centered*, text creates a ragged left and a ragged right line. Centered text can be difficult to read, so you should make sure that you center-align only short words and phrases. Also, you can leave extra line spacing between center-aligned lines of text, as in an invitation or in greeting card text.

The following are some advantages to using centered text:

✦ Provides even word spacing

✦ Is visually interesting

✦ Is formal and dignified

Centered headings work very well with left-aligned or justified body text. Centered text is seldom used for body text. You can, however, use it for short lists, announcements, or brief phrases in a flyer. Figure 17-4 shows the same flyer used in the preceding example, but with centered text instead of right-aligned text.

Figure 17-4: Centered text lends an air of dignity to the publication.

Justified text

Justified text is for use with body text only. It uses flush left and flush right edges. Justified text takes up less space than left-aligned text, because it uses the entire line; however, justified text also makes the page more gray, or dense. When you use justified text, make sure that you use extra margin and gutter space. Also, make sure that you use hyphenation.

> **Tip** Justified text is perfect for long publications, such as books, articles, and reports. A justified page appears organized and comfortable for the reader.

Figure 17-5 illustrates the same newsletter page as used in Figure 17-2; however, now the body text uses justified alignment. By using justified text, you can fit more text on the page. Justified text also makes the page seem dense, or gray. Note that the headlines use centered alignment, which helps add some white space to the page. Additionally, you should set the gutter space between columns a bit wider when you use justified text, to help keep the page from being so dense.

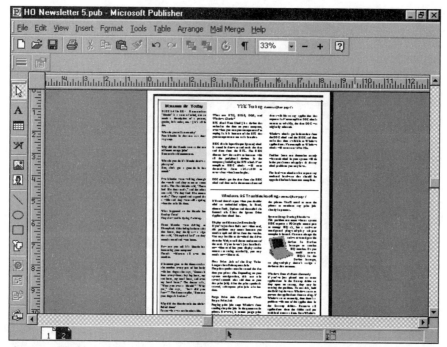

Figure 17-5: Justified text enables you to fit more copy on the page.

Note   Never use justified alignment for a heading or subhead. The spacing for large type that is justified in a frame may appear spotty, uneven, and unsightly. Left-align, right-align, or center headings for justified body text.

Applying text alignment

Publisher provides several methods by which you can align text in a document. The easiest methods are to use a keyboard shortcut or a toolbar button. Another way to apply text alignment is in the Indents and Lists dialog box.

To use keyboard shortcuts to align text, select the text and then press one of the following keyboard combinations:

Alignment Option	Keyboard Shortcut
Left-aligned text	Ctrl+L
Centered text	Ctrl+E
Right-aligned text	Ctrl+R
Justified text	Ctrl+J

To use the alignment buttons on the Formatting toolbar to align text, select the text and then press one of the following buttons:

Alignment Option	Button
Left-aligned text	
Centered text	
Right-aligned text	
Justified text	

To use the Indents and Lists dialog box, follow these steps:

1. Select the text.

2. Choose Format ➪ Indents and Lists. The Indents and Lists dialog box appears, as shown in Figure 17-6.

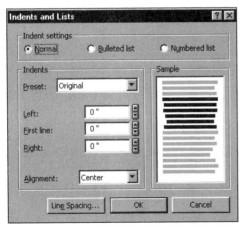

Figure 17-6: Set alignment at the same time that you set indents.

3. In the Indents area, click the down arrow beside the Alignment list box. Choose Left, Center, Right, or Justified.

4. Click OK.

Vertically aligning text

Thus far, you've learned to align text within the frame horizontally—between the left and right edges of the frame. Publisher also enables you to align text within a frame vertically—between the top and the bottom of a frame.

Figure 17-7 illustrates the three vertical alignments: top, center, and bottom.

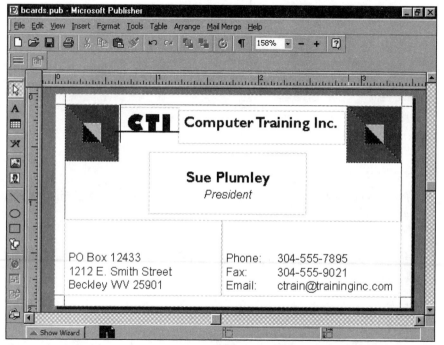

Figure 17-7: Aligning text between the top and bottom edges of the frame

Vertical alignment might be most useful when creating forms, captions, tables, and other such elements in a publication. However, you can vertically align any text in a frame, including single text frames, multiple-column text frames, tables, and connected text frames. As with horizontal alignment, all of the text in the frame follows the vertical alignment that you choose, not just the selected paragraph.

To align text vertically, follow these steps:

1. Select the text frame.
2. Choose Format ➪ Align Text Vertically. A cascading menu appears, as shown in Figure 17-8.

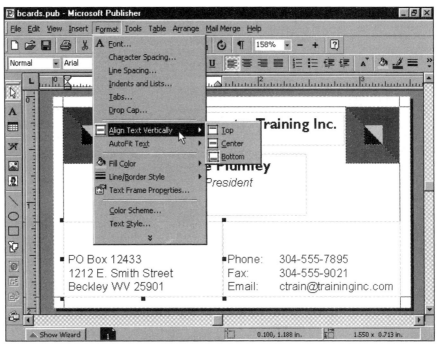

Figure 17-8: Choosing to align text vertically

3. Choose one of the following from the cascading menu: Top, Center, or Bottom.

Alternatively, you can right-click the text frame, choose Change Text ⇨ Align Text Vertically, and then choose Top, Center, or Bottom.

Quick Menus

Publisher uses several quick menus that offer shortcuts and commands to help you edit frames, text, and other items. To display a quick menu, right-click the object — text frame, drawing, table, or other object. The figure on the following page shows the Text and Frame quick menu. Each object's quick menu contains different commands.

This quick menu offers several editing commands, including Cut, Copy, Paste, Delete Text, and so on. You can also access several of the text-formatting commands by clicking the Change Text command. Change the font, character spacing, indents and lists, vertical alignment, tabs, and so on, by clicking this command.

Continued

(continued)

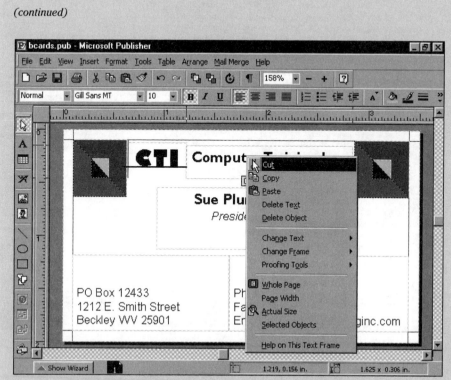

Use the quick menu to edit text, change the page size, and modify the frame.

To learn more about these quick menus, right-click a variety of objects in Publisher, such as clip art, drawing objects, page views, and so on. The commands that you see in the quick menu are similar to those that appear on the menus and toolbars in Publisher.

Using Line and Paragraph Spacing

Line spacing refers to the spacing between the lines of text in one paragraph. *Paragraph spacing* refers to the spacing between two or more paragraphs of text.

You're probably familiar with the single-spacing, one-and-a-half-spacing, and double-spacing used in most word processing programs and typewriters. Publisher enables you to set spacing between lines of text in the same way.

Paragraph spacing is extra space that you may add between two paragraphs of text. Unlike line spacing, paragraph spacing isn't necessarily required. Publisher enables you to measure line and paragraph spacing in any measurement unit that you want: spaces, inches, centimeters, points, or picas.

Tip

You can use any measurement unit within one dialog box by entering the unit's abbreviation after the number. For example, if your default measurement unit is inches, but for line spacing you prefer to use picas, you simply type **14 pi** in the text box, instead of typing **1 sp** or **1.2 in**. You can do this in any dialog box to change the measurement unit temporarily; Publisher converts the unit for you. The abbreviations are spaces (sp), inches (in), centimeters (cm), points (pt), and picas (pi).

As with any formatting that you perform in your publication, when you change line or paragraph spacing, apply the formatting to the entire document, for consistency. Occasionally, you'll want to change spacing for a bulleted or numbered list, a quotation, or even a special paragraph, but generally, keep line and paragraph spacing consistent throughout the document.

Note

If you want to use line or paragraph spacing for copyfitting purposes, reduce or expand all line or paragraph spacing in the document. Changing the line spacing in just one text frame, for example, makes that text stand out more than any other, and therefore disrupts the flow of your text.

Applying line spacing

Publisher determines line spacing, also called *leading* (pronounced "ledding"), by the size of the font that you're using. If you increase the size of the text, Publisher proportionately increases the amount of line spacing. When you reduce the type size, Publisher reduces the line spacing.

For most documents, you don't need to adjust line spacing; Publisher's defaults are fine. You may find times, though, when you want to change line spacing for the sake of readability or design.

Figure 17-9 illustrates text for which the line spacing was increased from 1 sp to 1.25 sp. The extra line spacing adds white space to the page and makes the text easier to read. It also takes up more space on the page.

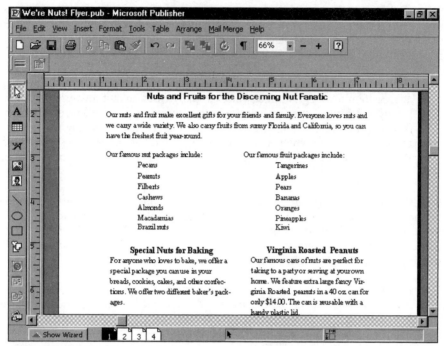

Figure 17-9: Added line spacing opens the page design to more white space.

Understanding line spacing

So, how do you decide how much line spacing to use? You need to understand how to calculate line spacing first. The tallest character in the font is the guideline for measuring line spacing. Uppercase letters, ascenders, and descenders must have enough space to keep them from overlapping with the line above and the line below them.

Generally, line spacing is equal to 20 to 30 percent of the size of the font. It's easy to measure line spacing in the same measurement unit that you use to measure type size — points. For example, 12-point type commonly uses 14-point leading, written as 12 on 14 or 12/14. Fourteen-point type uses 16-point leading; 18-point type uses 20- or 22-point leading, and so on.

Figure 17-10 illustrates four different leading measurements applied to text. The text is 12-point for all four paragraphs. The first paragraph uses 12-point leading; the second uses 14-point, the third uses 16-point, and the fourth uses 18-point. Publisher's default spacing for 12-point type is 12/14.

Another factor to consider is whether the type is serif or sans serif. Because a sans serif font has a vertical emphasis, you generally add more line spacing to improve readability. You can adjust line spacing to help fit copy, to enhance readability, or for the design's sake.

12/12   12/14

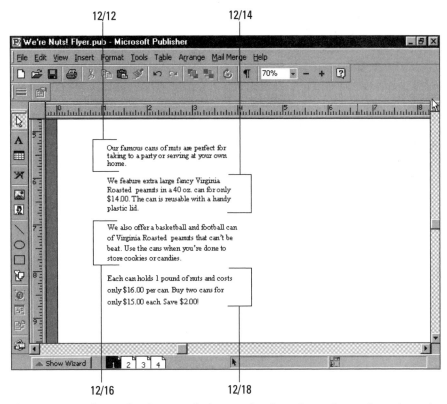

12/16   12/18

Figure 17-10: Change leading to suit the text, but keep it consistent throughout the document.

Applying line spacing to text

To apply line spacing to text, follow these steps:

1. Select a paragraph, all the text in a frame, or the entire story.

2. Choose Format ➪ Line Spacing. The Line Spacing dialog box appears, as shown in Figure 17-11.

3. In the Line spacing area, enter the amount of space that you want to add in the Between lines box.

4. Click OK.

Note

The Show Toolbar button displays the Measurements toolbar; that toolbar has no line spacing tools.

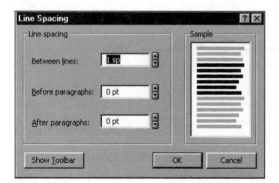

Figure 17-11: Use the Line Spacing dialog box to adjust both line and paragraph spacing.

Applying paragraph spacing

You use paragraph spacing to add white space to the document and to separate paragraphs. Remember, in Publisher terminology, a "paragraph" can consist of one word, a phrase, or several sentences. A hard return creates a paragraph.

Figure 17-12 illustrates different ways to use paragraph spacing. Bulleted text is easier to read when you use extra space between paragraphs. Also, numbered lists are easier to follow when they aren't separated only by line spacing.

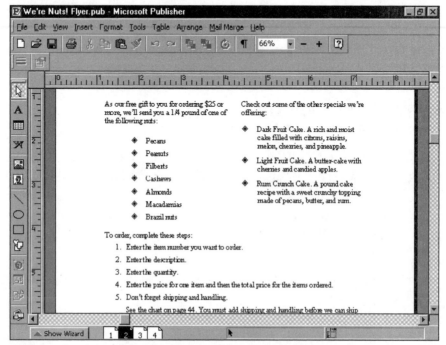

Figure 17-12: Use paragraph spacing to separate bullets and numbers.

Understanding paragraph spacing

You can use additional paragraph spacing when, for example, you don't indent the first line of the paragraph. The space works to help separate the paragraphs. You shouldn't, however, use indents and extra paragraph spacing on the same paragraphs. Also, after you choose one method or the other of separating paragraphs, you should use it throughout the entire text, for consistency.

Figure 17-13 illustrates the two different ways of separating paragraphs. The paragraphs on the left use extra paragraph spacing; the paragraphs on the right use indents.

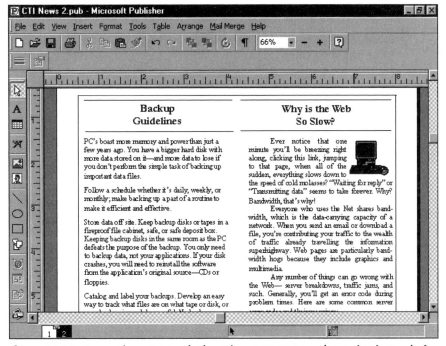

Figure 17-13: Separating paragraphs by using extra paragraph spacing instead of first-line indents

Naturally, adding more spacing between paragraphs takes up more space on the page, but it also adds that valuable white space.

Tip   Consider justifying the text on the page when you use the indented first line; it looks better than left-aligned text, and it's easier for the reader to find the line beginnings.

Publisher enables you to apply paragraph spacing above and below a paragraph. You could also add extra paragraph spacing below or above headings in your document, so that breathing room always exists between the heading and the text.

Applying paragraph spacing to text

To apply paragraph spacing to text, follow these steps:

1. Select a paragraph, all the text in a frame, or the entire story.

2. Choose Format ➪ Line Spacing. The Line Spacing dialog box appears (refer to Figure 17-11).

3. Enter the amount of space that you want to add before each paragraph in the Before paragraphs text box.

4. Enter the amount of space that you want to add after each paragraph in the After paragraphs text box.

5. View the sample. Click OK.

Tip

Generally, you'll want to add space after a paragraph that contains a heading, for example, so that breathing room exists between the heading and body text. You might want to add space before and after a paragraph when using it with body text, bullets, or numbered lists. Be careful when adding space both above and below a paragraph, however; you might end up with *too* much space between paragraphs, making the text difficult to read.

Understanding and Using Styles

Creating styles is an excellent method for formatting a document. A *style* is a collection, or set, of type characteristics that you can format once, but apply over and over again. These characteristics include font, font color, type size, character and line spacing, alignment, tabs, indents, and other such features that you've applied to the text.

You could, of course, format each individual paragraph of text in your publication. If the publication is long, however, you'll want to use styles, to save time and provide consistency in the document.

Additionally, after you apply styles to the text in your document, you can quickly and easily change the font or the spacing, for example, of any style and automatically change that characteristic throughout the document.

Understanding styles

Suppose that you want to apply a different font, type size, and paragraph spacing to the body text in your 12-page newsletter. You can accomplish this task in one of two ways:

✦ Select all the paragraphs on the first page and change the font, size, and spacing. Then, you can move to the second and third pages to make your modifications. You can continue modifying the body text to the end of the document.

✦ Change the font, size, and spacing for one paragraph, name that paragraph as a style, and then apply the style to all paragraphs in the report — quickly and easily. You format an element only once, and then you can use it over and over again.

Publisher includes some preset styles, such as Normal, which is 10-point Times New Roman, left-aligned text. Other styles appear in publications that you create with wizards. You can also define your own styles in Publisher, build on those styles, and copy them to other publications.

Creating styles

When you create a new style in Publisher, you can do it in one of two ways: create by example, or format the new style from scratch. If you create by example, you simply format the text on the page as you want it to look, and then you name the style. If you create a style from scratch, you name the style in the Create New Style dialog box, and then assign formatting to the style.

After you create styles, you can quickly and easily assign them to your documents, as shown in Figure 17-14. Styles that you create appear in the Style drop-down list box on the Formatting toolbar.

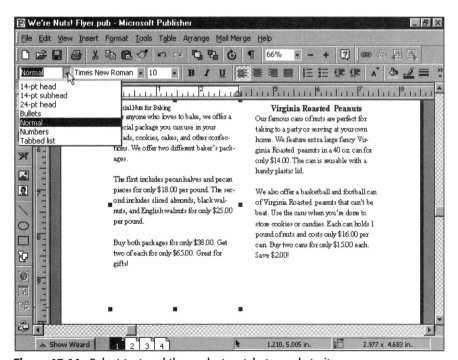

Figure 17-14: Select text and then select a style to apply to it.

When you create a style, you use another style as a base. For example, suppose that you have created a 14-point Arial, bold subhead. You applied center alignment and 4-point line spacing after the paragraph. Now, you can create a new style — say, a heading — that has all the same characteristics except a larger, 18-point type size. Then, repeat the creation process but make the type size 28-point. When you're finished, you have a set of headings to use in your document that are similar and consistently formatted.

Modifying styles

You can always add or delete styles to your publication. You can also modify the styles you've already created. You can change the font, type size, spacing, or any other attribute or characteristic about the style.

Publisher enables you to rename styles, as well. You might name a style "28-point head," for example, and then realize a 32-point head would work better. After you change the type size, you can change the name to "38-point head," to describe the heading accurately.

Tip   When naming styles, use the size, font, or attribute in the name, so that you can easily identify the style later. For example, "14-pt Arial" or "18-pt head" are descriptive ways of naming styles.

Using styles

Publisher makes creating and modifying styles easy. You can use the Text Style dialog box to create and edit styles. You can also create styles by example, which may make getting started using styles easier for you.

Creating a style

When you create a style, you choose the font, size, attributes, spacing, alignment, and any other formatting that you want to use over and over in a publication. If you plan to use a formatted style only one time, you don't need to save it as a style.

By example Create a style by example to use the formatted text in a publication quickly and easily.

To create a style by example, follow these steps:

1. Select the text that you want to format.

2. Apply any formatting that you want to the style: font, size, spacing, and so on.

3. Click in the Style box on the Formatting toolbar. The text in the box becomes selected.

4. Enter the name of the new style, as shown in Figure 17-15.

Enter the new style name

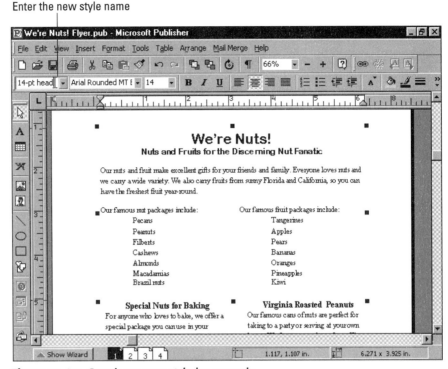

Figure 17-15: Creating a new style by example

5. Press Enter. The Create Style By Example dialog box appears, as shown in Figure 17-16.

Figure 17-16: Confirming the new style creation

6. Click OK. The style appears in the style box, so that you can apply it to other text in the document.

By dialog box Creating a style by using the Text Style dialog box is perfect for when you want to create and edit several styles at one time.

To create a style by using the Text Style dialog box, follow these steps:

1. Choose Format ➪ Text Style. The Text Style dialog box appears, as shown in Figure 17-17.

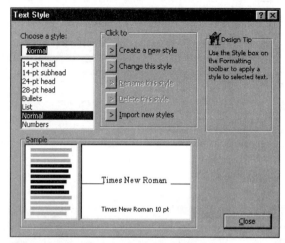

Figure 17-17: The Text Style dialog box offers options for creating and editing styles.

2. In the Choose a style list box, select the style on which you want to base the new style. If Normal is the only style in the box, choose it.

3. In the Click to area, click the Create a new style button. The Create New Style dialog box appears, as shown in Figure 17-18.

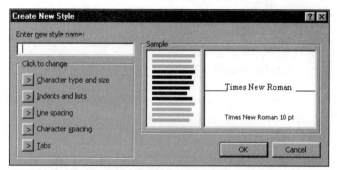

Figure 17-18: The Sample box shows the current style, but as you make changes, the Sample display changes as well.

4. In the Enter new style name text box, type the name of the new style.

5. Click any or all of the following buttons to make changes to the style:

- **Character type and size:** Displays the Font dialog box, in which you can change the font, style, size, color, and effects of the selected style. For more information about the Font dialog box, see Chapter 16.

- **Indents and lists:** Displays the Indents and Lists dialog box, in which you can apply indent settings, alignment, and bulleted and numbered list formatting. For more information, see Chapter 15.

- **Line spacing:** Displays the Line Spacing dialog box, in which you can adjust the space between lines of text, before paragraphs, and after paragraphs. For more information, see "Applying line spacing," earlier in this chapter.

- **Character spacing:** Displays the Character Spacing dialog box, in which you can change character scaling, tracking, and kerning. For more information, see Chapter 16.

- **Tabs:** Displays the Tabs dialog box, in which you can set tab stop positions, tab alignments, and leaders for tabs. For more information, see Chapter 15.

6. View the sample in the Sample box to make sure that it's what you want. Click OK to close the Create New Style dialog box. Click Close to close the Text Style dialog box.

Creating global styles

You can create a set of styles that you use repeatedly in multiple publications, so that you don't have to re-create those styles in individual documents. These styles, called *global styles,* automatically appear in a new publication when you open it. The text that you create, however, will be in the Normal style. You can either select the text and apply the styles, or select the style first and then enter the text as you go.

You don't have to use the text styles that you create, but they are readily available if you do want to use them. You might apply text styles such as 14-, 18-, and 24-point headings, body text, and any other generic formatting that you want to use.

To create global styles, follow these steps:

1. Create a new publication based on a blank publication.

2. Create the new text styles that you want to appear in all new publications.

3. Choose File ⇨ Save As. The Save As dialog box appears.

4. In the Save in text box, select your root drive, such as C:\. Go to Windows\ Application Data\Microsoft\Office.

Note If your operating system is Windows NT, you need to go to the following folder: Profiles*username*\\Application Data\\Microsoft\\Office.

5. Save the document as **Normal.pub** and then click the Save button.

Applying a style

After you create styles, you can easily apply them to any text within the same publication. You can apply a style by using the Style drop-down list on the Formatting toolbar.

To apply a style by using the Style drop-down list, select the text in the publication, click the drop-down arrow on the Style list box, and select the style to apply. For information about applying text styles to another publication, see "Import styles from other publications," later in this chapter.

Changing styles

After you create a style and apply it throughout the publication, you can make any changes to the style that you want. For example, you can change the size of body text or the font of your headings. When you change the style, all text formatted with that style changes automatically.

To change a style, follow these steps:

1. Choose Format ➪ Text Style to open the Text Style dialog box.

2. In the Choose a style list, select the style that you want to change.

3. Click the Change this style button. The Change Style dialog box appears, as shown in Figure 17-19.

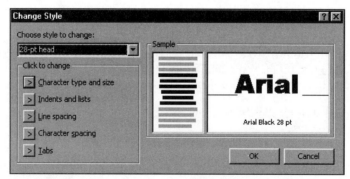

Figure 17-19: The options in the Change Style dialog box are similar to those in the Create Style dialog box.

4. Click the appropriate button in the Click to change area to change any of the text characteristics listed.

5. Click OK. Click Close to close the Text Style dialog box.

Note   When you change one instance of the text in your document—you select a heading and make it 2 points larger, for example—that change affects only the selected text, not the style. When you change a style in the Text Style dialog box, that change affects all text with that assigned style in the publication.

Renaming and deleting styles

You can rename a style, such as when you change the font size or some other characteristic, to make the name more descriptive. You can also delete any styles you no longer use.

To rename a style, follow these steps:

1. Choose Format ➪ Text Style to open the Text Style dialog box.

2. In the Choose a style list, select the style you want to rename.

3. In the Click to area, click the Rename this style button. The Rename Style dialog box appears, as shown in Figure 17-20.

Figure 17-20: Renaming the style so that it's more descriptive

4. Enter the new name for the style in the To text box.

5. Click OK.

To delete a style, follow these steps:

1. Choose Format ➪ Text Style to open the Text Style dialog box.

2. In the Choose a style list, select the style you want to delete.

3. In the Click to area, click Delete this style. Publisher displays a confirmation dialog box.

4. Click Yes. Click the Close button to close the Text Style dialog box.

Import styles from other publications

You might want to import styles from other publications, such as when you want consistency between your company documents. After you set up multiple styles in one publication, you can use those same styles in other publications, without going through the trouble of re-creating them, by importing the styles.

To import styles, follow these steps:

1. Choose Format ➪ Text Style to open the Text Style dialog box.
2. In the Click to area, click Import new styles. The Import Styles dialog box appears, as shown in Figure 17-21.

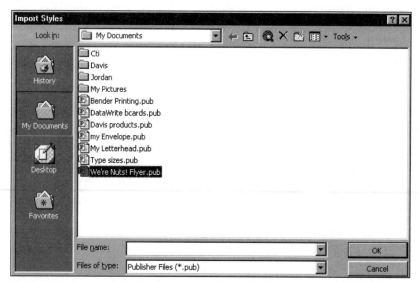

Figure 17-21: Import styles that you've already created and used in other publications.

3. Select the publication containing the styles that you want to import.
4. Publisher copies the styles to the Choose a style list, ready for you to modify, rename, or otherwise use in the new document.

Formatting Special Paragraphs

Publisher enables you to format text in various ways, to make better use of that text in your documents and to use text for design purposes. For example, you can rotate text in a document — to use it in a mailing list, table, or for another purpose — by turning or spinning the text to another direction. Publisher also enables you to create pull quotes and captions to suit your publication, add watermarks for design additions to letters or reports, and create text logos for your company.

Figure 17-22 illustrates a text logo used as a watermark for the company's letterhead. The CTI text is formatted with a light-gray, 400-percent scaling, and then is placed in the background of the document. The company could use the same watermark for all company documents.

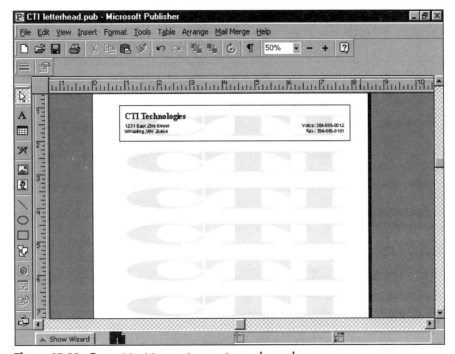

Figure 17-22: Format text to create a watermark or a logo.

Note   Publisher provides wizards for adding pull quotes, captions, calendars, and other text elements to your documents. For more information, see Chapter 24.

Rotating text

You can rotate any object, including text in a text frame, in Publisher. You can turn the text a specific number of degrees, or turn the object with the mouse until you like how it looks. Figure 17-23 illustrates a practical use for rotated text. The mailing panel of the brochure displays a return address that has been rotated.

You can edit rotated text, just as you would any other text. You can change font, type size, spacing, alignment, and character formatting, and perform other modifications.

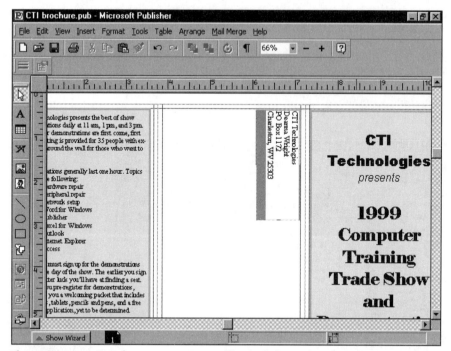

Figure 17-23: Rotated text to create a mailing panel on a brochure

To rotate text, select it and follow one of the following methods:

To rotate text 90 degrees to the left or right, choose Arrange ⇨ Rotate or Flip ⇨ Rotate Left or Rotate Right. The text in Figure 17-24 is rotated right.

To perform a manual rotation, position the mouse arrow over one of the selection handles. Press and hold down the Alt key; the mouse pointer changes to a Rotate pointer. Drag the frame to the rotation angle that you want, as displayed in Figure 17-24.

Tip

To rotate a selected text frame in 15-degree increments, hold down the Ctrl and the Alt keys as you drag the object with the selection handle and mouse.

Finally, you can use the Custom Rotate dialog box to rotate text. Select the text frame and then follow these steps:

1. Choose Arrange ⇨ Rotate or Flip ⇨ Custom Rotate. Alternatively, click the Custom Rotate button on the Standard toolbar. The Custom Rotate dialog box appears, as shown in Figure 17-25.

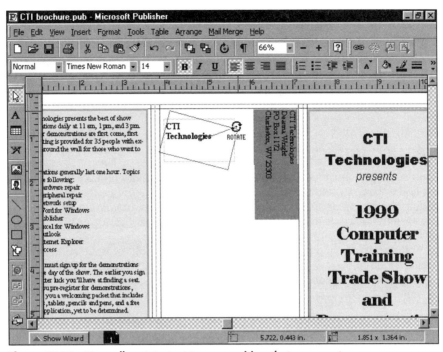

Figure 17-24: Manually rotate text to any position that you want.

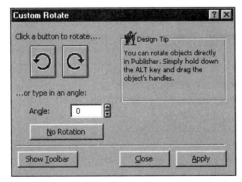

Figure 17-25: Rotating text to a specific degree

2. Click a button to rotate the selected frame left or right. As you click, the amount of the rotation appears in the Angle text box. Alternatively, enter in the Angle text box the amount of rotation that you want to apply.

3. Click the Close button to apply the rotation.

To remove the frame rotation, select the frame and follow these steps:

1. Choose Arrange ➪ Rotate or Flip ➪ Custom Rotate. Alternatively, click the Custom Rotate button on the Standard toolbar. The Custom Rotate dialog box appears.

2. Click No Rotation. The dialog box closes, and the text frame returns to normal.

Creating pull quotes

A *pull quote* is a short, effective statement or phrase that you take from the body text and enlarge to set it off from the rest of the text, to entice the reader into reading the article or story. You can create pull quotes, or *callouts*, to draw attention to an article in a newsletter or a quote in a report, for example.

Generally, you format a pull quote as 12- or 14-point bold or italic centered text. Placing a pull quote in a frame with a border or fill color makes it stand out from the text. You can place a pull quote in the middle of a column or between two columns in the publication.

Tip Try to position a pull quote at a natural break between sentences or paragraphs. Also, don't use more than one pull quote per page.

Figure 17-26 illustrates a pull quote centered between two columns. The text in the quote is 12-point Arial, centered, whereas the body text of the article is 10-point Times New Roman, justified. The pull quote stands out and looks attractive as well.

To create your own pull quote, follow these steps after you create the article or story:

1. Draw a text frame within the text or between columns.

2. Enter the text for the pull quote.

3. Select the text and center it horizontally and vertically.

4. Format the text with a 12- or 14-point font. You can use either the same font as the body text or the font you use for a heading.

5. Make the text either italic or bold. You might also add line spacing to the text. Instead of using 1 sp, for example, apply 1.5 sp to the pull quote text.

Tip Save the pull quote text as a text style, so that you can use it again in the current or other publications.

6. Add a fill or border to the frame. Figure 17-27 illustrates an example of another pull quote.

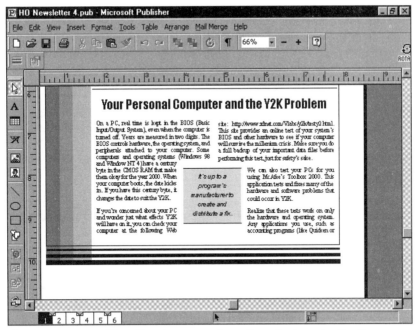

Figure 17-26: Use fill and borders around a pull quote, to grab attention.

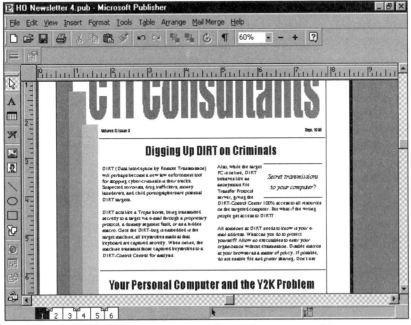

Figure 17-27: Add pull quotes to attract the reader to your articles.

Creating picture captions

A *caption* is text that briefly explains an illustration, artwork, photograph, or figure. Generally, readers look at the figure captions before they read the text in a publication. Captions are also tools for explaining illustrations to the reader.

Although the common position for a caption is beneath the illustration, you can place a caption next to or above the illustration or photograph; just make sure that you're consistent with the placement throughout the entire publication.

Caption text should be aligned the same as the body text, and the text frame should cover the length of the frame, if the caption is positioned above or below the frame. The text for captions is generally an 8- or 9-point sans serif — such as Arial or Lucida — bold or italic with a close leading, or line spacing. Figure 17-28 illustrates a caption for a photograph. The text is 9-point Arial, bold, and left aligned.

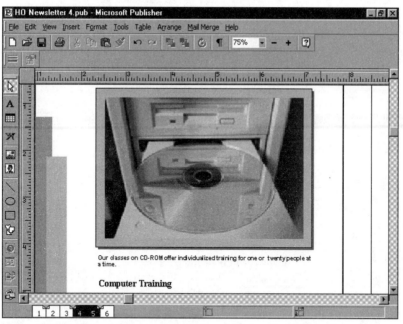

Figure 17-28: Use captions to explain the photograph or illustration.

To create a picture caption, follow these steps:

1. Create a text frame to hold the caption. Enter the text.

2. Format the text to 8- or 9-point bold or italic, using a sans serif font.

3. Change the line spacing for the caption to 1 point above the text size; for example, 8/9 or 9/10.

Adding a watermark

A *watermark* is a design that appears in the background of your document, such as a letterhead, report, or other publication. Watermarks are usually faded or grayed, so that whatever you type in the foreground is easy to read, even with the watermark on the page.

A watermark can be text, images or graphics, or both. A logo makes a nice watermark, as does the company's name. Figure 17-29 illustrates a watermark for the We're Nuts! Company. It can use this watermark on all company documents, to create consistency among its publications. The text is 96-point Showcard Gothic, with a line spacing of 1.5. The color of the watermark is light gray.

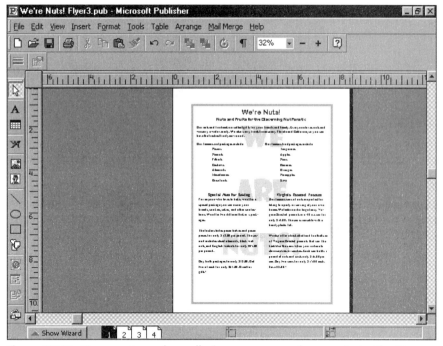

Figure 17-29: Use a watermark on all of your company documents, to identify your advertisements.

The following are a few guidelines to follow when creating a watermark:

✦ Place a watermark on the background of your document.

✦ Keep the text light in color.

✦ Keep the text very large (display text) so that it's not difficult to read.

✦ Don't let the watermark detract from the page design or the message of the text.

To create a watermark, follow these steps:

1. Go to the background of the publication.

2. Create a frame. You can use fill, borders, or both, if you want.

3. Create the text. Align it and format it as a large display font. You can add character scaling or tracking, any text effects or attributes, and line spacing.

4. Go to the foreground to create the text of the publication. Make sure that you use No Fill for any text or picture frames that you create, so that you can see the watermark.

Note

If you create a watermark that looks good onscreen but doesn't print correctly — that is, it prints solid black instead of gray — your printer uses the HPGL printer language. You can work around this problem. Cut the text frame, launch Paint, and paste the frame. Immediately copy the frame again, switch to Publisher, and paste the text frame back into the background. This procedure makes the text frame into a graphic that the HPGL printer language can print in gray.

If your printer uses PostScript or some other printer language, you'll have no problem with the watermark.

Formatting text logos

A *logo* is an identifier for a company or product. Most companies and products use some sort of logo that consists of text, graphics, or both. A logo projects an image — modern, formal, dignified, old-fashioned, and so on.

When designing a text logo, you can use any of Publisher's tools to modify the text and create a logo. Figure 17-30 illustrates some examples of various logos that you can create with the character and paragraph formatting tools of Publisher.

You also can use WordArt, an Office applet, to create text logos. For more information, see Chapter 21. In addition, you can use graphics with your logos; for information, see Part IV, "Adding Graphics, Objects, and Images." Figure 17-31 illustrates another set of logos that combines various text effects and characteristics with various frame formats.

Figure 17-30: Create logos for your product or company.

Figure 17-31: Use frame fills and borders to create different effects for the logos.

Summary

In this chapter, you learned how to format paragraphs, including the following:

✦ Setting alignment

✦ Using line and paragraph spacing

✦ Creating and using text styles

✦ Formatting special paragraphs

In the next chapter, you learn to define graphics, images, and other objects.

✦   ✦   ✦

Adding Graphics, Objects, and Images

A professional-looking document includes graphics and images. You might want to add lines and borders, clip art, pictures, or charts to a document. In this part you learn to add and format various graphics in Publisher. Depending on the document, you might want to add a color behind a text box or a border around a headline; alternatively, you might add sounds or animated pictures to a document. With Publisher's built-in tools you can add your own drawings and illustrations, clip art, fancy lettering and words, or tables of data. Publisher also supports linking and embedding, a method by which you can share data and graphics between various Windows and Office applications.

Understanding Objects

This chapter details the definition of graphics and objects, and shows you the best methods of combining text and objects in your documents.

Defining Graphics

Graphics can be a catch-all word, meaning any type of art, pictures, illustrations, charts, and other figures. It also includes various visual elements that you can add to the page, such as lines, boxes (a frame with a border), screens (a frame with a fill), borders, and so on. This section covers the visual elements that you might use in your publication; the following sections discuss images, pictures, and other illustrations.

Graphic elements add interest and diversity to the page. You can use a frame with a fill to attract attention and provide emphasis on the page. Frames with fills, borders, or lines also help to divide the page. Graphics should enhance the page, not ornament it. Excessive decoration may distract the reader from the text and the true message of the publication.

Using lines

Lines on the page help to divide articles or stories, emphasize headings or other text, direct the eye, tie certain elements together, and so on. In Publisher, you can use frame borders to supply left, right, top, and bottom lines around a story. You can also use the drawing line tool to create a line within the text, as shown in Figure 18-1. Horizontal lines at the top and bottom of the flyer help to define the page and stop the eye from wandering off the page; these lines are frame borders. The lines within the text help to divide the text by topic; these lines are drawn with the Line tool.

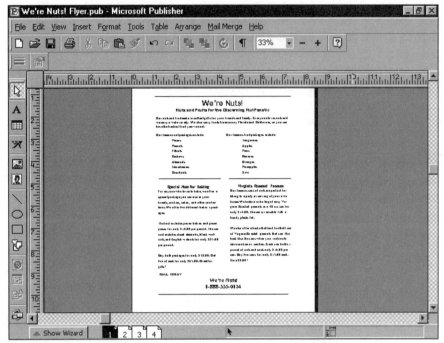

Figure 18-1: Use lines in your publications to enhance the page.

Understanding line use

When using a line to direct the eye, you might try a wide line above a major head, with smaller lines above subheads, for example. The lines show the reader where to look for the important topics. Figure 18-2 illustrates lines above the heads. As an alternative, you could place the lines below the head, but then the lines might *stop* the reader's eyes instead of leading them.

Vertical lines are useful in page design. Vertical rules can separate columns for left-aligned text, for example, to keep the reader's eyes from jumping to the adjacent column.

Tip
Make sure that you don't use a vertical line when you use justified text; doing so crowds the page too much.

You can also use rules — vertical, horizontal, or both — to divide lists and numbers, and columns in tables. (For more information about tables, see Chapter 22.) No matter where you use lines, however, make sure that you're consistent with the length and thickness, as well as the positioning and use.

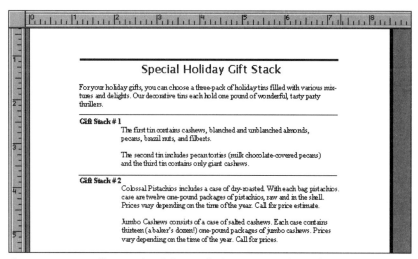

Figure 18-2: Use lines to lead the reader's eyes to main topics.

Applying lines

You can apply lines by using either frame borders or the Line tool. When you use frame borders, you can apply only a line that follows the size of the frame. Whether you use the Line tool or the frame border, you can control the width of the line and its color.

Frame lines When you apply lines to frames, you choose the sides to which you want to apply the line. Figure 18-3 illustrates the Border Style dialog box, with only the top line applied to the selected frame. You can also select the thickness and color of the lines that you apply.

To apply a frame line, follow these steps:

1. Select the frame.

2. Choose Format ➪ Line/Border Style ➪ More Styles. The Border Style dialog box appears.

3. In the Select a side area, click the sides to which you want to apply the line.

4. In the Choose a thickness area, select a preset thickness or enter a value for a custom thickness.

5. In the Color area, click the drop-down arrow next to Color and choose the color that you want to apply to the line.

6. Click OK.

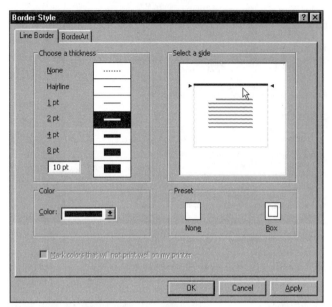

Figure 18-3: Select Box in the Preset area to add a line on all four sides of the frame.

Figure 18-4 illustrates a line applied to the left border of the frame, creating a vertical rule in the gutter. If you use this method, however, you must make sure that the line is not too close to the text in the frame. You can adjust the margin area in the Text Frame Properties dialog box (choose Format ➪ Text Frame Properties). (For more information about frames, see Chapter 10.)

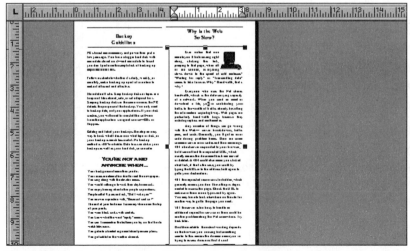

Figure 18-4: Creating a vertical line to separate text

Line tool The Line tool enables you to place a line anywhere in a document, regardless of the frame positioning. You can draw a line on the background, foreground, with or without a frame, in the margins — practically anywhere. The Line tool is on the Object toolbar. To use the Line tool, follow these steps:

1. Click the Line tool.

2. Press and hold down the Shift key to keep the line straight as you draw it.

3. Click the mouse where you want the line to begin, and then drag it to the end, as shown in Figure 18-5.

4. Release the mouse. Release the Shift key.

A selected line has two handles — one on each end. You can move and resize the line as you would any other object. If you resize the line, press and hold down the Shift key as you resize, so that the line remains straight. You can also copy, move, and delete a line as you would any other object. (For more information about drawing in Publisher, see Chapter 20.)

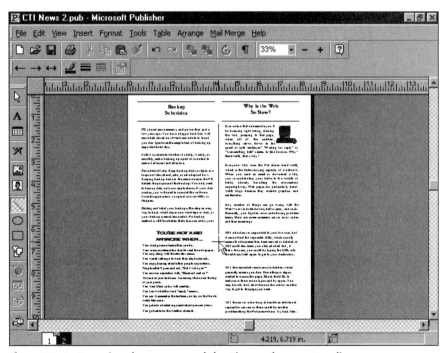

Figure 18-5: Dragging the mouse and the Line tool to create a line

Using borders

A *border* is a box that creates a boundary around text, pictures, or other objects. Borders draw attention to elements on the page or limit the reader's eyes to view only what's inside a page border, for example.

Understanding borders

Always be sure to include white space inside and outside the borders. Borders should never extend beyond a column's margins or a page's margins. Without white space, a border clutters the document. Figure 18-6 illustrates a page border with plenty of margins on the outside and extra white space inside the border. When using page borders, make sure that you use the exact same border on all pages of the document.

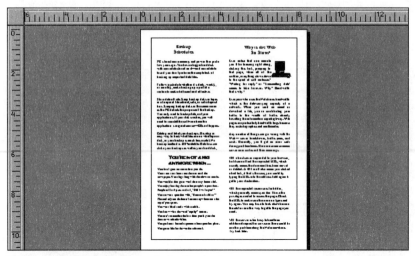

Figure 18-6: Page borders rein in the text.

You can use borders to isolate messages from the rest of the page or to draw attention to the text in the border. You can use page borders and text borders together, as shown in Figure 18-7, as long as you don't overdo it. The text border calls attention to the article, and sufficient space is left between the page border and text border.

Tip Using the Rectangle drawing tool, you can create double borders around a page. Simply draw a border and then draw another inside of it; use the rulers to measure the space between borders. You might try making the outside border thicker, for a nice effect. Make sure that you leave sufficient margin and white space on the page.

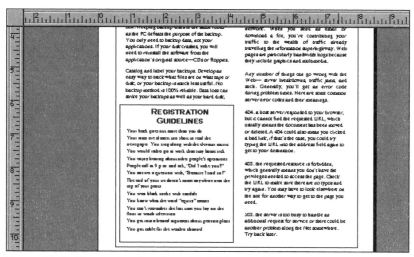

Figure 18-7: Using a text border to highlight specific text on a page

Applying borders

You can create borders around frames by using a frame border, or create borders around the page by using the Rectangle drawing tool.

Frame borders You can use frame borders to create various widths with which to frame a page or a text frame. You can even draw a blank frame with a border in the background, to use as page borders. To create a frame border, follow these steps:

1. Select the frame.

2. Choose Format ⇨ Line/Border Style ⇨ More Styles. The Border Style dialog box appears.

3. In the Preset area, select Box.

4. In the Choose a thickness area, select a preset thickness or enter a value for a custom thickness.

5. In the Color area, click the drop-down arrow next to Color and choose the color that you want to apply to the line.

6. Click OK.

Publisher also provides fancy borders in the BorderArt tab of the Border Style dialog box. For more information about border art and frames, see Chapter 10.

Rectangle tool You can draw a rectangle anywhere on the page, whether you're using frames or not. You can draw rectangles in the background of a document to create the same border on all pages. To create a rectangle, follow these steps:

1. Click the Rectangle tool.

2. Position the mouse near the upper-left corner of the page and drag the mouse to the bottom-right corner. Use the layout guides to help position the rectangle.

3. To apply another line width to the border, select it and click the Line/Border Style tool on the Formatting toolbar. Select the line thickness just as you would for a frame.

A rectangle has eight handles (just like a frame) when you select it. You can resize and move a rectangle as you would any other object. You can also move, copy, and delete a rectangle. (For more information about drawing in Publisher, see Chapter 20.)

Using fills

Fills add emphasis to the text or to your borders. If you're printing in color, fills, gradients, and patterns can really enhance your document. Figure 18-8 illustrates a simple fill in a page border. The border is dark gray and the fill is light gray. As with any fill or background, make sure that you can read the text through the fill.

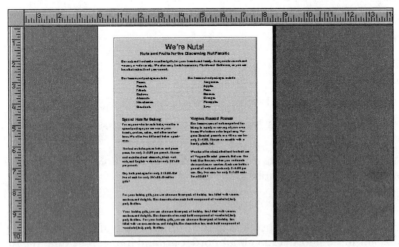

Figure 18-8: Using a simple fill and border for the entire page

Figure 18-9 illustrates the gradient fill used in a page border. The darkest area of the gradient is still light enough to read the text comfortably. The page is rather striking with the gradient; it attracts attention and provides a nice background and border.

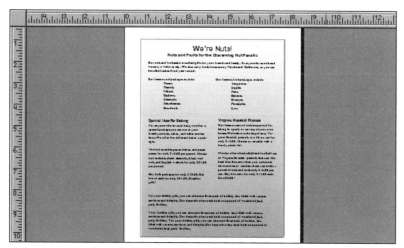

Figure 18-9: Using a light gradient as a background

You have to be careful when using patterns as fill. Most of the patterns are dark and busy — stripes, bricks, and so on. But you can apply a pattern and then select a light color, so that the pattern fades to the background instead of overpowering the text.

Figure 18-10 illustrates a basket weave pattern in the background of a frame. The fill attracts attention but doesn't overpower the text.

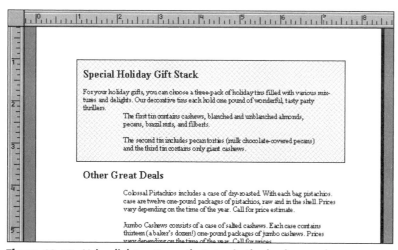

Figure 18-10: Using light patterns that stay in the background

Tip

You should observe margins and column guides when creating fills, just as you would with borders and lines. Avoid running text to the very edge of a filled rectangle or frame.

To apply a fill to a frame or a rectangle, select the box and then follow these steps:

1. Click the Fill Color button.

2. Select one of the following:

   • **Scheme colors:** Choose one of the colors already in the color scheme that you're using.

   • **More Color Schemes:** Displays the Color Scheme dialog box (see Figure 18-11), from which you can choose a color scheme to apply. Select a scheme and then click OK to display the new colors in the Fill Color menu.

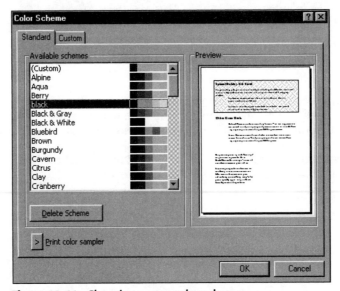

Figure 18-11: Choosing a new color scheme

   • **More Colors:** Displays the Colors dialog box, from which you can choose any color to apply to the fill.

   • **Fill Effects:** Displays the Fill Effects dialog box, from which you can choose Tints/Shades, Patterns, or Gradients to add to the rectangle or frame. Figure 18-12 illustrates the available Patterns, with a light color applied to them.

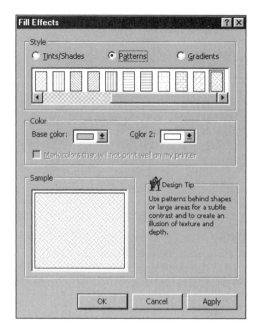

Figure 18-12: Choosing a pattern or other fill for the frame or rectangle

Note   For more information about using fills, see Chapter 10.

Looking at examples

Use graphics to enhance the document and attract attention to it. You can use a combination of lines and fills, or just use lines, borders, or a fill alone to strengthen the document.

Figure 18-13 applies fill in a checkerboard pattern that really catches the eye. The light-gray fill is applied only to the text areas, without borders of any kind. Using the fill changes the shape and impact of the white space in the document.

Use lines to divide areas of a form or document. You can also use fills in forms to draw attention to important areas and information. In addition, you can use patterned fills to designate areas the recipient should not fill in. Light patterns are fine when applied to any frame or rectangle. Figure 18-14 illustrates two fills applied to frames in a fax cover sheet, with lines that divide information areas.

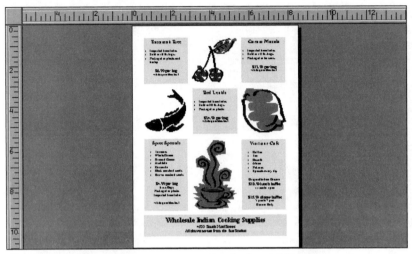

Figure 18-13: Using fills to create a pattern in the publication

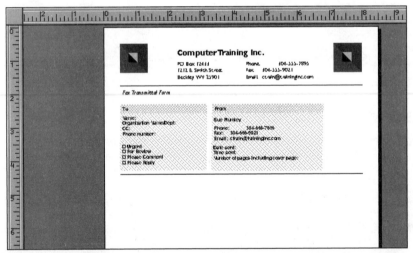

Figure 18-14: Use patterned fills and lines in a form, to separate information.

When using borders, lines, and fills in your publication, make sure that you balance the graphic elements. Figure 18-15 illustrates a newsletter in which a page border and various lines separate the text within the page. Also, two fills are used to enhance the page. The bottom fill balances with the top because of the clip art used in the frame. The gradient fills are opposite of each other, which adds a bit of excitement as well.

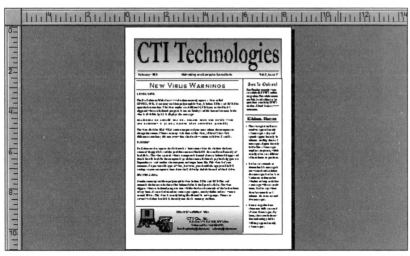

Figure 18-15: Combining lines, borders, and fills

Finally, use border art with fills to create an attractive and eye-catching page border. You can make the border art borders lighter in color, yet darker than the fill, to create a nice contrast that doesn't take over the document. Figure 18-16 illustrates a flyer using a dark-gray border art and a light-gray fill. Note that not much text is in the frame, and the text that does exist is quite large. You don't want to use large borders with small text, because the border will distract from the message.

Figure 18-16: Adjust the size and color of the border to match the text and the page design.

Defining Objects

Publisher enables you to insert a variety of objects in your publications. Anything that you add to a publication—whether a text frame, picture, or table—can be defined as an object.

The following are some common characteristics that all objects possess:

✦ You can select them, and they display a frame border plus eight selection handles.

✦ You can resize and move objects within the same page, to another page, or to another publication.

✦ You can delete objects.

✦ You can arrange layered objects by sending them to the back or front, or by sending them one or more layers backward or forward.

✦ Objects can snap to layout guides, ruler guides, or other objects.

✦ You can assign text to wrap around objects.

Understanding object types

Publisher includes an Object toolbar, as shown in Figure 18-17. You can use the Object toolbar to create a variety of objects, including text frames, pictures, lines, and rectangles.

Pointer Tool
Text Frame Tool
Table Frame Tool
WordArt Frame Tool
Picture Frame Tool
Clip Gallery Tool
Line Tool
Oval Tool
Rectangle Tool
Custom Shapes

Figure 18-17: Object toolbar in Publisher

Text frames are objects, because you can select, resize, move, and otherwise manipulate the frame. You also can create text frames that contain no text. (For more information about text frames as objects, see Chapter 10. For more information about text, see Chapter 13.)

A *table* is a collection of cells created by intersecting rows and columns; the table must be created within a table frame. You can enter information or pictures in a table cell. You can select, resize, delete, and otherwise manipulate a table frame, even though it contains text. (For more information about using tables, see Chapter 22.)

Figure 18-18 illustrates a table frame that's selected. The handles appear around the table so that you can resize and move the table. You can also format the text within a table, add a fill or border, and format and edit the table columns and rows.

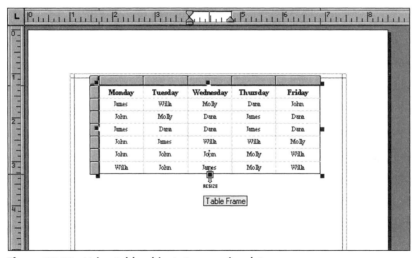

Figure 18-18: Using table objects to organize data

WordArt is an Office applet that creates a fancy word or letters in a frame. You can apply any font, type size, or attribute to a piece of WordArt; plus, you can apply various shapes and curves to the letters, as shown in Figure 18-19. Note that the WordArt is enclosed within a frame, which means that you can manipulate the object just as you can a text frame or other frame. (For more information about WordArt, see Chapter 21.)

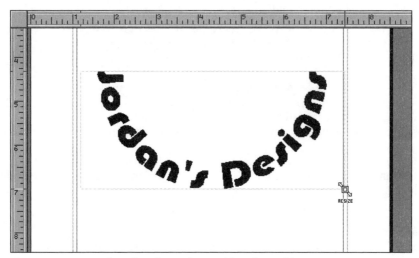

Figure 18-19: Any item in a frame is considered an object.

Pictures are objects, because you also create them in frames. You can insert a photograph or clip art picture into a picture frame. Again, you can add a background fill, a frame, or otherwise edit the picture frame as you would any other frame. (For more information about pictures and clip art, see Chapter 19.)

Figure 18-20 illustrates two picture frames — one containing a photograph and the other containing a piece of clip art. Note that the photograph uses a border, and the clip art frame uses a fill.

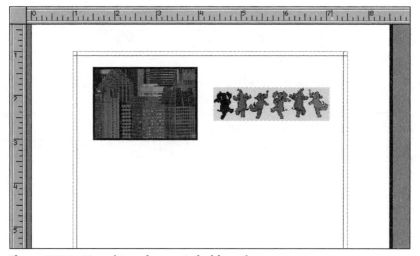

Figure 18-20: Use picture frames to hold any image.

The Clip Gallery frame can hold clip art, sounds, or motion clips. Figure 18-21 illustrates Microsoft's Clip Gallery. Office provides many clips, but you can also add your own from the Web or from other sources. (For more information, see Chapter 19.)

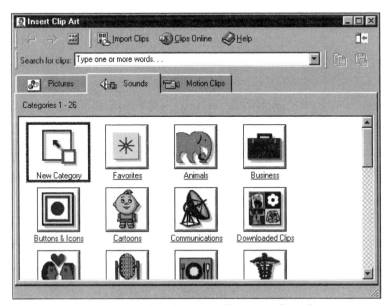

Figure 18-21: Insert sound and motion clips, as well as clip art.

Microsoft Draw objects — lines, ovals, rectangles, and custom shapes — are the only objects in Publisher that don't require a frame. Each item that you draw is an object unto itself, with handles for resizing, and characteristics that you can edit or format. Figure 18-22 illustrates a simple, abstract drawing of shapes and lines. Note that you can apply various line weights and fills to each object.

Note, too, that you can select one of the objects to edit or format it. Publisher also enables you to layer drawing objects, and group them together so that you can format, copy, or move them as one object instead of as multiple objects. (For more information about Microsoft Draw, see Chapter 20.)

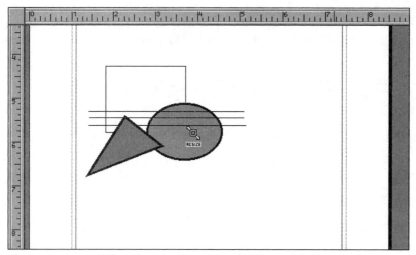

Figure 18-22: Each item in a drawing is an object unto itself.

Publisher also enables you to insert various objects from other Windows programs. These objects, called *OLE objects,* appear in a frame. OLE stands for *Object Linking and Embedding,* a Windows feature that enables many Windows applications to share information and data with one another.

You use the Insert Object dialog box, shown in Figure 18-23, to insert OLE objects. Note that you can insert pictures, charts, worksheets, slides, and other objects by using this technique. (For more information, see Chapter 23.)

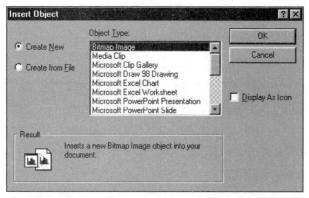

Figure 18-23: Use the Insert Object dialog box to insert a variety of objects created in other programs.

Following guidelines for object use

You can insert any object into a publication at any time. You can, for example, add pictures and clip art to an article or story to enhance or illustrate the text. Use tables or drawings for the same reason — to illustrate the text.

As with adding any text or object to the page, consider the page layout, white space, balance, and other design elements. For example, consider the headings, frame fills, and borders in conjunction with the entire page.

Adding tables

When using tables in your document, make sure that you follow the column or margin guides. The table shouldn't be larger or smaller than other elements on the page. Also, make sure that you use line thicknesses, fills, and text formatting that are similar to what you use on the rest of the page and publication.

Figure 18-24 shows a table inserted at the bottom of a page of text in a product flyer. The width and the weight of the table establish a base for the page. Horizontal lines that divide the text are the same width and thickness as the horizontal lines in the table. The text formatting for the table uses the same font as the body text. Finally, every other row in the table uses a light-gray fill, which adds some variety and emphasis to the page.

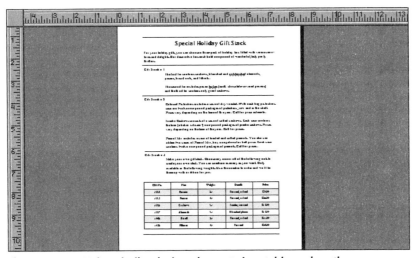

Figure 18-24: Using similar design elements in a table and on the page

Adding WordArt

WordArt creates distinctive text for display type, headlines, and logos. You can mold WordArt text into various shapes, or just present it in standard format. You have to be careful with your WordArt designs, to make sure that they fit the rest of the page design and text. You can easily create extravagant text that overpowers the rest of the document.

Figure 18-25 illustrates a WordArt heading that fits in with the rest of the text. The text presents a horizontal direction, because the text is short and reaches from margin to margin. Text on a curve or circle, for example, would not match the rest of the document so well.

Figure 18-25: Make sure that the text in the WordArt fits in with the rest of your publication.

Figure 18-26 illustrates another WordArt object. The shape of the text provides a top, of sorts, to the lines on the other three sides of the business card. Even though the logo is large, it still fits in with the rest of the card design.

Adding pictures and clip art

When adding pictures and clip art to a document, you must keep an eye on balance. Pictures are visually heavier than other graphics or text. When you use a picture on the page, you must make sure that it balances, even asymmetrically, with the rest of the page. For example, in Figure 18-27, the two pieces of clip art visually balance each other. The frame with the fill helps to equalize the rest of the page.

Figure 18-26: Use WordArt shapes in a publication, but make sure that the design fits the text.

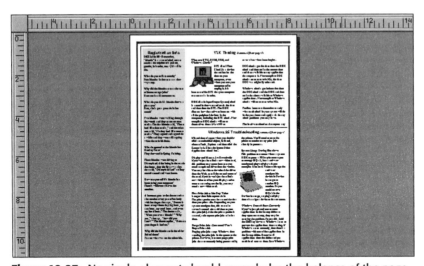

Figure 18-27: No single element should overwhelm the balance of the page.

Limiting your use and placement of pictures and other objects doesn't mean that you can't use large photographs or decorative objects. It simply means that you must make sure that the objects on the page are balanced. As an example, Figure 18-28 shows a large photograph that is well-balanced by the text at the top of the page. A large headline also helps to even up the visual weight on the page.

Defining Images

Images include clip art, line art, photographs, and drawings. *Line art* consists of any drawn image, whether drawn in Publisher using the Microsoft Draw tools or drawn in CorelDRAW or Adobe Illustrator, for example. You might also use an electronic scanner to scan in drawings or line art that you've created with a pen on paper.

Any of these objects can be inserted into Publisher by using the Picture Frame tool, except for Microsoft Draw objects, which can be drawn directly onto the page in Publisher. You treat images the same as any other object in Publisher; for example, you can select, move, resize, and otherwise manipulate the object.

Note, too, that the column width of the text is the same as the photograph. This helps to tie the photo in with the text so that it doesn't overwhelm it. Also, a fill and a border around the photograph repeat the page border and the design on the page background.

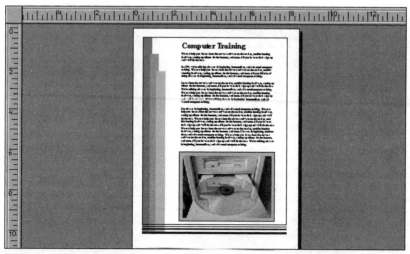

Figure 18-28: Consider the entire page's design when adding objects to it.

Adding drawings

When you add a drawing or an object from Microsoft Draw, make sure that it fits with the other elements on the page. Sometimes, you might want to use bright colors, for example, to make the drawing stand out; however, it must still conform to the overall design.

At the beginning of this chapter, you learned to use lines and rectangles to separate or emphasize text. You can also use the Microsoft Drawing tools to create illustrations for your publications. Figure 18-29 illustrates a drawing of networked computers that enhance an article about networking books. The lines and borders of the computers are the same thickness as the text division lines. The drawing doesn't overwhelm the text or the page.

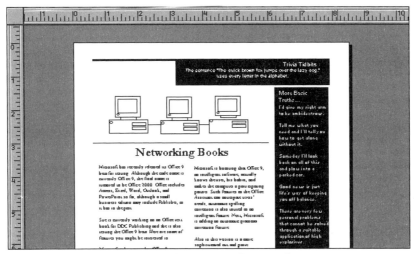

Figure 18-29: Add drawings to the page to illustrate the text.

Using Text and Objects Together

In the examples in this chapter, you've seen how to combine objects with the text on the page to make the design and page layout professional and attractive. Publisher offers several tools that help you to deal with the text and objects in your publication.

You can use text wrap, layering techniques, ruler and layout guides, the Snap To feature, and backgrounds and foregrounds when working with text and objects.

Using backgrounds and foregrounds

You use the background in Publisher to add any objects that should appear on all pages, such as logos, page borders, fills, page numbers or headers, and other objects. You can use the background to insert an object, and then, in the foreground, you can work around the object.

When using the background and foreground, remember these tips:

✦ Make sure that you make the frames in the foreground No Fill.

✦ Use layout guides and column guides when placing objects.

✦ Use the Ignore Background command for pages on which you do not want to view the object.

For more information about placing objects in the background, see Chapter 9.

Using text wrap

You can layer one frame on top of another and apply the text wrap feature so that text wraps around clip art, for example. Whether the frame that you're inserting is a text, picture, or other object frame, you can choose to wrap text around objects that are layered on top. Also, you can choose to wrap text around the frame or wrap it closer to the picture.

Tip   You can apply margins to the inside and outside of a frame to keep text from running into the borders of the picture frame.

Figure 18-30 illustrates the Text Frame Properties dialog box, in which you set the text wrap option. If you choose *not* to wrap the text around the frame, Publisher runs the text directly through the object frame; Publisher *does* wrap text around object frames by default. (For more information about wrapping text, see Chapter 10.)

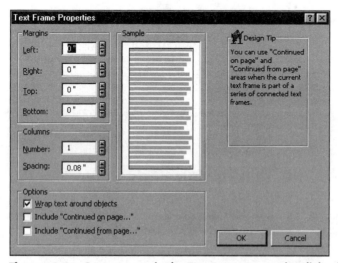

Figure 18-30: Set text wrap in the Text Frame Properties dialog box.

Figure 18-31 shows the text wrap options for a picture frame. If you choose to wrap the text around the entire frame (Publisher's default), you'll have more white space between the text and the picture. On the other hand, you can choose to wrap the text around the picture, to create an interesting effect.

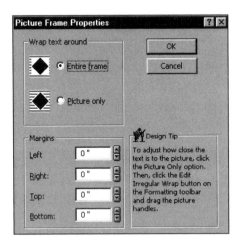

Figure 18-31: Choosing the text wrap options for the picture frame

Figure 18-32 illustrates the difference between wrapping text around the frame and wrapping it around the picture. You must set an outside margin around the picture if you plan to wrap text around the picture rather than around the frame. (For more information, see Chapter 10.)

Figure 18-32: Use only one type of wrap per publication, for consistency.

Applying layering

You can layer objects on top of other objects — text frames on top of pictures, or tables on top of drawings, for example. You might layer one frame on top of another to create various design effects. Whether you're layering frames or drawing elements (ovals, lines, and rectangles), you can easily switch the position of any object within the layer.

Using the Arrange menu, you can choose to bring an object forward or send it backward, to change its position in the stack by one object at a time. You also can send an object all the way to the back of the stack or all the way to the front of the stack.

Figure 18-33 shows a flyer that uses extensive layering. The colored shapes appear to be stacked one on top of the other, and then all shapes are stacked on top of the background frame. Additionally, the frame containing the Grand Opening text is stacked on top of everything.

Figure 18-33: Layering objects to create depth in a publication

For more information about layering, see Chapter 10.

Using guides and the Snap To feature

Publisher provides other tools to help you place objects in your publications. You can use guides and the Snap To feature.

Guides include ruler guides and layout guides. You use layout guides to make sure that your objects are within the margins and columns that you create in your publication. You can create ruler guides to line up certain objects on the page, as well.

The Snap To feature enables you to position an object easily. Snap To works like a magnet to pull the object closer to ruler marks, guides, or other objects on the page. (For more information about these features, see Chapter 8.)

Summary

In this chapter, you learned about using objects in your publications and making them fit the page design. You also learned about the following:

✦ The definition of graphics

✦ The definition of objects

✦ Using text and objects together in a document

In the next chapter, you learn how to add clip art and images to your Publisher publications.

✦   ✦   ✦

Adding Clip Art, Images, Sounds, and Motion Clips to a Publication

You can insert most any file—picture, sound, motion picture, animation, document, and so on—into your publication. Some files work well for the printed publication, such as pictures or clip art, whereas other files work well for Web page designs, such as animations and sound. For information about Web design, see Part VIII.

Clip art includes any drawn images. Cartoons, line art, realistic drawings that include shading, silhouettes, and more. Microsoft includes a clip art collection with Publisher, and even offers an online source for downloading more clip art files. You can also purchase third-party clip art collections; some include a variety of art, and others feature clip art about one subject, such as holidays or business.

Figure 19-1 illustrates two clip art files inserted in a flyer. You can find specific clip art pictures in Microsoft's Clip Gallery just by entering a word, such as **nuts**, in a search text box.

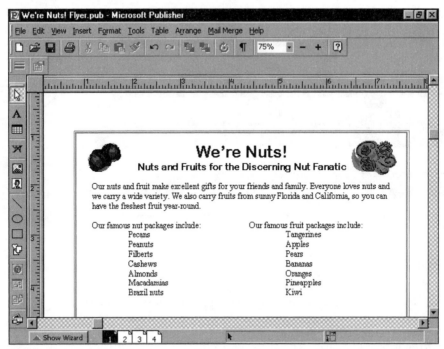

Figure 19-1: Add specific pieces of clip art to a document to enhance the page.

The term *images* refers to photograph files. You can scan photos, use photos provided by Microsoft, take your own photographs by using a digital camera, or use photos from a third-party program or supplier. Photograph files are generally in color and consist of very large files.

Figure 19-2 shows a photograph of a squirrel that has been added to the flyer in Figure 19-1. Photographs are sophisticated and elegant, whereas clip art presents a "fun" look to the publication.

Sound files are perfect to use in a publication that you send via any electronic method, such as e-mail or Web pages, or that you present on an intranet. You can include music clips, animal or mechanical sounds, singing, narration, and a host of other sounds in your publications. Microsoft provides many sound clips, but you can also record your own, purchase a third-party solution, or download sound clips from the Internet, a highly popular source.

Figure 19-3 illustrates the Sounds tab of the Clip Gallery dialog box. A small icon represents a sound in a publication when you insert the sound file. An online user clicks the speaker to hear the sound.

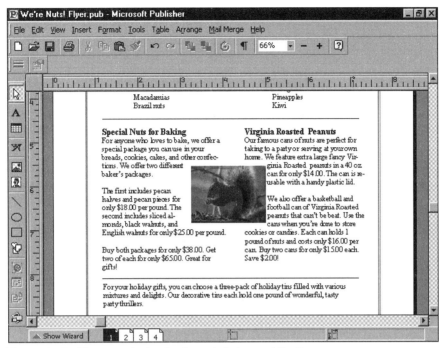

Figure 19-2: Photographs lend a formal air to a publication.

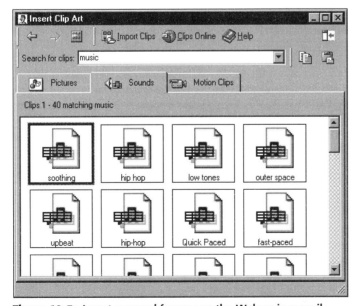

Figure 19-3: Insert a sound for use on the Web or in e-mail.

Animations and motion clips are also excellent for electronic publications. *Animations* include any drawn pictures that move when activated. For example, a cartoon character waving its hand, a line art animal running across the screen, a computer screen displaying a company logo, and so on.

Motion clips are generally thought of as motion picture clips, although they may also include drawn animated clips. Motion picture clips are not necessarily clips taken from an actual movie; they also include short clips made for electronic publication, computer animated photographs and clips, and so on.

Figure 19-4 illustrates the Motion Clips tab of the Clip Gallery dialog box. You can preview a motion clip; the window displays the motion clip so that you can choose whether to use it.

Figure 19-4: Preview motion clips before inserting them into an electronic document.

Using Microsoft's Clip Gallery

Microsoft's Clip Gallery includes clip art, sound clip files, and motion clip files. Microsoft includes many clips with Publisher, and you can add clips to your collection at any time. Clip Gallery makes it easy to add clips to your publications.

Tip   Because Clip Gallery includes so many files, the Gallery itself installs with Publisher, but many of the clips remain on the CD. To use the clips, you must access them from the CD.

When placing clip art or other clips in your publications, make sure that you follow the layout and column guides, as well as all the balance, white space, and consistency guidelines.

Finding and previewing a clip

Before you can preview the clip, you must insert a frame to hold the clip. You use the Clip Gallery tool to create a frame in your document. You can always resize, move, or otherwise manipulate and format the frame after you insert the clip. (See Chapter 10 for more information.)

Your first step is to find the clip. You can open Clip Gallery and choose the type of clip that you want — picture, sound, or motion. Next, you can search for specific clips by category or by subject. When you find the appropriate clip, you can insert or preview the clip. You can also place the clip in a special Favorites folder or search for clips that are similar to the one that you chose.

Creating the frame

To create a clip art frame, click the Clip Gallery tool. Drag the mouse to create the frame within the text. Clip Gallery opens with the Pictures tab of the dialog box showing, as shown in Figure 19-5. The Pictures tab includes photographs and clip art.

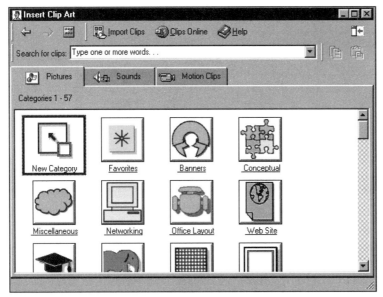

Figure 19-5: Search for just the right clip to insert into your publication.

Choosing the type of clip

You can choose the type of clip that you want in the Clip Gallery dialog box—
pictures, sounds, or motion clips. Click the tab representing the clip that you
want to use.

The Pictures tab lists 57 various categories, such as Cartoons, Business, Food &
Dining, Maps, Nature, Plants, and Web elements. You click a category to view related
clips, as shown in Figure 19-6. The Food & Dining category displays 60 clips.

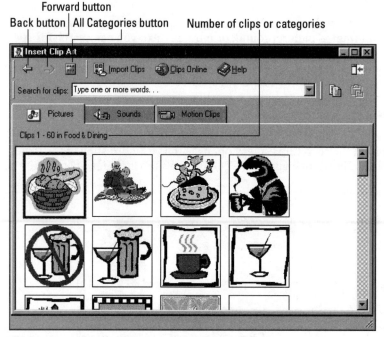

Figure 19-6: Viewing different categories of clips

If you want to go back to the previous category list in a tab, click the Back button.
You can, alternatively, click the All Categories button to view the categories in any
particular tab.

The Sounds tab contains categories such as Music, Household, Industry, Science
and Technology, and so on. Publisher offers a speaker icon to represent a sound,
and a musical staff icon to represent music, as shown in Figure 19-7.

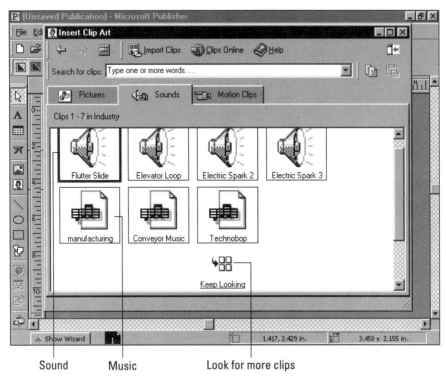

Figure 19-7: Searching through the sound clip categories

At the bottom of some pages of clips, a Keep Looking icon appears. Click this icon to search for more clips within the category that you chose.

The Motion Clips tab contains 50 categories, including Buildings, Government, Metaphors, People, and Places. The motion clips in any category may be based on either a piece of clip art or a motion picture clip.

Searching for clips

You can search for a specific topic in Clip Gallery by entering any word or phrase in the Search for clips text box. The search word that you enter may be very general, such as "business" or "computers," or it may be very specific, such as "laptop computer."

Figure 19-8 illustrates the Pictures tab of the Clip Gallery dialog box, with "laptop computer" in the Search for clips text box, and the search results shown in the window.

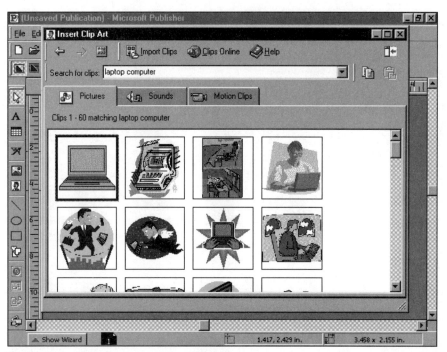

Figure 19-8: Find clips on very specific topics

Tip   If you choose a topic or category in one tab of the dialog box and then select a different tab, Publisher remembers the topic and displays related clips.

Previewing the clip

You can preview any clip in a separate window. The window displays the clip art in an enlarged format, so that you can see the picture better. It shows motion clips with full animation in the same type of window. Publisher displays sound clips in the media player so that you can listen to the clip.

To preview any clip, click on the clip, and a shortcut menu appears, as shown in Figure 19-9. The Preview clip choice appears on clip art only; the Play clip option appears on sound and motion clips. Both icons appear in the second position on the shortcut menu.

Clip art   When you preview a clip art picture, Publisher enlarges the clip in a separate window for you to view. You can select other clips to preview, and the Preview window remains open, displaying any clip that you choose.

To close the Preview window, click the Close (X) button.

Play or Preview Clip   Insert Clip

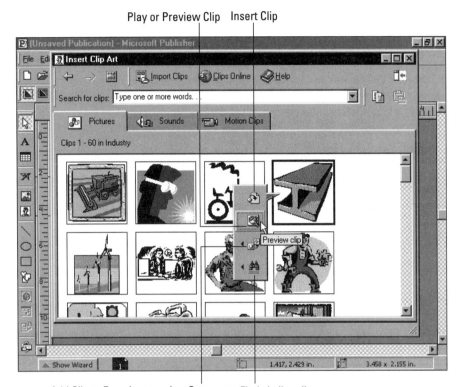

Add Clip to Favorites or other Category   Find similar clips

Figure 19-9: Preview or play a clip.

Sound clips When you preview a sound clip, Publisher displays the media player, as shown in Figure 19-10. The Clip Gallery dialog box remains onscreen. The player contains the name of the file in the title bar. Pause and Stop buttons appear on the media player; if you click the Pause button, it changes to a Play button. Click the Play button to resume play. When the sound has finished playing, the media player closes. If it doesn't close, you can click the Close button in the media player box.

Figure 19-10: Play a sound clip before you insert it into a publication.

Motion clips Each preview of a motion clip appears in its own window — the GIF Player window. The window remains open, and the clip plays over and over until you close it. Figure 19-11 illustrates a clip playing in the GIF Player window.

To close the clip, click the Close button.

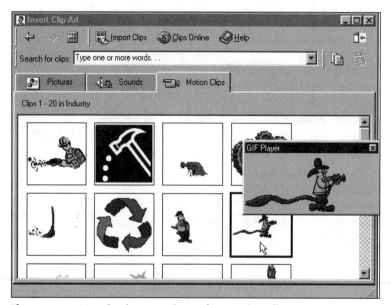

Figure 19-11: Previewing an animated or motion clip

Inserting the clip

You can insert any clip into your document. Click the clip and then choose the Insert Clip icon on the menu. Clip Gallery remains open. You can either close Clip Gallery by clicking the Close button, or minimize it to the Taskbar, if you want to use it again later.

When you close Clip Gallery, the chosen clip appears in your document. You can then resize, move, or change the frame containing the clip. Figure 19-12 illustrates a clip art, sound clip, and motion clip as they appear in a document.

You can double-click a clip in your publication to reopen the Clip Gallery dialog box. Any clip that you choose replaces the original one.

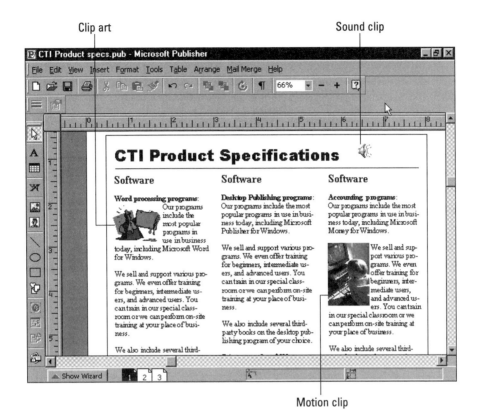

Figure 19-12: Apply any of various clips to a publication.

Editing a clip's frame

You can edit the frame of a clip just as you would any Publisher frame. You can resize the frame by selecting it and then moving one of the sizing handles. Move a frame by dragging it to a new position. You also can perform the following edits on a clip's frame:

✦ Add a background to a clip art frame by applying fill

✦ Add a border to the frame

✦ Increase inside margins to add a fill around the outer edge of a photograph

✦ Wrap text around the frame or the picture

Editing the clip art or photo

Besides editing the frame in which the clip is placed, you can edit the clip itself. Whether it's a photograph or a piece of clip art, you can recolor, scale, and crop any picture. Although any clip art or photograph looks good in a publication, editing the color, shape, or size might suit the material better than the original clip or photograph does.

Note You also can access commands for editing clip art by right-clicking the selected art piece.

Recoloring a picture

When you recolor a picture, you apply tints and shades of one color to the picture. The original clip art or photograph may be in multiple colors; however, Publisher changes the color to match the one that you choose.

For example, if you choose a shade of blue to apply to a photograph, Publisher changes the photo to tints and shades of that blue. You might use this technique for an artistic effect, to match other colors that you use in the piece, or to make the photograph look less real and more like a drawing.

Tip Use picture recoloring to create a very light picture in the background of a page, as in a watermark.

You also can choose to retain any of the black shading or lines in the picture, to highlight and define part of the picture. Figure 19-13 illustrates a color photograph recolored, with the black parts left black. The rest of the photo uses tints and shades of gray.

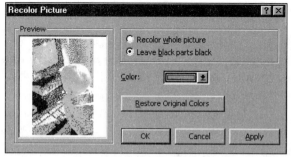

Figure 19-13: You can use any color—red, purple, blue, and so on—to recolor the photo.

When you recolor clip art, the effect is a bit different. Publisher uses the color that you choose plus some other, related colors in the art. You also can choose to leave the black parts black.

To recolor a picture, follow these steps:

1. Select the picture.

2. Choose Format ➪ Recolor Picture. The Recolor Picture dialog box appears, with the picture in the Preview area of the dialog box (refer to Figure 19-13).

3. In the dialog box, choose a Color from the drop-down dialog box, as shown in Figure 19-14. You can choose to use a scheme color, a recently used color, any color from the More Colors dialog box, or tints and shades from the Fill Effects dialog box.

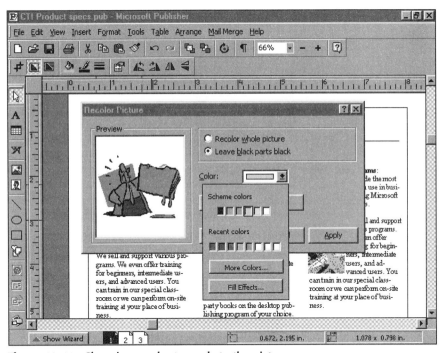

Figure 19-14: Choosing a color to apply to the picture

4. Choose either Recolor whole picture or Leave black parts black.

5. Check the preview. You can either change the color, or click the Restore Original Colors button to change the picture back to its original state.

 Tip   You can return at any time to the Recolor Picture dialog box to change the picture or restore the original colors. Coloring the clip art has no effect on the color in the original art; you're only coloring one copy.

6. Click OK.

Scaling a picture

Scaling a picture is a method of distorting it to change the *aspect ratio* (height versus width). Any original picture is proportioned correctly for its height and width. You can change the aspect ratio percentage to make the picture better fit the page or the text, or to create an artistic effect.

Figure 19-15, for example, applies to the figure on the left an aspect ratio of nearly two to one. The scale height is 25 percent and the scale width is 42 percent. On the other hand, the photograph at the right uses a different ratio. The scale height is 145 percent and the scale width is 95 percent.

You also can choose at any time to change the picture back to its original size.

Figure 19-15: Using scaling to make more decorative pictures

To scale a picture, follow these steps:

1. Select the picture.

2. Choose Format ⇨ Scale Picture. The Scale Picture dialog box appears, as shown in Figure 19-16.

Nature's Banquet

Color Plate 1: Contrasting colors and a WordArt design create a logo for a magazine.

WILD EDIBLES

Wild Grapes are Delicious

Wild grapes offer a variety of foods and uses for us. The fruit, leaves, and young shoots are all edible. The vines make wonderful wreaths, ornaments, and sculptures. And the leaves are often used in Middle Eastern foods as a wrap for some tasty meat and rice treats.

You can eat the grape leaves too, although they do have a slightly acidic flavor. Gather the leaves in the spring. You can freeze or can stacks of grape leaves for later use.

Stuff the grape leaves with lamb, veal, or ground beef mixtures. Rice is always a good addition, as are celery and marjoram. Bake the stuffed leaves with fresh tomatoes and basil poured over them for a wonderfully satisfying meal. You might try using game birds in place of the lamb or veal. Grouse is great with grape leaves.

Coriander as a Medicine

We all know about coriander's wonderful flavor in Indian, Japanese, and Chinese cooking. Whether you're crushing seeds for a strong, aromatic flavor or clipping leaves for that delicate hint of greenery, coriander is a useful and very edible herb.

Coriander is also a medicinal herb. The seed can be used as an antispasmodic, appetizer, and aromatic. Coriander has a settling effect on the stomach; you can also use it as a carminative and stomachic. Use coriander externally for rheumatism and painful joints. Or, use it to improve the flavor of other medicinal preparations.

Prepare medicines as an infusion by steeping 2 teaspoons of dried seeds in a cup of boiling water. Store the infusion in the fridge. Take 1 cup per day as needed.

Eucalyptus as Deodorant?

The eucalyptus, or blue gum, is an evergreen that is native to Australia. One species is the blue gum, which is grown here in the United States in California, Florida and other southern states. The eucalyptus is a tree also found in Tasmania.

You can use eucalyptus as a deodorant and you've probably seen many commercial deodorants based on the tree in the store. Make a cold extract from the eucalyptus leaves and use it externally. In addition to deodorant, you can use eucalyptus oil on wounds and ulcers.

Other medicinal uses of the eucalyptus include antiseptic, expectorant, and stimulant. You've likely seen cough drops and cough syrups made of the stuff. You also can use eucalyptus as an antiseptic bath for burns, indigestion, and reducing fevers.

Preparing for Fall

Now's the time to think about your fall collections. You should go out and search for the plants you want to gather in the fall now, while they are growing tall and easily recognizable. Some plants, like cattails, will be easy to spot in the fall. But other plants, such as chickweed and prickly pear may hide in the fall months when the foliage disappears. So get out there and find those plants—mark them with ribbons if necessary, make a map, whatever it takes to find them.

Color Plate 2: A magazine page uses a bleeding header in colors that match the page design, photos, and clip art.

Color Plate 3: Silhouettes of blue and red letters create a simple yet eye-catching logo.

Color Plate 4:
The colorful watermark provides the background for red and green type; the multicolored borders tie the piece together.

MANSON'S LANDSCAPING

MARCH SPECIALS:

All Bulbs	40% Off
Trees	10% Off
Shrubbery	10% Off
House Plants	20% Off
Mulch	20% Off

1244 East Main Street
Fayetteville
Hours: 9 am to 5 pm Daily

Color Plate 5: Recolor a picture to one tint and leave out the black parts to push the photo further into the background.

Oak Hill International Airport Restaurant

DIRECTORY

◆ Airport Info

◆ Specialties

◆ Hours

◆ Gift Shop

◆ Oak Hill

◆ Shopping

◆ Reservations

◆ Duty Free

If you think a lay-over is only a miserable delay in your trip, then plan your trip to include Oak Hill International Airport Restaurant, offering home made food served in a comfortable atmosphere. Relax as you dine in luxury atop the elevated restaurant overlooking Oak Hill's city lights.

Color Plate 6: The red, green, and purple attract browsers to this Web page; the plentiful white space provides a rest for the Net surfer's eyes.

HUMBLE OPINIONS
Computer Consultants

Vol. 2, Issue 5   May 1999

Whose Humble Opinions?

If you're new to our newsletter and services, you may not really know who we are here at Humble Opinions. And many of you may know some of us but are curious about the rest of us. This little introduction will help you get to know the members of our staff and the owners.

We provide outsourcing to help with your hurried deadlines...

As networking consultants, we can advise you about your hardware and software purchases, installation, and configuration. We also help you maintain your network and troubleshoot system problems.

Sue and Carlos are partners in Humble Opinions. Sue started the business in 1988 as a software training and consultant. She worked for multiple corporations and individuals.

In 1992, Sue began writing books for various publishers. Since 1992, Sue has authored 35 books and co-authored over 35 more.

Carlos joined Humble Opinions in 1994, after managing several computer stores. Carlos' exper-

tise is networking and equipment troubleshooting. He widened the customer base with new services. Carlos brings to the business a knowledge of various peer-to-peer and client/server networks; printer and hardware repair; and software installation and configuration.

Sue's expertise is in software configuration and operation, operating systems, most Windows products, desktop publishing, and training. Sue's degree, in fact, is in art education; so her skills lend themselves very well to teaching and producing publications and documents.

In addition to the owners, Humble Opinions includes several technicians. Mark has years of experience in hardware and printer repair. He also installs cables and networks, and configures various brands of client/server networks.

As consultants, we feel that selling products would be in direct conflict with our primary purpose. After all, if we sold a cer-

What about the Web?

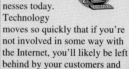

Many people ask about the use of the Internet in their businesses today. Technology moves so quickly that if you're not involved in some way with the Internet, you'll likely be left behind by your customers and your competition.

At the very least, you should have an Internet connection that provides your company with e-mail, a Web browser, and perhaps newsgroups.

Humble Opinions can help you install and configure an Internet browser and e-mail application. We also can provide you with information about area ISPs (Internet Service Providers), prices, on-line times, and such.

Finally we can provide you with information about more involved uses of the Web, such as e-commerce, VPNs, and more. Call today for more information.

Color Plate 7: The yellow appears as a background on which green frames float; the use of bright colors add pizazz to the newsletter page.

Many animals aren't as lucky as these...

Please contribute
to the

**Daines County
Animal Shelter**

304-555-4357
or
304-555-HELP

12211 S. Kanawha
Charleston, WV 25303

Color Plate 8: Use bright colors and large photos in a flyer to attract attention.

JADE'S PLANTS & SCULPTURES
Offering a wide variety of house plants, landscaping
trees and plants, and garden sculptures.

1136 E. Miller Street • Beckley • 800-555-3347

Color Plate 9: The large photograph attracts attention in this ad; the photo frame provides a border of color and text area.

Color Plate 10: Contrasting colors and vertical text help make this ad a standout.

DANCE LTD

Performances Nightly
8:00 PM

IntraTech Services is quickly becoming the largest Internet service provider in the United States. We want you to use us as a provider so we are offering more services for your business. Included in our services are e-mail, newsgroups, World Wide Web connection, intranet configuration, and extranets that reach across the world. We can supply you with Web page creation and space on our server for a personal or company Web site. We'll even help you design your Web page.

Color Plate 11: The MS Draw half-circle overlaps the photograph to create a space for the text and logo for this ad; matching colors make the ad unified.

Functional Pottery

Potters normally create perfectly symmetrical pots from solid pieces of clay. Turning the clay on a wheel lends itself to forming those hollow, round forms.

SJ Bender is no different. Some of her pottery is picture perfect—symmetrical, flawless, and wonderful. SJ's tour de force is functional pottery. Jars and covers, plates, vases, and other useful pots of all kinds are standard.

You'll not find more perfect pieces than in SJ's workshop in Fayetteville.

SJ also likes to play with her clay. She does a lot of hand-built pieces. SJ's famous fun boxes and sculptures are often bought by corporations as well as individuals. You can view her works at her studio in Fayetteville.

Raku

Raku is a form of firing pottery using an outside kiln. Ceremonial teabowls originating in Japan a few hundred years ago were made using raku. The pottery is glazed and then thrust into a red-hot kiln with tongs. The pots are left in the kiln just long enough for the glaze to melt.

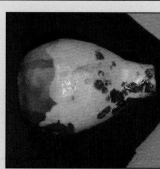

When removed from the kiln, the pottery is placed in dried leaves, straw, or other organic materials and covered to reduce the oxygen in the environment. Then the pots are removed from the natural materials and thrust into cold water. The effect is glorious—cracked glazes and oxidized ceramics. SJ's raku is among the very best. You'll have to see it to believe it.

Pottery
by
SJ Bender

Wheel-thrown and hand-built, stoneware, earthenware, raku— the pottery of SJ Bender is like none other.

Terrance Smythe

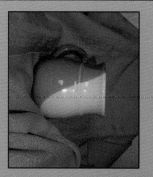

Visit the studio:
127 Old Miller's Road
Fayetteville, West Virginia
304-555-8115

Color Plate 12: Frame backgrounds present earthtone fills that match the photographs; notice the borders around the text frames repeat the photograph borders.

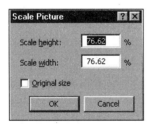

Figure 19-16: Scale a picture to add an artistic effect to it.

3. In Scale height, enter a percentage. In Scale width, enter a percentage.

4. Click OK to view the change.

You can always choose to Undo the scaling process (press Ctrl+Z), or choose to return the picture to its original size in the Scale Picture dialog box.

After you scale a picture, you can resize it by using the sizing handles. Publisher maintains the assigned aspect ratio only if you resize by using a corner handle. If you use a side handle, Publisher distorts the picture to fit the size.

Cropping a picture

You also can *crop* a picture (cut off a piece of the picture) to make it better suit your text or space. For example, you might want to cut some dead space off the top or bottom, or crop out an entire area of the picture.

To crop a picture, follow these steps:

1. Select the picture.

2. Choose Format ⇨ Crop Picture.

3. Position the mouse pointer over any one of the sizing handles to display the Cropping tool, as shown in Figure 19-17. Use the tool to drag the handle to crop a side or corner of the picture.

4. Drag the sizing handle toward the center of the picture until you've cropped off all you want. You can continue to crop from any side of the picture. You also can move the picture, if you want, while cropping; position the pointer to see the MOVE mouse pointer, and then drag the picture to a new position.

5. After you finish cropping, choose Format ⇨ Crop Picture again to deactivate the command.

Cropping Tool

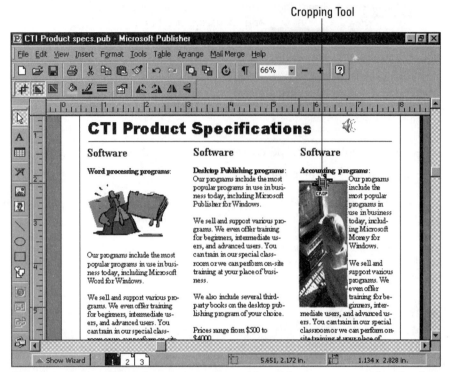

Figure 19-17: Crop from the top, bottom, or either side, or crop two sides simultaneously by dragging a corner handle.

Importing clips to Clip Gallery

You can import into Clip Gallery any picture, sound, or motion clips that you have on your hard drive or that you find on the Web. Any imported clips are then available for you to use at any time. Microsoft has a specific Web site for you to use to import clips, as well.

Importing local clips

Local clips are any files that you have on your computer. After you import the clip, it is easy to find in Clip Gallery and is available for use with other publications.

Publisher enables you to import clips from floppy disks, CD-ROM drives, and network drives. When you import a clip, you can copy or move it, or direct Clip Gallery to leave the clip where it is, and then access it when you want it.

To import local clips, follow these steps:

   1. In the Clip Gallery dialog box, click Import Clips, as shown in Figure 19-18.

Import Clips Clips Online

Figure 19-18: Add clips from your local drive to Clip Gallery.

2. In the Add clip to Clip Gallery dialog box (Figure 19-19), choose the location, folder, and picture file of the local clip that you want to import.

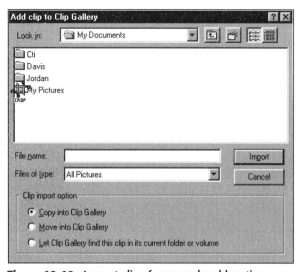

Figure 19-19: Import clips from any local location.

3. In the Clip import option area, choose one of the following options:

   • Copy into Clip Gallery

   • Move into Clip Gallery

   • Let Clip Gallery find this clip in its current folder or volume

4. Click Import. Clip Gallery adds the clip.

Importing clips from the Web

You also can import clips from the Web. You can use Microsoft's clip art site, or you can find other clips to import. You must connect to the Web before you can import clips; therefore, you need a modem, communications software, and an Internet connection. Microsoft's site is called Clip Gallery Live.

To import clips from the Web, follow these steps:

1. Connect to the Web.

2. Open the Clip Gallery dialog box.

3. Click the Clips Online button. Publisher displays the Connect to Web for More Clip Art, Photos, Sounds dialog box, shown in Figure 19-20.

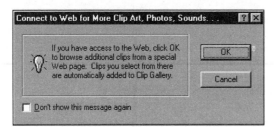

Figure 19-20: Connect to the Web to import clips.

4. Click OK. Publisher opens Microsoft Internet Explorer, or another installed browser, and locates the Microsoft page that supplies clips.

5. You must read and accept an end-user license agreement from Microsoft before you can access the clip art. Figure 19-21 illustrates Clip Gallery Live.

Choose type of clip

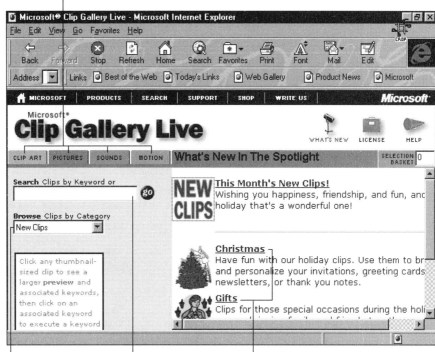

Search categories   Search for a subject   Use links to special topic

Figure 19-21: Search for clips on the Web from Microsoft's Clip Gallery Live.

6. Select the type of clip you want: Clip Art, Pictures, Sounds, or Motion.

7. Use the Search or Browse text boxes to find the clip you want. Clip Gallery Live displays a set of clips for which you're searching. Below each clip is the size of the clip, a Download Now arrow, and a check box, as shown in Figure 19-22.

Selection Basket

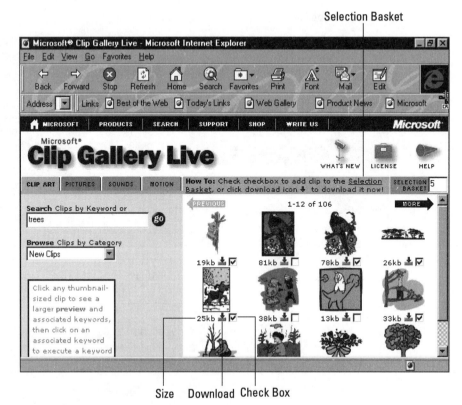

Size   Download Check Box

Figure 19-22: Choose the pictures that you want from Clip Gallery Live.

8. Click the Download Now arrow if you want to download clips one at a time. Click the check box to insert a check mark if you want to choose several clips and then download them all at one time. The Selection Basket keeps a record of the number of clips that you're choosing.

9. If you are downloading several clips, click the Selection Basket link after you finish choosing clips. Publisher displays the clips that you've selected, as shown in Figure 19-23.

10. Click Download to complete the process. Microsoft displays a progress dialog box as it downloads the clips.

11. When you're finished, exit the browser and disconnect from the Internet.

Publisher displays the new clips in the appropriate tab of the Clip Gallery dialog box, in the Downloaded Clips category.

Download

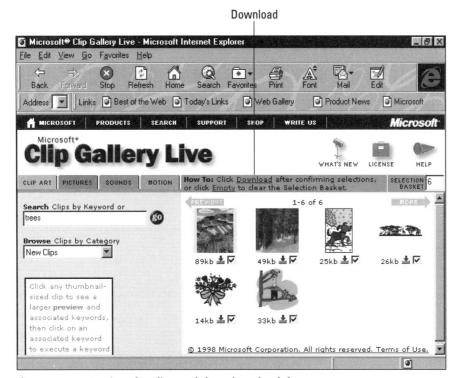

Figure 19-23: Review the clips and then download them.

Looking at Examples

You can use clip art and pictures in your publications, whether you plan to print them or use them online. You can use sounds and motion clips with any publication that will be viewed online, or you can use them with your Web documents.

You should use plenty of graphics in any electronic publication, such as a Web page, or a newsletter that you e-mail. You want to catch the reader's attention and take advantage of the technology. You don't, however, want to overdo it. Try to be consistent, use plenty of white space, and balance objects on the page.

Figure 19-24 illustrates a Web page that uses clip art, photographs, and motion clips for the home page. The CTI logo appears beside the name of the company. Text and art are divided on the page by horizontal lines. The four photos and clip art pictures at the bottom of the page are also links to other Web pages and sites.

Figure 19-24: Use clips for links in Web pages.

Figure 19-25 is a Web page within the same site as the one shown in the preceding figure. The logo and company name repeat, as do navigation buttons, to lead the viewer to various other pages in the site. The image consists of a motion clip linked to a music clip, so that when the page appears, both the sound and the animation play.

Note, too, in the figure how the image points into the page, to guide the reader's eyes. Also, white space on the page gives the reader's eyes a rest.

Figure 19-25: Use motion clips and sounds on Web pages.

Figure 19-26 illustrates page one of an electronic newsletter. The plant in the background is a recolored clip art. Also, note that the lower-right corner contains a sound clip. The recipient double-clicks the clip and then hears an announcement of a sale at the herb and plant store.

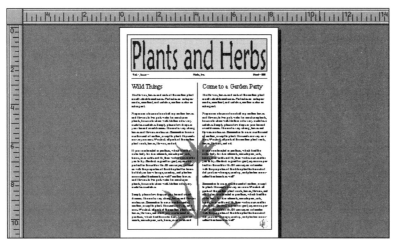

Figure 19-26: Include clips and sounds in electronic publications.

Figure 19-27 shows page two of the newsletter that's sent electronically. The placement of the pictures repeats the symmetrical balance. The size, shape, and formatting of the picture frames are similar, which helps to keep the elements on the page consistent. Two of the clips are motion clips that make the page more interesting.

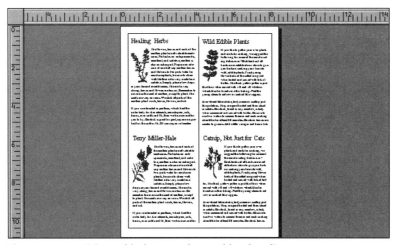

Figure 19-27: A formal balance enhanced by the clips.

Summary

In this chapter, you learned about using Microsoft's Clip Gallery to spice up your publications. Specifically, you learned about the following:

✦ Defining terms

✦ Inserting clip art and pictures

✦ Inserting sounds and motion clips

✦ Importing clips

In the next chapter, you learn about creating drawings with Microsoft Draw.

✦   ✦   ✦

Drawing with Microsoft Draw

Microsoft Draw is an Office applet included with Publisher. When you create a Microsoft Draw picture, you're drawing within Publisher by means of Draw tools. Publisher's menus and toolbars change to use Draw's menus and toolbars.

Some Draw tools exist on the Object toolbar—the Line, Rectangle, and Oval tools, for example. You can use these tools to create a quick line or box at any time, without creating a frame or opening the Draw applet.

Tip   Any drawing that you create in Draw is an object in Publisher. After you close the Draw program, you treat the Draw frame as any other in your publication.

When you want to create a more detailed or more complex drawing, however, or edit a drawing or piece of clip art, you can use the Draw toolbars to help you. Figure 20-1 illustrates Publisher when you open Microsoft Draw. Draw changes the menus to reflect commands related to drawing and formatting text in your drawings. A selected frame surrounds the drawing, and the AutoShapes and Drawing toolbars appear.

Using Microsoft Draw

When you draw lines, shapes, and so forth in Microsoft Draw, you work within the frame provided. If you click outside the frame, the Draw tools disappear and the Publisher window becomes active again. You can double-click any Draw frame to redisplay Draw's toolbars and work in a Draw frame.

Tip

You cannot change views or use Zoom within Microsoft Draw. Zoom to the view that you want to work in *before* you start the Draw applet.

Formatting toolbar   Standard toolbar   Microsoft Draw menus   AutoShapes toolbar

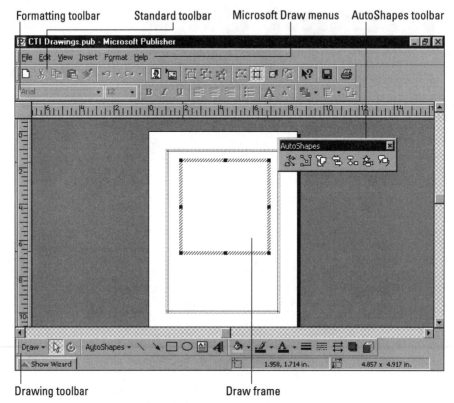

Drawing toolbar   Draw frame

Figure 20-1: Use the Microsoft Draw toolbars to help create a drawing.

To open Microsoft Draw, follow these steps:

1. Within Publisher, change to the view that you want to use, such as 66 percent.

2. Choose Insert ➪ Picture ➪ New Drawing. The Draw tools, menu, and frame appear.

3. Resize the frame to suit your working space. You treat the Draw frame just as you would a text or picture frame in Publisher; however, if you click outside of the frame, Draw closes and Publisher reactivates.

4. To close Draw, click anywhere outside of the draw frame. To edit a Draw picture, double-click the Draw frame.

Using Microsoft Draw menus

You'll also notice that Microsoft Draw replaces many of Publisher's menus with its own. Although the menu names are the same, the commands apply mainly to the Draw picture and program. The following list describes the Microsoft Draw menus:

✦ **File:** Contains Publisher's File menu commands, which include the New, Open, and Close publication commands, plus Save, Exit, Print, and so on.

✦ **Edit:** Contains commands that apply to your Draw objects. You can Undo, Cut, Copy, Paste, Clear, Select All, and Duplicate any drawing objects.

✦ **View:** Contains the Ruler and Toolbars commands. The available Draw toolbars include Standard, Formatting, Drawing, Picture, and WordArt.

✦ **Insert:** Contains commands to insert objects, such as clip art, WordArt, text boxes, and pictures, into a drawing, as well as commands to insert lines, basic shapes, block arrows, and other AutoShapes.

✦ **Format:** Contains commands to change text within your drawing. You can format fonts, paragraphs, bullets, colors, shadow settings, and other elements of the drawing.

✦ **Help:** Contains commands to get Draw-specific help. Help comes in Content and Index form and works similarly to Publisher's Help feature.

Using the Standard and Formatting toolbars

The Standard and Formatting toolbars include various buttons with which you already are familiar. The Standard toolbar, for example, has Copy and Paste buttons, Undo and Redo buttons, and other buttons that are the same as Publisher's Standard toolbar buttons. The Formatting toolbar includes Font and Font Size boxes, Bold and Italic buttons, and other options that the Publisher Formatting toolbar contains.

Both the Standard and Formatting toolbars have buttons that apply only to Draw. Figure 20-2 describes the toolbar buttons for both the Standard (top) and Formatting (bottom) toolbars.

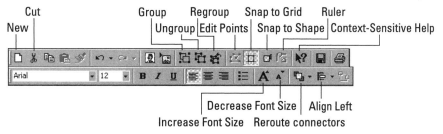

Figure 20-2: Use the Standard and Formatting toolbars with your drawing.

The following list describes those tools (buttons) on the Standard toolbar with which you may be unfamiliar:

✦ **New:** Creates a new publication.

✦ **Cut:** Moves the selected object to the Clipboard.

✦ **Group:** Joins selected objects and treats them as one, for editing and moving purposes.

✦ **Ungroup:** Separates grouped objects so that they no longer are treated as one object.

✦ **Regroup:** Rejoins previously grouped objects that currently are ungrouped.

✦ **Edit Points:** Changes the shape of the selected object or curve.

✦ **Snap to Grid:** When creating or moving a drawing object, this tool aligns it to an invisible grid.

✦ **Snap to Shape:** When creating or moving an object, this button aligns it to an invisible grid that goes through another object.

✦ **Ruler:** Displays or hides the ruler.

✦ **Context-Sensitive Help:** Similar to the Help feature in a dialog box, a specific Help box appears when you click this button and then click a tool or object about which you have a question.

The following list describes those tools (buttons) on the Formatting toolbar with which you may be unfamiliar:

✦ **Increase Font Size:** Increases the selected text by 2 points.

✦ **Decrease Font Size:** Decreases the selected text by 2 points.

✦ **Align Left:** Aligns all selected objects vertically along their left edges.

✦ **Reroute Connectors:** Changes the connector lines so that they take the shortest route between two shapes. *Connector lines* are lines that link, or join, two shapes, such as the lines connecting the rectangles in an organizational chart.

Using the Drawing toolbar

The Drawing toolbar supplies lines, shapes, colors, and formatting elements for you to use with your drawings. Figure 20-3 illustrates the Drawing toolbar. Many of the tools are shortcuts for the Draw menus.

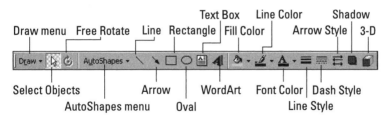

Figure 20-3: Use the Drawing toolbar to create and format lines and shapes.

The following list describes each tool on the Drawing toolbar:

✦ **Draw menu:** Contains commands that you can use as you create or edit your drawings, such as Rotate, Flip, Align, Group, and so on. Many of the commands also have buttons elsewhere in the window that you can use for shortcuts.

✦ **Select Objects:** Provides a mouse pointer that you can use to select, move, resize, and otherwise manipulate objects in the Draw program.

✦ **Free Rotate:** Enables you to turn, or spin, objects.

✦ **AutoShapes menu:** Contains the same AutoShape categories — Lines, Connectors, Basic Shapes, Block Arrows, Flowchart, Stars and Banners, and Callouts — that appear on the AutoShapes toolbar.

✦ **Line:** Creates a straight line.

✦ **Arrow:** Draws a line with an arrow point on one end.

✦ **Rectangle:** Creates a rectangle or a perfect square.

✦ **Oval:** Draws an oval or a perfect circle.

✦ **Text Box:** Enables you to create text in your drawing; this is *not* the same tool as a text frame in Publisher, although it does create a text frame, of sorts.

✦ **Insert WordArt:** Enables you to create a WordArt graphic within your drawing.

✦ **Fill Color:** Enables you to fill a shape with a color or pattern; works similarly to Fill Color in Publisher.

✦ **Line Color:** Enables you to color any line with any color or pattern; works similarly to Line Color in Publisher.

✦ **Font Color:** Enables you to apply color to any text that you create in the drawing.

✦ **Line Style:** Enables you to select from various line thicknesses and line styles.

✦ **Dash Style:** Enables you to select from various dashed-line styles.

✦ **Arrow Style:** Enables you to select from various styles of arrowheads and ends. Arrowheads appear at one end of a line and represent a pointer; ends appear at the opposite extremity of the line.

✦ **Shadow:** Enables you to select from multiple shadows to apply to your shapes.

✦ **3-D:** Enables you to select from various 3-D effects to apply to a shape.

Using the AutoShapes toolbar

The AutoShapes toolbar (as well as the AutoShapes menu) offers various common shapes that you can insert into your drawing. You can then edit, resize, format, and otherwise manipulate the shapes.

Figure 20-4 illustrates the tools on the AutoShapes toolbar. It also illustrates how the buttons on the toolbar work. When you click a button, a drop-down menu displays available tools.

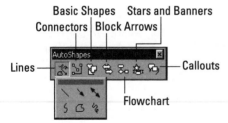

Figure 20-4: Use the AutoShapes toolbar to help you create various shapes.

The following list describes the tools on the AutoShapes toolbar:

✦ **Lines:** Choose a type of line — straight, arrow, curved, freeform, or scribble.

✦ **Connectors:** Draw connecting lines between two objects, such as when you're creating a flow chart.

✦ **Basic Shapes:** Create basic shapes, including squares, parallelograms, triangles, crosses, cylinders, hearts, and others.

✦ **Block Arrows:** Create arrows, including curved, double-headed, and various other arrow shapes.

✦ **Flowchart:** Create shapes similar to basic shapes, such as rectangles, diamonds, cylinders, triangles, and other shapes, and use them with the connectors to create a flowchart or other useful things.

✦ **Stars and Banners:** Use any of eight star shapes and eight banner shapes in your documents.

✦ **Callouts:** Use in your drawing and add text to the shapes. Callouts look like the comic strip balloons that indicate what cartoon characters are saying.

Note   To delete any line, shape, or AutoShape, select the object and then press the Delete key.

Working with Lines and Arrows

In Chapter 18, you learned a bit about drawing lines to separate text, create borders, and so on. You also use lines to create drawings in Publisher. Within the Draw frame, you can create the same lines, and then apply colors, thicknesses, and styles to them. You also can create lines with arrowheads on them.

Tip   To create a larger variety of lines, including scribbles, curves, and arrows, use Draw's AutoShapes. For more information, see the following section about AutoShapes.

Figure 20-5 illustrates a variety of horizontal lines that you can create with Draw. The thickness of the lines vary; the positioning of the lines creates an optical illusion, of sorts.

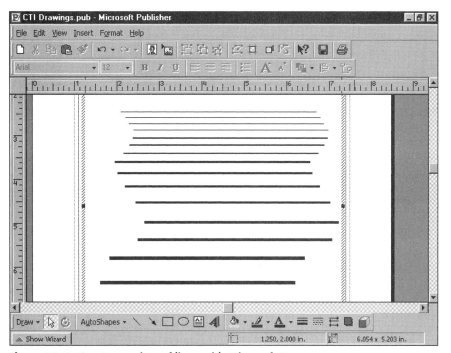

Figure 20-5: Create a variety of lines with Microsoft Draw.

Drawing lines and arrows

You can draw a line or arrow by using the same technique. Click the Line or Arrow button on the Drawing toolbar and then drag within the Draw frame. For a perfectly straight line, hold down the Shift key as you draw. Do not release the Shift key until after you release the mouse button.

Figure 20-6 illustrates several arrows drawn over the horizontal lines. You can draw a line or arrow in any direction within the frame.

To draw a curve, freeform, or scribble line, click any tool on the AutoShapes toolbar that represents the type of shape that you want to draw, and then draw the line.

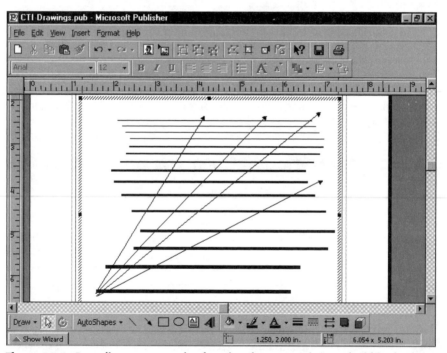

Figure 20-6: Draw lines or arrows by dragging the appropriate tool within the frame.

When drawing the curved line, draw a segment and then single-click the mouse when you want to change line direction; double-click the mouse when you want to stop drawing the curve. The same goes for the Freeform line — double-click the mouse to stop drawing the line.

Editing lines and arrows

You can change the position and length of any line or arrow. Select a line by clicking it. Both lines and arrows display selection handles that you can use to resize or edit them, as shown in Figure 20-7. Select multiple lines by holding down the Shift key as you click subsequent lines or arrows; or, you can draw a rectangular box around any number of objects by using the selection pointer.

To move an arrow or line, follow these steps:

1. Select the line or arrow.
2. Position the mouse selection pointer on the line, so that you see a four-headed arrow. Drag the line to where you want it.

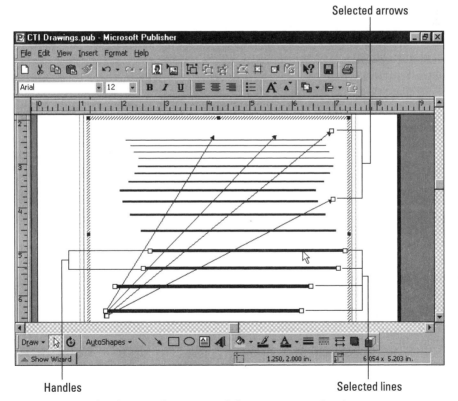

Selected arrows

Handles

Selected lines

Figure 20-7: Select lines and arrows, and then move or resize them.

To move multiple lines or arrows, follow these steps:

1. Select the lines or arrows.

2. Position the selection pointer over any one of the selected lines or arrows.

3. Drag the one line or arrow; the others move with it.

To resize a line or arrow, follow these steps:

1. Select the line or arrow.

2. Position the mouse selection pointer over one handle until it changes to a double-headed arrow.

3. Drag the handle to resize the line. To create a straight line, hold down the Shift key as you drag the handle.

 Tip To move or resize a line or arrow so that it rotates from a center point, select the line, press and hold down the Ctrl key, and then drag one end or the other. The line remains locked in the center position, rotating and resizing at the same time.

To resize or move an AutoShape line, follow these steps:

1. Select the line. Instead of handles appearing on the line ends, an invisible frame outlines the line, and handles appear around the edges of the frame.

2. Move the frame as you would any other frame.

3. Resize the line by dragging the handles to change the shape of the frame, and thus the length of the line.

Formatting lines and arrows

You can apply various line styles, colors, and arrowheads to lines and arrows. You can create a line, for example, change the thickness and color, and then apply an arrowhead to it.

Applying line styles

You can apply various line styles, such as $1/4$ point or 6 point, to lines and arrows. You also can apply a double or triple line to any line in your drawing, or apply various dotted and dashed line styles to any line or arrow.

To apply line styles to a line, AutoShape line, or an arrow, follow these steps:

1. Select the lines or arrows.

2. Click the Line Style or Dash Style button on the Drawing toolbar. The Line Style menu appears, shown in Figure 20-8.

3. Select the line style to change the selected lines or arrows.

If you want, you can choose More Lines at the bottom of the Line Style pop-up menu to display the Format AutoShape dialog box. Lines are also considered AutoShapes in Microsoft Draw. Figure 20-9 illustrates the Format AutoShape dialog box. Table 20-1 explains the options.

Note

The Format AutoShape dialog box applies to shapes, lines, pictures, and text, depending on the selected element. For example, if you choose the More Arrows command on the Arrow pop-up menu, you'll see the same options as displayed in the Format AutoShape dialog box. Some options may not apply to the selected object. If you're formatting lines, for example, the fill and text options don't apply. When you choose to format a picture, text, or other object, the name of the Format AutoShape dialog box changes to Format Picture, Format Text, and so on.

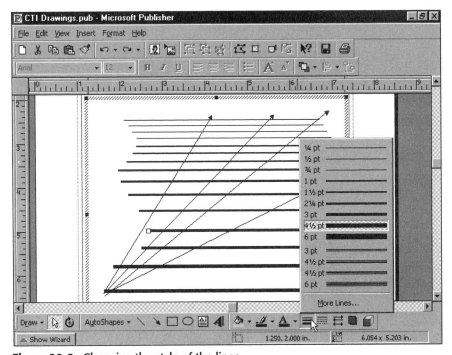

Figure 20-8: Changing the style of the lines

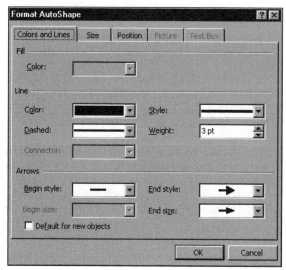

Figure 20-9: Format lines in more detail in the
Format AutoShape dialog box.

Table 20-1
Format AutoShape Dialog Box Options

Tab	Options
Colors and Lines	Choose fill or line color, line style and weight, connector style, arrowhead styles, and arrowheads and endings
Size	Enter the object's height and width, degrees of rotation, and scaling height and width, or reset to its original size
Position	Indicate the horizontal and vertical position within the Draw frame
Picture	Indicate cropping position from any one or more sides, and adjust the color and brightness of the image
Text Box	Indicate the vertical alignment of the text within the box, any internal margins, and the degree of text rotation

Tip   You can also double-click any Draw object to open the Format AutoShape
dialog box.

Applying arrowhead styles

You can apply various types of heads to an arrow, plus you can choose to insert an ending, such as a circle or diamond, to either end of the arrow. Figure 20-10 illustrates the Arrow pop-up menu. If you choose More Arrows at the bottom of the menu, the Format AutoShape dialog box appears (refer to Table 20-1 for available options).

To apply arrowhead styles to a line or an arrow, follow these steps:

1. Select the lines or arrows.
2. Click the Arrow Style button on the Drawing toolbar.
3. Select the style that you want to apply.

Applying line color

The process to apply line color in Draw is similar to the process in Publisher. The Line Color button includes a color and a menu. If you click the color, that color applies to the line. If you click the menu arrow next to the button, a pop-up menu appears. Figure 20-11 illustrates the button and its associated menu.

You can choose any color on the pop-up menu, or you can choose either of the following from the bottom of the menu:

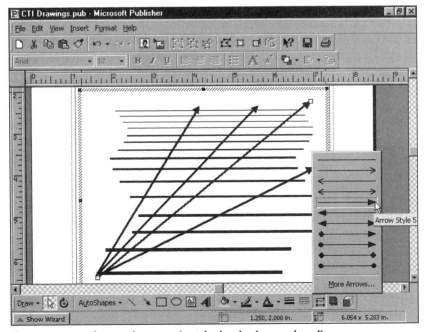

Figure 20-10: Change the arrow's style, beginning, and ending.

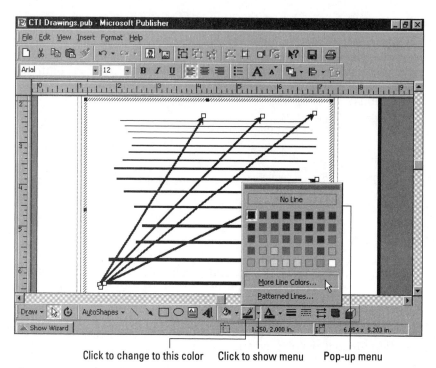

Click to change to this color   Click to show menu   Pop-up menu

Figure 20-11: Choosing a color for the lines

✦ **More Line Colors:** Displays the Colors dialog box, from which you can choose standard or custom colors. Figure 20-12 illustrates the options that you get when you choose the standard colors.

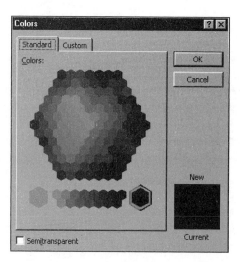

Figure 20-12: Selecting another color for the lines or arrows

✦ **Patterned Lines:** Select from a variety of patterns to apply to the line. You also can choose a foreground and a background color to change the look of the pattern. Unless the line is very thick, the pattern may not look right. Figure 20-13 illustrates the Patterned Lines dialog box.

To apply line color, follow these steps:

1. Select the lines or arrows.

2. Select the Line Color button on the Drawing toolbar.

3. Select either a color from the available colors, More Line Colors, or Patterned Lines.

Working with Shapes

You can draw various shapes in Draw, including circles, ovals, rectangles, squares, and a variety of AutoShapes. You can fill shapes and add a border in multiple colors and widths. You can use any shape to create an illustration or figure, or simply use a shape to add pizzazz to your publication.

Figure 20-14 shows a computer drawn in Draw. The drawing uses various shapes, AutoShapes, and lines to create the illustration.

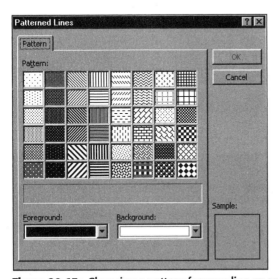

Figure 20-13: Choosing a pattern for your line or arrow

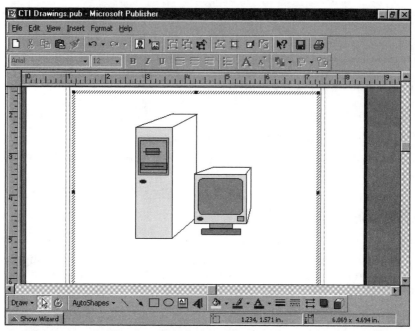

Figure 20-14: Using shapes and lines to create figures

Drawing shapes

You can draw any of the shapes in Draw by clicking the tool representing the shape and then dragging the mouse from the upper-left to the lower-right corner within the frame. After you draw a shape, you can resize it and move it.

Tip

You can use the Curve or Freeform AutoShape line tools to create a natural, less geometric shape. You can also fill a shape created with an AutoShape line tool.

To draw a rectangle or oval, click the tool button representing the shape and then drag the mouse within the Draw frame.

To draw a perfect square or circle, press and hold down the Shift key as you draw a rectangle or oval. Release the Shift key after you release the mouse.

To draw an AutoShape, follow these steps:

1. Display the AutoShapes toolbar (if it isn't already showing) by right-clicking any toolbar and choosing AutoShapes.

2. Select the tool and drag the mouse on the page as you would any other shape.

When you finish drawing a shape, it displays handles, as shown in Figure 20-15. The figure shows an AutoShape, a square, and a circle that's selected.

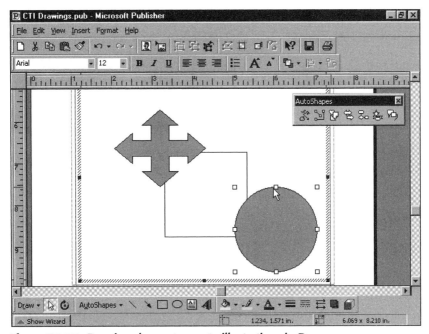

Figure 20-15: Drawing shapes to create illustrations in Draw

Editing shapes

You can select and edit any shape that you create. You can change its shape, size, and position. When you resize a perfect circle or square, you must hold down the Shift key while dragging the handle; otherwise, the shape reverts to an oval or rectangle, respectively.

Tip   When editing AutoShapes, holding down the Shift key while resizing makes the shape retain its proportions.

To resize a shape, select it and then drag one of the handles to change its shape or size.

To move a shape, select it and then position the selection pointer so that it appears as a four-headed arrow. Drag the shape to a new position.

Note   If you drag a shape or line off the edge of the Draw frame, any part of the shape not within the frame becomes hidden, as if it's behind the window. You can drag the shape back into the Draw frame or enlarge the frame so that you can see the entire shape or line.

Adjusting AutoShapes

In addition to resizing and moving AutoShapes, you can adjust each shape. Adjusting alters the edges of the shape. For example, if you draw a triangle, you can adjust it to a right triangle. If you draw a cylinder, you can adjust it so that you're looking at it from a different angle. Figure 20-16 illustrates a triangle and cylinder that have been adjusted.

Some shapes don't have the adjustment marker; other shapes have more than one marker.

Figure 20-17 shows the adjust markers on a block arrow. Onscreen, the adjustment marker appears as a green diamond. You can drag any adjustment marker only from left to right or from top to bottom.

To adjust a shape, drag the marker. If you don't like the results, press Ctrl+Z to undo the adjustment.

Formatting shapes

You can format a shape's line and fill. Change the border of a shape by applying a line style or dash style, change the line by using a color different from the fill, or apply any available color or pattern to fill a shape.

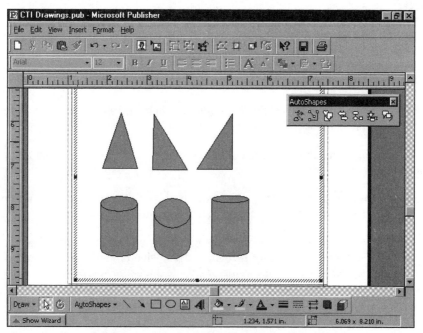

Figure 20-16: Adjusting an AutoShape to suit your drawing better

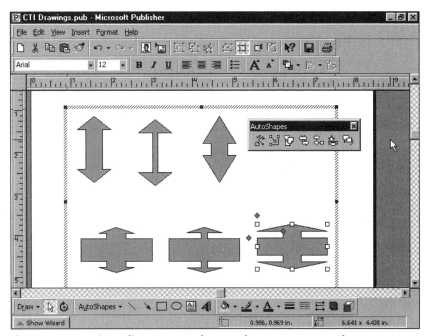

Figure 20-17: Using adjustment markers to change some AutoShapes

In Draw, you can also apply shadows and three-dimensional effects to the shapes. Shadows make shapes stand out from the page a little. Three-dimensional effects give the shape even more depth.

Changing line and fill

By default, shapes use a $^3/_4$-point outline or border and white fill. You can change the fill or line, however, just as you would any other frame or shape in Publisher. To change fill color, line color, and line style in Draw, use the buttons on the Drawing toolbar:

✦ Use the Line Style and Dash Style buttons to choose a line for any shape.

✦ Use the Fill Color and Line Color buttons to change fill and line color for shapes.

Figure 20-18 illustrates three shapes with fill color, line color, line style, and dash style applied. You might want to try adding a thick line to some shapes but change the line's style to dashed or dotted, as in the cloud in the figure. Also, consider using a light line around a darker shape; contrast these by layering onto another shape. For more information about layering, see "Layering objects," later in this chapter.

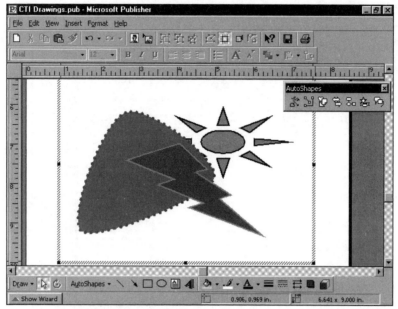

Figure 20-18: Using line and fill to change the shapes that you draw

Adding shadows

Adding shadows gives an object depth by making it look like it's casting a shadow. You can choose from a range of different shadows and then adjust the shadow to suit your purposes better.

Figure 20-19 illustrates the Shadow button on the Drawing toolbar and its associated pop-up menu. You can choose any shadow to apply to a shape. Note that Figure 20-19 has five different shapes, each with a different shadow.

To apply a shadow, select the shape and click the Shadow button on the Drawing toolbar. Select the shadow from the pop-up menu.

After you apply a shadow, you can adjust its depth and direction by using the Shadow Settings toolbar. To use the Shadow Settings toolbar, follow these steps:

1. Select the shape.

2. Click the Shadow button on the Drawing toolbar.

3. Choose Shadow Settings from the pop-up menu. The Shadow Settings toolbar appears, as shown in Figure 20-20.

4. Use the toolbar buttons to modify the shadow of the selected shape.

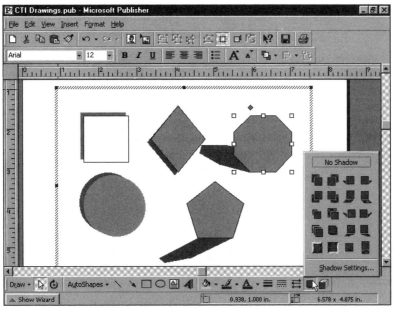

Figure 20-19: Applying shadows to shapes to give them some depth

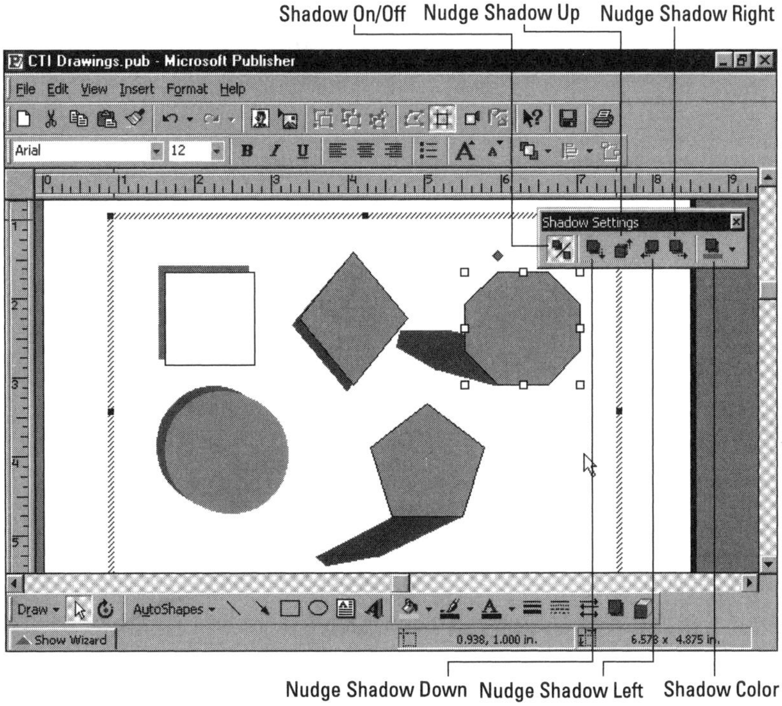

Shadow On/Off   Nudge Shadow Up   Nudge Shadow Right

Nudge Shadow Down   Nudge Shadow Left   Shadow Color

Figure 20-20: Modifying the shadow after applying it

Tip   You cannot use the shadow and 3-D effects on the same shape.

Adding 3-D effects

Three-dimensional effects give an extra depth to your drawings. You might want to use 3-D effects to create a more realistic-looking picture, for example, or to design a logo. You can apply various effects and then adjust them by modifying 3-D settings.

Figure 20-21 shows different 3-D effects with various AutoShapes. Note how applying a 3-D effect to an oval creates a cone.

To apply 3-D effects, select the object and then click the 3-D button on the Drawing toolbar. The pop-up menu shown in Figure 20-22 appears. Select the effect that you want to apply.

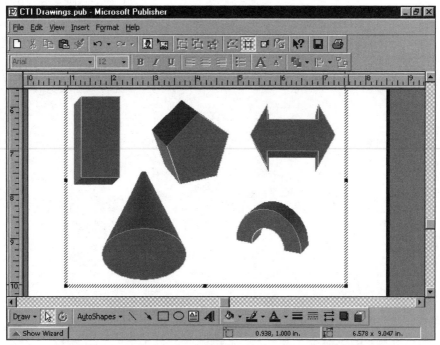

Figure 20-21: Applying various 3-D effects to shapes, for a realistic look

To modify the 3-D effect, follow these steps:

1. Select the object.

2. Click the 3-D button on the Drawing toolbar.

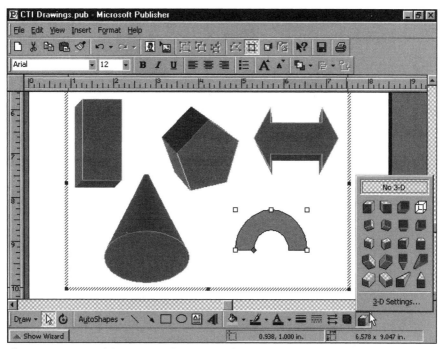

Figure 20-22: Applying a 3-D effect to an object

3. Choose 3-D Settings. The 3-D Settings toolbar appears, as shown in Figure 20-23.

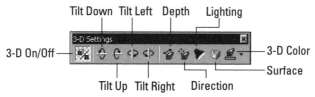

Figure 20-23: Modifying the 3-D settings

4. Click the toolbar button to adjust the setting; a slight change is made each time that you click the button. Table 20-2 explains each tool button on the 3-D Settings toolbar.

Figure 20-24 illustrates some of the 3-D effects from the 3-D Settings toolbar. All four shapes started out the same, but with modifications to the lighting, direction, depth, and tilt, four completely different shapes are created.

<table>
<tr><td colspan="2" align="center">Table 20-2
3-D Settings Toolbar Tools</td></tr>
<tr><td>**Tool**</td><td>**Description**</td></tr>
<tr><td>3-D On/Off</td><td>Turns the 3-D effect on or off</td></tr>
<tr><td>Tilt Down</td><td>Makes the object appear as if it is rotating down on the page, so that you see more of the top of the object</td></tr>
<tr><td>Tilt Up</td><td>Makes the object appear as if it is rotating up, so that you see more of the bottom of the object</td></tr>
<tr><td>Tilt Left</td><td>Turns the object to the left</td></tr>
<tr><td>Tilt Right</td><td>Turns the object to the right</td></tr>
<tr><td>Depth</td><td>Displays a menu from which you can choose a depth for the 3-D, in points</td></tr>
<tr><td>Direction</td><td>Displays a pop-up menu that enables you to choose the direction of the 3-D effect, such as up, down, up and to the right, and so on</td></tr>
<tr><td>Lighting</td><td>Displays a menu from which you choose where the light source originates and whether the source is bright, normal, or dim</td></tr>
<tr><td>Surface</td><td>Displays a menu from which you choose a finish for the object—wire frame, matte, plastic, or metal</td></tr>
<tr><td>3-D Color</td><td>Displays a color menu from which you choose a color for the 3-D effect</td></tr>
</table>

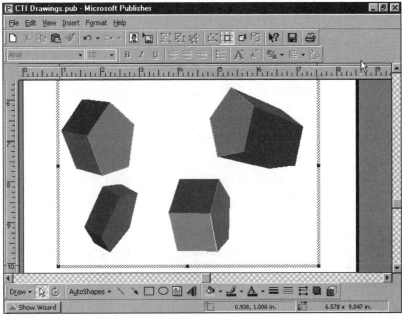

Figure 20-24: Use 3-D settings to create any version of a shape or object that you want.

Rotating and flipping an object

Rotate objects to make them fit into your drawing or to create a different effect. You might, for example, rotate an arrow to make it point in a different direction, or flip objects so that they face the other way.

You can rotate objects left and right or use free rotation for more control. You can flip objects horizontally or vertically. Figure 20-25 illustrates two arrows that were flipped or rotated, and what happens with each change. The arrow on the left was rotated right and left. The arrow on the right was flipped horizontally and vertically. The result of each rotation or flip appears below the original shape.

To rotate or flip an object, follow these steps:

1. Select the object.

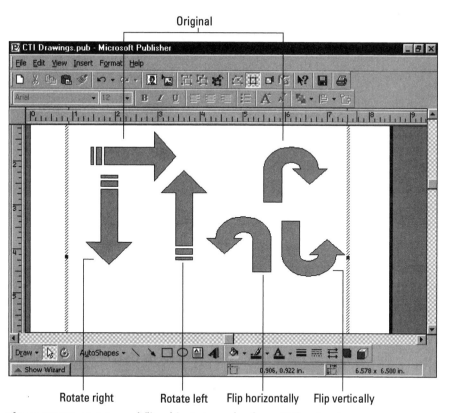

Figure 20-25: Rotate and flip objects to make them fit the drawing.

2. Choose Draw ➪ Rotate or Flip. Choose one of the following:

- Free Rotate
- Rotate Left
- Rotate Right
- Flip Horizontal
- Flip Vertical

If you choose Free Rotate, round handles appear on the corners of the object's frame. The selection pointer changes to the rotation pointer, as shown in Figure 20-26. Drag any round handle to rotate the object to the position you want.

After you finish rotating the object, click the Free Rotate button on the Drawing toolbar to deactivate the Free Rotate feature.

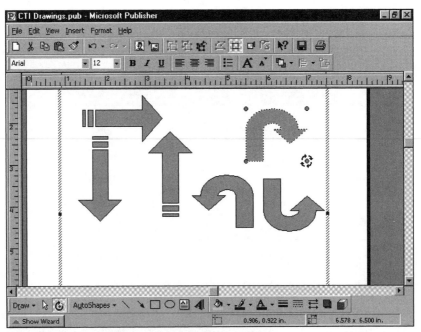

Figure 20-26: Using free rotation to rotate an object

Working with Multiple Objects

When you're drawing multiple shapes and lines to create an illustration or figure, you may need to perform some procedures to get the objects in the right position. Microsoft Draw provides various tools that you can use to position objects and layer them on the page.

When positioning objects, you might need to nudge, or push, a shape into place. You also can arrange objects by aligning them along a vertical or horizontal line, and distribute them evenly in the Draw frame.

Layering objects enables you to stack them, one on top of the other, to create depth or add a particular look to the drawing. You also can group, or join, objects together so that you can edit them as one.

Positioning objects

Microsoft Draw provides tools that you can use to nudge, align, or distribute objects within the Draw frame. Although these aren't tools that you're likely to use a lot, they may come in handy sometimes.

Nudge objects

Nudging is pushing or moving an object — shape, line, or group of objects — slightly to put it in the appropriate position. Sometimes, you might select an object and try to move it just a hair, but move it too far. Use the Nudge command to get the object in the perfect position.

To nudge an object, follow these steps:

1. Select the object or a group of objects.
2. Choose Draw ➪ Nudge.
3. Select one of the following: Up, Down, Right, or Left. The object moves in the direction that you choose.

You can press Ctrl+Z if you want to cancel the move. You can choose the Nudge command again and again until you get the object in the right position.

Align objects

You can align multiple objects so that they line up along their bottoms, tops, or sides. You can align objects horizontally or vertically. Figure 20-27 illustrates some of the alignments. The first row of boxes is aligned horizontally along the bottom, and the second row is aligned horizontally in the middle.

The boxes are also vertically aligned. The first two boxes align left, the second two align in the center, and the third pair of boxes align on the right.

To align multiple objects, follow these steps:

1. Select the objects.
2. Choose Draw ➪ Align or Distribute.
3. Choose one of the following: Align Left, Align Center, Align Right, Align Top, Align Middle, or Align Bottom. Table 20-3 describes the alignments.

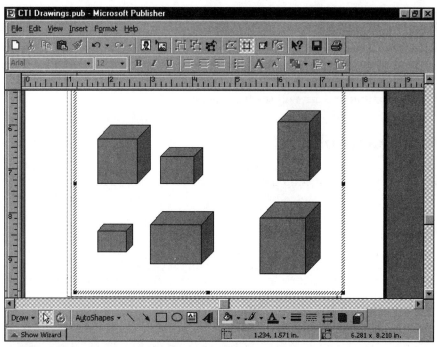

Figure 20-27: Aligning multiple objects in various ways

Table 20-3	
Object Alignment Options	
Alignment	**Description**
Align Left	Vertically align objects by their left edges
Align Center	Vertically align objects by their center
Align Right	Vertically align objects by their right edges
Align Top	Horizontally align objects along their top edges
Align Middle	Horizontally align objects along their middles
Align Bottom	Horizontally align objects along their bottom edges

Distribute objects

When you distribute multiple objects, you position them so that they have an equal amount of distance between them, horizontally or vertically. Figure 20-28 illustrates both horizontal and vertical distribution. Note that, within any one horizontal row of boxes, an equal amount of space exists between them. Also, in any vertical column of boxes, the space between the boxes is the same.

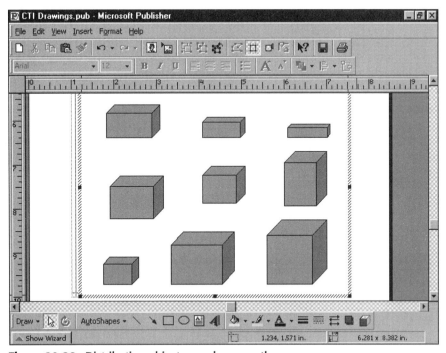

Figure 20-28: Distributing objects evenly across the page

To distribute objects, follow these steps:

1. Select three or more objects.
2. Choose Draw ➪ Align or Distribute.
3. Choose either Distribute Horizontally or Distribute Vertically.

Layering objects

By default, Microsoft Draw shapes use an opaque fill. When you create a drawing, the most recently drawn shape overlaps the ones before it. The overlapping, or *layering,* of objects enables you to create depth in your drawing. Also, overlapping means that you can hide parts of some shapes, if necessary, to add to the design.

When you layer objects, you might decide that an object in the background needs to be in the foreground, or vice versa. Microsoft Draw provides the tools to accomplish this change.

In addition, a drawing with a lot of lines and shapes in it can be difficult to move. If you don't select every line and shape, you'll leave some behind. Often, you'll want to format multiple lines or shapes simultaneously. To make moving, deleting, copying, and formatting objects easier, you can join the objects together in a group. When objects are grouped, Draw treats them as one object.

Order

Draw enables you to change the order in which objects appear on the page. You might, for example, draw several shapes and then decide that one shape needs to be on the bottom, or just one layer back. You can easily change the order of the objects in your drawing by using the Order command.

Figures 20-29 and 20-30 illustrate this process. The computer was created first, and then the table top was added. In Figure 20-29, the table top covers the computer.

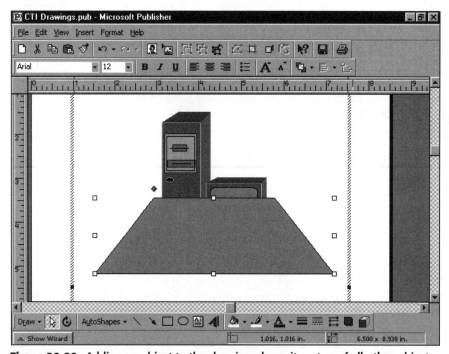

Figure 20-29: Adding an object to the drawing places it on top of all other objects.

In Figure 20-30, the table top object is sent to the back, so that it looks more like a table top.

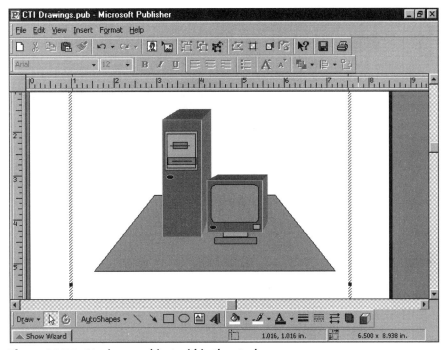

Figure 20-30: Moving an object within the stack

To order objects in Microsoft Draw, follow these steps:

1. Select the objects.
2. Choose Draw ➪ Order.
3. Choose one of the following:
    - **Bring to Front:** Places the selected object in front of all objects on the page
    - **Send to Back:** Places the selected object in the back of all objects on the page
    - **Bring Forward:** Brings the object one layer forward in the stack
    - **Send Backward:** Sends the object one layer back in the stack

Grouping

When you create an object with multiple pieces, it's difficult to edit the object without losing a piece here and there. Grouping makes editing and formatting pieces of the whole easier.

As an example, the computer in Figure 20-31 consists of many pieces — lines and various shapes — as shown when the pieces are all selected. If you choose to move the object or format the lines, for example, you have to select each piece of the whole.

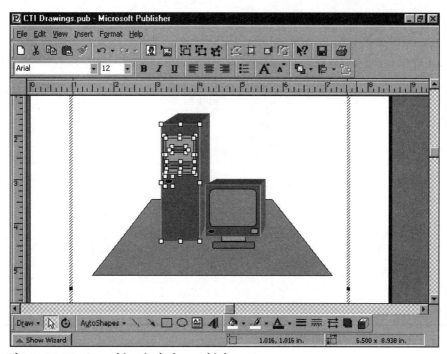

Figure 20-31: One object includes multiple parts.

By grouping the object, you can modify it more easily. When you group multiple objects, you can copy, move, or delete the objects more easily. Additionally, you can format the group of objects quickly. Suppose that you want to change the line thickness in the selected object. Change the lines only once for the group; otherwise, you have to change each individual line, one at a time.

Tip
You might want to create multiple groups in a drawing. In the computer drawing, for example, you can group all pieces to the CPU box, group all pieces to the monitor, and then select the box, monitor, and table and group them together, for easier moving, copying, and formatting.

When you group objects, you might need to ungroup them at times, to format one item differently from the rest or to delete or move one line or shape. You can ungroup items on these occasions. Draw also includes a Regroup command that enables you to regroup objects quickly after you make a modification.

To group objects, follow these steps:

1. Select all objects you want to group.

2. Choose Draw ➪ Group. The object appears with one set of handles, as shown in Figure 20-32.

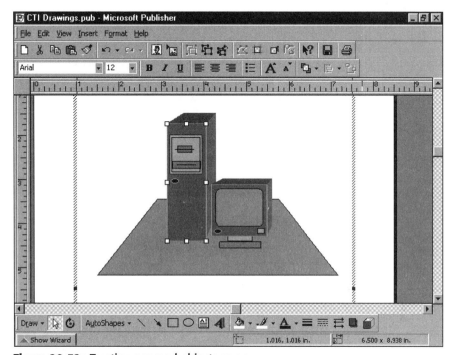

Figure 20-32: Treating grouped objects as one

3. To ungroup objects, select the object and then choose Draw ➪ Ungroup.

4. To regroup objects, select any one of the previously grouped objects and then choose Draw ➪ Regroup.

Working with Draw Text

You can add text to any drawing to help explain the drawing, to create callouts for the drawing, or to create logos, for example. After adding the text, you can format it as you would any other text, by changing font, size, attributes, color, alignment, and so on.

To add text to a drawing, follow these steps:

1. Click the Text Box tool.

2. Click the insertion point in the drawing or draw a frame, as shown in Figure 20-33. The text frame has selection handles, and a cursor appears in the frame for you to enter the text.

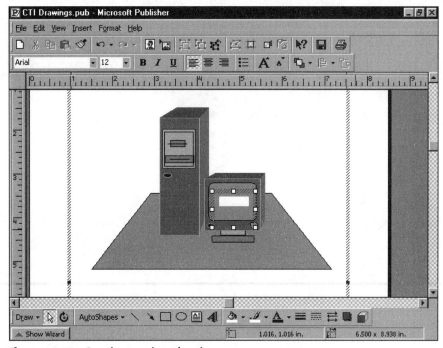

Figure 20-33: Creating text in a drawing

3. Type the text. You can resize and move the text frame, just as you would any object.

4. Select the text and use the Draw Formatting toolbar to apply any formatting that you want.

5. Choose Format ➪ Text Box to display the Format Text Box dialog box. Change the vertical alignment, internal frame margins, and rotate the text, if you want.

Figure 20-34 shows a drawing with text inserted. The text was formatted within a text frame and becomes a part of the drawing object.

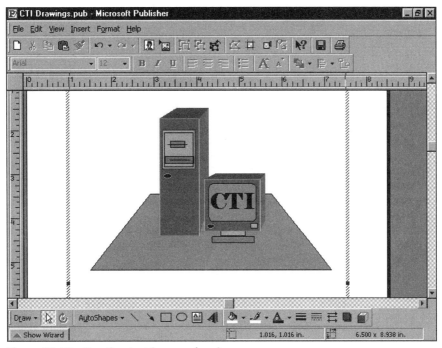

Figure 20-34: Creating text in your drawings

Editing Clip Art and Photographs

You can make changes to a piece of clip art by using Microsoft Draw. Changes that you can make include adjusting the brightness and contrast, cropping the clip, and applying image control. For example, you might want to change the color from the default to black and white or to grayscale. You can even change the picture to one that is suitable for watermarks. You can also change the image, brightness, and other characteristics of a photograph.

Note   A *watermark* is a low-contrast picture placed as a design in the background of the page. Changing a photo or piece of clip art to a watermark makes the picture fade into the background, so that you can read the text in the foreground.

Figure 20-35 illustrates clip art and a photograph that were edited in Draw. The clip art was made brighter and given additional contrast. The photograph was changed into a black-and-white picture that is more artistic than illustrative.

Understanding the editing tools

You use the Picture toolbar, shown in Figure 20-36, to modify and edit clip art or photos. With the toolbar, you can adjust brightness and contrast, add frames and fill, and crop the picture. Table 20-4 describes the tools in the Picture toolbar.

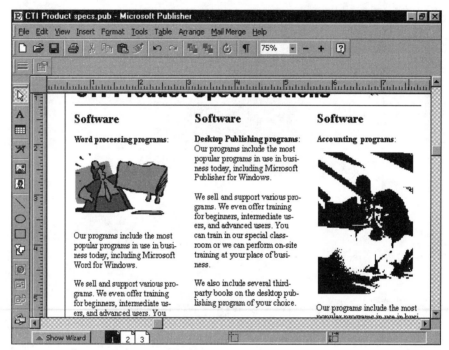

Figure 20-35: Create clearer pictures or artistic designs.

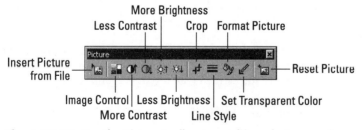

Figure 20-36: Use the Picture toolbar to modify a photo or a piece of clip art.

Table 20-4
Picture Toolbar Tools

Tool	Description
Insert Picture from File	Enables you to insert a different picture to edit.
Image Control	Displays a menu that enables you to set the image as it originally looked, to a grayscale, to black and white, or as a watermark.
More Contrast	Each click displays more contrast between light and dark in the picture.
Less Contrast	Each click displays less contrast between light and dark in the picture.
More Brightness	Each click brightens the picture.
Less Brightness	Each click darkens the picture.
Crop	Enables you to crop the picture by moving the picture around in the frame. If you move the picture to the left, for example, the left side hides behind the frame, or window, and therefore that side is cropped off.
Line Style	Applies a line style to a frame around the picture.
Format Picture	Displays the Format Picture dialog box, in which you can enter an amount to crop the picture, change image control, or reset the picture to its original state.
Set Transparent Color	Click the tool and then click a color to make that color transparent. This tool works only in a bitmapped image.
Reset Picture	Changes the picture back to the original formatting and color.

Editing the picture

You might want to experiment with editing clip art and photographs. To edit a picture using Draw, follow these steps:

1. Right-click the picture and then click Copy on the quick menu.

2. Choose Insert ⇨ Picture ⇨ New Drawing. Draw opens a frame that replaces the one in which your picture existed.

3. Choose Edit ⇨ Paste. Draw pastes the picture into the Draw frame.

4. If the Picture toolbar doesn't appear, right-click any toolbar and then choose Picture to display it.

5. Click the tool that you want to use on the picture.

6. Click anywhere outside of the frame to close Draw and return to Publisher.

7. Double-click the picture at any time to start Draw and edit the picture.

Summary

In this chapter, you learned how to use Microsoft Draw to create illustrations and edit pictures. Specifically, you learned about the following:

✦ Working with lines and arrows

✦ Working with shapes

✦ Working with multiple objects

✦ Working with text boxes

✦ Editing pictures

In the next chapter, you learn how to create WordArt objects.

✦   ✦   ✦

Using WordArt

WordArt is an Office applet that you can use within Publisher to create logos, special headings, display type, and other fancy type. You can format WordArt text, stretch it and apply other effects, place it on a curve or other shape, and otherwise manipulate the text.

You create WordArt in a WordArt frame. After you create the text, the frame acts like any other Publisher object. You can select the frame and then format, edit, or move it. When you open WordArt, the applet opens within Publisher but uses its own menus and toolbar, as shown in Figure 21-1.

Figure 21-2 illustrates various logos created in WordArt. Using different fonts as well as different effects makes each logo unique.

Note   Notice that when you're in Publisher, you can resize a WordArt frame, and the WordArt text generally adjusts to fit the new frame size while maintaining the design that you created. Sometimes, however, the design changes — by stretching or condensing, for example — making the WordArt text look strange.

Starting WordArt

You can start WordArt from any current publication and place a WordArt frame anywhere in the publication.

Tip   You cannot adjust your view after you open WordArt. Zoom to the view that you want *before* you draw the WordArt frame.

To start WordArt and create a new heading or logo, click the WordArt Frame tool on the Object toolbar in Publisher. Draw a new frame. The WordArt screen appears with the Enter Your Text Here box and a frame to hold the art.

To start WordArt so that you can edit an existing WordArt frame, double-click the WordArt frame.

Toolbar   WordArt menus   Rulers   WordArt frame   Enter Your Text Here box

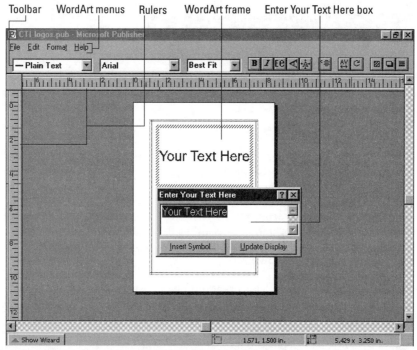

Figure 21-1: Use the WordArt applet to create fancy type.

Figure 21-2: Creating a variety of WordArt logos

Figure 21-3 illustrates the Enter Your Text Here box. The box must be open before you can enter or edit the text; however, you can format the text without using the Enter Your Text Here box.

Figure 21-3: Entering your Text in WordArt

Entering Text in WordArt

Use the Enter Your Text Here box to type your text. You can enter any keyboard character. You also can choose to enter one letter, a few words, or several sentences.

Use the Insert Symbol button to display the Insert Symbol dialog box. You can insert any symbol that you want, such as an accented letter or the trademark symbol. The Insert Symbol box, however, doesn't include the variety of fonts that the Symbol box in Publisher contains. For example, you will not find Wingdings or Transportation fonts in the Insert Symbol box in WordArt.

After you enter the text, click the Update Display button to change the text in the WordArt frame. To see the text onscreen, click the Close button in the Enter Your Text Here box. You can format the text onscreen by using the WordArt menus and toolbar.

You can display the Enter Your Text Here box at any time by choosing Edit ➪ Edit WordArt Text.

Using WordArt Menus

The WordArt menus appear when you open the WordArt applet. The menus supply various tools and commands related to your text in WordArt; however, the File menu remains Publisher's File menu. The following is a description of the WordArt menus:

✦ **File:** Publisher's File menu, which contains commands such as New, Open, Close, Save, and so on.

✦ **Edit:** Contains only one command: Edit WordArt Text.

✦ **Format:** Contains various formatting commands, including Spacing Between Characters, Border, Shading, and so on. Shortcuts for these commands also appear on the toolbar.

✦ **Help:** Contains help that is specific to the WordArt applet.

Using the WordArt Toolbar

The WordArt toolbar contains various tools to help you create your text. Figure 21-4 shows the toolbar buttons, and Table 21-1 describes each tool.

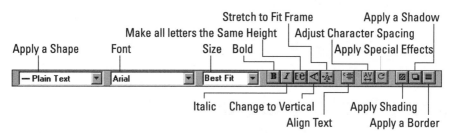

Figure 21-4: Use the toolbar to format the WordArt text.

Table 21-1
WordArt Toolbar Tools

Tool	Description
Apply a Shape	Displays a drop-down menu with 36 shapes—such as circles, waves, triangles, and so on—that you can apply to the text.
Font	Enables you to apply any font in your system to the text.
Size	Enables you to select a type size for the font. By default, Best Fit furnishes the best size to fit the frame.
Bold	Applies bold to the text. Click once to turn on the feature, and a second time to turn it off.
Italic	Applies italic to the text. Click once to turn on the feature, and a second time to turn it off.
Make all Letters the Same Height	Makes lowercase letters the same height as uppercase letters. Click once to turn on the feature, and a second time to turn it off.
Change to Vertical	Changes the text to read from top to bottom instead of left to right. Click once to turn on the feature, and a second time to turn it off.
Stretch to Fit Frame	Broadens and lengthens the text to the full size of the frame. Click once to turn on the feature, and a second time to turn it off.

Tool	Description
Align Text	Displays a drop-down menu that offers the following alignments: Center, Left, Right, Stretch Justify, Letter Justify, Word Justify.
Adjust Character Spacing	Displays the Spacing Between Characters dialog box, in which you can choose the tracking that you want to apply, such as Tight, Very Tight, Normal, Loose, and so on.
Apply Special Effects	Displays the Special Effects dialog box, in which you can set the Rotation and Slider controls. Rotation turns the text to the specified degree; Slider changes the shape of the WordArt effect.
Apply Shading	Displays the Shading dialog box, in which you can choose a pattern to apply to the text.
Apply a Shadow	Displays the Shadow dialog box, in which you can choose one of various shadows to apply to the text.
Apply a Border	Opens the Border dialog box, in which you choose a border to apply to the text, not to the frame.

Formatting Text

You can format text in WordArt as you would any other text. You can change fonts, type size, attributes, and alignment. You also can apply a shape to the text. WordArt enables you to change the formatting at any time; simply start WordArt by double-clicking the frame, and then change whatever you want.

Formatting fonts

Within the formatting of fonts, you can apply a new font, a type size, or an attribute. WordArt supplies all the fonts in your system, as does Publisher. Font sizes range from 12-point to 128-point, and you can opt to choose Best Fit. You also can create larger text. The attributes that you can apply are bold and italic.

 Tip
You do not need to select the text in WordArt. Any formatting that you apply affects all the text in the frame.

To apply a font to a WordArt, click the drop-down arrow beside the Font box on the toolbar, and select the font that you want to use.

To apply a size to the WordArt text, click the drop-down arrow next to the Size box and pick a size. Alternatively, you can choose Best Fit; WordArt makes the text as large as will comfortably fit in the frame. Also, you can enter a type size smaller or larger than those listed, by typing it into the Size text box.

To apply an attribute, click the Bold or the Italic button.

Figure 21-5 illustrates text that is 56-point Bauhaus 93. The text doesn't fill the entire frame, but you can adjust the frame later, if necessary.

Figure 21-5: Format the text any way that you want by changing font, size, and attributes.

Formatting alignment

You can center, left-align, right-align, or justify the text in a WordArt frame. When justifying text, you can use any of the following, each of which has a different effect:

- ✦ **Stretch justify:** Justifies the text by expanding the letters.
- ✦ **Letter justify:** Justifies by adding space between each pair of letters.
- ✦ **Word justify:** Justifies by adding space between the words.

Figure 21-6 illustrates letter-justified text. You can create a nice heading or logo by using this option or stretch-justified text. Word-justified text does not work so well, because of the huge white spaces left between the words; of course, the appearance of word-justified text depends on the number of words in the frame.

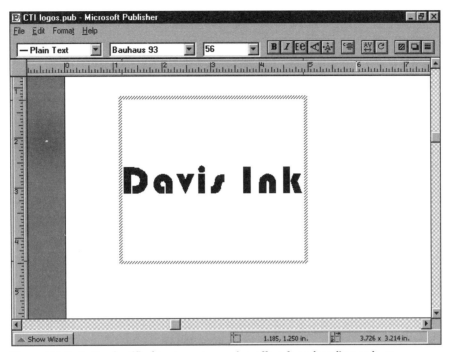

Figure 21-6: Letter-justified text creates a nice effect for a heading or logo.

To change the alignment of the text, click the Alignment button on the toolbar and choose the alignment that you want from the drop-down menu. A check mark appears beside the current alignment. The default alignment is centered.

Changing the shape of the text

WordArt provides various shapes that you can use to format your text. You can choose a triangle, circle, wave, or other shape in which to fit the text. Plain text is simply the text in a straight line with no shape effect added.

Figure 21-7 illustrates the available shapes. You'll discover that some shapes look better with longer words and some with shorter words. Also, certain fonts better suit certain shapes. You'll need to experiment to find the right size, shape, and font for your text.

To apply a shape to the text, click the Apply a shape drop-down arrow to display the drop-down menu. Choose any shape in the menu.

Figure 21-8 shows the Cascade Up shape with Bauhaus 93 font. If you have trouble finding the right font to go with a shape, try changing the size of the font, especially if you're using Best Fit. Sometimes, Best Fit stretches any text and makes it look strange in a shape.

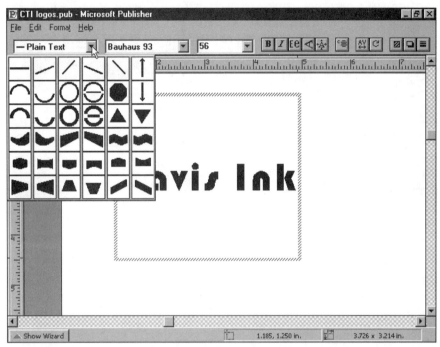

Figure 21-7: Apply various shapes to find the one that best suits the text.

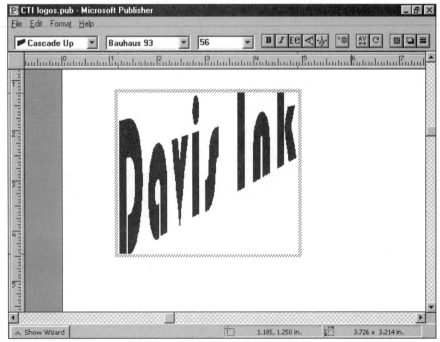

Figure 21-8: Try various shapes to find the one that you like.

Applying Special Effects

WordArt offers many different special effects that you can apply to your text, as previously described in Table 21-1. You can change letter height, direction, and how the font is stretched. You can rotate or slant the font, add shadows, and add borders. This section offers some suggestions for using the effects.

Changing letter height

When you change the letter height of the text, you make all uppercase and lowercase letters the same height, as shown in Figure 21-9. Fonts with a broader stroke, such as Elephant, Wide Latin, Impact, and so on, seem to work better with this effect.

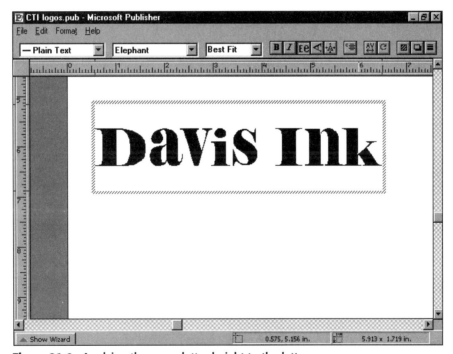

Figure 21-9: Applying the same letter height to the letters

You also can successfully use various shapes with the same letter height effect. For example, Wave 1 looks good with the Wide Latin font and the same letter height, as shown in Figure 21-10.

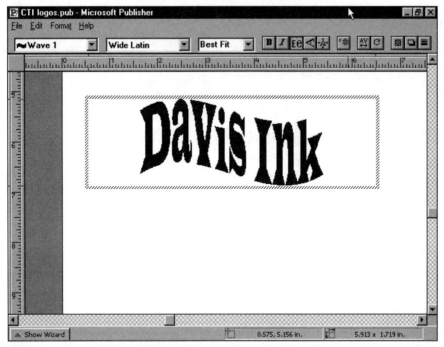

Figure 21-10: Applying a shape to the same letter height effect

Changing the direction to vertical

You can change the text of your WordArt from horizontal (the default) to vertical, as shown in Figure 21-11. The text in a vertical direction looks great in all uppercase. Some fonts automatically change to uppercase, but for others, you have to enter the text that way.

Once again, a wide font with a thick stroke is easier to read in vertical text than a thin-stroked font. Script doesn't work well with this feature, nor does an outline type. Also, some fonts use particularly large serifs, such as Goudy Stout; these types look better with horizontal direction than with vertical.

Stretching text to fit the frame

When you stretch the text to fit the frame in WordArt, the text expands to all sides of the frame. If you're using a plain text shape, you might end up with text similar to that shown in Figure 21-12. The uppercase letters and ascenders stretch to fit the frame, which creates a nice effect.

Note   When you use the Stretch to Fit feature and then return to Publisher, you can change the size and shape of the frame to create various changes in your text. The text stretches to fit the frame whether you're in WordArt or Publisher.

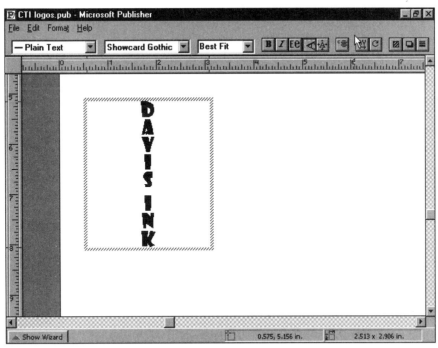

Figure 21-11: Vertical text reads from top to bottom.

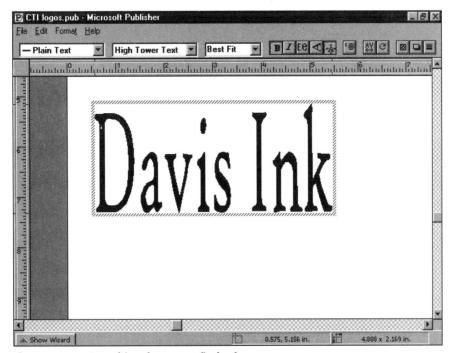

Figure 21-12: Stretching the text to fit the frame

If you also use a WordArt shape with text stretching, the text stretches to the shape as far as the frame edges, as shown in Figure 21-13. In this case, using a different font also changes the effect.

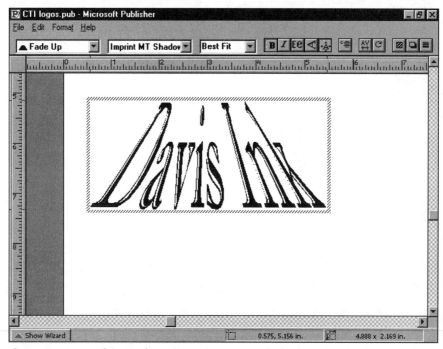

Figure 21-13: Applying a shape in conjunction with the stretching effect

Fonts with wide strokes look better stretched than do condensed or narrow fonts. Depending on the size of the frame and whether you're stretching the text's width or height, all uppercase letters may not be easy to read. For example, text stretched so that it is longer than it is tall looks best with initial caps, italic, or script, and any thick or heavy text, as shown in Figure 21-14.

Fonts with thin strokes or condensed type look good when you stretch their height, as shown in Figure 21-15. Sans serif fonts also look good stretched vertically.

Adjusting character spacing

As with characters in Publisher, you can adjust the spacing between the letters in WordArt text. Sometimes, you'll find that the combination of a font and a shape presses the text too close together. You can apply a loose or very loose character spacing to the text, or you can create your own custom character spacing. Also, WordArt text has automatic *pair kerning*, which automatically adjusts the space between certain letters, such as *A* and *V*, or *W* and *A*.

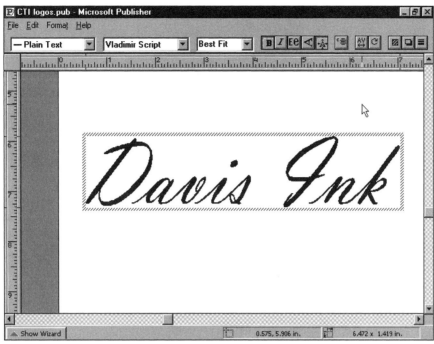

Figure 21-14: Script stretched horizontally looks good.

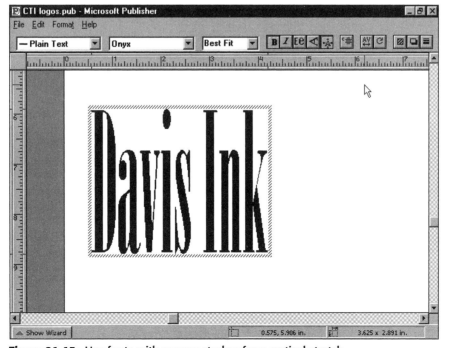

Figure 21-15: Use fonts with narrow strokes for a vertical stretch.

Figure 21-16 shows the Spacing Between Characters dialog box. Choose the spacing that best fits your text, font, and shape.

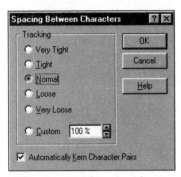

Figure 21-16: Changing character spacing, or tracking, of the WordArt

You might try changing the character spacing to Loose when you use the more bulbous fonts, such as Cooper Black. Also, fonts with wide strokes, such as Braggadocio, may require looser tracking. Use the tighter tracking for condensed type or fonts with narrow strokes. Figure 21-17 illustrates a condensed font with tight tracking.

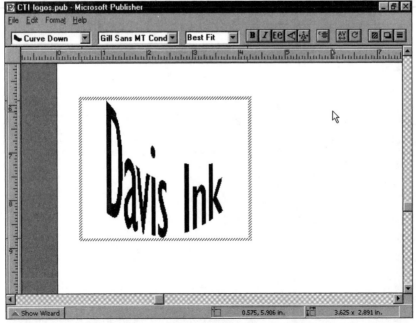

Figure 21-17: The goal is to make the text easy to read while creating a nice design.

Rotating and sliding text

You can rotate a piece of WordArt to change its look. You can even rotate the text when it's in a shape. *Sliding* the text is a change that you make to the WordArt effect. You can slide the WordArt to the left or to the right.

While you work with the Special Effects dialog box, you can view the effects onscreen so that you can change the Rotation or Slider as you work. Figure 21-18 shows the Special Effects dialog box beside a piece of WordArt. The Slider changed the triangle shape to a taller triangle. The ends of the triangle condense the *D* and the *K*. The text looks better in uppercase, in this situation, than in initial caps.

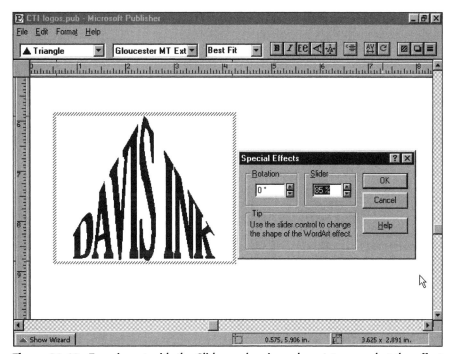

Figure 21-18: Experiment with the Slider and various shapes to see what the effects are.

Figure 21-19 illustrates the text-rotation feature. When rotating text, use initial caps so that the text is easier to read. Uppercase letters are difficult to read when rotated.

Applying shading

Shading consists of patterns that you apply to the text. WordArt offers a variety of patterns, including checks, horizontal stripes, bricks, basket weave, and clear. You can choose one color for the foreground and another for the background to create an exciting WordArt design.

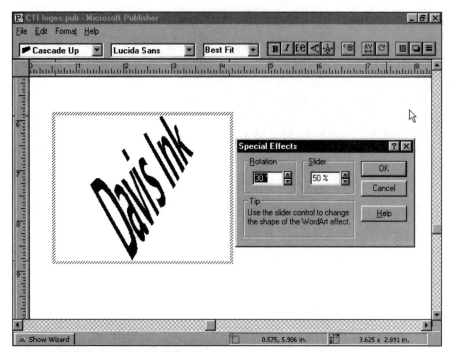

Figure 21-19: Rotating text to change its design

Use the Shading dialog box to apply color to your WordArt. For example, in the Style box, choose a solid color — white, the color, or a tint of the color. Then, in the Color area of the dialog box, choose the foreground color. You can create letters that are red, yellow, navy, teal, purple, and so on, without using a pattern at all.

Figure 21-20 illustrates a pattern, or shading, that fills the letters. To make the type readable, you might want to add a border to the letters, and some spacing between the letters, as shown in Figure 21-20. When using patterns and shading, use fonts with broad strokes, to make the type more readable.

Note   For more information about applying borders to WordArt, see the upcoming section, "Applying a border."

Figure 21-21 illustrates the Shading dialog box with the selected pattern in the Sample box. Be careful when using shadings: A pattern combined with the wrong font could be illegible.

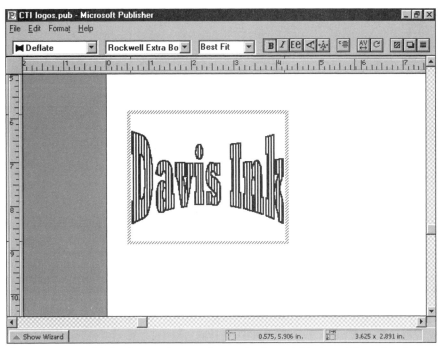

Figure 21-20: Add shading to the text, but make it readable by adding a border.

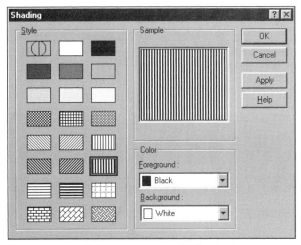

Figure 21-21: Using a pattern to fill the text

To open the Shading dialog box, click the Shading button on the toolbar. To use the dialog box, follow these steps:

1. In the Style area, choose a solid color, the clear style, or a pattern. View the sample in the Sample area.

2. In the Color area, choose a color for the Foreground.

3. If you're applying a pattern, choose a color for the Background.

4. Click OK.

Applying a shadow

You can apply a shadow to the type in your WordArt so that the text looks like it is three-dimensional. WordArt offers shadows that fall to the back, to the front, off to the side, and more. You also can apply a different color to a shadow.

Figure 21-22 illustrates the Shadow dialog box. You can apply a shadow and see how it looks onscreen, before you accept it in the dialog box. Change the shadows to see which best suits the font and shape of your text.

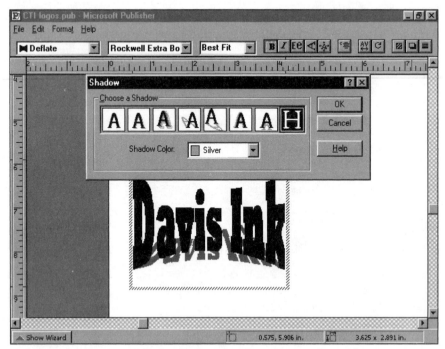

Figure 21-22: If you can't find a shadow that fits your text, change fonts or WordArt shape and try again.

If you want to turn off the shadow, open the Shadow dialog box and click the first selection in Choose a Shadow.

Applying a border

You can apply a border, or outline, to your text to make it stand out. Applying a black border to black text won't show up; however, you might want to use white text with a black border, or include a different color border for interest.

In general, apply a thin border to fonts with a narrow stroke; apply a thicker border when the font has a broad stroke or the type size is larger.

Figure 21-23 illustrates the Border dialog box. Apply a border while viewing the changes onscreen. You also can choose a color for the border in the Border dialog box.

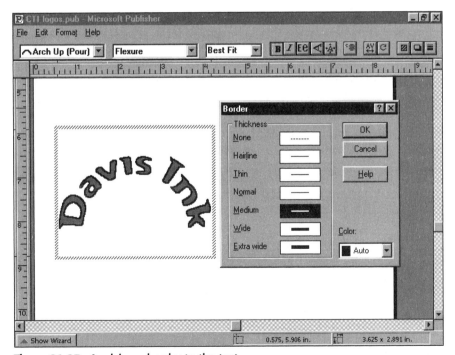

Figure 21-23: Applying a border to the text

Looking at Examples

The best thing about using WordArt formatting and special effects is that you can combine several effects to create a unique heading or logo. Again, make sure that you check your WordArt in Publisher while creating the text; sometimes, the text changes after you close WordArt.

Figure 21-24 illustrates two logos. The one on the left uses a pattern with a black border, to make the text show up. The logo on the right applies a shape and character spacing to the text.

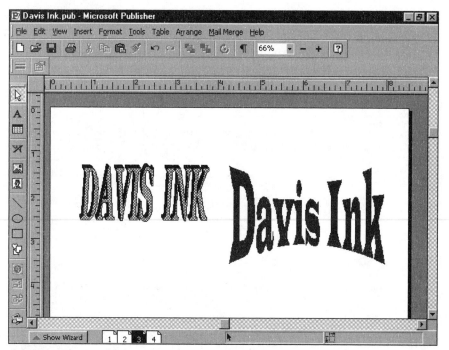

Figure 21-24: Combining techniques to create a logo

Figure 21-25 illustrates the use of WordArt text in a flyer. The font has a thin stroke, so an added border in the same color helps to thicken it a little. The lighter shadow also helps to define the font.

Figure 21-26 shows a newsletter nameplate created with WordArt. Sliding the Deflate shape and stretching the text helps to fit the WordArt into the allotted area. The font has a bold stroke, so custom tracking keeps the letters from running together.

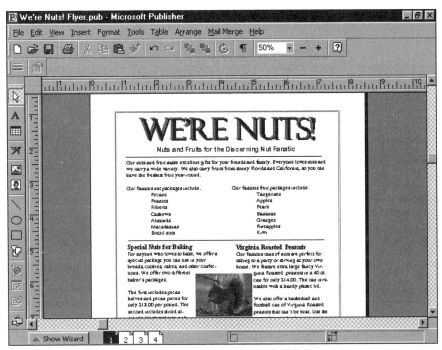

Figure 21-25: Using WordArt to attract attention in a flyer

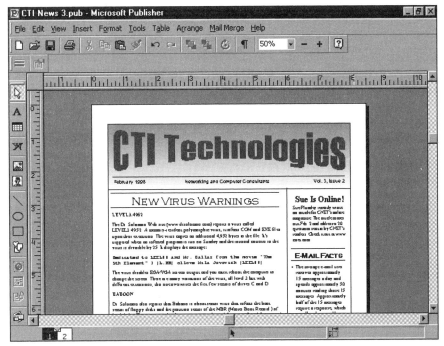

Figure 21-26: Using WordArt in a newsletter nameplate

Figure 21-27 illustrates the use of WordArt in a flyer. The shape of the WordArt echoes the page border design, making the flyer more eye-catching and interesting.

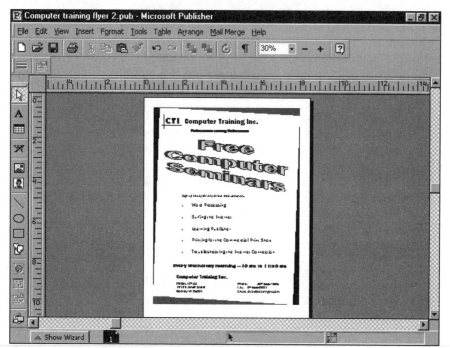

Figure 21-27: Using WordArt shapes in conjunction with the page layout and design

Summary

In this chapter, you learned about using the WordArt applet. You learned how to do the following:

✦ Create WordArt text

✦ Format the text

✦ Apply special effects to the text

In the next chapter, you learn about creating tables in your documents.

✦   ✦   ✦

Creating a Table

Publisher's Table feature is similar to Word's insofar as you can create a table with any number of rows and columns, format table borders, format individual cells, insert rows or columns, and delete rows and columns. Publisher includes a Table AutoFormat feature, from which you can select a border and fill format that suits your table. Alternatively, you can format the cells yourself.

You can enter text, numbers, and objects into any table cell. You can format font, alignment, spacing, and other characteristics of the table contents. Figure 22-1 illustrates a table in a document. The format is simple but serviceable.

Figure 22-2 shows the same table with a font change, fill added, and border changes. You can format the table any way that you want to make the data easy to read and understand.

Creating and Editing the Table

When you create a table in Publisher, you choose how many columns and rows you want to apply, and specify a format for the table. You can always add or delete columns and rows later. You also can change the table format at any time.

A table is an object in Publisher. It exists within a frame, which has selection handles and can be moved and resized.

Creating a table

You can create a table within any Publisher document. Publisher offers several table formats from which you can choose. You may also want to choose the default format, so that you can apply your own borders and fills.

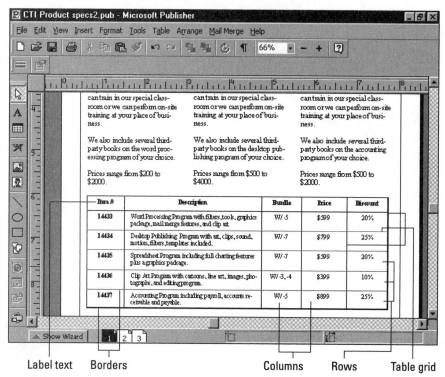

Figure 22-1: Creating a simple table for a publication

Some table formats are better suited for specific purposes. Table 22-1 explains the differences between the formats. Each table comes with specific text formatting, text alignment, shading or fills, and borders.

Table 22-1	
Table Formats	
Format	**Description**
None	Choose this option when you want to remove all line and fill formatting in a table.
Default	Provides an invisible table grid, but no formatting of border, text, or fill.
Checkbook Register	Provides a grid border with two shades of fill; helps you to follow the data in a long row. Row 1 contains formatted label text that is centered and bold; the rest of the text is left-aligned.

Format	Description
Lists 1 – 7	Provides various methods of distinguishing between rows and columns, using borders and fills. All lists supply a label row for row 1, with text that is bold and centered. Some lists also supply a label column with bold text. The rest of the table text is centered.
List with Title 1 – 3	Provides various table styles, each with one title row at the top, and row 2 as the label row. The labels are bold and vary in alignment from table to table. The label text also varies in alignment.
Numbers 1 – 6	Provides various table styles, each with labels in row 1, and labels in column 1. This format also includes a Total column. The number text is right-aligned in the Numbers format. Label text and table text varies from table to table.
Table of Contents 1 – 3	Provides a two-column table that is perfect for a table of contents list. The table style contains the title in row 1 and various shading and fill options. All table text in column 1 is left-aligned, and text in row 2 is right-aligned. Title text varies.
Checkerboard!	Provides a table with alternating dark and light cells, in a checkerboard pattern. The text in the light cells is black, and the text in the dark cells is white. All text is centered and bold.

To create a table, follow these steps:

1. Click the Table Frame tool.
2. Drag the tool along the page to create the table size that you want. The Create Table dialog box appears, as shown in Figure 22-3.
3. In Number of rows, either enter the number of rows that you want or accept the default.
4. In Number of columns, either enter the number of columns that you want or accept the default.
5. In Table format, choose a format. You can view the formats in the Sample box.
6. Click OK.

The table appears on the page, ready to enter data, as shown in Figure 22-4.

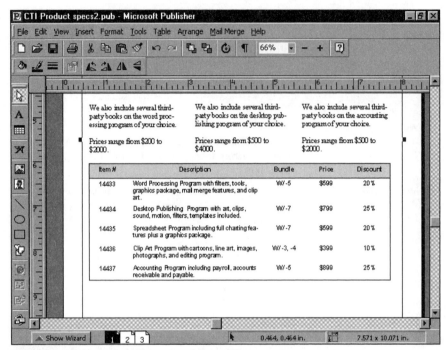

Figure 22-2: Modifying the text and the table

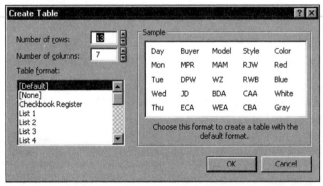

Figure 22-3: Enter the number of rows and columns that you want, and choose a format.

Note
When you select a table in Publisher, an extra row and column appear on the top and left edges of the table. These only appear when the table is selected, and they do not print. You can use the extra row and column to select rows and columns and to adjust the height of rows or the width of columns, as explained later in this chapter.

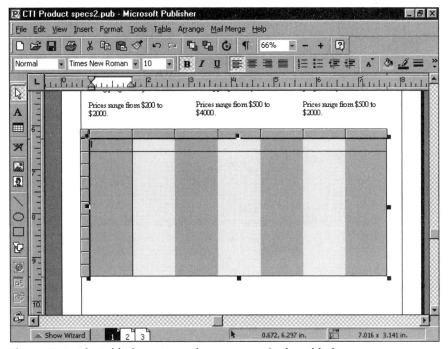

Figure 22-4: The table format you chose appears in the table frame.

Editing the table

When editing the table, you can change format, remove formatting, insert and delete columns and rows, and merge or join cells. You may also want to enter your data first and edit the table as you go. You can edit a table at any time. "Entering and Editing Data," later in the chapter, explains that process.

Changing AutoFormat

The first thing that you may want to do when editing is change the format, although you can change the table format at any time. You can decide, as you view each format, whether you want to keep the text formatting, text alignment, patterns or shading, or borders of that style. For example, you may see a table format that you like, except for its font or borders. You can choose to ignore the formats that you don't want, and apply only those formats that you do like.

To change the AutoFormat, follow these steps:

1. Select the table.

2. Choose Table ➪ Table AutoFormat. The Table AutoFormat dialog box appears with the format that you chose selected in the list.

3. Click the Options button. The AutoFormat dialog box enlarges to show the options illustrated in Figure 22-5.

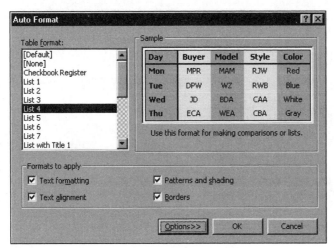

Figure 22-5: Choosing which formats to apply

4. In the Formats to apply area, clear the text box of the check mark if you don't want to apply these formats: Text formatting, Text alignment, Patterns and shading, and Borders. The Sample box reflects your choices.

Tip

Click [None] in the Table format list to remove all text, line, and fill formatting from the table. The rows and columns will still be present, and the default text (10-point Times New Roman) will be applied.

5. Click OK to accept the changes.

Selecting table elements

You select a table frame just like you select any other frame in Publisher. Clicking the frame displays the selection bars and the frame handles. To select one cell, click that cell. To select multiple cells, drag the I-beam over the cells that you want to select.

To select an entire row or a column, click the representative selection bar, as shown in Figure 22-6. The mouse pointer changes to a pointing hand when you pause it over the selection bar. Click the mouse to select an entire column or row.

Click here
to select row   Pointing hand

Click here
to select column

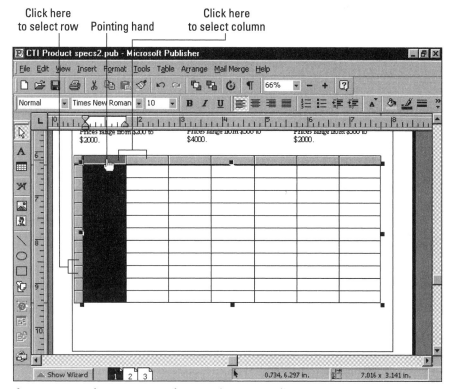

Figure 22-6: Select a row or column to format or edit it.

To select multiple rows or columns, click the selection bar and drag the pointing hand over the rows or columns that you want to select.

Working with rows and columns

When working with tables, you can insert or delete rows and columns, join or divide cells, and delete a table.

Inserting rows and columns   When you insert a column or row, you can choose whether to insert it before or after the selected row or column. You also can choose to insert multiple columns or rows at one time.

You can insert rows and columns by using either of two methods. Using the following method, you insert one or more rows or columns quickly; the row is inserted after the selected row, and a column is inserted to the right of the selected column. To insert a row or column, follow these steps:

1. Select the column or row. If you want to insert multiple rows or columns, select the number of rows or columns that you want to insert.

2. Choose Table ➪ Insert Columns or Insert Rows. Publisher inserts the element after the selected rows or columns.

You also can choose to insert rows before a specific row, or insert columns to the left of a specific column. To use the Insert dialog box, follow these steps:

1. Click the mouse in a cell within the row or column next to where you want to insert the new row or column.

2. Choose Table ➪ Insert Rows or Columns. The Insert dialog box appears, as shown in Figure 22-7.

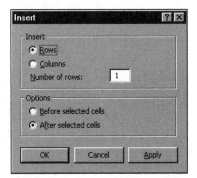

Figure 22-7: Insert multiple rows or columns before or after the selected cells.

3. In the Insert area, choose either Rows or Columns. Enter the Number of rows or columns that you want to insert.

4. In the Options area, choose either Before selected cells or After selected cells.

5. Click OK. Alternatively, click Apply to see the inserted rows or columns onscreen while the dialog box is still open.

Tip

If you leave the dialog box open, and decide that the result is not what you wanted, you can cancel the dialog box to reverse the action.

Deleting rows and columns   You can delete one row or column, or multiple rows or columns. You can delete rows or columns either by using a dialog box or by selecting them and then deleting them.

To delete rows or columns, follow these steps:

1. Select the rows or columns that you want to delete.

2. Choose Table ➪ Delete Row or Delete Column.

To delete rows or columns by using the Delete dialog box, follow these steps:

1. Click the mouse I-beam in a cell in the row or column that you want to delete.

2. Choose Table ➪ Delete Rows or Columns. The Delete dialog box appears, as shown in Figure 22-8.

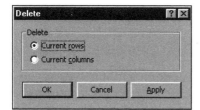

Figure 22-8: Delete the columns or rows

3. In the Delete area, choose Current rows or Current columns.

4. Click OK. Alternatively, click Apply to see the elements deleted onscreen while the dialog box remains open.

Adjusting column width and row height

When you create a table, the columns, by default, are 1-inch wide; rows are ¼-inch tall. You can adjust the height and width of these elements to fit your data into the table.

Although enlarging the frame automatically makes your columns wider and your rows taller, it makes all rows equal in height and all columns equal in width. When you want to expand all columns or rows, enlarge the table by using the selection handles.

When you want to vary the width or height of table elements, follow these steps:

1. Select the table.

2. Position the mouse pointer over the column or row line in the selection bar. The mouse changes to the ADJUST pointer, as shown in Figure 22-9.

Adjust pointer

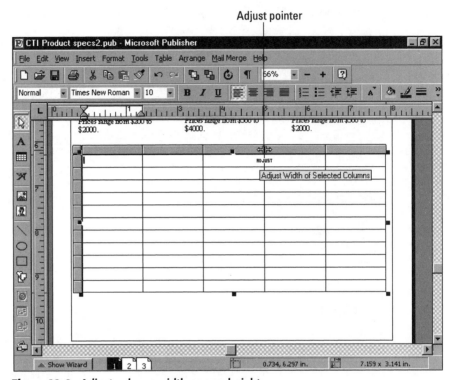

Figure 22-9: Adjust column width or row height.

3. Drag the ADJUST pointer to the new position. Note that the columns to the right or the rows below the line that you're adjusting also move.

Note

You also can adjust the width of the last column and the height of the last row in a table. You must slowly move the mouse over the line in the selection bar until it changes to the ADJUST pointer. Sometimes, locating the ADJUST pointer is difficult, because this area also produces the MOVE pointer, RESIZE pointer, and the Selection pointing hand.

Merging and dividing cells

Depending on the data that you're placing in the table, you may need to join several cells or divide cells. You can join, or *merge,* two or more cells together; for example, you might want to merge cells to fit in a table heading or to add a picture. You can also divide cells on a diagonal, to add various headings, or for other reasons.

Merging and splitting cells   Merge cells to prepare for specific headings or pictures. To merge cells, follow these steps:

1. Select the cells that you want to merge. The cells can be in one row or column, or reach across several rows and columns.

2. Choose Table ⇨ Merge Cells. Figure 22-10 illustrates merged cells.

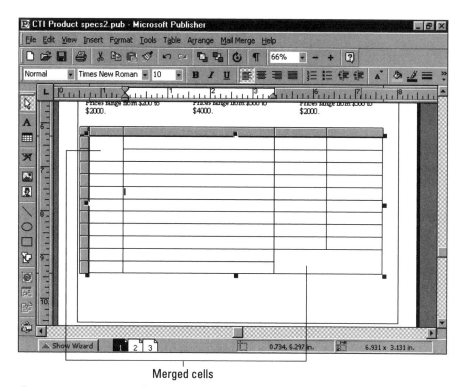

Merged cells

Figure 22-10: Merge cells to fit the data.

If you change your mind after you merge cells, you can split them up again. Follow these steps:

1. Select the merged cells.

2. Choose Table ⇨ Split Cells. Publisher returns them to their original formatting.

Using cell diagonals   Apply a cell diagonal to one or more cells. Splitting a cell diagonally offers multiple possibilities for entering data. When you split a cell, insertion points appear on either side of the diagonal division line.

To apply a cell diagonal, follow these steps:

1. Select the cell.

2. Choose Table ⇨ Cell Diagonals. The Cell Diagonals dialog box appears, as shown in Figure 22-11.

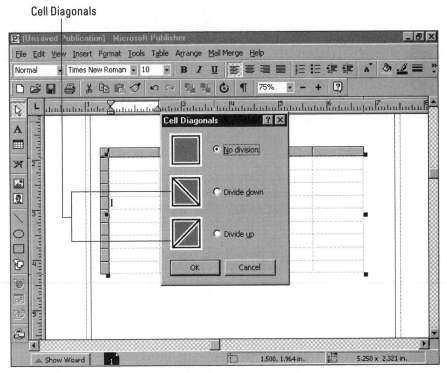

Figure 22-11: Dividing a cell to fit specific headings or data

3. Choose one of the following: Divide down or Divide up.

4. Click OK.

To remove the cell diagonal, open the Cell Diagonals dialog box and choose No division. Click OK.

Deleting a table

You can delete a table if you decide you no longer need it. To delete a table, right-click the table and choose Delete Object. Alternatively, you can select the table and press Ctrl+Shift+X.

Entering and Editing Data

You can enter text, values, and graphics in a table. You might want to enter column after column of numbers, for example; alternatively, you may want to enter words and phrases. You also can insert a picture or piece of clip art, to help add interest to the table.

After you enter text or data, you can format it just as you would any text in Publisher. You can apply fonts, text size, attributes, alignment, line spacing, color, and even create table styles. For more information about formatting text, see Part III, "Working with Text."

Navigating a table

You can enter text in any cell of the table. Click the cell to position the insertion point. Additionally, you can use the following keys and keyboard shortcut to move around in the table:

Tab	Move to next cell
Shift+Tab	Move to previous cell
Directional arrow keys	Move one cell up, down, left, or right

Tip If you press the Tab key while in the last cell of a table, you can add another row to the table.

Entering text

You type text into a table as you would into a frame — with only a few differences. When you press Enter in a table cell, the table enlarges by one line. When you continue to type at the end of a table cell, the text automatically wraps, and Publisher adds another line to the cell. You can continue to add text, and the cell expands to fit the text. When you expand one cell in a row, all the cells in that row expand.

Use the same editing keys — Backspace, Delete, and so on — to edit the text as you type. You can also insert special symbols into a table.

Formatting text

You format table text similarly to the way that you format any Publisher text.
However, a few shortcuts are available that you can use to format text more
quickly. Additionally, the following are some guidelines for formatting table text:

✦ When applying a font, text size, line spacing, alignment, or other format, you
  can select all table cells to which the formatting will apply, even if the cells are
  currently empty. Select the cells and then apply the format.

✦ You can apply vertical alignment to the text to center it vertically within a
  frame.

✦ You can use the ruler to set tabs and indents in a table. To enter a tab within a
  cell, press Ctrl+Tab.

✦ When formatting column or row labels, you generally make the text bold and
  centered, 10-point sans serif.

✦ Don't enter text right up against a column line; leave some margin or set an
  indent.

Filling down or right

Filling down or right repeats the text in a cell. For example, you can enter a value in
a row and then choose to fill down or fill right to repeat that value in all selected
cells.

To fill down or fill right, follow these steps:

1. Enter the value or text in a cell.

2. Select the cell containing the value, plus any cells in the following row or
   column that you want to contain the value.

3. Choose Table ➪ Fill Down or Fill Right.

Figure 22-12 illustrates the use of the Fill Down command. You type **Clip Art** once,
for example, and then select that cell and the next three cells, before selecting the
Fill Down command. Repeat with **Database** and **Desktop Publishing**. Note, too, how
the last two entries enlarged the cell height.

Adding pictures

You can add any pictures or objects to a table, just as you would to any Publisher
document. You can draw a clip art frame, for example, within the table and then
insert the picture. The frame overlaps the table, and the object that you insert
appears on top of the table.

Figure 22-13 illustrates a piece of clip art inserted into the table.

Filled down

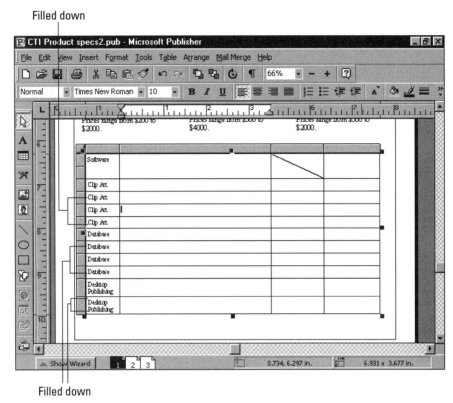

Filled down

Figure 22-12: Quickly enter repeated text or data.

For more information about inserting other objects, see Chapter 19.

Locking a table

Sometimes, the available space for a table is limited, and you might not want the table to expand as you enter text. You can *lock* a table so that the text won't wrap when it gets to the end of a cell; you have only a limited cell space in which you must fit the text. Locking the table also means that pressing Enter in a cell will not increase the row height. If you try to enter more text than the locked table allows, Publisher hides the text. You can unlock the table to view the hidden text.

To lock a table, follow these steps:

1. Select the table.

2. From the Table menu, click Grow to Fit Text so that the check mark disappears.

Insert clip art

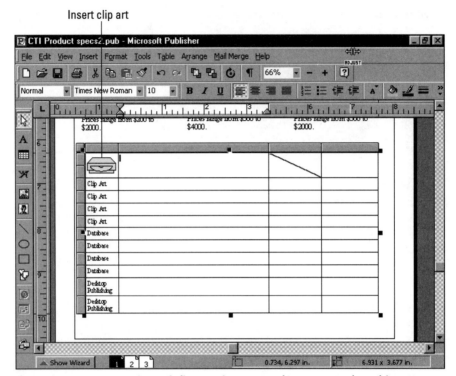

Figure 22-13: Insert a piece of clip art, picture, WordArt, or any other object.

To enable the table to expand with the text again, add the check mark to the Grow to Fit Text option.

Formatting a Table

When formatting a table, you can either use Publisher's AutoFormat (as described earlier in this chapter) or format the borders and fills yourself. For example, you might want to add a thicker border to the outline of the table, or just between the column labels and the rest of the data. You might want to fill certain columns, rows, or cells to make them stand out from the rest of the table.

Figure 22-14 illustrates a table with borders and fills applied. Use the Default or None options in the Table AutoFormat dialog box as a base when formatting your own table. Alternatively, you can use a Table AutoFormat and change it to look the way you want.

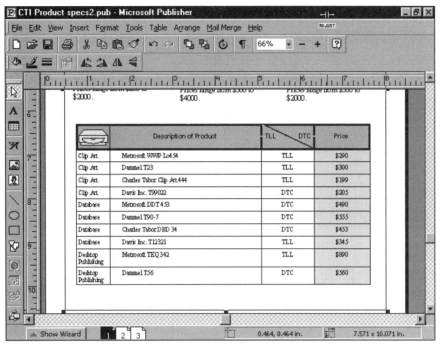

Figure 22-14: Apply specific formatting to your table.

Applying borders

You can apply a border to the outline of a cell or table. You also can apply a border to the entire cell, including the inside lines, or grid. If you want one cell to use a thicker border than any other cell in the table, you can apply a border to only one cell. Additionally, you can select a row or a column and apply a thicker or thinner border to those cells.

When you apply a border, you can choose either Grid or Box in the Border Style dialog box. If you choose Grid, the border applies to the outside and inside lines; if you choose Box, the border applies only to the outside border of the selected cells or table.

To apply the same border to all cells in a table, follow these steps:

1. Select the entire table either by choosing Table ⇨ Select ⇨ Table or by dragging the pointing hand over the selection bars.

2. Choose Format ⇨ Line/Border Styles ⇨ More Styles. The Border Style dialog box appears.

3. Select a line thickness and a color for the table border.

4. In the Preset area, select Grid, as shown in Figure 22-15.

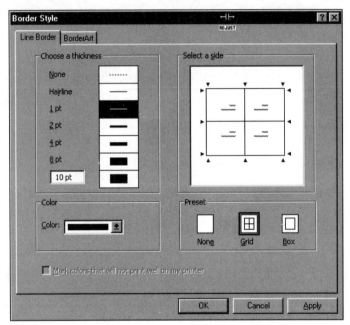

Figure 22-15: Applying a grid of borders to the table

5. Click OK.

To apply a border to just the outline of the table, choose Box instead of Grid in the Border Style dialog box.

To apply a border to just one cell, choose Format ➪ Line/Border Style, and then choose the border that you want to use.

To apply a border to specific cells, or to one or more columns or rows, select the cells and choose the border in the Border Style dialog box.

To apply a border to only one or two sides of the table or cell, select the table or cell and, in the Border Style dialog box, select the sides to which you want to apply the border.

For more information about borders and lines, see Chapter 10.

Applying fills

You can apply any color of fill or patterned fill that you want. You also can choose a fill for part of the table. Fill effects include tints and shades, patterns, and gradients.

To add a color, pattern, or gradient fill to a table, follow these steps:

1. Select the entire table or cells that you want to fill.
2. Choose Format ⇨ Fill Color; alternatively, click the Fill Color button on the Formatting toolbar.
3. Choose one of the following:
    - No Fill
    - Scheme colors
    - More Color Schemes
    - More Colors
    - Fill Effects
4. Choose the color or pattern that you want to use.

For more information about applying fills, patterns, color schemes, and such, see Chapter 10.

Summary

In this chapter, you learned about creating and formatting tables. You learned how to do the following:

✦ Insert a table

✦ Enter data

✦ Edit data

✦ Format text

✦ Edit the table

✦ Format the table

In the next chapter, you learn how to use object linking and embedding (OLE).

✦   ✦   ✦

Linking and Embedding Objects

Object Linking and Embedding (OLE) enables you to share information between Windows programs. You can create a chart or worksheet in Excel, for example, and then copy it and use it in any Publisher publication. Moreover, you can edit the chart or worksheet in Excel and have any changes that you make apply automatically to the object in Publisher. Using OLE means that your work is always up to date.

Other programs in which you can use linking and embedding include Word, PowerPoint, Access, WordPad, Paintbrush, and any other Windows application that supports OLE.

When linking and embedding, you start with a source program and a source document. The *source* is the program and document in which you create an object. An *object* is the picture, text, chart, or other element that you plan to share with Publisher. The source program, for example, might be Excel, and the source document might be a worksheet.

The other half of that coin is the *destination* program and document. Any Windows program that supports OLE can be a destination, but in this chapter, your Publisher publication is the destination document.

When linking and embedding, you can use one source and share it with one or more destinations.

Understanding Linking

Linking is one method of sharing information between two applications. *Linking* means that a connection exists between two programs. For example, you create a worksheet in Excel and then copy the worksheet to your Publisher document, but while copying, you also create a *link* between the two documents.

Figure 23-1 illustrates an Excel worksheet inserted into Publisher and linked to Excel. You can link either an entire file or only a portion of it.

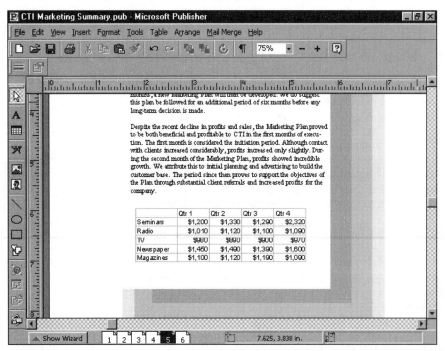

Figure 23-1: Link an Excel worksheet to your publications for automatic data updating.

When you link the object to its source application, you can quickly and easily edit the object in the source application and have any changes you make reflected within the Publisher document. Editing the object is easy, because OLE enables you to open a copy of Excel and edit the object simply by double-clicking the object in Publisher. Figure 23-2 illustrates the worksheet in its source document within Excel.

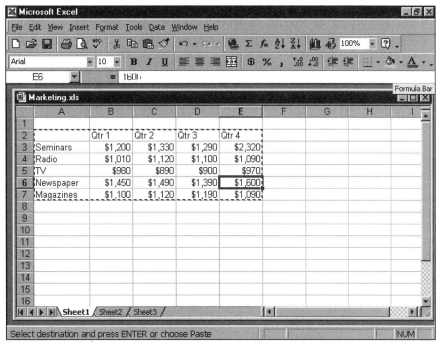

Figure 23-2: Editing a linked object within its source application.

Linking is handy when you have data that must always be current and that must be shared between multiple programs and multiple people. You can share data with coworkers and supervisors, for example, if you're connected to a network or the Internet. For instance, your boss could update your data within Excel, and the next time that you open your Publisher publication, you can choose whether or not to update links; if you do update links, the information that your boss changed automatically changes in your publication.

Additionally, you can link one worksheet or object to multiple documents, publications, and even programs. This technique is an efficient way to use OLE technology to keep all of your reports and other documents current.

Understanding Embedding

Embedding is a second method of sharing data between two Windows applications. *Embedding* is similar to linking, insofar as you create the object in a source application and then copy the object to a Publisher publication, but instead of linking, or connecting, the two applications, the object becomes part of Publisher.

Any changes that you make in the object appear only in Publisher; the changes do *not* affect the source document. Similarly, changes you make in the source document do not affect the embedded object.

Embedding is useful when you don't want the data constantly updated in both the source and the destination. When you want to update the data in the destination, you can double-click the object and edit it. Instead of opening the source application in a separate window, however, Windows opens it from within Publisher and your publication.

Figure 23-3 illustrates an embedded worksheet in Publisher after you double-click it to edit it. The object's frame looks like a small Excel worksheet. Note that the toolbar now contains several Excel tools and the formula bar. You edit the worksheet as if you were editing it in Excel. Any changes that you make are saved to the Publisher publication only, not to the source document.

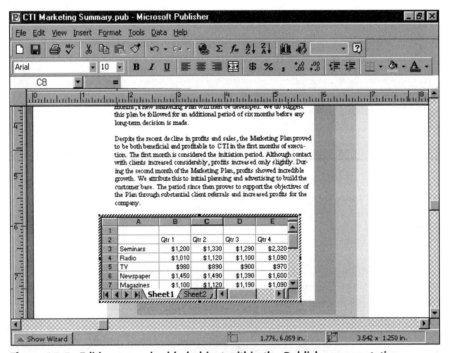

Figure 23-3: Editing an embedded object within the Publisher presentation.

Linking Objects

You can link a variety of objects to your Publisher document: a media clip, images, charts, worksheets, and so on. When you link the object, you also share the data with anyone else who can access the document. You might be connected to a network, for example, and share data files with others in your company. Linking objects to your publication guarantees that your data will be current.

You can only link objects that have been created in another program, such as Excel or PowerPoint. You create the object and then insert it into Publisher. Publisher provides two methods of inserting a link — you can insert an entire file and link it, or you can simply insert a selected object and link it. For example, you might not want to insert an entire worksheet, so you insert selected columns and rows. You might not want to insert an entire presentation, either, so you insert selected slides.

Linking an entire file

You can link any file to a Publisher publication as long as the source application supports OLE. Naturally, all Microsoft products do. Many other programs — word processing, database, spreadsheet, and so on — also support OLE. To find out whether a program supports OLE, read its documentation or consult the online Help system within the program.

OLE works similarly in most Windows applications. After you understand how to insert an object in Publisher, you'll be able to insert an object in most any program. Follow these steps to insert and link an object to a Publisher publication:

1. In Publisher, open the publication and go to the page on which you are inserting the linked object.

2. Choose Insert ⇨ Object. The Insert Object dialog box appears, as shown in Figure 23-4.

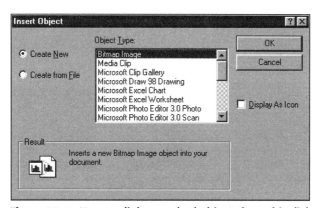

Figure 23-4: You can link or embed objects from this dialog box.

3. Choose the Create from File option. The dialog box options change to those shown in Figure 23-5.

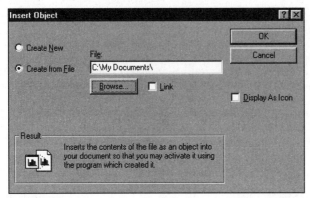

Figure 23-5: You must create from a file to link an object.

4. If you know the folder and filename of the file that you want to insert, enter the path in the File text box.

   Alternatively, click the Browse button. Figure 23-6 illustrates the Browse dialog box. Locate the folder containing the file that you want to insert, select the file, and then click the Insert button.

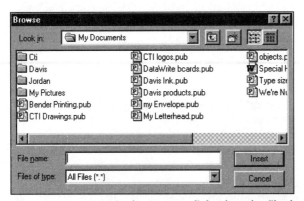

Figure 23-6: Locate in the Browse dialog box the file that you want to insert.

5. In the Insert Object dialog box, click the Link check box.

6. Click OK. The object appears in a frame in Publisher, as shown in Figure 23-7.

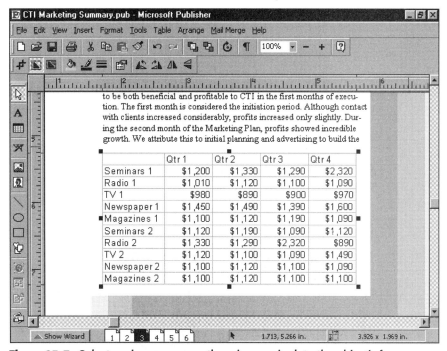

Figure 23-7: Select, resize, move, or otherwise manipulate the object's frame.

Linking part of a file

If you want, you can link to only part of a file, such as an Excel chart or a few slides from PowerPoint. To do so, you use a technique different from the Insert Object procedure. To link to part of a file, follow these steps:

1. Open the source application and the source document.

2. Select the items that you want to link to a Publisher document, as shown in Figure 23-8.

3. In the source application, choose Edit ➪ Copy.

4. Switch to Publisher and the destination document.

5. Choose Edit ➪ Paste Special. The Paste Special dialog box appears, as shown in Figure 23-9.

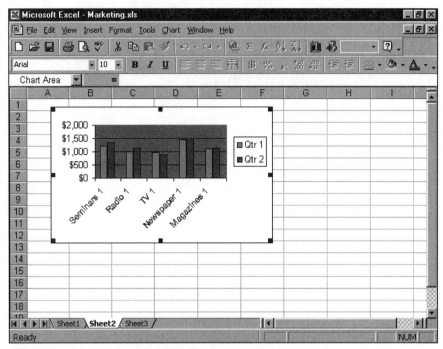

Figure 23-8: Select the part of the file that you want to link.

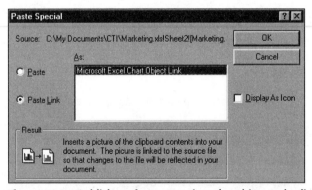

Figure 23-9: Publisher often recognizes the object to be linked.

6. Choose Paste Link.

7. Verify that the object is correct and then click OK. The selected object appears in your Publisher document.

Note that in both the Insert Object and Paste Special dialog boxes, an option offered is Display As Icon. If you have this option selected when you insert an object into your document, the object appears as shown in Figure 23-10. The icon is in a frame that you can resize or move. To view the object, double-click the icon. The document, chart, spreadsheet, or other object opens so that you can view it in its full size.

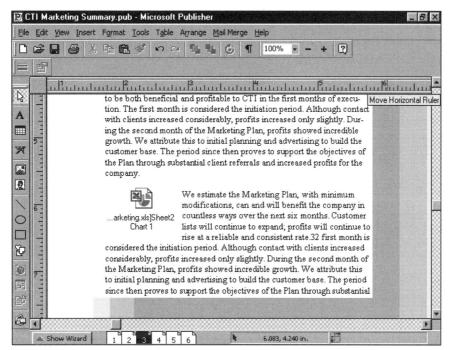

Figure 23-10: Displaying the object as an icon in your publication.

Editing the object

You can edit the object at any time from within Publisher. You double-click within the object's frame to edit the object in the source application. (If the object is displayed as an icon, as in Figure 23-10, double-click the icon to reveal the source application.) After you finish editing the file, save it as you normally would.

You can leave open the source application or close it. The changes to the linked file are made immediately. If you leave the source application open, however, and try to save the Publisher file, Publisher displays a message saying that you must update the link to continue. Click OK to update the link to an open source file.

Updating links

You can choose to update the links manually or automatically. By default, Publisher updates links automatically. When you open a publication, Publisher updates all links and adds any changes that may have been made to the linked files. When you save the file in Publisher, it saves the updated links. If you close the file without saving it first, Publisher asks whether you want to save the updated links or ignore them.

If you choose to update links manually, Publisher doesn't take care of the links for you. If a change occurs in a source file, the change will not be modified automatically in your Publisher document. You might choose to update links manually if you want to check changes in the document or wait on updates, for example.

To change a link to Manual Update, follow these steps:

1. In Publisher, choose Edit ➪ Links. The Links dialog box appears, as shown in Figure 23-11.

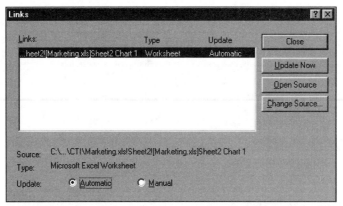

Figure 23-11: Use the Links dialog box to set options about the links in your document.

2. Select the link in the Links list.

3. Choose the Manual option and then click Close.

To update a manual link, follow Steps 1 and 2; click the Update Now button and then click Close.

Note   While the Links dialog box is open, you can select a link and click Open Source to open the source application. Click the Change Source button to choose a different file to link in place of the current one.

If you're planning to take your job to a commercial print shop, make sure that you take the OLE objects on disk so that the printer has access to them. See Chapter 31 for more information about commercial printing.

Embedding Objects

When you embed objects in your Publisher document, the changes that you make to the object appear only within that one publication, and don't affect the source document. You embed objects for the ease of editing the objects and for the choice of having various objects in your publications.

When you embed an object, you can open an abbreviated version of the source destination within Publisher to edit the object; any changes that you save are made *only* to the object in Publisher. You might want to embed an object, for example, that you do not want to update with the original source file.

Publisher offers three procedures for embedding files. You can embed existing files, embed part of an existing file, or create an embedded file within Publisher.

Embedding the entire file

You can embed an existing file similarly to the way in which you link an existing file. You use the Insert Object dialog box, without linking the file.

To embed an entire existing file, follow these steps:

1. In Publisher, open the destination document and go to the page on which you will embed an object.
2. Choose Insert ➪ Object. The Insert Object dialog box appears.
3. Select Create from File.
4. Enter the path and filename in the File text box, or use the Browse button to locate the file.
5. Do *not* click the Link check box to put a check mark in it.
6. Click OK. The file is inserted into your document, looking just as it would if you had linked it. You also can resize the frame and move it within the Publisher publication.

Embedding part of a file

You can embed part of a file, such as worksheet cells or a chart, into your Publisher publication. As with embedding an entire file, the embedded object is not linked to the source, but you can still use the source application to edit the object.

To embed part of a file, follow these steps:

1. In the source application, select the object or part of the file to be embedded.

2. Choose Edit ➪ Copy.

3. Switch to Publisher and the destination document.

4. Choose Edit ➪ Paste Special. The Paste Special dialog box appears.

5. Verify that the Paste option is selected, as shown in Figure 23-12.

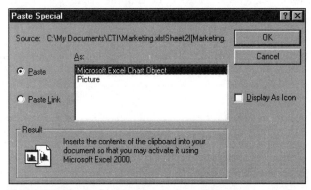

Figure 23-12: Embedding part of an object into your document.

6. In the As list, select the object type.

7. Click OK. The object appears in the Publisher document.

Creating an embedded object

You can create a new object and embed it by using the tools of the source application. Any program on your computer that supports OLE will work for creating an embedded object.

To create an embedded object, follow these steps:

1. In Publisher, choose Insert ➪ Object. The Insert Object dialog box appears with the default option of Create New, as shown in Figure 23-13.

2. In the Object Type list, select the source application that you want to use to create an embedded object.

3. Click OK. The source application opens within Publisher so that you can create the object, as shown in Figure 23-14. Note the PowerPoint menus and toolbars, as well as the Title slide AutoLayout.

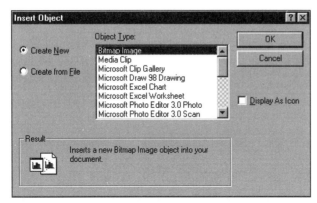

Figure 23-13: Select the object type you want to create.

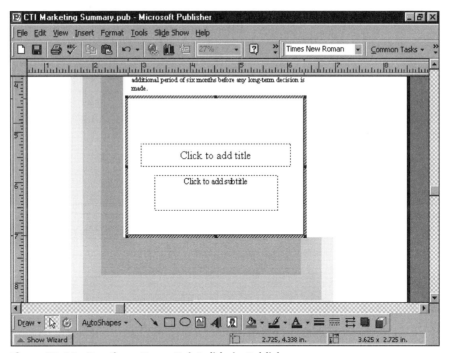

Figure 23-14: Creating a PowerPoint slide in Publisher.

4. Create the object just as you would in the source application, and then save your Publisher publication. Click outside of the object to return to Publisher.

Editing an embedded file

You edit an embedded file by double-clicking the object. The source application opens within Publisher to enable you to edit the object. Figure 23-15 illustrates an embedded chart ready for editing in Publisher, but using the Excel toolbars and menus. Note, too, that the object frame includes sheets as well as the Chart tab. The data for the chart is in Sheet 1, which is hidden when you're not editing the object.

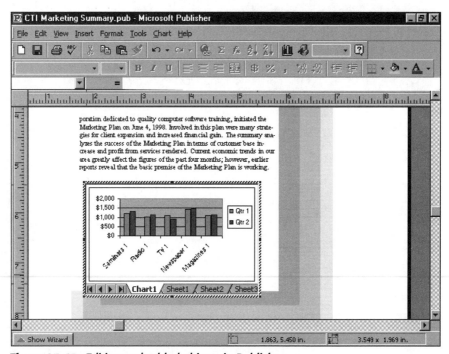

Figure 23-15: Editing embedded objects in Publisher.

Working with Specific Objects

You can link or embed a variety of objects in Publisher. Some objects may require different steps or procedures; others require special circumstances.

You already have learned to embed some objects in Publisher; for example, Word-Art and Microsoft Draw objects are embedded. You also know how to embed clip art and pictures into a Publisher publication.

In addition to these objects, you can embed media clips, photos, Word documents and pictures, a MIDI sequence, movie clips, Paint pictures, WAV sounds, and other objects. For a list of objects that you can insert into a document, scroll through the Object Types list in the Insert Object dialog box.

Embedding a media clip

You can embed any media clip, such as a sound, movie, animation, or other form. You can create the object from a file or create it new in Publisher, if you have the program and resources to do so.

When you use Microsoft Clip Gallery, you can easily embed clips into your documents. You can insert other clips, not associated with Clip Gallery, as linked or embedded objects, too, by using the same steps that you use for embedding other objects (choose Insert ⇨ Object). The only difference is that you must know the location and the filename of the file that you want to insert.

When embedding media clips, you might link or embed some of the following:

✦ Photos scanned or taken with a digital camera (JPEG, EPS, and so on)

✦ Clip art or pictures from a third-party program or the Internet

✦ Movie clips from the Internet (AVI, MPEG, MPE, MPG, MPA, ENC)

✦ MIDI sequences you create yourself (MID or RMI)

✦ CD audio files

✦ Sound files from CDs, the Internet, or third-party programs (WAV)

✦ Drawings from CorelDRAW, Paintbrush, Adobe Illustrator, or other art programs

Linking an embedded picture or clip art

If you plan to take your publication to a commercial print shop for printing, and plan to use photographs, clip art, drawings, and other color objects, you can link those objects to their originals, for better quality and resolution. When you embed a picture or color object into your publication, the quality of the picture degrades a bit. If you create a link in your publication to the original picture or object, you get a higher resolution to that object, and therefore the quality is better.

Tip

When you use a lot of pictures in your publication, you can speed up picture redrawing by choosing View ⇨ Picture Display. Then, in the Picture Display dialog box, choose either Fast resize and zoom or Hide pictures. Hiding pictures prints all images, but doesn't display them onscreen.

Linking to the object places the object in a separate file. Publisher copies a low-resolution copy of the object into your publication, but when you print it, Publisher uses the high-resolution source file for any linked objects.

Note

When you link to a picture so that you can take it to a commercial printer, make sure to include all linked files on disk for the printer. For more information about printing through a commercial print shop, see Chapter 31.

Understanding the link process

When you *link* the file to the object in your publication, you enable the best resolution possible for printing. When you insert a clip art, photograph, or other graphic, you're *embedding* it. For the best quality, linking the object to its original file is a better choice than embedding it.

Your first step is to insert the photographs or other art; the second step is to link them directly to their files. The Graphics Manager dialog box, shown in Figure 23-16, is the method by which you create and manage links to the photographs in your publication.

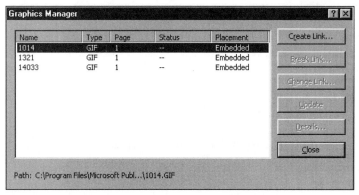

Figure 23-16: Creating links for your photographs.

In the Create Link dialog box (shown in Figure 23-17), you can choose one of the following:

✦ **Browse to locate the original file and link to it:** Links directly to the original file, offering the best quality and highest resolution.

✦ **Create a file from the full-resolution graphic stored in the publication and link to that:** Creates a file from the graphic in your presentation. Resolution might not be as good as with the preceding option.

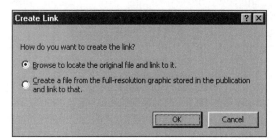

Figure 23-17: Choosing how you want to create the link

After linking a picture, you can view details about it at any time; for example, you can view the filename, file type and size, the color model, and so on. For more information about color models, see Chapter 31. Figure 23-18 illustrates the Details dialog box, in which you can view information about the graphic that is linked to your publication.

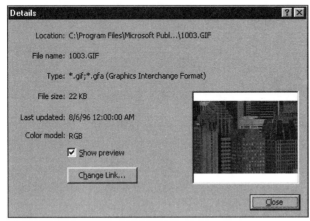

Figure 23-18: Viewing details about the graphic

You also can break the link to the graphic at any time, or change the link to another graphic.

Linking pictures

To link a picture, follow these steps:

1. Choose Tools ⇨ Commercial Printing Tools ⇨ Graphics Manager. The Graphics Manager dialog box appears (refer to Figure 23-16).

2. Select the first image and then click the Create Link button. The Create Link dialog box appears (refer to Figure 23-17).

3. Choose the method of creating the link: to the original file or to the embedded graphic in the publication.

4. Click OK to close the Create Link dialog box. The Link to Graphic dialog box appears, as shown in Figure 23-19.

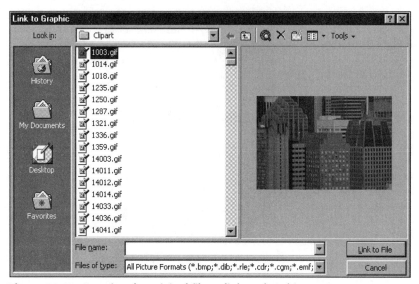

Figure 23-19: Locating the original file to link to the object.

5. Select the file and then click the Link to File button. Publisher links the file and returns to the Graphics Manager dialog box. The selected graphic is designated as Linked in the Placement column, and new buttons become available, as shown in Figure 23-20.

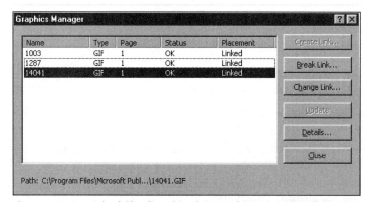

Figure 23-20: Linked files listed in the Graphics Manager dialog box.

6. Click the Close button to return to Publisher.

After you link a file, you can do any of the following:

✦ View its details by clicking the Details button in the Graphics Manager dialog box

✦ Break a link and return the file to embedded status by clicking the Break Link button in the Graphics Manager dialog box

✦ Change a link by clicking the Change Link button and choosing from the Link to Graphic dialog box another file to use in the link

✦ Update links by clicking the Update button in the Graphics Manager dialog box

Picture Formats and Publisher

Publisher provides numerous graphics filters to enable you to import pictures created in other applications. *Graphics filters* convert various file types so that they can be used in Publisher. The following is a list of file formats that you can import into Publisher:

✦ Windows Bitmap (BMP)

✦ CorelDRAW (CDR)

✦ CGM Graphics (CGM)

✦ Windows Enhanced Metafile (EMF)

✦ Encapsulated PostScript (EPS)

✦ Graphics Interchange Format (GIF)

✦ Joint Photographic Experts Group (JPEG or JPG)

✦ Kodak Photo CD and Pro Photo CD (PCD)

✦ PC Paintbrush (PCX)

✦ Macintosh Picture (PICT)

✦ Portable Network Graphics (PNG)

✦ Tagged Image File Format (TIFF or TIF)

✦ Windows Metafile (WMF)

✦ WordPerfect Graphics (WPG)

✦ Picture It! (FPX or MIX)

When you link a bitmapped object, Publisher saves it as a TIF file. When you link to an EPS or vector-based graphic, Publisher saves it as a WMF file.

The transparency of a bitmap isn't preserved. The transparency of a transparent GIF, however, is preserved. GIF files are saved as GIFs when linked in Publisher.

Summary

In this chapter, you learned about Object Linking and Embedding. You learned about the following:

✦ OLE terms

✦ Linking objects

✦ Embedding objects

✦ Editing linked and embedded objects

✦ Working with specific objects

In the next chapter, you learn to use some of Publisher's publication tools, such as Design Gallery and Publisher's wizards.

✦   ✦   ✦

Producing Publications

Publisher includes wizards and tools that enable you to quickly create documents of many kinds: letterhead, newsletters, signs, envelopes, labels, brochures, and more. This part shows you how to use Publisher's various design tools and wizards. You learn how to create different types of documents from wizards and from scratch—from planning to printing. In addition to creating common publications such as letterhead, newsletters, and flyers, you learn to create specialty documents and more complicated publications such as banners, booklets, and catalogs.

Using Publisher's Tools

T hree of the tools included with Publisher — production wizards, the Design Gallery, and the Design Checker — can aid you in creating and formatting your documents. Publication wizards enable you to base your publication on a particular type of document, such as a newsletter. The Design Gallery provides predesigned publication elements, such as logos or tables of contents, that you can customize as much as you like. Finally, the Design Checker can help you determine whether your publication's layout is error free. Read on to learn more about these useful tools.

Choosing Publication Wizards

Publisher provides numerous publication wizards on which you can base your documents. *Wizards* are tools that guide you, step by step, through creating a specific document type, such as letterheads, newsletters, signs, and so on. For more basic information about using Publisher's wizards, see Chapter 3, "Understanding the Catalog."

When using a wizard, you can let Publisher take the initiative and control the entire process, or you can choose the features that you want to apply from any one wizard. You can use a wizard to change a publication that you've already created, or to start a brand new publication.

Now that you understand about how to design a page, format fonts, create graphics, and otherwise create a publication in Publisher, you can use the wizards to help you create documents faster — and perhaps with more flair.

Using the wizard's defaults

When you first start Publisher, you have the choice of creating a new publication or opening an existing one, via the Catalog. You can also open the Catalog at any time to start a new publication (choose File ➪ New). Within the Publications by Wizard tab, shown in Figure 24-1, you can open any of more than 20 wizard categories. Each category represents common business and personal documents, and each is designed to help you quickly create a professional-looking publication.

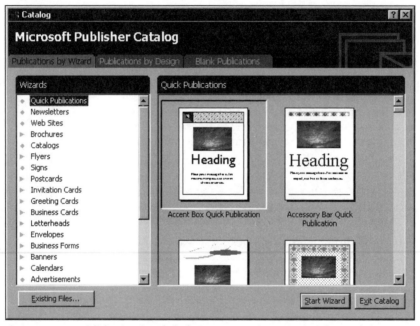

Figure 24-1: Publisher's wizards help you to create attractive documents.

Each wizard category contains multiple designs. Many categories contain multiple subcategories. For example, the Brochure categories offer the following subcategories from which to choose: Informational, Price List, Event, and Fund-Raiser. Within each subcategory are various designs based on Publisher's default color schemes and page layouts.

Figure 24-2 illustrates page 2 of a brochure using the Accent Box Price List layout. Publisher includes pictures, frames, and even sample text to help you complete the publication. You can accept or replace any of the design elements in the wizard.

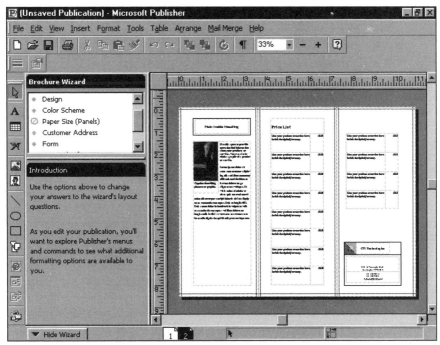

Figure 24-2: Use the brochure base to create your company publication.

Note

The wizards use your personal information to fill in any name, address, phone number, and other information. For more information, see Chapter 13, "Entering and Editing Text."

Using a wizard base

The Brochure base, as with any wizard, supplies you with the appropriate page size, layout guides, preformatted headings and body text, frames for text and pictures, and various designs and color schemes. The wizard creates a good foundation on which you can work; you simply modify the elements to suit your business or personal needs.

Figure 24-3 illustrates the text that Publisher supplies on the Price List Brochure; the text offers some suggestions for content. You replace the text with your own; however, Publisher provides the text frames, picture frames, table frames, and any other elements that you may need. You can easily delete or replace frames, plus you can move the elements around on the page, if you want.

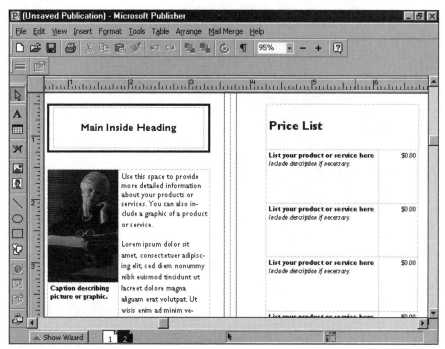

Figure 24-3: Take Publisher's suggestions for content, or create your own.

Many wizards ask questions as Publisher creates your document. For example, the wizard may ask the name of a newsletter or the date for your letterhead. The wizard then uses this information to fill in areas of the publication. You can turn off this step-by-step process if you prefer to fill in your own information.

To turn off the step-by-step question process, follow these steps:

1. Choose Tools ⇨ Options. The Options dialog box appears.

2. Select the User Assistance tab, as shown in Figure 24-4.

3. Remove the check mark from the Step through wizard questions check box to turn off the option.

4. Click OK.

After you turn off the option, it remains off for all wizards in all sessions until you turn on the option again. To turn on the option, follow Steps 1 and 2 in the preceding list, and then place a check mark in the Step through wizard questions check box.

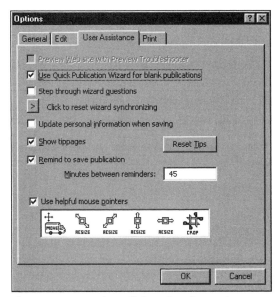

Figure 24-4: Turning off the wizard questions

Using the Quick Publication Wizard

The Quick Publication Wizard contains various layouts of text and pictures, with additional designs, borders, and backgrounds. The text is already formatted, and the colors are applied. You simply enter the text. You can choose the Quick Publication Wizard from the Catalog, or you can open a blank publication and apply various characteristics through the Quick Publication Wizard.

When you choose the Quick Publication Wizard from the Catalog, the documents are all 8½×11 inches, but you can change the size and orientation from the wizard box. The differences between the Catalog's presentations are in the formatting, layout, and design of the page.

Alternatively, you can choose a blank presentation, choose any size and shape from the Catalog, and then apply designs and color from the wizard box.

To use the Quick Publication Wizard, you can follow one of two sets of steps. The first set consists of the following steps:

1. Choose File ➪ New. The Catalog dialog box appears.

2. Select the Publications by Wizard tab and then choose Quick Publications.

3. In the Quick Publications window, select the design that you want to use. Click Create.

The following is the alternative set of steps:

1. Choose File ➪ New. The Catalog dialog box appears.
2. Select the Blank Publications tab and then choose the type of document that you want to create.
3. Click Create.

The publication that you chose appears in the work area. The Quick Publication Wizard box appears to the left of the document. You can use the options in the wizard box — Design, Color Scheme, Page Size, Layout, and Personal Information — to change the document in any way that you want. For more information about the Quick Publication Wizard, see Chapter 3, "Understanding the Catalog."

Altering a wizard's results

Publisher's wizards create professional-looking documents for you to use. Some characteristics of the document, however, may not suit your material or purposes. You might, for example, want to change fonts or enlarge the type to fit the copy better. You might need to add text boxes or pictures, change colors, or otherwise modify the document.

You can change the design of a publication by using the same wizard that you used to create it; or, you can select and change the characteristics of any frame or text within the publication.

Changing a design with a wizard

After you create a document with a wizard, you can use the wizard to change the publication. Use the wizard to change colors, layout, publication type, and other features of your publication.

When you create a publication with a wizard, the wizard box appears to the left of the work area. The wizard box contains various elements — design, color scheme, paper size, and so on — that apply to the current document. You can use any of the options in the wizard box to change the look of your publication.

Figure 24-5 illustrates the wizard box with the Design option selected for the Brochure Wizard. In the bottom half of the wizard box are the various design choices. You can click each choice to see how it affects the content and look of your publication. You should create the content first, so that you can see how it fits in different designs, layouts, or other modifications.

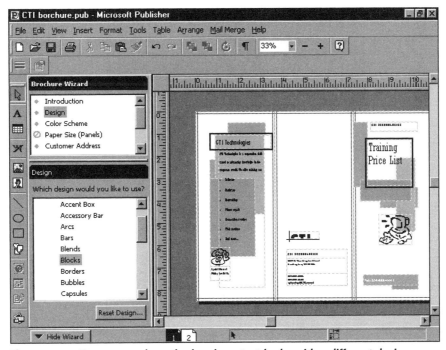

Figure 24-5: You can see how the brochure text looks with a different design.

Making your own changes

Using the wizard box changes only design and layout features. It normally doesn't change the font size and the placement of the frames on the page. To fit your copy, you may need to enlarge or reduce frames, change text size, or add or remove elements from the page. You can easily select and make any changes to text and frames in your publication by using the skills presented in the previous chapters of this book.

Looking at the design created by the wizard is important. Many designs look good and present an attractive document. Sometimes, however, the text is too small — for headlines, for example, or even for body text — for users to be able to read it comfortably. You can enlarge the text to fit the space and your copy.

You also might want to change the font of some publications created by wizards. Suppose that you regularly use a certain font for your company's publications, or that you don't like the look of the font used by the wizard. You can easily change fonts in the document, as well as alignment, color, placement, and so on.

Note   Most wizards apply the AutoFit Text option, which makes the text fit in the frame by resizing the text when you change the font. This is a handy feature that helps you to keep the frame size the same while enabling you to make changes to the fonts.

Figure 24-6 illustrates the brochure from Figure 24-5 with font and placement changes.

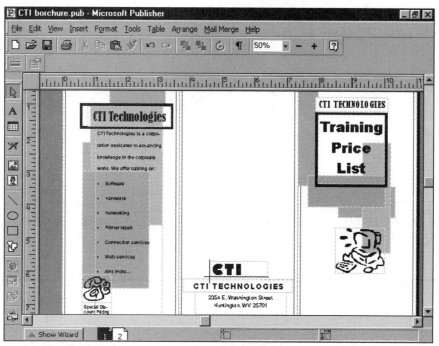

Figure 24-6: Enlarging the text makes it easier to read.

Adding Publication Elements with Design Gallery

You can add any type of element to your publications, such as a sidebar, logo, or coupon, by creating a text or graphic frame, formatting the text and frame, and so on. You also can add predesigned elements to a document by using Design Gallery, which enables you to add an object — to attract attention or add information — without having to create and format that object.

Design Gallery includes various elements that you can choose by object or by design. You can even create your own objects and insert those into documents that you create. Design Gallery's Objects by Category feature includes sidebars, advertisements, calendars, and so on; all you have to do is add the text.

Design Gallery's Objects by Design feature enables you to match the object to the design in your publication. Suppose that you chose the Blends or Southwest design for your document. You can add a calendar or other object using that same design, and thus keep the design in your publication consistent.

If you repeatedly use certain elements, such as a pull quote or caption, in various documents, you can save those objects so that you have to create them only once — but you can use them over and over.

To open Design Gallery, follow these steps:

1. Within your publication, choose Insert ⇨ Design Gallery Object. Alternatively, click the Design Gallery Object button on the Object toolbar. The Microsoft Publisher Design Gallery dialog box opens, as shown in Figure 24-7.

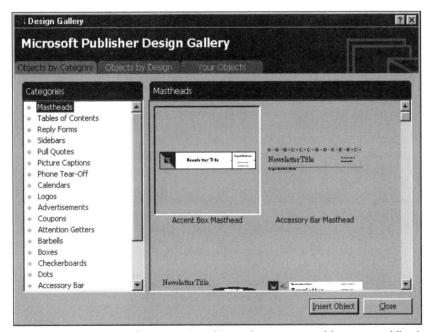

Figure 24-7: Design Gallery contains objects that you can add to your publications.

2. Choose the tab that you want to use (as explained in the following sections).
3. Select the category and then the design or object.
4. Click Insert Object.

Using Objects by Category

Design Gallery's Objects by Category feature offers a variety of objects that you can insert into your document, including mastheads for newsletters, coupons, and even various designs and borders. The following is a list of the categories and a description of the contents of each category.

✦ **Mastheads:** A *masthead* is a newsletter title, and often includes the volume, issue number, and the date the newsletter is produced. The mastheads in this category include various styles to fit Publisher's wizard design sets, such as Accent Box, Bubbles, Capsules, Marquee, and so on. Each masthead includes a graphic and formatted text.

✦ **Table of Contents:** Consists of a table with two columns, in which you enter the topic and the page number on which the topic appears. You can use a table of contents (TOC) in a report, newsletter, book, booklet, or other publication. The TOCs are preformatted for use in a plain document or with various design sets. Some TOCs don't match a design set but will work very well in most documents.

Figure 24-8 illustrates a TOC that was added to a newsletter. The TOC incorporates the same design as the newsletter, even though the newsletter wasn't created with a Publisher wizard.

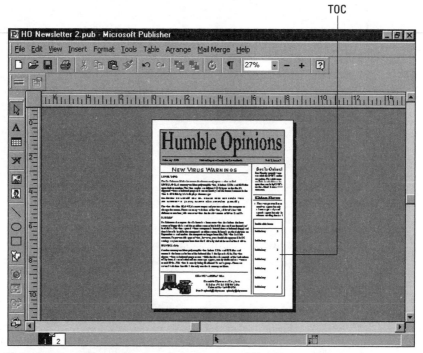

Figure 24-8: Add a table of contents to any publication.

✦ **Reply Forms:** Preformatted tables that you can add to a document for a response, order, or sign-up form. Inserting one of these tables, which all have lines and check boxes, is much easier than creating your own table. You can, of course, modify the form to suit your own needs.

✦ **Sidebars:** Use to insert related information in a report, book, newsletter, or even a flyer. A sidebar normally contains information that you want to stand out, so these designs make sure to attract attention. Many designs follow Publisher's design sets; others consist of boxes or screens of color. All use a bullet format for the text.

Figure 24-9 shows a sidebar added to a report. In this case, the report uses a simple design and layout, so the sidebar reflects that use. The sidebar uses a single vertical line to separate it from the rest of the text; also, the sidebar text is in a different font.

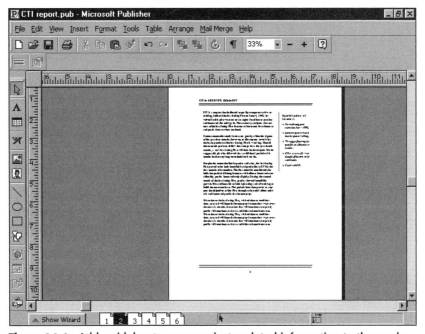

Figure 24-9: Add a sidebar to communicate related information to the reader.

✦ **Pull Quotes:** Attract attention to the text of a newsletter, such as by taking a quote from the text and enlarging it so that the reader notices it first (pull quotes also are referred to as *callouts*). The pull quote designs use design sets to create a box and text with screens and colors to attract attention.

✦ **Picture Captions:** Use to describe or label an illustration of any kind. When you select a caption, you're also selecting a picture frame to use with it. Naturally, you can change the frame, the frame's background, and the text of the caption.

✦ **Phone Tear-Off:** Add at the bottom of a flyer, for example, on which you put your phone number. People seeing the flyer can then tear off that part of the flyer to take home and call you later.

✦ **Calendars:** Although you can create a calendar by using the Table feature, Publisher makes adding a calendar to your publication easy with this object feature. Choose any calendar design, many of which are created with design sets, to insert a calendar into your document quickly and easily.

Figure 24-10 shows a calendar created in a publication by itself. When creating an object by itself, you can use any design or layout that you want. You also can make changes to the calendar to suit your own content and design.

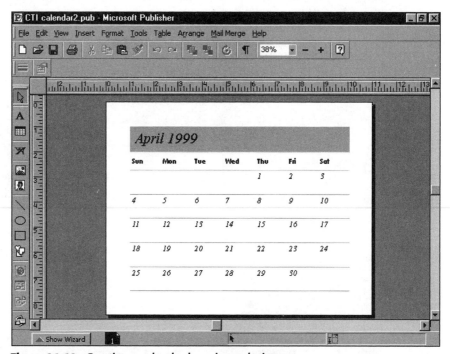

Figure 24-10: Creating a calendar by using a design set

Note

One of the wizard features that you can change for the calendar is the date. Scroll to select the year and the month, and then let the wizard enter the dates for you.

✦ **Logos:** If you're having trouble coming up with your own logo for your company, you can use one of these logos. Simply enter your company's name and use the graphics provided.

✦ **Advertisements:** Publisher offers several ads that you can use for newspaper or magazine advertisements. The designs are such that they will attract attention on a page with other ads. You simply add the copy.

✦ **Coupons:** Insert one of three different coupons into your publication, without the bother of designing your own. Figure 24-11 shows a coupon added to a flyer. Even though the coupon's design isn't the same as the flyer, it still fits into the layout and design.

Figure 24-11: Add a coupon to a flyer.

✦ **Attention Getters:** Shapes such as arrows, stars, and boxes with formatted text ready for you to type into. Add these to flyers or newspaper ads, for example, to grab the reader's attention.

✦ **Barbells:** Graphics that you can use as a partial border or separator on the page. A *barbell* is a line with a ball, or circle, on either end of the line.

✦ **Boxes:** Squares in alternating colors, which you can use as borders or separators.

✦ **Checkerboards:** Design consisting of white and black squares in a rectangle that you can add to a publication.

✦ **Dots:** Lines of dashes and dots that you can use for separators.

✦ **Accessory Bar:** Various designs that you can use as a border.

✦ **Accent Box:** These are various boxes and buttons you can add to a document.

✦ **Borders:** Page borders of different colors.

    ✦ **Linear Accent:** Various small designs and images that you can add to your publication.

    ✦ **Marquee:** More border or separator shapes and colors.

    ✦ **Punctuation:** Pairs of designs consisting of various shapes and colors to use at the top and bottom of a page, for example.

Using Objects by Design

Using Objects by Design to insert objects is similar to creating publications with Publications by Design. You choose the design set and then choose the object that you want to insert. For example, you can choose the Blends design set and then select a Masthead, Calendar, Pull Quote, or TOC. Each design set matches those in the Publications design sets, so you can match the objects that you insert to the design of your publications.

Figure 24-12 illustrates the first page of a newsletter that was created entirely by inserting objects from Design Gallery, using the Arcs design set, and the Sidebar, TOC, and Masthead. The text and headline were added in text frames. The formatting of some of the items was changed; for example, WordArt replaced the formatting for the name of the newsletter.

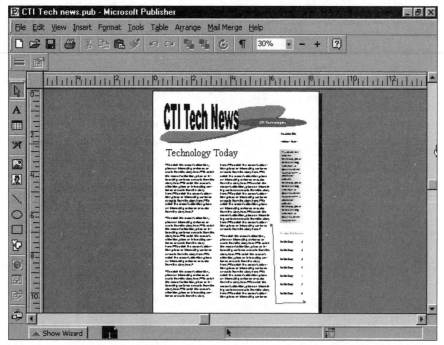

Figure 24-12: Create a publication by inserting objects within the same design set.

Editing objects

As with wizards, Publisher enables you to change the formatting, positioning, colors, and other characteristics of the objects that you insert into your document. You use the Wizard button that appears when you select one of these objects. Figure 24-13 illustrates the Wizard button, which appears on the right side of the screen, and the resulting wizard box, which appears on the left side of the screen.

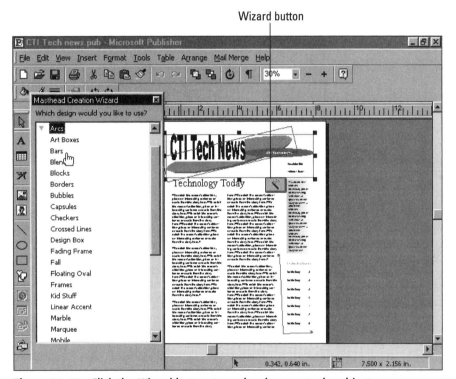

Figure 24-13: Click the Wizard button to make changes to the object.

Tip   Changing the design of one object in the publication, however, may make the other objects seem out of place. Remember to maintain consistency in your design.

Some items that you edit offer other characteristics that you can edit. The Calendar, for example, enables you to edit the date. Figure 24-14 shows the Change Calendar Dates dialog box. You can change the year and the month, and the wizard will position the dates appropriately.

Figure 24-14: Change the date, and let the wizard fix the calendar for you.

If you change a publication to another design and you have some objects left over that won't fit into that design, Publisher saves those objects to an Extra Content tab. If you happen to change your design back to the original, Publisher automatically inserts the leftover objects again. If your publication doesn't have any extra objects, you won't see the Extra Content tab.

Creating your own objects

You can create any object — such as a sidebar, a special frame for a picture, a logo, text design, or other object — and then save that object in Design Gallery, to use at will.

Using your knowledge of frame, object, and text formatting, create the object any way that you want. Then, after you insert it into Design Gallery, you can put it into other publications, which saves you time and effort and promotes consistency among your documents.

To create your own objects and save them in Design Gallery, follow these steps:

1. Create an object and then select it. Group the object if it consists of several smaller objects.

2. Choose Insert ➪ Add Selection to Design Gallery. The Add Object dialog box appears, as shown in Figure 24-15.

3. In the Object name box, enter a name for the object.

4. Choose a category name from the Category drop-down list, or enter a new one in the Category box.

5. Click OK.

The object appears in the Your Objects tab of Design Gallery, as shown in Figure 24-16. You can use the object in this and any other publication in Publisher.

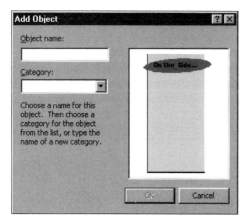

Figure 24-15: Add an object to Design Gallery.

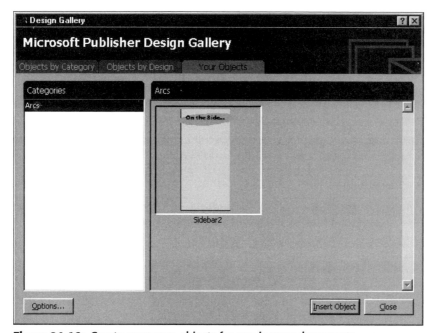

Figure 24-16: Create your own objects for use in your documents.

Note

The Options button that appears in the lower-left corner of Design Gallery's Your Objects tab enables you to delete objects that you've added, edit your categories, and browse other documents.

Using Design Checker

Design Checker is a tool that you can use to make sure that no problems exist with your completed publication. You can set Design Checker to look for empty frames, overflow text, objects in the nonprinting area, and so on. You also can check foreground and background pages, only specific pages in a publication, or all pages.

If Design Checker locates a problem, it displays a dialog box stating the problem and suggesting possible solutions. The following is a list of the problems that you can check for in your publications:

✦ **Empty frames:** Locates empty frames, which may overlap or hide other frames or objects, and may make printing or redrawing the screen take longer.

✦ **Covered objects:** Identifies objects that are covered by other objects, or frames that are hidden. If you *want* an overlapping effect, however, then turn off this option.

✦ **Text in overflow area:** Helps you to locate any text in the *overflow area* (the part of the frame that holds text when the frame is too small) before you print. You may occasionally miss text that has overflowed.

✦ **Objects in nonprinting region:** Notifies you if any text or pictures are in the *nonprinting region* of the page, which is the margin the printer can't reach. (In a laser printer, for example, the nonprinting area is ¼ inch around the edges.)

✦ **Disproportional pictures:** Notifies you if a picture is distorted in some way — too tall for its width, for example. However, if you want disproportional pictures in some documents, for artistic or other purposes, then turn off this option.

✦ **Spacing between sentences:** Notifies you when two spaces follow a period, or when you accidentally enter two spaces while typing.

Checking the design

Always save your document before checking the design. To check the design, follow these steps:

1. Choose Tools ➪ Design Checker. The Design Checker dialog box appears, as shown in Figure 24-17.

2. Choose the pages that you want to check.

3. Check the Check background pages option, if you want to check the background *and* the foreground.

4. Click OK.

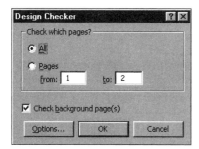

Figure 24-17: Checking the design elements on the page

Design Checker checks your document. If it finds a problem, it displays a different Design Checker dialog box, as shown in Figure 24-18. Note that Design Checker selects or highlights the problem area in the document.

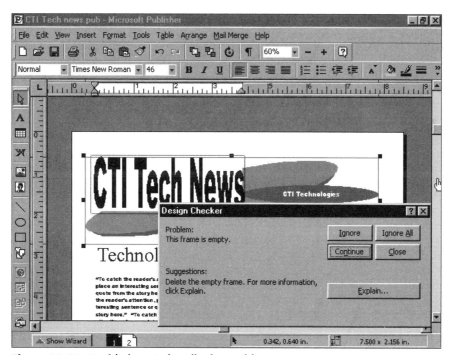

Figure 24-18: Decide how to handle the problem.

The options in the dialog box include the following:

✦ **Ignore:** Disregard this one instance of the problem

✦ **Ignore All:** Disregard all instances of this problem in the document

✦ **Continue:** Resume the design check

✦ **Close:** Stop the design check

✦ **Explain:** Publisher Help appears and explains how to correct the problem

You can click outside of the Design Checker box to fix the problem, and then click the Continue button when you're ready. When the check is complete, Publisher displays a dialog box telling you it is finished. Click OK.

Setting Design Checker options

You can choose which of the options you want Design Checker to look for. To set the Design Checker options, follow these steps:

1. Choose Tools ⇨ Design Checker.

2. In the Design Checker dialog box, click the Options button. The Options dialog box appears, as shown in Figure 24-19.

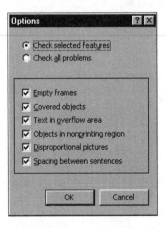

Figure 24-19: Choose the options that you want Design Checker to check.

3. Choose either Check selected features or Check all problems.

4. If you choose Check selected features, choose the problems you want to check for. If you do not want to check for a particular problem, clear that check box.

5. Click OK to return to the Design Checker dialog box.

Summary

In this chapter, you learned about using some of Publisher's tools for creating and formatting your publications. You learned how to do the following:

✦ Choose publication wizards

✦ Use Design Gallery

✦ Use Design Checker

In the next chapter, you learn how to create one-page publications by using Publisher's wizards.

✦　　✦　　✦

Creating One-Page Publications

✦ ✦ ✦ ✦

In This Chapter

Producing a letterhead

Creating an envelope

Making a flyer

✦ ✦ ✦ ✦

Your letterhead introduces you to the recipient of the letter. Before the recipient ever reads the letter, he or she gets a first impression from the letterhead. The letterhead design, the color of the paper, any logos, your name or the name of your company—all contribute to the first impression.

In addition to a name, address, and phone number, you should include other information the recipient might need to contact you. For example, you can include office and home phone numbers, toll-free numbers, e-mail addresses, the addresses of subsidiaries, and so on. Consider which information you want to make available to everyone receiving the letterhead, and then include it when designing the page.

You might also want to add a logo or photograph to a letterhead, or simply add some graphic lines, boxes, or other decorative effects. Publisher enables you to do all these things.

Producing a Letterhead in Publisher

Publisher offers a variety of letterhead designs. With the design sets—such as Accent Box, Accessory Bar, or the bars design—Publisher supplies graphic designs, font formatting, and placement of the text. Publisher also offers several designs based on PaperDirect predesigned papers.

Figure 25-1 illustrates a letterhead created with the Marquee design set and wizard.

The Letterhead Wizard, as well as other wizards in Publisher, uses your personal information to complete the information in the letterhead. For more information about filling out personal information, see Chapter 13.

Tip   You also may choose a color scheme with your personal information. When you use one color scheme for your company publications, you create a unity and consistency for your company.

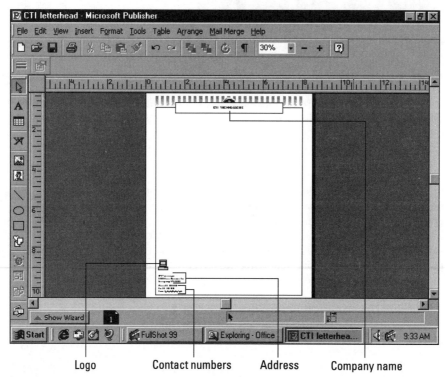

Logo   Contact numbers   Address   Company name

Figure 25-1: Use a design and color scheme for your letterhead that is consistent with other company documents.

Figure 25-2 shows the logo, address, and contact numbers in a close-up view. The font formatting and the placement of the text and logo are Publisher's choices — although you can easily change anything that you want.

Using the Letterhead Wizard

You can choose to create a letterhead on plain paper or on special paper. When you use a wizard to create a plain-paper letterhead design, Publisher includes the graphics — lines, boxes, color scheme, and so on — in the final, printed letterhead. When you use a wizard to create a special-paper letterhead design, Publisher prints only the text and logo. The special paper includes the preprinted graphic designs.

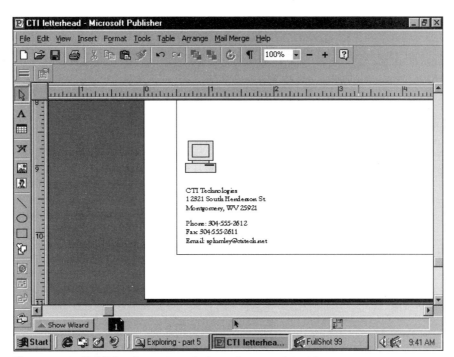

Figure 25-2: Publisher formats and places logos and text for you.

Note

In place of the Publications by Wizard tab, you can choose your document from the Publications by Design tab, if you want to choose a specific design set for all of your publications. Note, however, that you have more choices of documents from the Publications by Wizard tab.

When you use the Letterhead Wizard, Publisher automatically uses the information you enter in the Personal Information dialog box to fill in your company's name, address, and other information. If you use a logo with your company name, Publisher can also insert that into the letterhead.

As you use the wizard to create the letterhead, you can alter the design.

Choosing the letterhead design

The first step to using the Letterhead Wizard is to choose the basic design set and layout of the letterhead. To choose the letterhead design, follow these steps:

1. In Publisher, choose File ⇨ New or press Ctrl+N. The Microsoft Publisher Catalog appears.

2. In the Publications by Wizard dialog box, click Letterheads in the Wizards box. A variety of letterheads appear in the right pane of the window, as shown in Figure 25-3.

Figure 25-3: You can choose either Plain Paper or Special Paper letterhead designs.

3. Scroll through the designs and click the one that you want to use.

4. Click the Start Wizard button.

Note   You can choose to either run a wizard that asks you questions about your document's contents and design, or turn off this feature and use the wizard box to change these very same content and design elements. To turn off the feature, choose Tools ⇨ Options ⇨ User Assistance ⇨ Step through wizard questions. Remove the check mark from the check box beside the option.

Publisher displays the letterhead and the Letterhead Wizard onscreen, as shown in Figure 25-4. Publisher creates the letterhead design, using the personal information that you supplied.

If you like the look of the letterhead, you can accept it by clicking the Finish button in the Letterhead Wizard box. You then can edit the text or otherwise modify the letterhead on your own. Alternatively, you can modify the letterhead by using the Letterhead Wizard.

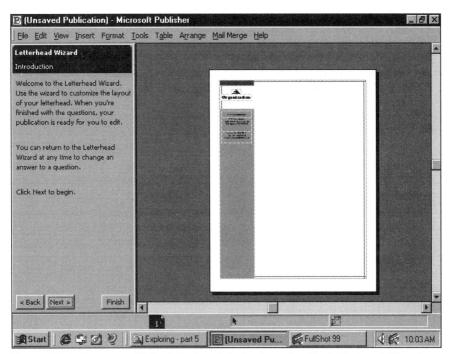

Figure 25-4: You can edit the letterhead design by using the Letterhead Wizard.

Stepping through the Letterhead Wizard

You can use the Letterhead Wizard to change design and layout characteristics of the letterhead. For example, you can apply a different color scheme, choose a new logo, or change personal information.

As you use the wizard, click the Next button to move to the next wizard box; use the Back button to return to the preceding box and make changes, if necessary. You can also click the Finish button at any time in the wizard to finish the design and take over editing it yourself.

Note   Each Letterhead Wizard offers similar design choices. Some letterhead designs, however, may present other design elements that you can modify.

To step through the Letterhead Wizard after creating a new letterhead, follow these steps:

1. In the Letterhead Wizard box, click the Next button. The Color Scheme box is one selection that may appear, as shown in Figure 25-5.

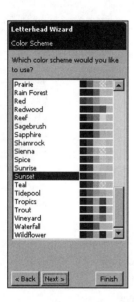

Figure 25-5: Choose the color scheme that suits your company's publications.

2. If you want to change the color scheme, choose one from the list. Click Next to continue. The logo is another element that you can add, remove, or change, as shown in Figure 25-6.

Note

You can add a logo to your letterhead at any time. Naturally, you can create your own logo and place it as you want in the letterhead. See Chapter 17 for more information. You can also use Publisher's Logo feature to add a logo to your letterhead. See Chapter 24 for more information.

3. Click Next to continue. The Personal Information box appears, as shown in Figure 25-7. You can change the Personal Information set to Primary Business, Secondary Business, Other Organization, or Home/Family by choosing the respective radio button.

4. Click Finish to complete the wizard. You should save your publication at this time.

Figure 25-6: Add or leave out a logo.

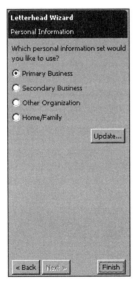

Figure 25-7: Changing the information displayed on the letterhead

After you close the wizard, Publisher displays the Letterhead Wizard box beside your publication. You can choose to change the design (as shown in Figure 25-8), color scheme, logo, or personal information at any time while you work on your letterhead.

Figure 25-8: Use the Letterhead Wizard as you work to make changes to the publication.

Tip   You can also choose to hide the Letterhead Wizard, to view more of the letterhead. Click the Hide Wizard button on the Publisher status bar.

Editing text or graphics

Publisher's wizards create professional-looking publications. The designs, color schemes, and logos are attractive and useful. You can easily create a letterhead from any of the wizards and use it without making any changes or modifications to the publication.

However, making changes to the text, design, and graphics is easy after you use the Letterhead Wizard to create the base document. You might want to change the letterhead, for example, to enter additional addresses or contact information.

You might also prefer to change the text formatting in a Publisher letterhead. Most of the text formatting in Publisher's wizards is too small. For example, in Figure 25-9, the name of the company is entirely too small. You can easily select and enlarge the text from 7-point to 10-point, for example, without changing the size of the frame.

Changing text formatting

You can change the size, font, style, alignment, color, and other characteristics of any text in a letterhead that you create with a Publisher wizard. You select the text and then use the Formatting toolbar to make the changes. (For more information, see Chapter 16.)

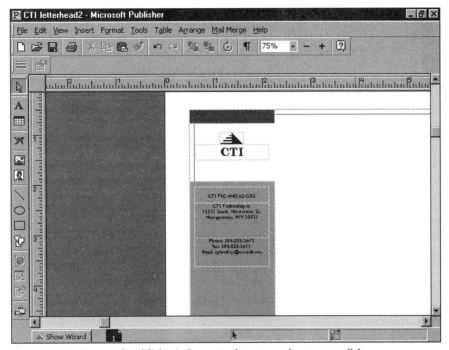

Figure 25-9: Some of Publisher's formatted text may be too small for your purposes.

You might want to create a style or two for use in your letterhead and other publications. Creating a style means that you can apply the same formatting to other paragraphs of text in the document, quickly and easily. (See Chapter 17 for more information.)

Naturally, you may need to enlarge the frames or otherwise alter frame formatting when you change the text. You can add frame fills and borders, layer and connect frames, and change frame properties. (For more information about frames, see Chapter 10.)

Figure 25-10 illustrates the letterhead with some changes to text formatting.

A wizard can serve as a starting point for your publication, or as a stopping point. It's all up to you.

Changing graphics

In addition to changing fonts and formatting, you can easily change the graphics in any letterhead. You can copy, move, or add lines and fills to graphic shapes and lines. You also can add line art, drawings, or clip art to the design. (For more information, see Chapter 18.)

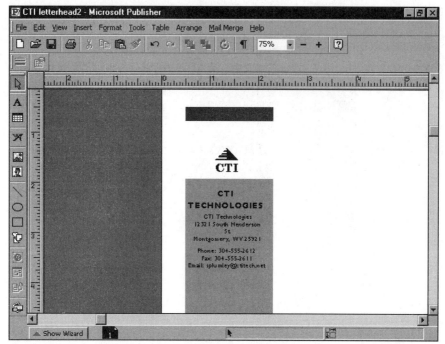

Figure 25-10: Use Publisher's tools to modify the letterhead to suit your needs.

If you added a logo to your letterhead, you can change the logo by editing text or by running the Logo Wizard, as shown in Figure 25-11. In the Logo Wizard, you can change the picture, design, graphic, and so on.

Note   You can even change the page layout of a letterhead. For example, you can modify the margins or orientation. See Chapter 7 for more information.

Creating your own letterhead design

You use letters in your personal life and in the business world. A letter might inform or request information, confirm a business transaction, or thank your mom for a gift. An attractive letterhead makes a letter more impressive and appealing. The letterhead might sell your business by creating a positive first impression.

When designing your own letterhead, you should remember a few guidelines. For example, don't allow a margin of more than one and a half inches at the top of the page; too much top margin detracts from the design of the letterhead and the body of the letter. Also, use at least a half inch or so for the bottom margin if you're planning to add the address or a graphic at the bottom of the page. In general, half-inch to one-inch margins all around the edge of the paper is a good guideline.

Logo Creation Wizard   Edit logo text   Click wizard button

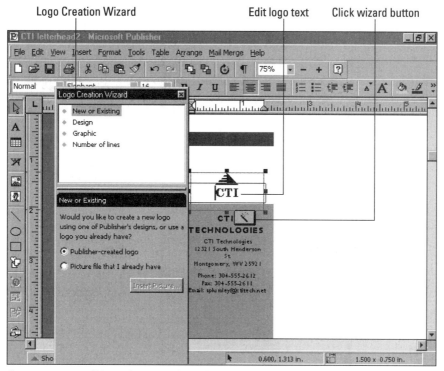

Figure 25-11: Editing a logo in a letterhead

Graphics may consist of page borders, lines, or shapes. You might even use a water-mark on the letterhead to attract attention. Ordinarily, you don't want to overpower the design with too many graphics or colors. Remember balance, consistency, and white space in your design.

When formatting your text, consider the overall look of the letterhead design. The text shouldn't be too large or too small. For example, a 36-point font for your com-pany name is most likely too large and overwhelming for the letterhead. Instead, try 18- to 24-point fonts for the largest text; use 9- or 10-point text for the address and other contact information.

Figure 25-12 illustrates a simple but interesting letterhead design. White text on a black frame makes the company name stand out, and the page frame repeats the frame around the contact information. Margins are .7 inch and provide enough space to keep the letterhead from looking crowded.

Figure 25-13 illustrates another design for the same company. This design uses a flourish as a watermark for the page. Printing in two colors — say, light blue for the flourish and red for the text — makes the letterhead impressive and attractive.

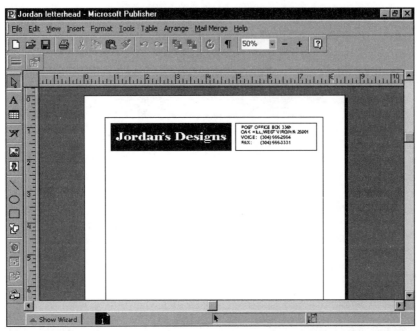

Figure 25-12: An uncomplicated design identifies the company and presents all the information.

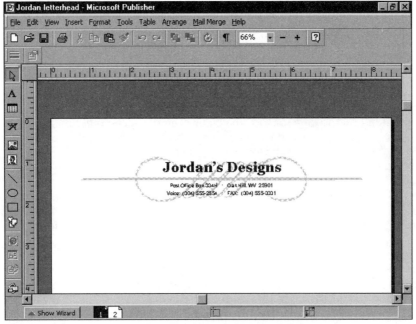

Figure 25-13: Use a watermark or other design to add pizzazz to the letterhead.

Creating an Envelope

Your envelope design should be coordinated with your letterhead. Use the same colors, fonts, and designs, for consistency. An envelope normally displays a name or company name and an address. You don't include any contact phone numbers or e-mail addresses on an envelope, although you might include a logo, graphics, or other small design to match the letterhead.

Figure 25-14 illustrates an envelope design that matches the previous letterhead design for Jordan's Designs (refer to Figure 25-13). The envelope uses the same watermark flourish with the same fonts in the return address; however, everything is on a smaller scale.

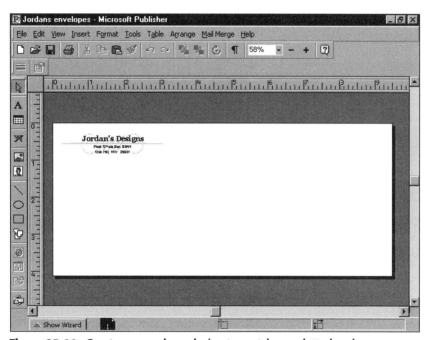

Figure 25-14: Create an envelope design to match your letterheads.

Publisher also enables you to create envelopes that match the letterhead that you created with a wizard. Figure 25-15 illustrates an envelope that matches the letterhead in Figure 25-10. Changes made in the letterhead were repeated in the envelope: the logo is smaller, the graphics were moved, and the name of the company was enlarged.

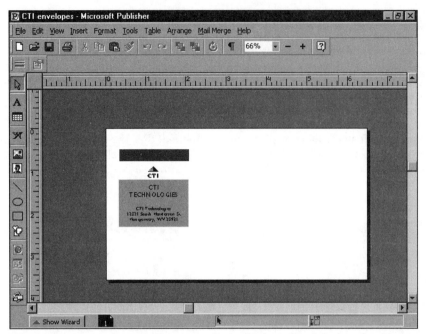

Figure 25-15: Any changes that you make to the letterhead design should also be made to the envelope.

Using the Envelope Wizard

As with letterhead designs, Publisher provides both plain- and special-paper envelopes. If you have envelopes from PaperDirect, for example, you can create an envelope design that fits well with the preprinted design.

Publisher provides its own designs and graphics when you choose to use plain-paper designs. Some of the designs look like miniature letterheads when printed to an envelope; in some cases, that's good, but in other cases, the designs leave something to be desired. Figure 25-16, for example, illustrates an envelope design for the Marquee design set. The return address and design take up too much room on the envelope; for instance, the margins are a half inch. Normally, margins for envelopes are only a quarter inch.

Additionally, the design in Figure 25-16 is a bit overpowering for an envelope. You can easily alter the design, however, if you don't like the way that it turns out after you run the wizard. Figure 25-17 shows the same envelope with the design altered to suit an envelope better. The new look is a bit more professional and tasteful.

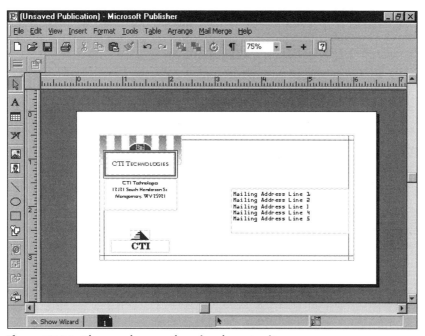

Figure 25-16: The envelope as the wizard creates it

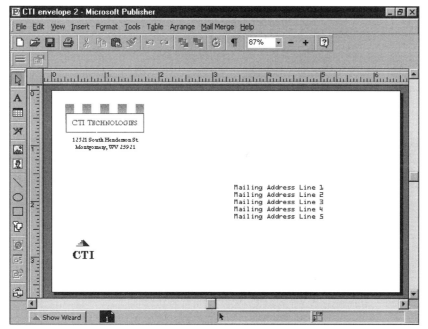

Figure 25-17: Removing some of the decorative graphics makes the design elegant instead of clumsy

Choosing the envelope design

You can choose an envelope design for plain paper or for special paper. Select the design that matches your letterhead design.

To use the Envelope Wizard, follow these steps:

1. Choose File ➪ New. The Microsoft Publisher Catalog dialog box appears.

2. In the Publications by Wizard tab, choose Envelopes from the Wizards pane.

3. Choose either Plain Paper or Special Paper and then scroll through the envelope designs.

4. Choose the one that you want and then click the Start Wizard button.

5. Publisher displays the selected design and the Envelope Wizard box, as shown in Figure 25-18.

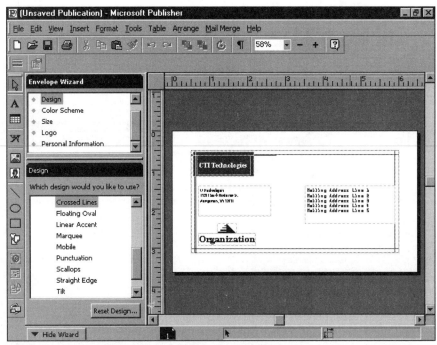

Figure 25-18: Use the Envelope Wizard to change the design, color scheme, and other characteristics of the envelope.

Editing the envelope using the Envelope Wizard

The Envelope Wizard offers editing tools that are similar to the Letterhead Wizard's tools. After you create an envelope, you can change the design, color scheme, and other characteristics.

The following is a description of the changes that you can make to the envelope by using the Envelope Wizard:

✦ **Design:** Change the design set to Floating Oval, Linear Accent, Mobile, or any other design listed in the Envelope Wizard.

✦ **Color Scheme:** Choose a new color scheme to use in place of the selected one.

✦ **Size:** Change the envelope from the default size to another size. Sizes generally are either #6 or #10. A #6 envelope is 3⅝×6½ inches; a #10 envelope is 4⅛×9½ inches.

✦ **Logo:** Add or remove the logo placeholder.

✦ **Personal Information:** Choose the type of personal information to insert, update the information, or insert a component for the mailing address.

Note For more information on addressing multiple envelopes automatically, see Chapter 32.

Naturally, you also can make any edits or changes to the envelope design, text, or formatting, just as you would with the letterhead design. Refer to the previous section, "Editing Text or Graphics."

Creating your own envelope design

When creating your own envelope design, you can use any font and formatting, graphics, or logo that you want in the return address. Make sure that the design matches your letterhead design. You also need to consider postal regulations when designing an envelope.

The United States Post Office recommends that you follow certain guidelines, to guarantee speedy and efficient delivery of the mail. The post office also requires you to follow certain regulations, for your mail to be processed.

Tip For more information about regulations and guidelines, ask your post office for complete and detailed booklets about preparing a mailing.

The following are some of the general guidelines and regulations:

✦ **Size:** The minimum size requirements for mailed pieces is 3½×5 inches; anything smaller won't pass through the machinery at the post office. Maximum sizes distinguish pieces that must be individually handled as opposed to processed mechanically. Any piece larger than 6⅛×10½ inches won't easily fit through automatic processing and thus may be delayed in delivery.

✦ **Boundaries:** The post office specifies certain boundaries for the return and delivery addresses, so that bar codes and facing identification marks (FIMs) are not obstructed by graphics or text. The post office uses FIMs and bar codes in business mailings, bulk mailings, and return replies.

Bar Codes and FIMs

The *bar code* is a system for encoding ZIP code information. A bar code appears in the lower-right corner of the mailed piece. Bar codes speed up the sorting process.

A facing identification mark, or FIM, is added to the bar code and located in the upper-right edge, along the top of the mailed piece. An FIM enables additional sorting information for business and courtesy-reply mail. If you do a lot of mailing, you can request the post office to assign your company a bar code and FIM, to help speed up processing of your mail.

The following are some regulations concerning placement of addresses and such. These regulations guarantee that the post office has the correct amount of space needed for bar codes and FIMs.

✦ **Return address:** The last line of the return address should not fall below the second line of the mailing address. Some of Publisher's envelope wizards *do* drop the return address, logo, or graphics below this line. You should check with your post office if you have any doubts about your envelope design.

✦ **Mailing address:** The mailing, or delivery, address should be indented at least one inch from the right and left margins of the envelope. The last line of the mailing address must also be at least $5/8$ inch from the bottom edge of the envelope; the first line of the mailing address should be no more than $2^3/4$ inches from the bottom of the envelope.

✦ **Bar code:** Place the bar code in the $5/8 \times 4^1/2$-inch area in the lower-right corner of the envelope.

✦ **FIM:** Place the FIM within $1/8$ inch of the top edge of the envelope, and between $1^3/4$ inch and 3 inches from the right edge.

✦ **Mailing address formatting:** When printing your mailing, or delivery, address, make sure that you observe a few guidelines for readability. Always left-align the text and use an easily readable typeface, such as a sans serif type. Don't use bold, italic, expanded, or condensed type for the mailing address. Also, be careful when applying line or character spacing; make sure that the text is readable.

Making a Flyer

A *flyer* is a tool for advertising, distributing information, announcing news, and so on. A flyer must attract attention and get the point across quickly to be effective. Flyers usually contain certain information:

✦ Include contact details, such as a name, address, and phone number.

✦ Add some sort of attention-getter. You can use a large graphic or a piece of WordArt to describe what it is you're selling or advertising. Large, bold, or colorful text grabs attention, for example.

✦ Use descriptive phrases, brief lists, or key words to help define the purpose of the flyer.

You can create a flyer on your own, or you can use one of Publisher's Flyer Wizards. The Flyer Wizards contain placeholders for the information that you need to include in a successful flyer. Together, preformatted headings and text areas, graphic designs, and even photographs form Informational, Sale, Event, or other flyers. You also can use plain-paper or special-paper flyer designs.

Figure 25-19 shows a Sale flyer created with a Flyer Wizard. The eye-catching graphics and large type attract attention. Listed in smaller type are items on sale and the address of the store. Note, too, that the CTI logo appears in the corner to add consistency and for identification.

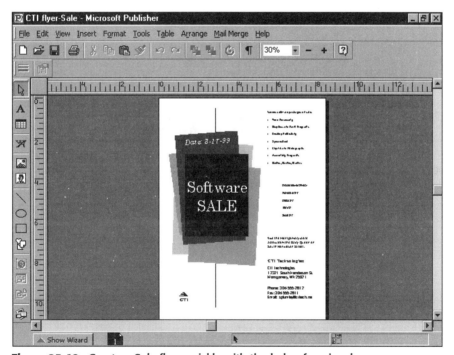

Figure 25-19: Create a Sale flyer quickly with the help of a wizard.

Using the Flyer Wizard

Publisher's Flyer Wizards offer a variety of subjects — such as informational, special offer, events, or even lost pets. As with other wizards, you can change the design or color scheme. You also can change the graphic, add tear-offs, and change the personal information used in the flyer.

You can use the Flyer Wizard to guide you, step by step, or you can simply use the wizard box to make your own changes.

Creating the flyer

You can choose a flyer design that corresponds to your other documents, or you can choose a completely different design to attract attention. Even though some flyers in the Wizard list specify certain information—such as a sale or announcement—you can always change the text later.

To create a flyer by using the Flyer Wizard, follow these steps:

1. Choose File ➪ New. The Catalog appears.

2. In the Publications by Wizard tab, select Flyers. Publisher displays a list of the available flyer types, as shown in Figure 25-20.

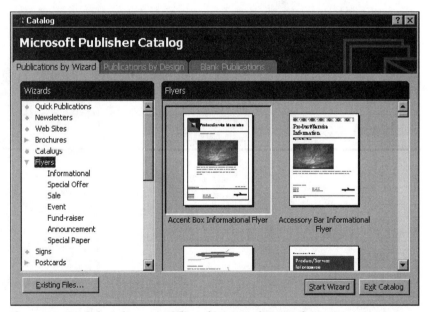

Figure 25-20: Select the type of flyer closest to the one that you want to use.

3. Select a category of flyer and then select the flyer design that you want.

4. Click the Start Wizard button. When you choose not to use the wizard's step-by-step instructions, Publisher displays the Flyer Wizard box and the document that you selected. Figure 25-21 illustrates the Promotional Wizard in the Blocks design, with the Flyer Wizard box on the left side.

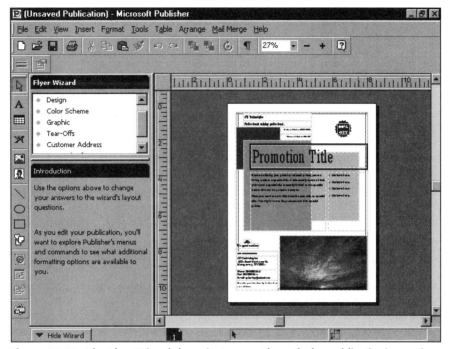

Figure 25-21: The Flyer Wizard doesn't step you through the publication's creation.

Editing the flyer

After you choose the flyer design and layout that you want, you can enter text as you would with any publication. You can delete text, reformat it, or add text; you also can change the frame sizes and formatting, and add, move, or remove graphics.

The Flyer Wizard box offers changes that you can apply to the flyer, as well. The following is a description of each characteristic that you can change from the Flyer Wizard box:

✦ **Design:** Change the design set to any available set, such as Blocks, Marquee, Tilt, and so on. Alternatively, change the design to a different type of flyer, such as Sale, Informational, Event, or Announcement; then, change the design set within the flyer type.

✦ **Color Scheme:** Choose a different color scheme to apply to the design.

✦ **Graphic:** Choose to remove or add a placeholder for a graphic. To edit the graphic, double-click the picture; this opens the Clip Gallery, from which you can choose another photograph or piece of clip art.

✦ **Tear-Offs:** Choose to add a coupon, phone tear-offs, order form, or other element to your flyer. When you choose to add an element, Publisher rearranges the existing elements and inserts the tear-off for you.

✦ **Customer Address:** Include a placeholder for a customer's address. Use this feature if you plan to do a mailing. Publisher includes a mail merge feature that will insert addresses for you. (See Chapter 32 for more information.)

✦ **Personal Information:** Change the personal information listed in the flyer to your business, other organization, or home and family information.

Figure 25-22 illustrates a promotional flyer created with the wizard. This flyer was changed to fit the content. The edited flyer has less text, so placeholders have been moved and the font size enlarged. Also, the graphic is different, and a sign-up form has been added.

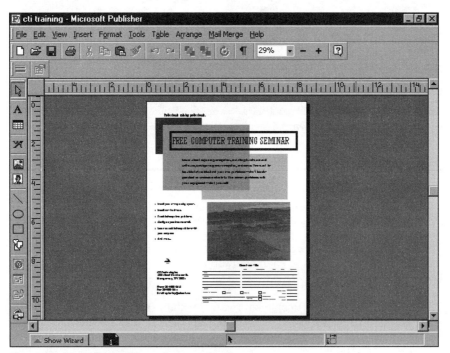

Figure 25-22: Editing a flyer after creating it

Creating your own flyer

You can create your own flyer by using the techniques for font formatting and graphic additions that you've already learned. Remember design basics, such as consistency, white space, and balance.

When creating content for a flyer, make sure that you add your company name and address, or other contact information. Also, add a point of emphasis — such as bright colors, large graphics, or large display type. Use short, descriptive phrases, lists, and images to get your point across.

Flyers are usually 8½×11 inches, but they can be larger, such as 11×17 inches. Orientation can be either portrait or landscape, whichever fits your content the best. Also, remember that a flyer can be double-sided. A menu, class descriptions, multiple-product flyer, or any document with many details can be printed on both sides of the paper.

Figure 25-23 illustrates a flyer for a nut sale. Large, colorful text (the word "Sale" and the name of the company are in red) and the large graphics attract the eye. Lists describe the nuts and fruit on sale. The company's address is at the bottom of the flyer.

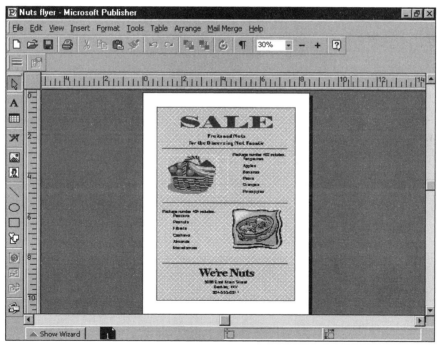

Figure 25-23: Colorful and eye-catching flyers sell your products.

Summary

In this chapter, you learned how to create one-page publications, both with the Publisher wizards and on your own. You learned how to create the following:

✦ Letterheads

✦ Envelopes

✦ Flyers

In the next chapter, you learn how to create specialty publications, such as certificates, calendars, and labels.

✦   ✦   ✦

Producing Specialty Publications

You can use Publisher to create specialty publications
such as certificates, calendars, business cards, labels,
and banners. This chapter explains how.

Producing Certificates

You can create a variety of certificates for your business or
personal use. Certificates of achievement, appreciation,
excellence, and even gift certificates are among the many
certificates that you can create with Publisher.

You can create certificates on plain paper, using Publisher's
graphics or your own, or you can use special certificate paper
to create your specialty publications.

Using the Certificate Wizard

Publisher includes a variety of certificates that you can use to
create award and gift certificates. Award certificates include
designs and backgrounds that you can apply to plain paper,
plus some designs for specialty papers.

The following are the types of award certificates for which
Publisher includes wizards:

+ On plain paper:
  • Best of Show
  • Certificate of Achievement
  • Certificate of Appreciation
  • Certificate of Excellence

- Certificate of Safety

- Employee of the Month

- Great Idea

- Sports Certificate

✦ On special paper:

- Certificate of Appreciation

- Certificate of Excellence

Figure 26-1 illustrates a Best of Show certificate, unaltered as to formatting and style. Note that you can fill in the certificate either by hand or on the computer. Publisher creates award certificates that are 11 × 8½ inches in landscape orientation.

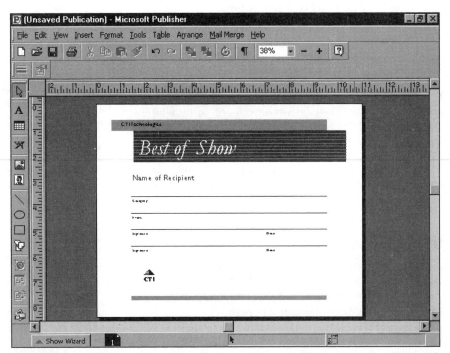

Figure 26-1: Publisher adds personal information, such as the company name and logo, to the certificate.

Publisher offers a variety of design sets for gift certificates, as well, including Accent Box, Accessory Bar, Blocks, Blends, and more. Gift certificates are 7 × 3⅝ inches in landscape orientation. Figure 26-2 illustrates a gift certificate created from the Straight Edge Wizard in Publisher. As with an award certificate, you can fill in a gift certificate either by hand or on the computer.

Figure 26-2: Create gift certificates for your products or services.

Naturally, you can change the wording and content of any certificate after you create it. You can also use the wizard to change color schemes, designs, and other characteristics.

Tip   Parchment paper is a nice type of paper to use for certificates; it gives the document a formal, sophisticated look.

Creating the certificate

Creating a certificate is easy in Publisher, even if you don't have the traditional certificate paper. The Plain Paper Wizards add designs to the certificate for you. Even though the Gift Certificate Wizards use the same design sets that you're accustomed to seeing in Publisher, the award certificates do not use design sets. Instead, award certificates use unique designs.

Note   You can either run a Publisher wizard that asks you questions about your document's contents and design, or turn off this feature and use the wizard box to change these very same content and design elements. To turn off the feature, choose Tools ➪ Options ➪ User Assistance ➪ Step through wizard questions.

To create a certificate by using a wizard, follow these steps:

1. Choose File ➪ New. The Catalog appears.

2. In the Publications by Wizard tab, select either Award Certificates or Gift Certificates.

3. In the right window pane, select the certificate and design that you want to use.

Note   If you did a standard installation, you may need to install the wizard for the certificate. Publisher prompts you if this is necessary, and it takes only a minute or so to install.

4. Click Start Wizard. The wizard either runs or the certificate appears onscreen with the Certificate Wizard on the left. You can proceed to edit the text or the certificate design characteristics.

Editing the certificate

You can edit text on the certificate as you normally would edit any other Publisher text. You can also edit design elements. The following is a list of the wizard elements that you can modify:

✦ **Design:** Apply one of the other certificate types, such as Safety or Sports, to the certificate.

✦ **Color Scheme:** Choose another color scheme to apply to the certificate.

✦ **Personal Information:** Choose or update your personal information for use with the certificate.

Creating your own certificate

You can create any type of certificate that you want, using a blank publication as your base. You need to set up your paper size and so on. Award certificates are commonly 11 × 8½ inches, and gift certificates are 7 × 3⅝ inches; both are landscape orientation. Margins should be at least 1 inch all around.

Publisher's BorderArt is an excellent element to add to a certificate. For more information about BorderArt, see Chapter 10.

Information that you may want to include on the certificate includes the company's name and perhaps a logo, and an area for the date, the recipient's name, and perhaps signature lines. Titles for certificates can be anything appropriate; you might use Certificate of Recognition or Certificate of Achievement, for example. Add any other text to describe the honor, if you want.

Often, the font used in a certificate title is center-aligned and in either a script or Old English font. Some TrueType fonts that you might consider include Olde English Text MT, Parchfont, Papyrus, Lucida Calligraphy, Freestyle Script, or Algerian. You also might want to try using WordArt for the certificate title. (For more information about WordArt, see Chapter 21.)

Tip   When using any script or decorative type, such as Old English, never use all caps. The text is harder to read in all uppercase.

Use a simple sans serif for the body of the certificate so that it is easy to read. Double-space between the lines of text to allow enough room for handwriting. Figure 26-3 shows a certificate that uses Olde English Text MT for the certificate title and Arial for the body of the text. Also added is a frame that uses BorderArt and a fill in red.

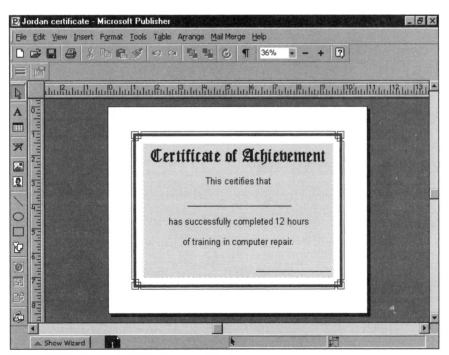

Figure 26-3: Create individualized certificates.

Figure 26-4 shows a certificate that uses WordArt for the title. Also, note the BorderArt frame and the clip art. You can apply company colors or any color to a certificate to add pizzazz.

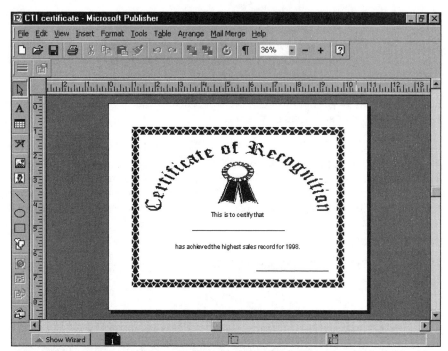

Figure 26-4: Create a certificate by using WordArt and BorderArt.

Producing a calendar

Calendars are most useful for business or personal purposes. With Publisher, you can make any size calendar that suits your purposes. You might publish a calendar for use in a monthly newsletter, flyers, advertisements, or other customer-related publications. You might also create calendars for your employees or for yourself, and publish important dates and deadlines.

Publisher's Calendar Wizard enables you to choose to create a calendar either by the month or by the year. You can also choose the date and year that you want for the calendar.

You formulate a calendar by creating a table. You can let Publisher create a full-page or wallet-size calendar for you, or you can create one yourself.

Using the Calendar Wizard

As with other documents, Publisher presents several calendar designs using design sets. The two different sizes Publisher offers are full page and wallet size. Each full-page calendar also includes other text and designs, but you can easily resize the calendar, move text, and otherwise modify the results from the Calendar Wizard.

You also can modify fonts, graphics, and table formatting. (See Chapter 22 for more information about formatting tables.)

Figure 26-5 illustrates a calendar created by using the Calendar Wizard. Changes in text placement and the table size and format, however, make the calendar more useful to the company. Altering and modifying the contents of any wizard is easy in Publisher.

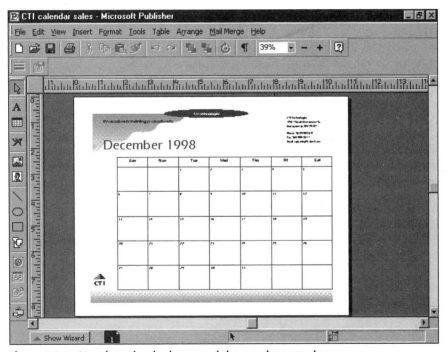

Figure 26-5: Use the calendar base, and then make your changes.

Creating the calendar

You can create a calendar by using the Calendar Wizard, and then later change design elements as well as dates and months.

To create a calendar by using the Calendar Wizard, follow these steps:

1. Choose File ➪ New. The Catalog appears.

2. In the Publications by Wizard tab, choose Calendars.

3. Select either Full Page or Wallet Size.

4. Scroll through the calendars and select the design that you want.

5. Click Start Wizard.

Tip The Understated Calendar under Full Page Calendars creates a good base on which you can build a calendar design of your own.

Editing the calendar

You can edit the design, color scheme, orientation, and personal information (if applicable) in the calendar, just as you would in any other document created by a wizard. The Calendar Wizard offers these choices and a few more.

You also can use the Calendar Wizard to edit a schedule of events, if you chose a design that lists the schedule. More important, you can change the date and month/year. The month/year option enables you to display either one month or the entire year.

Figure 26-6 illustrates a 1999 yearly calendar. Note that the Calendar Wizard option that appears in the left pane is Month/Year. Once again, you can move and resize the table to make the calendar any size that you want on the page.

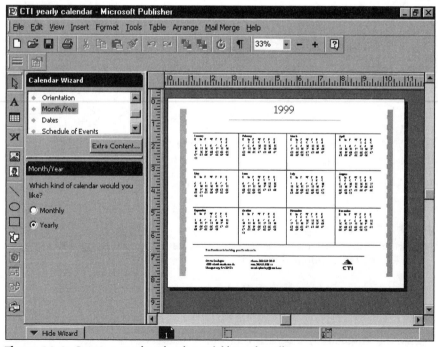

Figure 26-6: Create a yearly calendar quickly and easily.

The other handy change that you can do to the calendar through the Calendar Wizard is change dates. Using the Change Calendar dialog box, you can change the starting and ending month for a monthly calendar, or the year that you want to display if you're using the yearly calendar.

You can even display multiple months or years by changing the dates. For example, choose **January 1999** for the Start date and **December 1999** as the end date for a monthly calendar, and Publisher adds 11 pages to your document to display all 12 months.

Similarly, enter **1999** for the start date on a yearly calendar and **2001** for the end date, and Publisher inserts two extra pages, each page containing one yearly calendar.

To edit the calendar dates and setup, follow these steps:

1. Create the calendar by using the Calendar Wizard.

2. In the Calendar Wizard, choose Month/Year and select either Monthly or Yearly.

3. In the Calendar Wizard, choose Dates.

4. Click the Change Dates button. The Change Calendar dialog box appears.

5. Enter a Start date and year. Enter an End date and year.

6. Click OK. Publisher's Calendar Wizard creates the calendars.

Creating your own calendar

As you can tell, letting Publisher create a calendar for you is far easier than creating one yourself. Of course, you can use the Table feature to draw and format your own calendar. (See Chapter 22 for details.)

Alternatively, you can use Publisher's Understated Calendar as a base, add your own graphics and formatting, and then take advantage of the Calendar Wizard's Date, Month, and Year features. Figure 26-7 shows the Understated Calendar with customized designs added. Merged table cells create space for notes about important events and clip art. Color adds spice to the design.

Merged table cells

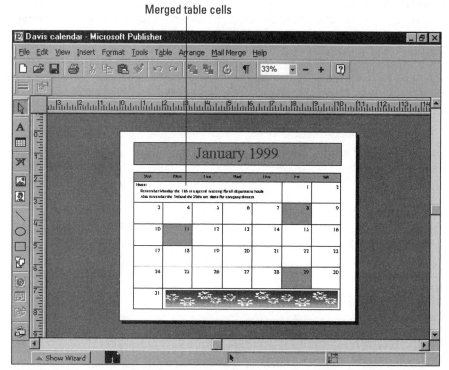

Figure 26-7: Customized calendar created by using a Calendar Wizard base

Building Business Cards

All companies use business cards to identify salespeople, managers, technicians, officers, and so on. Normally, you can have business cards printed at a commercial print shop for very little; but you also can print your own cards and customize them any way you want.

The nice thing about creating your own card design is that you have more control over the layout, design, and content. After you create the cards, you can either take them to a print shop or print them yourself. You also can customize certain cards to give to certain business associates.

When printing business cards yourself, you need to purchase perforated card stock or figure out some other way to cut them apart. Perforated card stock is 8¹/₂×11 inches, with eight to ten business cards per page. Publisher includes a wizard for this type of special paper.

If you design the cards on something other than the perforated card stock, use a heavy card stock with a nice vellum or linen finish. You can purchase this type of stock at a commercial print shop. You also can have the print shop cut the cards for you with a mechanical cutter, to ensure accuracy and consistency in card size.

Using the Business Card Wizard

Publisher's Business Card Wizard applies to both plain paper and special paper. The plain-paper cards use different design sets — such as Borders, Bubbles, Crossed Lines, and Floating Oval. The special-paper cards apply to specific designs created by PaperDirect. This special paper is perforated card stock.

Note   The perforations in the card stock are so fine that you cannot see any marks around the edge of each card. Your cards will look very professional if you print them on a laser or inkjet printer.

Figure 26-8 illustrates a business card created for special paper. You create one business card, and the wizard takes care of duplicating the card for printing on the paper. The graphic design appears only onscreen; only the text is printed, because the design is preprinted on the special paper.

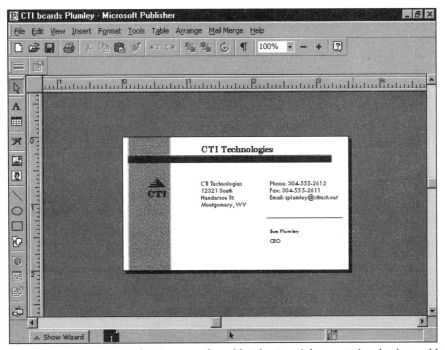

Figure 26-8: Design one business card, and let the Special Paper Wizard print multiples for you.

When you use the Special Paper Wizard, Publisher prints multiple cards to the page to fit the paper. When you use the Plain Paper option, you must tell Publisher how many cards to print to the page, or it will print only one by default. See the following section for more information.

Creating the card

Choose a design set that matches the other business documents that you use. A business card definitely should match your letterhead and envelope. Presenting a consistent look to your company's publications makes your business seem more organized and sophisticated.

To create a business card using the Business Card Wizard, follow these steps:

1. Choose File ➪ New. The Catalog appears.

2. In Publications by Wizard, select Business Cards.

3. Below Business Cards, choose either Plain Paper or Special Paper.

4. Scroll through the designs and select the one that you want.

5. Click Start Wizard.

Editing the card

You can edit the text on the business card to suit yourself. You may want to format some of the text to make it look more like your other business documents. You also can add or remove a logo and change the graphics, if you want.

Using the Business Card Wizard, you can change characteristics with which you are familiar, such as design, color scheme, logo, and personal information. You also can change the following characteristics:

✦ **Orientation:** Change the orientation to portrait, for example, to give the card a different look. The size remains the same, but the orientation may attract more attention than the usual landscape format.

✦ **Print Tiling:** Select to choose whether to print one business card on the page — say, for proofing purposes — or to print multiple cards on the page. When you print multiple copies per sheet, Publisher sets up ten business cards on an $8\frac{1}{2}$x11-inch page, by default.

Creating your own business cards

When you create your own business cards, you can use any design — font and graphics — that you want. You should match the business card design to other company documents to create unity in your presentation and image.

A business card's size is 3½×2 inches. Usually, business cards are landscape-oriented, but, as previously mentioned, portrait orientation adds a distinct look to the card. Margins should be at least ¼ inch, although you can use more or less margin, depending on your design and text.

To create your own business card, follow these steps:

1. Choose File ⇨ New. The Catalog appears.

2. Select the Blank Publications tab.

3. In the left pane of the tab, select Business Card.

4. Click Create. Publisher creates a blank business card and places it on the page beside the Quick Publication Wizard, which you can choose to use or not.

Figure 26-9 illustrates a business card in portrait orientation. The combination of the clip art and the script font gives the card a delicate look. The clip art reinforces the portrait orientation.

Figure 26-9: Create your own business cards, using graphics or clip art.

Printing business cards

When you print the business cards that you create, you can specify whether to print the card one per sheet or multiple cards per sheet. If you intend only to read the content or show someone the design, you can print one copy per page. If you plan to print multiple cards on your laser or inkjet printer, however, or take the design to a commercial print shop for printing, you should print multiple copies of the card per page.

Publisher figures out how many cards can print on each page, so that little or no paper waste occurs. If you use a wizard, Publisher sets up the cards for you, so you don't have to worry about printing; just make sure that you choose multiple cards through the wizard if you're printing to plain paper. If you're printing on special paper, Publisher prints multiple cards, by default.

If you want to change the number of cards to print per page, or set up your own business cards to print multiples, you can change the option in the Print dialog box. Follow these steps:

1. Choose File ➪ Print. The Print dialog box appears, as shown in Figure 26-10.

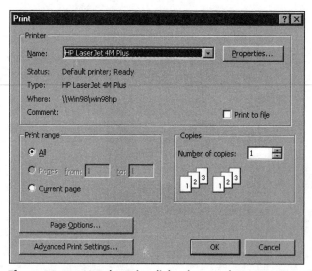

Figure 26-10: Use the Print dialog box to change page options.

2. Click the Page Options button. The Page Options dialog box appears.

3. Choose the Print multiple copies per sheet option, as shown in Figure 26-11.

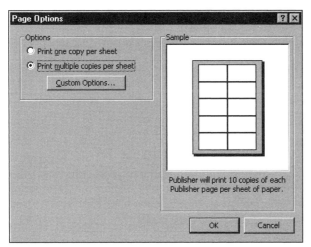

Figure 26-11: Let Publisher help you set up your business cards for printing.

4. Publisher displays a sample layout, depending on the orientation and size of your business card. By default, the 3¹/₂×2 landscape-oriented business card is displayed ten per page.

5. Accept this option by clicking OK. Click OK in the Print dialog box to print the cards.

Alternatively, click the Custom Options button to make changes to the margins and spacing that you want to apply to the cards. Figure 26-12 illustrates the Custom Options-Small Publications dialog box.

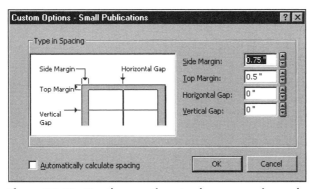

Figure 26-12: Use these options to change margins and gaps.

You might need to alter the top and side margins or the gaps between cards if you are using either a special paper that doesn't fit any of the existing Business Card Wizards or an uncommon size of business card. Make any changes in this dialog box and then click OK to return to the Page Options dialog box.

For more information about printing, see Chapter 30.

Making Labels

You can make labels for mailings, shipping, and even computer disks in Publisher. Publisher has various wizards that help you create labels for Avery brand products. Avery produces multiple labels on an 8½×11-inch sheet that you can peel off; they stick to envelopes, jars, disks, and other objects.

Each Avery label type has a corresponding number; Publisher lists the number in the wizards to make it easier for you to create labels that match the type that you've purchased. If you're using a brand other than Avery, it may provide the corresponding Avery number on its packaging. If not, you can create your own labels in Publisher.

Using the Label Wizards

Publisher includes a variety of Label Wizards. You create one label and, just as with business cards, the wizard takes care of duplicating the label and printing multiple labels on a page.

When printing labels created with the wizard, you can use the Page Options dialog box (choose File ➪ Print ➪ Page Options) to print only one copy of the label per page or multiple copies per sheet.

The following subsections provide descriptions of the types of labels that you can create with a wizard, and the corresponding Avery number.

Mailing labels

You might want to use mailing labels, in particular, when you use mail merge to prepare newsletters, flyers, or other publications for mailing. (For more information, see Chapter 32.) No designs are associated with these labels; you simply enter the mailing address, either manually, or automatically through mail merge.

Publisher Mailing Label Wizards include the following:

✦ Large Mailing Address
- Avery 5162
- Avery L7162

✦ Medium Mailing Address

- Avery 5161
- Avery L7159
- Avery L7161

✦ Small Mailing Address

- Avery 5160

Shipping labels

For shipping labels, Publisher includes the standard design sets, including Blocks, Borders, Tilt, and so on. Figure 26-13 shows the Mobile shipping label. You can change the text, graphics, and formatting as you would on any document. You also can fill in the mailing address manually or automatically.

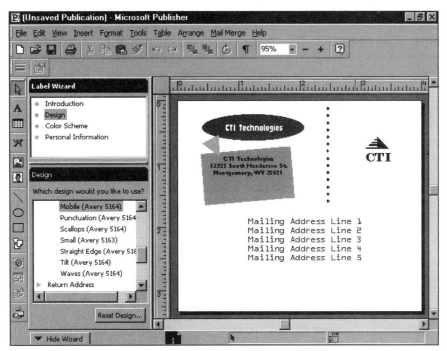

Figure 26-13: The Label Wizard enables you to change the design, color scheme, and personal information.

Publisher Shipping Label Wizards include the following:

- ✦ Shipping Label: Avery 5164
- ✦ Large Shipping Label: Avery L7167
- ✦ Small Shipping Label: Avery 5163

Return address labels

Return address labels are similar to other labels. These include no designs, only your personal information. Publisher's Address Label Wizards include the following:

- ✦ Large Return Address: Avery 5160
- ✦ Small Return Address: Avery 5267

Miscellaneous labels

Publisher also offers other Label Wizards, for cassette tapes, computer disks, and so on. Each wizard includes a unique design for the item. Publisher's miscellaneous wizards include these:

- ✦ Computer Disk Label: Avery 5196
- ✦ Cassette Label: Avery 5198
- ✦ Cassette Case Liner
- ✦ Compact Disc Case Liner
- ✦ Video Face Label: Avery 5199A
- ✦ Video Spine Label: Avery 5199B
- ✦ Jar/Product Label: Avery 5164, 5196, 5262, and 5163
- ✦ Binder Label
- ✦ Bookplate
- ✦ Equipment Tag: Avery 5160
- ✦ Luggage Tag
- ✦ Made By Tag: Avery 5160
- ✦ Name Tag: Avery 5096
- ✦ Sticker: Avery 3113

Note   If you did a standard installation, you may need to install the wizard for some or all of the labels. Publisher prompts you if this is necessary, and it takes only a minute or so to install.

To create labels by using the Label Wizard, follow these steps:

1. Choose File ➪ New. The Catalog appears.

2. In the Publications by Wizard tab, select Labels from the left pane.

3. Choose the type of labels that you want to create, and then select the label from the right pane.

4. Click Start Wizard.

Making your own labels

If you must create your own label in Publisher, you should first try to find a corresponding Avery number with the label sheets that you've purchased. If you have the size of your labels, you can look in the Page Setup dialog box (choose File ➪ Page Setup). Choose Labels, and view the list of Avery label sizes to see whether the size corresponds with your label type. Figure 26-14 illustrates the Page Setup dialog box. Note that it lists not only the Avery number and type of label, but the label size as well.

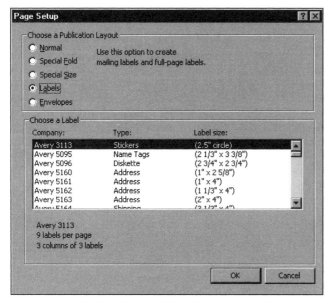

Figure 26-14: Match your label to the size, if it isn't an Avery label.

Another idea is to check the label package to see whether it suggests a layout. Most label packages include an instruction sheet that explains in detail how to create a label template to match their label sheets.

If all else fails, you can create your own label sheet by using a blank publication. Carefully measure the top and left margins of your label sheet and match those margins in the Layout Guides dialog box (choose Arrange ➪ Layout Guides) for your publication.

You also can set grid guides in the Layout Guides dialog box to help you create the label template. Figure 26-15 shows the Layout Guides dialog box, with margins and grids set. This template fits 12 labels on the page. Each label is $3^4/_5 \times 1^1/_2$ inches.

Tip   To adjust the label size further, you can go to the background and adjust the guides by pressing the Shift key and dragging the guides with the mouse.

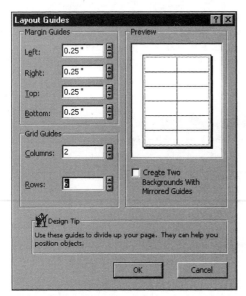

Figure 26-15: Create guides to help you create your labels.

You might also want to create one label and then copy it repeatedly to fill in the rest of the labels.

Creating a Banner

Banners are large messages created to string across a doorway, window, wall, or other large area. You might welcome home someone with a banner, for example, or indicate a point of entry, registration, or some other information. Banners are usually between five and ten feet long. Their height can be 11 or $8\frac{1}{2}$ inches.

To create a banner in Publisher, you gather and fasten together multiple sheets of paper. Generally, you print to multiple sheets of $8\frac{1}{2}\times11$-inch paper. Then, you collect the pages and tape or glue them together to create the long banner.

Publisher provides various templates for creating a banner, including several design sets and preformatted text. Alternatively, you can use a blank banner publication to create your own banner in Publisher.

Using the Banner Wizard

Publisher's Banner Wizards include various topics — such as Informational, Sale, Event, Birthday, Welcome, Congratulations, Holiday, Romance, and Get Well. Each wizard includes a border, or other graphic, and preformatted text. Naturally, you can edit the text if you prefer to use different wording or phrases.

Creating the banner

Use the Banner Wizard to create the banner, and then edit the text and graphics.

To use the Banner Wizard, follow these steps:

1. Choose File ➪ New. The Catalog appears.

2. In the Publications by Wizard tab, choose Banners. Then, choose the type of banner that you want to create.

3. Select the style of banner in the right window pane.

4. Click the Start Wizard button.

Figure 26-16 illustrates a banner in which the text and the clip art were changed to suit the situation better. Note that the view of the banner is seven percent. The text is 234 points. This particular banner will be 5 feet by $8\frac{1}{2}$ inches.

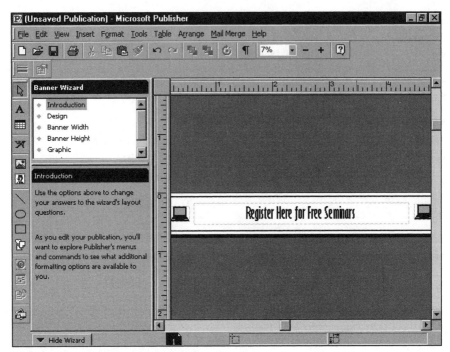

Figure 26-16: Create a banner to advertise your service or product.

Editing the banner

To edit a banner, you can change the text and graphics as you would with any other document. You also can change text formatting and color. Using the Banner Wizard, you can change design, graphics, and the border.

Additionally, you can change the banner width and height from the Banner Wizard box. If you choose to change the banner width, you can choose either 8½ or 11 inches. If you choose to change the banner width, you can choose 5, 6, 8, or 10 feet for the width. Naturally, the longer that you make the banner, the more paper it takes to print it.

Figure 26-17 illustrates one page from the banner in the preceding figure. The letters are 3¼-inches tall in this example. You need to cut and paste the pages together. Note in the figure that the printer margins limit the image from printing all the way to the edge of the page. The remainder of the image prints on the next page.

Figure 26-17: Print out multiple pages to create the banner.

Creating your own banner

You also can create your own banner by using a blank publication. Publisher includes a banner in the Blank Publications tab of the Microsoft Publisher Catalog dialog box. When you choose this publication as a base, the default size of the banner is 5 feet by 11 inches. You can change the size by opening the Page Setup dialog box and choosing the 10- or 15-foot banner. You also can choose to print in landscape format, which changes the height to $8\frac{1}{2}$ inches.

Set the layout guides and margins any way that you like. You can add graphics, frames, and text, as you can with any publication. Design the banner as you would any publication, and print it as you normally would. The banner automatically tiles, and you need to cut down each page and then tape or glue together the banner pieces.

Figure 26-18 illustrates an 11 inch by 5 foot banner advertising an Internet seminar. BorderArt borders work very well in a banner, as does large type. When designing your own banner, start with a font that is 256 points and work from there. Depending on the font that you use, you may need to adjust the size. Make the type as large as fits in the frame. For the BorderArt, make the border at least 56 points to begin with, so that it shows up on the large page. Adjust that size, if necessary.

Figure 26-18: Create your own banner by using Publisher's BorderArt and display type.

Summary

In this chapter, you learned how to produce some specialty publications. You learned how to create the following:

✦ Certificates

✦ Calendars

✦ Business cards

✦ Labels

✦ Banners

In the next chapter, you learn how to create small publications, such as invitations and booklets.

✦　　✦　　✦

Creating Small Publications

Folding a publication is a finishing technique. Many of your publications will require folding, including brochures, newsletters, even letters you're about to mail. Generally, you'll fold your own publications and stuff the envelopes yourself. However, if you have numerous publications — 800 or 2,000, for example — you may want to take your job to a commercial print shop for printing and finishing. Whether you fold your own publication or not, you need to understand how the folds in certain jobs affect the publication's design.

Signatures refer to laying out the pages in books or booklets so that when they are folded, the pages are in the proper page order. Even if you don't take your booklet to a commercial printer, you need to consider signatures if you print four or more pages.

Understanding Folds

You need to understand several folds when designing your publications. Some publications, such as invitations and booklets, are folded to create the final piece. Other publications are folded for easier mailing.

Letters and newsletters, for example, must be folded twice (into thirds) to fit in an envelope. Flyers and brochures may also be folded in this manner. This parallel fold is the most common fold and the easiest one to make.

The French fold is another common fold. Used for note cards and invitations, the French fold consists of two folds. The first fold is lengthwise, and the second is at a right angle to the first. In Publisher, the French fold is also called the Side Fold Card, as shown in Figure 27-1.

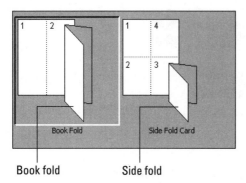

Book fold   Side fold

Figure 27-1: Use a French fold for invitations and note cards.

An $8^1/_2 \times 11$-inch page folded in a French fold creates a finished note card that is $5^1/_2 \times 4^1/_4$ inches. Envelopes that match this card size are called A2 envelopes, and the envelope size is $5^3/_4 \times 4^3/_8$ inches.

The book fold is a common fold used in booklets and books. A book fold consists of one fold in the middle of the page. In Publisher's Catalog (refer to Figure 27-1), the Book Fold applies to portrait orientation. If you change the orientation to landscape, however, the fold makes more sense.

The final piece then ends up being $8^1/_2 \times 5^1/_2$ inches, a common size for church programs and bulletins, play programs, and the like. Figure 27-2 illustrates the results of changing the default Book Fold to landscape orientation.

You also can use the Top Fold Card for invitations and note cards. The Top Fold Card also uses the A2 envelopes.

Figure 27-3 illustrates the Top Fold Card. Also in the figure is the Tent Card, which you can use to define or identify a product on a table, for example, or for announcements.

Understanding Signatures

You don't need to be concerned with signatures unless you plan to create a publication with four or more pages. Suppose that you plan to produce a booklet. You set up the booklet as an $11 \times 8^1/_2$-inch landscape-oriented page. When you fold the booklet in half, as in a book fold, you end up with four pages. Pages one and four are on one side of the sheet; pages two and three are on the other side of the sheet. Now, if you add four more pages to that booklet, the numbering becomes confusing.

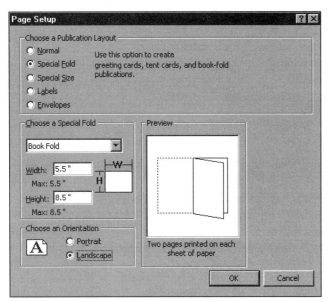

Figure 27-2: Use the Book Fold for programs.

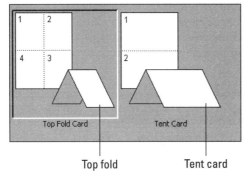

Top fold   Tent card

Figure 27-3: Top Fold Cards are less common, but still useful for some publications.

When you create a booklet in Publisher, Publisher takes care of numbering the pages for you. You can add 4, 8, 12, 16, or more pages to the publication, and Publisher correctly numbers and prints the signatures needed to make the publication work. In Publisher, instead of working with an 11×8½-inch sheet of paper, you work with the final size of the booklet—5½×8½ inches.

Tip   You might want to make a dummy of the publication, to help you place the pages. For example, to produce the 5½×8½-inch booklet, fold an 11×8½-inch sheet of paper in half. You then can sketch out your booklet plan, images, headings, and so on before creating the booklet in Publisher.

Figure 27-4 illustrates pages two and three of a four-page booklet. The program's text is simple, listing only speakers, rooms, and topics. The mirrored background makes the program more interesting.

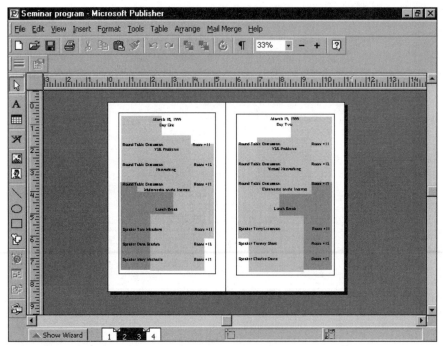

Figure 27-4: Pages two and three of a four-page program

If you take your booklet to a commercial print shop, the printer lays out the publication in signatures, to ensure that the correct pages fall in the proper order. Luckily, Publisher takes care of all those details for you.

Making Invitations and Cards

Invitations and greeting cards are easy to create in Publisher. Using a French or top fold with an 8½×11-inch sheet of paper, you can create professional and attractive cards for any occasion — a party, dinner, fundraiser, thank you, announcement, and more.

Publisher includes more than 170 Invitation and Greeting Card Wizards from which you can choose to create just the right card for any occasion. Many of the cards use design sets, but numerous unique designs also are available that you can use.

Figure 27-5 illustrates one card design from Publisher. Naturally, you can change text or graphics to make the card unique. Note that only the front of the card shows; three other pages represent the inside and back of the card in a French fold.

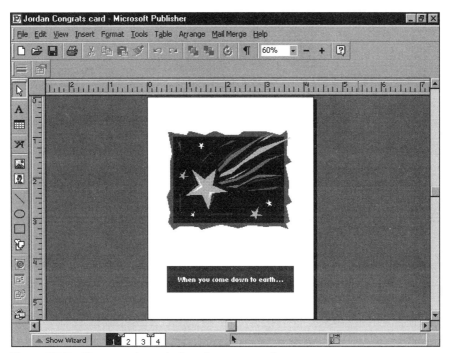

Figure 27-5: Choose unique designs for any occasion

Figure 27-6 illustrates a Top Fold Card used for a housewarming announcement. Note that the Top Fold Card works well with landscape orientation. The card's size is $5\frac{1}{2} \times 4\frac{1}{4}$ inches; the illustration shows only the front of the card. Four additional pages include the inside and back of the card.

Tip   You can apply artistic effects to photos by using Microsoft's PhotoDraw, included with the Office 2000 package.

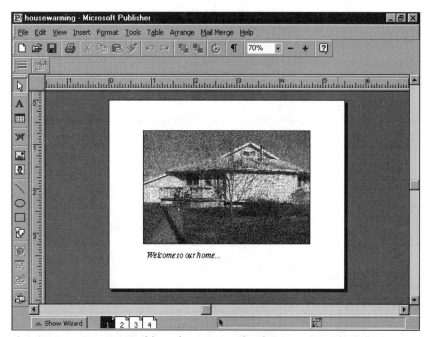

Figure 27-6: Use a Top Fold Card to create a landscape-oriented card.

Using the Card Wizard

Publisher includes many wizards for both invitations and greeting cards. Many of the cards use the same design sets — Accent Box, Blocks, Bubbles, and so on — and many of the cards apply unique designs to the card. Most of the Card Wizards create text — and often, graphics — for all four pages of the card.

The following figures show all four pages of one greeting card. Figure 27-7 illustrates the front, or page one, of the card. You can easily change the verse, font formatting, or graphic design of any card created in Publisher's wizards.

Figure 27-8 shows pages two and three of the greeting card. The inside pages contain a graphic and text; however, you can add anything to the card that you want. Publisher even gives you a choice of different text that you can use.

Figure 27-9 illustrates page four, or the back cover, of the card. You might want to leave the last page blank, use Publisher's text, or add text or graphics of your own. Note that the text in the figure identifies the creator of the card.

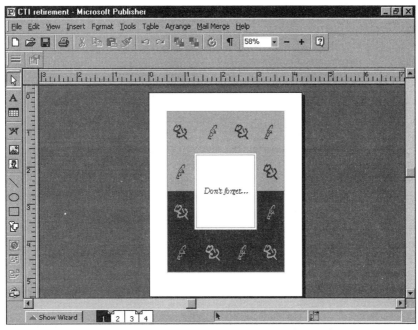

Figure 27-7: A design and text appear on page one of the card.

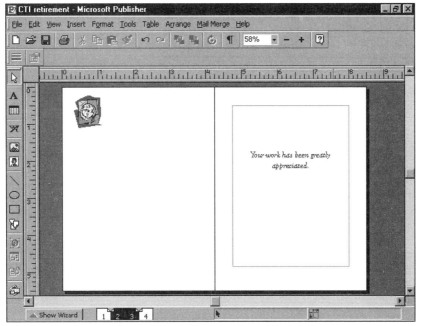

Figure 27-8: Use Publisher's suggested text, or make up your own for the inside of the card.

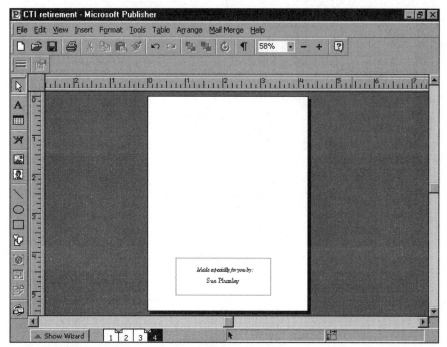

Figure 27-9: Put your name or your company's name on the back of the card.

Note   If you performed a standard installation, you probably need to install the Card Wizards as you use them. Have the Microsoft Office 2000 CD-ROM handy. It takes only a few seconds to install the Card Wizards.

Creating the card

Publisher supplies more than 180 Card Wizards that you can use, listed in two separate categories: Invitation Cards and Greeting Cards. Invitation Cards offer designs and verses for parties, housewarmings, showers, events, celebrations, and fundraisers.

Greeting Card topics include thank you notes, announcements, reminders, holiday and birthday cards, congratulations, apologies, get well cards, and sympathy notes. Publisher presents several cards in various design sets, as well.

Note   You can either run a Publisher wizard that asks you questions about your document's contents and design, or turn off this feature and use the wizard box to change these very same content and design elements. To turn off the feature, choose Tools ➪ Options ➪ User Assistance ➪ Step through wizard questions.

To create a card from the Card Wizard, follow these steps:

1. Choose File ➪ New. The Catalog appears.

2. In the Publications by Wizard dialog box, choose Invitation Cards or Greeting Cards from the Wizards pane.

3. From the list of card topics, select the card and design that you want.

4. Click Start Wizard.

Editing the card

The Invitation and Greeting Card Wizards either take you through the wizard step by step or present the card onscreen with the Card Wizard box beside the card. With the Card Wizard, you can change the design, color scheme, and personal information.

Most cards also enable you to change the suggested verse; thus, you can use the design and layout of any card with the verse from another card. Of course, you can always change the text yourself, as well as change font formatting, graphics, and other card elements. Some cards also enable you to change the layout, size, and fold of the card.

When you choose to change the suggested verse, use the Suggested Verse dialog box. You can choose the category first and then choose from the available messages in that category. Categories include either the type of invitation or the type of greeting card.

If you choose a Greeting Card Wizard, for example, you can choose from these categories: Anniversary, Birth Announcement, Bon Voyage, Easter, Engagement Announcement, and so on.

In each category is a list of available messages. If you choose a Thank You note, you can choose from more than 35 verses. Figure 27-10 illustrates the Suggested Verse dialog box with the list of available messages. When you choose a message, the dialog box displays both the front and the inside message.

Creating your own card

You can, of course, create your own greeting card or invitation. Publisher makes designing your own cards easy, by presenting you with a Side Fold and a Top Fold template in the Blank Publications folder of the Catalog. The templates present four pages that represent the front, back, and inside of the card. After you create the card, Publisher arranges it on an $8^{1}/_{2} \times 11$-inch page and prints it, without any worry on your part about signatures.

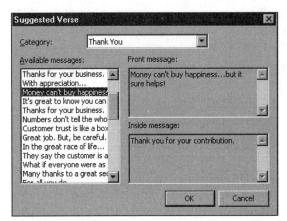

Figure 27-10: Choose an appropriate message for your card.

When you create a greeting card or invitation, consider the type of fold that you use. Generally, you use a Side Fold Card for a card in portrait orientation; use a Top Fold Card for a card in landscape orientation. These are standard uses for the folds, and they make your card look more professional.

You can use any graphic, clip art, photo, WordArt, font formatting, or any other features in Publisher to create your card. You can use text and graphics on any page or on all pages.

To create a card base, follow these steps:

1. Choose File ➪ New. The Catalog appears.

2. Select the Blank Publications tab.

3. Choose either Side Fold Card or Top Fold Card.

4. Click the Create button.

5. Publisher displays a dialog box asking whether you want it to insert pages automatically. Choose Yes, so that you have the four pages needed to complete the card.

Publisher inserts the card in portrait orientation, by default, and opens the Quick Publications Wizard. If you chose a Top Fold Card and want to change the orientation to landscape, you can use the Card Wizard or the Page Setup dialog box.

Figure 27-11 shows a simple yet elegant Thank You card created with WordArt and a photograph. Creating your own cards means that you can individualize the verse and message in each card that you send.

Figure 27-11: Create a specialized card for someone special.

Creating a Program or Booklet

You might need a program to describe events, demonstrations, speakers, or other scheduled activities. You might want to produce a booklet on safety regulations, for example, or an employee handbook, guide to procedures, or other information that you can distribute to employees, customers, or vendors.

You can print a program or booklet on both sides of the page or on one side only. The design of the publication is flexible; design and length depend on the content of the publication. The size of the program or booklet depends on copy, printer capabilities, paper, and so on.

The page size can be $8\frac{1}{2} \times 11$ inches, $5\frac{1}{2} \times 8\frac{1}{2}$ inches, or some other size. The most common size for programs is $5\frac{1}{2} \times 8\frac{1}{2}$ inches. Many booklets are also that size. Using the Book Fold in Publisher, the program is printed on both sides of a landscape-oriented $8\frac{1}{2} \times 11$-inch sheet and then folded in half to create four $5\frac{1}{2} \times 8\frac{1}{2}$-inch pages. After the fold, the document is in portrait orientation.

Booklets and programs commonly consist of multiple pages. Because of the way signatures work, you use 4, 8, 12, or any other multiple of four for the number of pages in a booklet or program.

Tip   If you plan to produce more than 50 or 100 programs or booklet copies, you should, depending on the number of pages in each document, take the job to a copy or print shop.

Creating programs

You can create your own programs or use one of Publisher's Program Wizards. The programs, by default, have four pages; however, you can add more pages, if necessary. When you add more pages, you add a signature of four pages. So, if you start with four pages, adding another signature creates four additional pages.

If you do need to make a program more than four pages, Publisher automatically arranges the pages onscreen in order and prints them as they should be, in signature, for you.

Using the Program Wizard

Publisher contains three Program Wizards that produce 5½×8½-inch publications: the Music Program, Religious Service, and Theater Program. Naturally, you can change the graphics and text in any of these programs to suit your own purposes.

After you create the program, you can make changes to the design, color scheme, and personal information used in the program. The inside pages of the program present formatting consistent with the topic. For example, the Theater Program Wizard includes an area for the play title, director, and a description of the play acts on page two, as shown in Figure 27-12. Page three offers an area for the author's biography. Page four lists the crew and those who have contributed to the play in some way.

To use a Program Wizard, choose File ➪ New and then choose Programs in the Wizards pane of the Publications by Wizard tab. Program Wizards offer either step-by-step instructions or display the Program Wizard box, from which you can change the design, color scheme, and personal information. You also can change text, format the fonts, and add or remove graphics, as appropriate for your program.

Creating your own program

Publisher offers only three Program Wizards, so you very likely may want to create your own program. Publisher makes creating a program easy, using the Book Fold blank publication. The pages that you design represent the front, back, and inside of the program as it will look when printed.

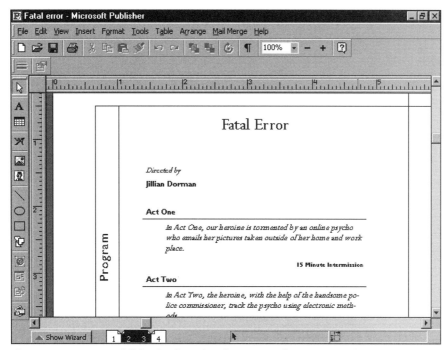

Figure 27-12: Use Publisher's Play Wizard to create the programs for your next event.

To create a program by using the Book Fold blank publication, follow these steps:

1. Choose File ⇨ New. The Catalog appears.

2. Select the Blank Publications tab.

3. Select Book Fold and then click Create.

4. Choose Yes to insert pages automatically.

5. By default, the Book Fold uses portrait orientation. You can change it to landscape by using the Page Setup dialog box or by using the Page Size option in the Quick Publications Wizard.

You can adjust layout guides to create the appropriate margins. Add text and graphics as you want.

Figure 27-13 shows page one of a conference and trade show program. The simple design presents a silhouette that is repeated on the inside of the program.

Figure 27-14 shows the repeated image used as a watermark over pages two and three of the program. Over the top of the watermark is a list of events, times, speakers, and room numbers. The design is elegant and the text is easy to read.

Figure 27-13: A simple program cover attracts attention.

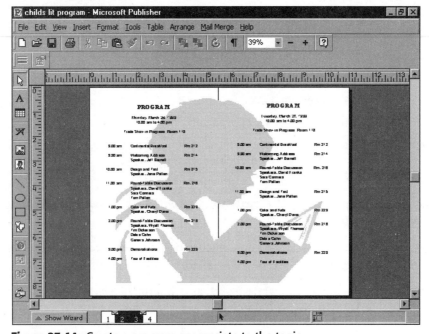

Figure 27-14: Create a program appropriate to the topic.

Figure 27-15 shows the back cover of the program. Note that the page border from the front page is repeated to tie the publication together, even though the layout of the page is different from the other pages.

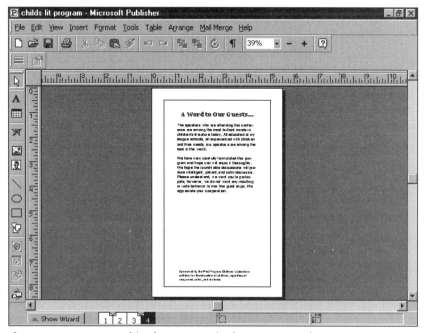

Figure 27-15: Use graphic elements to tie the pages together.

Creating booklets

Booklets are small books that contain 4 to 20 or so pages, and outline information that you distribute to several people. For example, you might want to create an Employee Handbook, outlining details of employment rights and guidelines, termination information, benefits, and so on. A booklet such as this might contain 8 or 12 pages, for example, and be given to everyone in your company.

A booklet might contain a title or topic page, an introduction, pages divided into topics, and perhaps a summary page. You might also add forms, tables, graphics, and contact information. You could add a glossary, appendix, notes area, index, bibliography, and other information, depending on the topic of your booklet.

After gathering your content, you should decide how long the booklet will be and how many pages you need. An excellent size for a booklet is 5½×8½ inches. The size is easy to store and use. Of course, an 8½×11-inch page might better suit your content.

Make sure that you number the pages in a booklet if the publication consists of more than four pages. You can use Publisher's page-numbering feature to accomplish this task. (For more information, see Chapter 12.)

The following are a few additional considerations in the design and formatting of booklets, as well as references to the chapters in this book that discuss those considerations:

✦ Use headers or footers (or both) to help identify page contents and page numbers. (Chapters 7, 12)

✦ Consider the facing pages in your design and formatting. Pages two and three, for example, should complement each other in design and layout, rather than oppose each other. (Chapter 7)

✦ Don't number the first or the last page of the booklet. Start your page numbering with the first right-hand page after the cover, which should be page one. (Chapter 12)

✦ Don't forget about balance, white space, and consistency in your design. (Chapter 5)

✦ Use plenty of margin space so that the pages aren't too crowded. (Chapter 7)

✦ Use 10-, 11-, or 12-point type for the body; use 14-, 18-, and 24-point type for subheadings and headings. Left-align the text for easier reading. (Chapter 16)

✦ Add some clip art or photographs for interest. (Chapters 18, 19)

✦ Consider starting your booklet by creating an outline of the topics and heads, to keep yourself organized. Then, proceed with writing the book.

To create a booklet, choose File ➪ New. In the Catalog, select the Blank Publications tab and choose either Full Page or Book Fold. Click Create. You may want to change the orientation to suit your publication.

Figure 27-16 shows the cover of an Employee's Computer Guidelines Handbook. The CTI logo appears in the background of right pages only. The simple gradient on the page makes it interesting, without detracting from the text.

Figure 27-17 shows the second and third pages of the booklet. The gradient repeats on all pages, with the CTI logo appearing only on right pages. A footer identifies the page number and the name of the booklet; note that page one is the right page, and that the left page contains text but isn't numbered. Clip art adds interest to the text.

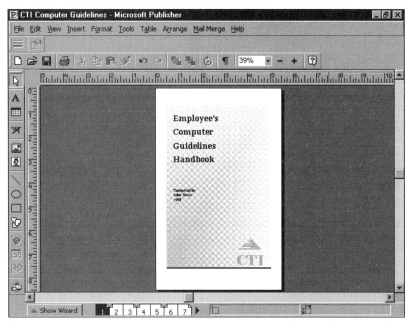

Figure 27-16: Design your own booklets by using Publisher's features and tools.

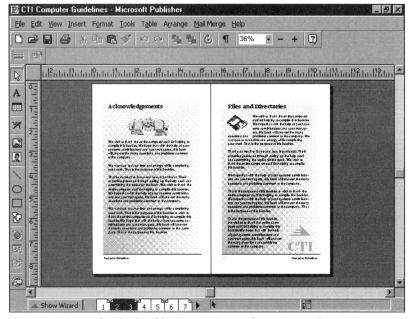

Figure 27-17: Make the booklet interesting and easy to read.

Summary

In this chapter, you learned about creating small publications. In addition to learning about folds and signatures, you learned about the following:

✦ Making invitations and cards

✦ Creating programs

✦ Creating booklets

In the next chapter, you learn about producing business publications, such as newsletters, brochures, and business forms.

✦   ✦   ✦

Producing Business Publications

◆   ◆   ◆   ◆

In This Chapter

Creating a newsletter

Forming a brochure

Working with business forms

◆   ◆   ◆   ◆

Newsletters, brochures, business forms — these can be easily created in Publisher, either through one of its wizards or from scratch. In this chapter, you learn how to use Publisher to produce such types of business publications.

Creating a Newsletter

Newsletters can help your business by introducing you to prospective customers, informing current customers, selling products or services, introducing new employees, and more. You can send newsletters to your customers, or you can send them to your employees and vendors. Newsletters can keep your staff informed of changes in policies and upcoming events, or they can inform vendors of new services and needs in your company.

Newsletters can contain any type of information that your audience may want to read. You might include articles that inform and articles that sell. Add a few humorous stories to make sure that your audience won't want to miss a thing. You can use graphics, photos, tables, and other elements to add interest. And don't forget to advertise periodically, as well, by including articles about your company, services, and products.

Planning a newsletter

Your first consideration is the size and number of pages your newsletter will contain. Newsletters can consist of one page, two pages, four, six, or even eight pages. Common sizes are $8^1/_2 \times 11$ inches, $8^1/_2 \times 14$ inches, and 11×17 inches. The 11×17-inch page is folded to create a four-page $8^1/_2$×11-inch newsletter; to use this paper size, of course, you need a printer that can print 11×17-inch paper or you need to take your job to a print shop.

Figure 28-1 illustrates a newsletter laid out on an 11×17-inch page. The pages that you see are pages two and three, the inside of the newsletter. Page one is on the back of page two, and page four is on the back of page three. Folding this newsletter in half reduces the size to $8^1/_2 \times 11$ inches.

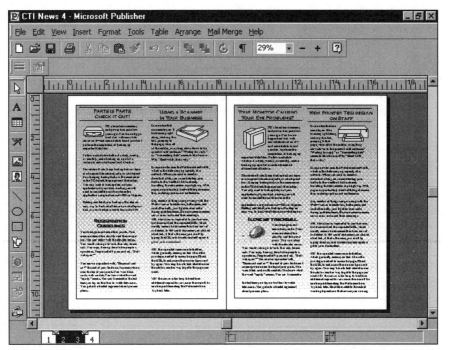

Figure 28-1: You can print on an 11×17-inch page only if your printer is capable of handling that size of paper.

The standard newsletter sizes are $8^1/_2 \times 11$ inches and $8^1/_2 \times 14$ inches. A two-page newsletter (front and back) works well with either size. You can even create a four-page newsletter (two sheets of paper, printed front and back) without needing to use a fastening technique, such as staples. Do remember, however, that $8^1/_2 \times 14$ inches might be an odd size to store; $8^1/_2$×11-inch paper is easier to file, place in a binder — or even stack, for that matter.

When planning size and page count, consider how you'll distribute the newsletter. If you're planning to mail it, you may want to make sure that the weight of the entire newsletter is less than one ounce, so that you don't have to pay so much postage.

Consider the folded size of the newsletter and the thickness of the document after it's folded. Consider the weight of the paper that you use, as well. For example, you need to use at least a 24# paper so that you can print on both sides. A heavier paper might add too much weight to the mailing.

Understanding the parts of a newsletter

You can make a newsletter as simple as one article on one page, or you can add elements to make the newsletter more interesting, to help your readers, and to identify the newsletter as your company's publication.

Mastheads, nameplates, tables of contents, headers and footers, mailing panels, and so on are parts of the newsletter that you may want to add. You can add one or several elements, depending on your content, the size of the newsletter, and your company's style.

Using columns

A newsletter may consist of only one column, or two, three, or even four columns. The columns can be even in width or of varying widths. You might want to use vertical lines to separate columns, or you can use white space. You can even use columns formatted within frames. Chapter 7 discusses columns, gutters, and balancing page elements. Chapter 10 discusses columns in frames.

Creating a masthead and dateline

A *masthead* is the title of your newsletter. The *dateline* is the text below the masthead that lists the date, often the volume and issue number of the newsletter, the editor's name, and perhaps even a catchy phrase.

You might name the newsletter after your company, or you could give it another, descriptive name. You can use WordArt, clip art, display type, and other graphics to create the masthead. Any text in the masthead is most often a different typeface from the body text and headings.

The masthead is usually located at the top of the front page, although it can be located anywhere on the front page. Figure 28-2 illustrates a masthead created with WordArt. The name of the newsletter is the name of the company. Note that additional contact information is also available at the bottom left of the newsletter, including the street address, telephone numbers, and e-mail addresses.

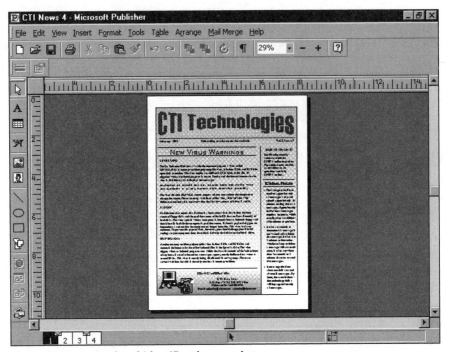

Figure 28-2: A masthead identifies the newsletter.

When creating a dateline, use type no larger than 9- or 10-point, and use a plain font. For example, use a sans serif font (Arial) if your masthead font has serifs, or use a serif font (such as Times New Roman) if your masthead font is sans serif.

Figure 28-3 illustrates several mastheads and their corresponding datelines. The first and second mastheads are formal and sophisticated. The third masthead is informal, even amusing.

Creating a nameplate

A *nameplate* is a small box added to the newsletter that lists the name of the publication, the editor, perhaps the circulation editor, advertising information, and so on. Most newsletters don't use a nameplate, and it's really not necessary, unless your newsletter accepts advertising from outside interests. In that case, your advertisers might want to know the circulation, subscription prices, contact names, and so on.

Figure 28-3: Design a masthead that suits your company.

Nameplates are usually located on page two of the publication, although a nameplate also can be placed on the last page of the newsletter. Figure 28-4 illustrates a nameplate in a quarterly newsletter. You can include advertising, subscription, and contact information. You may want to include a disclaimer, to limit your legal liability.

Figure 28-5 shows a different sort of nameplate. This box, located on page one of the newsletter, lists only the contact information, including the company's name, address, voice and fax numbers, and Internet e-mail addresses.

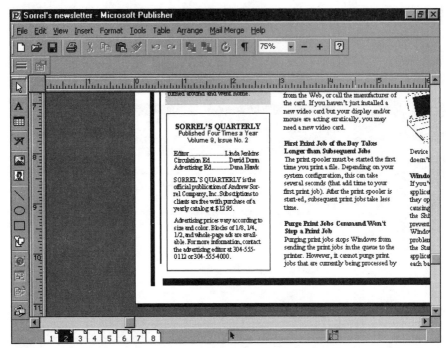

Figure 28-4: Create a nameplate to add information for subscribers and advertisers.

Using a table of contents

You might want to add a table of contents (TOC) when your newsletter is more than four pages. You use a table of contents to direct readers to important information that you want them to find easily.

Use a right leader tab to separate the page number, as shown in Figure 28-6. You can enclose the TOC in a box to make it stand out from the rest of the page. The TOC should be located on page one of the newsletter.

Adding a mailing panel

Add a mailing panel to the last page of a newsletter so that you can attach labels to the newsletter for mailing. If your newsletter is 8½ × 11 inches, for example, you can add a mailing panel to the lower half or lower third of the last page, as shown in Figure 28-7. In this example, you fold the newsletter into thirds to display only the mailing panel on one side. You also should fasten or staple the newsletter closed so that it doesn't come apart or open in the mail.

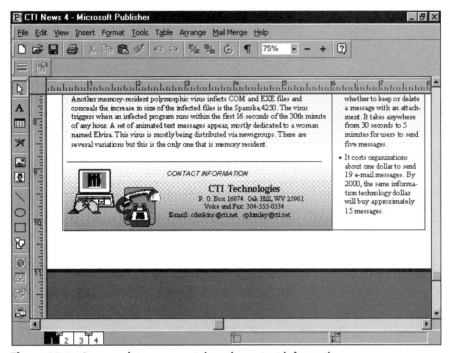

Figure 28-5: A nameplate may contain only contact information.

If your newsletter contains several pages, such as 8 or 16, you might create a mailing panel that takes up half of the last page. Folding a thick newsletter in half is easier than folding it into thirds. You also should fasten the newsletter so that it remains closed.

All you really need in a mailing panel is your company's return address (see Figure 28-8). You also may want to add a bar code, FIM, or bulk postage permit, depending on your method of mailing your newsletters. For more information, see Chapter 25.

Tip　　You might want to skip the mailing panel and mail your newsletter in an envelope with first class mail, to make sure that the recipient gives your newsletter his or her personal attention.

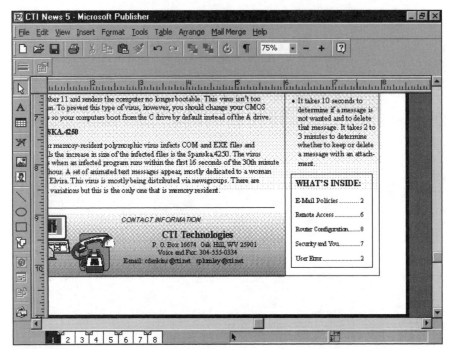

Figure 28-6: Add a table of contents when you have more than four pages in your newsletter.

Adding miscellaneous items

You can add other miscellaneous items to a newsletter, including a calendar of events, pull quotes, page borders, lines to divide stories, page numbers, and headers and footers to describe content or page count.

Don't forget about using Design Gallery to add items to a newsletter. You can insert various predesigned mastheads, tables of contents, forms, sidebars, pull quotes, captions, calendars, and more.

Using the Newsletter Wizard

Publisher's Newsletter Wizards use many varied designs. Some have a TOC, others have graphics, and still others have borders. All have a nameplate of some sort, and each applies a design set, such as Accent Box, Design Box, Fading Frame, and so on.

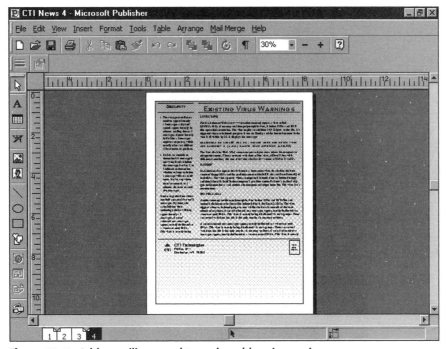

Figure 28-7: Add a mailing panel to make addressing easier.

You should match the newsletter format and design set with your company's other documents. However, you can use the basic foundation of any newsletter design that you like and, by changing color schemes and modifying the design yourself, come up with a unique newsletter that is still reminiscent of your other company documents.

Creating the newsletter

Nearly all of Publisher's newsletter styles contain four columns. Sometimes, one column contains only a graphic or a small amount of text; other times, one column contains a TOC. You can, however, change the number of columns by using the Newsletter Wizard.

The design sets for newsletters are similar to those for other documents. The graphics often become a part of the nameplate or act as a page border. Photographs and clip art are also included; the frames act as placeholders, so you can change the graphics as you like. You also can edit the text, graphics, borders, and columns, as well as other elements of the newsletter.

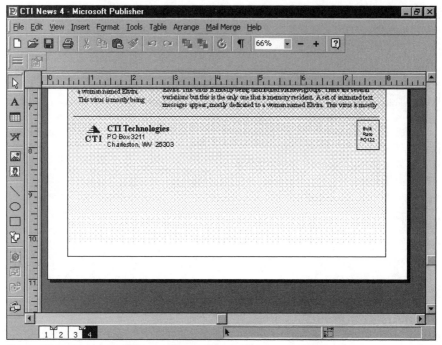

Figure 28-8: Use a mailing panel to make mailing a newsletter easy.

Note

You can either run a Publisher wizard that asks you questions about your document's contents and design, or turn off this feature and use the wizard box to change these very same content and design elements. To turn off the feature, choose Tools ➪ Options ➪ User Assistance ➪ Step through wizard questions.

To create a newsletter by using the Newsletter Wizard, follow these steps:

1. Choose File ➪ New. The Catalog appears.

2. In the Publications by Wizard tab, choose Newsletters in the left pane.

3. The available newsletters in design sets appear in the right pane.

4. Scroll through the newsletters to find one that you want, and then select it.

5. Click Start Wizard.

Editing the newsletter

As with any wizard publication, after you create a newsletter with a wizard, you can enter and edit the text; add, replace, or remove graphics; move stories and headings around; and otherwise edit the newsletter.

The Newsletter Wizard steps you through a series of questions and design choices, or simply displays the wizard box, whichever option you choose. Additionally, each newsletter design contains suggested text, headings, and information about building a newsletter.

You can change the design, color scheme, and personal information, just as you can with other publications. You also can change the following with the Newsletter Wizard box:

✦ **Inside Page Content:** When working on the inside pages of a newsletter, you can add a calendar, order form, response form, or sign-up form, and alter the positioning and number of stories and graphics.

✦ **Number of Columns:** Change the number of columns in a newsletter to one, two, three, or four.

✦ **Insert Page:** Insert any number of pages.

✦ **Customer Address:** Insert a placeholder on the last page of the newsletter for a mailing panel.

✦ **One- or Two-Sided Printing:** Changes the layout of the newsletter so that you can print on only one side of the paper or on both sides.

✦ **Convert to Web Site:** Publisher copies the newsletter content to create a Web site.

Figure 28-9 illustrates the inside of a newsletter created from a wizard. This example uses several of the wizard changes — number of columns, calendar, color scheme, and mailing panel (which is on page four).

Note You can easily create your own newsletter from scratch by starting a blank publication and adding elements as you go. However, using a wizard as a base may be easier, because making changes by using the wizard box is so easy.

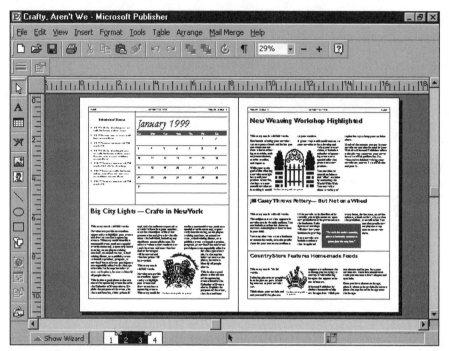

Figure 28-9: Start with a Newsletter Wizard and then modify the document to make it unique.

Forming a Brochure

Brochures are a form of advertising that details information about your services, your products, or your company. In addition to this type of information, you can add other useful details to a brochure, such as maps, department phone numbers, company history or goals, organizational charts, or price lists and product descriptions. You always should include your company's logo, name and address, and any other contact phone numbers.

Deciding on a brochure format

Brochures come in many shapes and sizes; the standard, conventional brochure format, however, is landscape, 11 × 8½ inches, with two parallel folds that create three panels on the font and three on the back. Figure 28-10 illustrates the layout of this brochure format. Note that the layout guides indicate the panel divisions and folds.

A mailing panel makes the brochure easy to distribute to the public; you can use Publisher's Mail Merge feature to create mailing labels for the brochure. (See Chapter 32.)

Folds

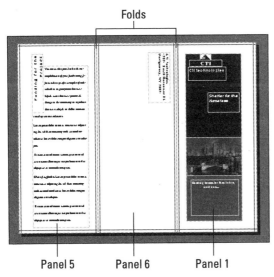

Panel 5   Panel 6   Panel 1

Figure 28-10: The outside of the brochure creates the front and back panels.

The inside panels — two, three, and four — are on the back side of the page. Figure 28-11 illustrates the inside of the brochure. Graphics, subheads, and repeated colors help to tie together the panels and lead the reader's eyes through the text.

Folds

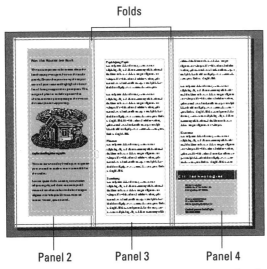

Panel 2   Panel 3   Panel 4

Figure 28-11: Inside panels describe more-detailed information.

Other common size formats for brochures include the following:

✦ 14 × 8½ inches, with three parallel folds to create four panels on the front and four on the back

✦ 11 × 8½ inches, folded once to create a 5½×8½-inch finished piece

✦ 8½ × 11 inches (portrait orientation)

✦ 8½ × 14 inches (portrait orientation)

✦ 11 × 17 inches, folded to 8½× 11 inches

Brochure Design and Layout

When planning your brochure's graphics, use lines, borders, images, and other graphics to lead the eye through the brochure in a methodical way. Use the text to make the reader want to open the brochure and read on.

The front panel should contain a graphic, an interesting, attention-getting heading, or both. The three inside panels might list general services or benefits to the customer. Try to persuade the reader to read on. Add graphics and images to maintain interest and explain details.

Panel five might contain a bulleted list of items that will interest the reader—product benefits, sales items, tips and tricks, or some information the reader can use. The last panel, number six, can be used for either a mailing panel (similar to one in a newsletter) or the contact numbers and other company information.

Make sure that your brochure's design matches other company publications. Use similar design elements or the same design sets. You can, of course, change the design somewhat, but you want to keep some sort of consistency between documents.

Tip   Don't use vertical lines to indicate the fold in a brochure. It is very difficult to fold exactly on the line. You can, however, use vertical lines, boxes, and other graphics within the layout guides.

Using a Brochure Wizard

Publisher supplies numerous brochure designs in most of the design sets used in other publications and documents. You can choose from an Informational, Price List, Event, or Fund Raiser brochure for plain paper. You also can create an Informational or Price List brochure on special paper.

The design sets include the Accent Box, Accessory Bar, Borders, Bubbles, and others. Publisher also has added a few design sets specifically for brochures, such as the Quadrants and Even Break designs.

Creating a brochure

You can choose to create a brochure on plain paper or special paper. Publisher takes you through the wizard questions and supplies the Brochure Wizard box to help you with your design. Publisher also includes informational text within the brochure that might give you ideas for content.

To create a brochure by using the Brochure Wizard, follow these steps:

1. Choose File ➪ New. The Catalog appears.

2. In the Publications by Wizard tab, select Brochures in the left pane.

3. Choose the brochure that you want from the right pane.

4. Click the Start Wizard button.

Publisher displays the brochure base and the Brochure Wizard onscreen.

Editing the brochure

You can edit the text and graphics in a brochure just as you do in any other document. You also can use the Brochure Wizard to make changes to the design. In addition to the Design, Color Scheme, and Personal Information elements, the Brochure Wizard offers the following:

✦ **Paper Size (Panels):** Some wizards enable you to change the page size from 11 × 8½ inches to 14 × 8½ inches, in which case you can change from three to four panels.

✦ **Customer Address:** Add a mailing panel to the brochure.

✦ **Form:** Add an order, response, or sign-up form to the brochure.

✦ **Convert to Web:** Convert the information in the brochure to Web content for your Web site. When you choose this option, Publisher asks whether you want to use the Web Site Wizard, to create the Web design automatically, or whether you prefer to add your own hyperlinks and do your own Web layout. (For more information about designing for the Web, see Chapter 33.)

To give you an idea of the outcome, Figure 28-12 illustrates the brochure from Figures 28-10 and 28-11 as a Web page. Starting a Web page with information that you've already typed is much easier than starting from scratch.

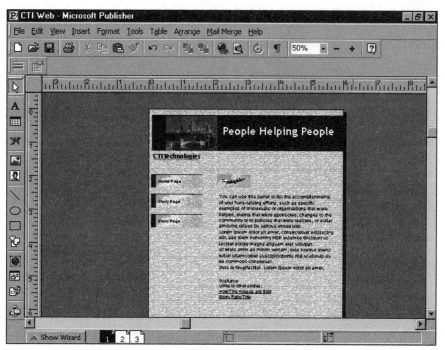

Figure 28-12: Create a Web page quickly from your brochure.

Creating your own brochure

Publisher doesn't include a blank publication on which you can base your own brochure automatically. Still, you can easily create your own brochure by using the full-page blank publication and making some changes.

First, create a new publication with a blank 8½×11-inch page. In Page Setup, change the orientation to landscape.

Next, set the layout guides. Your margins should be at least ⅓ or ⅜ inch all around. You need to create three columns, as well. Now, if you create text and graphic frames using the layout guides as they are, the folds will fall exactly on the lines of the text frame. To fix this problem, you need to add ⅜ inch (or whatever margin you created on the edges) to either side of the gutter line.

Draw some extra vertical ruler guides, as follows:

1. Choose Arrange ➪ Ruler Guides ➪ Add Vertical Ruler Guide.

2. Position the mouse over the guide and then press and hold down the Shift key. Drag the ruler guide into position. Using the pink layout guide for measurement purposes, move the ruler guide to the left by ⅜ inch.

3. Add another guide and position it ⅜ inch to the right of the pink layout guide.

4. Repeat with the other inside gutter margin. Figure 28-13 illustrates the layout guides in the brochure. Note how the first text frame fits in between the guides.

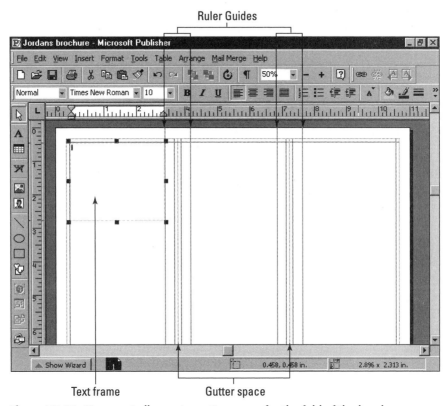

Figure 28-13: You must allow extra gutter space for the fold of the brochure.

Note
Naturally, you could make your margins and gutters wider, say ⅖ or ½ inch. White space in any document is always a benefit.

After you create the brochure's guides, you can create a design and add text as you want. Figure 28-14 illustrates a sample design. The brochure offers the reader information about security for their network and servers, and for the Internet. The graphic and text on panel one attracts the attention of anyone who's worried about their business and computer network safety.

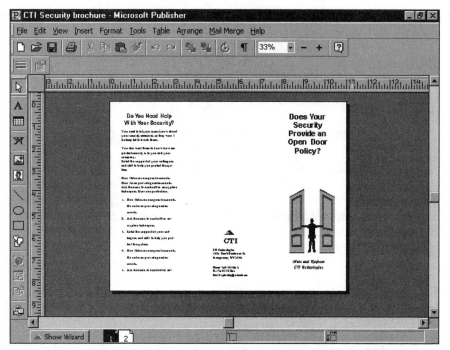

Figure 28-14: Design a brochure using graphics and eye-catching headlines.

Figure 28-15 shows the inside of the security brochure. Repeating the graphic from panel one ties together the front and back, and using that graphic as a watermark draws attention to the content of the brochure. Even with the graphic and the text, plenty of white space remains to help make the brochure readable.

Working with Business Forms

Companies use business forms every day—fax cover sheets, expense reports, order forms, purchase orders, invoices, and more. You can create your forms within Publisher and then either reproduce them or customize them as necessary.

All forms have common elements, such as the company's address and contact information, a place for the date and perhaps a form number, and tables consisting of rows and columns in which certain information must go. Depending on the form that you need, the table of cells differs.

You can use Publisher's Business Forms Wizards to create many different form types. If you can't find the appropriate form in a wizard, you can use one of these forms as a base, and then alter it to suit your needs.

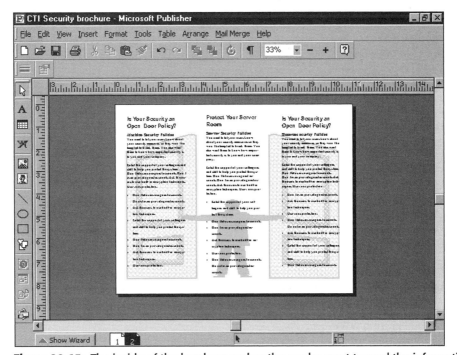

Figure 28-15: The inside of the brochure makes the reader want to read the information.

Figure 28-16 shows one of the tables in a form. The table is pretty basic. The rows and columns were adjusted, and borders were applied to most, but not all, of the cells. You can see the nonprinting gridlines of the cells that are left unused.

You can use Publisher's Table feature to create your own forms. The Table feature enables you to insert rows and columns, merge cells, lock cells, format headings and margins, use borders and fills, and more. (For more information about tables, see Chapter 23.)

Tip   You can design your forms so that they can be filled out by hand, by typewriter, or on the computer.

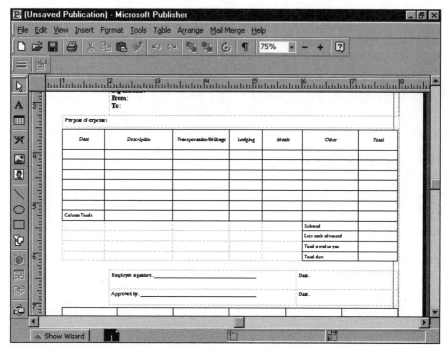

Figure 28-16: The major component of a form is the table.

Planning a Form

Forms must contain certain information, such as contact information, the name of the form, and other such data. Most forms also ask for information, such as names, addresses, dates, prices, descriptions, product numbers, and so on. When you create a form, you must provide spaces for each type of information.

Two types of information are found in forms:

✦ **Label information:** Any text that is constant, such as the words Date, Description, Quantity, and so forth.

✦ **Variable information:** The text that a person fills in, such as the date and his or her name and address.

Tables are great for creating a framework for the form. You can use a table to hold both label and variable information. Frames are also handy for structuring a form. Furthermore, you can apply borders, fill, and formatting to both frames and tables to help you divide and organize the information within the form.

When you're ready to create a form, make note of the variable and label text that you need. If you're not sure, ask the people who will use the form both what information they need to complete the form, and in what order the label text should be presented to make using the form easiest.

After you create the form, pass it out to those who will use it and let them experiment with it for a while. Let them make suggestions on how to improve it, before you print a large quantity of the forms. The following are some additional suggestions:

✦ When you plan your form, consider line spacing. If the form will be filled in by hand, you need to add more space between lines, either inside or outside a table. Use at least 1/4-inch line spacing for handwritten forms.

✦ You also must add more length to lines in which the recipient will write the response by hand. Column widths and information boxes also should provide enough room for handwriting.

✦ If a form will be used with a typewriter, you must use typewriter spacing, so that the typewriter hits the appropriate space when the user hits the Return key. One, one-and-a-half, and double-line spacing all are suitable for use with a typewriter.

Using a Business Form Wizard

Publisher provides many Form Wizards for you to use. All the Form Wizards are based on a design set, but the headings and borders are a small piece of the form design. The biggest part of the form is the table created to hold the necessary information.

As with any document that you create from a wizard, you can edit the text, move or remove graphics, and edit the design. With forms, you also can edit the tables.

Publisher provides the following Business Form Wizards:

✦ Expense Report

✦ Fax Cover

✦ Inventory List

✦ Invoice

✦ Purchase Order

✦ Quote

✦ Refund

✦ Statement

✦ Time Billing

✦ Weekly Record

Creating the form

You can select any design set under the form category to create your form. Your forms should match your company's other documents.

To use the Business Form Wizard, follow these steps:

1. Choose File ⇨ New. The Catalog appears.

2. In the Publications by Wizard tab, select Business Forms.

3. Select the type of form that you want in the left pane and then choose the form design in the right pane.

4. Click the Start Wizard button.

Figure 28-17 illustrates the top half of a fax cover sheet, created with the help of the Fax Cover Wizard. Note that the wizard inserts your personal information. Naturally, you can edit and format the text and change the design at any time.

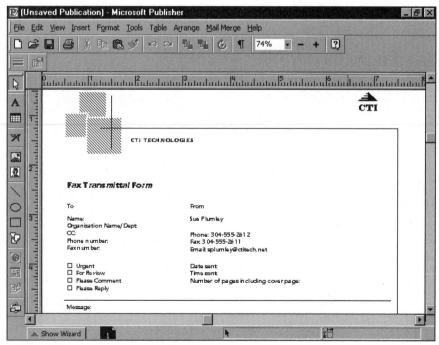

Figure 28-17: Create a fax cover sheet in a matter of minutes.

Editing the form

After you create a form, you can change the text, reformat fonts, move frames, and otherwise edit the document. Using the Business Form Wizard — either the steps or the wizard box—you can change the design, logo, and personal information in any form.

You can change the color of elements, add color and borders to the tables, alter the tables, and even copy or move tables. When editing tables, you can add or delete rows and columns, merge cells, and lock a table. When formatting tables, you can apply borders to some cells and not others, add color or patterns to certain cells, and even add clip art or other graphics to the cells.

Figure 28-18 shows an invoice created from a wizard but altered to conform better to the company's needs.

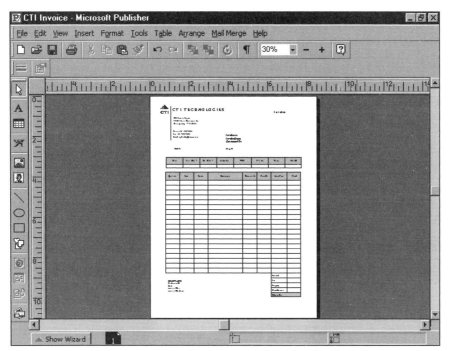

Figure 28-18: Insert rows, move elements around, and make the form conform to your needs.

Creating your own form

If you can find a similar form in the Business Form Wizards, you can alter it to make it fit what you want. However, if you can't find the form that you need in the wizards, you can create your own form:

1. Start with a blank publication and set your layout guides.

2. Create the table or tables that you need for the form. (See Chapter 23 for more information about creating tables.)

3. Determine how much space on the form the necessary data will take, and then use the leftover space to fit in your company's name and address, the name of the form, and other supplementary information.

Tip

After you create one form, you can copy the table and elements from that form into another, different form. For example, invoices and purchase orders often use the same type of tables. Copying a table that is already formatted may be easier than starting from scratch.

You also might want to use Design Gallery when you create your form. A part of your form may require a reply or order form, for example, which you can insert from Design Gallery and change in any way necessary to make it fit your needs. (For more information about Design Gallery, see Chapter 24.)

Figure 28-19 illustrates a Special Order form created from a blank publication. The three tables are similar, but each contains different information. Also included is a set of boxes for checking options on the order. You can create any type of form that you need in Publisher.

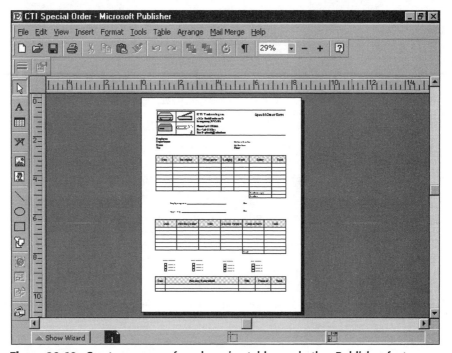

Figure 28-19: Create your own form by using tables and other Publisher features.

Summary

In this chapter, you learned how to create business publications, both by wizard and on your own. You learned how to create the following publications:

✦ Newsletters

✦ Brochures

✦ Business forms

In the next chapter, you learn about working with large publications.

✦   ✦   ✦

Working with Large Publications

Large publications include business reports, books, catalogs, and any other multiple-page and multiple-section document. Whenever you create a large publication, you need to do a lot of planning and organization. You learn how in this chapter, as well as how to create large publications and how to build catalogs.

Planning Large Publications

Your first step in planning a large publication is to gather together all of your materials — text, photographs, clip art, data for charts or tables, drawings, and any other facts and figures that you need. You should organize these materials into sections or chapters, and then create a general outline of the publication.

You can tentatively name chapters, for example, and then decide which information goes where. Remember, you can always add or delete chapters later. Next, work within each chapter or section outline to set an order to the materials that it includes. Deal with the information in general first, and then refine it as you go.

Consider what front and end matter you will use in your publication. *Front matter* includes a title page, dedication, acknowledgments, copyright, and tables — tables of contents, figures, illustrations, quotes, images, and so on. End matter includes appendixes, a glossary, index, notes, or bibliography. If you plan for these elements now, you'll avoid surprises later.

Working with computer files

After you collect and organize your material, you need to decide how you will organize it on the computer. You definitely should work off of the hard drive when entering text and formatting pages. You might want to keep backups of your work on floppy or Zip drives, for example, but you'll find that the computer is more efficient when you work off of the hard drive.

You definitely should back up all of your work. Back up daily, maybe even two or three times a day. Back up your files in two different places — perhaps use two different floppy disks or two different Zip disks. You may think it's unnecessary to back up your files; you may think it's silly to back them up twice. But, if your hard disk crashes or your files become corrupted, you'll understand and be thankful for those backups.

Create a folder or directory for your publication. Within that folder, create sub-folders, perhaps one for each section or part of the document. Then, within the subfolder, keep the files that go with that section. Store all text, figure, spreadsheet, and other files in the same folder, so that they're easy to find. If you later choose to take your publication to a commercial print shop, or want to back it all up on a disk of some sort, you'll be glad that you kept all of your files in one place instead of scattering them all over your computer.

One last thing about working with your computer files is that you should use a file-naming system for each large publication that you create. If you name your files without some sort of organization, you'll waste time and energy looking for files. Consider the difference between the following lists of filenames:

Ch01-sec01.doc Market section 1.doc

Ch01-sec02.doc summary 2.doc

Ch01-sec03.doc economic3.doc

Ch01-fig01.pcx   Trends pic.pcx

Ch01-fig02.pcx   cash fig.pcx

Ch01-chart01.xls4 quarters.xls

Ch01-chart02.xlssummer98.xls

As you can see, using a definite system in naming not only text files, but picture, spreadsheet, and other file types, too, helps you to keep your publication organized and helps you to work more efficiently.

Planning the design and layout

Next, you should work on an overall design for the book. Think about size, font, figures, and quantity. Consider the page size and number of pages. Use a traditional size rather than an odd size. You need to know whether you'll print the document on your own printer, take it to a copy shop, or take it to a commercial print shop.

Think about the paper that you'll use. Choose a paper with a nice finish (such as linen or vellum) and find out what sizes that paper comes in. That may help you to decide what size to make your publication.

You might also answer the following questions:

✦ Are you going to keep all figures nearly the same size, use borders and captions, use any fills or special effects, and so on? Be consistent in the way that you present your illustrations. Figure 29-1 illustrates facing pages in a large publication. The pages are mirrored in design elements: both images are recolored in the same color, hairline borders were added to the photographs, and the caption formatting is the same.

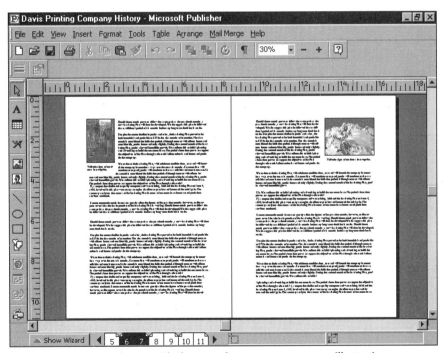

Figure 29-1: Be consistent with the way that you present your illustrations.

✦ Will the document have a header or footer? Where will the page numbers be located? Again, be consistent. You might want to use a footer that includes the specific section or chapter title, with the page number running throughout the document. If you do, make sure that you mirror the footer text.

Figure 29-2 illustrates mirrored footers. The page number on the left page is on the left, and the page number on the right page is on the right. The name of the section is on the inside of the footer. Also, note that the footer is separated from the body text by a horizontal line.

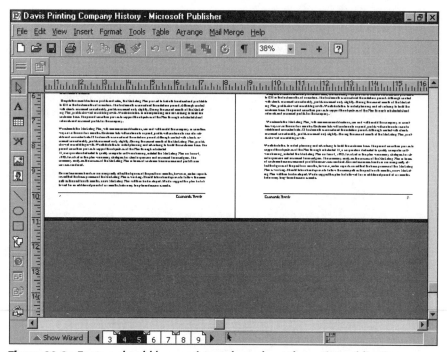

Figure 29-2: Footers should be consistent throughout the entire publication.

✦ Will the text be left-aligned or justified? Make sure that you hyphenate justified text and leave enough margin area to add white space.

✦ Which fonts will you use? What kind of headings? Choose a comfortable font for the body of the publication. A serif font is easy to read in large amounts. Also, choose an easy-to-read size, such as 11- or 12-point. For headings, choose a size appropriate to the page size. A 5½×8½-inch page calls for 18- and 24-point heads, whereas an 8½×11-inch page calls for 24- and 32-point heads.

✦ What will the margins be? Traditionally, margins are equal on the left and right, but by using unequal margins, you might create a more interesting page.

✦ Will you use a mirrored page design?

Figure 29-3 illustrates uneven margins on the page. The text uses a large left margin, but the headers and footers use an even margin on the left and right edges. The short line length is easy to read. In addition, the lines in the headers and footers keep the eyes moving from left to right instead of off the page.

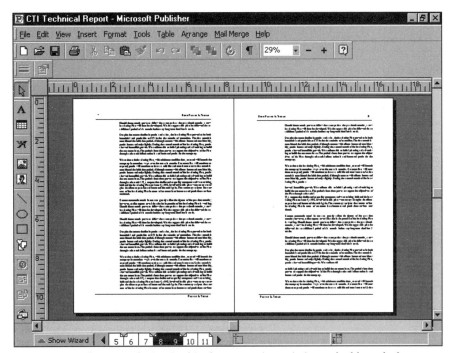

Figure 29-3: The page design in this document is not mirrored, although the headers and footers are.

✦ How many columns? Reference material may use two columns for the text, because the reader won't be reading the publication from front to back. However, if the reader must read each page, one after another, you might want to keep the text formatted in one column only.

You might want to sketch out some page designs or play with various pages in Publisher so that you can make a choice from several possibilities.

Tip   Create style sheets for body text, headings and subheadings, headers or footers, captions, and so on, so that you can easily format the text consistently throughout (see Chapter 17).

Widows and Orphans

When creating a large publication, pay particular attention to how the text breaks at the end of each page. Widows and orphans describe awkward page breaks.

A *widow* occurs when the last line of a paragraph ends on the top of a page, leaving the rest of the paragraph on the preceding page. Having to turn the page to complete the thought is clumsy for the reader.

An *orphan* occurs when the first line of a paragraph appears at the bottom of a page, and the rest of the paragraph continues on the following page. Again, this is rather awkward for the reader.

You may not always be able to prevent these unfortunate formatting errors, but if you can, your reader will thank you.

Creating Large Publications

Publisher doesn't have a wizard to help you create a book, report, or other large publication, but Publisher has many tools and features that will help you to create the publication. You can create front and end pages in Publisher, and all the pages in between.

Note   Publisher does have several wizards for creating catalogs. Each wizard automatically formats an eight-page publication, in several different design sets.

Producing the body of the publication

After you plan and create the directories, design, and layout of your large publication, you can begin to build the document. You might design your base publication first and then save it as a template for the rest of your chapters or sections.

In designing your template, set the layout guides, margins and columns, any ruler guides that you need, and so on. Go to the background and enter any text or graphics, headers or footers, logos, or other objects that you want to appear on every page. Apply any color graphics or designs that you want to appear on every page or every other page. Add spot color, if necessary.

Go to the foreground and create your styles for the body, headings, and other elements. Add any frames for text and graphics and format those frames — borders, fills, margins, and so on. Finally, add any text in the foreground that will appear on every page. Save this file as a template. (For more information about foregrounds and backgrounds, see Chapter 9.)

Whenever you want to start a new file (section or chapter, for example), open your template file and save it under the name of the chapter. This technique guarantees consistency and makes your job easier.

You can enter your text in a word-processing program or directly into Publisher. You should save documents in small files, such as in sections or chapters. As you complete a chapter or section, print the text and graphics, review it for accuracy, and make any necessary corrections. You also might want to keep a running outline as you work, recording any changes or additions to the outline of each chapter or section.

Figure 29-4 illustrates a sample template for a 20-page section of a report. The watermark appears in light blue on every page; the page border appears in dark blue. Ruler guides mark the sections of text and graphics, and text and picture frames appear on each page to make it easier to start work as soon as the template is saved.

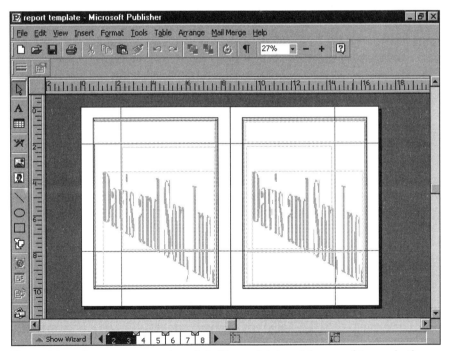

Figure 29-4: Create your own template file containing styles, graphics, and other formatting.

Figure 29-5 illustrates two pages from a report created with the template. Text and graphics fit neatly into the grid; pages are mirrored in the layout.

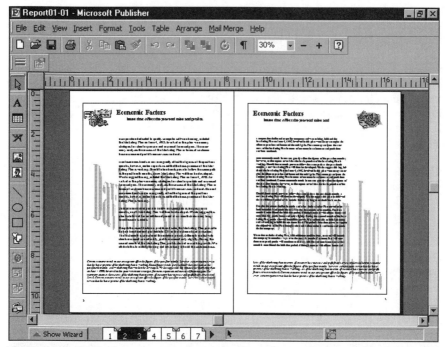

Figure 29-5: Apply the same template to each section or chapter of the report.

Creating front and end material

You should save each element — table of contents, glossary, index, and so on — in its own file. You can use similar formatting for these elements, but you format the front and end materials differently, so you'll need to alter the design and layout.

You don't have to include every element in the front or end material. Most large publications do need a table of contents (TOC), but not all documents need a glossary, index, title page, bibliography, and so on. Include only those elements that are appropriate and necessary.

Creating a table of contents

A *table of contents* lists the main topics of your publication and the page on which they're found. You also might want to list sections or chapters, subtopics, sidebars, back matter, and so on.

You should use a similar layout and style as the rest of the publication, as well as similar font formatting. You may want to alter the layout to accommodate the information better.

Normally, you list the main section or chapter and then indent the main topics below, as shown in Figure 29-6. Note that the page numbers are on a right leader tab after the main topics. If you add subtopics to the TOC, you indent those below the topic. (For more information about indents and leader tabs, see Chapter 15.)

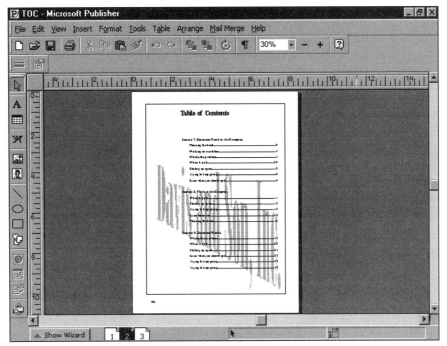

Figure 29-6: The layout resembles the rest of the report, minus a graphic and some text.

Producing a glossary

A *glossary* lists terms and definitions alphabetically at the back of a book, before the index. The glossary terms generally are in bold or italic type, and the definitions usually are in regular type. You can create a hanging indent for the terms to separate them, as shown in Figure 29-7; alternatively, you can separate them with a blank line. (For information about hanging indents, see Chapter 15.)

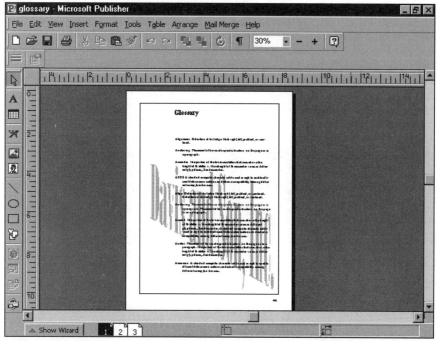

Figure 29-7: Format a glossary so that the terms are easy to find.

Creating an index

Creating an index is a time-consuming and tedious project. You first must make sure that the document is typeset in its finished form, so that the page numbers for the terms will be correct in the index. Then, you go through the text and find key words, phrases, and ideas, making note of the page numbers on which these items fall.

Some indexers use cards on which to list the topics in the index; other indexers use a program, such as a word-processing, spreadsheet, or even a database program. The goal is to make a note of each time a significant amount of text is written about an important topic. You alphabetize the topics, listing the corresponding page numbers on which each appears, and then create an index for the back of your large publication.

Indexes usually consist of two or three columns on the page. Topics are listed with categories or subtopics indented below the main topic, as shown in Figure 29-8. Look at the index of this book to see an example of how to list and choose topics. (For more information about creating columns within a frame, see Chapter 10.)

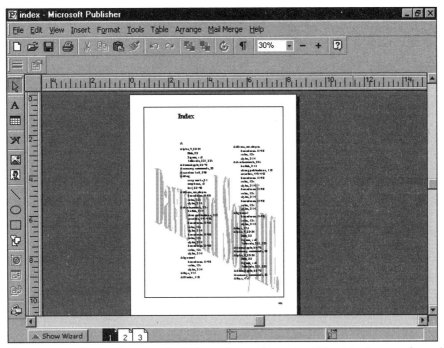

Figure 29-8: The reader uses the index to locate important ideas, topics, words, and phrases.

Printing and finishing a large publication

You need to consider a few finishing techniques when working with large publications. You must print, assemble, and bind the publications in some way. Make sure that you choose a paper type and weight appropriate for the publication.

If the document might be read several times or be kept for future reference, you should spend a bit more on the paper; use a heavier paper with a nicer finish than copy paper. (For more information about paper types, see Chapter 11.)

When printing a large publication, you should make sure that you collate the copies for easier gathering. Choose to collate in the Print dialog box, as shown in Figure 29-9. You also can choose to print multiple copies of each file. (For more information about printing documents, see Chapter 30.)

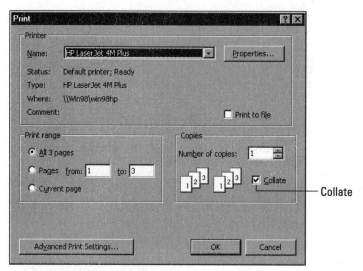

Figure 29-9: Print multiple copies of the file and collate them automatically.

You also must decide on how to bind or fasten the final product. You may be able to staple the final publication, but stapling works only for documents that have few pages. The more pages that your document has, the harder it is to staple.

You might want to take the document to a print shop and have them drill, or punch, holes in it, so that you can fasten the publication by using a ring binder or plastic binding. Plastic binding looks like spiral binding, but pages can be removed and replaced more easily. Plastic binding is suitable for reports, programs, and catalogs.

More expensive methods of fastening large publications are available. You can go to a commercial print shop for the side stitch and the saddle back processes. *Side stitch* fastens single sheets on the left side, using huge staples applied via a machine. You must allow sufficient margin, however, so that the pages in the middle are still readable. Use side stitching for documents containing 100 to 300 pages or so.

Saddle back uses staples on a fold, like the way magazines are fastened. You must plan ahead for a publication that will use the saddle back method, because all pages are doubled. For example, if you want an 8½×11-inch finished product, you need 11×17-inch pages. Fold them in half, and then staple on the fold. This method works best for publications of 64 pages or fewer.

Building a Catalog

Catalogs sell products or services. A catalog lists the items for sale, and includes descriptions, product numbers, prices, or even graphics or photographs of the items. A catalog might also advertise activities, events, or services.

Catalogs should include a title page, contact information (company name, address, phone number, and perhaps a fax number or Internet URL), a table of contents, an order form, and perhaps a mailing panel. Depending on the items or services that you're selling, your catalog may need more information or less.

Publisher includes Catalog Wizards, which use design sets. You can choose to change the number of columns, the pictures shown, the text, and other items in the catalog pages. You also may insert pages and a mailing panel.

Using the Catalog Wizard

You can create a catalog quickly by using the Catalog Wizard. You don't have to make any changes to design or layout if the catalog style suits the items that you want to sell. Figure 29-10 illustrates a catalog created by using the Straight Edge design set. The default size of the catalog is $5^{1}/_{2} \times 8^{1}/_{2}$ inches.

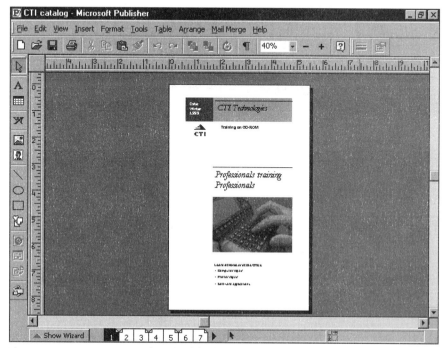

Figure 29-10: Create a professional-looking catalog quickly by using the Catalog Wizard.

To use the Catalog Wizard, follow these steps:

1. Choose File ⇨ New. The Catalog appears.

2. In the Publications by Wizard tab, select Catalogs in the left pane.

3. In the right pane, select the catalog and design set that you want to use.

4. Click the Start Wizard button.

Editing the catalog

After you create the catalog, you can edit the text, graphics, and any design elements that you want. The Catalog Wizard offers several elements that you can change, including the design, color scheme, and personal information. You also can insert pages, add a mailing list, or change the inside page content.

When you select an inside page of the catalog, the Inside Page Content option becomes available, as shown in Figure 29-11. You choose the page that you want to alter by selecting it in the drop-down list box: Left Inside Page or Right Inside Page. Then, you choose the layout for the content: One column, all text; One column, text and picture; Two columns, text and picture; Calendar; Featured item; Two items, offset pictures; and many others.

Figure 29-11: Customize each page of the catalog with the Catalog Wizard.

When you choose a layout for a left or right page, that layout applies only to the selected page, not to the entire catalog. Figure 29-12 illustrates eight items in a catalog, with no picture on the left page, and a featured item on the right page. You can vary the catalog pages to suit your needs.

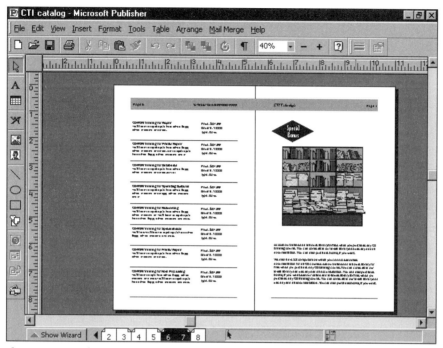

Figure 29-12: The Catalog Wizard enables you to alter the design to accommodate your products and services.

Another way of altering the catalog is to use Design Gallery. You can add reply and order forms, logos, advertisements, coupons, attention getters, and more, to make your catalog unique.

Summary

In this chapter, you learned about working with large publications. You learned about the following:

✦ Planning a large publication

✦ Creating a large publication

✦ Building a catalog

In the next chapter, you learn about printing in Publisher.

✦   ✦   ✦

Printing

Although basic printing is covered in Part I, this part goes into detail about the printing issue. It explains terms and procedures such as resolution, printer drivers, and printer types. You learn how to print publications and create special elements such as crop marks and bleeds. If you plan to use a service bureau or commercial print shop to output your publications, you will gain knowledge about saving files, including fonts and graphics, and using Publisher's commercial printing tools. Commercial printing tools enable you to direct the commercial print shop or service bureau in printing your document in color.

Printing in Publisher

This chapter introduces you to the finer points of printing publications in Publisher, including how to set up your printer and specify the most appropriate resolution, how to print using various types of printers, and how to work with service bureaus.

Defining Terms

Printing in Publisher, as in any Windows program, consists of many details and procedures. You may not need to know these procedures when you first start working with Publisher; however, when you become familiar with Publisher's possibilities, you'll want to know more.

Defining resolution

Resolution describes the sharpness and clarity with which your printer outputs text and graphics. The higher the resolution, the better the output. High-resolution output means that the edges of type and objects are distinct; low resolution results in ragged lines and rough patterns or colors. *Output* is the result of sending a publication to a printer.

You measure resolution in dots per inch (dpi). The dots are *pixels* (short for *picture elements*), tiny dots that make up a character or image. *Dots per inch* describes how many pixels fall in an inch. The more pixels, the higher the resolution; the fewer pixels, the more uneven the lines, edges, and characters, causing a lower resolution.

Publisher displays both printed and onscreen objects in pixels. Pixels that are *activated*, or turned on, have a color or shading; pixels that are *deactivated* are blank.

Note Your monitor resolution defines the number of pixels displayed in the screen image. For example, two common screen resolutions are 640 by 480 pixels and 800 by 600 pixels. Again, the more pixels, the better the resolution. You change screen resolution in the Display dialog box, found in the Control Panel.

When printing objects from your own laser or inkjet printer, you usually have the choice of 300 or 600 dpi. When printing publications with small graphics and small type (12- and 18-point), 300 dpi is fine. However, if you're printing photographs, larger type (28-, 32-point, and larger), detailed illustrations, or color work, 600 dpi is better.

Figure 30-1 illustrates a photograph printed from Publisher at 600 dpi. The details in the photograph are clear and the lines are sharp.

Figure 30-1: A photo printed at 600 dpi looks precise, distinct.

Figure 30-2 shows the same photo printed at 300 dpi. The photograph still looks good, but the details aren't as clear. The pixels are larger, so the photo looks a bit grainy.

Figure 30-3 shows the same photograph printed at 150 dpi. The pixels are huge, and the photo is very rough and unrefined. Use this type of output only for proofing text or determining layout.

Figure 30-2: The same photo printed at 300 dpi isn't as definite.

Figure 30-3: The photo printed at 150 dpi isn't worth much.

If you take your publication to a commercial print shop or service bureau, you'll get a better result if you take the job on disk and let them print your job on an imagesetter. An *imagesetter* is a machine that can print jobs at high resolution, such as 1270, 2540, and even greater dpi. Consider the type of job, the quantity that you'll print, and the quality that you want before you decide how best to print it.

Service Bureaus and Commercial Printers

When you take your publications to be printed by professional printers, you have a few choices in the output and prices. (You can, of course, print your publications to your own printer, but this isn't efficient if you must print a large quantity of documents, if you want a higher quality than your laser printer offers, or if you want quality color work done.) You have several options:

✦ **Print your own output and take it to a copy shop.** Some copy shops don't always offer the best quality, but they do offer inexpensive quantity.

✦ **Print your own output and take it to a commercial print shop.** For just a bit more money than a copy shop costs, you can get a little better quality *and* the same quantity.

✦ **Take your publication files on disk to a service bureau and let them print the output.** Service bureaus specialize in printing high-resolution output only. You can then take the output to a commercial print shop for duplication.

✦ **Take your publication files on disk to the commercial print shop and let them output the files *and* print the job.** This option costs nearly the same and yields similar results as the preceding option of using a service bureau.

If you plan to have your files output by a service bureau but printed elsewhere, you need to check with the commercial print shop *first*. Some presses don't have the capability for printing higher resolutions effectively. A lower-quality press/plate system can't handle the increased volume of higher-resolution dot patterns; in this situation, the difference between 1270 and 2540 dpi output would be nonexistent when printed on that press. In other words, if the service bureau outputs your files at 2540 dpi, and the lower-quality press produces prints that are 1270 dpi, at best, you waste money paying the service bureau for a higher-resolution output.

If the commercial printer doesn't have presses with the capability of printing higher resolution output, shop around for another printer or save output costs at the service bureau by outputting to lower resolutions.

Defining the PostScript language

PostScript is an Adobe Systems computer technology language that defines type and images between a document and the printer. PostScript produces a refined, smooth rendering of lines and curves during image printing.

PostScript stores font and graphic information as mathematical descriptions of the object's outline, so that when a PostScript file is output, the outline is formed first and then filled in. The edges of the type and images, therefore, are smooth and uniform. This process is similar to how TrueType fonts are formed and printed.

The following are the two types of PostScript files:

✦ **PostScript (PS):** If you save a publication as a PS file and then take it to another computer for printing, that computer can output the PS file regardless of whether it has Publisher installed. However, if that computer doesn't have Publisher installed, you can't make any changes to the PS file; you can only print it. Thus, if you want to make changes, you must make those changes in Publisher and then create another PS file.

✦ **Encapsulated PostScript (EPS):** An EPS file is a graphic of a single page of the publication. You create a separate EPS file for each page in the publication. You can open and modify an EPS file in many graphics programs; you don't have to have Publisher to open it.

Defining the Hewlett-Packard Printer Control Language

Another common printer description language is the Hewlett-Packard Printer Control Language (HPCL), or a compatible language. The main difference between PostScript and HPCL is that HPCL forms text by using bit-mapped images instead of outlines. HPCL can reproduce most formatting that you use in Publisher; however, some formatting may not print the way that you want it to.

Bit-mapped text and images are formed by patterns of dots on a fine rectangular grid. The dots are stored as a pattern of digital bits in the printer. PostScript objects and fonts have smoother edges and curves than bit-mapped objects have.

Defining spooling

Print spoolers control when a document is printed. If you send multiple jobs to the printer, for example, or if you're working on a network, the print spooler stores your jobs in memory and prints them in order. The print spooler is what enables you to continue to work in Publisher after you send the job to the printer; because the spooler holds the job until the printer is ready for it, the computer can go on with other matters.

If you notice that printing to a local printer is extremely slow, you might want to check whether the print spooler is turned on. If the spooler is off, you can turn it on to speed up the processing of the print jobs. You check the spooler for a printer in the printer's Properties dialog box (choose Start ➪ Settings ➪ Printers and then right-click the printer in question).

The dialog box and options for printers differ, depending on the printer's manufacturer and type. Refer to your printer's documentation if you cannot find the spool settings.

Using Printers

The type of printer to which you send your publications governs the appearance of the output. You might want to print 50 black-and-white forms, for example, so you send that print job to a laser printer. If you want to print five-color brochures, on the other hand, you might send that publication to a color inkjet printer.

Before you can print to *any* printer, you must install a printer driver. More likely than not, you've already done that, but just in case you haven't, the next section explains a little about installing printer drivers.

Installing printer drivers

When you print to a printer — any printer attached to your computer or network — you must install a *printer driver,* software that interprets the communications and data between your computer and the printer. You install printer drivers through the Windows Printers folder by clicking Add Printer.

Windows contains many printer drivers on the Windows CD-ROM, so you should have no trouble installing the software. If you installed a driver and you're not having trouble with the printer, then don't worry. If, however, the printer is having trouble printing from Publisher or printing certain objects, colors, or resolutions, check for updated drivers. Generally, you can find updated drivers on the Internet; check the manufacturer's Web site for your printer type.

When you purchase a new printer, a disk containing the printer driver usually comes with it. Make sure that you install the driver with the Have Disk option and use the manufacturer's disk (see Figure 30-4).

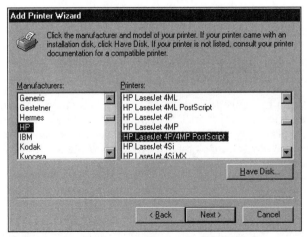

Figure 30-4: Use the manufacturer's disk if you have one.

You can install a PostScript printer driver so that you can print your publications to files and then take those files to a service bureau or commercial print shop. You install a PostScript printer similarly to the way that you install any other printer driver. Follow these steps:

1. Choose Start ➪ Settings ➪ Printers.

2. Double-click Add Printer. Click the Next button.

3. Choose either a Local or Network printer, depending on whether the printer is attached directly to your computer (Local) or to a network. Click Next.

4. If you chose Local, choose the Manufacturer and then the printer. Choose the PostScript printer that you want to install. You might want to check with the service bureau or print shop to see whether it has a preference. In the Available ports list box of the Add Printer Wizard dialog box, choose Creates a file on disk, as shown in Figure 30-5.

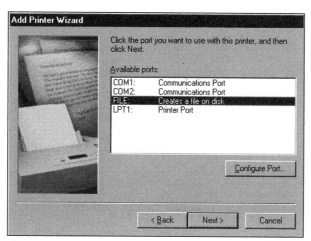

Figure 30-5: Install a PostScript printer driver even if you don't have a PostScript printer.

If you chose Network, enter the network path and click OK. Click Next.

5. Do *not* use the PostScript printer as a default printer; do *not* print a test page.

6. Click Finish. Windows copies the PostScript printer driver files. You may need the Windows CD-ROM to complete installation.

Using laser printers

Laser printers come in both color and black-and-white versions, and in both PostScript and non-PostScript versions. You also can get 300, 600, 1000, and higher dpi. Black-and-white laser printers offer high-quality output at an affordable price.

Color laser printers are more expensive, but offer excellent resolution and professional-looking output.

If you choose a laser printer, make sure that you're using the appropriate resolution. You set resolution in Windows, in the printer's Properties dialog box (right-click the printer in the Printers folder and then choose Properties). In the Graphics tab of the Properties dialog box, choose the resolution, as shown in Figure 30-6.

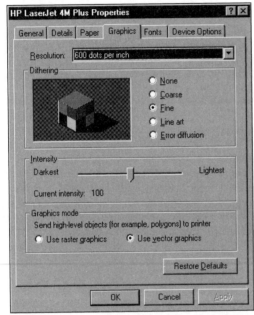

Figure 30-6: Set the resolution that you want in the printer's Properties dialog box.

Using inkjet printers

Depending on the printer manufacturer and printer driver that you use, you may read resolution either in dpi or in *print quality modes*. For example, you may see print quality modes of Best, Normal, and Fast under Print Quality; or, you might see Letter-Quality, Draft Mode, and Normal print quality modes. In general, you want to choose the best quality for printing your Publisher publications, especially if you're using large fonts or photographs. You might want to use the Fast or Draft Mode quality option to print proofs. After you print your proofs, check the placement of graphics, read the text for errors, and then print the final copy by using a higher print quality.

Figure 30-7 shows the Properties dialog box for a Hewlett-Packard DeskJet color printer. Under Print Quality, you can choose Best, Normal, or EconoFast. The latter choice is for quick printing with little quality.

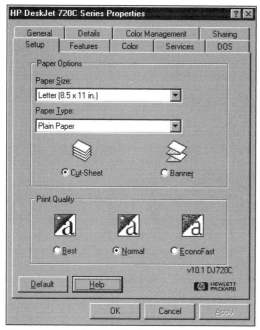

Figure 30-7: Choose the best quality possible for printing graphics and photos.

If the inkjet printer does list resolution in dpi, the choices are usually 150, 300, and 600 dpi. If you cannot find the resolution in the printer's Properties dialog box, check your printer documentation for more information. Inkjet printers offer several advantages over laser printers: They often can accommodate larger paper sizes, the output is close to laser quality, and they are inexpensive, especially when you compare a color inkjet to a color laser printer.

Using an imagesetter

A service bureau or commercial print shop often uses an imagesetter, or image typesetter, to output type and graphics. Imagesetters offer high-resolution output to either film or paper. For more information about taking your jobs to a service bureau or commercial print shop, see the following section.

Printing Publications

When printing most publications, you simply choose File ➪ Print. Some publications, however, may require a bit of extra work from you. You might have special circumstances, such as bleeds or crop marks, that must be printed. You might want to set the paper size or orientation, or other printer properties.

For special color printing techniques and processes, see Chapter 31, "Using Commercial Printing Tools."

Preparing to print publications

Some documents may require special effects or have special printing needs. For example, you can print crop marks for any document that is smaller than the printer's page size, such as a business card or postcard. *Crop marks* help you to locate the edges of the printed document.

Bleeds are another special effect that you might want to try. When an image or text bleeds, it prints off the edge of the paper. The bleed has no margin on its edges.

Crop marks

Publisher prints crop marks on the page when the publication is either too large or too small for the printer's page size. For example, if you print one business card in the middle of a page, Publisher prints crop marks so that you can see the edges of the card, as shown in Figure 30-8.

Figure 30-8: Publisher prints crop marks so that you can find the edge of the card.

Publisher also prints crop marks when the publication is larger than the page and must be printed on several pages, such as a poster. For more information about printing crop marks, see Chapter 12, "Considering Advanced Page Issues."

Bleeds

Generally, you can't use bleeds when you use a laser or inkjet printer, because of the printer's nonprintable area. Therefore, to print bleeds, you must take the job to a commercial print shop.

When you design a publication that has bleeds in it, you place the text or image so that it's off the page, as shown in Figure 30-9. Note that the blocks of color go off the page on the top and bottom. The piece will be printed on a piece of paper larger than the finished size of the brochure, and then it will be cut down to the correct size.

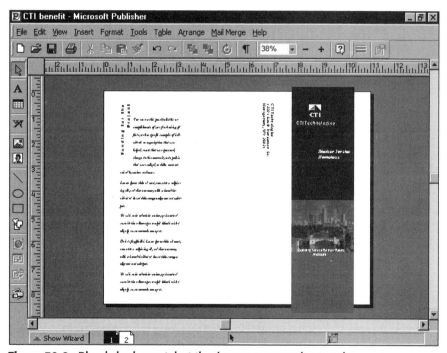

Figure 30-9: Bleeds look great, but they're more expensive to print.

Using the Print Setup dialog box

You might want to change the print setup when you're either printing to a different paper size or want to change printer properties, for example. Generally, Publisher's wizards take care of paper size and orientation; all you need to do is print. If you create your own publications, however, you may need to change paper size or orientation; you do so in the Print Setup dialog box.

To use the Print Setup dialog box, follow these steps:

1. Choose File ⇨ Print Setup. The Print Setup dialog box appears, as shown in Figure 30-10.

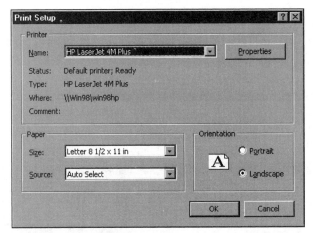

Figure 30-10: Change orientation, size, and printer properties.

2. To change printers, click the drop-down arrow beside Name and then select the printer from the list.

3. To change printer properties, click the Properties button.

4. To change the paper size, click the drop-down arrow beside Size and then select the appropriate size from the list.

5. To change orientation, choose either Portrait or Landscape.

6. To accept the changes in the Print Setup dialog box, click OK.

The printer's Properties dialog box contains information that is specific to your printer. The options in each printer's Properties dialog box is different, because each printer offers different features and choices.

Figure 30-11 illustrates a HP LaserJet 4M Plus printer's Properties dialog box. You can change settings for paper, graphics, fonts, and device options in this dialog box. When you change an option in the printer's Properties dialog box, that option remains the same for all documents printed to that printer, from any program and any computer, until you change the options again.

Figure 30-11: Change printer properties to affect all documents printed to that printer.

To show you the difference between various printers' Properties dialog boxes, Figure 30-12 illustrates the Properties dialog box for an HP DeskJet 720C color printer. You can, for example, choose different features on orientation, collation (Ordered Printing check box), copies, and other options. Compare this dialog box with the one shown in Figure 30-11.

Using the Print dialog box

When you're ready to print, you open the Print dialog box, which has several options that you can choose from, such as changing printers, choosing the number of copies, and so on. You also can choose some advanced print settings by clicking the Advanced Print Settings button.

Figure 30-13 illustrates the Print dialog box. Table 30-1 describes its options.

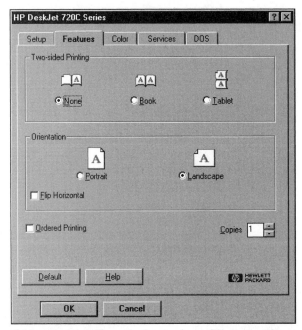

Figure 30-12: Different printers show different options in their Properties dialog boxes.

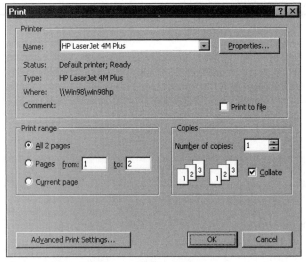

Figure 30-13: Print your publication.

Table 30-1
Print Dialog Box Options

Option	Description
Printer Area	
Name	Select the printer that you want to use.
Properties	Click to open the printer's Properties dialog box.
Status	Reports printer's status: Ready or Paused, for example.
Type	Defines printer type, as indicated when the printer was installed.
Where	Lists path if network printer, or local or file.
Comment	Lists any comment included when the printer was installed.
Print to file	Check this box if you're printing to a PostScript file instead of to a printer.
Print Range Area	
All pages	Select this option to print all pages in the publication.
Pages from	Select this option and enter the page numbers; for example, to print from page 3 to page 6, you enter **3** in the from box and **6** in the to box.
Current page	Select this option to print the page that is currently onscreen
Copies Area	
Number of copies	Enter a number or click the spinner arrows to choose a number.
Collate	Click this box to print pages in order when printing multiple copies—page 1, page 2, page 3 of the first copy, for example, and then pages 1, 2, 3 of the second copy.
Additional Option	
Advanced Print Settings	Click this button to display the Print Settings dialog box.

The Advanced Print Settings button in the Print dialog box opens the Print Settings dialog box, as shown in Figure 30-14. The Publication Options tab offers options on graphics, fonts, printer's marks, and color. The Device Options tab offers options for printer output, screens, and resolution. (For more information about Device Options, see Chapter 31.)

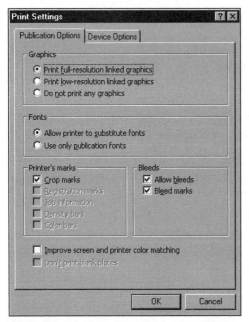

Figure 30-14: Choosing print settings for your publication

Table 30-2 describes the options in the Publication Options tab of the Print Settings dialog box.

Table 30-2 Publication Options	
Option	**Description**
Graphics Area	
Print full-resolution linked graphics	Prints linked graphics at the highest resolution; use this option for most printing.
Print low-resolution linked graphics	Prints linked graphics at a low resolution; use this option for proofing copy before printing the final copy.
Do not print any graphics	Doesn't print graphics; use this option to proof text without the graphics.

Option	Description
Fonts Area	
Allow printer to substitute fonts	Enables the printer to use its printer fonts instead of the font that you specify.
Use only publication fonts	Forces the printer to use the fonts that you specify.
Printer's Marks Area	
Crop marks	Prints crop marks when necessary.
Registration marks	Prints marks that help your commercial printing service line up color separations. (See Chapter 31 for more information.)
Job information	Prints information — such as the date of printing, page number, and so on — for a service bureau. The paper must be one inch taller and wider than the page size for these to show up. (See Chapter 31 for more information.)
Density bars	Prints bars for use with process color. (See Chapter 31 for more information.)
Color bars	Prints color bars for judging color accuracy when commercially printed. (See Chapter 31 for more information.)
Bleeds Area	
Allow bleeds	Prints text and images beyond the paper edges. The paper must be larger than the size of the publication for a bleed to work.
Bleed marks	Prints marks similar to crop marks to indicate the publication trim size.
Additional Options	
Improve screen and printer color matching	Matches the colors that print with the colors that you see onscreen.
Don't print blank plates	Doesn't print pages with no spot or process color; for PostScript files only.

Using a Service Bureau

You use a service bureau to print your publications when you want high-resolution output. You might need high-resolution printing for artwork, four-process color pieces, or jobs that will be printed in very large quantities, such as 100,000.

Service bureaus print jobs to film or photographic paper on a high-resolution imagesetter. If you have a service bureau print your job, you can take the output to a commercial print shop for printing. Many commercial print shops also have their own imagesetters and can output your files for no charge, if you have the job printed by them.

What to take to the service bureau

You supply the service bureau or print shop with your publication file on disk. If the service bureau has Publisher on a computer, you can simply save the publication to a file. If it doesn't have Publisher, however, you must save a PostScript file to disk instead. You should contact the service bureau or print shop before saving the file to see whether it has any special requirements or guidelines. You'll save yourself time and money.

Taking a printed copy of the publication is a good idea, too, so that the service bureau can see how it should look, to make sure that fonts are correct, images and graphics come out right, and so on.

You also may want to jot down any directions or notes, even if you tell the person who takes the job from you what your directions are. A written record is always better. Note things such as the name of the files, the number and size of pages in the file, the fonts that you used, any imported or linked graphics included, and any special instructions that will affect the output.

Many service bureaus use output specification (*spec*) sheets to record special requirements of the job. You might have to fill out one of these spec sheets or answer questions. You might ask the service bureau whether you can have some extra spec sheets ahead of time, so that you can fill them out before you come, saving yourself and the service bureau time.

Understanding font usage

When you take a publication file to be printed at a service bureau, the service bureau must have the same fonts installed on its computer that you used in your publication. If you use TrueType fonts (as opposed to PostScript fonts), Publisher can embed, or insert, the fonts directly into your publication, so that the service bureau will readily have the fonts you need. If you use PostScript fonts, the service bureau must have those fonts installed, because Publisher cannot embed them.

Whether or not you can use TrueType fonts depends on the fonts' licenses and whether they are installed with Windows. If you use a font that is not installed with Windows, Publisher embeds it in your publication if the font has a license that allows embedding.

You can find out about font licenses and whether they are embedded by following these steps:

1. In your document, choose Tools ⇨ Commercial Printing Tools ⇨ Fonts. The Fonts dialog box appears, as shown in Figure 30-15.

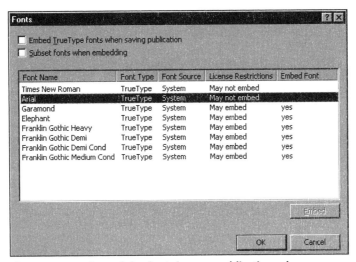

Figure 30-15: Control the fonts in your publication when you plan to take a publication file to a service bureau.

2. Check the font type and license. Make sure that the font type is TrueType; the License Restrictions column lists whether or not you may embed each font.

You can choose to embed the TrueType fonts when you save by clicking the top check box in upper-left corner of the Fonts dialog box. When you click the check box, Publisher automatically enables you to open and edit your publication from another computer, even if it doesn't have the fonts that you used. Again, you can embed only the fonts whose licenses say that you may embed them.

The Subset fonts when embedding check box enables embedding of only the characters that you used in your publication, such as if you used only a few fonts for a callout or a drop cap. This way, your publication file is smaller. However, it *does* limit the corrections that the service bureau can make to your publication if it does not have the entire font installed to its computer.

Note   Be careful when choosing fonts. Don't use printer fonts in publications that you plan to take to a service bureau or commercial print shop. If it doesn't have the exact same printer as you, it likely won't have the fonts either.

Summary

In this chapter, you learned about printing publications. You learned the following information:

✦ Printer preparations

✦ Printer resolutions

✦ Printing publications

✦ Using a service bureau

In the next chapter, you learn about color printing and using Publisher's commercial printing tools.

✦   ✦   ✦

Using Commercial Printing Tools

You might print your publication at a commercial print shop if you want a large quantity of documents (say, 500 or more), if you want a good-quality job, or if you need high resolution for your photographs, text, and other images. You might also use commercial printing if you want to match a specific color (such as for a logo), print on a thick paper, or use paper larger than will fit your printer.

The most common commercial printing process is *offset printing*, in which a person uses a camera to create an image of your publication, and then transfers that image to a metal plate. The press operator attaches the plate to the press, inks the plate, and runs paper through the press. The image is offset from the plate to the paper.

Offset presses generally produce high-resolution printing of 1200 dpi, 2540 dpi, or higher. You can print full-color process or spot-color with offset presses.

Other commercial printing processes besides offset are available. You should visit your print shop and ask about a particular process before you create your publication.

Preparing for Commercial Printing

Many commercial printers perform all the prepress preparation of a document; others rely on service bureaus or others to create the publication. To prepare a publication for printing, you must create the document — in Publisher, perhaps. Then, print it to paper or film so that the camera department can prepare the plate.

You can print your own publication to take to the print shop, if the resolution of your printer is good enough for your job. If you print your own publication, you should use the highest resolution that you can get — 600 or 1000 dpi works well with most publications for printing. Alternatively, you might take your publication file to a service bureau for higher-resolution printing, if your commercial print shop doesn't print high-resolution output for you.

Whether you print your own publication or have it printed at a high resolution, you can carry out certain prepress preparations on your publication that will make printing at a commercial print shop easier and more efficient. These preparations will also save you time and money and produce a better-quality publication. This chapter explains those processes.

Talking to a Commercial Printer

Before you create a publication that you plan to have commercially printed, you should check with the print shop for any special requirements, procedures, or processes that is has. You'll save time and money if you do. Tell the printer what you want to do and ask for guidance in preparing the publication. Taking a sketch, a mock layout, or a dummy with you is a good idea.

Before you go to the printer, make sure that you know the following:

✦ How many pages do you estimate the publication to have and what will its final trim size be?

✦ How many copies of your job will you want? Knowing the number of copies will help the printer decide the process for creating a plate and printing the job.

✦ What type of paper do you want to use? Depending on the paper's weight, size, and finish, you may have different options available to you regarding the process.

✦ Are you using color? How many colors? Ask the printer how best to distribute the color throughout your publication.

✦ What level of quality are you looking for? The quality of printing for flyers, for example, doesn't need to be as high as the quality of printing for brochures.

✦ How much are you willing to pay for the job? Limits on your resources also change the available options for the commercial printing process.

✦ How quickly do you need the job? Often, asking for a quick turnaround costs more.

Understanding Color Printing

When you print your publication at a commercial print shop, you can use as many colors to print the job as you want. You might want only black, for example, or black and red, or even black, red, and blue. The colors that you choose may apply to the type, graphics, clip art, photographs, and other illustrations.

If you use color photographs or artwork in your publication, you'll likely use *process-color printing* (also called *full-process color*), which applies the color to photographs, for example, so that the images look real, as if you used a camera to take the photograph and then placed that photo in the publication. Applying process colors to artwork makes the artwork look as it does in real life. The printer can match the specific colors to correspond with the artwork.

You need to decide which type of printing you want for a publication and then design the document to match the color printing.

Understanding spot-color printing

You generally use *spot-color printing* to add color to logos, type, borders, lines, headlines, clip art, and other objects in your publication. Spot-color printing uses standard, premixed colors of semitransparent ink that you can choose from a chart (called a *color-mixing guide*). Using this color-mixing guide is good, because that makes colors consistent from printing to printing. If you choose a color to use for your logo and you know that color number in the mixing guide, you can always get the very same color for your logo, no matter where it is printed or when.

Naturally, you also can choose specially mixed colors for spot-color printing. You don't have to use a standard color from the mixing guide. Specially mixed colors cost more than standard colors, however.

When you use spot color in a publication, you usually use fewer colors than with process-color printing. Process-color printing always uses four colors. The fewer colors you use, the less expensive the printing.

Spot-color printing is also less expensive than full-process color because the printer makes fewer plates. Suppose that you want to print a newsletter in black and red. The printer makes one press plate that contains only the black type and images, and one that contains only the red. The press operator then runs the paper through once to print the red, and a second time to print the black. That's only two plates, compared to four plates in full-process color printing (see the next section).

Defining Separations

When you use a color photograph or artwork in a publication, the print shop's camera operator cannot reproduce the color image without first separating the colors from each other. Generally, commercial print shops don't do their own color separations, because that is a very complex and involved process. Most print shops send away their color photos to be separated.

Process-color printing is such a detailed and expensive operation that the camera operator usually creates a composite of the colors from the plates before sending the plate on to the press. A *composite* is a proof that combines all plates (and colors) to print on one page, to check for any revisions.

You can print separation proofs—a copy of each color on a separate sheet of paper—in Publisher for both process- and spot-color printing.

Understanding process-color printing

Process-color printing uses four colors—cyan, magenta, yellow, and black—in combination to create a wide variety of colors. Process-color printing is also called *four-color printing* or *four-color process printing*. The process-color inks are *semitransparent*, meaning that one color shows through the next to produce the different colors. Use process-color printing for photographs, artwork, and other special images.

Note   Some digital methods of printing color don't necessarily require separations. Ask your commercial printer about the methods it uses for process-color printing.

When a commercial print shop prepares a process-color printing, the camera operator must make four plates—one each for each color—and the press operator runs the paper through the press four times. The press operator must be very careful to set the plates in the exact same position and to print each sheet precisely, so that the colors register with each other.

Registration is a method of lining up each plate and printing each color so that they match exactly. You've seen newspaper photographs, comics, or advertisements in which the colors do not exactly line up. These colors aren't registered properly.

Because of the registration process, the cost of process-color printing is higher than spot color. Not only does the press operator need to line up the plates perfectly, but the camera operator must make the plates so that they register correctly, too.

Other reasons the cost of process-color printing is higher include the type of press that is used, the press operator's experience and skill, and the complexity of the design. If your publication includes two colors that are very close together and require exact registration, it is a more difficult job for the camera and press operators, thus requiring more time and costing more money. Something as simple as hairline borders around your photographs are more difficult to print and also cost more.

Understanding process-color inks

The CMYK (cyan-C, magenta-M, yellow-Y, and black-K) process inks create full-process colors. The inks are semitransparent, so one color can print over another to form any color needed to reproduce color photographs and artworks. The press operator mixes the inks by percentages to create the exact mixture.

Different systems are used to mix process colors. The PANTONE Matching System (PMS), which Publisher uses, is one standard way to specify process colors.

CMYK is a color model used for commercial process-color printing. Other color models include RGB (red, green, and blue) and HSL (hue, saturation, and luminosity). These color models define how your computer monitor displays color.

It's important to remember that the colors you get with CMYK may not exactly match the colors that you see on the screen, and vice versa. Your screen may not accurately represent the colors as they print. When you create objects in Publisher by using the RGB model, you need to set up the publication for process-color printing. Publisher automatically converts RGB to CMYK when you do this procedure, as explained later in this chapter.

Color Printing in Publisher

If you're printing to your printer — laser or inkjet — you can use the composite RGB color model for printing. This is the Publisher default, so you need not change a thing. If you plan to use spot-color, black-and-white commercial printing, or process colors, you need to set up your publication for that specific process.

Setting up for commercial printing simply defines the color model and the colors that you want to use for printing.

Setting up for black-and-white printing

Even though printing in black isn't really printing in "color," you need to set up for black-and-white printing if you plan to take your job to a commercial printer. If you're printing to your own laser or inkjet printer, you can use the default color model with no trouble. Setting up the publication for a commercial printer makes the resolution higher and generates a richer black and richer grays for printing from a plate.

To set a publication up for black-and-white printing, follow these steps:

1. Open the publication.

2. Choose Tools ⇨ Commercial Printing Tools ⇨ Color Printing. The Color Printing dialog box appears, as shown in Figure 31-1.

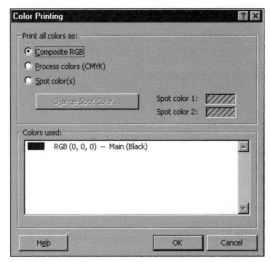

Figure 31-1: Use the Color Printing dialog box to set up your publication for commercial printing.

3. In the Print all colors as area, choose Spot color(s).

4. Click the Change Spot Color button. The Choose Spot Color dialog box appears.

5. Choose the Black and white only option, as shown in Figure 31-2.

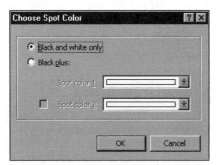

Figure 31-2: Setting up the publication to print in black and white

6. Click OK.

7. Click OK to close the Color Printing dialog box.

8. Save the document.

All color photos or images, clip art, and text in the document appear in black, white, and grays.

Setting up for spot-color printing

When you set up your publication for spot-color printing, you choose black plus one color. You can choose a second spot color, as well. Publisher changes the colors in your publication to either the selected spot colors or blacks and grays. If your document has photographs, clip art, or images, for example, Publisher changes these to black and gray, unless you specifically assign a spot color to them.

You can manually assign spot colors to objects, however. Suppose that you have photographs in your publication and want to change them to blues rather than grays and black. Simply select the photo (or clip art, or image of any kind) and choose Format ➪ Recolor Picture. The Recolor Picture dialog box appears with the image as it will look in the spot color, as shown in Figure 31-3. Note that you can click the Color drop-down menu to change the color to any tint of the spot color.

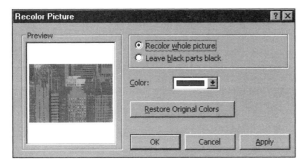

Figure 31-3: Changing images to the spot color for printing

You also can change fonts, lines, fills, and such to the selected spot colors. After you set up the spot color for printing, you can select text and change the color to any spot color or tint of that color. Figure 31-4 illustrates the Font dialog box; click the Color drop-down arrow to change to a tint of the spot color.

Figure 31-4: Change the font quickly and easily to the spot color.

Applying one or two spot colors

You can apply one or two spot colors. To set up for spot color, follow these steps:

1. Choose Tools ➪ Commercial Printing Tools ➪ Color Printing. The Color Printing dialog box appears.

2. Choose Spot color(s), as shown in Figure 31-5.

3. To choose a second spot color, click the Change Spot Color button. The Choose Spot Color dialog box appears.

4. Click the check box beside Spot color 2.

5. Click the drop-down arrow beside the second color, and choose the color that you want to apply.

6. Click OK. The second color appears in the Colors used area of the Color Printing dialog box.

7. Click OK.

8. Save the publication.

Tip

When you apply a second spot color, Publisher applies that color only to colors in your document that match it 100 percent. So, if you choose red as your second color, Publisher only applies red to any exact red in the document; it doesn't apply the red to red-oranges, pinks, or maroons, for example. You can, however, apply the first or second color to any type, picture, fill, or border after you set up for spot color.

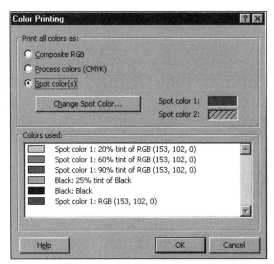

Figure 31-5: Choosing one spot color applies tints of that color to all colors in your publication, except for black.

Using the PANTONE Matching Systems

After you set up a publication for spot color, you can choose the appropriate color from the PANTONE Matching System. Remember that Publisher uses the RGB color model (for your screen colors) by default.

When you choose the PMS color model, Publisher displays PANTONE Solid and PANTONE Process colors, from which you can choose. Publisher matches your original color to a PMS color, which you then can adjust if you want. Publisher also gives you the PANTONE color reference (number) so that you can give that to your commercial print shop.

Further, Publisher offers you the choice of choosing the PMS color for either coated or uncoated paper:

✦ **Coated paper:** Covered with a shiny surface that gives a glossy look to the paper; represents the color as more vivid, or bright.

✦ **Uncoated paper:** Has a dull, or matte, finish; absorbs more of the ink and gives the color a duller look.

To use the PANTONE color model, follow these steps:

1. Choose Tools ➪ Commercial Printing Tools ➪ Color Printing. The Color Printing dialog box appears.

2. Choose Spot color(s).

3. Click the Change Spot Color button. The Choose Spot Color dialog box appears.

4. Click the drop-down arrow beside the color in Spot color 1. The color menu box appears.

5. Click the More Colors button. The Colors dialog box appears.

6. In the Show Colors area, click All colors.

7. Click the drop-down arrow beside the RGB Color model, as shown in Figure 31-6.

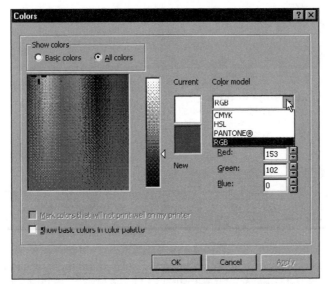

Figure 31-6: Changing the color model for commercial printing

8. Select PANTONE. The PANTONE Colors dialog box appears, as shown in Figure 31-7. The color that you selected appears onscreen with the closest match to a PMS color.

9. In the Color Type drop-down list box, choose either Coated Paper or Uncoated Paper.

Tip   If you want to use a process color, click the PANTONE Process tab and make a note of the process color. You might want to use a process color to match a specific logo color, for example.

10. Click OK to select the PANTONE color.

11. Click OK in the Colors dialog box to accept the changes.

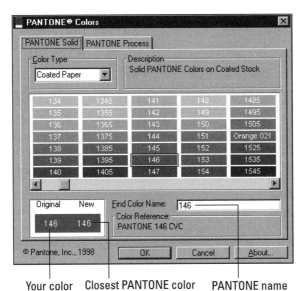

Figure 31-7: Using the PANTONE color model

12. Click OK two more times to close the Choose Spot Color and Color Printing dialog boxes, unless you need to change the second spot color to PANTONE.

13. Save the publication.

Note If you chose two spot colors, you must also change the second spot color to PAN-TONE. Publisher won't change it automatically.

Setting up for process-color printing

When you set up a publication for process-color printing, you simply choose the option and let Publisher do the rest. Blacks remain black, and all other colors change to percentages of CMYK. Color photographs do not show up in the process colors and do not change. The commercial printer needs to get separations of those before printing.

To set up a publication for process-color printing, follow these steps:

1. Choose Tools ➪ Commercial Printing Tools ➪ Color Printing. The Color Printing dialog box appears.

2. In the Print all colors as area of the dialog box, choose Process colors (CMYK). The colors are displayed in the Colors used area. Note that the colors may not look the same onscreen as they do in the CMYK color model.

3. Click OK.

4. Save the publication.

Printing Separation Proofs and Composites

You can print separation proofs in Publisher for both process- and spot-color printing. You can print separation proofs on a black-and-white printer; one proof is used for each color, showing only the objects to be printed in red, for example, or blue. If you have a color printer, such as an inkjet, however, you can print the separations or composite on that printer.

You print separation proofs to confirm that the appropriate colors will print as you want them, and to show the printer, when you take in your publication file for printing. You print composites to see what the final product looks like.

Printing for process-color

When you print separations for process color on a color printer, each color appears as it is: cyan, magenta, yellow, and black. When you print the separations to a black-and-white printer, the colors show up as blacks and grays, but at least you can get an idea of the separation-printing process.

Figure 31-8 illustrates an advertisement created in color with a full-color photograph. You can see the color ad in the color signature of this book. The left half of the circle is the photograph; the right side is text on an orange background. The background is black.

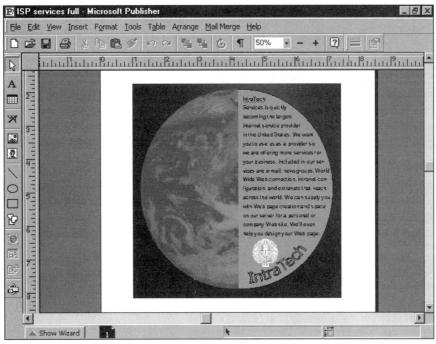

Figure 31-8: An advertisement that will be printed by means of four-color process

Figure 31-9 illustrates the black separation for the process-color. Note that the background, type, and shading show up as black. The other colors are filtered out.

Figure 31-9: The black separation after setting up the publication for process-color printing

To print separation proofs or a composite for process-color printing, follow these steps:

1. Choose File ⇨ Print. The Print dialog box appears, as shown in Figure 31-10.

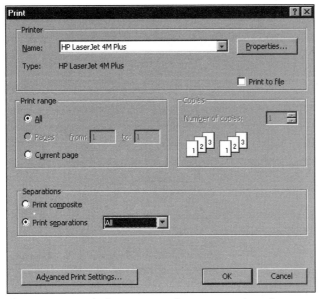

Figure 31-10: Printing a composite or separations for your color publication

2. In the Separations area, choose one of the following:

   • Print composite

   • Print separations

3. Select All, Black, Cyan, Magenta, or Yellow from the Print separations drop-down list.

4. Click OK. Publisher prints the publication.

Printing for spot-color

When working on spot-color, you can choose to print a composite or separations. Separations print for black and either one or two spot colors, depending on your setup.

Figure 31-11 illustrates a flyer for a grand opening. The flyer uses black and two spot colors: yellow and brown. The text appears in black, the background rectangle is yellow, and the squares and rectangles are tints of brown.

Figure 31-12 illustrates the black separation. Note that only the type appears on the page.

Watkins mall spot - Microsoft Publisher
File Edit View Insert Format Tools Table Arrange Mail Merge Help
38%
GRAND OPENING
Watkin's Antique Mall
Saturday, March 20
from 8 am to 8 pm
440 East 22nd Street
Charleston Town Mall
Show Wizard

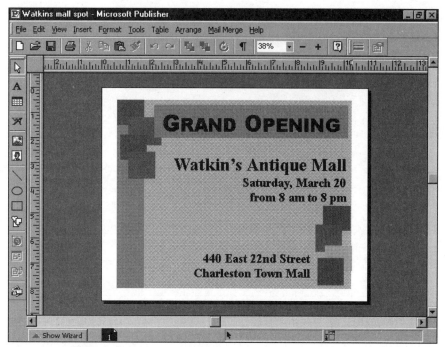

Figure 31-11: This flyer uses two spot colors and black.

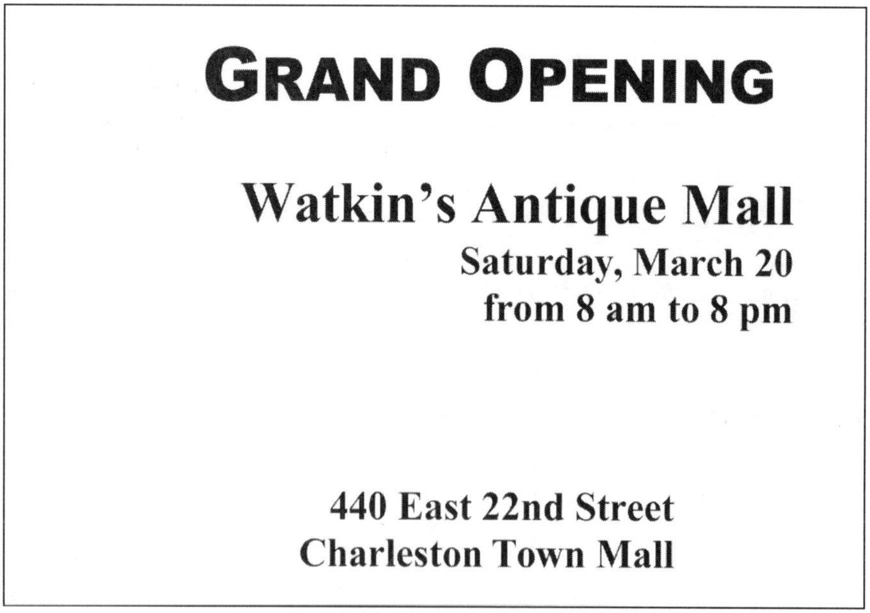

GRAND OPENING
Watkin's Antique Mall
Saturday, March 20
from 8 am to 8 pm
440 East 22nd Street
Charleston Town Mall

Figure 31-12: The black separation contains only text that will print with black ink.

Figure 31-13 shows the separation for the browns, spot-color 1. The variances between the tints are negligible in the printout; the important thing is to make sure that all the pieces are there before you take it to a printer.

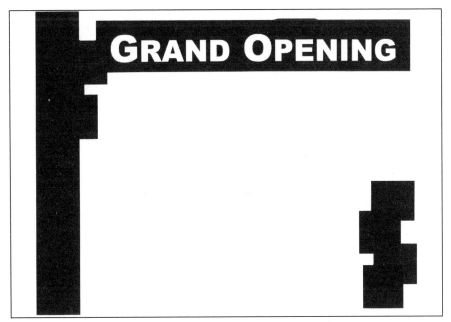

Figure 31-13: The spot-color 1 separation represents tints of brown.

Figure 31-14 illustrates spot-color 2, the yellow. An interesting point to note is how the other colors — black and brown — are "knocked out" of the background to make a space for the color. This is a good example of where registration is important when printing. If the registration is off, even a little, the black or brown may not fill in the white area. This will show up on the final piece.

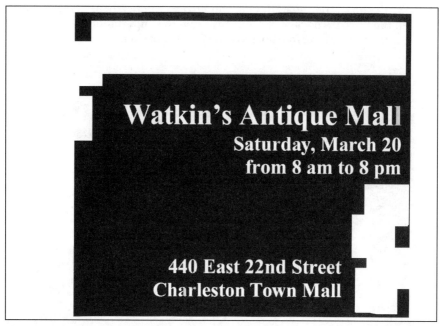

Figure 31-14: The second spot color shows positioning for the first spot color and black.

 Note   The knocked-out area in the preceding figure provides a great example of trapping. See the next section for more information.

Understanding Trapping

Registration, as previously noted, is the process of exactly and precisely lining up two colors in a publication so that one doesn't overlap the other. As you can see in Figure 31-14, text, and often objects, provides a very small space in which a second color can be printed. If the color doesn't fit exactly into the area that is knocked out, it's called *misregistration*.

Many things can cause misregistration: shifting plates, stretched paper, even poorly produced publications or plates, for example. If two colors are misregistered when printed, small rifts appear around the text or objects. Publisher offers two solutions to this problem:

✦ **Overprinting:** Places objects and text on top of the background color. Publisher overprints objects by default when dark objects or text are printed on top of light objects or backgrounds. This doesn't work, however, when the background is dark and the objects or text on top are light. Trapping works in this instance.

✦ **Trapping:** Diffuses, or spreads, lighter colors into darker colors so that a slight overlap fills in the rifts in case misregistration is present. Not all publications require trapping, and often it depends on the type of press and paper the commercial print shop uses. Ask your printer beforehand whether trapping is necessary; also, ask the printer whether you should do the trapping or whether the printer will do it.

If you choose to do your own trapping, you can use Publisher's Automatic Trapping feature.

How Publisher traps

Publisher turns off trapping by default, but you can turn on automatic trapping for any publication. Publisher creates traps only when printing separations, which must be set up for process- or spot-color printing.

The program uses certain internal rules for trapping. The trapping rules work from the foreground objects, through the layers, to the background. The program traps the borders first, and then the fills, and traps the text last. You also can set values to your traps for objects or selected parts of an object. Publisher determines the placement and size of a trap from the *luminance* (the amount of light) of each object.

The program assigns spreads, chokes, or centerline traps to objects, depending on their luminance. A *spread* is when the color extends beyond an object's outline. A lighter foreground object is spread to trap a darker background object.

When the foreground object is darker and the background is lighter, Publisher uses a *choke* to trap the foreground to the background. The lighter background is extended into the darker color.

A *centerline* trap applies when two objects have similar luminance values. Publisher extends both colors to the centerline by one half of the default trap width.

Publisher doesn't trap the contents of imported objects created in illustration programs. If you create traps in the illustration program and then import the object, however, Publisher maintains that trap.

Other objects that Publisher doesn't trap include objects that are the same color and overlapping, gradients, patterns, and some objects that are similar in color to the ones that they overlap.

Trapping objects and text

You can set general trapping preferences that will apply to all objects in a publication. You must set trapping for each publication, and you must first set up the publication for commercial printing. Table 31-1 describes the options in the Preferences dialog box (shown in Figure 31-15 later).

Table 31-1
Trapping Preferences

Trapping Preference	Description
Trapping Settings Area	
Automatic trapping	Add a check mark in the check box to turn on the option. By default, automatic trapping is not active.
Width	The default trap width is .25 points for all objects that Publisher can trap; you can change the width of the trap.
Indeterminate	This default trap width is for objects such as WordArt, BorderArt, and Microsoft Draw objects.
Thresholds	Click this button to set the starting points for certain trappings, such as when two objects are close in color or luminance.
Only allow spread traps on text glyphs	Depending on the font, a choke or centerline trap may show where the character strokes overlap; using only spreads on this type of font is neater and more attractive.
Spot Color Options — Luminance Area	
Spot color 1	Sets the value for the luminance of the first spot color; Publisher uses the value when analyzing traps.
Spot color 2	Sets the value for the luminance of the second spot color.
Trap white as a color	Sets the program to use a spread when white is in the foreground, and to use a choke when white is in the background. Normally, Publisher doesn't consider white a color; you have to set it here.
Black Overprinting Area	
Text below	Enter the size at which you want Publisher to begin knocking out the background; all smaller sizes of text will be overprinted.
Overprint threshold	Describes the amount of black ink, or the size of the object. If the object has less than this percentage of black ink, Publisher knocks out the objects behind it instead of overprinting.
Lines	Check this option to overprint lines automatically. Clear the check box to knock lines out.
Fills	Check this option to overprint fills automatically. Clear the check box to knock fills out.
Imported pictures	Check this option to overprint automatically all imported pictures that can't be color-separated.

Trapping all objects in a publication

You can set your preferences to trap all objects in a publication. To change trapping preferences, follow these steps:

1. Choose Tools ➪ Commercial Printing Tools ➪ Trapping ➪ Preferences. The Preferences dialog box appears.

2. Click the check box beside Automatic trapping, as shown in Figure 31-15.

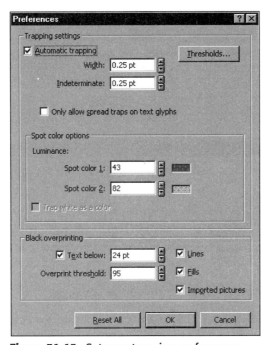

Figure 31-15: Set your trapping preferences.

3. Set any options, as described in Table 31-1.

4. Click OK when you're finished. Your publication will not be visibly different, unless you print the separations and very carefully examine them.

5. Save your document.

Trapping individual objects in a publication

You can set preferences for trapping parts of objects or text. When you select an object — such as a border, fill, or text — you can change the following:

✦ **Setting:** Choose whether the value you set will apply to overprinting or knockout, or create a custom setting.

✦ **Placement:** Choose the placement for the trap: centerline, choke, or spread.

✦ **Width:** Enter a value between .01 and 20 points, to override Publisher's default trap setting.

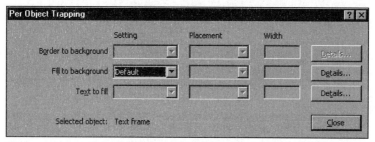

Note

If a setting is unavailable, you must first select the object before setting the trap.

To set per-object trapping, select the object and then follow these steps:

1. Choose Tools ⇨ Commercial Printing Tools ⇨ Trapping ⇨ Per Object Trapping. The Per Object Trapping dialog box appears, as shown in Figure 31-16.

Figure 31-16: Select the setting, placement, and width for each object that you want to trap.

2. Choose the options that apply to the selected object, as described previously.

3. Click the Details button to display the Trapping Details dialog box, as shown in Figure 31-17.

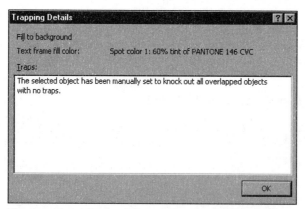

Figure 31-17: Viewing information about the selected object's traps

4. Click OK to close the Trapping Details dialog box.

5. Click Close to accept the changes in the Per Object Trapping dialog box.

Using Pack and Go

Publisher includes a feature called Pack and Go, which enables you to condense, gather, and bundle a publication's files to take to another computer. When you use the Pack and Go feature, your publication looks exactly the same on the second computer as it does on your computer, because you include all graphics, images, and even the fonts with the Pack and Go file. (For more information about embedding fonts, see Chapter 30, "Printing in Publisher.")

You might want to use the Pack and Go feature when you:

✦ Use TrueType fonts that the other computer may not have

✦ Want to make sure that your linked pictures and images appear in your publication

✦ Take your publication to a commercial printer

Publisher compresses your publication files when you Pack and Go. Also, if a file is too large for one floppy disk, Publisher divides the file appropriately so that it can span over two or more disks. Publisher even includes an executable file that enables you to unpack the publication file when you get to the other computer.

Packing your publication

You can pack your publication to take to any computer, as long as that computer has Publisher installed on it.

To pack your publication, follow these steps:

1. Open the publication.

2. Choose File ➪ Pack and Go ➪ Take to Another Computer. The Pack and Go Wizard steps you through the process.

3. Click the Next button to continue to the next step.

4. Save the publication when prompted.

5. When prompted to choose a location for the Pack and Go file, choose the appropriate floppy disk drive, Zip drive, or other storage medium. Click OK.

6. When prompted, choose to embed TrueType fonts and to create links for embedded graphics. Click Next.

7. If prompted to insert another disk, do so and then click OK. Make sure that you label the disks and use numbers to identify the first disk, second disk, and so on. You need to unpack the files in the same order as you pack them.

8. Click OK when you're finished.

Unpacking your publication

The files that Publisher saves as it creates your Pack and Go disks are compressed and must be unpacked by using the executable file that Publisher includes on the first disk of the packed files. The filename is Unpack.exe. If you have trouble unpacking the file, Publisher also includes a Readme file on disk that gives you complete information and instructions.

To unpack the files and open the publication on another computer, follow these steps:

1. Insert the first disk in the drive of the second computer.
2. Open Windows Explorer or My Computer, and then locate the drive in which you inserted the disk.
3. Double-click the Unpack.exe file.
4. The program prompts you for a path to the computer to which it can unpack the files. You might want to create a special temporary folder that you can delete later. Enter the path to the folder.
5. Click OK.
6. If multiple disks are involved, insert them when prompted and click OK.
7. Publisher notifies you when it's finished unpacking. Click OK.
8. To open the publication, switch to the designated folder on the hard drive and then double-click the publication's name. Note that the publication's filename has PNG added to the name before the .pub extension.

Summary

In this chapter, you learned about preparing a publication for commercial printing. You learned about the following items:

✦ Understanding color printing

✦ Printing color publications in Publisher

✦ Printing separation proofs and composites

✦ Understanding trapping

✦ Using Pack and Go

In the next chapter, you learn how to use Publisher's mail merge.

✦　　✦　　✦

Using Mail Merge

Most publications are created for distribution to others: co-workers, customers, friends, and so on. If you want to mail your publications, you can use Publisher's mail merge feature to create a mailing list and make your mailing duties easier. You learn how to create the list of names and addresses and integrate this list with any Publisher document to personalize letters and create mailing panels.

Merging an Address List with a Publication

You use mail merge when you're creating bulk mailings, such as mailing 100 or 1000 newsletters to your customers. You can use mail merge to personalize publications, as well. Suppose that you want to send a letter introducing a new salesperson or product to your customers. You can use mail merge to insert each customer'sname and title, for example, and other individualized information about them.

Figure 32-1 shows a letter in which a customer's name and address have been inserted into fields. Note that the name appears in the salutation as well as the recipient's address. You can personalize letters and other publications by inserting the appropriate fields throughout the document.

The process of merging mail begins with two documents: a main publication, such as a letter or envelope, and an address list. You use *field codes* to identify address information, such as Name, Address 1, City, and so on. You then can insert the field codes into the publication. When you perform the mail merge, Publisher inserts the address information into the publication to replace the field codes.

After you perform the preliminary work, Publisher can automatically insert any information that you want into any publication.

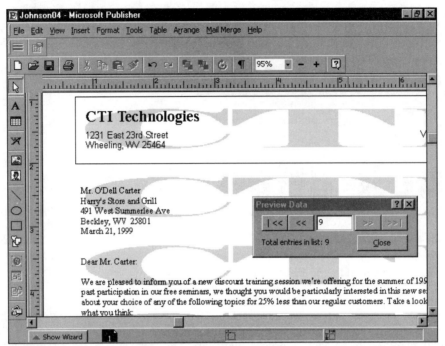

Figure 32-1: Print multiple, personalized documents by using Publisher's Mail Merge feature.

Defining Terms

Publisher's Mail Merge feature uses the following terms to identify the process and the elements involved. You need to know these terms to perform a mail merge.

✦ **Data source:** Your address list, although you can add other information, as well, such as a person's title or a price list of products. The data source is a database, of sorts, that you can create in Publisher; alternatively, you can create a data source in Excel or Word, or another program. You define the type of information — Name, Address, City, State, and Zip, for example — and then fill in the information for each individual or each item that you want in the address list.

✦ **Publication:** Can be a letter, newsletter, brochure, invoice, or any other publication that you want to mail. You print a mailing label for those documents with a mailing panel, or you print envelopes for others.

✦ **Fields:** Areas in which you enter the information in the data source. So, if the information type is Name, you would enter **Sue Plumley**, for example, in that field or category.

✦ **Field codes:** Placeholders in the publication. When Publisher sees the field code, it knows to insert information from the data source. Field codes might look like this in a publication: <<Title> <<First Name> <<Last Name>. You can format the text in a field code, just as you would format other text in a publication. You also can move, copy, and delete a field code.

✦ **Records:** Consist of all the information relating to one person or company. A person's name, title, company, address, phone number, and comments about that person are all information in one record.

Overviewing Mail Merge

Publisher's Mail Merge feature enables you to address labels, envelopes, postcards, and such automatically, as well as personalize letters to customers, employees, acquaintances, and others. After you create a data source, you easily can insert any of the information that you've entered into any publication that you've created.

Creating a mail merge takes several steps. The following is a summary of each step. More-detailed directions for completing these steps follow in the next sections.

1. Create a data source, by entering in a file the names and addresses, plus any other information that you want to include. Within the file, you divide each record of information into fields. All records use common fields.

   You also can use a data source from another program, such as Excel or Word.

2. Create the publication, either by opening an existing publication or by creating a new one in Publisher. The publication might be a letter, envelope, mailing label, or something else. You should save a copy of your publication for use with mail merge.

3. Insert fields of your data source into the publication, using the handy shortcut provided by Publisher. You insert each field into one publication (such as a letter), and Publisher uses that publication to create a duplicate for each address in your data source.

4. Merge the address list and publication. After you create the publication and insert the fields, you merge the two onscreen, so that you can view, filter, and correct any mistakes.

5. Filter, or sort, the merged documents, to locate names, addresses, cities, or other records.

6. View the merged documents, to make sure that all is right before you print them.

7. Print the merged publications, when you're sure that you're ready.

Creating a New Data Source in Publisher

When you create a data source, you enter the information that you'll use later in the mail merge. Before you create a new data source, you should gather all the information that you need, so that you can enter most of the text at one time. Of course, you can always open a data source and edit, add, or remove names and information, after you create the source.

Publisher's Address List feature enables you to edit and customize the list. Working within Publisher to create a data source is easy. Naturally, you don't have to use a Publisher address list; you can use a database, contact list, or other data from another source. See the next section for more information.

Creating a data source

Publisher's Data Source feature is the same thing as its Address List feature. After you create the data source, you can use it repeatedly, and you can even add, remove, or edit the information in the data source.

Before you can create a data source in Publisher, you need to open or create a new document, create a text frame, and select that frame. You can later use this document as the publication for the merge. Alternatively, you can open the document that you plan to use for the mail merge, and then create or select a text frame in that publication.

The New Address List dialog box includes many different fields. You can use either all or only some of the fields listed. Also in the New Address List dialog box are tools to help you find entries, customize and create new entries, filter entries, and otherwise edit the entries.

To create a data source in Publisher, follow these steps:

1. Click the text frame.

2. Choose Mail Merge ➪ Create Publisher Address List. The New Address List dialog box appears, as shown in Figure 32-2.

3. Enter the address information for the first record. Use the vertical scroll bar to the left of the Enter Address Information box to reveal more fields for your record. You can press the Tab key, the Enter key, or the directional arrow to move from field to field.

4. When you're finished with the record, click the New Entry button. The information is saved, and a new record with cleared fields appears.

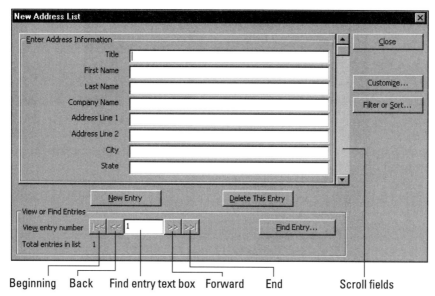

Beginning Back Find entry text box Forward End Scroll fields

Figure 32-2: Use the fields that you want to use, and leave the other fields blank.

Editing the data source

As you create your address list, or after you save it, you can view any entry and edit or delete its contents. You also can customize the address fields. After you finish creating and editing the source, you can save it. Then, you can open and edit it at any time, or you can use it to create your mail merge.

Viewing and finding entries

Use the View or Find Entries area of the New Address List dialog box to display specific entries, or each entry in the file, by doing one of the following:

 ✦ Click the Back or Forward button

 ✦ Click the Beginning or End button

 ✦ Enter the entry number in the View entry number text box

 ✦ Click the Find Entry button

If you click the Find Entry button, the Find Entry dialog box appears, as shown in Figure 32-3.

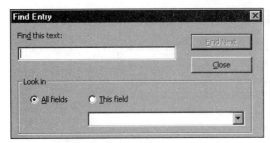

Figure 32-3: Find an entry by searching for a name or other specific text.

To find an entry by using the Find Entry dialog box, follow these steps:

1. Enter the text in the Find this text box, such as the name of the person, city, or company for which you're searching.

2. Specify a field, if you want, to speed up the search.

3. Click Find Next to search for the record.

4. Click Close when you're finished.

Deleting entries

You also can delete an entry by displaying the entry in the New Address List dialog box and then clicking the Delete This Entry button.

Customizing the address information

You can add, remove, rename, or move field names in the Enter Address Information box to suit your needs better. In the New Address List dialog box, click the Customize button. The Customize Address List dialog box appears, as shown in Figure 32-4.

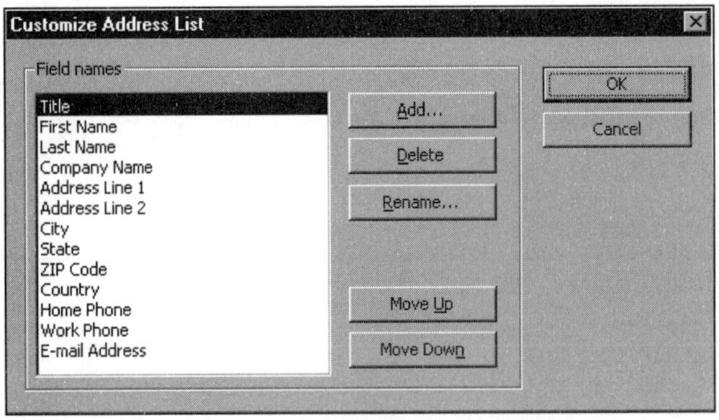

Figure 32-4: Customize the fields in each record.

To customize the address list, follow these steps:

1. Open the Customize Address List dialog box.

2. To add a field name, select one of the fields beside which you want to insert the new field. Click the Add button to add a field to the list. The Add Field dialog box appears, as shown in Figure 32-5.

Figure 32-5: Creating a new field to add to the address list

3. Enter the name that you want to use for the new field, and then choose whether to add the new field before or after the currently selected field. Click OK.

4. To delete a field name in the Customize Address List dialog box, select from the Field names list the field name that you want to delete, and then click the Delete button. Click Yes in the confirmation dialog box.

5. To rename a field name in the Customize Address List dialog box, select from the Field names list the field name that you want to rename, and then click the Rename button. The Rename Field dialog box appears, as shown in Figure 32-6.

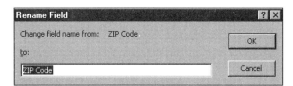

Figure 32-6: Renaming the field

For your convenience, you can select any field name in the Customize Address List dialog box and move it up or down on the list by using the Move Up or Move Down button. Moving the field name doesn't affect how the field appears in your publication, only how it appears in the Enter Address Information dialog box. For example, if moving the Company Name field and entering it before entering the contact person's name is easier for you, you can move it in the Customize Address List dialog box.

Saving the data source

You must save the data source to be able to use it in a merge, or to edit or open it again.

To save the data source, follow these steps:

1. Click the Close button in the New Address List dialog box. The Save As dialog box for saving Publisher address lists appears, as shown in Figure 32-7.

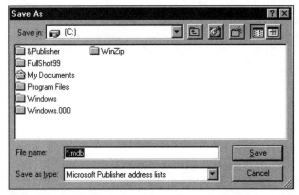

Figure 32-7: Saving the address list

2. Locate the appropriate folder and enter a filename for the address list. Note that Publisher automatically assigns the .mdb extension to the filename.

3. Click the Save button. Publisher saves the file and returns to the Publisher screen and your document.

Note   You now have an existing data source to use with any publication.

Reopening and editing the data source

The following steps enable you to reopen the data source at any time to edit it:

1. Choose Mail Merge ➪ Edit Publisher Address List. The Open Address List dialog box appears, as shown in Figure 32-8.

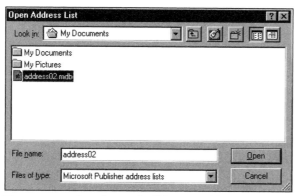

Figure 32-8: Opening and editing an address list

2. Locate the folder, and either enter the filename or select it from the list.

3. Click Open. Publisher opens the Address List dialog box with the information that you entered.

Sorting and filtering

You can sort and filter an address list to help you find certain records. When you filter, you can view or print those addresses that appear in certain cities, in certain ZIP codes, or with certain names, for example. When you sort, you change the order of the names and addresses to either ascending or descending order, according to field.

Filtering

You filter to find specific records that conform to specific criteria. For example, you can find all records whose title is "Mr." or "Ms.," all people who work at a certain company, or all companies in one state.

Figure 32-9 shows the Filter tab of the Filtering and Sorting dialog box. Note that the first filter definition says to find all records in which the state is equal to WV. After you fill in the first filter definition, the second definition becomes available.

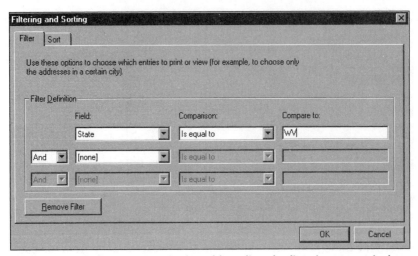

Figure 32-9: Finding everyone in the address list who lives in one particular state

Not only can you choose the field that you want to search, but you also can choose a comparison statement. The available comparison statements include the following:

✦ **Is equal to:** Use to name the exact state, name, or other field that you want to find.

✦ **Is not equal to:** Use to exclude a field from the results.

✦ **Is less than:** Use to enter a value.

✦ **Is greater than:** Use to enter a value.

After you choose a field and a comparison statement, you enter a value or text in the Compare to text box. After you fill in the first filter definition, the second one becomes available, and after you fill in the second filter definition, the third one becomes available. Both the second and third filter definitions offer the same choices as the first: Field, Comparison, Compare to.

The additional And/Or box between the first and second and the second and third definitions enables you to modify the statements. Figure 32-10 shows a filtering search that will locate all records with the title of *Ms.* in the states of WV or VA.

When you click OK, the filter goes into effect for the next mail merge — and all mail merges that you perform — until you open the Filtering and Sorting dialog box again and click the Remove Filter button.

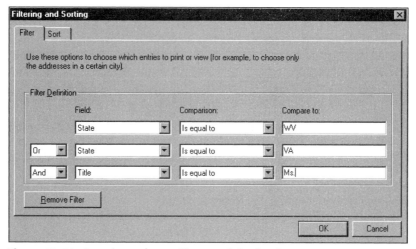

Figure 32-10: Locating only specific records in the data source

Sorting

The Sorting feature of mail merge enables you to arrange the records — either all the records or only the filtered ones — in order by field. You can, for example, choose to sort company names in ascending order (from A to Z or 0 to 9). Or, you can choose to sort all last names in descending order (from Z to A or 9 to 0).

As with filtering, after you create the first sort criterion, you can add a second, and then a third, criterion by which to sort. Figure 32-11 shows the Sort tab of the Filtering and Sorting dialog box. This sort first arranges the records in ascending order by last name, and then in ascending order by company name.

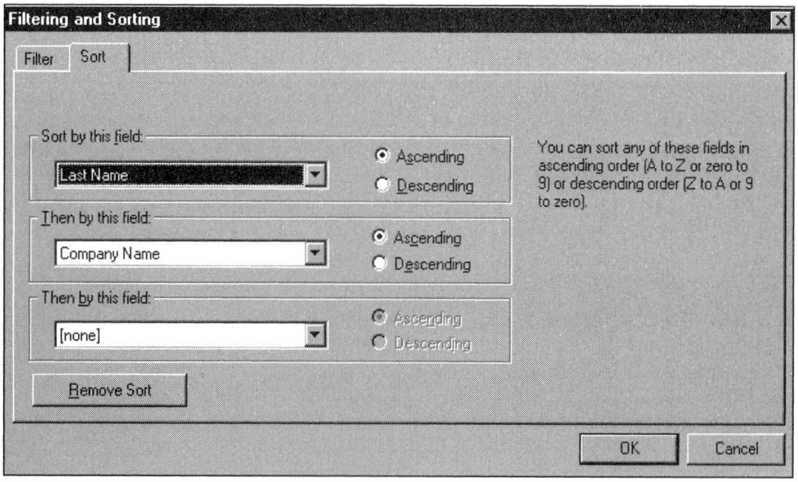

Figure 32-11: Sort your records to make your job easier after you print.

As with filtering, the sort appears when you merge the data source with your publication, and the sort remains set for all merges until you click the Remove Sort button in the Filtering and Sorting dialog box.

Using an Existing Data Source for Mail Merge

You use an existing data source to merge with your publication. The data source may be a Publisher address list that you just created or one that you created last week or last month, for example. You also can use an Outlook contact list, a database file, or a file from another program, such as Excel or Word.

After you open the data source, you insert the fields into your publication, to prepare for the merge. When you insert fields, you can insert them into any publication — a letter, labels, envelopes, and such.

Designating the source

When you create a data source in another program, make sure that you use field names — such as First Name, Last Name, Address 1, and so on — in the first row of your file. Figure 32-12 illustrates an Excel file, with the entries in the first row acting as field names.

To use an existing data source, follow these steps:

1. Open the publication and then click a text frame.

2. Choose Mail Merge ⇨ Open Data Source. The Open Data Source dialog box appears, as shown in Figure 32-13.

3. Choose Merge information from another type of file. You use this option if you either have a data source that was created in another program or already created an address list in Publisher. The Open Data Source dialog box appears, as shown in Figure 32-14.

Note

The following are two other choices for creating or opening a data source: **Merge from an Outlook contact list:** Choose if you plan to use your contact list of names and addresses from Outlook. **Create an address list in Publisher:** Choose if you haven't created a data source yet and want to use Publisher to create one.

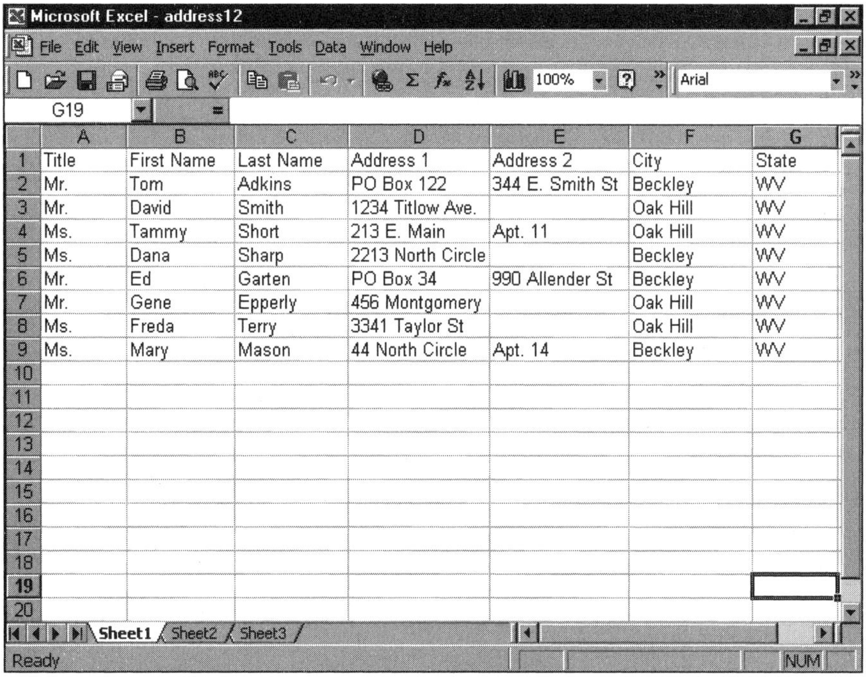

Figure 32-12: Assign field names in your data source

Figure 32-13: Choosing your data source

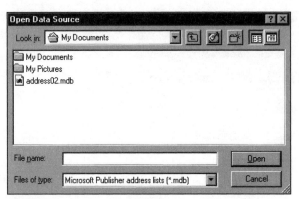

Figure 32-14: Choosing the file that you want to use as a data source.

4. In the Open Data Source dialog box, you can open either your Publisher address list or another file. To open the Publisher address list, locate the folder and the file. Make sure that Microsoft Publisher address lists (*.mdb) appears in the Files of type drop-down list box, as shown in Figure 32-14. Publisher also provides the following file types:

- Microsoft Access (*.mdb)
- Microsoft Word address lists (*.doc)
- Microsoft Works database (*.wdb)
- Microsoft Excel (*.xls)
- Paradox (*.db)
- Text files (*.txt, *.csv, *.tab, *.asc)
- dBASE III, IV, 5 (*.dbf)

To choose another file type in the Open Data Source dialog box, follow these steps:

1. In the Open Data Source dialog box, choose the file type that you want to open from the Files of type drop-down list box.

2. Locate the folder and file that you want to open, and then select the file.

3. Click the Open button. A confirmation box similar to the one in Figure 32-15 might appear.

4. Choose Yes to use the first row entries as field names.

5. The Insert Fields dialog box appears, so that you can insert the fields into your publication. The following section explains how to insert fields.

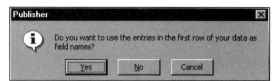

Figure 32-15: When using an Excel file as a data source, you get this confirmation dialog box.

Inserting fields

You insert the fields of your data source into the publication by using the Insert Fields dialog box. When you insert fields, you must also insert spaces, punctuation, and any other text that you need around the fields. You also must add paragraph returns when inserting multiple lines of field names. For example, if you insert the City, State, and ZIP code fields, you should insert the City field, enter a comma and space, insert the State field, insert one or two spaces, and then insert the ZIP code field, as follows:

> **<<City>, <<State> <<ZIP>**

You can click and enter text into your document; the Insert Fields dialog box remains onscreen until you close it. Click the dialog box title bar to activate it.

Tip   You can copy, format, and delete inserted fields just as you would any other text.

To insert fields into a publication, follow these steps:

1. Position the insertion point in the text box within your publication. You can draw a new text box, if necessary.

2. Click the first field that you want to insert from the Insert Fields dialog box. Click the Insert button.

3. Add any spaces or punctuation, and then click the next field name.

4. Continue to insert the field names until you're finished.

5. Click the Close button when you're finished with the Insert Fields dialog box.

6. Save your document.

Figure 32-16 shows a letter with the field names inserted. Note that spaces, punctuation, and paragraph returns have been added. Note, too, that you can use the fields throughout the publication, if you want.

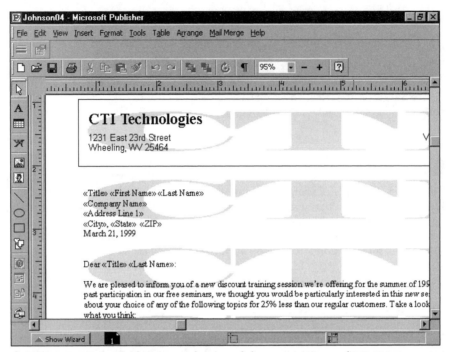

Figure 32-16: Insert fields into one letter and then merge to send 50, 100, or more individualized publications.

Tip   You can always insert fields into the document, even after you close the Insert Field dialog box. Choose Mail Merge ⇨ Insert Field, or press Ctrl+Shift+I.

Merging the Data Source with the Publication

When you first perform the merge, Publisher displays your publication with the names, addresses, and other information as it will appear when printed. You can view each record as it will look in the publication, or you can view selected records in the publication.

You can view the publication with the merge results, or view it with field codes so that you can make changes or adjustments, if you like. You also can cancel the merge at any time and start over.

When you merge, Publisher doesn't create a file with 10, 50, or 1000 documents in it. The file contains only the original number of pages. If you save the document, it still contains only the original number of pages.

The merge, however, acts as a *link* between the publication and the data source. Publisher inserts the records from the data source into the publication, and when you print the merged files, Publisher changes the data for each copy that is printed.

You also can filter and sort the records that you use in your merged document. For more information, see the earlier section, "Sorting and filtering."

Performing the merge

Performing the merge is amazingly simple. Publisher automatically inserts the data in the designated places. You can view the merged data in the publication and print the merged file.

To perform the merge, follow these steps:

1. Open the publication in which you've inserted the fields to a specific data source.

2. Choose Mail Merge ➪ Merge. Publisher performs the merge by inserting the records from the data source into the publication. Publisher also displays the Preview Data dialog box, as shown in Figure 32-17.

3. Using the Preview Data dialog box, preview each record, or spot check if you have a lot of records. Make sure that they are right.

   When you close the Preview Data dialog box, Publisher displays the field codes in the publication rather than the actual names and other data.

   You can view the merged information again at any time by choosing Mail Merge ➪ Show Merge Results.

Note   If you want to change a record, field name, or the inserted fields in any way, you should cancel the merge, correct the elements that you want to change, and then perform the merge again.

To cancel a merge, choose Mail Merge ➪ Cancel Merge.

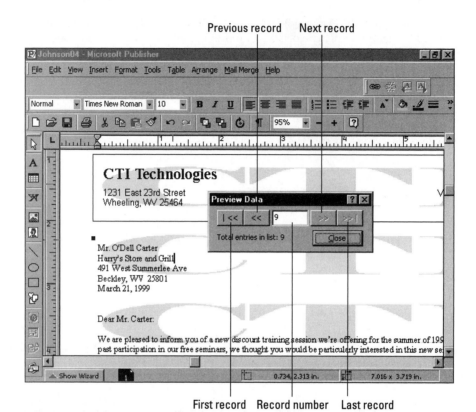

Figure 32-17: Preview the records with the Preview Data dialog box, to make sure that they're correct.

Printing the merged file

After you merge the data source with the publication, you can print the merged documents with the appropriate information inserted. Depending on how you entered your information, you may have empty fields that appear in some of the records. Suppose you have two lines for addresses: Address 1 and Address 2. Some addresses, however, contain only one line, which means that one line appears blank in the publication. You can remove this empty line in the Print Merge dialog box. To print the merged documents, follow these steps:

1. Choose File ➪ Print Merge. The Print Merge dialog box appears, as shown in Figure 32-18.

2. Click the check box for Don't print lines that contain only empty fields, if your publication has any blank lines caused by empty fields.

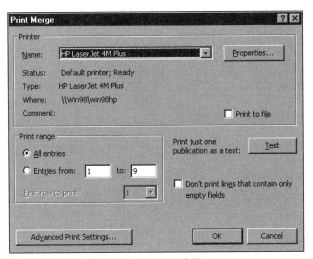

Figure 32-18: Printing the merged file

3. You should print one publication as a test. To do this, click the Test button in the Print Merge dialog box. The Print Merge dialog box returns to the screen. Check the test to make sure all is right.

4. When you're ready to print, enter the Print range. You can print all entries (records), or choose only the ones that you want to print.

5. Click OK.

Summary

In this chapter, you learned how to merge an address list with any Publisher publication. Specifically, you learned about the following:

✦ Understanding mail merge

✦ Creating data sources

✦ Using a data source

✦ Merging the data source with the publication

In the next chapter, you learn about preparing a Web page.

✦   ✦   ✦

Designing for the Web

Microsoft Office 2000 boasts new and improved Web integration features. Publisher includes most of these features to help you create Web publications such as Web pages and Web sites. This part explains the procedures, as well as offers advice for creating content and designing Web pages. You learn about creating an efficient site and about the elements that make up a successful Web site. Finally, you learn how to publish your Web site to your local Internet Service Provider or your own Web server.

Preparing a Web Page

This chapter shows you how to create a Web page in Publisher, either by using the Web Wizard or by adding elements to a blank publication page. But first, let's take a look at what elements you need to gather before you can start putting together your Web page.

Gathering and Creating Content

Before you can create your Web page, you must gather together graphics, images, text, and any other content that you want to use for the Web page. You can enter your text directly into Publisher. You can use clip art, photographs that were scanned or taken with a digital camera, drawn images, and so on.

Figure 33-1 illustrates a Web page design that includes eye-catching colors, a digital photograph, links to other pages, and more. The links enable the Web surfer to jump to the pages that interest him or her.

You want to make sure that you have all legal rights to anything that you publish on the Web. Don't use someone else's text or images unless you have express permission to do so. Copyright and patent laws apply to business over the Internet, just as they do elsewhere.

Figure 33-1: Make the Web page attractive and interesting.

Considering legal and ethical issues

Other legal issues exist that you should consider when dealing with the Internet. If you plan to sell products or services, consider whether any international limits or export laws might govern those products. Remember, the Internet has no state or national boundaries.

You also should consider the ethics of publishing pages on the Web. Business pages are fine, because users come to you if they want. Spamming—sending junk e-mail over the Web—generally isn't accepted, however. Sending advertisements to large mailing lists often aggravates and alienates the prospective customers.

Considering content and design

Consider the Web surfer when you're designing your page. Most users surf the Internet quickly, skipping from page to page without spending much time at any one site. For this reason, you want your Web page design to attract and keep the attention of anyone who visits your page.

One major reason most users skip a Web page is that the page takes too long to download, or appear. Many surfers don't want to wait more than a couple of seconds to view the page. If your page takes too long to appear, the user moves on. Figure 33-2 illustrates a Web page that displays five images; however, each image is small and loads quickly. Note, too, the underlined links and the small amount of text on the page.

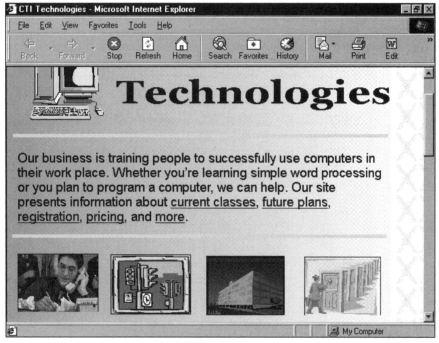

Figure 33-2: Use small graphics rather than large ones, for faster downloading.

You can help speed up the display of your Web page by designing for speed. The following are a few ways to design for speed:

✦ **Don't use large graphics.** The larger a graphic is, the longer it takes to appear on the page. You can use smaller, postage-stamp-sized graphics that load quickly. If you want to give the reader a chance to see the larger picture, you can do that, too, by adding an option on the page: Click here to view the full-sized version of the image.

✦ **Use JPEG and GIF as the standard Internet formats for photographs and other images, respectively.** If you compress JPEG (Joint Photographic Experts Group) and GIF (Graphics Interchange Format) figure files adequately (but not *too* much), both formats use small amounts of disk space, load quickly, and look good as finished images.

✦ **Don't fill the page with too much text or graphics.** If the page is too full (too busy), the reader might become easily distracted and miss your message. Also, try to be consistent with your formatting. Just as with professional-looking publications, you don't want to use too many different fonts, designs, patterns, and such on a Web page. Remember to apply consistency, white space, and balance.

✦ **Present large amounts of text in lists and tables rather than in long paragraphs.** Readers are in a hurry to click another link; don't make them stop and read large amounts of text, because they usually won't do so.

Figure 33-3 shows a Web page that uses very little text. Buttons that refer the reader to other pages keep the busy surfer jumping from page to page. A small, animated graphic captures attention, and the text gets the point across instantly.

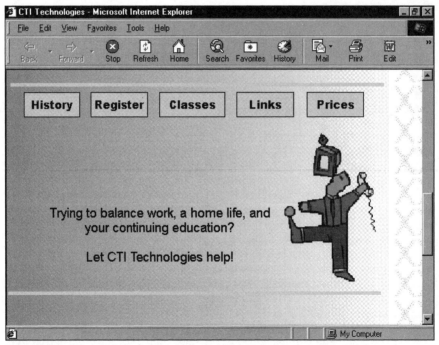

Figure 33-3: A simple yet eye-catching Web page helps the surfer find the appropriate information.

About Web Servers

When you create a Web page or Web site, you need a Web server on which you can display your work to the world. You might want to run your own Web server, or you might want to rent space on someone else's Web server.

It's fairly common for businesses to run their own Web servers these days. When you use your own server, you have more available space than an Internet Service Provider (ISP) might have, you have instant access to your data, and you can publish the kind of data that you want without having to adhere to someone else's policies.

Running your own server also has disadvantages. The cost and maintenance of the hardware is completely up to you. You must pay for the server, software, routers, firewalls, and the dedicated line to the Internet. You also have to troubleshoot connection problems, breaches in security, and server failures.

If you plan to rent space from an ISP's Web server, before you decide which service and which ISP to use, you need to ask potential ISPs some specific questions. Naturally, you want to ask how much server space you'll be allotted, the costs, and the speed of the ISP's lines. You also might want to ask about the server security and the backup system that the ISP uses, what support it supplies, any special requirements to connect to the server, and whether the ISP supplies the connection equipment or you must purchase it yourself.

Whether you run your own Web server or use someone else's, you need to obtain a domain name and IP (Internet Protocol) address. An ISP can help you to obtain these. The *domain name* is a text name that represents your IP address. Thus, whereas an IP address might be 192.33.159.1, its domain name would be easier to remember: mydomain.com, for example. You can use either the IP address or the domain name to get to a Web page.

Using a Web Wizard

Publisher contains many wizards that you can use to create a Web page or Web site. The difference between the two is that a Web site *contains* multiple Web pages. Publisher's Web Wizards use the same design sets used with other types of publications—Accent Box, Accessory Bar, Bars, Blends, and so on.

In addition, Publisher offers some unique designs for Web Wizards, including Blackboard, Circles, Frames, Kid Stuff, and more. Figure 33-4 illustrates a Web page created by using the Kid's Stuff Web Wizard. Publisher's background, colors, and font style fit the subject matter. In this example, the text was changed, moved, and reformatted somewhat.

Figure 33-4: Use a wizard as a base for your design, but make changes to text formatting, graphics, and so on.

Any Publisher Web Wizard produces a page that measures 6×14 inches, which creates a Web page in your browser that covers three and a half screens. Figure 33-5 illustrates one screen of the Web page design in Internet Explorer. As you design your Web page, you want to adjust your design to accommodate the browser's screen.

Tip   No animation, movie, or sound clip works in Publisher, but you can preview them in your browser by choosing File ⇨ Web Page Preview, or by pressing Ctrl+Shift+B.

Running the Web Wizard

You can run the Publisher Web Wizard and either use the Web page as is or make adjustments to it. Choose a design that matches your company's other documents, if possible.

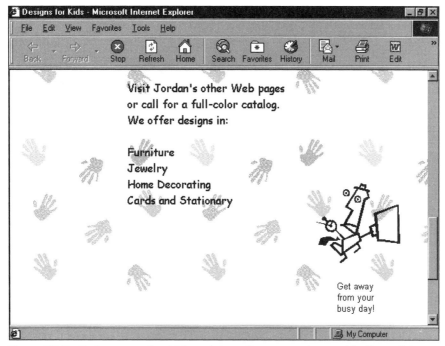

Figure 33-5: Each screen should have interesting text and a graphic, if possible.

To run the Web Wizard, follow these steps:

1. Choose File ➪ New. The Catalog appears.

2. In the Publications by Wizard tab, select Web Sites from the left pane.

3. In the right pane, select the design you prefer.

4. Click the Start Wizard button. The document and the Web Site Wizard box appear onscreen.

Editing the Web Wizard

You can edit the text and graphics in the Web Wizard, just as you can with any publication. You also can change the text formatting and frame placement, add or remove elements, and so on.

The Web Site Wizard box enables you to change color schemes, design, and personal information. The Web Site Wizard box also enables you to do the following:

✦ **Forms:** Insert one of the following forms: Order, Response, or Sign-Up. Alternatively, you can add no form.

✦ **Navigation bar:** Links the pages of the Web site. If you're designing just one page, you don't need the bar. If you want to add the bar, you can choose it here.

✦ **Insert page:** Insert any number of pages to create a Web site, if you want.

✦ **Background sound:** Add a sound to the Web site from any sound file in Publisher or Office. Publisher includes more than 35 sounds. You also can download sounds over the Internet from Microsoft Live Gallery, or create your own sounds with a microphone and the right software.

Figure 33-6 illustrates the Web Properties dialog box, from which you can choose a background sound. Click the Browse button to view and hear available sounds.

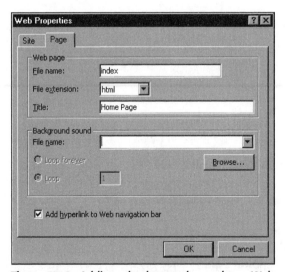

Figure 33-6: Adding a background sound to a Web page

Figure 33-7 illustrates the Background Sound dialog box. After you choose a sound, you can decide whether to play it once, several times, or repeatedly in a loop. The path to the sound files is C:\Program Files\Common Files\Microsoft Shared\Clipart\Pub60Cor. (For more information about the Web Properties dialog box, see Chapter 34, "Preparing a Web Site.")

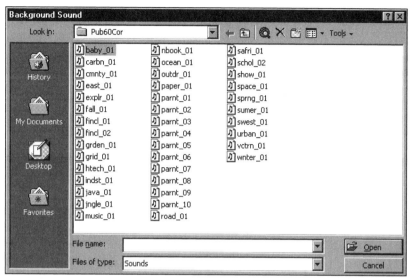

Figure 33-7: Choosing a sound from Office clip files

✦ **Background Texture:** The Color and Background Scheme dialog box appears when you click the Select Texture button in the Web Site Wizard box. You can choose to use a different color scheme for the entire Web page, but you also can choose to add a background.

Figure 33-8 illustrates the Color and Background Scheme dialog box. In the Standard tab, locate the Background area. Choose a solid color from the drop-down color menu. If you want to add a texture instead, place a check mark in the Texture check box.

You can accept the default texture that appears in the Sample box, or you can click the Browse button to apply another texture from the Web Backgrounds dialog box. To view each background, click the drop-down arrow beside the View button, and then choose Preview, as shown in Figure 33-9.

Publisher includes more than 150 background files. The path to the background files is C:\Program Files\Common Files\Microsoft Shared\ Clipart\Publisher\Backgrounds.

✦ **Convert to Print:** You can use the Web page contents to create a brochure or a newsletter. Publisher converts the content for you.

Figure 33-10 illustrates a Web page design that was edited after the Web Wizard created it. You can add graphics, change colors, use bullets, and move text around to make the design fit your needs.

Figure 33-8: Adding a solid color or a textured background to the Web page

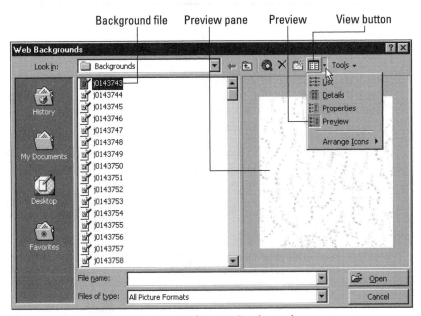

Figure 33-9: Selecting a background to use for the Web page

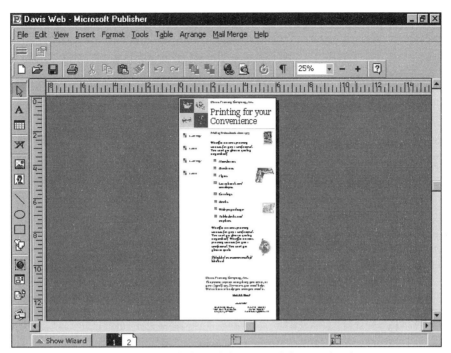

Figure 33-10: Start with the Web Wizard design and then make changes.

Previewing a Web page

You can preview a Web page at any time and then go back to Publisher to make changes in design or content.

To preview the Web page, follow these steps:

1. Choose File ➪ Web Page Preview or press Ctrl+Shift+B.

2. If you have more than one page in the Web site, the Web Page Preview dialog box appears, asking whether you want to preview the Web site or the Current page. If you view only one page, links to other pages won't work. Click your choice.

3. Click OK. The Web page or Web site opens in Internet Explorer or another default browser.

4. Click the Close button in the browser to close the preview.

Hypertext Markup Language (HTML)

HTML is a set of codes used to create pages of text and graphics for the World Wide Web. Internet browsers interpret the HTML code to make the text appear formatted and the graphics appear the way you want them to on your Web page. Hypertext enables the creation of links between pages within a Web site, as well as between Web sites all around the world.

HTML uses *tags* to define the page's appearance, text formatting, and links between pages. When you view an HTML page in Word or Notepad, for example, all you see is a stream of codes and text with no formatting. When you view that same HTML page with a browser, you see the Web page as it should be, with color, font formatting, images, and more.

Although you can learn to format your Web pages in HTML, using Publisher to create the pages for you is much easier. You can format a Web page as you would any other publication, and Publisher converts the page to HTML behind the scenes. You never have to view the HTML page or deal with the codes.

Creating Your Own Web Page

You can create a Web page on your own, without the help of the Web Wizard, if you like. You can add ready-made navigation bars and icons, or you can create your own. You can add hyperlinks, images, backgrounds, and other designs to make the Web page your own.

Using a blank publication

You can use a blank publication page to start your Web page. Publisher includes a blank Web page that is 6×14 inches with no margins. By default, Publisher sets the width of the Web page to fit a monitor that has VGA or higher resolution. You can make a change, however, in the page width, if you want.

Create a blank Web page

You can create a standard blank Web page that fits all video displays with horizontal scrolling. To create a Web page, follow these steps:

1. Choose File ➪ New. The Catalog appears.

2. Select the Blank Publications tab. In the Blank Publications pane, choose Web Page.

3. Click the Create button. Publisher creates the page and displays it onscreen.

Change the Web page width

You can change the Web page width to 7½×14 inches or to your own custom width. You might want to change the width of the Web page to fit higher-resolution video displays, such as SVGA. If you use the larger page width, VGA users must scroll the page horizontally as well as vertically, which is inconvenient. If you make a custom width, users may have to scroll, depending on the size that you make the page.

To change the page width, follow these steps:

1. Choose File ➪ Page Setup. The Web Page Setup dialog box appears, as shown in Figure 33-11.

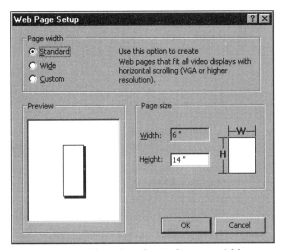

Figure 33-11: Changing the Web page width

2. Choose one of the following, depending on what you want to do:

   • **Wide:** Changes the Web page width to 7½×14 inches.

   • **Custom:** Enter your own Width and Height.

3. Click OK to accept the changes.

Designing the page

You can use any of Publisher's tools and features to design your Web page. Consider all the design elements — white space, balance, and emphasis, for example — as you create the page.

You can apply margin guides and grid guides to aid in your design. Figure 33-12 illustrates a Web page layout that uses a one-inch left margin, with grids set up in two columns and four rows.

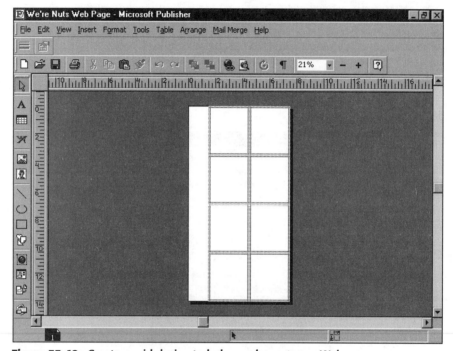

Figure 33-12: Create a grid design to help you lay out your Web page.

The following are some features and procedures that you can use to format your own Web page:

- ✦ Add a background (choose Format ➪ Color and Background Scheme)
- ✦ Use WordArt for the Web page title (see Chapter 21, "Using WordArt")
- ✦ Add clip art and animated clip art, movie and sound clips, and photographs (see Chapter 19, "Adding Clip Art, Images, Sounds, and Motion Clips to a Publication")
- ✦ Use frame borders and fills for text and graphics, and use shapes and lines to help divide and decorate the page

✦ Apply color to fonts, graphics, backgrounds, fills, and so on

✦ Format text, use bullets, change attributes, and use drop caps or other special text formatting

✦ Add line art or drawings of your own

✦ Create tables for organizing information (see Chapter 22, "Creating Tables")

✦ Add elements from Design Gallery, such as navigation bars or buttons (see Chapter 24, "Using Publisher's Tools")

✦ Add buttons or icons from Clip Gallery, as shown in Figure 33-13

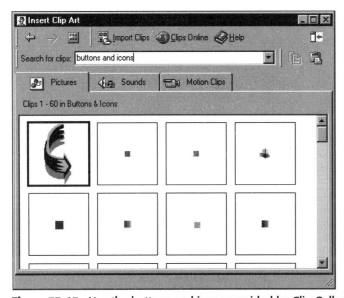

Figure 33-13: Use the buttons and icons provided by Clip Gallery.

Figure 33-14 shows a Web page previewed in Internet Explorer. This page uses the wide page setup (7¹/₂×14). Note that the design uses a background, graphic lines, clip art, and WordArt.

Figure 33-14: Design your own Web page from scratch.

Figure 33-15 shows the second quarter of the screen. Remember, the layout guides divide the page with a one-inch left margin plus four rows and two columns (refer to Figure 33-12). You can see how the rows and columns apply in this figure.

Figure 33-16 illustrates the third quarter of the Web page. Varying the use of the columns helps to make the page interesting, while using rows maintains consistency.

Figure 33-17 shows the last quarter of the page, the contact information. The arrow came from the Buttons & Icons clip art in Clip Gallery, adding a nice point of emphasis.

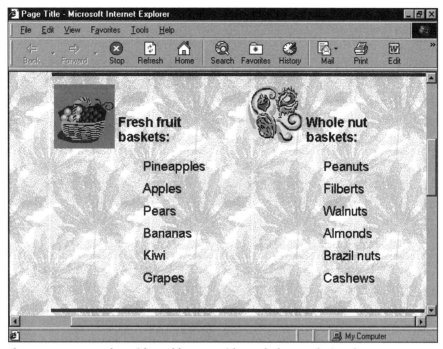

Figure 33-15: Use the grids and layout guides to help you design the page.

Creating hyperlinks

Hyperlinks are text or graphics that perform some sort of action when you click them. That action may be a leap to another Web site, for example, or it may display another part of your own Web site or a graphic. Usually, Publisher changes the color of the text that you link and underlines it for easy recognition.

Tip

If you create a hyperlink for a graphic, image, or clip art, you should add text below the graphic instructing the user to "Click here for . . ." (fill in the blank), so that the reader knows that it represents a link.

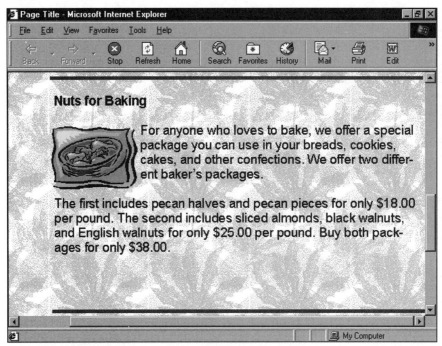

Figure 33-16: Vary the design of your Web page, for interest.

Inserting the link

You can insert a link to another page, address, or file. You should check your links in the browser, though, to make sure that they work.

To create a hyperlink, follow these steps:

1. Select the text or graphic to which you want to link.

2. Click Insert ⇨ Hyperlink or press Ctrl+K. The Hyperlink dialog box appears, as shown in Figure 33-18.

3. In the Create a hyperlink to area, choose the option that you want, as described in Table 33-1.

4. Enter any additional information.

5. Click OK.

Figure 33-17: Don't forget to add contact information to your Web page.

Figure 33-18: Inserting a hyperlink into your Web page

Tip

Hyperlinks work only when you view the page in a browser. Preview the Web page to see the links.

Table 33-1 describes the options in the Hyperlink dialog box. Note that whichever radio button you select in the Create a Hyperlink To area causes a corresponding change to the name of the list box in the Hyperlink information area.

	Table 33-1 **Hyperlink Options**
Option	**Description**
Create a Hyperlink To Area	
A Web site or file on the Internet	Choose to link the selected text to an Internet Web site address (URL). Enter the URL in the Hyperlink information area.
Another page in your Web site	Choose this option, and then select the specific page in the Hyperlink information area.
An Internet e-mail address	Choose to have e-mail sent to you or someone else in your company, perhaps. Enter the e-mail address in the Hyperlink information area.
A file on your hard disk	Link to a file, such as a Word or Excel file, a graphic, an image, or a sound file.
Hyperlink Information Area	
Internet address of the Web site or file	Appears when you choose to link to a Web site or file on the Internet. Enter the address of the site or the path to the file.
Favorites	Click to open the Favorites folder, from which you can choose a URL.
First, Previous, Next, or Specific page	These options appear when you choose to create a hyperlink to another page in your Web site. Choose the page to link to.
Internet e-mail address	This option appears when you choose to create a hyperlink to an Internet e-mail address. Enter the address here.
Path of the file	This option appears when you choose to create a hyperlink to a file on your hard disk. Enter the path and filename, or click the Browse button to locate the file.

To remove a hyperlink, select the linked object. Open the Hyperlink dialog box and then click the Remove button.

Viewing a link

You should view all links to make sure that they work. Also, after you place your Web page on the Web server, check all links. Finally, check links periodically, in case an address has changed or the link fails for some other reason.

When you preview your Web page, check the links by clicking the text or graphic that you linked. Figure 33-19 illustrates the File Download dialog box generated by the hyperlink. The user who clicks the link can download the file and save it to a local computer, or view the file from its current location.

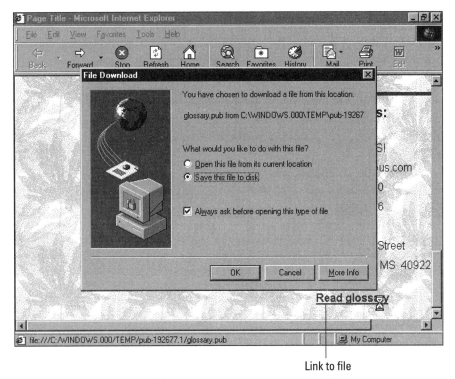

Link to file

Figure 33-19: Check your links in the browser to make sure that they work.

Tip

You might want to run the Design Checker (choose Tools ➪ Design Checker) to make sure that everything is appropriate for use on the Web. Design Checker looks for disproportionate images, fonts that might not look right on the Web, overlapping frames, and other problems with the document.

Creating a Web page from another document

You can open nearly any document in Publisher and create a Web page from it. Publisher converts the formatting to HTML, so that the publication can be displayed by a Web browser. Naturally, changing a publication to a Web page may involve some design problems; however, Design Checker automatically analyzes the publication and gives you hints about fixing the problems.

The main problem with most documents is that they're too large for the browser screen. The browser does, however, apply the vertical and horizontal scroll bars, so that the user can view the entire page.

Figure 33-20 illustrates a flyer as a Web page. Note the horizontal scroll bar; when a page doesn't fit the screen, Internet Explorer (and other browsers) automatically displays the scroll bar.

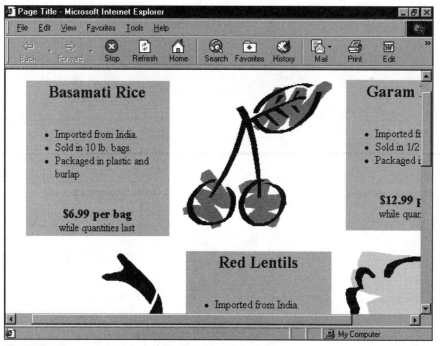

Figure 33-20: Convert any publication to a Web page.

If your publication has one page, Publisher creates a Web page. If the publication contains more than one page, Publisher creates a Web site.

To create a Web page from another publication, follow these steps:

1. Open the publication that you want to convert.

2. Choose File ➪ Create Web Site from Current Publication.

3. Publisher asks whether you want to run Design Checker now. You should run Design Checker, in case you're using a font, design, or layout that doesn't work well with the World Wide Web. Choose Yes to run Design Checker.

Note   Design Checker checks whether the page will download quickly, or be slow because of large graphics. It also checks your fonts to make sure that they'll look right in browsers.

4. Save your document under a new name, because it's now a Web page.

5. Preview the page in your browser.

Summary

In this chapter, you learned to create Web page designs in Publisher. You learned how to do the following:

✦ Create and gather content

✦ Use the Web Wizard

✦ Create your own Web page

In the next chapter, you learn how to prepare a Web site.

✦   ✦   ✦

Preparing a Web Site

Even though a Web site may contain just one page, generally, a Web site contains multiple Web pages that are linked together. The pages are usually related in some way; for example, a company might create a Web site of its products and services, company history, staff, forms, or other information to share with the visitors to the site. You can even create a personal Web site that tells about your family, hobbies, friends, and pets.

Before you create your own Web site, you should spend some time looking at other sites on the Web. Note the type of content presented, design and layout of the site, methods of linking, and so on. Figure 34-1 illustrates the home page of a Web site. The navigation bar helps the visitor find other Web pages; other links throughout the page also guide the visitor.

You need to plan your Web site carefully before you publish it to the Internet. You'll save time and energy, as well as additional costs, if your site is exactly the way that you want it, before it goes to the Web server. If you don't plan ahead, your site may be filled with content that's difficult to locate, update, and maintain.

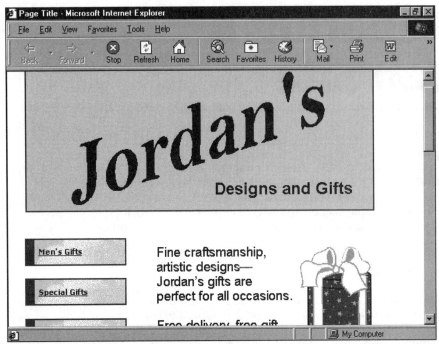

Figure 34-1: Use links and a navigation bar to move from one Web page to another.

Planning Your Web Site

When planning your Web site, enlist the help of your coworkers and staff. You might want help deciding on the content type, choosing design and layout, and gathering information. If you get opinions before you start, and apply some or all of the suggestions to the site, you'll receive fewer complaints later.

If you want to take it a step further, you can enlist your coworkers to help you create and maintain the site. Create a consultant group to help you plan and implement the Web site. Create a design or template that each person can use as a base for the Web page, and then assign each person one document or Web page to create and maintain, for example. Assign another person to oversee all Web pages for consistency of design and content.

If you run your own Web server, assign a small group of people to maintain the content, software, and perform troubleshooting procedures on the Web server. Have your group help you to decide the answers to the following questions:

✦ What are the goals of your Web site? Do you want to sell products or services, supply information, or gather information? Form the goals as your first step toward planning the content.

✦ Who is your primary audience? The design of your site depends on your target audience. Consider colors, graphics, content wording, and so on. Do you want the site to be formal, fun, exciting, low-key?

Tip

Use styles for font consistency from page to page, and create a template on which you can build each page, to ensure that all pages contain the same color scheme, layout, and design elements.

✦ How will you organize your site? You should create a map, or outline, of the site, so that you can plan your links and the overall framework of the site.

E-Commerce and Credit on the Web

E-commerce, or *electronic commerce,* enables you to reach millions of potential customers and increase your sales through electronic marketing. When you plan to sell your products and services over the Web, you must consider exactly how the transactions will take place.

How will the people who visit your site pay for your products? You should, of course, include a phone number and address, an e-mail address for questions or comments, and other contact information that will help the customer feel more comfortable purchasing over the Web.

Will you accept credit cards over the Internet? This is a question that's bounced around a lot these days. Some customers are afraid to provide their credit card information; others have no reservations. If you run a secure server, taking credit card information over the Internet shouldn't be a problem. Let customers know that you have security measures in place, so that they feel more comfortable providing their credit card information.

Secure servers process orders by using *Secure Sockets Layer* (SSL) session-encryption technology. The card information is encrypted both in transfer and as it is stored on the server, so that it's not subject to hackers, crackers, and other unscrupulous predators on the Internet.

SSL and *Secure Electronic Transaction* (SET) are standard technologies in merchant servers. A *merchant server* is a piece of complex software that enables you to set up a secure server, order forms, invoicing, inventory systems, and other such business necessities for use on the Web. SET requires credit card users to receive digital certificates for authentication. VISA and MasterCard even offer reduced rates when your company uses SET-enabled merchant server software.

If you plan to sell on the Web, but plan to take money by snail mail or credit over the phone or fax, then you don't need to worry about a secure server. If, however, you want to perform transactions over the Web, look into running your own secure Web server.

Organizing the Site

When organizing your site, you should first create an outline of the content that you want to include. List the pages, for example: home page, contact page with forms, products, history, fun links, customer information, and so on. Next, outline the contents for each page: heading, links, e-mail address, graphics, text, and so on.

You also must decide how to organize your files and folders. You could create one folder for the entire site and then create other folders as subfolders. You might save all items — text, graphics, and such — for each page in a folder. Alternatively, you can save all graphics in one folder, all text in a folder, and so on. Try to organize all files by using the same criterion, however, so that you can easily find files when you need them.

Figure 34-2 shows Windows Explorer with the Jordan's Web folder contents. Saving the files in various folders helps you to keep your files together and organized.

Figure 34-2: Use folders to arrange your Web site files.

Creating a Web Site

You can create your Web site by using a wizard or from scratch. Basically, you create Web pages (as described in Chapter 33, "Preparing a Web Page") and then continue to add pages to the publication. Alternatively, you can create a Web site from another publication type (also described in Chapter 33).

Common Mistakes to Avoid

When you create a Web site for selling your products or services, you should avoid making some common business mistakes. For example, make sure that you find out about sales tax in the states in which you'll be selling. You also may want to check international laws on selling, on selling certain products, and so on, because the Internet does reach many other countries.

A good example affected by varying international laws is that some herbal supplements in the United States are prescription-only, or illegal, in other countries. Whereas herbal supplements is a huge business in the United States, you may get in trouble for shipping such products to other countries.

Be careful when asking visitors for information about themselves — such as names, addresses, and so on. People may not be willing to give you that information without good reason. On any forms you use to collect information, explain how you will use the information. You also should publish a privacy policy on your site, stating, for example, that any information provided by users is kept confidential, is not used for any other purpose than those previously stated, and is not sold or traded.

Keep the content, and especially the links, on your site up to date. Always respond to customer inquiries and e-mail. Continue to improve your site by adding chat, video, and technologies that make the site more effective.

Register your site with as many search engines as possible. Offer your site's address to other sites who have related products or philosophies so you can swap hyperlinks. Publish your site address in all of your paper publications, advertisements, and so on.

You can use many of Publisher's features to create the Web site, including fonts and formatting, graphics, tables, clip art, WordArt, and more. Create your Web pages in a publication, and then you can add the elements that make your individual Web pages into a Web site: the navigation bars, buttons, and hyperlinks.

Creating a home page

The first page of your Web site usually is the *home page,* which introduces the site and your company, product(s), service(s), and so on. Your home page usually has links that connect it to the other pages in your site. You might also use a navigation bar on the home page.

Using a navigation bar

Navigation bars or other links help users move between the pages. Often, Back and Forward (or Next Page and Previous Page) buttons appear on the Web pages to make navigation easier. Users must have a way to move between the pages. Figure 34-3 illustrates a navigation bar on a home page in Publisher. The navigation bar makes going from page to page easier for users.

Navigation bar

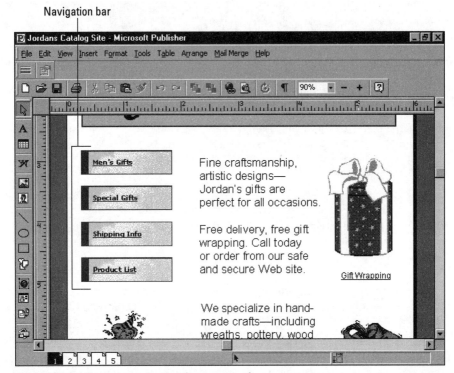

Figure 34-3: Create a navigation bar on your home page.

A *navigation bar* is a collection of links to the other pages in your site. You can add a navigation bar from Publisher's Design Gallery. It will update automatically as you add or remove pages.

Publisher supplies two types of navigation bars: vertical and horizontal. The vertical bar appears along the left side of the page and contains a decorative design, but you can change the graphics and text for the bar. The horizontal bar is text-only and appears at the bottom of the page. You can't change the text in the horizontal bar; instead, the text for the horizontal bar changes when you change the text in the vertical bar.

You want to use only one vertical navigation bar in your site; do not add one bar for each page in the site. For more information about hyperlinks, see Chapter 33.

Note   Alternatively, you can create your own navigation bar in Publisher. Create a frame with borders or fill, format the text as you want it, and then copy the frame repeatedly to supply the links that you need. Publisher's bars don't supply the links, you do.

To add a navigation bar to your Web page, follow these steps:

1. Display the Web page on which you will place the navigation bar.

2. Create your own bar.

   As an alternative, you can create a bar from the Design Gallery Objects. Figure 34-4 shows the Microsoft Publisher Design Gallery categories for 0Web additions.

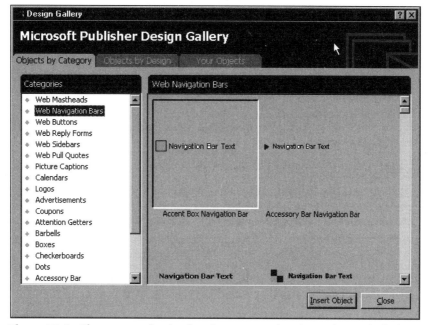

Figure 34-4: Choose a navigation bar, button, masthead, or other Web design element.

3. Enter the text in the bar or box, replacing *Navigation Bar Text.* Select the text.

4. Choose Insert ⇨ Hyperlink. The Hyperlink dialog box appears, as shown in Figure 34-5.

5. In Create a hyperlink to, choose Another page in your Web site.

6. In Hyperlink information, select the page to which you want to link the text.

7. Click OK to close the Hyperlink dialog box.

Repeat the preceding process with any other links that you want in your navigation bar. The links will not work until you preview the publication in the browser.

Figure 34-5: Create the link to another page in your site.

Adding other links

You might want to include other links on the home page. You can link any text or graphic to another page in the site, a file on the server (or in your Web site folder), or to a Universal Resource Locator (URL) on the Web, as described in Chapter 33, "Preparing a Web Page."

Publisher offers buttons that you can use to create links for e-mail or other links. Use Design Gallery to insert those buttons, or create your own button designs. Figure 34-6 illustrates an E-mail button. Clicking the button automatically addresses a message to the e-mail address that you indicate.

Tip   You might want to add the text of your e-mail address in a frame close to the E-mail button, in case the visitor prefers to write down the address and e-mail you later.

To create an E-mail button and link it, follow these steps:

1. Insert the E-mail button from Design Gallery.

2. Right-click the button. A shortcut menu appears.

3. Choose Hyperlink, and the Hyperlink dialog box appears.

4. In Create a hyperlink to, choose An Internet e-mail address.

5. In Hyperlink information, enter the address in the Internet e-mail address text box, as shown in Figure 34-7.

6. Click OK.

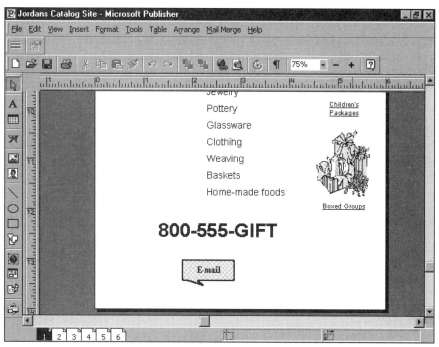

Figure 34-6: Use an E-mail button to link to your e-mail address.

Figure 34-7: Creating a hyperlink to your e-mail address enables your site's visitors to e-mail you easily.

Linking other pages

In addition to the links that appear on your home page, you must add links to the other pages in your site, so that visitors can easily move around within your site. You might want to add links to text or graphics, to an e-mail button — as you did on the home page — or to another link button.

Publisher provides other link buttons, besides an e-mail button, that you can insert into your Web page. You might want to insert a home page link on every page, so that visitors can quickly go back to the home page. Or, you can create other links by using the Design Gallery buttons — such as Next or Previous — or lead visitors to a specific page in your Web site.

Figure 34-8 illustrates two additional buttons that you can add to your Web page. The Home button takes visitors to the home page; the Special Gifts button takes visitors to another page of gifts. Note that the table above the buttons acts as a table of contents for the site; visitors can find the gifts that they want in the catalog on the Web.

You also can provide Previous and Next, or Back and Forward, links for each page. Figure 34-9 illustrates the arrows and text used to create these buttons on a Web page in Publisher.

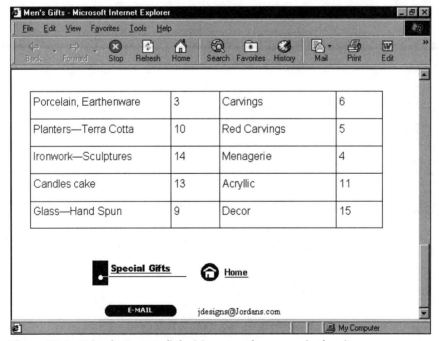

Figure 34-8: Using buttons to link visitors to other pages in the site

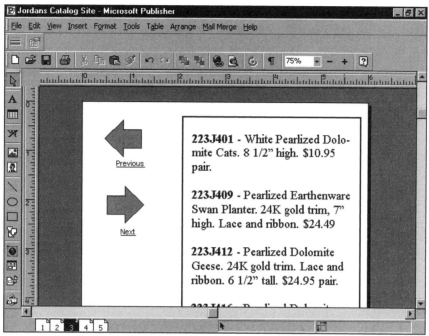

Figure 34-9: Make your own buttons and links.

You can create any type of button that you want for the links on your Web pages. To create arrows like those in the figure, use custom shapes to create the arrows. Fill them, and then rotate the arrow to point backward or forward. You can add text and then link both the text and the arrow.

In the Hyperlink dialog box, choose to hyperlink to another page in the Web site and then choose the previous or next page as the link. Make sure that you link both the text and the arrow, or other graphic, so that your visitor won't have to click everything on the screen to navigate the site.

Changing the home page name

By default, Publisher names your home page Index.html. You can change that name to anything that you want if you're using your own Web page. Most ISPs, however, require that your home page name be Index.html for use on their servers. You should ask your ISP, however, because some may have different requirements for the name of the home page.

You use the home page name in your URL. A sample URL is `www.Jordans.com\`
`Publications\Index.html`. This address takes you to the Jordan's server, Publications folder, and the Index.html file that contains the home page.

Preventing Linking Errors

Checking to make sure that the links you use are good is important, especially if you link to other Web sites. Often, you may click a link in your browser while on the Internet and receive an error, such as "Server Can't Connect" or the popular "404-Not Found" error.

You can prevent these kinds of errors on your own Web site by testing your links frequently. You don't want your users to find useless links and become aggravated with your site as a result.

Web sites often move or shut down, usually without leaving any other message than an error. Often, the site's address, or URL, changes because of a folder or server change; a moved site may not leave a forwarding address. You must check regularly for changes of address in the URLs linked to your site.

You may receive connect and 404 errors for other reasons, too. If the Internet or a specific server is busy at the time that you connect, your request may get lost or overlooked; if the ISP or the server in the URL is having problems, you may not be able to connect. These problems, however, aren't your fault and are beyond your control. You can tend only to those elements that are within your control—your links.

You can assign each page a name and title. The title appears in the browser's Title bar; remember, search engines use the title for indexing Web pages. You can change the name or title of a page at any time. Some ISPs may require a specific name or extension (such as .htm instead of .html), as well. If you need to change your home page name or extension, follow these steps:

1. Display the Web page in Publisher.

2. Choose File ➪ Web Properties. The Web Properties dialog box appears, as shown in Figure 34-10.

3. Select the Page tab.

4. In the Web Page area, enter the new filename in the File name text box.

5. Select either html or htm in the File extension drop-down box.

6. Enter a title in the Title text box.

Figure 34-11 illustrates the title of the home page in Internet Explorer's Title bar. Title pages help surfers locate your Web site.

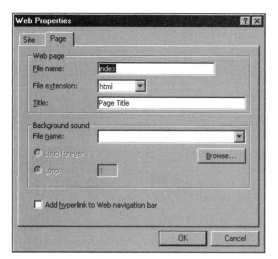

Figure 34-10: Use the Page tab to change the Web page name, extension, or title.

Creating Electronic Forms

Publisher provides three Web reply forms for you to use in your Web site. Publisher supplies an Order Form, a Response Form, and a Sign-Up Form in Design Gallery. If you use a Web Wizard to create your Web site, you also can add any of these forms from the Web Site Wizard box.

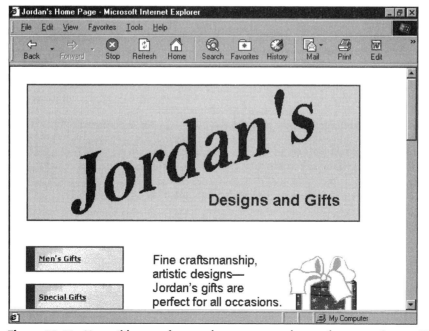

Figure 34-11: Use a title page for your home page and any other pages in your Web site.

You also can create your own forms by using Publisher's Form Control button on the Object toolbar. Using Form Control, you can insert the parts of a form that you need, and provide your own label text.

Using Publisher's forms

Naturally, you could also create your own form in table format; however, using one of Publisher's forms is easier, if you can make one of them fit your needs. Figure 34-12 shows a Sign-Up Form from Design Gallery.

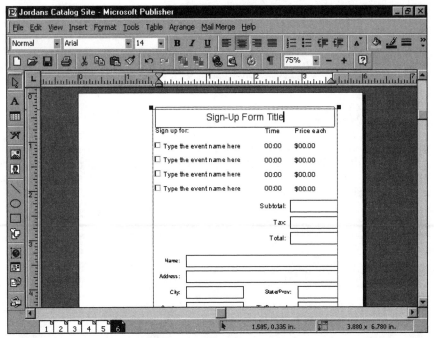

Figure 34-12: Insert a form and then change it to suit your purposes.

In Publisher, you can enter and modify text in the form, move sections, add lines or boxes, and otherwise edit the forms. Figure 34-13 shows an unlocked form and all of its pieces. Make sure that you select only one element or section at a time after unlocking the form, to prevent losing the entire form.

Figure 34-14 illustrates a Sign-Up Form modified to let the visitor sign up for free newsletters. Note the page title; it helps surfers find this site.

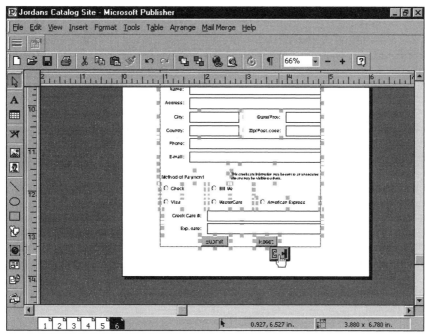

Figure 34-13: Unlock a form to move its elements or delete certain ones.

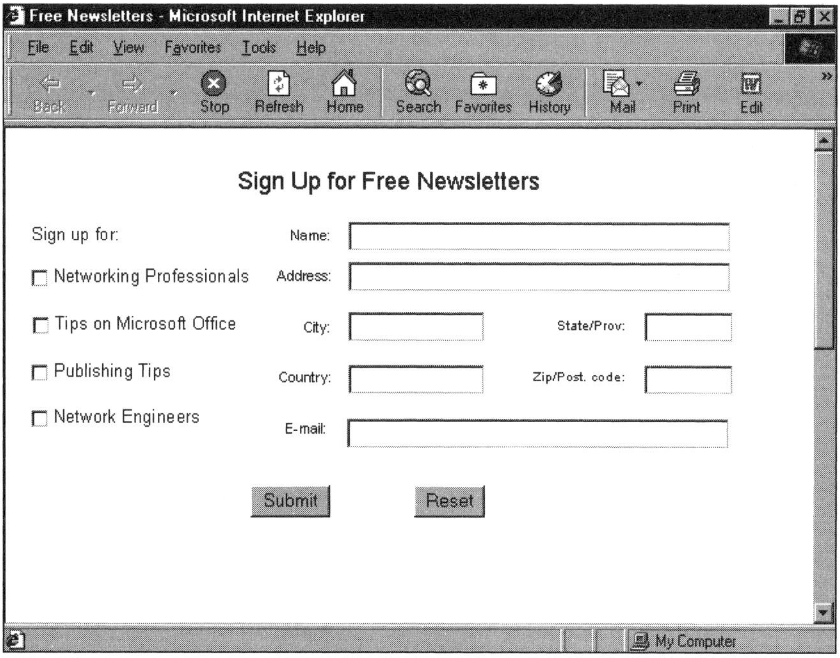

Figure 34-14: Use forms on your Web pages, for the visitor's convenience.

Creating your own form

You can use Publisher's forms for many purposes. If you prefer, however, you can create your own forms. Publisher provides a Form Control feature that enables you to insert the type of form element that you need. You can enter your own labels for each element. When you click the Form Control button, the mouse changes to a crosshairs cursor that you use to draw the element on the page.

The following is a list of the Form Control elements that Publisher provides:

✦ **Single-Line text box:** Creates a box that is as long as you want, but only the height of one line of text.

✦ **Multiline text box:** Creates a box as long and as tall as you want; adds scroll bars to the box so that users can view the text if they type more information than can be displayed in one screen.

✦ **Check box:** Creates a small square and includes an area for your label text.

✦ **Option button:** Creates a small circle for options and includes the label text.

✦ **List box:** Creates a drop-down box in which you can enter multiple items.

✦ **Command button:** Creates a Submit or Reset button.

Figure 34-15 shows each of these elements. Note that the figure also displays the Form Control Tool toolbar and button.

Each Form Control object has its own Properties dialog box, in which you can enter text and set options for the form. The following sections describe the available options for each object after you click its button on the Form Control Tool toolbar. To display the Properties dialog box for any Form Control object, draw the object and then double-click it.

Single-Line text box

Use a Single-Line text box to have visitors enter their name or address, or some other information that is no more than 255 characters long. You also can change the number of characters allowed by making it less than 255, as in a password or phone number, for example. Figure 34-16 shows the Single-Line Text Box Properties dialog box.

Enter any default text, such as a label, in the Default text area. You can't enter text in the Single-Line text box otherwise.

Another option is to use asterisks instead of characters to represent onscreen the text that the user enters. Use this option, for example, if the user is entering a password.

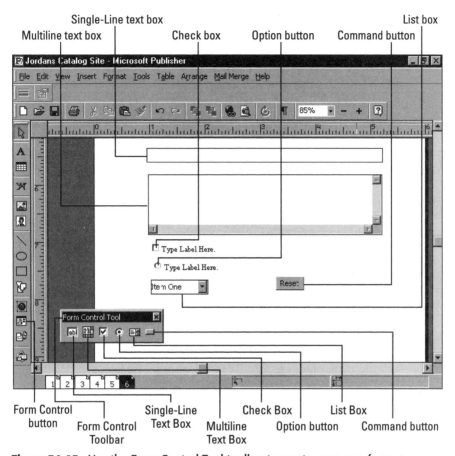

Figure 34-15: Use the Form Control Tool toolbar to create your own form.

Figure 34-16: Set the properties for the Single-Line text box.

The data processing label that you enter in the Data processing area of the dialog box identifies the text when it's returned to you. You can use labels such as Name, Address, E-mail, and so on, or other labels that fit the information better.

Use the last check box in the dialog box, This control must be filled in by user, to specify that the user can't continue unless he or she fills in the information.

Tip   Each Single-Line text box that you create can have different properties.

Multiline text box

Enter default text, such as a label or instructions, in the Default text area. You also can add a return data label for the text, and choose whether the user must enter information into the box. Figure 34-17 shows the Multiline Text Box Properties dialog box.

Figure 34-17: Enter properties for the Multiline text box.

Check box

When you create a check box for your form in Publisher, you can choose whether to show the box with a check (selected) or without a check (not selected) as the default. Then, the user must click the check box to change the default.

You also can label the data for sorting when you receive it from users. Enter a value for the label; you might want to use the default Yes, or No, or any other value that you want. The value that you enter here is part of the data returned to you when the user submits the form.

Figure 34-18 illustrates the Check Box Properties dialog box.

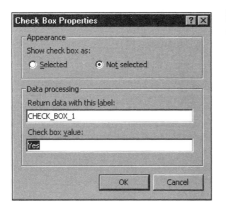

Figure 34-18: Create your own check boxes in your forms.

Option button

Option buttons enable users to check only one option in any group of options. Using the Option Button Properties dialog box, you can set whether the option is selected or not, enter a label for the return data, and apply a value to the option button. Figure 34-19 shows the Option Button Properties dialog box.

Figure 34-19: Enter the values and choices for the option buttons.

List box

The List Box Properties dialog box, shown in Figure 34-20, offers you a place to enter the information that you want to include in the list box. In addition to a return data label, you can enter each item, its value, and whether or not to show the item as selected. You can format the list box to use two, three, or more items in the list.

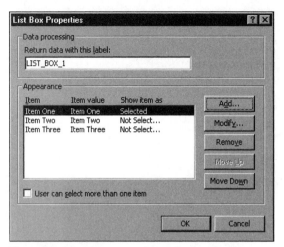

Figure 34-20: Name your items in the List Box Properties dialog box.

To use the List Box Properties dialog box, follow these steps:

1. Draw and then double-click the list box. The List Box Properties dialog box appears.

2. In the Appearance area, select an item and then click the Modify button. The Add/Modify List Box Item dialog box appears.

3. In the Appearance area, enter a name for the first item.

4. Choose whether to display the item as Selected or Not Selected in the list box. You can have only one item selected initially in the list box; that item is usually the first item, but you can change it to another by using this dialog box.

5. For the purpose of data processing, set the item's value to be the same as your item name, or enter a new value.

6. Click OK to close the dialog box.

Note   You can view the items in a list box only in the browser.

Command button

You can label a command button with Submit or Reset. Reset erases all the information the user entered into the form fields, and prepares the form for new information. Submit relinquishes the data to you in one way or another. In the Command Button Properties dialog box, shown in Figure 34-21, you can set the button to either command. You also can change the button label text, if you prefer not to use the words Reset and Submit.

Note   For some data-retrieval methods to work, your Web server or ISP, depending on where your Web site is located, must support FrontPage Server Extensions (FSE). If you've installed Microsoft Office 2000 and FrontPage, you'll have no problem. See the online documentation for more information.

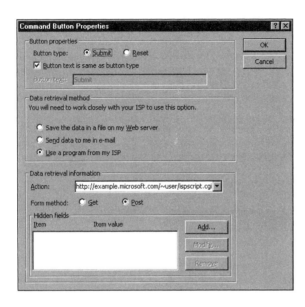

Figure 34-21: Set the options for the command buttons.

If you choose the Submit option in the Command Button Properties dialog box, you have a few other decisions to make. Table 34-1 explains these options. Note that whichever radio button you select in the Data retrieval method area causes a corresponding change to the name of the options in the Data retrieval information area.

Table 34-1
Command Button Properties for Submit

Option	Description
Data Retrieval Method Area	
Save the data in a file on my Web server	Writes the data to a file on the same server as your Web site.
Send data to me in e-mail	Enter an e-mail address for the data to be mailed to you in a message.
Use a program from my ISP	Use this option if your ISP supplies a program that you can use to receive your Web form data.

Continued

Table 34-1 *(continued)*

Option	Description
Data Retrieval Information Area	
Name of data file	Appears when you choose Save the data in a file on my Web server. Enter the name of the data file to create.
File format	Also appears when you choose Save the data in a file on my Web server. Enter the extension that you want to attach to the data file.
Send data to this e-mail address	Appears if you choose Send data to me in e-mail. Enter the entire address in this text box.
Subject of e-mail	Also appears if you choose Send data to me in e-mail. Enter the subject, so that you always know which information you're receiving.
Action	Appears when you choose Use a program from my ISP. Enter the URL of the program on your ISP's Web server.
Form method	Also appears when you choose Use a program from my ISP. Ask your ISP for the form in which the data is sent.
Hidden fields	Also appears when you choose Use a program from my ISP. Some programs require hidden fields. Ask your ISP for more information.

Inserting an HTML Code Fragment

An HTML *code fragment* is code that you add to your Web page so that you can display a special feature, animation, object, or such. You might add a visitor counter, for example, or a scrolling marquee. You also can use standard HTML, ActiveX, VBScript, or Java applets.

You set the HTML code fragment in Publisher, but in the browser, you see the feature or animation. You need to know the HTML code to use this feature. Publisher doesn't check the HTML code that you enter, so you must double-check it yourself.

To add an HTML code fragment, click the HTML Code Fragment button on the Object toolbar. The mouse changes to crosshairs; draw the frame in which the fragment will appear. The HTML Code Fragment Properties dialog box appears, as shown in the following figure. Insert the code that you want, and then click OK.

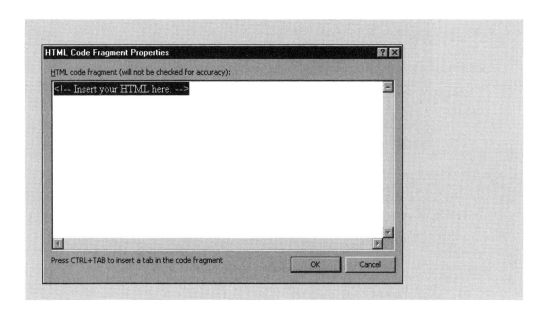

Figure 34-22 shows a simple form created with Form Control elements. You can make your form as long or as complicated as you want.

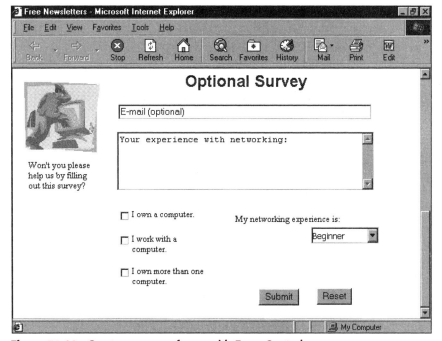

Figure 34-22: Create your own forms with Form Control.

Publishing the Web Site

When you publish to the Web, you transfer your Web site to an ISP's server or to your own Web server. You publish a site by using a Web folder. When you save by using Save As, Publisher offers the Web folder in your Places bar. This folder acts as a shortcut, or link, to a location on the Web server.

You can save to your Web server or to an ISP's server by using this method. However, the server must support Microsoft FrontPage 97 or later extensions. If you've installed Microsoft Office 2000 and FrontPage, you are okay.

Note   FrontPage is Microsoft's Web-site management software. It includes the tools for creating a site, formatting pages, managing links, editing pages, and organizing the entire site. FrontPage uses its FrontPage Server Extensions (FSE) to help you manage your Web site. You need FSE installed to use certain Web features in Publisher.

Publisher includes the Microsoft Web Publishing Wizard to help you publish your Web site. With the right information from your ISP, the Web Publishing Wizard can connect you to the ISP's server over the Internet and upload your files for you.

If you (or your ISP) don't use FSE, you still can publish your Web site by using File Transfer Protocol (FTP). You need to contact your ISP or system administrator for more information about the FTP addresses.

Setting site properties

The properties of your Web site include search engine information and settings to make your site suitable for specific browsers. A search engine, such as Yahoo! (www.yahoo.com), is an Internet resource that helps you find key words or phrases, people, and other online resources. *Search engines* are servers that gather the titles of Web pages and sites, index them, and then search through the index to help you find topics on the Internet.

You set site properties to help search engines locate your pages on the Internet. To set site properties, follow these steps:

1. Choose File ➪ Web Properties. The Web Properties dialog box appears with the Site tab displayed, as shown in Figure 34-23.

2. In the Keywords text box, enter any words or phrases that describe your Web page. Use a comma and space between each word.

3. In the Description text box, enter phrases or sentences that will help a search engine describe the content of the page.

Figure 34-23: Use site properties to set keywords for search engines and to target your viewers' browsers.

4. In the Target audience area, select the versions of browsers to which you want to publish.

Note

You should use Microsoft Internet Explorer or Netscape Navigator 3 or later if you're publishing to the Internet; that way, more people can view your Web page. You should use Microsoft Internet Explorer or Netscape Navigator 4 or later if you're targeting a specific audience, such as on an intranet. The latter option targets only newer browsers.

5. Use the Language option only if you created the Web site in another language. This option sets the appropriate characters for a language other than English.

6. Click OK to accept the changes.

Using Web folders

Web folders are shortcuts to the place on a Web server where your Web site will appear. You might, for example, get a URL from your ISP and create a shortcut to that by using a Web folder. On the other hand, you might have your own Web server and use the Web Folders feature to create a shortcut to your own server.

Contact your ISP or system administrator to find out the address of the Web server on which you can save files. The server must support Web folders, which means that it must also support FSE. If your ISP or Web server doesn't support these extensions, you can publish your site by using FTP or the Microsoft Web Publishing Wizard.

To create a Web folder, connect to the Internet or intranet. Make sure that the Web server is available. Then, follow these steps:

1. Double-click My Computer. The My Computer window appears, as shown in Figure 34-24.

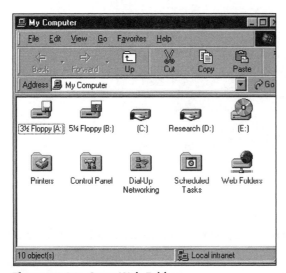

Figure 34-24: Open Web Folders

2. Double-click Web Folders. The Web Folders window appears, as shown in Figure 34-25.

Figure 34-25: The Web Folders window acts as a shortcut to the Web server.

3. Double-click Add Web Folder. The Add Web Folder Wizard appears. You must enter a URL for your company's Web server, an ISP's Web server, or other Web server — wherever your Web site will be located. Figure 34-26 illustrates the Add Web Folder dialog box.

Figure 34-26: Follow the Add Web Folder Wizard's steps to create a Web folder.

4. Follow the instructions of the Add Web Folder Wizard. Your new folder appears in a list under Web folders.

After you create a Web folder, you can publish your Web site to that folder and then to the Web server. To publish your Web site to the Web, follow these steps:

1. In Publisher, choose File ⇨ Save As. The Save As dialog box appears, as shown in Figure 34-27.

2. On the Places Bar (on the left side of the dialog box), select Web Folders.

3. Select the folder to which you want to publish.

4. Click Save.

Web folders

Figure 34-27: Save the publication to a Web folder.

Using the Web Publishing Wizard

To use the Web Publishing Wizard, you need to get the following information from your ISP or system administrator, or know the following about your own Web server:

✦ The URL of the Web site

✦ The title of your home page

✦ Whether the ISP's required title or extension is different from yours

If your home page title needs to be changed, see the earlier section, "Changing the home page name."

Note If you did not install the Web Publishing Wizard when you installed Publisher, you must reinstall Microsoft Internet Explorer 5. Choose Custom Install, and then select the Web Publishing Wizard.

To start the Web Publishing Wizard, follow these steps:

1. Choose Start ➪ Programs ➪ Microsoft Web Publishing ➪ Web Publishing Wizard.

   If you cannot find the Wizard there, try choosing Start ➪ Programs ➪ Internet Explorer ➪ Web Publishing Wizard.

2. Follow the Web Publishing Wizard's instructions to get online and publish your Web pages.

Using FTP locations

You must have access to the Internet or an intranet to create a Web site. After you create the site, you can publish your site to the Web via the FTP location shortcut.

To create a site via an FTP location, follow these steps:

1. In Publisher, choose File ⇨ Open.

2. In the Look in drop-down box, select Add/Modify FTP location in the Look in box. The Add/Modify FTP Locations dialog box appears, as shown in Figure 34-28.

Figure 34-28: Add FTP locations

3. In the Name of FTP site box, enter the name of the FTP site, as given to you by your ISP or system administrator.

4. In the Log on as area, select one of the following:

   • **Anonymous:** If you want to log on to a site that uses anonymous logins.

   • **User:** If you have privileges on the FTP site. You must enter a password if you choose User.

Note   The FTP Sites list box displays the sites that you've added. You may select a site that you previously added and then modify it.

5. Click Add.

6. Click OK.

Summary

In this chapter, you learned about working with Publisher and Web sites. You learned about the following:

◆ Understanding the Web site

◆ Creating a Web site

◆ Publishing the Web site

✦　　✦　　✦

Publisher and Windows 95/98

APPENDIX

◆ ◆ ◆ ◆

In This Appendix

Working with basic
Windows tools

Finding files

Organizing files and
folders

Using the browser

Understanding Dial-
Up Networking

◆ ◆ ◆ ◆

This appendix shows you how to use Windows tools in
conjunction with Publisher to extend its capabilities.

Working with Basic Windows Tools

Many of Windows' basic features and functions can help you
while working in Publisher. Mouse actions, the Taskbar,
manipulating windows, and so on make working with
Publisher easier and more efficient.

Note
For information about printing with Windows, adding print
drivers, and viewing print properties, see Chapter 30,
"Printing in Publisher."

The more advanced Windows features also can make your
work in Publisher easier. Use these features to find and
organize folders, copy files, print files, create folders, and
more. If you're familiar with Windows 95/98, you only need to
scan this appendix to make sure that you're not missing a
valuable Windows tool. If you're not familiar with Windows,
this appendix can help you use it to its fullest potential when
working with Publisher.

Using the mouse and working with Windows

Windows provides many tools and features that you use every
day in your work. The mouse, menus, Minimize and Restore
buttons, Taskbar — all of these help you to work in any open
Windows program. You're probably familiar with Windows'
basic tools, but you may have forgotten about some that you
can use to your advantage in Publisher.

Using the mouse

Obviously, you know how to use the mouse, but don't forget about the actions that you can perform with the mouse that make your job easier. Use the quick menus in Publisher. Drag and drop, double- and triple-click—just as you would in other programs—to get your work done in Windows.

A useful mouse feature to use with Publisher and Publisher objects is right-clicking to display a quick (or *shortcut*) menu. Right-click a text frame to display the menu shown in Figure A-1. Use shortcuts to copy, paste, and delete the text or frame; change the text or frame; proofread the text; change the view; and get help with the text frame—all from the right-click of a mouse.

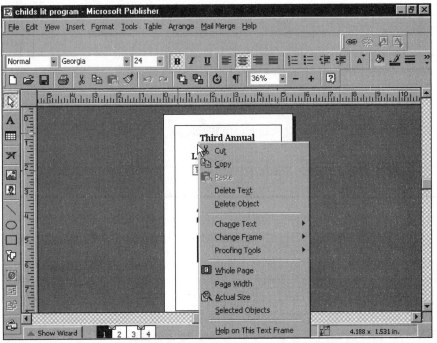

Figure A-1: Using the shortcut menu in Publisher

You can right-click graphics, images, borders, pages, toolbars, and even the workspace. Use this mouse feature to speed up your work and improve efficiency.

Working with Windows

Windows, the program, supplies windows in which your programs reside. The windows onscreen provide many tools that you can use to make your work in Publisher more effective. Make sure that you take full advantage of the tools found in every window—Minimize and Restore buttons, Title bar, Taskbar, and so on.

Title bar and buttons

You can use the Title bar and its features to display the Publisher window onscreen, for example, or to minimize, maximize, and restore the Publisher window. You can drag the Title bar of a restored window to move it around on the desktop.

Restore a window so that you can view two programs onscreen at one time. For example, you might want to display a graphic or paint program, a screen capture program, or two Publisher programs open simultaneously, as illustrated in Figure A-2.

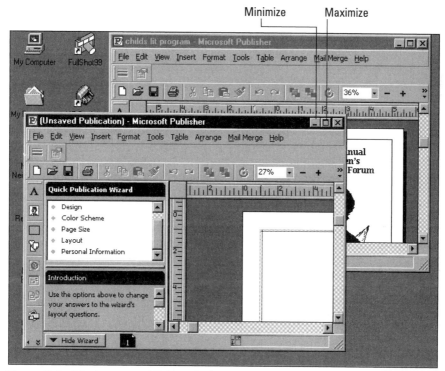

Figure A-2: Display two Publisher windows so that you can compare, share, copy, or cut text and graphics between them.

Taskbar

Use the Windows Taskbar to arrange the windows onscreen. Right-click the Taskbar to display a shortcut menu; choose to cascade or tile the windows to help you work between them. Figure A-3 shows two Publisher windows tiled horizontally. Click the program window in which you want to work to activate that window.

Even after you tile or cascade the two program windows, you can use the mouse and the window border to resize the windows when necessary. When the window is active, you can use all the Publisher tools and features in either program window.

Figure A-3: You can work with two open Publisher programs simultaneously, to share information between them.

Multitasking with Windows and Publisher

Multitasking is the Windows capability of handling multiple processing tasks, apparently at the same time. I say "apparently" because Windows cannot really perform many tasks at the same time; what it *can* do is perform these tasks at nearly the same time—and very quickly.

Windows applications are designed to break down their operations into a series of small tasks. Windows switches between these tasks from several applications so quickly that it seems the processes are running simultaneously.

Because you can run multiple applications at the same time, you can take advantage of multitasking when using your Publisher program. For example, open Excel and Publisher. Add Word and Access to the mix, if you want. You can switch between programs by using the Taskbar, or arrange the various program windows onscreen simultaneously.

Share information between programs, use OLE, cut and paste, and so on. Print from one program while working in another. Windows' multitasking most likely is quicker than you when working with multiple programs.

Starting Publisher and opening publications

You already know that you can start Publisher by using the Start menu. You have several other methods available to start Publisher and open Publisher documents:

✦ Create a shortcut for Publisher on your desktop — it's a great way to open the program quickly, without going through the menus.

✦ Open Publisher and its publications from Windows Explorer or My Computer.

✦ Open a Publisher document — and thus Publisher — by choosing Start and then selecting the file from the Documents menu.

✦ Open Publisher automatically when you open Windows.

Using Windows Explorer or My Computer

You can open Publisher and documents from either Windows Explorer or My Computer. By default, Publisher saves its publications in your My Documents folder. By default, Publisher's program file is located in the C:\Program Files\Microsoft Office\Office folder.

My Computer

Open My computer by double-clicking the My Computer icon on the desktop, and then double-click the hard drive icon. Figure A-4 shows the My Computer window, with the hard disk selected. After you open the hard disk, you must locate the program or publication file that you want to open.

Figure A-4: Opening the hard disk in the My Computer window

Figure A-5 illustrates the My Documents folder in the My Documents window. Open any publication file by double-clicking the file. When you open a publication file from the My Computer window or Windows Explorer, Windows opens Publisher and the publication and displays them both onscreen.

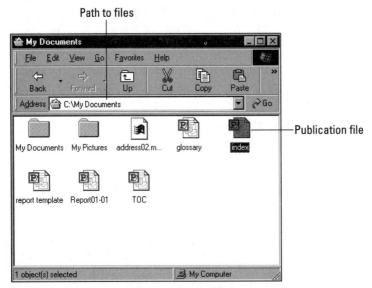

Figure A-5: Open a publication and Publisher by double-clicking a file.

If Publisher is already open, Windows opens a second Publisher program. If you double-click a third publication, Windows opens a third Publisher program. Be careful when using this technique, however. You do not want more than two Publisher programs open at the same time. More than two programs will tax your Windows resources and slow down all open programs. It may even crash your system.

Windows Explorer

You can use Windows Explorer to open publications and the Publisher program, just as you can use the My Computer window. Windows Explorer might be a bit easier to use, though, because you can see the entire directory structure, as well as all files, simultaneously.

Figure A-6 illustrates Windows Explorer with the My Documents folder open. Note that you see the folder and any folders that it contains in the left pane. In the right pane, you see the files of the selected folder.

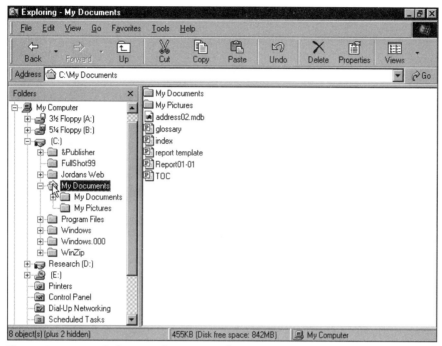

Figure A-6: Use Windows Explorer as an alternative to the My Computer window.

Open Windows Explorer by choosing Start ⇨ Programs ⇨ Windows Explorer. When you double-click a publication in Explorer, you open both the publication and the Publisher program. Just as with the My Computer window, don't have open more than two Publisher program windows simultaneously.

Using shortcuts

You can create shortcuts for your Publisher program, or any Publisher publication, on your desktop. The shortcut is simply an icon with a link to the file. The Publisher shortcut links to the MS Publisher executable file in the C:\Program Files\Microsoft Office\Office folder. A publication shortcut links to the publication file. Just as when you double-click the publication file in Explorer, double-clicking the shortcut opens both the publication and Publisher.

Figure A-7 shows the Publisher shortcut and a publication shortcut on the Windows desktop. Place a publication shortcut on the desktop when you work in that publication daily, for example.

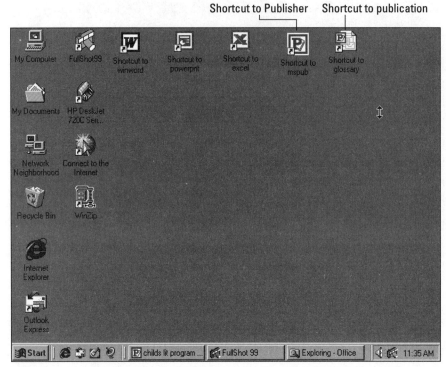

Figure A-7: Add shortcuts to your desktop to make opening regularly used programs faster.

You can create a shortcut from a publication by right-clicking the publication and then choosing Create Shortcut. The shortcut appears in the right pane of the Explorer window. Drag the shortcut to the desktop (you must restore Explorer's window to see the desktop).

You also can create a shortcut from the mspub executable file. To create a shortcut of the program's executable file, follow these steps:

1. In Windows Explorer or in My Computer, go to the folder C:\Program Files\Microsoft Office\Office.

2. Locate the mspub file, as shown in Figure A-8.

3. Right-click the file and then choose Create Shortcut from the quick menu.

4. The shortcut appears in the right pane of the window as the last file. Drag the shortcut to the desktop.

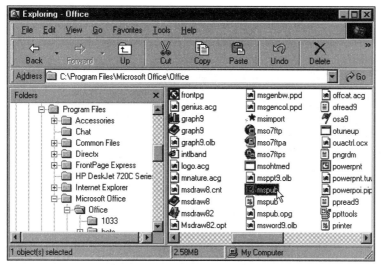

Figure A-8: Locate the file for which you want to create a shortcut.

You can move a shortcut around on the desktop. You also can delete a shortcut when you're finished with it, as in a publication shortcut. Select the shortcut and press the Delete key. Deleting a shortcut doesn't remove the publication or program from your hard disk; deleting a shortcut only removes the shortcut icon from the desktop.

Using the Documents menu

You can open a Publisher publication by using Windows' Documents menu. The menu displays the 15 most recent documents and publications that you opened, as shown in Figure A-9. Files other than Publisher publications — Excel, Word, and so on — also appear in the list when you use programs other than Publisher.

Once again, selecting a publication to open by using this method also opens a copy of Publisher. Note, too, that the My Documents folder appears at the top of the Documents menu. Clicking the folder opens the My Documents window from My Computer.

Finding Files

When working with Windows and Windows applications, it's difficult to organize files and folders so that you can readily find the files you need. Windows includes a feature called Find Files, which can help you to locate lost or misplaced files. For information about organizing your files, see the later section, "Organizing Files and Folders."

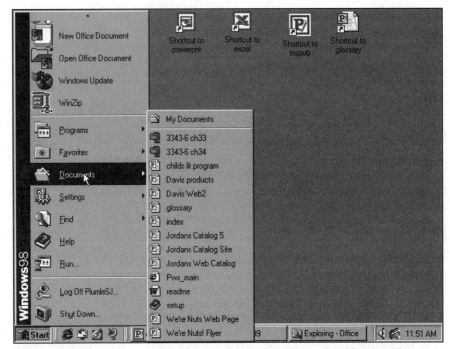

Figure A-9: Use the Documents menu to open recently used publication files.

Figure A-10 illustrates the Find dialog box, with the files that it found from the criteria given. The search parameters are to find all files on drive C that start with CTI and end with a .pub extension. Note the list at the bottom of the dialog box. Find has located 44 files that fit that description.

You can set the search parameters for the filename, file location, the date the file was created or modified, size, contents, and more. You can search for a file type in general, a file created on one particular date, or a file with a specific name. You can widen or narrow the search to result in one or hundreds of files.

When Windows finds the specified files or folders, it displays the filename or folder name, the folder in which the file is located, the size of the file, the file type, and the date the file was last modified. You can use this information to choose the file that you want. You also can copy or cut files, open or print them, and perform other file management tasks on the files in the Find dialog box.

Open the Find dialog box by choosing Start ➪ Find ➪ Files or Folders. When you want to start a new search, make sure that you click the New Search button to clear the old search parameters.

Search for   On drive C

Number of found files

Figure A-10: Finding specific files on the hard disk

Using the Name & Location tab

Generally, you use the Name & Location tab to locate files or folders on the hard disk, a floppy disk, Zip disk, or CD-ROM. You can search any or all drives, a specific folder, or all subfolders. You can name a file, or use wildcards to find certain file types. You can even include certain text that appears in a file.

Finding named files or folders

When you name the files for which you're searching, you can enter an exact name of the file or folder and then click the Find Now button. For example, you can enter Office and find all files or folders that contain the word "Office," including Microsoft Office, Office folders, Office 2000 setup files, and so on. Find doesn't know the difference between a file and a folder; it displays them all.

You also can use wildcards to locate files. *Wildcards* are the asterisk (*) and the question mark (?). The asterisk finds all characters, and the question mark finds only single characters. Using a wildcard widens the search by adding more possibilities.

Suppose that you want to find all Publisher files. You can enter ***.pub** in the Named text box, and Find will locate all files that end in a .pub extension—that's all Publisher files. If you want to find all files that start with certain text, such as CTI or Davis, you can. The following are some examples of using the asterisk in a file search:

Example	File Search Result
.	Finds all files.
*.doc	Finds all files with a .doc extension.
Davis*.pub	Finds all files starting with Davis and ending with the .pub extension, such as Davis letterhead.pub and Davis flyer.pub.
D*.*	Finds all files that start with *D*.
Davis*.*	Finds all files that start with Davis, no matter what the extension.
02.	Finds all files. This one is a trick: you can't specify text after the asterisk. The asterisk cancels text after it.

Using the question mark, you can limit the file search more than with an asterisk. Question marks represent *one character* in a filename or extension. For example, *.p?? finds all files with a *p* starting the extension, such as .pub, .pcx, and .ppd files. The question mark wildcard doesn't always work well in the Find dialog box. For example, ??? 02.* finds a lot of unrelated files, following no rhyme or reason. You might want to use some of the other criteria described in this section to help narrow your search.

Figure A-11 illustrates the files found with *.p?? added to the Named text box. All the .pcx and .pub files appear in the Find dialog box.

Finding files containing text

The text box labeled Containing text enables you to enter text that you know will appear only in certain files, such as a company or person's name, a logo phrase, or other text. Enter as much or as little text as you need to indicate the file that you want to find.

Enter, for example, **professionals training professionals**. That logo phrase represents the CTI Technologies training department. Only those publications with that phrase in the file will appear in the Find dialog box.

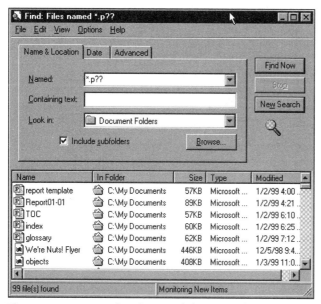

Figure A-11: Narrowing the search by using the ? wildcard

Look in

The Look in drop-down box presents the desktop, My Computer, hard drives, floppy drives, and so forth for the search. You can look in only the Document Folders on your computer, or you can look on all hard drives. Click the drop-down arrow to display the available drives and folders. By default, Document Folders is the first place Windows looks for files.

Using the Date tab

By default, the Date tab is marked to find all files, no matter what date the file was last modified. You can, however, modify the search parameter to find files created, modified, or accessed on a particular date or in the last month or so, for example.

Figure A-12 illustrates the Date tab of the Find dialog box. Instead of the default All files option, the figure shows the Find all files list box set to Modified, with the relevant dates set between 10/12/98 and 1/10/99.

The following are the options on the Date tab:

✦ **All files:** Choose to find all files using search parameters set in other tabs of the Find dialog box.

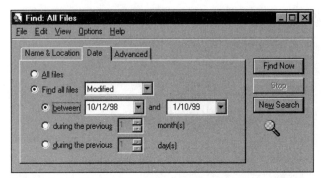

Figure A-12: Finding files that were created or accessed on a specific date

- ✦ **Find all files:** Choose Modified, Created, or Last accessed. When you choose this option, you can narrow the search further by choosing one of the following options:

  - **Between:** Enter the date or select from the drop-down calendar box. You can choose today, this month, last year, or any date from either drop-down box. Enter the date, such as **3/14/99**, in the appropriate text boxes.

  - **During the previous/month(s):** Choose this option and then enter the number of months.

  - **During the previous/day(s):** Choose this option and then enter the number of days.

Using the Advanced tab

Use the Advanced tab to specify a file type or file size, or both. In Of type, you can choose all files and folders, address book files, application files, cabinet files, help files, configuration settings, GIF images, JPEG images, Excel, Word, movie clips, system files, and so on. Depending on your computer and the files that you've installed, you can choose from more than 100 file types.

You also can choose to narrow the search by specifying the size of the file. In the Size is drop-down box, choose At least or At most and then enter the size of the file. This comes in handy, for example, when you're looking for a small image file for your Web page, as shown in Figure A-13.

Setting Find options and views

In finding files, you can use several Find options, features, and views to help in your search. You can copy files, print files, change the way the Find box displays files, and even save search parameters for use later.

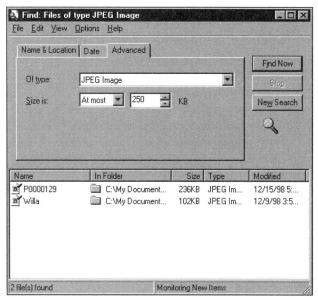

Figure A-13: Finding files of a specific type and size

Saving a search

If you perform a particular search a lot — say, searching for JPEG files of a certain size for your Web publications, you can save that search and use it whenever you need to. Save a search by setting the search parameters and then choosing File ⇨ Save Search.

Editing and printing files

You also can cut or copy any files that you find in a search. When you locate files in the Find dialog box, right-click the file for which you want to display the shortcut menu. You can open, print, cut, copy, delete, and even rename the file, as shown in Figure A-14.

Changing the view

You can change the way that you view files in the Find dialog box. Choose to view the files in Large Icons view, as in the My Computer window, or in Small Icons view, List view, or Details view. Details view provides the filename, folder name and path, size, type, and the date last modified. The other views provide only the filename and an icon for the type of file.

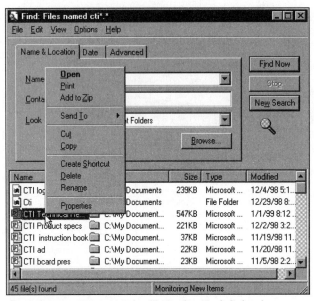

Figure A-14: Managing the file in the Find dialog box

To change the view, choose View and then choose the view that you want to use.

Tip   If you need further help with the Find dialog box, use the online help topics by clicking the Help menu.

Organizing Files and Folders

When you're creating Publisher publications, you often save them to the default folder, My Documents. After you create many files, you might decide that you need a better way to organize your files, so that you can find them more easily.

You can create your own folders, copy or move folders and files, delete and rename files and folders, and otherwise manage the content of your hard disk (or any disk attached to your computer), so that your work is more effective and efficient.

You can use My Computer or Windows Explorer to mange your files and folders. Both work the same way except for the view. My Computer displays one window at a time; Windows Explorer displays two panes, which enables you to view folders in one pane and files in the other. I prefer Windows Explorer, so that's the one I outline in this section.

Displaying files and folders

When you open Windows Explorer, you see your desktop, drives, folders on those drives, the Network Neighborhood, and other items in the left pane of your Windows Explorer window. In the right pane, you see the contents of whatever drive or folder is selected in the left pane.

Figure A-15 illustrates the contents of the desktop and My Computer on the left, and the contents of My Computer on the right.

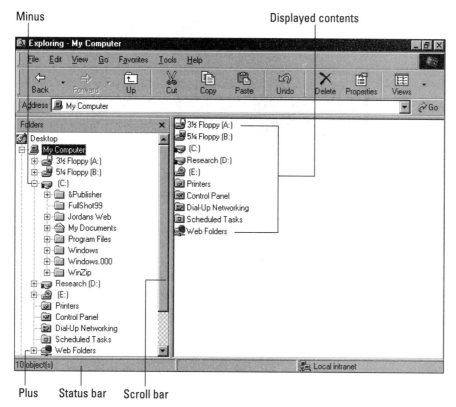

Figure A-15: Viewing the contents of your computer

Note in the figure that some items have a plus sign (+) to their left, some have a minus sign (-), and others have no symbol to the left. The plus sign indicates that the drive or folder contains more folders. The minus sign indicates the contents are already displayed. No symbol to the left means that no subfolders exist to display, even though that folder may contain files.

Click the plus sign to open and view the contents of a drive or folder. Click the minus sign to collapse the view of the contents. Alternatively, you can double-click a folder or drive in the left pane to display its contents.

Using scroll bars

You can use the scroll bars to scroll the windows for more folders or files. The left pane uses a vertical scroll bar; the right pane uses vertical and horizontal scroll bars, depending on the view, as shown in Figure A-16. You can change the view to Large Icons, Small Icons, List, or Details by using either the Views button on the toolbar or the View menu.

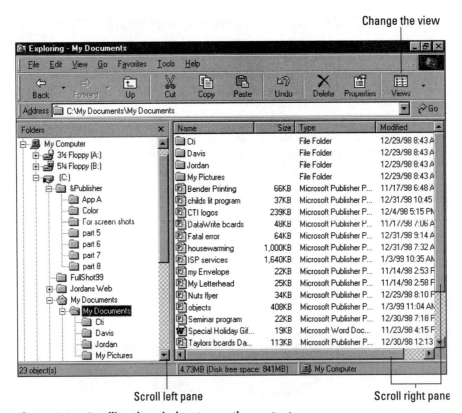

Figure A-16: Scrolling the window to see the contents

Using the status bar

The status bar appears at the bottom of the Windows Explorer window. On the status bar, you can view the number of files in any folder, the amount of space used by a folder or file, and the amount of free disk space left on the selected drive. When you select a drive or folder in the left pane, the status bar shows information about it.

Managing folders

As you work in Publisher, you'll need to use the Folders features to keep your files in order. You can organize your files and folders by creating new folders, and by deleting, renaming, moving, copying, and otherwise managing your existing folders.

Creating a new folder

You can create a new folder anywhere on your drives quickly and easily. When you create a new folder, you can name it anything you want. You might name a folder after a company, customer, date, or by its contents — letters, envelopes, images, and so on. You need to build a folder structure that makes sense to you; you're the one who will use the directory structure.

Tip Windows displays folders in alphabetical order in Windows Explorer. Additionally, Windows displays folders with symbols — such as !, @ , #, and & — at the top of the folder list. If you want to position a folder at the top of the list so that it's easy to find, start its name with one of these symbols.

To create a new folder, follow these steps:

1. In Windows Explorer, select the drive or folder in which you want to create a new folder. For example, selecting drive C places the new folder in the root of that drive; selecting the My Documents folder places the new folder in the My Documents folder.

2. Choose File ➪ New ➪ Folder. The new folder appears at the end of the list of files and folders, with the name New Folder, ready to be changed, as shown in Figure A-17.

3. Enter a name for the new folder and then press Enter.

Tip If you want to see the new folder at the top of the window, where it normally appears, choose View ➪ Refresh to change the view.

Renaming a folder

You can easily rename a folder. Select the folder and then click it a second time to display a rectangle around the name. The current name appears selected; if you type, you automatically replace the current name with the new name. Alternatively, you can click the mouse in the name box and add to or edit the current name. You also can select a file, choose File ➪ Rename, and then enter the new name in the name box.

Be careful to not double-click the folder name instead of clicking twice, slowly. Double-clicking opens the folder. Clicking twice, slowly, enables you to rename the folder.

Another way to rename a folder (or a file) is to right-click it, and then enter the new name to replace the current file name that is highlighted.

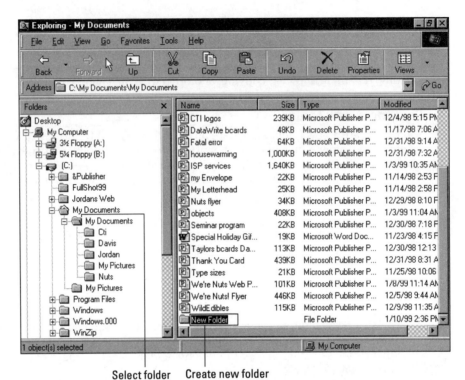

Select folder   Create new folder

Figure A-17: Enter a name for the new folder.

Deleting a folder

Delete any folder (and its contents) by selecting the folder and then pressing Delete. Windows asks whether you're sure that you want to move the folder to the Recycle Bin. Alternatively, you can choose File ⇨ Delete. You must confirm the deletion to move the folder to the Recycle Bin.

Copying or moving a folder

You can move or copy a folder to another drive or to another folder. Windows supplies two methods of copying and moving:

✦ **Drag the folder from the left pane to the right pane:** To move a folder in Windows Explorer, drag the folder from the right pane to the left. In the left pane, hold the folder over the drive or folder to which you want to move it, so that the new folder is highlighted. Release the mouse button, and the original folder moves to the new one. To copy, you do the same thing as moving a folder, except that you press and hold down the Ctrl key before you drag the folder to be moved.

✦ **Use the Cut and Copy commands:** You can use the Edit commands, keyboard shortcuts, or toolbar tools to move or copy folders. Use Cut and Paste to move a folder from the right pane to the left pane, and use Copy and Paste to copy the folder, as you would any other item or text in Windows or Publisher.

Managing files

File management is similar to folder management. You can copy and move files in the same way that you copy and move folders. You can rename files, delete files, and otherwise manage the files in Windows Explorer. Refer to the previous section, "Managing folders," for information about deleting, renaming, copying, or moving files.

You also can sort files in Explorer, to help you locate files more easily. You can sort the files alphabetically by name or by type, sort them by size (smallest to largest), or sort them by the date they were last modified (oldest to newest).

To sort files, follow these steps:

1. Using Details view, display the files that you want to sort.
2. Choose View ⇨ Arrange Icons. Select by Name, by Type, by Size, or by Date, according to what you want to do.

Using Internet Explorer

The Windows default browser is Internet Explorer. Using this browser, you can view your Web publications before you put them on a Web server, or you can connect to an intranet or the Internet to view your Web publications. Use the browser to view the Web page (created in HTML) so you can see what others will see over the Internet.

Opening Internet Explorer

You can open Internet Explorer from the Windows desktop, from the Programs window, or from Publisher to preview a Web page or site.

To open Internet Explorer from the Windows desktop, double-click the Internet Explorer icon, as shown in Figure A-18.

To open Internet Explorer by using the Start menu, choose Start ⇨ Programs ⇨ Internet Explorer. To open Internet Explorer with it showing the Web site from Publisher, choose File ⇨ Web Page Preview or press Ctrl+Shift+B.

Figure A-19 illustrates Internet Explorer with a Publisher Web site onscreen.

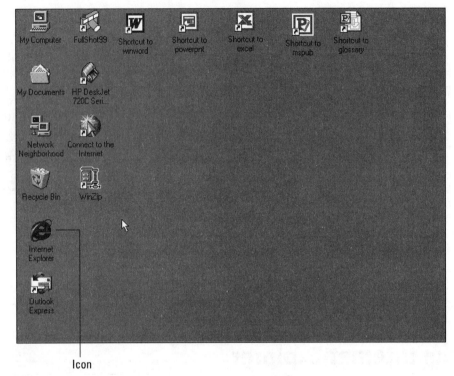

Icon

Figure A-18: Opening Internet Explorer from the desktop

You can turn on or off any of the toolbars by choosing View ⇨ Toolbars, and then choosing Standard Buttons, Address Bar, or Links, as appropriate.

Navigating Internet Explorer

To navigate a Web site, you can use the standard buttons on the toolbar, the links and buttons in a Web document, or a combination of both. Because the standard buttons always work the same way, no matter which Web site you're visiting, you might want to use them more frequently.

Figure A-20 illustrates the standard buttons on the Internet Explorer toolbar. The following list describes the buttons:

Toolbar with standard buttons   Address bar

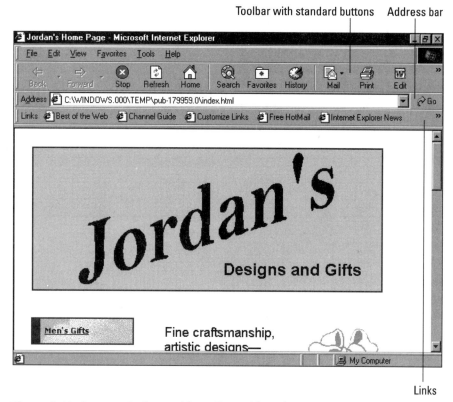

Figure A-19: Internet Explorer with toolbar, address bar, and links onscreen

Figure A-20: Using the toolbar to navigate the Web

- ✦ **Back:** Go to the previous Web page
- ✦ **Forward:** Go to the next Web page
- ✦ **Stop:** Stop transferring the current Web page, image, or text
- ✦ **Refresh:** Renew the view of the current Web page
- ✦ **Home:** Jump to your home page — by default, the home page is www.microsoft.com
- ✦ **Search:** Use Microsoft's search engine to search the Web

+ **Favorites:** Store site addresses that you like and want to visit repeatedly

+ **History:** Display the sites that you've visited recently, as shown in Figure A-21

+ **Mail:** Send an e-mail, read a message, send a page or link to a friend, or read the news

+ **Print:** Print the current page

+ **Edit:** Modify the current publication text in Microsoft Word 2000

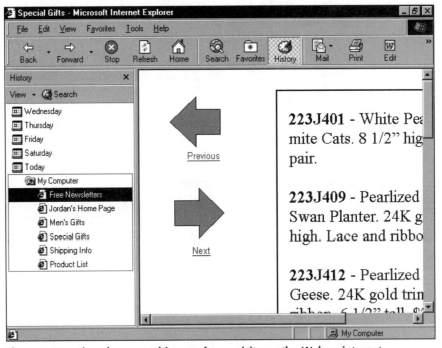

Figure A-21: View the recent history of your visits on the Web or intranet.

Tip

If you need more help with Microsoft Internet Explorer, use the online help by choosing Explorer's Help menu.

Understanding Dial-Up Networking

Windows enables you to reach beyond your local computer to use files, information, images, and other data over various networks. You can attach your computer to a local area network (LAN) or to the Internet, all with Windows tools and features.

When you're using Publisher, you may want to use networking in Windows. For example, you can save your publication files to a local network drive so that your coworkers can use them. Also, you can send your Web page to your ISP's server over the Internet, use files and images from other servers over the Internet, share data with coworkers, and so on.

Using Windows networking can help you attach your computer to your office, corporate headquarters, or the world.

Note If you're connected to a LAN, ask your network administrator to attach your computer to the network and configure it for you. Each network is set up differently, and only your administrator knows how to configure your computer for that network.

Dial-Up Networking (DUN) is a feature that enables you to attach to an outside network — such as the Internet — via a modem and a telephone line. Your computer may be connected to a line other than a telephone line — for example, ISDN, T1, Fractional T1, and T3 are high-speed lines that connect many corporations to the Internet. Depending on the line that you use, you may or may not use a modem; your company may use different equipment to attach to the network.

Setting up a DUN connection

No matter what the line or the equipment, you still use Dial-Up Networking to attach to an external network. Windows enables you to set up DUN from the My Computer window. If you have the information that you need to configure DUN, you can attach to the Internet or to a corporate Extranet.

Here's what you need:

✦ Modem, router, terminal adapter, or other equipment for sending information from your computer to the cable or line that leads to the external network

✦ A line or cable to the external network

✦ Information from your ISP, or other external network provider, including the phone number of the server

To set up the Dial-Up Networking connection, follow these steps:

1. Open My Computer.

2. Double-click Dial-Up Networking, as shown in Figure A-22. If you do not see the Dial-Up Networking folder, you must install that feature from the Windows CD-ROM.

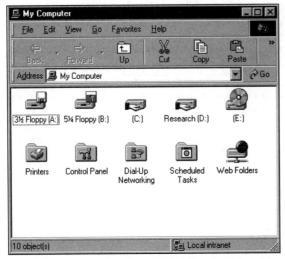

Figure A-22: Opening the Dial-Up Networking folder

3. Double-click the Make New Connection icon. The Make New Connection Wizard appears. If you have not installed a modem, the Modem Installation Wizard appears first. Follow the directions to install the modem, and then follow the wizard's instructions to create a new connection.

4. When you're finished, the connection icon appears in the Dial-Up Networking dialog box, as shown in Figure A-23.

Configuring a protocol

If you're connecting to the Internet, you need to install TCP/IP (Transmission Control Protocol/Internet Protocol) to attach to the ISP. *TCP/IP* is the protocol used for communication on the Internet. You also need more information about the configuration, such as the IP address of the server. If you're connecting to an external corporate network, ask the network systems administrator for information on how to proceed.

To configure TCP/IP for the Internet, follow these steps:

1. Choose Start ➪ Setting ➪ Control Panel.

2. In Control Panel, double-click the Network icon. The Network dialog box appears, as shown in Figure A-24.

3. In the Configuration tab, click the Add button. The Select Network Component Type dialog box appears, as shown in Figure A-25.

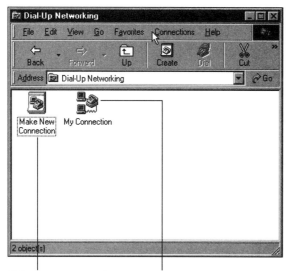

Make a new connection   New connection

Figure A-23: Make a new connection to identify the server and phone number of the external network.

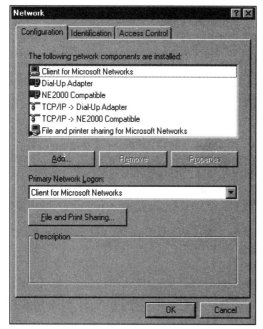

Figure A-24: Your dialog box may or may not have entries as the one shown; it depends on whether you're connected to a network (as in this case).

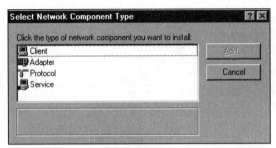

Figure A-25: You'll be adding the TCP/IP protocol to your configuration.

4. Select Protocol, and then click Add. The Select Network Protocol dialog box appears, as shown in Figure A-26.

5. In the Manufacturers list box, select Microsoft. In the Network Protocols box, select TCP/IP. Click OK.

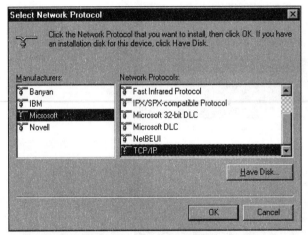

Figure A-26: Select the TCP/IP protocol.

6. In the Network dialog box, select Dial-Up Adapter. Click the Properties button. The Dial-Up Adapter Properties dialog box appears, as shown in Figure A-27.

7. Click the Bindings tab and make sure that the check box for TCP/IP has a check mark in it. Click OK.

8. In the Network dialog box, select TCP/IP – Dial-Up Adapter, and then click the Properties button. If you receive a warning or confirmation, click Yes to continue.

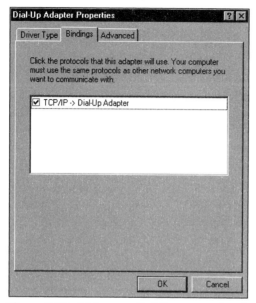

Figure A-27: Make sure that the protocol and adapter are bound together.

9. In the TCP/IP Properties dialog box, choose the IP Address tab. Enter the information that you received from your ISP.

   The ISP probably has specific instructions regarding the IP address and Subnet Mask, which appear in the same dialog box. Follow the ISP's directions carefully. You also may need to use the DNS Configuration tab in this same dialog box. Refer to the ISP's instructions.

10. When you're finished, click OK to close the dialog box. Click OK again to close the Network dialog box. You'll be prompted to restart your computer. When it starts up again, you're ready to call the Internet.

Summary

This appendix covered some of the more useful Windows features for use with Publisher. If you need more help with Windows, refer to the online help.

✦   ✦   ✦

Index

B

background sound for Web page, 770, 771
Background view, 168
backgrounds
    designing publications with, 184–190
    hiding elements in, 182–184
    types of items placed in, 179–180
    using background feature, 180–182
    viewing, 181
    for Web pages, 771, 772
Backspace key, 266
backup copies
    making, 92–93
    opening, 97
balance, 139–140, 141, 142
banners, 627–630
    creating a banner with Banner Wizard,
        627–628
    creating your own, 630
    defined, 627
    wizards for, 68, 627
bar codes, 599, 600
barbells from Design Gallery, 573
basic design considerations
    audience, 108
    color, 115, 118–119
    document purpose, 108
    format choices, 109–112
    method of distribution, 109
    paper size, 113
basic design strategies
    balance, 139–140, 141, 142
    consistency, 113
    emphasis, 113–114
    white space, 115, 116, 117
basic information for getting started
    closing a publication, 36
    creating a new publication, 20–21
    exiting Publisher, 36

    saving a publication, 35–36
    starting Publisher, 17–19
    understanding program window, 21–22
    using dialog boxes, 28–30
    using menus and commands, 24–28
    using Quick Publication Wizard, 22, 34,
        61–66
    using scroll bars, 30–31
    using status bar, 33–34
    using Title bar, 23–24
    using toolbars, 32–33
BestFit copyfitting feature, 277, 279
binding margins, 145
black-and-white printing, 719–721
blacks and grays, 254
blank publications
    examples of designs from scratch, 80–82
    starting, 79–80
Blank Publications tab, Catalog dialog box,
    21, 60, 79–80
blank Web page, 774
bleeds, 247, 704, 705
body text, 338
bold text, 349, 350
bond paper, 243
book fold, 634, 635
book fold layout, 230, 231, 232
book paper, 243
book production
    body of publication, 682–683
    computer files, 678
    design and layout, 678–681
    end matter, 677
    front matter, 677
    glossary, 685, 686
    index, 686, 687
    printing and binding, 687–688
    table of contents, 684–685
    widows and orphans, 682

continued

S

saddle back, 688

sans serif typefaces, 336

Save As dialog box, 35

saving a publication

    backup copies, 92–93

    basic method, 35–36

    file types, 91–92

    filenames, 85, 90–91

    locations for, 88–90

    with Save As dialog box, 86–88

scaling characters, 364–365

scaling pictures, 448–449

screen fonts, 344

screens, 407. *See also* fills applied to
        frames

ScreenTips, 45, 129, 130

scroll bars, 22, 30–31

search engines, 810–811

Secure Electronic Transaction. *See* SET

secure servers, 789

Secure Sockets Layer. *See* SSL

Selected Objects view, 153, 154, 155

selecting

    deselecting after, 50–51

    frames, 196–198

    multiple items, 49–50

    objects, 48

    texts, 48–49

selling on the Web

    e-commerce and credit, 789

    legal and ethical issues, 764

    mistakes to avoid, 791

semitransparent inks, 718

separation proofs and composites, 718,
        726–732

separator, defined, 318

serif typefaces, 336

servers, Web, 767

service bureaus, 698, 712–714

SET (Secure Electronic Transaction), 789

shade, defined, 215

Shadow Settings toolbar, 478, 479

shapes, 473–484

    adjusting, 476

    drawing, 474, 475

    editing, 475

    formatting, 476–484

sharing files, 95–97

shipping labels, 623–624

shortcuts

    for opening publications, 823–825

    for opening Publisher 2000, 19, 823–825

shortcuts, keyboard

    for alignment of text, 376

    for boldface text (Ctrl+B), 353

    for centered text (Ctrl+E), 376

    for commands, 27, 28

    for copying text (Ctrl+C), 53

    for cutting text (Ctrl+X), 53

    for italic text (Ctrl+I), 353

    for justified text (Ctrl+J), 376

    for left-aligned text (Ctrl+L), 376

    for pasting text (Ctrl+V), 53

    for printing (Ctrl+P), 102

    for Redo command (Ctrl+Y), 52

    for right-aligned text (Ctrl+R), 376

    for saving files (Ctrl+S), 36

    for underlining text (Ctrl+U), 353

    for Undo command (Ctrl+Z), 52

Shrink Text on Overflow feature, 277, 279

side stitch, 688

sidebars from Design Gallery, 571

side-fold card, 232, 233, 633–634

signatures, 633, 634–636

signs, wizards for, 67

sizing frames, 221

sliding text, 511

continued

(continued)

my2cents.idgbooks.com

Register This Book — And Win!

Visit **http://my2cents.idgbooks.com** to register this book and we'll automatically enter you in our fantastic monthly prize giveaway. It's also your opportunity to give us feedback: let us know what you thought of this book and how you would like to see other topics covered.

Discover IDG Books Online!

The IDG Books Online Web site is your online resource for tackling technology — at home and at the office. Frequently updated, the IDG Books Online Web site features exclusive software, insider information, online books, and live events!

10 Productive & Career-Enhancing Things You Can Do at www.idgbooks.com

- Nab source code for your own programming projects.

- Download software.

- Read Web exclusives: special articles and book excerpts by IDG Books Worldwide authors.

- Take advantage of resources to help you advance your career as a Novell or Microsoft professional.

- Buy IDG Books Worldwide titles or find a convenient bookstore that carries them.

- Register your book and win a prize.

- Chat live online with authors.

- Sign up for regular e-mail updates about our latest books.

- Suggest a book you'd like to read or write.

- Give us your 2¢ about our books and about our Web site.

You say you're not on the Web yet? It's easy to get started with IDG Books' *Discover the Internet,* available at local retailers everywhere.